Free Radicals
in
Solution

Cheves Walling

Professor of Chemistry
Columbia University

Free Radicals
in
Solution

NEW YORK · JOHN WILEY & SONS, INC.

London · Chapman & Hall, Ltd.

Library of Congress Catalog Card Number: 57–10818

PRINTED IN THE UNITED STATES OF AMERICA

Dedication

To Morris S. Kharasch and Frank R. Mayo, pioneers of free radical chemistry, who first aroused and then maintained my interest in this subject.

Preface

The chemistry of organic free radicals in solution as a significant field of study is now some twenty years old, and, judging by the volume of publications, is receiving increasing attention throughout the world. Unfortunately, the subject is treated only briefly in most advanced organic chemistry texts and no comprehensive survey of the field has appeared in approximately ten years. It is in the hope of filling this gap that this book has been written. In writing I have attempted to use a level of exposition which should be comprehensible to readers with a basic knowledge of college-level organic and physical chemistry, although, in later sections, many of the principles developed in earlier chapters are assumed. Accordingly, the non-specialist wanting to look up a particular topic may wish to refer to some of the earlier development.

A subject as complicated as the whole field of free radical chemistry requires considerable arbitrariness on the part of the author as to organization and emphasis. My own interest in reaction kinetics and in radical chain processes as the most illuminating and synthetically attractive types of radical reactions has largely guided the organization of this book. Accordingly, after a brief historical introduction and consideration of the general physical and chemical properties of free radicals, I have attempted to summarize present knowledge of bond dissociation energies which determine the overall thermodynamics of radical reactions.

In Chapters 3–5 vinyl polymerization has been chosen as the first class of radical reaction for detailed consideration and is used to develop the basic ideas of the kinetics of radical chain processes and the relations between structure and reactivity in radical reactions. This may appear as a rather specialized and intractable field to many organic chemists, but it deserves a larger share of their attention, and at present it certainly provides the largest body of reliable kinetic data on liquid-phase radical chain reactions.

Next, in Chapters 6–9 I have tried to apply the ideas developed in the discussion of polymerization to other radical chains—chiefly additions to double bonds, halogen substitutions, and autoxidation processes.

Finally, in the last two chapters I have discussed a variety of non-chain processes in which radicals are produced by thermal dissociation of weak bonds, photochemical reactions, and oxidation-reduction processes, and in other ways. The treatment afforded these topics is perhaps less thorough than that in earlier sections, partly because the mechanisms of some of the reactions are still largely conjectural, and partly because some of these topics lie in fields such as radiation chemistry which are treated in detail elsewhere (and with which, it must be admitted, I am relatively unfamiliar).

One important aspect of radical reactions is that, in spite of their overall variety, they all break down into relatively few kinds of individual steps involving a limited variety of types of radical. All this helps in applying a unified treatment to the field, but also, as a consequence, regardless of the manner in which a book of this sort is organized, similar types of reaction intermediates and reactions will occur at widely separated points in the discussion. As an aid to the reader in tracking down topics which have been arbitrarily divided in this way, I have made frequent use of cross references between sections. Beyond this point I can only hopefully refer him to the subject index.

Next there is the question of coverage and critical discussion. I have attempted to cover the literature appearing in major journals and *Chemical Abstracts* through June, 1956, and have included a number of subsequent references of particular significance. However, the literature on radical chemistry is now so voluminous that on many topics I have made no attempt to present a detailed historical development, and have restricted myself to citing recent references which summarize the field. Again, in many cases it has been necessary to omit considerable supporting data, and I hope that authors to whom full justice has not been done will recognize the necessity of holding a book of this sort to manageable dimensions. (Here I might remark that, at the present rate of scientific publication, the author of a half-finished book in an active field has to keep writing at a brisk rate just to keep where he is.) As to critical discussion, on topics where there are differences of opinion and where I feel qualified I have not hesitated to indicate which interpretation I prefer, nor, where it seemed appropriate, have I shunned a certain amount of speculation. I hope this treatment will be recognized for what it is, a suggestion for future work rather than any sort of final word on the subject.

Finally, I am happy to acknowledge the assistance of my many friends who have helped in the preparation of this book by making material available to me in advance of publication and reading portions of the manuscript. My especial thanks go to Professor W. H. Urry who carefully and deliberately read the entire manuscript and made many valuable suggestions.

CHEVES WALLING

April, 1957
Columbia University

Contents

xii   Contents

CHAPTER 1

Introduction

The Structure and Physical Properties

of Free Radicals

1 · 1 Introduction

Words have the common property of changing their meaning with use, and the terms used in chemistry are no exception. In fact, such changes are almost inevitable as our knowledge of the phenomena

1

that the words were coined to describe develops and grows. The term *radical* is a case in point, and, if we follow the changes in connotation that this word has undergone, we are led through the whole development of the ideas of theoretical organic chemistry.

Originally, the word *radical* was employed to designate a group of atoms that preserve their integrity and endure as a unit through a series of chemical reactions, a sense in which the word is still widely used today. During the first half of the nineteenth century, a number of such radicals were recognized as components of organic compounds, and attempts were made to isolate them in a free state, in a manner more or less analogous to the separation of metals from their salts. Several such endeavors, initially believed successful, later proved to have yielded dimers of the expected radicals. Nevertheless, the results obtained served as important additions to the expanding body of chemical knowledge. Thus Gay-Lussac in 1815 prepared cyanogen, the dimer of the cyanogen (cyano) radical CN, by heating mercuric cyanide, and so introduced this substance to chemistry.[1] Similarly, in 1842 Bunsen prepared the dimeric cacodyl from cacodyl chloride and zinc [2] via the reaction

$$2(CH_3)_2AsCl + Zn \rightarrow (CH_3)_2As\!-\!As(CH_3)_2 + ZnCl_2 \qquad (1)$$

Employing the analogous reaction of sodium with methyl and ethyl iodides, Wurtz in 1854 prepared gases with the empirical formulas CH_3 and C_2H_5.[3] Again, although subsequent work showed that the products were respectively, in fact, ethane and butane (admixed with ethane and ethylene), Wurtz's researches led to a new reaction which still bears his name and remains one of the (more moss-covered) cornerstones of elementary organic instruction.

At about the same time, similar presumed radicals were described by Frankland [4] as the result of heating ethyl iodide with zinc in a sealed tube. Again the experiment produced important results; for, on distilling the residue in his tubes, Frankland was led to the discovery of the spectacular class of organozinc compounds, a versatile group of reagents which found considerable synthetic use until superseded by the more tractable Grignard reagents some fifty years later.

[1] H. L. Gay-Lussac, *Ann. chim.*, **95**, 172 (1815).

[2] R. H. Bunsen, *Ann. Chem. Justus Liebigs*, **42**, 27 (1842).

[3] C. A. Wurtz, *Compt. rend.*, **40**, 1285 (1854).

[4] E. Frankland, *Ann.*, **71**, 171, 213 (1849).

Around 1860 two concepts entered chemistry which had a profound effect upon the search for organic free radicals. One was the vapor-density method of determining molecular weights, which conclusively identified earlier "radicals" as dimers. The second was the valence theory. Although this served to clarify the issue by identifying earlier postulated radicals as essentially derivatives of trivalent carbon, its success in interpreting the growing array of observations in organic chemistry solely in terms of structures involving tetravalent carbon really brought to a halt attempts to isolate or detect organic free radicals as such. In fact, by the end of the nineteenth century, although metal vapors were considered to be monatomic and high-temperature dissociations such as

$$I_2 \rightleftharpoons 2I \cdot \tag{2}$$

were recognized,[5] the majority of organic chemists were convinced that, except for such anomalies as carbon monoxide and the isocyanides, only compounds of tetravalent carbon were capable of existence.

This viewpoint was rather violently upset at the turn of the century by Gomberg's description of his attempts to prepare hexaphenylethane by treating solutions of triphenylmethyl chloride with silver powder or zinc dust.[6] The resulting yellow solutions reacted instantly with air, iodine, and a variety of other reagents, properties which he could only explain on the basis of dissociation of the hexaphenylethane into triphenylmethyl radicals, i.e.:

$$\phi_3C-C\phi_3 \rightleftharpoons 2\phi_3C \cdot \tag{3}$$

In short, the goal which had eluded numerous investigators a half century and more before had been achieved.

Once the initial scepticism of other workers was overcome, a number of laboratories turned to the problem of stable free radicals, and a large variety of such species were prepared, identified and their properties studied. However, because their structural requirements for existence are possessed by only rather complicated molecules, they have remained a rather esoteric branch of organic chemistry, considered in more detail in Chapter 10.

The development of the concept of the electron pair bond, beginning with Lewis's suggestions in 1916,[7] and elaborated by the devel-

[5] V. Meyer, *Ber.*, **13**, 394 (1880).

[6] M. Gomberg, *ibid.*, **33**, 3150 (1900); *J. Am. Chem. Soc.*, **22**, 757 (1900).

[7] G. N. Lewis, *J. Am. Chem. Soc.*, **38**, 762 (1916).

opment of quantum mechanics, gave more specific meaning to the term *radical* or *free radical* (here used interchangeably). Thus the (then hypothetical) methyl radical

$$
\begin{array}{c}
\text{H} \\
\ddot{\text{H}}:\ddot{\text{C}}\cdot \\
\text{H}
\end{array}
$$

consisted of a carbon atom surrounded by three electron pairs and an additional unpaired or odd electron. By extension, any structure containing an atom with an unshared electron might be considered a radical, as may molecules containing two or more unpaired electrons (di- and polyradicals), and this definition of a *free radical as a molecule or atom with one or more unpaired electrons* will be employed here. As will be seen, although the largest number of radicals are those with an odd electron associated with a carbon atom, halogen atoms and radicals with odd electrons on O, N, P, S, and Si play important roles in many reactions. Finally we may note that, although most of the radicals with which we are concerned are electrically neutral, radical ions also exist and are sometimes important either as stable products or reactive intermediates in certain systems.

The next step in the development of the chemistry of free radicals, the establishment of the role of radicals as transient intermediates in chemical reactions, first received serious attention in quite a different branch of chemistry, the investigation of pyrolytic and photochemical reactions in the gas phase. This field became an increasingly active branch of physical chemistry in the 1920's, and the possibility of free radical intermediates in such processes was seriously suggested as early as 1925 by Taylor.[8] Nevertheless, a number of alternative hypotheses continued to be advanced to interpret experimental results,[9] and it was not until the publication of the work of Paneth and Hofeditz in 1929 [10] that conclusive evidence became available. These investigators, in an elegant series of experiments, studied the pyrolysis of tetramethyl lead under conditions of low pressure and rapid flow, in an apparatus shown schematically in Fig. 1·1. A carrier gas such as hydrogen, saturated with tetramethyl lead

[8] H. S. Taylor, *Trans. Faraday Soc.,* **21,** 560 (1925).

[9] For an interesting discussion of the early evolution of this field, cf. F. O. Rice and K. K. Rice, *The Aliphatic Free Radicals,* The Johns Hopkins Press, Baltimore, 1935, Chapter II.

[10] F. Paneth and W. Hofeditz, *Ber.,* **62,** 1335 (1929).

(contained in A at some predetermined temperature), passes through a quartz pyrolysis tube B at a pressure of 1–2 mm and a velocity of 10–15 meters/sec and through a trap C maintained at liquid nitrogen temperature. If B is heated strongly at some point a, the tetramethyl lead is completely decomposed, depositing a lead mirror at that point. Once such a mirror is deposited (alternatively by heating a small piece of metal previously introduced into the tube) the significant part of the experiment may be performed. If the mirror at a is allowed to cool and the tube is now heated at a new point b, upstream from the first, a new mirror is deposited at b, and, simul-

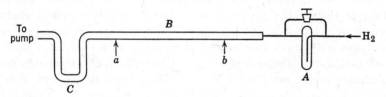

FIG. 1·1 Apparatus for the detection of methyl radicals in the pyrolysis of tetramethyl lead.[10]

taneously, the mirror at a disappears and tetramethyl lead collects in C. Evidently the pyrolysis yields reactive fragments which have very short lives, since the rate of removal of the mirror at a decreases as the distance between a and b is increased. These same fragments also remove mirrors of zinc and antimony, in the former case yielding dimethyl zinc as the product in C. These observations led the authors to conclude that the reactive intermediates being swept down the tube were methyl radicals formed by the reaction

$$(CH_3)_4Pb \rightarrow Pb + 4 \cdot CH_3 \tag{4}$$

which rapidly combined to form ethane but still had half-lives of the order of 10^{-3} sec during which they could react with a cold metal mirror by the reverse of reaction 4.

Paneth's conclusions soon received additional experimental support, and, subsequently, the whole field of gas-phase radical reactions has had notable development. However, since it has recently been reviewed in detail [11] and lies outside of the proper scope of this book, gas-phase reactions will be mentioned here only when they

---

[11] E. W. R. Steacie, *Atomic and Free Radical Reactions*, second edition, Reinhold Publishing Corp., New York, 1954.

A shorter discussion is given by W. A. Waters, *The Chemistry of Free Radicals*, second edition, Oxford University Press, London, 1948.

have direct bearing on similar radical processes in solution. Actually, as we will see, organic radical reactions comprise one of the fields of chemistry where a close parallel indeed exists between phenomena in the gas and liquid state. Such differences as arise are usually accounted for by concentration differences and the intrusion of heterogeneous processes on vessel walls in the gaseous state reactions.

The idea of free radicals (in the modern sense) as intermediates in liquid-phase reactions has had a largely independent and somewhat more recent development. The parallel between autoxidation of aldehydes and of sulfite ion was pointed out in 1927 by Bäckström,[12] who recognized the chain nature of both processes, and in 1934 postulated the aldehyde autoxidation as a free radical chain reaction.[13] Although this appears to be the first specific liquid-phase reaction involving a free radical chain to be identified, it is interesting that Staudinger had suggested in 1920 that polymerization processes might involve trivalent carbon,[14] and Haber and Willstätter had considered free radical chain mechanisms for a number of organic reactions in solution.[15] However, most of their schemes, like most of Nef's much earlier reaction mechanisms involving divalent carbon "radicals," [16] have not survived subsequent detailed investigation.

In 1937 Hey and Waters published a most significant review,[17] interpreting a number of reactions, which had hitherto proved stumbling blocks in the development of the electronic theory of organic reactions, as being free radical processes. Among these were the reactions of aromatic nuclei with benzoyl peroxide, decompositions of aromatic diazonium salts as in the Gomberg-Bachmann reaction, and the "abnormal" addition of hydrogen bromide to olefins. At the same time and independently, Kharasch [18] proposed the present accepted free radical chain mechanism for the "abnormal" addition, a reaction first demonstrated by Kharasch and Mayo four years before.[19] Finally, in the same year, Flory [20] published a brilliant and

[12] H. L. J. Bäckström, *J. Am. Chem. Soc.,* **49,** 1460 (1927).

[13] H. L. J. Bäckström, *Z. physik. Chem.,* **25B,** 99 (1934).

[14] H. Staudinger, *Ber.,* **53,** 1073 (1920).

[15] F. Haber and R. Willstätter, *ibid.,* **64,** 2844 (1931).

[16] J. U. Nef, *Ann.,* **298,** 202 (1897).

[17] D. H. Hey and W. A. Waters, *Chem. Revs.,* **21,** 169 (1937).

[18] M. S. Kharasch, H. Engelmann, and F. R. Mayo, *J. Org. Chem.,* **2,** 288 (1937).

[19] M. S. Kharasch and F. R. Mayo, *J. Am. Chem. Soc.,* **55,** 2468 (1933).

[20] P. J. Flory, *ibid.,* **59,** 241 (1937).

prescient paper on the kinetics of vinyl polymerization, treated as a free radical chain reaction, and outlining the framework into which much subsequent work has been fitted.

Inevitably, the full significance of these publications was not immediately recognized, nor the conclusions everywhere accepted. Nevertheless, 1937 is a convenient date to mark the beginning of our present recognition of the role of free radicals as reactive intermediates in ordinary temperature, liquid-phase reactions, just as the publication of Rice and Rice's *The Aliphatic Free Radicals* [9] two years earlier marked a turning point in the study of free radicals in gas-phase photochemistry and pyrolysis.

Since 1937 knowledge of organic reactions involving free radicals has increased at a steadily accelerating pace. New synthetic methods such as radical addition reactions to double bonds have come into being, and old reactions of halogenation and autoxidation have been rendered more versatile and efficient by a recognition of their reaction paths.

In fact, whole new industries, notably that of vinyl polymerization, have arisen based upon free radical processes. Along with these developments has come a much more detailed understanding of the mechanism and characteristics of free radical reactions.

The balance of this and the next chapters will be devoted to an introductory survey of some of this knowledge. Subsequent chapters will consider the kinetics of radical processes in more detail and take up the specific properties of individual radical reactions. Actually, as we will see, in spite of the great volume of data now available, the whole subject of organic radical reactions is a rather closely integrated one, involving only a few types of reactions and rather a limited number of types of radical. Furthermore, because the species involved are, in general, uncharged, many of the complexities of polar reactions (effects of ionic strength, acidity and basicity, ionizing power of the media, etc.) are largely avoided. A happy consequence is that the tie-up between theory and experiment is often gratifyingly clear-cut and direct.

1 · 2   Magnetic Properties of Free Radicals

An organic free radical, like any other molecular species, has its own distinctive physical properties—molecular weight, absorption spectrum, dipole moment, melting point, etc. In addition, free radicals, as a class, have a group of characteristics due to a unique structural feature: the presence of one (or more) unpaired electrons. These characteristics are of great importance as means of detecting the presence of free radicals, quantitatively estimating their concentrations, and learning something of their structures.

Of the characteristics arising from the presence of unpaired electrons, the most significant are those affecting the magnetic properties of molecules, and, in fact, these are the only ones which provide a general tool for demonstrating the free radical nature of molecules.

1·2a Magnetic Susceptibility

Since a number of comprehensive reviews are available,[21-24] the basis of magnetic susceptibility measurements need only be discussed briefly. When a substance is placed in a magnetic field of strength H, the resulting intensity of magnetization per unit volume, I, is given by the relation

$$I/H = \chi \tag{5}$$

where χ (also sometimes written as K or κ) is the magnetic susceptibility of the material per unit volume. Similarly, a molar susceptibility may be defined as

$$\chi_M = \chi M/\rho \tag{6}$$

where M is the molecular weight and ρ the density. Experimentally, it turns out that χ (and hence χ_M) may be either positive or negative. When χ is positive, a substance is *paramagnetic;* whereas if χ is negative, it is *diamagnetic.* In addition, a few materials such as iron, nickel, and certain alloys show extremely large positive susceptibilities and are known as *ferromagnetic.* In terms of the classical model, it is convenient to think that, in a magnetic field, the magnetic lines of force are concentrated within a paramagnetic substance and partially excluded from a diamagnetic one. Magnetic susceptibility is thus equivalent to electric susceptibility in electrical theory, which, in turn, is related to the dielectric constant.

From quantum mechanics and statistical mechanics, the molar sus-

[21] J. H. Van Vleck, *Electric and Magnetic Susceptibilities,* Oxford University Press, New York, 1932.

[22] E. C. Stoner, *Magnetism and Matter,* Methuen, London, 1932.

[23] P. W. Selwood, *Magnetochemistry,* Interscience Publishers, New York, 1943.

[24] L. Michaelis, *Technique of Organic Chemistry,* A. Weissberger, editor, Volume I, Interscience Publishers, New York, 1949, Chapter 29. This is probably the most useful account for the organic chemist.

ceptibility χ_M may be divided into two parts, which in most cases may be expressed in the form

$$\chi_M = N(\alpha_0 + \mu_M{}^2/3kT) \tag{7}$$

where N is Avagadro's number, k, Boltzmann's constant, α_0 the induced moment, and μ_M the permanent magnetic dipole moment of a single molecule. The quantity α_0 arises chiefly from electronic motion within a molecule. Since electrons are charged particles, imposition of a magnetic field distorts their motion and this change in motion produces a countermagnetic field. This consequence, in turn, decreases the effective magnetic field in the region of the molecule. The result is that χ_M is negative, and molecules without permanent magnetic dipole moments are diamagnetic.

In all cases of significance to us here, permanent magnetic dipole moments arise from electron spin.[25] With paired electrons, the net moment is zero, since the pairing is between electrons of opposite spins. However, for an unpaired electron this moment is not zero, and may be calculated from quantum theory to have the value $\sqrt{3}$ Bohr magnetons. As a consequence, since $\mu_M{}^2$ is positive, χ_M will contain a positive term. In fact, since $N\mu_M{}^2/3kT$ has a value of 1260×10^{-6} cgs units at 20°C, and since the diamagnetic term for typical organic molecules is generally less than 10% of this, it appears that *paramagnetism is a unique property of free radicals*, a prediction first made by Lewis in 1923.[26] It should be noted that, provided other sources of magnetic moment can be neglected, the magnitude of the paramagnetic term in χ_M is independent of the molecule involved, but is temperature dependent, increasing as the temperature is lowered. In the case of molecules with more than one unpaired electron, μ_M is given, in Bohr magnetons and for n electrons, by the relation

$$\mu_M = \sqrt{n(n + 2)} \tag{8}$$

providing that the electrons involved occupy orbitals which may interact with one another. However, if they are isolated, the expected relation is $\mu_M = n\sqrt{3}$.

[25] Two other sources of permanent magnetic dipoles may exist in molecules: angular momenta of the orbital electrons and nuclear spin. However, in organic molecules, the effect of the former appears to be "quenched" by the strong internal electric fields, and the moment due to the latter is less than $\frac{1}{1000}$ of that due to the spin of a free electron.

[26] G. N. Lewis, *Valence and Structure of Atoms and Molecules,* Chemical Catalog Co., New York, 1923, p. 148.

Finally, we may note that the ions of many transition-state metals may possess as many as several unpaired electrons. By our definition, such ions are properly free radicals, but they differ so in bond-forming properties from organic radicals that the definition is of little utility here. Nevertheless, studies of the magnetic properties of such ions and their coordination complexes have proved very valuable in connection with the determination of their structures.

The determination of the magnetic susceptibilities of molecules is most commonly carried out by investigating their behavior in inhomogeneous magnetic fields. A material placed in a magnetic field of strength H acquired a potential energy per unit volume.

$$E = \chi H^2 / 2 \qquad (9)$$

Accordingly, if the field is inhomogeneous in some direction x, it follows that it will be acted upon by a force per unit volume

$$F = \chi H \, dH / dx \qquad (10)$$

From eq. 10 it is evident that paramagnetic substances will be subject to a force drawing them into a magnetic field, whereas diamagnetic materials will be repelled, and, in fact, this distinction provides the original definition of the terms.

The simplest method of determining χ by measuring H is probably that of Gouy, first employed in 1889,[27] and shown schematically in Fig. 1·2. If a long sample of uniform cross section, A, is suspended between the poles of a powerful magnet, so that one end is in a uniform field of strength H, and the other lies essentially in field zero, the force acting upon the sample is given by

$$F = \chi H^2 A / 2 \qquad (11)$$

and may easily be determined by weighing the sample in the presence and absence of the magnetic field. In practice, a number of refinements are necessary, for example the use of a double-ended compensating tube, so that χ is always determined relative to some known standard, but the procedure is basically as described. For liquids, a thin-walled container may be employed, or the force may be determined by measuring the difference in level of the liquid in two arms of a U tube, one of which is placed in a magnetic field. This technique, originally developed by Quincke,[28] is shown schematically in Fig. 1·3. It has had a number of modifications and appears very well

[27] L. G. Gouy, *Compt. rend.*, **109**, 935 (1889).
[28] G. Quincke, *Ann. Physik*, **24**, 347 (1885); **34**, 401 (1888).

adapted for the study of solutions of stable organic radicals.   It is quite sensitive, but temperature control becomes difficult if it is used at high or low temperatures.

Probably the most sensitive modification of the Gouy method is the Theorell balance.   Here the sample is suspended horizontally as

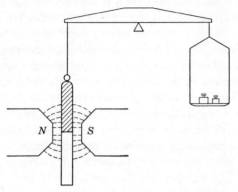

Fɪɢ. 1·2   Schematic diagram of Gouy balance for determining magnetic suscep-tibilities.

a pendulum in the magnetic field, and its displacement is measured with a microscope.[29]   With such a device, displacing forces as small as 10^{-6} gram may be detected with samples of about 100 mg.

Although a number of measurements have been made on organic radicals in the solid state, the most important application of magnetic

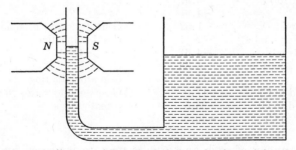

Fɪɢ. 1·3   Schematic diagram of Quincke technique for determining the magnetic susceptibility of liquids.

susceptibility measurements has been in the detection and quantitative estimation of free radicals in solution.   Determination of the degree of dissociation of hexaphenylethane is a typical example of

[29] H. Theorell, *Arkiv Kemi, Mineral. Geol.*, **A16**, 1 (1943).

such an application and illustrates well the utility and limitations of magnetic susceptibility measurements. The major problem in interpreting measurements in such a system is separating the paramagnetic contribution of the radicals from the diamagnetic contribution of all the components of the system. In principle, this might be done by employing measurements over a temperature range and separating out the temperature-dependent paramagnetic term, but this procedure is not feasible in most systems since radical concentrations are also temperature dependent. Accordingly, solvent diamagnetism is usually corrected for, either by using a compensating-tube apparatus, or by direct measurement in the same apparatus and some method of estimating the diamagnetism of the other components (e.g., hexaphenylethane and the radicals themselves in the system mentioned).

Fortunately, diamagnetism proves to be a closely additive property, and the diamagnetism of a molecule may be estimated by summing the expected contributions of its atoms plus certain constitutional corrections. The validity of this method was first established by Pascal, and a table of such Pascal constants or atomic diamagnetic increments are given in Table 1·1.

TABLE 1·1   ATOMIC DIAMAGNETIC INCREMENTS IN CGS UNITS ($\times 10^{-6}$)

(After Michaelis [24])

H	−2.93	S	−15.0
C	−6.00	Se	−23.0
N (open chain)	−5.57	P	−26.3
N (ring)	−4.61	As	−43
N (monoamides)	−1.52	Constitutional Corrections	
N (diamides, imides)	−2.11	C=C (aliphatic)	+5.5
O (single bond)	−4.61	C=C—C=C	+10.6
O (double bond)	−3.36	C≡C	+0.8
F	−11.5	C in aromatic ring	−0.24
Cl (bonded to C)	−17.0	C common to 2 aro-	
Br (bonded to C)	−26.5	matic rings	−3.1
I (bonded to C)	−40.5		

The accuracy of such an estimate may be increased by directly measuring χ_M for a molecule of similar structure and then making the necessary corrections (e.g., χ_M for hexaphenylethane should be twice that for triphenylmethane less the value for two hydrogens).

An illustration of the actual magnitudes of the quantities involved is given in the following, calculated from the data of Roy and Marvel on the dissociation of 0.1 molar hexaphenylethane in benzene solution at 20° [30] employing the Quincke technique.

Calculated Diamagnetic Contributions

Benzene	-0.668×10^{-6} cgs units
Solute	-0.037
χ (calculated)	-0.705
χ (observed)	-0.700 ± 0.002
Paramagnetic contribution	0.005 ± 0.002

The result corresponds to some 2% dissociation or to a radical concentration of 4×10^{-3} molar. Since the paramagnetic contribution is a small difference between large numbers, and approaches the accuracy with which they are known, it is evident that experimental error is considerable and one is nearing the capabilities of the technique. This sensitivity limit of 10^{-3} molar as we will see (Chapter 3 et seq.) lies far above the actual concentrations in many systems in which radical reactions are in progress, but greater sensitivity is sometimes possible. The most delicate measurement of organic radical concentrations by magnetic susceptibility measurements to date is that of Lewis, Calvin, and Kasha.[31] These workers demonstrated the paramagnetic properties of the phosphorescent state of fluoroscein using a modified Theorell balance, capable of determining approximately 2×10^{-8} moles of free radicals in a volume of 0.02 cc with an accuracy of $\pm 10\%$, i.e., detecting a 10^{-4} molar concentration.

1·2b Paramagnetic Resonance Spectra

The fact that paramagnetic substances may show characteristic absorption spectra when placed in a magnetic field provides a relatively new and potentially very valuable technique for detecting and studying organic free radicals, and recent reviews of the topic have been written by Wertz [32] and Fraenkel.[33] Compared with magnetic susceptibility measurements, the technique is more sensitive and may provide information concerning electronic structure. On the other hand, the apparatus is relatively elaborate, and as a test for free

[30] M. F. Roy and C. S. Marvel, *J. Am. Chem. Soc.*, **59**, 2620 (1937).
[31] G. N. Lewis, M. Calvin, and M. Kasha, *J. Chem. Phys.*, **17**, 804 (1949).
[32] J. E. Wertz, *Chem. Revs.*, **55**, 829 (1955).
[33] G. K. Fraenkel, *Ann. N. Y. Acad. Sci.*, **67**, 546 (1957).

radicals it may fail because, for various reasons, the radical may show no absorption.

The theory of paramagnetic absorption spectra is complex, and, in fact, many of the features of spectral fine structure are not understood. The qualitative basis of the theory, however, is as follows. An unpaired or free electron in a magnetic field is acted upon by a force which tends to orient its spin in relation to the field (this is the origin of the paramagnetic term in eq. 7). Two such orientations are possible, "with" or "against" the field, which differ in energy by an amount proportional to the external field. From quantum theory this difference amounts to

$$E = g\beta H \tag{12}$$

where g is the spectroscopic splitting factor, 2.0023 for a free electron, and β the Bohr magneton, 0.927×10^{-20} ergs/gauss. The existence of such a phenomenon has long been known and is related to the Zeeman effect, or splitting of atomic spectral lines in a magnetic field. If such a system is exposed to electromagnetic radiation of appropriate frequency so that

$$h\nu = g\beta H \tag{13}$$

electrons in the lower level may absorb energy and "flip over" to the higher state.

Substitution of numerical values into eq. 12 shows that, at any feasible field strength, the energy involved in the transition is very small, amounting to about 2.4 cal/mole at 9000 gauss. Indeed, the corresponding absorption would occur in the microwave region at 2.5×10^{10} cycles/sec, and necessarily the study of paramagnetic resonance spectra is normally carried out in this region, the first published observation being by Zavoisky in 1945.[34]

The required microwave and magnetic equipment for paramagnetic resonance work is necessarily elaborate,[32, 35, 36] and any description would be out of place here. However, the method consists essentially in placing a sample in a suitable microwave system which is also in a strong magnetic field, and determining the effect of the sample on the microwave power absorbed or reflected in the system. Since it is

[34] E. Zavoisky, *J. Phys. U.S.S.R.*, **9**, 211 (1945).

[35] B. Bleaney and K. W. H. Stevens, *Reports on Progress in Physics*, **46**, 107 (1953).

[36] J. M. Hirshon and G. K. Fraenkel, *Rev. Sci. Instruments*, **26**, 34 (1955).

more convenient to change magnetic field than microwave frequency, the resulting power absorption commonly is obtained as a function of field strength, and line widths are measured in gauss rather than frequency units. Samples may be introduced in thin-walled glass tubes of capillary size or larger, and the system under examination may be heated, cooled, or irradiated during examination without too much difficulty. A notable feature of this technique is the sensitivity. The theoretical quantity of radicals detectable by a suitably designed instrument has been calculated as 2×10^{-14} moles,[33, 37] and, experimentally, 5×10^{-11} moles of the stable radical diphenylpicrylhydrazyl have given observable spectra.[37] Since the sample employed was a solid, diluted with inert material to a volume of approximately 0.1 cc, this corresponds to a 5×10^{-7} molar radical concentration. By using larger samples, lower radical concentrations should be detectable, but the sensitivity of the method decreases with increasing width of the observed absorption bands.

Aside from the sensitivity of the method, paramagnetic resonance spectra have two other significant properties which add to their usefulness. First, the spectra observed are independent of the diamagnetic properties of the system, and thus require none of the corrections needed in magnetic susceptibility measurements. Second, although spectra of all radicals with a single odd electron have their band centers at approximately the same frequency at a given field strength (corresponding to that expected for a free electron), band widths vary widely, and, in addition, some radicals show hyperfine splitting to give a number of peaks. Evidently, in favorable cases these differences permit the identification of individual radicals. They also provide information on radical processes and structures.

Under suitable conditions, band widths may be correlated with radical lifetimes, the width in gauss being approximately $10^{-7}/\tau$, where τ is the lifetime in seconds. This provides a technique for measuring radical lifetimes in the range of 10^{-6} to 10^{-10} sec and has been used to determine the rate of reaction between the naphthalene radical ion and naphthalene,[38] and also of radical displacements occurring in molten sulfur (cf. Section 7·3c).

Hyperfine splitting appears usually to arise from interaction between the odd electron of a radical and neighboring atoms possessing nuclear magnetic moments. It thus gives information about the

[37] J. M. Hirshon, thesis, Columbia University, 1954.
[38] R. L. Ward and S. I. Weissman, *J. Am. Chem. Soc.*, **76**, 3612 (1954).

extent of delocalization of the unpaired electron and the electronic structure of the radical. Since the proton has a nuclear spin of ½, interaction with neighboring hydrogen atoms can be detected, and, for a single hydrogen, leads to a splitting of each electron-spin level into two symmetrically displaced levels. The transitions observed

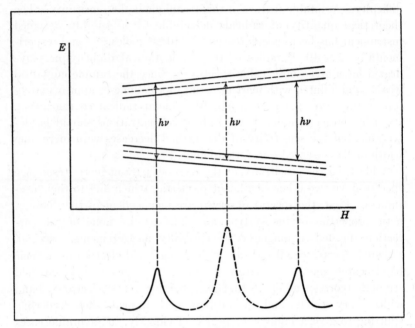

FIG. 1·4   Plot showing the hyperfine splitting of a paramagnetic resonance absorption line due to interaction of an electron with a single proton. The lower half of the figure shows the observed absorption. Dotted lines refer to the energy levels and spectra in the absence of interaction.

in paramagnetic resonance experiments cause a reorientation of the electron without change in nuclear orientation and are indicated in Fig. 1·4 by solid arrows, with the energy levels and absorption in the absence of a proton shown by dashed lines. In solution the width of splitting is proportional to the average density of the odd electron at the hydrogen nucleus and thus indicates the intensity of the interaction.

Such a two-peak absorption is actually observed [33] with the tri-chlorosemiquinone radical ion (I) and indicates the extensive de-

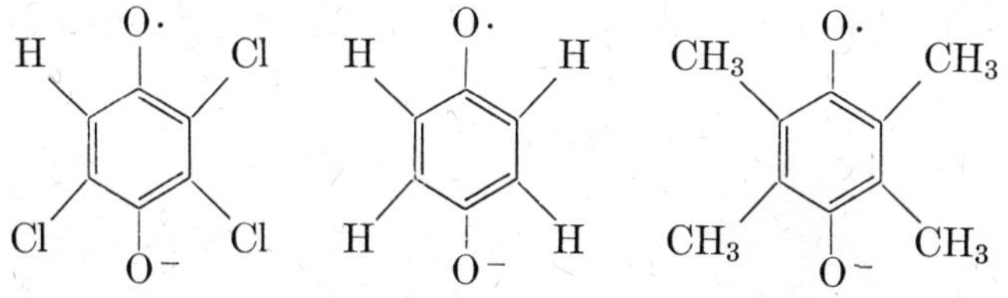

$$\text{(14)}$$

I   II   III

localization of the odd electron which must contribute to the stability of the semiquinone.

With a larger number of equivalent protons, $n+1$ equally spaced peaks will be produced with relative intensities corresponding to the coefficients in a binomial expansion. Thus, with semiquinone ion (II) and duroquinone ion (III), five and thirteen peaks have been reported.[39] The latter case is particularly interesting since, in resonance terminology, it corresponds to contributions from structures such as

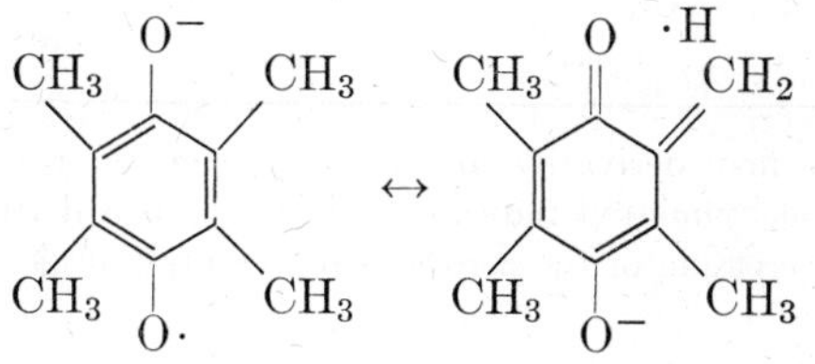

$$\leftrightarrow \qquad \text{(15)}$$

and amounts to an experimental demonstration of radical hyperconjugation.

With non-equivalent protons more elaborate spectra result. Although some of the simpler ones have been interpreted, some are highly complex; see Fig. 1·5 showing the first derivative of the absorption curve for triphenylmethyl.[40]

Up to the present, paramagnetic resonance absorption spectroscopy of organic free radicals has been largely limited to species which are stable in solution, or which may be preserved in the solid state (cf. Section 1·3). However, the sensitivity of the method is such that it also presents the possibility of detecting transient radical intermediates in reactions. Thus spectra have been observed for free radicals involved in vinyl polymerization,[41] the first direct detection

[39] B. Venkataraman and G. K. Fraenkel, *ibid.*, **77**, 2707 (1955).

[40] H. S. Jarrett and G. J. Sloan, *J. Chem. Phys.*, **22**, 1783 (1954).

[41] G. K. Fraenkel, J. M. Hirshon, and C. Walling, *J. Am. Chem. Soc.*, **76**, 3606 (1954).

by physical means of radicals involved in liquid-phase radical chain processes.

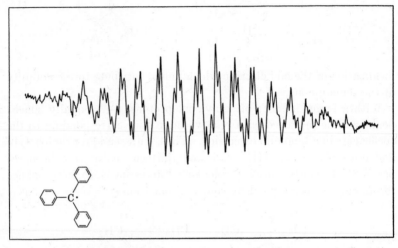

Fɪɢ. 1·5   Plot of first derivative of the paramagnetic resonance absorption spectra of the triphenylmethyl radical.[40]   Since this is a derivative curve, each crossing of the zero axis represents a peak.

1·2c   Other Magnetic Properties

Two other properties arising from the magnetic moment of free radicals may be employed for their detection. These are the catalysis of the *ortho-para* conversion of hydrogen and the behavior of radicals in the form of molecular beams when exposed to strong inhomogeneous magnetic fields.

The hydrogen molecule exists in two states, designated *ortho* and *para* and distinguished by the fact that in *ortho* hydrogen the nuclear spins of the hydrogen atoms are symmetric, whereas in *para* hydrogen they are antisymmetric.[42] This difference in structure is enough to produce slight but significant differences in physical properties, notably specific heat, which may be used as a basis for analysis. The composition of equilibrium mixtures of *ortho* and *para* hydrogen varies with temperature, the *para* fraction decreasing from 99.82% at 20°K to a limiting value of 25% at room temperature and higher. Normally, the interconversion of *p*- to *o*-hydrogen is a very slow process, so that gaseous *p*-hydrogen can be kept for weeks at room

---

[42] A good review of this topic is given by A. Farkas, *Orthohydrogen, Parahydrogen and Heavy Hydrogen,* Cambridge University Press, Cambridge, 1935.

temperature in clean glass vessels. However, various catalysts readily effect equilibration, even at very low temperature. Among these are charcoal, and a number of metals, e.g., nickel, effective as hydrogenation catalysts. Thus, the usual way of preparing pure p-hydrogen is by adsorbing hydrogen on charcoal or other catalyst held at liquid hydrogen temperatures. A mixture containing 50% p-hydrogen may be prepared similarly by cooling the catalyst in liquid nitrogen. More interesting to us here is the conversion in homogeneous systems, since Wigner, in 1933, calculated that the strong magnetic field of paramagnetic molecules should be able to bring about the equilibration.[43] This prediction has been abundantly confirmed. In the gas phase, the paramagnetic molecules O_2, NO, and NO_2 produce rapid conversion; e.g., at 20°C with oxygen at 10-mm pressure the half-life of p-hydrogen is only 143 minutes, whereas diamagnetic gases are without effect. Similarly dissolved oxygen or the presence of paramagnetic ions brings about the rapid isomerization of p-hydrogen dissolved in a solvent. The effectiveness of paramagnetic ions decreases with the number of unpaired electrons and the corresponding magnetic moment.

As we would expect, the p-hydrogen conversion can also be used to detect organic free radicals, triphenylmethyl [44] and more complex radicals [45] bringing about the equilibration. Solid organic free radicals, e.g., diphenylpicrylhydrazyl, are also effective.[46]

As a technique for detecting radicals the p-hydrogen conversion is usually carried out by shaking a solution with hydrogen enriched with p-hydrogen and withdrawing gas samples from time to time for analysis, e.g., by thermal conductivity measurements which require only a few cubic millimeters. Accordingly, the technique is not too difficult, although it has had little application since about 1941. Its limitations seem to be two. First, the effectiveness of a radical in bringing about conversion according to Wigner's theory is given by a complex expression involving $\mu_M{}^2$ and the inverse sixth power of the separation between the radical and hydrogen during collision. This distance can hardly be known with sufficient precision to give any absolute value for the radical concentration involved, although ob-

[43] E. Wigner, *Z. physik. Chem.*, **B23**, 38 (1933).

[44] G. M. Schwab and E. Agallidis, *Z. physik. Chem.*, **B41**, 59 (1938).

[45] G. M. Schwab and E. Schwab-Agallidis, *Naturwissenschaften*, **28**, 412 (1940).

[46] J. Turkevich and P. W. Selwood, *J. Am. Chem. Soc.*, **63**, 1077 (1941); L. G. Harrison and C. A. McDowell, *Proc. Roy. Soc. London*, **A220**, 77 (1953).

served results are of the expected order of magnitude and relative measurements are entirely feasible. Second, even diamagnetic solvents produce a slow p-hydrogen conversion, through interactions between the hydrogen and solvent atoms (chiefly protons) having nuclear spins, giving rise to a very small paramagnetism. Table 1·2

TABLE 1·2   HALF-LIVES OF p-HYDROGEN IN VARIOUS SOLVENTS AT 20°C

(Farkas;[42] p. 84)

Solvent	Half-Life, min
H_2O	134
C_6H_6	350
$C_6H_5NH_2$	270
CH_3OH	230
C_6H_{12}	452
CS_2	1000

lists half-lives for the conversions in several solvents. This obviously limits the sensitivity of the method, which has been estimated at about 10^{-4} molar radical concentration in water by Farkas,[47] of the same order of magnitude as magnetic susceptibility measurements.

A final consequence of the magnetic properties of free radicals, necessarily restricted to radicals in the gas phase, is observed in the so-called Stern-Gerlach experiment. If a molecular beam containing free radicals is passed through a magnetic field, as we have seen, the ground state will be split into two levels with the odd electron spin oriented with and against the field. If the field is inhomogeneous, molecules in which the spin is oriented "with" the field will be accelerated towards the region of high field strength, and those oriented against the field will be accelerated in the opposite direction. In consequence, the beam is split into two parts. The relation between this phenomenon and the magnetic susceptibility measurements we have discussed is worth pointing out. Since the two levels of the odd electron in a magnetic field differ in energy, at equilibrium their population will therefore differ. In a magnetic susceptibility measurement on a solid or liquid, when the differently oriented species are not free to separate, the resulting force on the sample is proportional to the difference in concentration of the two oppositely oriented species. Since this difference decreases with increasing temperature, the origin of the temperature dependence of the paramagnetic susceptibility becomes evident.

[47] L. Farkas, *Ann. N. Y. Acad. Sci.*, **40**, 129 (1940).

Molecular beam experiments have been carried out in an apparatus shown schematically in Fig. 1·6. Molecules from a source S are passed into an evacuated chamber through collimating slits A and B, and then between the poles of a magnet M, and on to a detector D. The pole pieces of M are so designed as to yield a strongly inhomogeneous field, e.g., by slotting one and making the other wedge shaped. A number of techniques may be used to detect the deflection of the resulting beam; for example, by collecting the impinging molecules on a cold surface, or, better, by the use of a manometer which determines

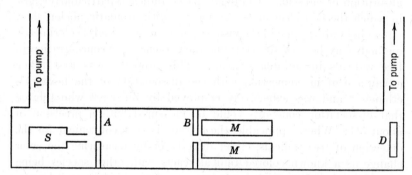

Fig. 1·6   Schematic diagram of apparatus for molecular beam experiments.

the gas pressure a particular region in space by the loss of heat from a hot wire.

Molecular beam experiments have been used to show the presence of unpaired electrons in atoms of the alkali metals, copper, silver, gold, and a number of other metals and simple molecules such as O_2 and NO.[48] The method is very sensitive and in recent years has been used to investigate the very much smaller *nuclear* magnetic moments of a number of elements.[49]

A further refinement in molecular beam experiments is the molecular beam resonance technique developed by Rabi, in which the beam is also subjected to a rapidly oscillating magnetic field, superimposed upon a strong homogeneous one. At characteristic frequencies, energy absorption occurs (as in paramagnetic resonance spectroscopy experiments) which changes the position of the beam at the detector.[49]

Actually, although molecular beam experiments have been very

[48] W. A. Waters, *The Chemistry of Free Radicals*, second edition, Oxford, 1948, pp. 21–25.

[49] A review of this topic is given by N. F. Ramsay, *Nuclear Moments*, John Wiley & Sons, New York, 1953.

valuable in the study of electronic and nuclear structure, they have not so far been applied to the study of systems containing organic free radicals, probably because of the elaborate apparatus required and the complexities connected with interpreting the results.

1 · 3   Other Physical Properties of Free Radicals

Of the physical properties of individual radicals, distinguished from free radicals as a class, the most useful are those connected with light absorption or emission. Conjugated free radicals, particularly those in which the odd electron is conjugated with aromatic nuclei, show strong light absorption in the visible region. Accordingly, colorimetric methods may be used to determine the presence and concentration of free radicals in suitable systems. This property was first taken advantage of in connection with the dissociation of the hexaaryl-ethanes [50] and was extensively employed by Ziegler,[51] who showed that dissociation constants could be measured with a precision of about 5%. Where applicable, the method is very convenient for the detection of free radicals, either directly or by measuring the color change as a known colored radical reacts with other species being formed in the system. A noteworthy example of this second technique is the use of diphenylpicrylhydrazyl. This violet-colored stable radical reacts with many other free radicals to yield colorless products, so that, by measuring the rate of color fading, the rate of radical production in a system may be determined.[52] This technique, although it suffers from certain complications (Section 3·3c), would appear to have wide application since a number of other colored stable radicals are known.

In a more qualitative manner, the transient appearance of color has often been taken as evidence for the presence of radical intermediates in oxidation-reduction reactions; e.g., in the autoxidation of benzoin in alkaline solution a transient violet color appears which has been identified with an intermediate radical ion.[53] Similar measurements may also be employed in the ultraviolet region of the spectrum and should permit the detection of simpler radicals. Thus the absorption spectrum of the benzyl radical (and the analogous ϕ-O· and ϕ-NH

[50] J. Picard, *Ann.*, **381,** 347 (1911).

[51] K. Ziegler and L. Ewald, *ibid.,* **473,** 163 (1929).

[52] P. D. Bartlett and H. Kwart, *J. Am. Chem. Soc.,* **72,** 1051 (1950).

[53] A. Weissberger, H. Mainz, and E. Strasser, *Ber.,* **62,** 1942 (1929).

species) at near 3000 A have recently been described by Porter and Wright.[54]

Absorption spectra measurements, of course, presume that non-radical species with similar spectra are not present, and such a presumption may lead to difficulties. Thus Marvel et al.[55] have shown that solutions of hexa-(p-ethylphenyl)-ethane remain yellow on standing but entirely lose their paramagnetic properties in a few hours. It is evident that colorimetric methods of radical counting must be used with care. There is, as well, a limit to the sensitivity of the method, depending upon the molecular extinction coefficient of the radicals involved. Assuming optimum conditions, $\log \epsilon = 5$, in a 10-cm cell as little as 10^{-7} molar radical concentrations might be detected, but $\log \epsilon$ values are more commonly in the range of 2–4.

Two recent developments are of particular interest in the application of spectroscopy to the study of organic free radicals and are discussed further in Section 11·1. One is the development of the technique of flash photolysis, notably by Norrish, Porter, and co-workers at Cambridge.[56] If a very intense flash of light is sent through a suitable system, a very high concentration of free radicals may be momentarily produced. With the appropriate equipment, absorption spectra of these radicals may be observed over a period of a few milliseconds, and both the species and their rate of disappearance determined. Although only a limited number of results have been published, the technique seems to offer a great deal of promise.

The second approach involves the study of spectra in glassy media, initiated by Lewis and Kasha.[57] If a wide variety of unsaturated molecules are incorporated in a rigid glass, e.g., a boric acid glass at room temperature or alcohol-hydrocarbon mixtures at liquid air temperature, and then irradiated, radicals are produced which are effectively trapped for long periods (minutes or hours) during which their absorption spectra can be observed. In addition, many unsaturated molecules may be excited to diradical triplet states which show characteristic phosphorescent emission spectra. Recently, Porter and Windsor have even been able to observe these spectra in ordinary

[54] G. Porter and F. J. Wright, *Trans. Faraday Soc.*, **51**, 1469 (1955).

[55] C. S. Marvel, M. B. Mueller, C. M. Himel, and J. F. Kaplan, *J. Am. Chem. Soc.*, **61**, 2771 (1939).

[56] R. G. W. Norrish and G. Porter, *Nature*, **164**, 658 (1949), and subsequent papers.

[57] M. Kasha, *Chem. Revs.*, **41**, 401 (1947).

solutions, where the species have half-lives of 10^{-4} sec, by means of their flash-photolysis technique.[58]

Two final physical measurements which may be used in the study of radicals may be noted briefly. One is the measurement of molecular weight to detect dissociation of molecules into radicals. In the liquid phase, this is limited to rather highly dissociated species such as hexaphenylethane, the usual techniques being by freezing point depression or boiling point elevation of solvents, which will detect dissociation of the order of 5% or greater. In the gas phase, vapor density measurements may be used, the example of iodine having been already mentioned.[5]

A variant of gas-phase molecular weight measurements which is of considerable promise in studying gas-phase radical reactions involves passing the radicals into a mass spectrometer and identifying them by their fragmentation patterns. As an example, Ingold and Lossing have used the technique to follow the rate of recombination of methyl radicals arising from the decomposition of $Hg(CH_3)_2$.[59] The most important application of the mass spectrometer to radical reactions occurring in solution, however, has been in the determination of bond dissociation energies, discussed in the next chapter.

1·4 Structure and Stereochemistry of Radicals

It is appropriate to close this section with some comments on the physical structure and stereochemistry of organic free radicals. The development of quantum mechanical concepts of chemical bonds[60] has given us a clearer idea of the reasons behind the stereochemistry of organic molecules. Thus, the tetrahedral configuration of a saturated carbon atom is associated with an sp^3 hybridization of the orbitals of its bonding electrons, and the planar structure of the ethylene molecule arises from a trigonal sp^2 hybridization. However, quantum mechanics gives no clear-cut answer as to the hybridization and stereochemistry of a simple alkyl radical such as $\cdot CH_3$. Boron halides and alkyls with electron sextets are known to be planar, and extensive evidence shows that carbonium ions (which are isoelectronic with the trialkyl borons) also strongly prefer a planar configuration. On the other hand, in ammonia and amines the config-

[58] G. Porter and M. W. Windsor, *J. Chem. Phys.,* **21**, 2088 (1953).

[59] K. V. Ingold and F. P. Lossing, *J. Chem. Phys.,* **21**, 368 (1953).

[60] A comprehensive discussion which is still intelligible to the non-specialist is given by C. A. Coulsen, *Valence,* Oxford University Press, Oxford, 1952.

uration about nitrogen (which has eight electrons in its outer shell) is that of an (easily inverted) pyramid. Alkyl radicals, with seven electrons, occupy an intermediate position, and their transient existence has so far precluded attempts to determine their structure by the usual methods of spectroscopy, electron diffraction, etc.

Chemical evidence, to date, has also been mainly inconclusive. Production of free radicals by various techniques at asymmetric centers in optically active molecules have generally produced optically inactive products, a result which fails to distinguish between a planar molecule and an easily inverted pyramid (cf. the failure of many workers to resolve unsymmetrically substituted amines). A few cases where optical activity has been preserved through presumed radical processes at an active center, e.g., in the decomposition of 2-methylbutyryl peroxide, Section 10·2c, favor the pyramidal formulation but, as pointed out, may have special explanations.

Similarly, the stereospecificity of certain radical additions to double bonds, Sections 6·2c, 7·1a, and 7·2, are probably determined more by steric hindrance, polar interactions, and the ease of rotation around single bonds than by radical planarity.

In short, chemical evidence appears incapable of distinguishing between a planar radical and a pyramidal one able to undergo inversion during its (usually short) life. The only positive evidence would be the preservation of optical activity by a radical at an asymmetric center, and results to date are still equivocal.

As we have seen in our discussion of paramagnetic resonance spectra, Section 1·2b, the odd electron in *conjugated* radicals is extensively delocalized, a phenomenon which contributes strongly to their resonance stabilization. In the usual resonance picture this should also favor a planar configuration for such conjugated radicals which (taking the benzyl radical as an example) should be hybrids of the sorts of structure [61] shown in eq. 16.

$$ (16) $$

[61] For a similar argument involving resonance stabilization of non-radicals, cf. G. W. Wheland, *Resonance in Organic Chemistry*, John Wiley & Sons, New York, 1955.

Similarly, in the molecular orbital picture of molecular structure, overlap between an odd electron and a neighboring π electron system

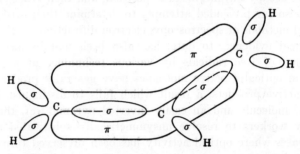

FIG. 1·7   Molecular orbital picture of the structure of the allyl radical
$$CH_2{=}CH{-}\dot{C}H_2.$$

would be favored by sp^2 hybridization and a planar structure, Fig. 1·7. In short, it is quite possible that the nearness to planarity (and perhaps ease of inversion) of a particular radical may depend upon its interaction with neighboring substituents, a topic discussed further in Section 2·3c.

CHAPTER 2

Chemical Reactions of Radicals

Bond Dissociation Energies

2·1   Chemical Reactions of Free Radicals

2·1a   The Classification of Chemical Reactions

The investigations of theoretical organic chemistry in the past twenty-five years have demonstrated that the reactions of organic chemistry, in spite of their manifold forms and complexities, can be broken down into relatively simple steps, involving most commonly only one or two molecular species. Further, these individual steps turn out to be of only a limited number of types. Although it is true that a number of reactions remain stubbornly mysterious, this classification and organization, together with the recognition of the structural characteristics which render the electron shells of molecules susceptible to attack by particular reagents, are undoubtedly both the major objective and the outstanding achievement of this branch of chemistry.

It is now well recognized that these individual reaction steps fall into two, or possibly three; broad classes.

1. *Polar, ionic,* or *heterolytic reactions.* In these, the most familiar class of organic reaction, a bond is formed by one species donating and the other accepting the necessary electron pair. Similarly, in bond breaking, the electron pair remains with one of the fragments. Such reactions encompass the majority of the familiar phenomena of organic chemistry and may be symbolized very generally by a type equation:

$$A: + B \rightleftharpoons A:B \qquad (1)$$

where A: is an electron-donating or *nucleophilic* species, and B is *electrophilic,* or able to accept an electron pair. Mechanisms of such reactions are discussed specifically in a number of books and have been the subject of most organic reaction mechanism studies.[1,2]

2. *Radical* or *homolytic reactions,* in which species with odd electrons are involved. Here, both species donate a single electron to bond-forming processes:

$$A\cdot + B\cdot \rightleftharpoons A\!-\!B$$

It is with such reactions that we are here concerned.

3. *Molecular reactions.* A number of reactions are known in which two or more bonds are formed and broken simultaneously as in the bimolecular decomposition of HI,

$$2HI \rightleftharpoons I_2 + H_2 \qquad (2)$$

[1] E. R. Alexander, *Principles of Ionic Organic Reactions,* John Wiley & Sons, New York, 1950.

[2] C. K. Ingold, *Structure and Mechanism in Organic Chemistry,* Cornell University Press, Ithaca, New York, 1953.

28

It has been suggested that such reactions, characterized in general by bimolecular kinetics and insensitivity to catalysis or major solvent effects, belong in a separate class.[3] In organic chemistry, the Claisen rearrangement and perhaps the Diels-Alder reaction are examples of this group.

Each of these classes, in turn, may be divided into a number of types depending upon the consequences of bond forming and breaking on molecular structure, and we now turn to these typical forms of radical reactions.

2·1b Types of Radical Reactions

It is convenient to classify radical reactions under four general headings:

1. *Radical-Forming Reactions.* (a) *Thermal cleavage of covalent bonds.* The covalent bonds in a number of organic and inorganic molecules are weak enough so that they dissociate more or less rapidly into free radicals at or near room temperature. The case of hexaphenylethane has already been cited, but probably the most useful source of free radicals in solution are the organic peroxides which undergo a ready scission of the relatively weak $O—O$ bond, e.g., for the case of di-t-butyl peroxide:

$$(CH_3)_3C—O—O—C(CH_3)_3 \rightarrow 2(CH_3)_3C—O \cdot \qquad (3)$$

Numerous other examples of such weak bonds are known, organic azo compounds, certain organometallics, disulfides, etc., so that a wide variety of radical sources of this sort are available. At higher temperatures (500–1000°), in fact, even simple hydrocarbon molecules may dissociate, and the reactions of high temperature pyrolyses are, in consequence, essentially radical processes.

(b) *Photochemical cleavage.* The energy associated with a quantum of light, 48 kcal/mole at 6000 A, 96 kcal/mole at 3000 A, is of the same order of magnitude as that of most covalent bonds. Accordingly the energy transferred to a molecule by light absorption is often dissipated through bond rupture. Most of the molecules which are convenient thermal radical sources at slightly elevated temperatures may be induced to dissociate photochemically by near-ultra-

---

[3] P. D. Bartlett in H. Gilman's *Organic Chemistry,* Volume III, John Wiley & Sons, New York, 1953, p. 4.

The term "four center reactions" has also been proposed for these processes, J. Hine, *Physical Organic Chemistry,* McGraw-Hill Book Co., New York, 1956, p. 453.

violet radiation at room temperature or below. In addition, many other molecules which are thermally quite stable are easily dissociated photochemically. Thus biacetyl yields acetyl radicals

$$CH_3CO\text{—}COCH_3 \rightarrow 2CH_3\overset{\displaystyle O}{\overset{\|}{C}}\cdot \tag{4}$$

and halogens are dissociated to halogen atoms.

$$Cl_2 \rightarrow 2Cl\cdot \tag{5}$$

The easy control of such photolyses make them particularly valuable in the study of the kinetics of radical reactions.

(c) *Oxidation-reduction processes.* Numerous (but by no means all) oxidation-reduction processes occur by one electron transfer steps. When organic substrates are involved, organic radicals are produced. Such reactions are both important and varied, examples being the reaction of an organic hydroperoxide with ferrous ion [4]

$$Fe^{++} + ROOH \rightarrow Fe^{+++} + OH^- + R\text{—}O\cdot \tag{6}$$

and of molecular oxygen with the duroquinone dianion.[5]

$$O_2 + \quad\rightarrow\quad + O_2\cdot^- \tag{7}$$

(d) *Other radical-forming processes.* The energy required to dissociate covalent bonds may be supplied in other, if less clear-cut, ways.

Exposure of organic materials to high-energy particles, e.g., α, β, and γ rays, results in the introduction of energy locally far in excess of that associated with ordinary chemical bonds. Although the processes by which such energy is degraded are complex and obscure, a large portion of it goes into a rather indiscriminate breaking of chemical bonds. As a result, the consequences of such exposure are largely radical reactions, although often of a very complicated kind. In some cases, particularly in polymer systems, bonds can

[4] M. S. Kharasch, A. Fono, and W. Nudenberg, *J. Org. Chem.*, **15**, 763 (1950).
[5] T. H. James and A. Weissberger, *J. Am. Chem. Soc.*, **60**, 98 (1938).

apparently be broken by essentially mechanical processes, brought about by very rapid stirring,[6] ultrasonic vibrations,[7] and even osmotic swelling forces.[8]

Finally, there is quite conclusive evidence that, in a few instances, radicals may be produced thermally by polymolecular processes in which the energy required to break some bonds is partially supplied by forming others. Thus, in the purely thermal polymerization of styrene, initial radical formation involves a reaction between at least two, and perhaps three, styrene molecules.[9]

2. *Radical Transformations.* Radicals formed in reactions are frequently unstable in respect to other molecular arrangements of the same atoms and may decompose or rearrange.

(a) *Radical decompositions.* The characteristic radical decomposition is one in which a radical breaks down into a simpler radical and an unsaturated molecule, e.g., in the case of the *t*-butoxy radical formed in eq. 3 above. In general, such decompositions become

$$CH_3-\underset{\underset{CH_3}{|}}{\overset{\overset{CH_3}{|}}{C}}-O\cdot \ \rightarrow \ \cdot CH_3 + CH_3\overset{\overset{O}{\|}}{C}CH_3 \qquad (8)$$

increasingly important as the temperature is raised, and are very important in high-temperature reactions in the gas phase.

(b) *Radical rearrangements.* Rather than coming apart, radicals may rearrange to more stable structure, as an example:[10]

$$\phi_3C-\dot{C}H_2 \ \rightarrow \ \phi_2\dot{C}-CH_2\phi \qquad (9)$$

Such rearrangements have not been extensively investigated, but aromatic nuclei and halogen atoms appear to be most commonly involved in the migrations.

3. *Radical Attack on Substrates.* (a) *Radical additions.* Free radicals characteristically attack the π electrons of unsaturated systems to form new radicals, e.g.,

$$Br\cdot + CH_2{=}CH-CH_3 \ \rightarrow \ Br-CH_2-\dot{C}H-CH_3 \qquad (10)$$

[6] P. Alexander and M. Fox, *J. Polymer Sci.,* **12,** 533 (1954).

[7] G. Schmid and O. Rommel, *Z. physik. Chem.,* **A185,** 98 (1940).

[8] The continued growth of certain polymer gels (cf. Chapter 5) may be brought about by bond rupture through such swelling forces.

[9] F. R. Mayo, *J. Am. Chem. Soc.,* **75,** 6133 (1953).

[10] D. Y. Curtin and M. D. Hurwitz, *ibid.,* **74,** 5381 (1952).

An important property of such additions is that they are frequently *reversible,* the reverse being a radical decomposition analogous to eq. 8. Such reversibility often leads to important consequences.

(*b*) *Radical displacements* are another characteristic form of attack, e.g.,

$$CCl_3CH_2CH_2 \cdot + Cl\text{—}CCl_3 \rightarrow CCl_3CH_2\text{—}CH_2Cl + \cdot CCl_3 \quad (11)$$

We may note that, whereas polar displacements are commonly on carbon atoms in the center of molecules, with a resulting Walden inversion of the molecule, radical displacements are typically on the peripheral atoms, particularly univalent hydrogen or halogen as in the example given. A number of displacements on divalent atoms are known, but there are very few apparent examples of radical displacements on carbon.

(*c*) *More complex attacks.* It has been proposed that some radical-substrate reactions may involve more than two molecules in the transition state,[11] and it appears that a few radical-substrate reactions exist which do not fit clearly into *a* and *b* above.

4. *Radical-Destroying Processes.* (*a*) *Radical combination or coupling.* The reverse of the dissociation of a covalent bond into two radicals is the combination of two radicals to form a bond. As the driving force for such reactions is large, being the energy of bond formation (up to 100 kcal/mole), such combinations are characteristic of almost all radicals with which we are concerned and occur with great rapidity. In the gas phase, methyl radicals combine at almost every collision [12] by the reaction

$$2 \cdot CH_3 \rightarrow C_2H_6 \quad (12)$$

and in solution, rates of typical radical combinations vary from the velocity of diffusion down to reactions with rate constants of the order of 10^6 liters/mole/sec. In fact, even in the case of triphenylmethyl, which is appreciably dissociated at equilibrium, the equilibrium is very mobile with a rate constant for combination of about 200 liters/sec.[13]

(*b*) *Radical disproportionation.* In spite of the rapidity of radical coupling, a competing reaction which is sometimes of importance is that of disproportionation into saturated and unsaturated mole-

[11] G. S. Hammond and A. Ravve, *ibid.,* **73,** 1891 (1951).

[12] R. Gomer and G. B. Kistiakowsky, *J. Chem. Phys.,* **19,** 85 (1951).

[13] Calculated from measured equilibria and rates of dissociation of hexaphenylethane.

cules. Thus, reaction 13 is found [14] to take two paths, in about the proportions indicated. In general, coupling appears to be favored,

$$
2 \underset{CH_3}{\overset{CH_3}{\underset{\diagdown}{\diagup}}} C \cdot
\quad
\begin{cases}
\xrightarrow{\sim 60\%} & \underset{CH_3\ \ CH_3}{\overset{CH_3\ \ CH_3}{CH_3OCOC \!-\!\!-\! CCOOCH_3}} \\[2em]
\xrightarrow{\sim 40\%} & \underset{CH_3}{\overset{CH_3}{CH_2\!\!=\!\!C\!-\!COOCH_3}} + \underset{CH_3}{\overset{}{CH_3\!-\!CHCOOCH_3}}
\end{cases}
\tag{13}
$$

but there is dispute as to the relative importance of the two processes in a number of cases.

(c) *Oxidation-reduction reactions.* Just as radicals may be formed by one-electron transfer processes, they may similarly be destroyed. Thus, eq. 6 is frequently followed by

$$
R\!-\!O \cdot + Fe^{++} \rightarrow R\!-\!O^- + Fe^{+++} \tag{14}
$$

unless some competing process intervenes. The avoidance of such radical destruction processes is an important problem in the use of oxidation-reduction systems to produce free radicals.

2·1c Sequences and Chains of Radical Reactions

In the study of both polar and radical reactions, an overall experimental observation often turns out to be the consequence of a whole series of reaction steps. In radical reactions this is almost necessarily so, for, where radicals exist only as transient intermediates in going from one stable substance to another, both radical-forming and radical-destroying reactions must be involved, between which additional steps may also be sandwiched. A typical example is the gas-phase decomposition of di-t-butyl peroxide, in which the chief products are ethane and acetone,[15] formed by the sequence of reactions 4, 8, and 12 already mentioned. Obviously a great number of such combinations of type steps are possible. In practice, sequences may involve both polar and radical reactions combined, as in the thermal decomposition of benzoyl peroxide in the presence of iodine investi-

---

[14] A. F. Bickel and W. A. Waters, *Rec. trav. chim.*, **69**, 312 (1950).

[15] J. H. Raley, F. F. Rust, and W. E. Vaughan, *J. Am. Chem. Soc.*, **70**, 88, 1336 (1948).

gated by Hammond.[16] Benzoyl hypoiodite is formed by a radical reaction, but the products isolated are the results of its subsequent polar decomposition. In fact, to take a supremely complicated example, combinations of radical and polar steps have been suggested for certain enzyme reactions.[17]

The most interesting and important sequences to us here are those involving radical-substrate reactions. There are two reasons for this. First, substances which react with radicals are a much larger class than materials which readily produce radicals, so that such processes greatly extend the range of radical reactions. Second, attack of a radical on a substrate transfers an odd electron to a new site, rather than destroying it by pairing, and the new radical produced may in turn attack another substrate. In short, such sequences may be strung together into long chains and a single radical lead to the reactions of hundreds or thousands of molecules. Such *radical chain reactions* are undoubtedly the most important group of radical reactions in solution, both because of their synthetic utility and because of the information they give about radical processes and radical kinetics. Accordingly they will receive particular attention in the next few chapters.

The radical-substrate reactions which make up the propagation steps in our radical chain reactions commonly occur in typical sequences, giving rise to specific types of product as follows.

Successive addition reactions to unsaturated molecules produce long chains of covalently bonded atoms and are the propagation step in radical polymerizations.

$$-CH_2-\underset{\underset{H}{|}}{\overset{\overset{R}{|}}{C}}\cdot + CH_2{=}\underset{\underset{H}{|}}{\overset{\overset{R}{|}}{C}} \rightarrow -CH_2-\underset{\underset{H}{|}}{\overset{\overset{R}{|}}{C}}-CH_2-\underset{\underset{H}{|}}{\overset{\overset{R}{|}}{C}}\cdot \qquad (15)$$

Successive displacement reactions lead to substitution reactions, as in the side-chain halogenation of toluene.[18]

$$Br\cdot + HCH_2\phi \rightarrow H-Br + \cdot CH_2\phi \qquad (16)$$

$$Br-Br + \cdot CH_2\phi \rightarrow Br\cdot + BrCH_2\phi \qquad (17)$$

[16] G. S. Hammond, *ibid.*, **72**, 3737 (1950); G. S. Hammond and L. M. Soffer, *ibid.*, **72**, 4711 (1950).

[17] W. A. Waters, *The Chemistry of Free Radicals*, second edition, Oxford, 1948, Chapter XII.

[18] M. S. Kharasch, P. C. White, and F. R. Mayo, *J. Org. Chem.*, **3**, 33 (1938).

Here, obviously two different displacement reactions must occur alternately if there is to be any difference between products and reactants.

Alternate displacement and addition reactions are involved in radical additions to double bonds. Thus the "abnormal" or radical addition of hydrogen bromide to an olefin involves the alternate propagation steps.

$$Br\cdot + CH_2\!\!=\!\!CH\!\!-\!\!CH_3 \rightarrow BrCH_2\!\!-\!\!\overset{\cdot}{C}H\!\!-\!\!CH_3 \qquad (18)$$

$$BrCH_2\!\!-\!\!\overset{\cdot}{C}H\!\!-\!\!CH_3 + H\!\!-\!\!Br \rightarrow BrCH_2\!\!-\!\!CH_2\!\!-\!\!CH_3 + Br\cdot \qquad (19)$$

Radical decompositions and rearrangements may also be involved in radical chain processes. The decomposition to trimethylacetaldehyde to isobutane and carbon monoxide,[19] for example, proceeds via the steps:

$$(CH_3)_3C\cdot + H\!\!-\!\!COC(CH_3)_3 \rightarrow (CH_3)_3CH + (CH_3)_3C\!\!-\!\!\overset{\cdot}{C}O$$
$$(CH_3)_3C\!\!-\!\!\overset{\cdot}{C}O \rightarrow (CH_3)_3C\cdot + CO \qquad (20)$$

Such chains, incidently, are of particular interest, and often lead to quite complex products, a striking example being the reaction of diazomethane and carbon tetrachloride to yield pentaerithrytol tetrachloride described by Urry,[20] in which an eight-step cycle of reactions is repeated.

2·1d Some General Characteristics of Radical Reactions

Having reached this point, it may be a good idea to summarize some of the properties of radical reactions which are useful both in identifying radical processes and choosing experimental conditions for carrying them out.

1. Since (with the exception of some oxidation-reduction systems) the intermediates in radical reactions are non-ionic and not highly polarized, radical reactions turn out to be generally insensitive to the ionizing power of solvents, and in fact (as has been mentioned) occur very similarly in the liquid and gas phase. In this connection, the statement that radical reactions occur in non-polar solvents, although generally correct, nowise implies that they fail to take place in polar, ionizing solvents including water. However, non-polar solvents are sometimes preferred media, e.g., in the study of halogenation reactions, since they tend to suppress competing polar processes.

[19] J. B. Conant, C. N. Webb, and W. C. Mendum, *J. Am. Chem. Soc.*, **51**, 1246 (1929).

[20] W. F. Urry and J. R. Eiszner, *ibid.*, **74**, 5822 (1952).

2. In contrast to many polar reactions, radical processes (again excepting certain oxidation-reduction systems) rarely show catalysis by acids or bases. On the other hand, acceleration by light is almost invariably an indication of a radical process, the quantum efficiency indicating whether or not a chain process is involved. Similarly, acceleration by typical radical sources (peroxides, etc.) is reliably taken as evidence for a radical chain process.

3. Since, in a radical chain reaction, formation of a single radical normally leads to the reaction of a large number of molecules, anything which is capable of interrupting the chain will lead to a decrease in reaction rate or even a virtual halt in the reaction. A number of such characteristic interrupters (termed *inhibitors* or *retarders*, depending upon their effectiveness) are known. In general they are either stable free radicals, e.g., nitric oxide or diphenylpicrylhydrazyl, or non-radical substrates which react readily with free radicals to yield other radicals which are too unreactive to propagate a chain. Typical are benzoquinone, sulfur, and aromatic polynitro compounds, although the effectiveness of an inhibitor varies markedly with the system in which it is employed. Such inhibitors are important both in the study of radical chains and in suppressing unwanted radical reactions.

2·2   Rates and Energetics of Radical Reactions

The products actually obtained in a chemical reaction are the result of the relative rates of a number of possible competing reactions. In organic chemistry it is a common experience that these rates lie close enough together so that a mixture of products is obtained, and, further, the composition of this mixture may be profoundly influenced by apparently trivial changes in reaction conditions. This generalization is certainly true of radical reactions, and, accordingly, in this book we will give much attention to kinetics, and the factors affecting these competing rates, particularly in radical chain reactions. It has been remarked that chemists often forget that the laws of mass action apply to chemical synthesis as well as in investigations of mechanism.

2·2a   The Time Schedule of Radical Processes

The kinetics of radical chain reactions will be treated in detail in the next and succeeding chapters. However, it is reasonable to say that the dominant characteristic of the chain processes with which we are concerned is the universal presence of extremely rapid radi-cal-destroying processes. Thus, to take a hypothetical but typical example of a reaction in which radicals are produced at a rate of 2×10^{-8} moles/liter/sec (about the rate observed in a 5×10^{-3} molar solution of benzoyl peroxide at 60°C) and subsequently disap-pear by bimolecular coupling with a rate constant of 10^7 liter/mole/sec, simple calculation shows that the radical concentration in such a system is 3.3×10^{-8} molar, and the average lifetime of a free radical is about 1.65 sec.

The very low radical concentration illustrates why extraordinarily sensitive techniques would be required to detect free radicals in such systems, and the radical lifetime points up what we may call the rigid *time schedule of radical chain processes*. Obviously, if a chain process of 2000 steps were to occur in such a system, individual re-actions would have to follow each other at intervals of less than 10^{-3} sec, corresponding, for a 1-molar reactant, to a rate constant of 10^3 liter/mole/sec. Although radical lifetimes can be somewhat lengthened, and we can put up with somewhat shorter chains, it is plain that our consideration of radical-substrate reactions will be perforce restricted to fast reactions and competition between fast reactions, all of which have necessarily numerically large rate con-stants (>1 liter/mole/sec), if we are going to observe chains at all.

2·2b   Rates and Activation Energies of Radical Reactions

So much has been written about the theory of reaction rates and the relation of rate and activation energy that the subject, being very familiar to most readers,[21] needs only a brief introduction. As energy required to bring about chemical reactions is normally sup-plied by the kinetic energy of the molecules in the system, the rela-tion between this energy and the rate constant for a reaction may be expressed in terms of one of two equations.

$$k = PZe^{-E/RT} \qquad (21)$$

$$k = \frac{\kappa T}{h} e^{\Delta S\ddagger/R} e^{-\Delta H\ddagger/R} \qquad (22)$$

The first is derived from the kinetic theory of gases and the second from transition-state theory. Both equations divide the rate constant

---

[21] Good recent reviews are given by A. A. Frost and R. G. Pearson, *Kinetics and Mechanism,* John Wiley & Sons, New York, 1953, and by R. Livingston, *Technique of Organic Chemistry,* Volume VIII, S. L. Friess and A. Weissberger, editors, Interscience Publishers, New York, 1953.

into two parts. One is a temperature-dependent term containing the "activation energy" E, or the essentially equivalent quantity $\Delta H^{\ddagger}$, the "heat of activation," and representing the fraction of molecules at any instant possessing the necessary energy for reaction. The other portion of the rate constant is an almost temperature-independent term which, in the collision theory, consists of the collision number Z and the probability P that a collision of molecules with sufficient energy will lead to reaction. In the transition-state theory this term is divided into the quantity $\kappa T/h$ (6×10^{12} at room temperature), about equal to Z,[22] and an exponential containing the entropy of activation, $\Delta S^{\ddagger}$. It is evident that negative values of $\Delta S^{\ddagger}$ correspond to small values of P.

The advantage of the transition-state theory is that it relates a rate process to an equilibrium one (the equilibrium between reactants and transition state) susceptible, at least in principle, to thermodynamic and statistical mechanical treatment. Accordingly, it is sometimes possible to draw plausible conclusions in regard to $\Delta S^{\ddagger}$ and the temperature-independent factor in the rate expression.[23]

Among radical reactions, unimolecular thermal dissociations commonly show "normal" PZ factors of 10^{10}–10^{12}. However, other radical reactions often show rather small PZ factors, 10^{6}–10^{9}. The origin of these small values, corresponding to values of $\Delta S^{\ddagger}$ of -20 to -34 entropy units (cal/degree/mole), has been ascribed[24] to the "forbidden" nature of the electron pairing and unpairing processes involved. However, in many cases they may arise for precisely the same reason that many non-radical processes show large negative values of $\Delta S^{\ddagger}$, namely that a rigid transition state is involved which has lost many of the degrees of freedom formerly available to the reactants. In fact, in most cases this seems the preferred explanation. Individual examples of such low PZ factors will appear in later chapters.

[22] Since $\kappa T/h$ is proportional to T and, from the kinetic theory of gases, Z varies with $T^{1/2}$, it is evident that $\Delta H^{\ddagger}$ and E are not quite equivalent. However, the difference is smaller than the precision of most experimental determinations, and we shall use the terms interchangeably.

[23] Often it is not, and calculation of $\Delta S^{\ddagger}$ and $\Delta H^{\ddagger}$ from experimental data amounts to nothing more than an erudite method of describing empirical temperature dependence of k. Some of the difficulties in untangling the contribution of factors to the $\Delta S^{\ddagger}$ and $\Delta H^{\ddagger}$ terms in eq. 22 have been admirably pointed out by L. P. Hammett, *Physical Organic Chemistry*, McGraw-Hill Book Co., New York, 1941, Chapter VII.

[24] J. L. Magee, W. Shand, and H. Eyring, *J. Am. Chem. Soc.*, **63**, 644 (1941).

The major variable, however, in producing the wide range of rate constants observed in chemical reactions, is the activation energy. In rapid radical reactions, it is evident that this activation energy must be small (<15 kcal) and must lie far below the energies required to dissociate the chemical bonds involved (60–100 kcal). The basic explanation of such a phenomenon is that the driving force required to break one bond is in large part supplied by the energy

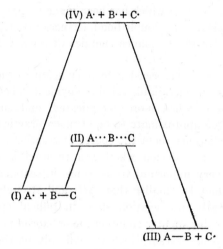

Fig. 2·1   Energy diagram for radical displacement process A· + B—C → A—B + C·.

liberated in forming another.   For a bimolecular displacement the situation may be symbolized as

$$A· + B—C \rightleftharpoons A···B···C \rightleftharpoons A—B + ·C \qquad (23)$$

where A···B···C represents the *transition state* in which B is partially bonded to both A and C and the reaction has been indicated as reversible for purposes of discussion below.

Energetically, the situation is depicted in Fig. 2·1 where II − I represents the activation energy of the forward process, IV − I the dissociation energy of the B—C bond, and III − I the heat of reaction ΔH.

Many efforts have been made to predict the magnitude of the activation energy in such processes in terms of the dissociation energies of the bonds involved.   A much-quoted example are the Hirschfelder rules,[25] which predict that the activation energy for an *exothermic* reaction such as 23 taken in the forward direction (as indicated in Fig. 2·1) will be about 5.5% of the energy required to break the B—C bond, i.e., 5.5% of IV − I. For an *endothermic* process in which the products contain more energy than the reactants, e.g., the back reaction of 23, it will be the energy change in the overall reaction plus 5.5% of the strength of the bond broken, i.e., I − III + 0.055 (IV − III).

Another generalization which has been made is that, for the attack of a series of radicals on a double bond, changes in activation energies are proportional to the resonance energies of the attacking radicals, multiplied by a constant $\alpha \cong 0.4$.[26]

Although we will have occasion to refer again to such treatments, the more data become available the more evident it becomes that the actual situation is much more complicated, and such theoretical treatments are too approximate to be of much practical use in making detailed predictions about the course of reactions.

Nevertheless, the question whether a reaction is exothermic or endothermic is very important to us, since, inescapably, the activation energy cannot be smaller than ΔH, and strongly endothermic processes cannot be propagation steps in radical chain reactions. Whether a particular slightly endothermic or exothermic process may be such a step, is a question which we will only partially be able to unravel in the course of this book.

Referring again to Fig. 2·1, we see that III − I = (IV − I) − (IV − III); ΔH is given by the difference in the dissociation energies of the B—C and A—B bonds. Evidently, the problem of bond dissociation energies is of critical importance in radical chemistry, and it will be our next topic of discussion.

2·3   Bond Dissociation Energies

2·3a   *Definition*

The importance of bond dissociation energies has long been recognized, but their accurate measurement has presented a particularly knotty problem which is only now approaching a satisfactory solution. The considerations involved have recently been treated in

[25] J. Hirschfelder, *J. Chem. Phys.,* **9,** 645 (1941).
[26] M. G. Evans, J. Gergely, and E. C. Seaman, *J. Polymer Sci.,* **3,** 866 (1948).

detail by Cottrell,[27] who also gives a critical discussion of available data upon which much of this section is based. An earlier review by Szwarc [28] is also available.

One difficulty in treating bond dissociation energies arises because, in polyatomic molecules, two related quantities exist which must be distinguished. If one selects a molecule such as methane, we may imagine a process by which it is, as it were, expanded into a gaseous carbon atom and four hydrogen atoms:

$$CH_4 \rightarrow C + 4 \cdot H \tag{24}$$

and we may associate one-quarter of the energy involved in such a process with each C—H bond. This quantity is at present usually referred to as the C—H *bond strength* or *average bond strength* in methane and is important in the quantum mechanical treatment of the electronic binding energy of molecules. In more complicated molecules, however, its exact meaning becomes somewhat indefinite.[29]

An alternative process would be the dissociation of a single C—H bond to give gaseous fragments

$$CH_4 \rightarrow \cdot CH_3 + H \cdot \tag{25}$$

and the energy associated with it is the *bond dissociation energy*, conveniently symbolized as $D(CH_3—H)$. It is with this latter quantity that we are obviously concerned here. With diatomic molecules, the two processes are identical, but in polyatomic molecules they may (and often do) differ significantly in energy. Unfortunately, this difference has often been overlooked. In fact, the early extensive table given by Pauling [30] is still occasionally used in discussions of radical reactions, in spite of the fact that they refer to bond strengths (as defined here) many of which, indeed, have had to receive subsequent revision.[27, 31]

Another factor which must be kept in mind in discussing bond dissociation energies is that, for theoretical purposes, the process should be that occurring at $0°K$ in the gas phase at zero pressure. In prac-

[27] T. L. Cottrell, *The Strength of Chemical Bonds*, Butterworth, London, 1954.

[28] M. Szwarc, *Chem. Revs.*, **47**, 75 (1950).

[29] M. G. Evans and M. Szwarc, *J. Chem. Phys.*, **18**, 618 (1950).

[30] L. Pauling, *The Nature of the Chemical Bond*, Cornell University Press, Ithaca, N. Y., 1939.

[31] A revised table is given by K. S. Pitzer, *J. Am. Chem. Soc.*, **70**, 2140 (1948).

tice, of course, measurements are made under different conditions, and, in general, dissociation energies are 1–2 kcal/mole higher at ordinary temperatures. The reason for this is that, in the dissociation process, the products lose degrees of freedom and have lower heat capacities than the undissociated molecules. For our purposes, actually, it is more convenient to employ dissociation energies at ordinary temperatures (25°C), and we shall do so in this book, although the correction is, more often than not, smaller than the experimental errors in determining D's.

2·3b The Measurement of Bond Dissociation Energies

A number of techniques for determining bond dissociation energies, such as measuring the temperature coefficient of a dissociation equilibrium constant or spectroscopic measurements on diatomic molecules,[32] have been available for some time. Unfortunately, they are not applicable to most of the bonds of interest to the organic chemist, and, in recent years, new techniques have had to be devised.

One of these is essentially chemical and involves the measurement of the activation energies for the forward and backward processes in a radical displacement reaction. The classical example is the determination of $D(CH_3—H)$ for methane by Kistiakowsky and his associates [33–35] by measuring activation energies for the reactions

$$CH_4 + Br\cdot \rightarrow \cdot CH_3 + HBr \quad E = 17.8 \text{ kcal/mole} \quad (26)$$

$$\cdot CH_3 + HBr \rightarrow CH_4 + Br\cdot \quad E = 2.0 \text{ kcal/mole} \quad (27)$$

The energetics of such a system correspond to the situation shown in Fig. 2·1, and it is evident that ΔH for reaction 26 is given by the difference in the two activation energies, namely, 15.8 kcal/mole.

Reaction 26 may be realized by an alternative path,

$$CH_4 \rightarrow CH_3\cdot + H\cdot \quad (\Delta H = 102.8) \quad (28)$$

$$H\cdot + Br\cdot \rightarrow HBr \quad (\Delta H = -87.0) \quad (29)$$

$$\overline{CH_4 + Br\cdot \rightarrow \cdot CH_3 + HBr \quad \Delta H = 15.8} \quad (30)$$

[32] A comprehensive review of this topic is given by A. G. Gaydon, *Dissociation Energies and Spectra of Diatomic Molecules,* Chapman & Hall, London, 1950.

[33] H. C. Andersen, G. B. Kistiakowsky, and E. R. Van Artsdalen, *J. Chem. Phys.,* **10,** 305 (1942).

[34] H. C. Andersen and G. B. Kistiakowsky, *ibid.,* **11,** 6 (1943).

[35] E. R. Van Artsdalen and G. B. Kistiakowsky, *ibid.,* **12,** 28 (1944).

so, as ΔH for reaction 29 is known from spectroscopic data, ΔH for reaction 28, i.e., $D(CH_3-H)$, is obtained by Hess's law as 102.8 kcal/mole. Kistiakowsky's measurements were carried out in the neighborhood of 180°; the corresponding value at 25°C is 102 kcal/mole. A number of other C—H dissociation energies have subsequently been measured by the same technique.[36]

Once a direct measurement of a dissociation energy is available, related quantities may be obtained by thermochemical calculations. For this purpose, tabulated values of heats of formation are convenient.[37] By convention, heats of formation, ΔH_f, of substances are referred to the elements in their normal state at 25°C at 1 atmosphere pressure, and this must be kept in mind when such tabulations are used. Thus, the heat of formation of the methyl radical (at 25°C) is obtained from the cycle

$$\Delta H, \text{ kcal/mole}$$

$$CH_4 \rightarrow \cdot CH_3 + \cdot H \qquad\qquad 102 \qquad\qquad (28)$$

$$\cdot CH_3 \rightarrow C\ (s.) + \tfrac{3}{2}H_2\ (g.) \qquad 32. \qquad\qquad (31)$$

$$H\cdot \rightarrow \tfrac{1}{2}H_2\ (g.) \qquad\qquad -52 \qquad\qquad (32)$$

$$CH_4 \rightarrow C\ (s.) + 2H_2\ (g.) \qquad 82 \qquad\qquad (33)$$

ΔH for reaction 32 appears in such a tabulation as $-\Delta H_f$ for a gaseous hydrogen atom, and ΔH for reaction 33 as $-\Delta H_f$ for methane. Since ΔH for reaction 28 has been measured, $-\Delta H_f$ for the methyl radical is obtained as 32 kcal/mole. The values of ΔH_f for H· and CH_4 were obtained respectively by spectroscopy and by heat of combustion measurements.

Calculation of the dissociation energy for any CH_3-X bond for which the heats of formation of ·X and CH_3X are known proceeds as follows for methyl chloride:

$$
\begin{aligned}
D(CH_3-Cl) &= 80.6 \text{ kcal/mole} \\
-\Delta H_f\ CH_3\cdot &= -32.0 \\
-\Delta H_f\ Cl\cdot &= -29.0 \\
\hline
-\Delta H_f\ CH_3Cl &= 19.6
\end{aligned}
\qquad (34)
$$

[36] B. H. Eckstein, H. A. Scheraga, and E. R. Van Artsdalen, *ibid.*, **22**, 28 (1954).

[37] For this purpose the tabulation of F. D. Rossini et al., "Selected Values of Thermodynamic Properties," *Nat. Bur. Standards U.S. Cir.* 500, 1952, have been used in this book.

Similarly the dissociation energy of the C—C bond of ethane may be obtained

$$D(CH_3—CH_3) = 84.2$$
$$2\Delta H_f \cdot CH_3 = -64.0 \tag{35}$$

$$\overline{}$$

$$-\Delta H_f \; C_2H_6 = 20.2$$

A modification of the chemical method, and in principle the most direct method of all, is to measure the activation energy for the thermal cleavage of a particular chemical bond in a molecule, making the assumption that the reverse reaction has an activation energy of zero as in the case of the recombination of methyl radicals.[12] For simple organic molecules, this assumption is probably valid. Nevertheless, the actual experiments are difficult to carry out. Very high temperatures (up to 800–900°C) are required, and in every case it is necessary to establish that the expected bond is undergoing scission, that one is dealing with a truly homogeneous unimolecular decomposition, and that no subsequent chain processes are being set up. The most successful measurements of this sort have been carried out by Szwarc and his collaborators.[28, 38] In their technique, pyrolyses are carried out in the presence of large excesses of toluene vapor which react rapidly with the resulting radical fragments to yield benzyl radicals. These subsequently dimerize without introducing kinetic complications. By this means, dissociation constants for a considerable number of bonds (chiefly C—H and C—halogen) have been determined, with results which are self-consistent and usually agree well with dissociation energies measured by other means when these are available. Figure 2·2 shows a typical plot of log k versus $1/T$ for toluene and the three xylenes from which dissociation energies may be calculated.[38]

A quite different and independent means of determining dissociation energies is the *electron impact method* and involves the behavior of molecules in a mass spectrometer.[39] When molecules at low pressures in the gas phase are bombarded with electrons, they are broken up into charged and uncharged fragments, and the mass spectrometer is essentially an instrument for determining the rela-

---

[38] M. Szwarc, *Nature*, **160**, 403 (1947), and subsequent papers.

[39] A good discussion of this method is given by Cottrell, Chapter 5 of the reference cited in footnote 27.

tive number of these particles of any particular charge per mass ratio by passing them through suitable electric and magnetic fields.[40] If, in such an instrument, the energy of the bombarding electrons is gradually increased, any particular charged species is first observed at a characteristic *appearance potential*, and its concentration in-

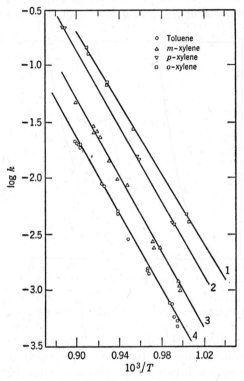

Fɪɢ. 2·2 Determination of $D(R—H)$ from pyrolysis data (after Szwarc [38]).

creases from that point on. Thus, in the mass spectra of methane, the first appearance of CH_3^+ corresponds to the reaction

$$CH_4 + e \rightarrow CH_3^+ + H\cdot + 2e \qquad (36)$$

[40] In recent years, mass spectrometers have been greatly refined in precision and utility, and they find extensive application in chemistry, particularly for analytical purposes: cf. D. W. Stewart, "Mass Spectrometry," in *Physical Methods in Organic Chemistry*, Volume I, Part II, A. Weissberger, editor, Interscience Publishers, New York, 1946; G. P. Barnard, *Modern Mass Spectrometry*, The Institute of Physics, London, 1953.

and there is evidently a relation between the measured appearance potential of $CH_3{}^+$ and ΔH for reaction 36. Two uncertainties must be disposed of before this measured appearance potential can be taken as ΔH for the reaction. The first is experimental and involves the difficulty in extrapolating the instrumental observations back to the first appearance of $CH_3{}^+$. Thus, Fig. 2·3 represents a typical plot of experimental data,[41] and it is evident that there is some un-

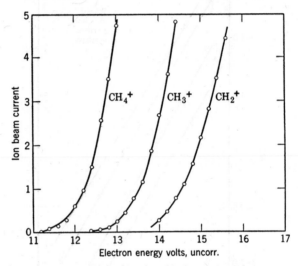

FIG. 2·3   Appearance potential plots for the formation of $CH_4{}^+$, $CH_3{}^+$, and $CH_2{}^+$ from methane (after McDowell and Warren [41]).

certainty as to the exact value of the appearance potential. The second uncertainty is that, for the appearance potential to be actually ΔH for the reaction involved, the products must be left with no excess kinetic energy, or otherwise the calculated ΔH will be too large. It is evident that appearance potentials thus give maximum possible values for the ΔH's of the corresponding processes, although it now appears that in many instances this excess energy is negligible.

In order to get from appearance potentials to bond dissociation energies, a *direct* [42] and an *indirect* [43] method are available. For the determination of $D(CH_3{-}H)$ by the direct method, the appearance potential of $CH_3{}^+$ is measured for methane, and for a system known

[41] C. A. McDowell and J. W. Warren, *Discussions Faraday Soc.*, **10**, 53 (1951).

[42] J. A. Hipple and D. P. Stevenson, *Phys. Rev.*, **63**, 121 (1943).

[43] D. P. Stevenson, *J. Chem. Phys.*, **10**, 291 (1942).

to contain methyl radicals. $D(CH_3—H)$ is then obtained by the cycle

$$CH_4 \rightarrow \cdot CH_3 + H \cdot$$
$$CH_3 \cdot + e \rightarrow CH_3^+ + 2e \qquad (37)$$

$$\overline{CH_4 + e \rightarrow CH_3^+ + H \cdot + 2e}$$

The indirect method involves combining heats of formation with appearance potentials as in the following cycle:

$$CH_4 \rightarrow \cdot CH_3 + H \cdot$$
$$2H \cdot \rightarrow H_2$$
$$2H_2 + C \text{ (s.)} \rightarrow CH_4$$
$$3H_2 + 2C \text{ (s.)} \rightarrow C_2H_6 \qquad (38)$$
$$C_3H_8 \rightarrow 4H_2 + 3C \text{ (s.)}$$
$$C_2H_6 + e \rightarrow C_2H_5^+ + H \cdot + 2e$$

$$\overline{C_3H_8 + e \rightarrow C_2H_5^+ + \cdot CH_3 + 2e}$$

A number of similar combinations are possible, and, in fact, a total of eight independent electron impact determinations give $D(CH_3—H)$ as 102 ± 1 kcal/mole [44] in excellent agreement with the chemical method. It should be noted that, in such calculations, appearance potentials are expressed in electron volts per molecule, and must be converted to kcal per mole, 1 ev $= 23.06$ kcal.

2·3c   Values of Bond Dissociation Energies

Tables 2·1–2·3 summarize available data on bond dissociation energies for molecules of the types involved in organic free radical reactions, taken, in general, from the reviews of Szwarc,[28] and Cottrell,[27] and the thermochemical tables of Rossini et al.[37]   One change has been made, however, from the usual tabulations in that, where differences are significant, values are given for 25°C, rather than the more abstract 0°K.   Even so, it should be kept in mind that they refer to gas-phase processes, so some unknown (but probably small) correction should be made in applying them, as we must, to liquid-phase reactions.   Table 2·1 lists dissociation energies for a variety of inorganic molecules, arranged in order of increasing atomic number.   Dissociation energies which are considered reliable (± 1–3 kcal) are printed without parentheses.   Those with parentheses are less certain.   Methods of measurement are indicated as spectroscopic (S.), electron impact (El.), kinetic measurements (K.), equi-

[44] D. P. Stevenson, *Discussions Faraday Soc.*, **10**, 35 (1951).

TABLE 2·1   DISSOCIATION ENERGIES FOR INORGANIC MOLECULES IN KCAL/MOLE AT 25°C

Bond	D	Method [a]	Bond	D	Method [a]	Bond	D	Method [a]
H—H	104.2	S.[27]	O_2N—NO_2	13	Eq.[27]	PBr_2—Br	(69)	(B.E.) [27]
BF_2—F	(153)	(B.E.) [27]	ON—O	73	T.[27]	S_n—S_m	33.4[c]	Eq.[45c]
BCl_2—Cl	(103)	(B.E.) [27]	ON—Cl	37	Eq.[28]	HS—SH	(80.4)	El.[45]
BBr_2—Br	(81)	(B.E.) [27]	O_2N—Cl	30	K [45a]	ClS_2—Cl	(71)	(B.E.) [27]
NH_2—H	102	K., T.[28]	ON—Br	28	Eq.[28]	Cl—Cl	58.0	S.[37]
HO—H	120	S., T.[37]	O=O	118.2	S.[27]	$TiCl_3$—Cl	(112)	(B.E.) [27]
HOO—H	89.5	El.[45b]	HO—OH	52	T.[37]	$AsCl_2$—Cl	(77)	(B.E.) [27]
F—H	135	T.[27]	PCl_3—O	122	T.[27]	Br—Cl	52	T.[27]
SiH_3—H	(84)	(B.E.) [27]	HO—Cl	60	T.[27]	$SnCl_3$—Cl	(84)	(B.E.) [27]
PH_2—H	(85)	(B.E.) [27]	HO—Br	56	T.[27]	I—Cl	50	S.[27]
HS—H	(90)	El.[45]	HO—I	56	T.[27]	Hg—Cl	80.5	T.[27]
Cl—H	103.2	S., T.[37]	F—F	37	S.[27,b]	ClHg—Cl	23	S.[27]
AsH_2—H	(65)	(B.E.) [27]	F—Cl	60.5	S.[27]	$BiCl_2$—Cl	(74)	(B.E.) [27]
HSe—H	(72)	(B.E.) [27]	Si—O (silica)	(114)	(B.E.) [27]	Se—Se (Se_6)	(45)	(B.E.) [27]
Br—H	87.4	S., T.[37]	$SiCl_3$—Cl	(96)	(B.E.) [27]	Br—Br	46.1	S.[37]
I—H	71.4	S., T.[37]	$SiBr_3$—Br	(77)	(B.E.) [27]	Br—I	42	S.[27]
N_2	171	S.[27]	P—P(P_4)	(53)	(B.E.) [27]	I—I	36.1	S.[37]
H_2N—NH_2	60	K.[28]	PCl_2—Cl	(87)	(B.E.) [27]			

[a] See text.
[b] This is a significant revision of the earlier value (63.5 kcal).
[c] In molten sulfur.

[45] J. L. Franklin and H. E. Lumpkin, *J. Am. Chem. Soc.*, 74, 1023 (1952).
[45a] H. F. Cordes and H. S. Johnston, *ibid.*, 76, 4269 (1954).
[45b] S. N. Foner and R. L. Hudson, *J. Chem. Phys.*, 23, 1364 (1955).
[45c] D. M. Gardner and G. K. Fraenkel, *J. Am. Chem. Soc.*, 78, 3279 (1956).

librium measurement (Eq.) or thermochemical (T.). Details of the measurements are given in the reviews or original articles cited. For several substances of interest, only average bond energies are available and dissociation energies have been taken as the average bond energy + 10%. Such values are always included in parentheses, and the method is indicated as B.E. The basis of this rather arbitrary method is that, in a number of symmetric covalently bonded molecules with no lower stable valence state, where both quantities are known (e.g., H_2O, NH_3, and CH_4) the dissociation energy for the first bond is found to be 5–20% larger than the average bond energy. Accordingly it is likely that the majority of the estimates given here are correct within ±5 kcal. Some of the individual cases are discussed in more detail when we take up specific radical reactions involving the dissociation energies in question.

Table 2·2 lists dissociation energies for a number of methane derivatives. Whenever possible, these have been calculated via a thermochemical cycle as indicated in the previous section, but, in addition, some have been measured directly, and occasionally it has been necessary to estimate the values from average bond energies.

TABLE 2·2   BOND DISSOCIATION ENERGIES OF METHANE DERIVATIVES
IN KCAL/MOLE AT 25°C

Bond	D	Method
CH_3—H	102	K., [33-35] El. [44, 48]
CH_3—$B(CH_3)_2$	(74)	(B.E.) [27]
CH_3—CH_3	84.2	T. [37]
CH_3—OCH_3	77	T. [50a]
CH_3—NH_2	75	T. [28]
CH_3——N=N—CH_3	46	K. [46]
CH_3—NO_2	57.3	T. [50]
CH_3—ONO	56.2	T. [50]
CH_3—OH	90	T. [37]
CH_3O—H	100	T. [50a]
CH_3O—NO	36.4, 38.9	K., [27] T. [50]
CH_3O—NO_2	40	K. [27]
CH_3—$Al(CH_3)_2$	(58)	(B.E.) [27]
CH_3—SiR_3	(62)	(B.E.) [27]
CH_3—SH	74.2, 67	El., [45] K. [49]
CH_3—SCH_3	73.2	El. [45]
CH_3S—H	88.8	El. [45]
CH_3S—SCH_3	73.2	El. [45]
CH_3—Cl	80.6	T. [37]
CH_3—Br	67.2	T. [37]
CH_3—I	52.6	T., [37] El. [48]
CH_3—Hg	6	T. [47]
CH_3—$HgCH_3$	52	K. [47]
CH_3—$CdCH_3$	(24)	(B.E.) [27]

[46] M. Page, H. O. Pritchard, and A. F. Trotman-Dickenson, *J. Chem. Soc.*, **1953**, 3878.

[47] B. G. Gowenlock, J. C. Polanyi, and E. Warhurst, *Proc. Roy. Soc. London*, **A218**, 269 (1953).

[48] C. A. McDowell and B. G. Cox, *J. Chem. Phys.*, **20**, 1496 (1952).

[49] A. H. Sehon and B. de B. Darwent, *J. Am. Chem. Soc.*, **76**, 4806 (1954).

[50] P. Gray, *Trans. Faraday Soc.*, **51**, 1367 (1955).

[50a] P. Gray, *ibid.*, **52**, 344 (1956).

A very important property of bond dissociation energies in organic molecules is their variation with the structure of the organic radical produced in the dissociation.   Table 2·3 lists available data on dissociation energies of H—, CH_3—, Cl—, Br—, and I— bonds for a series of organic radicals.   The sources of the halogen data, and most of the allyl, benzyl, and phenyl values, are the pyrolysis studies of Szwarc and collaborators; most of the balance come from electron impact measurements.   Recent original references are indicated, and the balance of the cases are discussed by Cottrell.   The accuracy of the values in most cases appears to be better than ±3 kcal/mole, and

TABLE 2·3   VARIATION OF R—X DISSOCIATION ENERGIES WITH STRUCTURE OF R

R—X	—H	—CH₃	—Cl	—Br	—I	"Resonance Energy" of R
Methyl	102 [33-35, 44, 48]	84.2 [3l]	80.6 [1l]	67.2 [37, 52, 56]	53 [37, 48]	0
Ethyl	98 [44, 54, 62]				51.5 [28]	4
Isopropyl	94 [44, 54]		73 [62]	59 [62]	(46), [28] 42 [62]	8
t-Butyl	90 [44, 54]				(45), [28]	12
Vinyl	(104–22) [27, 61]	109 [61]	104 [61]		(55) [28]	0
HC≡C—	121 [27]					0
Allyl	77 [59]	61.5 [59]		47.5, [51] 45.4 [65]	36 [28]	25
Benzyl	77.5 [28, 51, 60]	63 [28]	68 [64]	50.5 [51]	39 [28]	24.5
Phenyl	102 [55]	88.6 [55]	85.6 [55]	71 [55]	57 [55]	0
CH≡C—CH₂—				58 [62]	46 [62]	(10–15)
—CN	115 [53]	103 [58]				0
HC— (=O)	78 [27]	75 [27]				10–15
CH₃C— (=O)		72 [66]				12
φC— (=O)			73.2 [64]	57 [5l]		...
CF₃	102, [63] 103 [62a]	(117) [55]	83 [62a]	64.5 [52]		...
CH₂Cl				61 [52]		
CHCl₂				53.5 [52]		...
CCl₃	90, [28] 89 [62a]		68 [62a]	49, [52] 49.5 [62a]		12
CH₂Br	99 [35]			62.5 [52]		...
CHBr₂				55.5 [52]		...
CBr₃				49 [52]		...
·CH₂—CH—	40 [l]					58 [a]
HC=CH—					8–11 [27]	...
·CO—	26 [27]	17 [27]				...
·CH₂—	(92) [53]					...
:CH—	(88) [53]					...
:Ċ—	80 [3l]					...

[a] See text.

[51] M. Szwarc, B. N .Gosh, and A. H. Sehon, *J. Chem. Phys.*, **18**, 1142 (1950).
[52] M. Szwarc and A. H. Sehon, *ibid.*, **19**, 656 (1951).
[53] F. H. Field, *ibid.*, **19**, 793 (1951).
[54] C. H. Leigh and M. Szwarc, *ibid.*, **20**, 844 (1952).
[55] M. Szwarc and D. Williams, *ibid.*, **20**, 1171 (1952).
[56] V. H. Diebler, R. M. Reese, and F. L. Mohler, *ibid.*, **20**, 761 (1952).
[57] M. Ladacki and M. Szwarc, *Proc. Roy. Soc. London*, A219, 341 (1953).
[58] C. A. McDowell and J. W. Warren, *Trans. Faraday Soc.*, **48**, 1084 (1952).
[59] A. H. Sehon and M. Szwarc, *Proc. Roy. Soc. London*, A202, 263 (1950).
[60] D. O. Schissler and D. P. Stevenson, *J. Chem. Phys.*, **22**, 151 (1954).
[61] F. H. Field, *ibid.*, **21**, 1506 (1953).
[62] J. B. Farmer and F. P. Lossing, *Can. J. Chem.*, **33**, 861 (1955).
[62a] J. B. Farmer, H. S. Henderson, F. P. Lossing, and D. G. H. Marsden, *J. Chem. Phys.*, **24**, 348 (1956).
[63] G. O. Pritchard, H. O. Pritchard, H. I. Shiff, and A. F. Trotman-Dickenson, *Chemistry & Industry*, 1955, 896.
[64] M. Szwarc and J. W. Taylor, *J. Chem. Phys.*, **22**, 270 (1954)
[65] A. Maccoll, *J. Chem. Soc.*, 1955, 965.
[66] M. Szwarc and J. W. Taylor, *J. Chem. Phys.*, **23**, 2310 (1955).

frequently confirmatory evidence for a particular value is available, usually via thermochemical cycles. Thus, the very important D(benzyl—H) has been obtained by pyrolysis of toluene,[28] and indirectly from pyrolysis of benzyl bromide [51] and electron impact measurements,[60] all of which are in agreement within 3 kcal/mole. A kinetic measurement involving the bromination of toluene, however, gives a value of 89 kcal.[67] There is good reason to think that

[67] H. R. Anderson, H. A. Scheraga, and E. R. Van Artsdalen, *J. Chem. Phys.*, **21**, 1258 (1953).

this value is in error, and the matter is considered further in Section 8·4b.

The usual basis for accounting for the variation in dissociation energies within each column of Table 2·3 is in terms of the resonance or delocalization energy of the radicals produced, and we have already discussed the types of structures contributing to the benzyl and allyl radicals, Section 1·4.

Substitution of a CH_3 for an H of the methyl radical decreases dissociation energies by about 4 kcal/mole. One way of accounting for such a decrease is in terms of hyperconjugation:

$$
\begin{array}{ccc}
\text{H} \quad \text{H} & & \cdot\text{H} \\
| \quad\quad | & & \\
\text{HC}\!-\!\text{C}\cdot & \rightarrow & \text{HC}\!=\!\text{CH}_2 \\
| \quad\quad | & & | \\
\text{H} \quad \text{H} & & \text{H}
\end{array}
\qquad (39)
$$

and, as we have seen, Section 1·2b, paramagnetic resonance spectra give clear evidence of interaction between odd electrons and protons attached to carbons for which such structures can be drawn. Halogen atoms and carbonyl groups are also effective in decreasing dissociation energies. For the halogens hybrid radical structures may be written

$$
\begin{array}{ccc}
\text{H} & & \text{H} \\
| & & | \\
\text{R}\!-\!\text{C}\!-\!\text{Cl} & \leftrightarrow & \text{R}\!-\!\text{C}_-\!-\!\text{Cl}\cdot^+ \\
\cdot & &
\end{array}
\qquad (40)
$$

with carbonyl groups comparable structures are

$$
\begin{array}{ccc}
\text{O} & & \text{O}\cdot^+ \\
\| & & \| \\
\text{R}\!-\!\text{C}\cdot & \leftrightarrow & \text{R}\!-\!\text{C}^- \\
\end{array}
\qquad (41)
$$

Although bond dissociation energies are not available, chemical data show that carbonyl groups on neighboring atoms also weaken C—H bonds, and here structures analogous to allyl radicals may be envisioned.

$$
\begin{array}{ccc}
\text{O} & & \text{O}\cdot \\
\| & & | \\
\text{R}\overset{\cdot}{\text{C}}\text{HC}\!-\!\text{R} & \leftrightarrow & \text{R}\!-\!\text{CH}\!=\!\text{CH} \\
\end{array}
\qquad (42)
$$

Obviously, ascribing differences in dissociation energies solely to radical stabilization is rather a superficial treatment. For one thing, changes in the organic radical may also alter the properties of the bond involved. Indeed, changes in bond length and in the force constants for bond stretching with changes in R are well known. Such an effect probably accounts for most of the discrepancies between columns of Table 2·3. Thus, the "resonance energy of the benzyl radical" is obtained as 24.5, 21.2, 17, and 14 kcal respectively depending upon whether X is H, CH_3, Br, or I. Presumably, in the benzyl halides, appreciable overlap occurs between the π electrons of the benzene ring and the unshared electron pairs of the iodine atom, resulting in a bond strengthening which must be overcome in the dissociation process although, even with this argument, D(benzyl—Cl) appears high. Similarly, vinyl, $HC \equiv C$, and CN radicals all show D(C—H) values greater than D(CH_3—H) although there is some doubt of their exact values. All these molecules are known to have somewhat shorter, stiffer C—H bonds than methane, a phenomenon which, again, has been ascribed to hyperconjugation.

Another factor which may influence bond dissociation energies is the relief of steric strain as dissociation occurs. Such an effect might arise from repulsion between the radicals dissociating, or by relief of crowding of substituents on the carbon radical as it goes from a tetrahedral configuration towards a more planar one.

Such steric effects are believed to contribute to the easy dissociation of hexaarylethanes (Chapter 10) and have been suggested by Szwarc [52] as a factor in determining the dissociation energies of the polyhalomethanes. They may also contribute to the apparent "resonance energies" of secondary and tertiary alkyl radicals. Finally, electrostatic attraction or repulsion between groups may affect bond dissociation energies. Although this is generally a second-order effect it apparently plays a role in some of the thermal dissociations discussed in Chapter 10.

Since both conjugation leading to increased bond strengths and steric effects should be least for C—H bonds, we will find it convenient to take the differences between D(CH_3—H) and D(R—H) as our measure of the *resonance energy of the R radical*, recognizing here the limitations of the definition, and such quantities are listed in the last column of Table 2·3. Resonance energies of some more complicated radicals (obtained in the same way) are also available and will be mentioned in the appropriate place.

The bottom six rows of Table 2·3 contain bond dissociation energies of some radicals. Particularly important is D($\dot{C}H_2CH_2$—H), obtained thermochemically from the heats of formation of ethylene and the ethyl radical. Its value, 40 kcal, is 58 kcal less than D(C_2H_5—H), and, since the products of dissociation are ethylene and a hydrogen atom, it is convenient to think of this difference as the energy required to "open" the π bond of ethylene. In fact, we will use this value later in calculating probable activation energies for radical addition and disproportionation processes. The last three figures in Table 2·3 are the remaining bond dissociation values for methane. $D(\text{C--H})$ is accurately known from spectroscopy, and the others are from electron impact measurements and are somewhat uncertain.[68] Since their average is about 90 kcal, they show clearly the difference which may exist between a dissociation energy of a particular bond and an average bond energy in a molecule.

Finally, we may note that our $D(\text{C--H})$ values for radicals are low compared to those of saturated molecules. In short, *the presence of an odd electron in a molecule has a weakening effect on the surrounding bonds*. This phenomenon seems to account for the ease of radical decomposition, rearrangement, and disproportionation reactions to which we will frequently have occasion to refer.

[68] Somewhat different values are given by A. Langer, J. A. Hipple, and D. P. Stevenson, *ibid.*, **22**, 1836 (1954).

CHAPTER 3

Free Radical Polymerizations

The Kinetics

of Radical Chain Processes

3 · 1   Introduction

If you will take a bottle of styrene or methyl methacrylate and place it on your desk, with a little patience you can observe one of the most interesting reactions of organic chemistry. Little by little, the clear liquid shrinks in volume and increases in viscosity, turning finally to a glassy solid. Generally, this last transformation begins at the bottom of the vessel, but eventually, in a matter of days or weeks, the whole sample is converted to a hard transparent glass which you can obtain only by breaking the bottle. The process which you have observed is the reaction of *vinyl* or *addition poly-merization*, in the course of which the molecules of olefin are trans-formed into a smaller number of essentially saturated molecules of very high molecular weight.[1] This reaction is of enormous technical importance. It supplies the basis of the synthetic rubber industry and is important in the manufacture of many plastics and synthetic fibers. It is also usually (but not always) a free radical reaction. Both because of its simplicity and its freedom from side reactions and because of the relation between polymer structure and the sequence of reactions involved in polymer formation, it provides our best intro-duction to the detailed mechanism and kinetics of free radical chain processes in solution.

Reactions such as we have described have been known for over a century,[2] and in fact were first described as "polymerizations" by Berthelot in 1866.[3] During most of this time, their study was scrupu-lously avoided by most chemists, since the polymers obtained are non-crystalline, non-distillable, form no crystalline derivatives, and, in general, are quite resistant to the methods of classical organic chemistry. Accordingly, polymers, when they were formed, were regarded as tars or annoying by-products and discarded. In recent years, this situation has been profoundly altered. Chemical methods applicable to high molecular weight substances have been developed, physical chemists have become intrigued with their properties, and the role of polymeric substances in natural and biochemical systems has become widely recognized. However, it must be admitted that the greatest stimulus to the field of polymer chemistry in general,

[1] A comment on nomenclature: Olefins which undergo polymerization are commonly known as *monomers;* the resulting polymer is designated by the prefix *poly* attached to the name of the monomer, e.g., *polymethyl methacrylate*. A more systematic nomenclature has been suggested, *J. Polymer Sci.*, **8**, 257 (1952), but has received little general use.

[2] E. Simon, *Ann.*, **31**, 265 (1839).

[3] M. Berthelot, *Bull. soc. chim. France*, (2) **6**, 294 (1866).

and addition polymers in particular, has been their industrial importance. Accordingly, we now find, in place of a few wary investigators, whole groups of synthetic chemists busily preparing new monomers and polymers, teams of physical chemists struggling with the relationships between molecular structure and physical properties, and staffs of engineers searching for new applications and drawing up plans for new plants. As a result, a whole forest of publications has sprung up in this field of polymer chemistry. From this profusion we will try to select information which illuminates, in this chapter, the nature and kinetics of radical chain processes in solution; in Chapter 4, relations between structure and reactivity in radical reactions, and, finally, in Chapter 5, some features of free radical reactions which are peculiar to high-polymer systems. For readers who are interested in the more technical aspects of addition polymerization, a number of recent treatments are available.[4-6]

3·2   The Structure of Addition Polymers

The general field of the properties and physical chemistry of addition polymers is quite beyond the scope of this book.[7] Nevertheless, some aspects of their structure and physical properties are so closely related to the polymerization reaction that they need brief discussion.

Our recognition of the chemical structure of addition polymers, and, in fact, of high molecular weight organic molecules in general, is largely the result of studies initiated over thirty years ago by Hermann Staudinger, which led to a series of investigations that earned him the Nobel Prize in 1953.

In 1920,[8] Staudinger proposed that the polymerization reaction might be written as

$$n\text{CH}_2{=}\text{CHR} \rightarrow -(-\text{CH}_2-\text{CHR}-)_n- \qquad (1)$$

[4] C. E. Schildknecht, *Vinyl and Related Polymers,* John Wiley & Sons, New York, 1952.

[5] G. F. D'Alelio, *Fundamental Principles of Polymerization,* John Wiley & Sons, New York, 1952.

[6] R. H. Boundy and R. F. Boyer, *Styrene,* Reinhold Publishing Corp., New York, 1952.

[7] An excellent recent treatment, which also covers polymerization kinetics, is given by P. J. Flory, *Principles of Polymer Chemistry,* Cornell University Press, Ithaca, N. Y., 1953. This book also contains an engaging account of the early development of polymer chemistry.

[8] H. Staudinger, *Ber.,* **53,** 1073 (1920).

i.e., that a typical addition polymer was essentially a saturated linear molecule, with the monomer units connected by ordinary covalent linkages, and strung in a head-to-tail fashion along the polymer chain. Although this suggestion provided the key to the whole problem of the formation and properties of addition polymers, it was many years before it was generally accepted, and in particular before the nature of the end groups in the product of reaction 1 and the value of n in typical polymers were understood. In fact, until after 1930, no very good ways of determining polymer molecular weights were available, and many workers considered them not as covalent molecules at all, but rather as some sort of association compound.

By now, this essentially linear, head-to-tail structure of vinyl polymers is firmly established on a basis of both chemical and physical evidence. The chemical evidence consists primarily of degradation studies.[9] Thus, Staudinger and Steinhofer [10] observed that the pyrolysis of polystyrene at about 300°C yields, in addition to monomeric styrene, the molecules shown (2),

$$
\begin{array}{cc}
\phi \quad \phi \quad \phi & \phi \quad \phi \quad \phi \quad \phi \quad \phi \\
| \quad\ | \quad\ | & | \quad\ | \quad\ | \quad\ | \quad\ | \\
CH_2-CH_2-CH_2 & CH_2-CH_2-CH_2-CH_2-CH_2
\end{array}
$$

$$(2)$$

but no products having phenyl groups on adjacent carbons. In a more extensive series of studies, Marvel and his students [11] have shown that polyvinyl chloride, polyvinyl acetate, and polyvinyl methyl ketone must have head-to-tail structures. More recently polymethyl α-bromoacrylate [12] and the copolymer of propylene and sulfur dioxide [13] have also been shown to have head-to-tail struc-

[9] Early work on this subject has been reviewed by C. S. Marvel, *The Chemistry of Large Molecules*, R. E. Burk and O. Grummit, editors, Interscience Publishers, New York, 1943, Chapter VII. Also in H. Gilman, *Organic Chemistry*, Volume I, John Wiley & Sons, New York, 1943, Chapter 8.

[10] H. Staudinger and A. Steinhofer, *Ann.*, **517**, 35 (1935).

[11] C. S. Marvel and C. L. Levesque, *J. Am. Chem. Soc.*, **60**, 280 (1938), and subsequent papers.

[12] C. S. Marvel, E. D. Weil, L. B. Wakefield, and C. W. Fairbanks, *ibid.*, **75**, 2326 (1953).

[13] C. S. Marvel and E. D. Weil, *ibid.*, **76**, 61 (1954).

tures, although earlier anomalous results [9] had suggested that they were put together in a head-to-head, tail-to-tail fashion.

Physical evidence of polymer structure can be derived from X-ray diffraction patterns of polymers which can be obtained in a semi-crystalline condition. Addition polymers do not, in general, form macroscopic crystals. However, when molecules have sufficient symmetry and, preferably, where there are strong polar forces between chains, crystalline regions exist in polymer samples within which the polymer chains lie in ordered patterns. Thus, X-ray spacing measurements of the crystalline regions of polyvinylidene chloride, polyisobutylene, and polyvinyl alcohol (obtained by hydrolyzing polyvinyl acetate) indicate that the polymer consists of linear chains with head-to-tail arrangements of monomer units.[14]

In spite of this essentially linear, head-to-tail structure, it should not be inferred that other arrangements do not occasionally occur. Flory and Leutner [15] have investigated the occurrence of widely separated head-to-head structures in polyvinyl acetate by hydrolyzing the polymer, treating with periodic acid to cleave any 1,2-glycol structures which might be present, reacetylating, and determining

$$-CH_2-\underset{\underset{H}{|}}{\overset{\overset{OAc}{|}}{C}}-\underset{\underset{H}{|}}{\overset{\overset{OAc}{|}}{C}}-CH_2- \rightarrow -CH_2-\underset{\underset{H}{|}}{\overset{\overset{OH}{|}}{C}}-\underset{HIO_4}{\overset{}{\vdots}}-\underset{\underset{H}{|}}{\overset{\overset{OH}{|}}{C}}-CH_2 \quad (3)$$

the change in molecular weight. Their results indicate 1–2% of head-to-head linkage, the exact amount increasing with temperature. In addition to such reversals of order, under suitable conditions some chain branching may also occur in addition polymers. In the case of dienes, a much more complicated situation arises, since vinyl groups pendant from one polymer chain may become included in another, to yield finally a cross-linked structure in which the entire polymer may become essentially a single giant molecule. These phenomena are all considered further in Chapter 5.

The second problem in the Staudinger structure of addition polymers is that of their size, i.e., the value of n in eq. 1. This quantity, known as the degree of polymerization of a polymer, and the related

[14] Page 237 of the reference in footnote 7.

[15] P. J. Flory and F. S. Leutner, *J. Polymer Sci.*, **3**, 880 (1948); *ibid.*, **5**, 267 (1950).

polymer molecular weight, n times the molecular weight of the monomer, are of such obvious importance in polymer chemistry that they have received much investigation. In fact, it is the very large values of $n(10^2-10^5)$ which are encountered in typical addition polymers which give them their distinctive properties.

To a limited extent, polymer molecular weights may be determined by methods of end-group analysis. However, with many addition polymers, the molecular weights involved are so high that one must turn to more sensitive physical methods, carried out upon dilute polymer solutions. Of these, the most important are measurements of osmotic pressure, light scattering, sedimentation and diffusion (employing an ultracentrifuge), and intrinsic viscosity. Again, these methods will only be briefly discussed.[16]

The first three methods, when properly carried out, yield absolute values of molecular weight, although with the complication that, where the polymer sample consists of molecules with a range of molecular weights (so-called *polydisperse systems*), they give different sorts of averages.[17] Judging by the agreement between different methods, their accuracy approaches $\pm 5-10\%$. The intrinsic viscosity method, in contrast, is essentially empirical and requires calibration against one of the other techniques. However, once this relation is known for a system, its simplicity makes it the preferred technique. The intrinsic viscosity $[\eta]$ of a substance is defined as

$$[\eta] = \lim [(\eta_r - 1)/C]_{C \to 0} \tag{4}$$

where η_r, the relative viscosity of a solution, is the ratio of its measured viscosity to that of the solvent and C is the concentration of solute, usually measured in grams per 100 cc. The existence of a relationship between $[\eta]$ and polymer molecular weight was again first pointed out by Staudinger,[18] and subsequent work has shown that the relationship is of the form

$$[\eta] = K'M^\alpha \tag{5}$$

[16] Cf. Chapter VII of reference cited in footnote 7.

[17] Osmotic molecular weight measurements yield the usual or *number* average, i.e., $\overline{M}_n = \Sigma N_i M_i / \Sigma N_i$, where N_i is the number of molecules of species i, and M_i is the molecular weight of species i. Light-scattering measurements yield the *weight* average, $\overline{M}_w = \Sigma N_i M_i^2 / \Sigma N_i M_i$, whereas ultracentrifuge measurements may yield various higher averages.

[18] H. Staudinger and W. Heuer, *Ber.*, **63**, 222 (1930); H. Staudinger and R. Nodzu, *ibid.*, **63**, 721 (1930).

where K' and α are constants for any particular polymer-solvent system.[19] Since α is positive, it is implicit in eq. 5 that addition polymers show high intrinsic viscosities compared with low molecular weight compounds, and that the relative viscosities of even their dilute solutions are large. Thus, a 1% solution of polystyrene (mol. wt 10^6) in benzene has approximately four times the viscosity of benzene alone. Ordinary rubber cement is another good example of a dilute solution of a linear polymer. The detailed theory of this

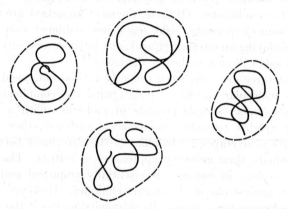

FIG. 3·1   Schematic drawing of a solution of a linear high polymer showing loosely coiled conformation of polymer chains.

high viscosity is very complex, but, qualitatively, it can be illustrated in terms of Fig. 3·1. In dilute solution a linear polymer molecule exists as a loose random coil which entraps solvent and gives the molecule an effective volume many times that which it would have if the molecule were compact. When such a system is subjected to a shearing force, these loose coils serve to prevent the free movement of solvent molecules past one another. Looked at this way, the viscous behavior of polymer solutions constitutes an additional proof of the linear nature of addition polymers. In fact, the major achievement in the physical chemistry of high polymers and their solutions has been in accounting for a great many of their properties in terms of linear molecules arranged in such loose, ran-

[19] Since α is found to have values varying between 0.5 and 0.8, intrinsic viscosity measurements on polydisperse systems yield *viscosity average* molecular weights, lying between $\overline{M}_n$ and $\overline{M}_w$, but usually approaching the latter. Accordingly, in using eq. 5 on any particular system it is necessary to know with what sort of a molecular weight distribution one is dealing.

dom coils, and application of such a structural picture to the polymerization process will again appear in Chapter 5.

We may now come back to the remaining uncertainty in the Staudinger formulation of an addition polymer—the nature of the end groups. Initially [8] it was suggested that these might be free radicals rendered unreactive by the high molecular weight of the molecules to which they are attached, and, in fact, we now know of circumstances where this is at least partially the case. However, in most systems the chain ends turn out to be ordinary, covalently bonded groups, the nature of which is determined by the particular reaction sequence by which the polymer was formed. These end-groups will be of considerable importance to us in connection with unraveling the nature of these sequences.

To summarize this section, the basic Staudinger formulation of the structure of an addition polymer as a chain of hundreds or thousands of monomer units, strung together in a linear, head-to-tail fashion, is now firmly established by a variety of chemical and physical methods, as are techniques for determining the number of units in such chains. Since the evidence is quite independent of the reactions by which such polymers are formed, we may use these structures, and any knowledge we may gain about end groups and imperfections in this linear chain structure, as evidence for the mechanism of polymerization processes without fear of circular reasoning. In fact, *it is the relation between the physical structure of polymer molecules and the course of the reaction by which they are formed that makes the study of polymerization particularly useful in working out the path of radical chain reactions in solution.*

3·3   The Kinetics of Free Radical Polymerizations

3·3a   General Properties of the Polymerization Reaction

If we attempt a more systematic study of the polymerization reaction described at the beginning of this chapter, we soon find that it has a number of characteristic features. First, out of the variety of substituted olefins available, only a rather limited number yield polymers of high molecular weight. Table 3·1 lists the commoner examples, and it may be seen that the majority are substances which have the structure $CH_2=C\langle$, i.e., with one end of the double bond unsubstituted, and which are free from allylic C—H bonds. The basis of this structural requirement will be of considerable interest to us, as

TABLE 3·1   SOME COMMON POLYMERIZABLE MONOMERS

Name	Formula
Ethylene	$CH_2=CH_2$
Vinyl chloride	$CH_2=CHCl$
Vinyl acetate	$CH_2=CHOAc$
Vinylidene chloride	$CH_2=CCl_2$
Tetrafluoroethylene	$CF_2=CF_2$
Acrylonitrile	$CH_2=CHCN$
Methacrylonitrile	$CH_2=C(CH_3)CN$
Methyl acrylate	$CH_2=CHCOOCH_3$
Methyl methacrylate	$CH_2=C(CH_3)COOCH_3$
Styrene	$CH_2=CHC_6H_5$
Butadiene	$CH_2=CH-CH=CH_2$
2-Chlorobutadiene	$CH_2=CCl-CH=CH_2$

will be the explanation of such exceptions as tetrafluoroethylene and methyl methacrylate.

Second, we find that the rate of polymerization of any particular monomer is subject to wide variability. It is not only increased by heat but, more significantly, by a wide variety of other agents. Among these are light and the whole series of initiators [20] (organic peroxides, azo compounds, etc.) which we have already mentioned as undergoing thermal cleavage into free radicals. Another class of reagents, quinones, aromatic polynitro compounds, sulfur, and oxygen, characteristically inhibit, or at least retard, such polymerizations. For this reason, kinetic studies of polymerization reactions need to be carried out in the scrupulous absence of air.

These observations of acceleration and inhibition are our primary reason for regarding radical polymerizations as radical chain processes, but we should note that other conditions for addition polymerization exist as well. Many olefins are polymerized by strong acids, and a few examples, e.g., styrene and isobutylene, yield high polymers through a non-radical, carbonium ion process which has received considerable study.[21]

Again, a few monomers, notably styrene and certain carbonyl conjugated olefins,[22] yield high polymers in the presence of metallic

---

[20] Such initiators are also frequently referred to as *catalysts;* however, as they are, in fact, slowly consumed in the reaction, the term is not strictly correct.

[21] P. H. Plesch, editor, *Cationic Polymerization and Related Complexes,* W. Heffer and Son, Cambridge, 1953.

[22] R. G. Beaman, *J. Am. Chem. Soc.,* **70,** 3115 (1948); H. Gilbert, F. F. Miller, S. J. Avrill, R. F. Schmidt, F. D. Stewart, and H. S. Trumbull, *ibid.,* **76,** 1074 (1954).

sodium or strong bases. Here the active center appears to be a carbanion. A technique for distinguishing between radical and non-radical polymerization processes on the basis of copolymerization behavior in homogeneous systems is presented in Chapter 4.

In addition to these homogeneous phase reactions, a series of heterogeneous polymerizations of intense interest both from the scientific and practical points of view have recently been developed by Ziegler, Natta, and others.[23] Although the mechanism of these processes (like most heterogeneous reactions) is obscure and they may follow more than one path, some sort of heterogeneous polar process (probably involving the growing polymer chain as a nucleophilic species) seems plausible. In any case they differ too much from conventional reactions to be fitted into any simple scheme at present.

A third significant property of a radical-induced polymerization may be observed by periodically examining the reaction mixture during the polymerization process. It is found that, at any time, the system consists solely of monomer and high polymer, and, although the *amount* of polymer increases with time, over a considerable extent of reaction its *molecular weight* remains constant. Hence, it is evident that the process which produces each completed polymer molecule occurs very rapidly and is over in a time which is very short compared to that required for conversion of the whole system to polymer. This observation will be of critical importance to us in considering the course of the overall reaction.

3·3b   Overall Kinetics of Initiated Polymerizations

It is now convenient to attempt to set up a kinetic scheme for addition polymerization as a radical chain process, bringing in additional experimental observations as opportunity arises. The simplest such scheme, following the arguments of the preceding chapter, is one in which three processes are involved: radical formation, radical addition to a double bond, and radical destruction. If we choose a system containing a typical radical initiator such as benzoyl peroxide, these steps may be symbolized as follows, using both explicit structural formulas and a shorter notation which will be convenient in kinetic developments.

[23] No attempt will be made here to discuss these in detail or to review the literature. However, cf. K. Ziegler, *Angew. Chem.*, **67**, 541 (1955); G. Natta, *Chemica e Industria*, **37**, 888 (1955).

Initiation:

$$\phi-\overset{\overset{O}{\|}}{C}-\overset{\overset{O}{\|}}{C}-\phi \xrightarrow{k_d} 2\;\phi-\overset{\overset{O}{\|}}{C}-O\cdot \qquad (6a)$$

$$In \xrightarrow{k_d} 2R\cdot \qquad (6b)$$

followed by

$$\phi-\overset{\overset{O}{\|}}{C}-O\cdot + CH_2=CHR \xrightarrow{k_i} \phi-\overset{\overset{O}{\|}}{C}-O-CH_2-\overset{\overset{H}{|}}{\underset{R}{C}}\cdot \qquad (7a)$$

$$R\cdot + M \xrightarrow{k_i} M_1\cdot \qquad (7b)$$

Chain propagation:

$$\phi-COO-(CH_2-CHR-)_{n-1}-CH_2-\overset{\overset{H}{|}}{\underset{R}{C}}\cdot + CH_2=CHR \xrightarrow{k_p}$$

$$\phi-COO-(CH_2-CHR)_n-CH_2-\overset{\overset{H}{|}}{\underset{R}{C}}\cdot \qquad (8a)$$

$$M_n\cdot + M \xrightarrow{k_p} M_{n+1}\cdot \qquad (8b)$$

Chain termination:

$$\phi-COO(CH_2-CHR)_{n-1}-CH_2-\overset{\overset{H}{|}}{\underset{R}{C}}\cdot$$

$$+ \;\overset{\overset{H}{|}}{\underset{R}{C}}-CH_2-(CHR-CH_2)_{m-1}-OCO\phi \xrightarrow{k_{tc}}$$

$$\phi-COO-(CH_2-CHR)_{n-1}-CH_2-\overset{\overset{H}{|}}{\underset{R}{C}}-\overset{\overset{H}{|}}{\underset{R}{C}}-CH_2-(CHR-CH_2)_{m-1}-OCO\phi$$

$$(9a)$$

$$M_n\cdot + M_m\cdot \xrightarrow{k_{te}} P_{m+n} \qquad (9b)$$

or

$$\phi-COO-(CH_2-CHR)_{n-1}-CH_2-\overset{\displaystyle H}{\underset{\displaystyle R}{C}}\cdot$$

$$+\ \cdot\overset{\displaystyle H}{\underset{\displaystyle R}{C}}-CH_2-(CHR-CH_2)_{m-1}-OCO\phi \xrightarrow{k_{td}}$$

$$\phi-COO-(CH_2-CHR)_{n-1}-CH{=}CHR$$
$$+\ CH_2R-CH_2-(CHR-CH_2)_{m-1}-OCO\phi \quad (10a)$$

$$M_n\cdot + M_m\cdot \xrightarrow{k_{td}} P_m + P_n \quad (10b)$$

Equations 9 and 10 correspond to chain termination by radical *combination* and *disproportionation* respectively.[24] There is some question as to the relative importance of the two processes, and, in fact, the formulation of the disproportionation reaction given is based entirely upon analogy to non-polymer systems. However, for kinetic purposes the two are equivalent, and it is usually convenient to combine them as

$$M_n\cdot + M_m\cdot \xrightarrow{k_t} P_{m+n} + P_m + P_n \quad (11)$$

vith

$$k_t = k_{tc} + k_{td}$$

In order to develop tractable kinetic expressions from eqs. 6–11, it is necessary to introduce certain simplifying assumptions. The first of these is that k_p and k_t are independent of the length of the growing polymer chain. This follows from our picture of a polymer molecule in solution as a loosely coiled chain in which the "growing end" has considerable freedom of movement, with the result that its reaction properties are influenced only by the immediately adjacent monomer units. It is also supported by experimental measurements of polymerization rates in different solvents in which molecular weights vary considerably, by molecular weight distribution studies, and by actual determination of k_p and k_t in polymerizing systems of different average chain length, all of which are treated in more de-

[24] We eliminate consideration of any termination process $R\cdot + M\cdot \to X$ since, if k_i is of the same order of magnitude as k_p, for any long-chain process $[M\cdot] \gg [R\cdot]$, and the probability of such a reaction becomes vanishingly small.

tail below. Apparently, this constancy extends down to chains of as few as 3–5 monomer units. However, as polymerization proceeds and polymer chains become increasingly entangled, the situation becomes more complex, and rate constants, particularly k_t, vary with both chain length and polymer concentration with consequences considered further in Chapter 5. For the present, however, we will be concerned only with the initial stages of polymerization processes, and, because rate constants will be taken as independent of polymer chain length, it is convenient to omit subscript m and n's from subsequent equations.

From eqs. 6–11 the rate of monomer disappearance in a polymerizing system is given as

$$\frac{-d[\text{M}]}{dt} = k_i[\text{R}\cdot][\text{M}] + k_p[\text{M}\cdot][\text{M}] \tag{12}$$

For a long-chain process producing high polymer, $k_i[\text{R}\cdot][\text{M}] \ll k_p[\text{M}\cdot][\text{M}]$, and we obtain

$$\frac{-d[\text{M}]}{dt} = k_p[\text{M}\cdot][\text{M}] \tag{13}$$

Similarly, we may write

$$\frac{d[\text{M}\cdot]}{dt} = k_i\text{R}\cdot\ [\text{M}] - 2k_t[\text{M}\cdot]^2 \tag{14}$$

Since monomer concentrations and polymerization rates are directly measurable, and radical concentrations are not, our next problem (and a general one in treating any radical chain process) is to eliminate radical concentrations from our equations, and, for the purpose, it is convenient to introduce the so-called *steady-state assumption*, namely, that in any reaction involving an intermediate present in only very low concentrations, *the rate of change of concentration of such an intermediate is small compared to its rates of formation and disappearance*. Since the time to form any one polymer molecule, and accordingly the lifetime of any radical, is short compared to the whole polymerization process, it is evident that our radicals fall into the class of such low-concentration intermediates. Accordingly, to a good approximation, eq. 14 may be equated to zero, yielding

$$k_i[\text{R}\cdot][\text{M}] = 2k_t[\text{M}\cdot]^2 \tag{15}$$

Similarly we may write

$$\frac{d[\text{R}\cdot]}{dt} = 2fk_d[\text{In}] - k_i[\text{R}\cdot][\text{M}] = 0 \tag{16}$$

where f represents the fraction of initiator fragments formed by initiator decomposition which are successful in initiating the polymerization process. This question of *initiator efficiency* is frequently an important one in treating radical chain processes and is discussed further below. However, in many systems, initiation is apparently quite efficient with $0.5 < f < 1.0$.

Combining eqs. 13–16 one obtains

$$\frac{-d[\text{M}]}{dt} = k_p[\text{M}](k_d f[\text{In}]/k_t)^{\frac{1}{2}} \tag{17a}$$

which may be written in a shorter form

$$R_p = k_p[\text{M}](R_i/2k_t)^{\frac{1}{2}} \tag{17b}$$

where R_p and R_i represent rates of polymerization and of polymer chain initiation respectively.[25]   Equation 17 is a typical rate expression for a radical chain process, but, before discussing it further, some remarks on the steady-state assumption are in order, since we will use it repeatedly in treating radical reactions, and because it is treated rather briefly in most discussions of kinetics.

The basis of this steady-state assumption may be most readily visualized by considering a process of two consecutive first-order processes

$$\text{A} \xrightarrow{k_1} \text{B} \xrightarrow{k_2} \text{C} \tag{18}$$

with

$$\frac{d[\text{A}]}{dt} = -k_1[\text{A}] \tag{19a}$$

$$\frac{d[\text{B}]}{dt} = k_1[\text{A}] - k_2[\text{B} \tag{19b}$$

$$\frac{d[\text{C}]}{dt} = k_2[\text{B}] \tag{19c}$$

[25] Writers on polymerization kinetics have not always been consistent (or even clear) on the use of a factor of 2 in writing rate expressions for processes producing or destroying radicals in pairs. Here we have used the convention of Flory, Matheson, and others, of writing the expression to correspond to the number of radicals formed or consumed; cf. eqs. 14 and 17.

in which $k_2 > k_1$ so that [B] remains small compared to [A] and [C] during most of the reaction. Equations 19 may be integrated without simplifying assumptions, and Fig. 3·2 indicates the variation of [A], [B], and [C] during reaction, choosing $k_2 = 10k_1$. The slope of line A in Fig. 3·2 is equal to either side of eq. 19a and the slope of line C to either side of eq. 19c, whereas the slope of B is their *difference*, or eq. 19b.

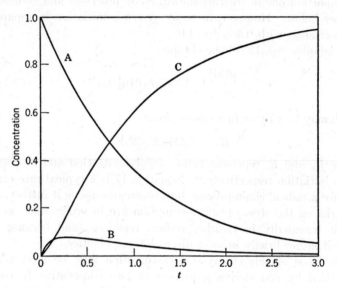

Fig. 3·2 Change in concentration with time for consecutive first-order reactions $A \xrightarrow{k_1} B \xrightarrow{k_2} C$ (case where $A_0 = 1$, $k_1 = 1$, $k_2 = 10$).

Since, except for the brief initial period, B is almost flat, never departing far from the axis, it is evident that this difference between eqs. 19a and 19c is very close to zero over all but the beginning of the reaction, hence, to a good approximation [26]

$$\frac{d[B]}{dt} = k_1[A] - k_2[B] = 0 \qquad (20)$$

Similar arguments apply to cases involving more complex kinetics, and, for radical reactions in which the concentration of intermediates

[26] Solution of eq. 14 for the case given yields $[B]_{max} = 7.9\%$ $[A]_0$ at the point where 12% of A has reacted. The error in [C] here in using eq. 20 will here be over 50% of its actual value, but the percentage error decreases steadily as the reaction proceeds.

is very low, the approximation becomes very good indeed. The initial portion of Fig. 3·2 indicates a small induction period in the appearance of C, since it must wait for the initial formation of B. However, as the ratio of k_2/k_1 increases, so that less and less B is present, this induction period grows shorter and shorter (measured in terms of the total reaction). In this region, obviously, eq. 20 does not apply,

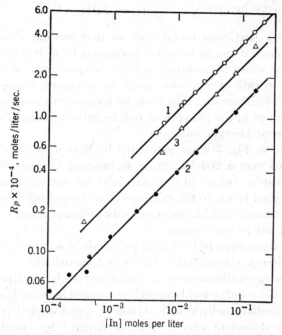

FIG. 3·3 Plot of polymerization rate versus initiator concentration: 1, methyl methacrylate–azobisisobutyronitrile (50°); [29] 2, styrene–benzoyl peroxide (60°); [27] 3, methyl methacrylate–benzoyl peroxide (50°) [28] (after Flory [7]).

and we will have occasion to consider radical reactions under such *non-steady-state* conditions. However, in typical polymerizations this induction period is of the order of, at most, a few seconds, providing additional evidence of the very low radical concentrations involved.

Returning now to eq. 17, in many cases experiments employing initiators which undergo spontaneous unimolecular decomposition give excellent agreement with the predicted relationship. Figure 3·3, taken from Flory [7] shows a log-log plot of initial polymerization rate against initiator concentration for styrene initiated with benzoyl peroxide,[27] and methyl methacrylate, initiated with benzoyl peroxide [28] and azobisisobutyronitrile.[29] This latter compound, which decomposes into free radicals via the process,[30, 31]

$$\underset{\underset{CH_3}{\diagup}\overset{CH_3}{\diagdown}}{C} \overset{CN\quad NC}{\diagdown\diagup} \underset{\underset{N=\!\!=\!\!N}{\diagup}\overset{CH_3}{\diagdown}}{C} \rightarrow 2 \;\; \underset{\underset{CH_3}{\diagup}}{C\cdot} \overset{CH_3\quad CN}{\diagdown\diagup} + N_2 \qquad (21)$$

belongs to a particular useful class of initiators for radical chain processes, since it and its homologs decompose by a strictly unimolecular process which is essentially solvent independent, but which can be varied in rate over a wide range by structural changes in the azonitrile. Furthermore, they show no tendency to undergo induced decompositions in the presence of free radicals, a common complication with peroxide-type initiators.

The data of Fig. 3·3 are well fitted by lines with the theoretical slope of 0.5 over a 200-fold range in initiator concentration. The slight curvature below 10^{-3} molar initiator concentration in the styrene system is due to the existence of a thermal initiation process with this monomer, which undergoes slow polymerization, even in the absence of any added initiator.

Similar dependence of the initial polymerization rate on the square root of initiator concentration has been observed with a variety of other monomer-initiator systems, vinyl acetate–benzoyl peroxide in benzene,[32] d-sec-butyl-α-chloroacrylate–benzoyl peroxide in dioxane,[33] and azobisisobutyronitrile with styrene [34, 35] and diethyl fumarate,[36] both in the absence of solvent. Further, Arnett [29] has shown that the rates of polymerization of methyl methacrylate, using different azonitrile initiators at the same concentration and temperature, is proportional to $k_d^{0.5}$ over a hundredfold range.

[27] F. R. Mayo, R. A. Gregg, and M. S. Matheson, *J. Am. Chem. Soc.*, **73**, 1691 (1951).

[28] G. V. Schulz and F. Blaschke, *Z. physik. Chem.*, **B51**, 75 (1940).

[29] L. M. Arnett, *J. Am. Chem. Soc.*, **74**, 2027 (1952).

[30] F. M. Lewis and M. S. Matheson, *ibid.*, **71**, 747 (1949).

[31] C. G. Overberger, M. T. O'Shaughnessy, and H. Shalit, *ibid.*, **71**, 2661 (1949).

[32] S. Kamenskaya and S. Medvedev, *Acta Physicochim. U.R.S.S.*, **13**, 565 (1940).

[33] C. C. Price and R. W. Kell, *J. Am. Chem. Soc.*, **63**, 2798 (1941).

[34] D. H. Johnson and A. V. Tobolsky, *ibid.*, **74**, 938 (1952).

[35] B. Baysal and A. V. Tobolsky, *J. Polymer Sci.*, **8**, 529 (1952).

[36] C. Walling and E. A. McElhill, *J. Am. Chem. Soc.*, **73**, 2819 (1951).

Equation 17 implies that polymerization rates should be proportional to $R_i^{1/2}$, even when other initiation processes are involved. The best data are on photoinduced processes, both vinyl acetate [37, 38] and methyl methacrylate [39] showing a polymerization rate proportional to the square root of light intensity in polymerizations directly induced by ultraviolet irradiation. In addition, a number of monomers show similar behavior in photosensitized reactions, a subject considered further in our discussion of the evaluation of individual rate constants below. These observations all support the idea of the generality of bimolecular termination processes in free radical polymerizations yielding high polymers, but a few exceptions occur. Thus the photochemical polymerization of vinyl chloride in tetrahydrofuran, sensitized by azonitriles, is proportional to $R_i^{1/2}$ at $25°$, but to $R_i^{0.63}$ at $55°$,[40] and the polymerization of acrylonitrile, induced by the thermal decomposition of either benzoyl peroxide or azobisisobutyronitrile, shows a rate proportional to the 0.8 power of initiator concentration.[41] In this last case, the situation is complicated by the insolubility of the polymer in monomer, and systems of this sort are discussed further in Chapter 5. Later we will consider some important cases where intervention of other steps into the kinetic chain leads to both shorter chains and a change in the $R_p - R_i$ relationship.

The dependence of polymerization rate upon monomer concentration is somewhat less clear-cut than its relation to initiator concentration. Figure 3·4 is a plot of R_p versus [M] in benzene solution, corrected for changes in initiator concentration, for styrene [27] and methyl methacrylate initiated with benzoyl peroxide,[42] and methyl methacrylate initiated with azobisisobutyronitrile.[29] In all systems the reaction is evidently rather close to first order in respect to monomer. The relation for benzoyl peroxide-initiated styrene in toluene at 80° has recently been determined with excellent precision by Horikx and Hermans,[43] who find that the apparent order in respect to monomer increases from 1.18 at [M] = 1.8 moles/liter to 1.36 at [M] = 0.4. Their experimental technique, incidentally, using a stirred flow reactor, should be very useful in the study of radical chain

[37] G. M. Burnett and H. W. Melville, *Proc. Roy. Soc. London,* **A189,** 456 (1947).

[38] G. M. Burnett and H. W. Melville, *ibid.,* **A189,** 494 (1947).

[39] K. S. Bagdasaryan, *J. Phys. Chem. U.S.S.R.,* **21,** 25 (1947).

[40] G. M. Burnett and W. W. Wright, *Proc. Roy. Soc. London,* **A221,** 28 (1954).

[41] W. M. Thomas and J. J. Pellon, *J. Polymer Sci.,* **13,** 329 (1954).

[42] G. V. Schulz and G. Harborth, *Makromol. Chem.,* **1,** 106 (1947).

[43] M. W. Horikx and J. J. Hermans, *J. Polymer Sci.,* **11,** 325 (1953).

processes, although it has so far been employed by only a few investigators.

The origin of this high order of the polymerization reaction in respect to monomer is, so far, rather hard to pin down in particular cases. However, it appears that at least three factors may be in-

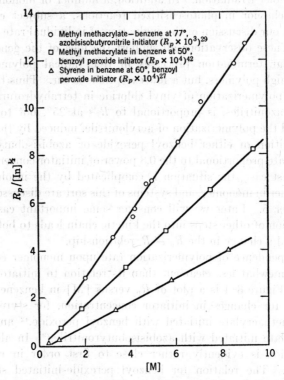

Methyl methacrylate—benzene at 77°, azobisisobutyronitrile initiator ($R_p \times 10^3$)[29]

Methyl methacrylate in benzene at 50°, benzoyl peroxide initiator ($R_p \times 10^4$)[42]

Styrene in benzene at 60°, benzoyl peroxide initiator ($R_p \times 10^4$)[27]

FIG. 3·4 Variation in polymerization rate (corrected for changes in initiator concentration) with monomer concentration.

volved. The first is variation in k_d and f with medium as discussed in the next section. The second is the presence of adventitious retarders in the solvents employed. This may seem unlikely, but recently Mayo[44] has shown that even carefully fractionated bromobenzene contains impurities which retard the polymerization of styrene and which are only removed by polymerizing styrene in the bromobenzene and then recovering the solvent for use. Finally, a small amount of reaction between polymer radicals and solvent is known to occur in almost all polymerizing systems, and, if the re-

[44] F. R. Mayo, *J. Am. Chem. Soc.*, **75**, 6133 (1953).

sulting radicals are less reactive than those of the growing polymer chain, the result may be a retardation of the polymerization process beyond that predicted by eq. 17.

3·3c Details of the Initiation Process; Initiator Efficiencies

Although the majority of studies of polymerization kinetics have been carried out using benzoyl peroxide, or, more recently, azobisisobutyronitrile and its homologs, a great number of other substances and combinations of substances have been shown to induce the polymerization of typical monomers. However, although such reactions provide additional evidence of the radical chain nature of the polymerization process, they contribute little additional to our picture of polymerization kinetics, and discussion of them will be deferred to Chapter 10, where the properties of various initiator systems and their rates of radical production are treated in more detail.

One property of the initiation process, as indicated in eqs. 6 and 7, however, needs mention here, and that is the inclusion of initiator fragments in the polymer which the formulation demands. Polystyrene and polymethyl methacrylate, prepared using various halogenated benzoyl peroxides, contain bound halogen which cannot be removed by repeated precipitation.[45-52] Fragments from N-nitroso-acetanilides used as initiators have also been found in polystyrene, polymethylmethacrylate, and polyacrylonitrile.[53] The use of initiators labeled with radioactive isotopes is a particularly sensitive means of detecting initiator inclusion in polymers, and has been employed to detect fragments of potassium persulfate containing S^{35} [54] and azobisisobutyronitrile containing C^{14}.[55-57] A modification of this tracer

[45] W. Kern and H. Kammerer, J. prakt. Chem., 161, 81 (1942).
[46] C. C. Price, R. W. Kell, and E. Krebs, J. Am. Chem. Soc., 64, 1103 (1942).
[47] C. C. Price and B. E. Tate, ibid., 65, 517 (1943).
[48] P. D. Bartlett and S. G. Cohen, ibid., 65, 543 (1943).
[49] H. F. Pfann, D. J. Dallen, and H. Mark, ibid., 66, 983 (1944).
[50] J. W. Breitenbach and H. Schneider, Ber., 76B, 1088 (1943).
[51] S. G. Cohen, J. Polymer Sci., 2, 511 (1947).
[52] L. Horner and H. Pohl, Ann., 559, 48 (1947).
[53] A. T. Blomquist, J. R. Johnson, and H. J. Sykes, J. Am. Chem. Soc., 65, 2446 (1943).
[54] W. E. Mochel and J. H. Peterson, ibid., 71, 1426 (1949); W. V. Smith, ibid., 71, 4077 (1949).
[55] L. M. Arnett and J. H. Peterson, ibid., 74, 2031 (1952).
[56] J. C. Bevington, H. W. Melville, and R. P. Taylor, J. Polymer Sci., 12, 449 (1954).
[57] J. C. Bevington, J. H. Bradbury, and G. M. Burnett, ibid., 12, 469 (1954).

technique which has also been employed is to use bromobenzoyl peroxide, and subsequently activate the halogen in the polymer by neutron bombardment.[49]

Although some of the measurements cited above have been purely qualitative, the more precise determinations indicate one to two initiator fragments per polymer molecule, and thus provide further evidence for the correctness of the chain mechanism given.

We may now turn to the question of initiator efficiency, the value of f in eqs. 16 and 17. If one selects an initiator for which the rate of decomposition can be accurately measured (e.g., by nitrogen evolution with azobisisobutyronitrile, or by titration with peroxides) three methods are available for determining this efficiency. The first involves comparing the rates of initiator decomposition and production of polymer molecules. Thus, if every initiator molecule produces two radicals which may start chains, and all chains end by radical combination, if $f = 1$, each initiator molecule which decomposes will produce one molecule of polymer, and a lower number indicates a lower initiator efficiency. This technique requires the accurate measurement of number average polymer molecular weight, and it also requires both that we know the relative importance of radical combination and disproportionation in the chain termination process, and that no induced decomposition of the initiator is taking place. This last appears to be a safe assumption with azonitrile initiators, although not with many peroxides. However, when one corrects for such induced decomposition, f for the benzoyl peroxide-induced polymerization of styrene and methyl methacrylate appears to be between 0.6 and 1.0.[34, 35, 58]

The second method involves comparing the amount of initiator combined with polymer with the amount decomposed. This method again requires knowledge of the rate of the *uninduced* decomposition of the initiator. Arnett and Peterson,[55] using azobisisobutyronitrile labeled with C^{14}, have obtained initiator efficiencies varying from 0.5 to 1.0 for methyl methacrylate, vinyl acetate, styrene, vinyl chloride, and acrylonitrile (increasing in that order), and Bevington et al., with the same initiator, have reported efficiencies of 0.5–0.55 with methylmethacrylate,[57] styrene,[59] and styrene-butyl acrylate mixtures.[60]

[58] A. V. Tobolsky and R. B. Mesrobian, *Organic Peroxides,* Interscience Publishers, New York, 1954.

[59] J. C. Bevington, *Trans. Faraday Soc.,* **51,** 1392 (1955).

[60] J. C. Bevington, J. H. Bradbury, and G. M. Burnett, *J. Polymer Sci.,* **12,** 469 (1954).

The third method involves the use of an inhibitor such as the stable free radical diphenylpicrylhydrazyl which efficiently halts radical chains, apparently [61] via the process

If a measured small quantity of this substance is included in the polymerization system, the rate of chain production may be followed, either by colorometric methods (the hydrazyl is violet, and its reaction products light yellow or colorless), or by determining the length of the induction period by dilatometry.[62]

This method involves the assumption that the inhibitor reacts quantitatively and solely with growing polymer chains, and, while it has had considerable use, its quantitative nature has been seriously questioned by Hammond, Sen, and Boozer.[63] For one thing, olefin-diphenylpicrylhydrazyl systems are remarkably oxygen sensitive, and, further, the hydrazine derivative formed in reaction 22 may conceivably be subject to further radical attack.

Duroquinone [62] and benzoquinone [64] have also been used to determine rates of chain initiation, although here the inhibition process is more complicated, involving radical attack on the quinone, apparently to yield a radical product which is too unreactive to propagate the polymerization chain; cf. Section 4·3. The effectiveness of the inhibitor may depend upon the polymerization system involved, and it is also necessary to know the number of chains stopped by each inhibitor molecule.

If we take the results of all these various methods, we are led to the conclusion that the efficiency of the initiation process in vinyl

[61] A. Henglein, *Makromol. Chem.*, **15**, 188 (1955).

[62] P. D. Bartlett and H. Kwart, *J. Am. Chem. Soc.*, **72**, 1051 (1950).

[63] G. S. Hammond, J. N. Sen, and C. E. Boozer, *ibid.*, **77**, 3244 (1955).

[64] S. G. Cohen, *ibid.*, **67**, 17 (1945); **69**, 1057 (1947).

polymerization with usual initiators approaches, but often falls significantly short of, unity and may vary appreciably with the initiator, monomer, and medium involved.

The origin of this phenomenon becomes evident from a more detailed consideration of the initiation process and the diffusion processes of molecules in solution. The first step in the chain initiation process is, as we have seen, the cleavage of an initiator molecule into two fragments. However, in the liquid phase, these fragments cannot immediately separate, since they are surrounded by a "cage" of solvent molecules.[65] Accordingly they undergo a number of consecutive collisions with each other, and, during this time, they may well recombine. In fact, even after they have diffused out of this initial cage there is still an appreciable probability of their diffusing back together again, and it is evident that both of these processes may compete with the initiation of polymerization. This situation is indicated by the following equations:

$$\text{In} \rightarrow (2\text{R}\cdot) \tag{23}$$

$$(2\text{R}\cdot) \rightarrow \text{X} \tag{24}$$

$$(2\text{R}\cdot) + \text{M} \rightarrow \text{R}\cdot + \text{M}\cdot \tag{25}$$

$$(2\text{R}\cdot) \rightleftharpoons 2\text{R}\cdot \tag{26}$$

$$\text{R}\cdot + \text{M} \rightarrow \text{M}\cdot \tag{27}$$

in which $(2\text{R}\cdot)$ represents radicals confined next to each other within the same cage. Equation 24 which we will call *primary recombination* may represent either regeneration of initiator, or the formation of stable products, e.g., phenyl benzoate and carbon dioxide from benzoyl peroxide, or tetramethylsuccinonitrile and nitrogen from azobisisobutyronitrile.

The reverse reaction in eq. 26 represents the rediffusion together of two fragments from the same initiator molecule, and may be followed by eq. 24 leading to *secondary recombination*. It is significant that this sequence is time dependent, for the average separation of two fragments will increase with time, with a corresponding decrease in the probability of their ever re-entering the same solvent cage.

If we now look at the relative rates of the processes involved, the basis of initiator efficiencies becomes reasonably clear. In ordinary solutions, the average time that fragments will be confined within a solvent cage is 10^{-11} to 10^{-10} sec, and, by the time that they have

[65] J. Franck and E. Rabinowitch, *Trans. Faraday Soc.*, **30**, 120 (1934).

separated by a few molecular diameters, their probability of redif-fusion back together has become negligible.[66] Thus, if either primary or secondary recombination is to occur, it must be fitted into a time cycle of perhaps 10^{-9} sec. Known rate constants for radical combi-nations range upward from 10^7 liter/mole/sec, so, if we realize that, within a solvent "cage," the effective radical concentration is of the order of 10 molar (admittedly, applying such a bulk concept to our discreet picture is only an approximation), there is good likelihood of reaction 24 taking place. On the other hand, known rate con-stants for radical addition processes usually lie in the range of 10–10^5 liter/mole/sec, so that, even in a system containing almost pure monomer (about 10 molar), reaction 25 will not compete with recombination.

This analysis of the situation was first given by Flory.[7] It indi-cates that initiator efficiency will be independent of monomer con-centration (down to the point where so little monomer is present that fragments from *different* initiator molecules begin to combine, rather than starting chains) and will depend essentially upon the competi-tion between reactions 24 and 26.

Earlier, Matheson had discussed the cage effect in terms of the competition between reactions 24 and 25,[67] but it seems hard to recon-cile this picture with the known rates of the processes involved, unless the initiation process involves participation of the monomer in the initiator cleavage, for example, by a *simultaneous* cleavage of the initiator and bond formation between an initiator fragment and a monomer molecule. Such a process is unlikely for azonitrile initia-tors, since their decomposition rate is essentially independent of sol-vent, but it is conceivable with other initiators, e.g., hydroperoxides, which undergo an accelerated primary decomposition in the presence of olefins; cf. Section $10\cdot2d$.

Recently, further information has become available upon the effect of changes of medium upon the extent of radical recombination in typical initiator systems. The rate of decomposition of azobisiso-butyronitrile decomposition may be followed either by nitrogen evo-lution or by the rate of reaction with diphenylpicrylhydrazyl. The

[66] R. M. Noyes, *J. Am. Chem. Soc.*, **77**, 2042 (1955).

[67] M. S. Matheson, *J. Chem. Phys.*, **13**, 554 (1945). Matheson's treatment, incidently, was devised originally to provide an alternative to an earlier kinetic scheme of G. V. Schulz and E. Hussmann, *Z. phys. Chem.*, **B39**, 246 (1938), which postulated initiation by decomposition of a peroxide-styrene complex and which now appears to be without foundation.

first method measures the rate of reaction 23. The maximum rate of the second reaction, however, is determined by diffusion. Taking its bimolecular rate constant as 10^{10} liter/mole/sec, the approximate rate of diffusion together of small molecules in a non-viscous solvent, for

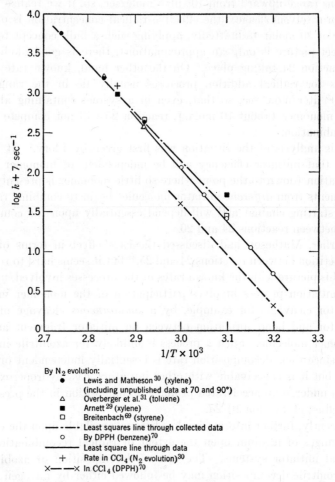

By N_2 evolution:
- Lewis and Matheson [30] (xylene)
  (including unpublished data at 70 and 90°)
- △　Overberger et al.[31] (toluene)
- ■　Arnett [29] (xylene)
- □　Breitenbach [69] (styrene)
- —·—·— Least squares line through collected data
- ○　By DPPH (benzene) [70]
- —— Least square line through data
- +　Rate in CCl_4 (N_2 evolution) [30]
- ×——× In CCl_4 (DPPH) [70]

Fig. 3·5 Decomposition of azobisisobutyronitrile in aromatic solvents.[68]

10^{-3} molar diphenylpicrylhydrazyl (above the concentration usually employed) the average time before reaction of an initiator fragment will be 10^{-7} sec, and it is evident that diphenylpicrylhydrazyl will count only those fragments which escape primary and secondary recombination. In Fig. 3·5,[68] data on the decomposition are plotted,

[68] C. Walling, *J. Polymer Sci.*, **14**, 214 (1954).

measured by both N_2 evolution [29-31, 69] and by means of diphenylpicryl-hydrazyl.[70] In typical aromatic solvents at 60°, apparently about 75% of the fragments escape recombination, but in carbon tetra-chloride the fraction is much lower, about 30%. A more direct com-parison has been carried out by Hammond, Sen, and Boozer,[63] who simultaneously measured N_2 evolution and diphenylpicrylhydrazyl fading in the presence of azobisisobutyronitrile in various solvents with similar results. They also determined efficiencies of radical pro-duction (obtaining results they consider more reliable) of 0.44 in CCl_4 and 0.6–0.7 in various aromatic solvents using iodine as a radi-cal trap.

Alternately, the yield of available radicals formed from azobisiso-butyronitrile can be checked by determining the yield of tetramethyl-succinonitrile (the expected coupling product of the initial radicals) in the presence of reactive substrates, and it is significant that 10–30% is still isolated, either in the presence of high concentrations of mer-captans [63] or excess diphenylpicrylhydrazyl.[71]

Similar variations are also observed in other systems in which radicals are produced in pairs. Data on benzoyl peroxide are less reliable due to the necessity of correcting for induced decomposition; but, again, in benzene diphenylpicrylhydrazyl indicates a rate of radical formation only 25–50% of that calculated for the primary reaction.[68] A more striking result is noted in the photodissociation of I_2,[72] a reaction discussed further in Section 11·1a. The origin of these variations may lie partly in the time available for primary recombination, while fragments are confined to the same solvent cage, and this time would be accordingly related to their rates of diffusion, but the variation may also depend upon the orientation of the radi-cals and their ability to lose the energy liberated in recombina-tion.[72]

Finally, we should note that even the foregoing may be too simple a picture of the process of chain initiation, since a radical source may simultaneously decompose by radical-forming and non-radical-form-ing paths. Additional comments on this situation appear in Chapter 10, but, for the moment, we will not attempt to differentiate further between recombination of initial radical pairs and non-radical wast-age of initiator.

[69] J. W. Breitenbach and A. Schindler, *Monatsh.*, **83,** 724 (1952).

[70] C. E. H. Bawn and S. F. Mellish, *Trans. Faraday Soc.*, **47,** 1216 (1951).

[71] J. C. Bevington, *Nature*, **175,** 477 (1955).

[72] F. W. Lampe and R. M. Noyes, *J. Am. Chem. Soc.*, **76,** 2140 (1954).

3·3d Kinetic Chain Length, Molecular Weight, and Chain Termination

We have already seen the importance of polymer molecular weights in demonstrating the long-chain nature of free radical polymerization processes, and their use in determining polymerization initiation rates. We may now consider their relation to polymerization rate and to the kinetic chain length ν, the average number of monomer molecules consumed by every radical which starts a polymerization chain. This quantity is evidently given by the ratio of R_p to R_i (or R_t):

$$\nu = R_p/R_i = R_p/R_t \qquad (28)$$

From eqs. 13–17 this becomes

$$\nu = k_p[M]/2k_t[M\cdot] \qquad (29)$$

or, eliminating radical concentrations,

$$\nu = k_p{}^2[M]^2/2k_t R_p \qquad (30)$$

Equations 29 and 30 illustrate an important general property of radical chain processes involving bimolecular propagation and termination: the inverse relationship between chain length, and either radical concentrations or overall reaction rates. They also indicate that the chain length at constant reaction rate is not dependent on the particular means of initiating the reaction, but is a characteristic of the particular monomer system involved.

If only the reactions discussed so far are taken into account, the relation between ν and polymer molecular weight (or the average degree of polymerization $\bar{P}$) obviously depends upon the relative importance of chain termination by disproportionation and combination, the former giving $\bar{P} = \nu$ and the latter $\bar{P} = 2\nu$.

At present, the majority of the evidence indicates that most polymerization processes terminate primarily by radical coupling processes. Thus the polymerization of styrene initiated by radio-active persulfate [54] or azobisisobutyronitrile [56] contains two initiator fragments per molecule. Further, data on many simple radicals, e.g., ethyl radicals in the gas phase [73] and α-alkyl benzyl radicals in solution,[74] show that in many cases combination is certainly the major result of radical interaction. The only polymerization system for

---

[73] E. W. R. Steacie, *Atomic and Free Radical Reactions,* second edition, Reinhold Publishing Corp., New York, 1954.

[74] M. S. Kharasch, H. C. McBay, and W. H. Urry, *J. Org. Chem.,* **10,** 401 (1945).

which there is any good evidence for extensive disproportionation is methyl methacrylate, although even here results are somewhat contradictory. Bevington, Melville, and Taylor,[56] using radioactive azobisisobutyronitrile, have made the most extensive study and report approximately 1.2 initiator fragments per molecule. On the other hand, Arnett, in a similar experiment, has found approximately two

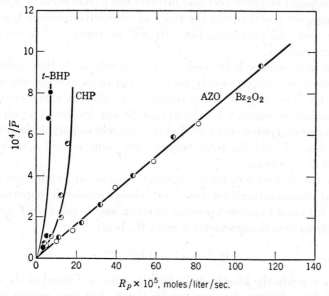

FIG. 3·6   Plot of $1/\bar{P}$ versus R_p for methyl methacrylate at 60° in the presence of various initiators: AZO, azobisisobutyronitrile; Bz$_2$O$_2$, benzoyl peroxide; CHP, cumene hydroperoxide; t-BHP, t-butyl hydroperoxide (after Baysal and Tobolsky[35]).

fragments per molecule,[55] and has also concluded that termination is by combination on kinetic grounds.[29]   An intermediate result is given by experiments on the decomposition of methyl α-azobisisobutyrate, which yields radicals which may be thought of as simple structural analogs of polymethacrylate radicals. Here, coupled and disproportionated products occur in a ratio of about 3:2; cf. Section 2·1b.

Regardless of the relative importance of disproportionation and coupling, it is evident that, for systems in which only the reactions so far considered are important, $\bar{P}$, like ν, will be inversely proportional to R_p and independent of the particular initiator involved. For a number of monomer-initiator systems this is true, but, in others, polymer molecular weights are lower than expected; cf. Fig. 3·6. A similar lowering of molecular weight occurs in the presence of many solvents, and certain monomers, e.g., vinyl acetate, give polymers with molecular weights essentially independent of R_p. All these results point to an additional process, leading to an increase in the number of polymer molecules without the interruption of kinetic chains. This is the process of *chain transfer* (with initiator, solvent, and monomer respectively) and involves the introduction of a radical displacement reaction into the chain of successive addition reactions which make up polymerization. It will be considered in detail in the next chapter.

The molecular weights and degrees of polymerization which we have discussed have properly been referred to as average quantities. Since the possibility of chain termination exists at every step of a polymerization chain, it is evident that, at any instant in a polymerization process, polymers of all different degrees of polymerization are being formed, and the total polymer has some sort of a molecular weight distribution.

The simplest such distribution arises when chain termination is via radical disproportionation (or where chain transfer is important).[75] Here, if k_p and k_t are independent of chain length, the weight fraction of polymer containing exactly n units W_n is given by

$$W_n = n(1 - 1/\nu)^2 \nu^{1-n} \tag{31a}$$

Here ν is again the kinetic chain length or the reciprocal of the probability of a chain undergoing termination rather than growth at any step. Similarly, if chains end by radical combination, the distribution becomes

$$W_n = n(n - 1)\nu^{2-n}(1 - 1/\nu)^3/2 \tag{31b}$$

Equation 31b indicates a considerably narrower distribution than 31a, and, in principle, determination of molecular weight distributions by some sort of fractionation procedure might be used to determine the nature of the termination process. An attempt to do this on polymethyl methacrylate has been made by Evans and co-workers [76] with results in rough agreement with eqs. 31. However, the difficulties of obtaining adequate fractionation are such that the results may be of only qualitative significance in indicating the actual existence of polymer with a range of molecular weights.

[75] Chapter 8 of reference cited in footnote 7.

[76] J. H. Baxendale, S. Bywater and M. G. Evans, *Trans. Faraday Soc.*, **42**, 675 (1946).

3 · 4   Evaluation of Individual Rate Constants
in Polymerization

3·4a   The k_p^2/k_t Ratio; Limitations of Steady-State Kinetics

Equation 17 may be rewritten as

$$k_p^2/k_t = (R_p/[M])^2/R_i \qquad (32)$$

Since R_p and $[M]$ are directly measurable and R_i may be determined essentially by the methods discussed in connection with the evaluation of initiator efficiencies (polymer molecular weights, rate of initiator decomposition, with f known or assumed, or inhibitor consumption), it is evident that the ratio of k_p^2/k_t can, in principle, be determined for any polymerizing system obeying the kinetics which we have outlined. Further, if the ratio is known, the polymerization rate may be predicted for any value of R_i, and a comparison of k_p^2/k_t ratios gives the relative rates of polymerization of different monomers at a given rate of chain initiation.

A comparison of different determinations of k_p^2/k_t for styrene by several groups of investigators [43, 77–81] is shown graphically in Fig. 3·7, and provides a very good measure of the general reproducibility and reliability of polymerization kinetics. The most consistent set of data, collected over the widest temperature range, are those of Tobolsky and Offenbach,[81] and, by the usual Arrhenius relationship:

$$k_p^2/k_t = [(PZ)_p^2/(PZ)_t]e^{-(2E_p-E_t)/RT} \qquad (33)$$

yield the relationship

$$k_p^2/k_t = 1.74 \times 10^5 e^{-12,740/RT} \qquad (34)$$

Tobolsky, incidently, has investigated the k_p^2/k_t ratio for a number of systems via the relation between polymer molecular weight and polymerization rate and has found it convenient to express his results in terms of the parameter

$$A' = (2k_{td} + k_{tc})/k_p^2 \qquad (35)$$

[77] M. S. Matheson, E. E. Auer, E. B. Bevilacqua, and E. J. Hart, *J. Am. Chem. Soc.*, **73**, 1700 (1951).

[78] F. R. Mayo, R. A. Gregg, and M. S. Matheson, *ibid.*, **72**, 1691 (1950).

[79] G. V. Schulz and E. Husemann, *Z. physik. Chem.*, **B39**, 246 (1938).

[80] H. W. Melville and L. Valentine, *Trans. Faraday Soc.*, **46**, 210 (1950).

[81] A. V. Tobolsky and J. Offenbach, *J. Polymer Sci.*, **16**, 311 (1955).

In converting to k_p^2/k_t above, chain termination by radical coupling has been assumed, and the major uncertainties in values of k_p^2/k_t calculated from eq. 34 arise from this assumption and possible error in molecular weight determinations.

Ferrington and Tobolsky [82] have recently made a similar investigation of methyl methacrylate polymerization, correlating data ob-

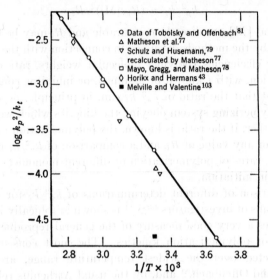

FIG. 3·7 Variation of k_p^2/k_t with temperature in the polymerization of styrene.

tained between 20 and 100°C. Assuming now chain termination by disproportionation, the data are well fitted by the relation

$$k_p^2/k_t = 6.67 \times 10^3 e^{-8180/RT} \tag{36}$$

From eqs. 34 and 36 k_p^2/k_t for styrene and methyl methacrylate at 60° are 0.0007 and 0.028 respectively. The corresponding value for vinyl acetate is 0.185, indicating that, at a given rate of chain initiation, polymerization rates increase markedly in the order styrene < methyl methacrylate < vinyl acetate.

Although the ratio k_p^2/k_t is a useful quantity, it is of greater interest to know the individual values of k_p and k_t, and these quantities cannot be obtained from any measurements of ordinary, steady-state reaction kinetics. Rather, it is generally necessary to go to systems in which non-steady-state conditions prevail. Photochemical tech-

[82] T. E. Ferrington and A. V. Tobolsky, *J. Colloid Sci.*, **10**, 536 (1955).

niques provide the most convenient way of setting up such conditions (since radical production may be abruptly started and stopped).

3·4b *Non-Steady-State Kinetics; The Rotating Sector Method*

If we consider a photoinduced polymerization (either with or without some photosensitizing agent present) we may write, for the radical concentration, analogous to eq. 14:

$$d[\mathrm{M}\cdot]/dt = 2fI_{abs} - 2k_t[\mathrm{M}\cdot]^2 \tag{37}$$

where I_{abs} represents the quanta of light absorbed in moles/liter/sec by the system, and f is the chain-starting efficiency of the photochemical process. Once steady-state conditions are reached, eq. 37 may be equated to zero, giving

$$2fI_{abs} = 2k_t[\mathrm{M}\cdot]_s^2 \tag{38}$$

but obviously at the very onset of irradiation eq. 38 is not a valid expression. We may now consider this period, and to do so it is convenient to rewrite eq. 37 as

$$d[\mathrm{M}\cdot]/dt = 2k_t([\mathrm{M}\cdot]_s^2 - [\mathrm{M}\cdot]^2) \tag{39}$$

and introduce the concept of the average lifetime of a growing polymer chain under steady-state conditions τ_s. This quantity is evidently equal to the radical concentration at the steady state, divided by the rate of disappearance of radicals:

$$\tau_s = [\mathrm{M}\cdot]_s/2k_t[\mathrm{M}\cdot]_s^2 = 1/2k_t[\mathrm{M}\cdot]_s \tag{40}$$

or, using eq. 13,

$$\tau_s = (k_p/2k_t)[\mathrm{M}]/(R_p)_s \tag{41}$$

Integration of eq. 39 and combining with eq. 40 gives us

$$\tanh^{-1}([\mathrm{M}\cdot]/[\mathrm{M}\cdot]_s) = (t - t_0)/\tau_s \tag{42}$$

where t_0 represents the time at which $[\mathrm{M}\cdot] = 0$. Similarly, the polymerization rate at any time t is given by

$$R_p/(R_p)_s = [\mathrm{M}\cdot]/[\mathrm{M}\cdot]_s = \tanh(t - t_0)/\tau_s \tag{43}$$

If $[\mathrm{M}\cdot]$ is not zero but, say, $[\mathrm{M}\cdot]_2$ at the beginning of illumination, the expression takes the form:

$$\tanh^{-1}([\mathrm{M}\cdot]_1/[\mathrm{M}\cdot]_s) - \tanh^{-1}([\mathrm{M}\cdot]_2/[\mathrm{M}\cdot]_s) = t/\tau_s \tag{44}$$

where $[M \cdot]_1$ is the radical concentration after a time of illumination t. If the light is turned off in such a system at time t, radical decay sets in by the relation

$$d[M \cdot]/dt = -2k_t[M \cdot]^2 \qquad (45)$$

giving a radical concentration $[M \cdot]$ after a further time interval t' of

$$1/[M \cdot] - 1/[M \cdot]_1 = 2k_t t' \qquad (46)$$

Again it is convenient to introduce steady-state concentrations and rewrite eq. 46 as

$$[M \cdot]_s/[M \cdot] - [M \cdot]_s/[M \cdot]_1 = t'/\tau_s \qquad (47)$$

or

$$(R_p)_s/R_p - (R_p)_s/(R_p)_1 = t'/\tau_s \qquad (48)$$

If we continue to alternate light and dark periods in this manner, $[M \cdot]$ and R_p will vary with time as indicated in Fig. 3·8,[83] with

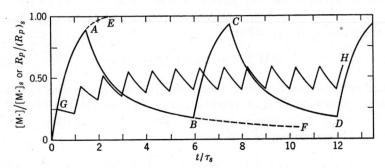

Fig. 3·8　Variation in radical concentration in photochemical experiment with alternate light and dark periods of time t and $3t$. Curve $OABCD$ for case $t/\tau_s = 1.5$; OGH, $t/\tau_s = 0.25$ (after Flory [7]).

radical concentrations rising and falling in a saw-tooth manner.

The study of the rate of polymerization in such flickering light as a function of the rate of flickering provides the basis of an important method of determining τ_s, from which the individual rate constants may be derived.

The limiting cases for very slow and very fast flickering are easily discussed. Let us take a specific example, with the length of a dark period, t', as equal to r times a light period, t, and set $r = 3$. From Fig. 3·8, it is evident that, if we take our flickering cycle very *long*

[83] Page 151 of reference cited in footnote 7. Flory's symbols are used throughout this section.

compared with τ_s, $R_p = (R_p)_s$ during essentially all of every light period, and $R_p = 0$ during essentially all of every dark period. Hence over a complete cycle

$$(R_p)_{avg} = (R_p)_s/4 \qquad (49)$$

On the other hand, if the flickering cycle is sufficiently *short* compared to τ_s, we are essentially conducting an experiment in steady light with $(I_{abs})_{avg} = (I_{abs})/4$. Here, since R_p is proportional to $(I_{abs})^{1/2}$

$$(R_p)_{avg} = (R_p)_s/4^{1/2} = (R_p)_s/2 \qquad (50)$$

and we see that, somewhere as the time of the flickering cycle passes through τ_s, a significant change in polymerization rate will occur. Such variations in rate with rate of flickering will occur, in general, whenever chain propagation and chain termination reactions are of different order in respect to the active centers involved.

The detailed form of this relationship, which permits the evaluation of τ_s, was first worked out by Briers, Chapman, and Walters,[84] and may be obtained as follows. After a number of cycles, it is evident that the saw-tooth shape of the radical concentration in Fig. 3·8 will assume a steady shape with the same radical concentration $[M \cdot]_1$ at the end of each consecutive light period, and also a constant value $[M \cdot]_2$ at the end of each dark period. Under these conditions, the *average* radical concentration is given by

$$[M \cdot]_{avg}(t + rt) = \int_0^t [M \cdot]\, dt + \int_0^{rt} [M \cdot]\, dt' \qquad (51)$$

where $[M \cdot]$'s in the integrals are given by eqs. 44 and 46, respectively. Evaluation of these integrals gives

$$\frac{[M \cdot]_{avg}}{[M \cdot]_s} = (r + 1)^{-1} \left\{ 1 + \frac{\tau_s}{t} \ln \left[\frac{[M \cdot]_1/[M \cdot]_2 + [M \cdot]_1/[M \cdot]_s}{1 + [M \cdot]_1/[M \cdot]_s} \right] \right\} \qquad (52)$$

Elimination of $[M \cdot]_1$ and $[M \cdot]_2$ from eq. 52 by the use of eqs. 44 and 45 gives $[M \cdot]_{avg}/[M \cdot]_s$ [or $(R_p)_{avg}/(R_p)_s$] as a function of τ_s/t for any value of the ratio of dark to light period, r. A plot of this relationship for $r = 2$ is shown in Fig. 3·10, and an extensive table of values $(R_p)_{avg}/(R_p)_s$ as a function of τ_s/t for various values of r has been given by Burnett and Melville in a recent review of this entire

[84] F. Briers, D. L. Chapman, and E. Walters, *J. Chem. Soc.*, **562** (1926); cf. W. A. Noyes, Jr., and P. A. Leighton, *The Photochemistry of Gases*, Reinhold Publishing Corp., New York, 1941, p. 202.

topic.[85] The more complex equations for the cases in which an appreciable dark reaction occurs have also been worked out,[85, 86] as have those for situations where the intensity of illumination has a trapezoidal form, and where chain termination is a combination of first- and second-order procesess.[40, 85]

Once τ_s is known, k_p and k_t may be obtained via eqs. 32 and 41. Experimentally, the desired intermittent illumination is usually obtained by placing between the light and the reaction system a rotat-

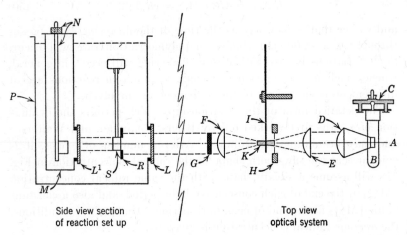

Side view section
of reaction set up

Top view
optical system

Fig. 3·9 Schematic diagram of apparatus used by Kwart, Broadbent, and Bartlett [89] for the polymerization of vinyl acetate with intermittent illumination.

ing disk from which sectors of suitable size have been cut. For this reason, this technique of determining rate constants is commonly known as the *rotating sector method*. It was first applied to liquid-phase radical reactions in 1945 by Bartlett [87] in the United States, and by Melville [88] in Great Britain. At present it appears to be the most accurate and dependable method of determining the rate constants in polymerization processes.

A diagram of the apparatus used by Kwart, Broadbent, and Bart-

[85] G. M. Burnett and H. W. Melville, *Technique of Organic Chemistry*, Volume VIII, A. Weissberger, editor, Interscience Publishers, New York, 1953, pp. 133–169.

[86] M. S. Matheson, E. E. Auer, E. B. Bevilacqua, and E. J. Hart, *J. Am. Chem. Soc.,* **71,** 497 (1949).

[87] P. D. Bartlett and C. G. Swain, *ibid.,* **67,** 2273 (1945) ; *ibid.,* **68,** 2381 (1946).

[88] G. M. Burnett and H. W. Melville, *Nature,* **156,** 661 (1945) ; *Proc. Roy. Soc. London,* **A189,** 456 (1947).

lett [89] is shown in Fig. 3·9.   Radiation from an 85-watt mercury arc B is focused by the quartz lenses D and E, passes through the iris H and the sectored disk I, and is collimated by the lens F, reaching the thermostatted quartz reaction cell S.   The image of the arc B is focused at K in order to give as sharp a transition from light to dark period as possible. G is a filter to isolate the desired portion of the spectrum, L and L^1 are transparent windows, and N is a photocell for monitoring the intensity of the light employed.

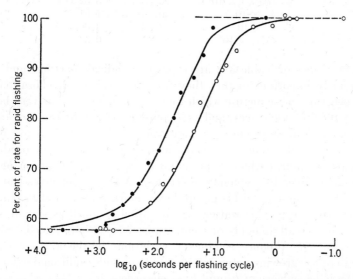

FIG. 3·10   Relative rates of polymerization of vinyl acetate at 25° as a function of rotating sector speed $(r = 2)$.[89]

The polymerization rate in such a system is conveniently followed dilatometrically, taking advantage of the large (known) difference in density between monomer and polymer.

Data obtained with this apparatus on the photopolymerization of vinyl acetate at 25° using di-t-butyl peroxide as a photosensitizer, are shown in Fig. 3·10, in which experimental points for runs at two light intensities are matched against the theoretical curve.   By displacing this calculated curve sideways to give the best fit to the data, τ_s is obtained, and the results are summarized in Table 3·2.   Di-t-butyl peroxide was used as a photosensitizer, and the ratio of k_p^2/k_t was obtained by the inhibitor technique using duroquinone.

[89] H. Kwart, H. S. Broadbent, and P. D. Bartlett, *J. Am. Chem. Soc.*, **72**, 1060 (1950).

TABLE 3·2   RATE CONSTANTS IN THE POLYMERIZATION OF VINYL ACETATE
AT 25°

(After Kwart, Broadbent, and Bartlett [89])

	Run 2	Run 3
$R_i \times 10^9$	1.11	7.29
$(R_p)_s \times 10^4$	0.450	1.19
$(k_p^2/k_t) \times 10^2$	3.17	3.37
τ_s, sec	4.00	1.50
$(k_p/k_t) \times 10^5$	3.35	3.32
$k_p \times 10^{-3}$	0.94	1.01
$k_t \times 10^{-7}$	2.83	3.06
$[M\cdot] \times 10^8$	0.44	0.54

The values of Table 3·2 are typical of radical reactions and are extremely important in that they provide detailed corroboration of the general kinetic picture which we have developed. k_t is very large (3×10^7 liter/mole/sec), and as a consequence the lifetimes of radical chains are short (1–4 sec), and radical concentrations are only about 0.5×10^{-8} molar. Nevertheless, since k_p has a value of about 10^3, every radical which is produced leads to polymerization of an average of over 10^4 monomer molecules. A number of investigators, notably Matheson and his group, have shown that k_p and k_t remain constant when polymerization rate is varied as much as sixfold, and also when small amounts of chain transfer agents are added. Since these changes produce significant variations in the average chain length of the growing polymer, the results provide additional evidence of the independence of k_p and k_t of chain length.

3·4c   Other Methods of Determining Rate Constants

An alternative scheme for determining τ_s in a photoinitiated system is by measurement of the *photochemical aftereffect,* or the rate of decay of the radical concentration after illumination is interrupted. Thus, from eq. 48, if $(R_p)_s/R_p$ is plotted against t', the slope of the line will be equal to $1/\tau_s$. Although the theory of this method is relatively simple, experimental techniques are very difficult. This is because either very slow reaction rates must be measured, in order to obtain large values for τ_s, or else extraordinarily rapid methods of measuring rates must be available. In either case, very small changes in the extent of reaction must be detected.

A most ingenious solution to this problem has been attempted by Bamford and the group at Courtaulds, Ltd., who have carried out polymerizations in a combination reaction cell–viscosimeter. Since the relation of both reaction rate and intrinsic viscosity to molecular weight are known and means are available for extrapolating relative viscosities to intrinsic viscosities, such a device makes it possible to follow changes in polymer concentration amounting to a very small fraction of a per cent. Accordingly, the dying out of radicals as measured by changes in R_p can be followed for many minutes and even hours. A number of assumptions are involved in converting the measured relative viscosities into reaction rates, and the computations are highly complex, so it is perhaps not surprising that results which have been obtained on styrene,[90] methyl methacrylate,[91] and vinyl acetate [92] are in only fair agreement with those obtained by the rotating sector method.

Another technique is to use a very accurate dilatometer. This has been done by Burnett [93] to investigate the *induction period*, i.e., the buildup in radical concentration, in styrene photopolymerized by very weak irradiation, using essentially eq. 43. Since the steady state was reached at a few hundredths per cent reaction, a dilatometer sensitive to about $10^{-3}\%$ reaction was required.

The alternative approach is to use a very rapid method of following small changes in the extent of reaction during the first few seconds following the cessation of irradiation. Techniques have been described for doing this by following changes in dielectric constant,[94] index of refraction,[95] and temperature changes.[96, 97] In the first two methods it turns out that the most convenient way of making such measurements is under essentially adiabatic conditions, so that all three methods depend upon the temperature rise (a few thousandths of a degree) occasioned by the heat liberated by the polymerization. An interesting modification of these rapid methods is to produce the desired radicals by a single intense pulse of light from a discharge tube (flash photolysis). Results to date show reasonably good agreement with the rotating sector method for several monomers, and the whole photochemical aftereffect method seems to show a great deal

[90] C. H. Bamford and M. J. S. Dewar, *Proc. Roy. Soc. London,* **A192,** 309 (1948).

[91] *Ibid.,* **A197,** 356 (1949).

[92] G. Dixon-Lewis, *ibid.,* **A198,** 510 (1949).

[93] G. M. Burnett, *Trans. Faraday Soc.,* **46,** 772 (1950).

[94] T. G. Majury and H. W. Melville, *Proc. Roy. Soc. London,* **A205,** 323, 496 (1951).

[95] N. Grassie and H. W. Melville, *ibid.,* **A207,** 285 (1951).

[96] W. I. Bengough and H. W. Melville, *ibid.,* **A225,** 330 (1954).

[97] W. I. Bengough and H. W. Melville, *ibid.,* **A230,** 429 (1955).

of promise for the study of radical reactions, particularly since expressions equivalent to eq. 48 may be obtained, and rate constants determined, even when chain growth and chain termination are both of the same order in respect to radical concentration, so that the rotating sector method is inapplicable.

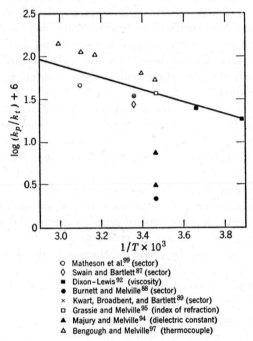

FIG. 3·11   Summary of values of k_p/k_t for vinyl acetate.

Another method of determining photochemical aftereffects and radical lifetimes would be by flow methods. Such a technique has been described by Goldfinger,[98] although results so far have been qualitative in nature. In Chapter 5 we will also see that in emulsion polymerization systems a method exists for determining k_p without the application of non-steady-state kinetics.

3·4d   Summary of Polymerization Rate Constants

We may now turn to a consideration of the reliability of the determination of polymerization rate constants by the methods we have described, and attempt to summarize what appear to be the best values for monomers upon which data are available. From the preceding discussion it is evident that determination of individual rate constants depends upon combining two different measurements, one giving k_p^2/k_t, and the other k_p/k_t, and it is the latter which is derived from non-steady-state experiments of some sort or another. Accordingly, in considering the reproducibility of this latter measure-

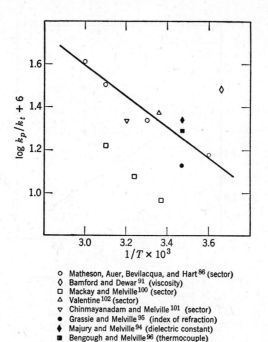

O   Matheson, Auer, Bevilacqua, and Hart[86] (sector)
◊   Bamford and Dewar[91] (viscosity)
□   Mackay and Melville[100] (sector)
△   Valentine[102] (sector)
▽   Chinmayanadam and Melville[101] (sector)
●   Grassie and Melville[95] (index of refraction)
◆   Majury and Melville[94] (dielectric constant)
■   Bengough and Melville[96] (thermocouple)

FIG. 3·12   Determinations of k_p/k_t for methyl methacrylate.

ment, it is convenient to compare various determinations of the k_p/k_t ratio rather than the individual rate constants themselves. Figure 3·11 summarizes data on vinyl acetate obtained in eight different studies.[87–89, 92, 94–95, 97, 99] The most reliable results are probably the sector experiments of Matheson [99] and Bartlett,[89] and are in excellent agreement. It is worth noting that vinyl acetate is a particularly difficult monomer with which to obtain reproducible polymerization since it stubbornly retains traces of impurities which behave as polymerization retarders. Similar summaries for methyl methacry-

[99] M. S. Matheson, E. E. Auer, E. B. Bevilacqua, and E. J. Hart, *J. Am. Chem. Soc.*, **71**, 2610 (1949).

late [86, 91, 94-96, 100-102] and styrene [90, 94-95, 103-105] appear in Figs. 3·12 and 3·13 with eight and six sets of determinations respectively. With methyl methacrylate, Matheson's [86] measurements (the most extensive series) lie close to the average of all determinations, and, although they differ somewhat from those of Mackay and Melville,[100] lines through the two sets of data show approximately the same

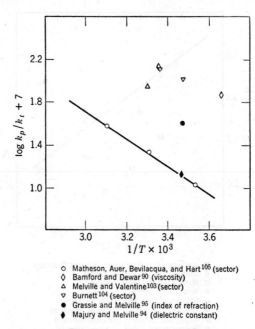

○ Matheson, Auer, Bevilacqua, and Hart [105] (sector)
◊ Bamford and Dewar [90] (viscosity)
△ Melville and Valentine [103] (sector)
▽ Burnett [104] (sector)
● Grassie and Melville [95] (index of refraction)
◆ Majury and Melville [94] (dielectric constant)

FIG. 3·13 Determinations of k_p/k_t for styrene.

slope and thus yield the same activation energy difference for k_p and k_t. The situation with styrene is rather more puzzling since Matheson's [105] data lie significantly below almost all other determinations. The possible sources of this discrepancy have been discussed at some length by Matheson [105] but still remain somewhat obscure.

[100] M. H. Mackay and H. W. Melville, *Trans. Faraday Soc.*, **45**, 323 (1950).

[101] B. R. Chinmayanandam and H. W. Melville, *ibid.*, **50**, 73 (1954).

[102] L. Valentine, thesis, Aberdeen, 1949, quoted by H. W. Melville and G. M. Burnett, *J. Polymer Sci.*, **13**, 417 (1954).

[103] H. W. Melville and L. Valentine, *Trans. Faraday Soc.*, **46**, 210 (1950).

[104] G. M. Burnett, *ibid.*, **46**, 772 (1950).

[105] M. S. Matheson, E. E. Auer, E. B. Bevilacqua, and E. J. Hart, *J. Am. Chem. Soc.*, **73**, 1700 (1951).

From the spread in the data displayed in Figs. $3 \cdot 11$–$3 \cdot 13$ and the further experimental error involved in the determination of k_p^2/k_p, it is plain that considerable uncertainty still surrounds the exact values of k_p and k_t for even the most carefully investigated monomers. The basic parameters from which k_p and k_t are determined are R_i, R_p and τ_s, and, if we express them in these terms, it is instructive to consider the effect of errors in these parameters on the final result. Via eqs. 17 and 41 we may write

$$k_t = 1/2R_i\tau_s{}^2 \tag{53}$$

$$k_p = R_p/[\mathrm{M}]R_i\tau_s \tag{54}$$

It is evident that a positive error in τ_s will give too small values of both k_p and k_t, but it will introduce a larger error into k_t. Similarly, a positive error in R_i will make both k_p and k_t too small, whereas R_p will only affect k_p. The greatest uncertainty arises in determining τ_s, and we should note that, although workers have frequently reported k_p and k_t to three figures, the actual values in the best cases are probably uncertain to at least 20%, and, in single determinations, as much as one power of 10. Nevertheless, it is desirable to summarize what seem to be the best values, and this is done in Table $3 \cdot 3$, where k's at 30 and 60° are listed (interpolating or extrapolating from data at other temperatures when necessary).

TABLE $3 \cdot 3$ ABSOLUTE RATE CONSTANTS FOR CHAIN PROPAGATION AND TERMINATION IN VINYL POLYMERIZATION

Monomer	k_p 30°	60°	E_p, kcal	$PZ_p \times 10^{-7}$	$k_t \times 10^{-7}$ 30°	60°	E_t, kcal	$PZ_t \times 10^{-9}$
Vinyl acetate [a]	990	2,300	6.3	3.2	2.0	2.9	3.2	3.7
Methyl methacrylate [a]	350	705	4.7	0.087	1.5	1.8	1.2	0.11
Styrene [a]	49	145	7.3	0.45	0.24	0.30	1.9	0.058
Methyl acrylate [106]	720	2,090	~7.1	~10	0.22	0.47	~5	~15
Butyl acrylate [107]	14				0.0009			
Vinyl chloride [108]	6800	12,300	3.7	0.33	1200	2300	4.2	600
Methacrylonitrile [109]	29	184	11.5	600	~1.1	2.3	5.0	45
4-Vinylpyridine [110]	12 (25°)				0.3 (25°)			
Butadiene [b, 111]	25	100	9.3	12				
Isoprene [b, 111]	11	50	9.8	12				

[a] See text for source of data.
[b] In emulsion system, cf. Section $5 \cdot 3a$.

[106] M. S. Matheson, E. E. Auer, E. B. Bevilacqua, and E. J. Hart, *J. Am. Chem. Soc.*, 73, 5395 (1951).
[107] H. W. Melville and A. F. Bickel, *Trans. Faraday Soc.*, 45, 1049 (1949).
[108] G. M. Burnett and W. W. Wright, *Proc. Roy. Soc. London*, A221, 28, 37, 41 (1954).
[109] N. Grassie and E. Vance, *Trans. Faraday Soc.*, 52, 727 (1956).
[110] P. F. Onyon, *ibid.*, 51, 400 (1955).
[111] M. Morton, P. P. Salatiello, and H. Landfield, *J. Polymer Sci.*, 8, 215, 279 (1952).

In the case of vinyl acetate, k_p/k_t has been taken as

$$8.7 \times 10^{-3} e^{-3100/RT} \tag{55}$$

a weighted average of all but the lowest results, indicated by the solid line in Fig. 3·10, and combined with Matheson's value of k_p^2/k_t. For methyl methacrylate and styrene, Matheson's values of k_p/k_t have been combined with Tobolsky's extensive correlations [81-82] of k_p^2/k_t. With the other monomers fewer sets of determinations are available; so there is both less choice and also less reliability in the results.

Matheson's data on methyl acrylate are listed, although k_p/k_t have also been determined by Melville's group.[94, 95] A serious difficulty arises with this monomer since τ_s increases rapidly with conversion, and results must be extrapolated to less than 1% reaction (cf. Section 5·2a). Results on butyl acrylate and vinyl chloride appear anomalous. In the first case, the low values of both k_p and k_t have been suggested as arising from steric hindrance, but subsequent determinations of τ_s vary by 15-fold,[94, 96] and the system is probably subject to the same difficulties as methyl acrylate. With vinyl chloride, the polymer is insoluble in monomer, so measurements have been carried out in tetrahydrofuran to give a homogeneous system. Both first- and second-order termination processes are important, and one suspects that k_p and k_t are both too large.

Estimates of activation energies and PZ factors are also included in Table 3·3 and certainly support the picture of radical chain processes developed here. Chain propagation is a rapid process with a rate constant of 10–10^4 and an activation energy of 4–10 kcal. Chain termination is still faster (k_t's of the order of 10^7 and E_a's < 5 kcal) so that in all of these systems radical concentrations are low and chain lives short.

A more detailed discussion of the variation of k_p with structure is given in the next chapter, but we may note that the experimental errors in E_p and E_t are actually too large for differences to have much significance. A similar uncertainty attends differences between PZ factors, but in general $PZ_p \sim 10^7$ and $PZ_t \sim 10^9$. The low value for the former probably arises here from the large overall entropy decrease on polymerization due to loss of vibrational degrees of freedom.[112]

[112] J. H. Baxendale and M. G. Evans, *Trans. Faraday Soc.*, **43**, 210 (1947). Cf. also Section 5·4.

CHAPTER 4

Copolymerization,
Chain Transfer, and Inhibition
in Polymerization

The experiments and techniques described in the last chapter have been successful in establishing the radical chain nature of vinyl polymerization, setting up a general kinetic scheme which accounts for overall polymerization rates and polymer molecular weights, and even in determining the individual rate constants of the steps involved in the radical chains. However, except for establishing the facts of the ready addition of radicals to a variety of olefins, and the general rapidity of radical chain termination processes in solution, they have told us little about the critically important problem of the effect of changes in structure on radical reactions. The basic reason for this is that, as we go from one olefin to another, we change the structure of both radical and substrate, producing effects upon the rate processes involved which are largely compensatory. In order to learn something more about the relation between structure and reactivity, it is necessary to devise systems in which we compare the relative reactivity of two or more substrates towards the same radical, or (a more difficult procedure) two radicals towards the same substrate. As we will see, the most successful, and the simplest, way of carrying out such comparisons is by measuring the relative rates of competitive reactions in which one of the reactions being compared (and that which we will usually take as our standard) is the chain propagation step in polymerization. Actually, it turns out that such measurements are often simpler and more reliable than the determination of overall rates of chain processes. The most important series of such comparisons are found in the study of copolymerization and chain transfer reactions, inhibition reactions representing, in general, a special case of one or the other of these. The method, furthermore, has broad application and will find frequent use in subsequent chapters.

4 · 1   Copolymerization [1,2]

4·1a   The Reaction of Copolymerization

If a polymerization is carried out on a mixture of two (or more) olefins, fractionation experiments on the resulting product often show that it consists not of a mixture of polymers arising from independent polymerization of the individual olefins but of a new material in which all types of monomer units are distributed along each polymer chain.[3,4] Such a product is known as a *copolymer*, and the reaction by which it is formed is termed *copolymerization*. Since the physical properties of a polymer are determined by the nature, relative quantities, and arrangement of monomer units along the chain, the copolymerization reaction is of great technical importance, as it permits altering the composition of a polymer to fit a particular practical use. Thus, although the bulk of the synthetic rubber manufactured is a general-purpose product consisting of a 75% butadiene–25% styrene copolymer (GR-S), replacement of the styrene by acrylonitrile yields a product with specifically high oil and solvent resistance. Similarly, the introduction of a small amount of vinyl chloride units into poly-vinylidene chloride gives a product with much improved physical properties for use as a plastic (Saran).

This technical interest in the reaction of copolymerization has led to its intensive study, and it was early recognized [1,2] that the composition of a copolymer might be quite different from that of the monomer mixture (or feed) from which it was being formed. Further, the relative tendencies of monomers to be incorporated into polymer chains did not correspond at all to their relative rates of polymerization alone, i.e., to $k_p^2/2k_t$. In fact, a number of monomers, e.g., maleic anhydride, readily enter into certain copolymers, while showing no tendency whatever to form high polymers by themselves. These observations point to the important problem of copolymer compositions as being a topic quite distinct from that of overall polymerization kinetics, and such proves to be the case. As we will see, its study,

[1] F. R. Mayo and C. Walling, *Chem. Revs.*, **46**, 191 (1950). Much of the material in this section is based directly upon this review.

[2] T. Alfrey, Jr., J. J. Bohrer, and H. Mark, *Copolymerization*, Interscience Publishers, New York, 1952. The subject is also discussed in the general references on polymer chemistry given in Chapter 3.

[3] H. Staudinger and J. Schneiders, *Ann.*, **541**, 151 (1939).

[4] F. R. Mayo and F. M. Lewis, *J. Am. Chem. Soc.*, **66**, 1594 (1944).

originally undertaken for purely practical purposes in order to determine the conditions under which copolymers could or could not be formed, has provided the largest body of information on the relation between structure and reactivity in radical reactions, and has led to the recognition of principles which appear to have very general applicability to a very wide variety of radical processes.

4·1b   Copolymer Compositions; the Copolymerization Equation

As we have seen, recognition that the rate constants of the polymerization process are independent of chain length provides one of the critical steps in formulating usable kinetic expressions for the polymerization process. A similar key to the problem of copolymer compositions lies in the recognition that the reactive properties of a growing polymer chain depend primarily upon the monomer unit at the growing end, and not upon the length and composition of the chain as a whole. If this assumption is introduced, it is plain that, in a polymerizing system containing two monomers, essentially two types of radical are present, and copolymer is formed as the result of four competing chain propagation reactions:

$$M_1 \cdot + M_1 \xrightarrow{k_{11}} M_1 \cdot$$
$$M_1 \cdot + M_2 \xrightarrow{k_{12}} M_2 \cdot$$
$$M_2 \cdot + M_1 \xrightarrow{k_{21}} M_1 \cdot \tag{1}$$
$$M_2 \cdot + M_2 \xrightarrow{k_{22}} M_2 \cdot$$

where $M_1 \cdot$ and $M_2 \cdot$ represent chains ending in monomer units M_1 and M_2 respectively.[5]

Under such conditions the rates of disappearance of M_1 and M_2 are given by

$$-d[M_1]/dt = k_{11}[M_1 \cdot][M_1] + k_{21}[M_2 \cdot][M_1] \tag{2a}$$
$$-d[M_2]/dt = k_{12}[M_1 \cdot][M_2] + k_{22}[M_2 \cdot][M_2] \tag{2b}$$

Also, since we are dealing with radicals as low-concentration intermediates, and since chains are long so that the major path by which radicals $M_1 \cdot$ and $M_2 \cdot$ are formed and destroyed is by interconversion of one into the other, we may write the steady-state expression

$$d[M_1 \cdot]/dt = k_{21}[M_2 \cdot][M_1] - k_{12}[M_1 \cdot][M_2] = 0 \tag{3}$$

Dividing eq. 2a by eq. 2b, eliminating radical concentrations via eq. 3, and introducing the parameters $r_1 = k_{11}/k_{12}$, $r_2 = k_{22}/k_{21}$, yields

[5] H. Dostal, *Monatsh.*, **69**, 424 (1936).

$$\frac{d[M_1]}{d[M_2]} = \frac{[M_1]}{[M_2]}\frac{r_1[M_1] + [M_2]}{[M_1] + r_2[M_2]} \tag{4}$$

by straightforward algebra. Equation 4 is the *copolymerization equation* first published in 1944 by Alfrey and Goldfinger,[6] by Mayo and Lewis,[4] and by Wall.[7] A similar derivation has subsequently been given by Melville, Noble, and Watson;[8] and Goldfinger and Kane[9] have also obtained eq. 4 by a statistical method which assumes reactions 1 and long chains formed from a monomer mixture of constant composition but which makes no explicit steady-state assumption. Equation 4 relates the composition of the copolymer being formed at any instant from a polymerizing mixture of monomers at concentrations $[M_1]$ and $[M_2]$ to the feed composition by means of the two parameters r_1 and r_2, the *monomer reactivity ratios* characteristic of the particular monomer pair. Each r, it may be seen, is the ratio of the rate constants for the reaction of a particular active center with the monomer corresponding to the end unit in the chain and with the other monomer in the system. This ratio is taken in such a way that a value of $r > 1$ indicates that an active center should react more readily with its own type of monomer, whereas $r < 1$ indicates that it will prefer the other species. Thus, in the copolymerization of styrene (M_1) with methyl methacrylate (M_2) at $60°$, $r_1 = 0.52$ and $r_2 = 0.46$,[1,4] indicating that each radical reacts about twice as readily with the monomer of opposite type. Further, it is evident that the form of eq. 4 is such that r's are independent of the particular concentration units employed, and that the copolymer composition depends only upon the *relative* monomer concentrations in the feed and will accordingly be independent of dilution.

The validity of eq. 4 was first demonstrated for the radical copolymerization of styrene–methyl methacrylate,[4] and it has subsequently been tested for over one hundred additional monomer pairs. In general it appears to be obeyed within the limits of experimental accuracy for all except a few systems (considered later) in which the preceding monomer unit affects the reactivity of the end group, or in which reversibility of a step (either chain propagation or the formation of an intermediate complex) complicates the kinetics. It has also been shown to describe the behavior of non-radical copolymeri-

[6] T. Alfrey, Jr., and G. Goldfinger, *J. Chem. Phys.*, **12**, 205, 322 (1944).

[7] F. T. Wall, *J. Am. Chem. Soc.*, **66**, 2050 (1944).

[8] H. W. Melville, B. Noble, and W. F. Watson, *J. Polymer Sci.*, **2**, 229 (1947).

[9] G. Goldfinger and T. Kane, *ibid.*, **3**, 462 (1948).

zations proceeding through carbonium ion or carbanion active centers,[1,2] although these will not be considered here.

Since rate constants for chain initiation or chain termination do not appear in the copolymerization equation, it predicts no dependence of copolymer composition on the overall rate of the polymerization process, nor upon the particular initiator starting the radical chain. This independence has been confirmed for styrene–methyl methacrylate initiated thermally,[4,10] photochemically,[10] by benzoyl peroxide,[4] and by β-ray irradiation,[11] and indirectly for many other systems. The question of the dependence of monomer reactivity ratios on medium is of more interest, since, in general, rate constants (and ratios of rate constants) refer to some specific environment. However, results here again confirm the general insensitivity of radical reactions to changes in the medium in which they take place. Again with styrene–methyl methacrylate no change in monomer reactivity ratios have been detected upon the addition of small amounts of water, ethyl benzene, dodecyl mercaptan, or hydroquinone, or the presence or absence of air,[4] nor by changing the reaction medium from mixtures of pure monomers to monomer solutions in ethyl acetate, benzene, or acetonitrile, or even to methanol, a solvent from which the polymer precipitates as it is formed.[4,12,13,14] Actually, since the customary method of determining monomer reactivity ratios is to select single values of r_1 and r_2 which predict the composition of the copolymers obtained from a wide variety of monomer ratios (and accordingly a wide range of media), the fact that eq. 4 applies at all to actual systems affords a general demonstration of this insensitivity. Because of the practical importance of emulsion polymerization, discussed in the next chapter, considerable attention has been given to the comparison of monomer reactivity ratios determined in emulsion and homogeneous systems. Again, the copolymerization equation is obeyed, and such changes in copolymer composition as occur apparently arise because monomer distribution between the phases preferentially removes one monomer from the reaction site.[15]

[10] C. Walling, E. R. Briggs, W. Cummings, and F. R. Mayo, *J. Am. Chem. Soc.*, **72**, 48 (1950).

[11] W. H. Seitzer, R. H. Goekermann, and A. V. Tobolsky, *ibid.*, **75**, 755 (1953).

[12] K. Nozaki, *J. Polymer Sci.*, **1**, 455 (1946).

[13] F. M. Lewis, C. Walling, W. Cummings, E. R. Briggs, and F. R. Mayo, *J. Am. Chem. Soc.*, **70**, 1519 (1948).

[14] C. C. Price and J. G. Walsh, *J. Polymer Sci.*, **6**, 239 (1951).

[15] Detailed discussions of such systems, with numerous original references, are given on pp. 224–225 of the reference cited in footnote 1, and in Chapter V of the reference cited in footnote 2.

Similar changes may be observed in the presence of a complexing agent which preferentially ties up one monomer,[16] or when the co-polymerization properties of an ionizable monomer like methacrylic acid are compared in aqueous solution at different values of pH.[17] Although such changes represent possible experimental complications, they contribute little more to our picture of free radical reactions. However, it is significant that monomer reactivity ratios in *ionic* polymerizations are usually notably different from those determined in the radical reaction. Accordingly, copolymerization experiments are often a very simple and convincing way of demonstrating whether a particular initiator system induces a radical chain reaction.[18]

4·1c   The Copolymer-Feed Relationship in Copolymerization

The copolymerization equation is so important in our study of the relation between structure and reactivity in radical reactions (in fact, equivalent expressions describe the feed-product relationship for any radical chain reaction with alternative, irreversible propagation steps) that its properties warrant rather detailed discussion. The manner in which copolymer compositions may vary with changes in the values of the monomer reactivity ratios is illustrated in Figs. 4·1 and 4·2. Figure 4·1 depicts the relatively simple case of $r_1 r_2 = 1$, i.e., the two monomers showing the same relative reactivities towards growing chains ending in either type of radical. In such a case the copoly-merization equation takes the relatively simple form.

$$d[M_1]/d[M_2] = r_1[M_1]/[M_2] \qquad (5)$$

This situation has been termed an "ideal" copolymerization by Wall,[7] who pointed out the analogy between plots such as Figs. 4·1 and 4·2 and liquid-vapor diagrams. Figure 4·2 illustrates a series of systems where r_2 remains constant at 0.5, and r_1 varies between 2 and 0. Here a chain ending in M_2 preferentially next adds M_1 and, as r_1 decreases, there is also an increasing tendency for a chain end-ing in M_1 to next add M_2 as well. The formation of such *alternating copolymers* is perhaps the most important and significant feature of

---

[16] H. C. Haas and E. R. Karlin, *J. Polymer Sci.*, **9**, 588 (1952).

[17] T. Alfrey, Jr., C. G. Overberger, and S. H. Pinner, *J. Am. Chem. Soc.*, **75**, 4221 (1953); A. Drucker and H. Morawetz, *ibid.*, **78**, 346 (1956).

[18] Again, styrene–methyl methacrylate make a convenient pair for such experi-ments, since a 1:1 feed gives an approximately 1:1 copolymer by radical poly-merization but essentially pure polystyrene and pure polymethacrylate respec-tively by carbonium and carbanion mechanisms; [10] cf. also R. L. Dannley and E. L. Kay, *ibid.*, **77**, 1046 (1955).

radical copolymerizations and is discussed in detail below. The extent of this alternating tendency in a system is conveniently measured by the magnitude of the r_1r_2 product, where both r's are finite, which approaches zero with increasing alternation. It should be noted that, for the limiting case of $r_1 = 0$, it is implied that M_1 is incapable of polymerizing alone.

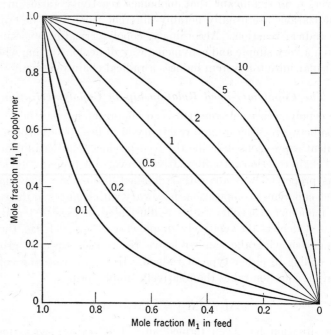

FIG. 4·1   Relationship between copolymer and feed compositions for "ideal" copolymerizations for indicated values of r_1 $(r_1r_2 = 1)$.[1]

Figure 4·2 indicates an interesting property of alternating copolymerizations. For values of $r_1 < 1$, the curve of copolymer composition crosses the line representing the composition of the feed. At this point, feed and copolymer compositions are identical. Wall,[7] again in analogy to distillation, has termed the reaction under such conditions an *azeotropic copolymerization*. From eq. 4 it is easily shown that the feed composition at this crossing is given by

$$[M_1]/[M_2] = (r_2 - 1)/(r_1 - 1) \qquad (6)$$

Since r_1 and r_2 are both necessarily positive, the condition for the existence of an azeotropic copolymerization is that both monomer reactivity ratios be simultaneously larger or smaller than unity. The former case, which would indicate a tendency of both monomers to polymerize concurrently but *independently*, has not been observed experimentally.

Inspection of Figs. 4·1 and 4·2 shows that, for an approximately "ideal" copolymer, if monomers differ appreciably in reactivity, the

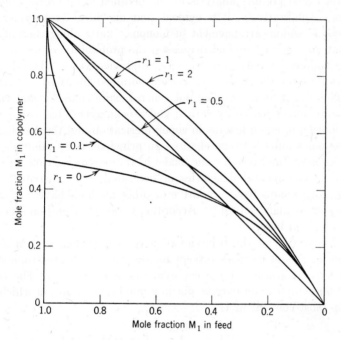

FIG. 4·2 Effect of increasing alternation on relation between feed and copolymer compositions ($r_2 = 0.5$ for every system).[1]

initial copolymer will consist almost entirely of the more reactive component. In fact, in such a system it is evident that continued reaction will yield first essentially a pure polymer of the more re-active monomer and, after this component is exhausted, essentially pure polymer of the other. Styrene–vinyl acetate provides a good example of such a system, the initial polymer from a 1:1 feed being about 98% polystyrene. On the other hand, if the system shows a strong tendency to alternate, the polymer composition will approxi-mate the azeotropic copolymer composition over a wide range of initial feeds. Styrene–maleic anhydride is a good example of such behavior, giving an almost 1:1 copolymer for almost any monomer ratio in the feed. This alternating tendency is thus of great practical importance, as it permits the preparation of copolymers from a wide variety of monomers which, if they showed "ideal" behavior, would differ too much in reactivity for both components to be included in the polymer chain in significant amounts.

The picture of the copolymerization reaction from which eq. 4 was obtained also permits analysis of the detailed structure of polymer chains. Qualitatively, it is evident that an "ideal" copolymer will possess a random arrangement of monomer units along the polymer chain. As the $r_1 r_2$ product decreases, the probability of an M_1 unit being followed by M_2 will increase, and vice versa. Distribution expressions for the "ideal" case were obtained by Wall;[7,19] Alfrey and Goldfinger[6] have worked out general expressions for any values of the monomer reactivity ratios; and Stockmayer[20] has treated the distribution of chain lengths in copolymerization and the distribution of monomer units between chains. In principle, these analyses provide an additional test for our model of the polymerization reaction, but the experimental difficulties of determining the distribution of units along chains by degradative or other methods have so far not been convincingly solved.[21] Accordingly the distribution functions are not given here.

Consideration of the behavior of a copolymerizing system as reaction progresses requires (except for the case of an azeotropic composition) integration of the copolymerization equation. The result is rather complex and may be put in a number of forms, of which one of the most convenient is

$$r_2 = \frac{\log \dfrac{[M_2]_0}{[M_2]} - \dfrac{1}{p} \log \dfrac{1 - p[M_1]/[M_2]}{1 - p[M_1]_0/[M_2]_0}}{\log \dfrac{[M_1]_0}{[M_1]} + \log \dfrac{1 - p[M_1]/[M_2]}{1 - p[M_1]_0/[M_2]_0}} \qquad (7)$$

where $p = (1 - r_1)/(1 - r_2)$.

However, if it is desired to calculate the change in copolymer composition with conversion for a system in which r_1 and r_2 are known, the most convenient method is a numerical or graphical one devel-

[19] F. T. Wall, *ibid.*, **62**, 803 (1940).

[20] W. H. Stockmayer, *J. Chem. Phys.*, **13**, 199 (1945).

[21] Alfrey et al. give a detailed discussion of the state of this problem, Chapter 7 of the reference cited in footnote 2; cf. also F. W. Morthland and W. G. Brown, *J. Am. Chem Soc.*, **78**, 469 (1956).

oped by Skeist.[22] For the purpose, eq. 4 may be expressed in the form

$$\frac{d[M_1]}{d([M_1] + [M_2])} = F_1 = \frac{r_1 f_1^2 + f_1 f_2}{r_1 f_1^2 + 2 f_1 f_2 + r_2 f_2^2} \tag{8}$$

where f_1 and f_2 are now mole fractions of monomers in the feed. If we consider a mixture such that the polymer being formed contains more of monomer M_1 than the feed, i.e., $F_1 > f_1$, and in which there are a total of M moles of monomers present, when dM moles have polymerized the polymer will contain $F_1 dM$ moles of M_1. At the same time, the number of moles of M_1 in the feed will have been reduced to $(M - dM)(f_1 - df_1)$. Consequently the material balance for M_1 gives

$$f_1 M - (M - dM)(f_1 - df_1) = F_1 dM \tag{9}$$

whence

$$dM/M = df_1/(F_1 - f_1) \tag{10}$$

or

$$\ln M/M_0 = \int_{(f_1)_0}^{(f_1)} df_1/(F_1 - f_1) \tag{11}$$

If the quantities F_1 and $1/(F_1 - f_1)$ are computed from eq. 8 at suitable intervals for $0 < f_1 < 1$, the fraction of total monomers which must react to change the composition of residual monomers from any value to any other value may be obtained by determining $\ln (M/M_0)$ by graphical or numerical integration of eq. 11 between the desired values of f_1. The corresponding value of F_1 (the composition of the polymer being formed at that point in the reaction) is then given by eq. 8. The average composition of the total polymer formed at that point follows by graphical integration of a plot of F_1 versus M_1, or as the difference between the composition and amount of residual monomers and those originally present. Figures 4·3 and 4·4, taken from the review by Mayo and Walling,[1] illustrate the manner in which the composition of the copolymer being formed varies with conversion for two typical systems: styrene–2-vinylthiophene ($r_1 = 0.35, r_2 = 3.10$), an almost ideal system in which the monomers differ threefold in reactivity, and styrene–diethyl fumarate, a strongly alternating pair ($r_1 = 0.30, r_2 = 0.07$). In the first system, all initial copolymers are richer in 2-vinylthiophene than the feed, but the final copolymer is almost pure polystyrene. In the second system, which

[22] I. Skeist, *J. Am. Chem. Soc.*, **68**, 1781 (1946); cf. I. H. Spinner, B. C. Y. Lu, and W. F. Graydon, *ibid.*, **77**, 2198 (1955).

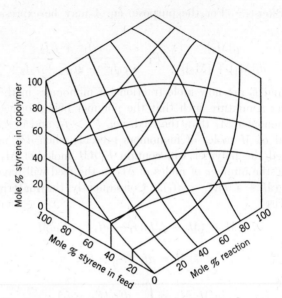

Fig. 4·3 Styrene–2-vinylthiophene: variation in instantaneous composition of the copolymer being formed with initial feed and per cent reaction.[1]

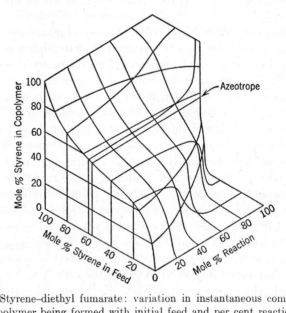

Fig. 4·4 Styrene–diethyl fumarate: variation in instantaneous composition of copolymer being formed with initial feed and per cent reaction.[1]

forms an azeotropic copolymer containing 57 mole % styrene, the picture is more complicated but substantiates the qualitative description of such systems given in a preceding paragraph.   By similar graphical procedures, integrated copolymer compositions and copolymer composition distributions may be obtained as a function of conversion, and a number of such plots are given in the reference cited.[1]

4·1d   The Determination of Monomer Reactivity Ratios

The usual procedure for evaluating r_1 and r_2 for a given monomer pair involves the determination of the composition of the copolymers formed from two or more feeds of different composition.   Such experiments require considerable care and must usually be carried out for this particular purpose.   Feed compositions must be accurately known, and conversions kept low enough so that significant quantities of both monomers are left unreacted.   In fact, it is usually desirable to keep conversions under 10% so as to avoid the necessity of using the integrated form of the copolymerization equation in the subsequent evaluation of data.   (It is common practice, after the polymer has been isolated and analyzed, to correct the feed to its average value during the course of the reaction.)

Polymer isolation and analysis also require particular care in order to yield significant results.   The polymer must be completely separated from unreacted monomer, initiator, etc., by several precipitations from a solvent by a non-solvent, and then dried to constant weight, preferably in a finely divided form or by "freeze drying" from a solvent such as benzene.[23]

Polymer compositions have usually been determined by ultimate analysis, but, in some cases, functional group determination (i.e., of acetoxy groups in vinyl acetate copolymers) or spectroscopic methods are applicable.

Once copolymer and feed compositions are known, essentially three procedures are available for determining r_1 and r_2 for the system. One is basically the reverse of the technique by which Figs. 4·1 and 4·2 were drawn.   Experimental points are entered on a plot of copolymer composition versus feed, and values of r_1 and r_2 selected by trial and error until the best fit of eq. 4 is obtained.   Obviously, this method is tedious, and it is difficult to tell when the best fit has been reached.   Further, the method is only applicable to low-conver-

[23] F. M. Lewis and F. R. Mayo, *Ind. Eng. Chem. Anal. Ed.,* **17,** 134 (1945).

sion experiments where the differential form of the copolymerization equation is valid. From the figures it is evident that the fit will be most sensitive to changes in r's near either end of the curves, i.e., at very high or very low $[M_1]/[M_2]$ ratios. Unfortunately, this is often the region in which it is most difficult to get sufficiently reliable analytical values for calculating copolymer compositions.

A second method for determining r_1 and r_2 is to substitute experimental values of feed and copolymer composition for a single experi-

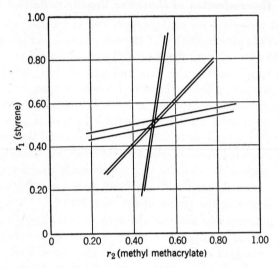

Fig. 4·5　Graphical solution of copolymerization equation for styrene–methyl methacrylate (six experiments).[1, 4]

ment into eqs. 4 or 8, and then plot r_2 as a function of r_1. The result is a straight line, and plots for a series of such experiments at different initial feeds should, in principle, intersect at a point, the desired values of r_1 and r_2 for the system. In practice, of course, some scatter is observed, and the center of intersection is taken as the best values of r_1 and r_2. Figure 4·5 shows such an intersection, taken from the original paper of Mayo and Lewis,[4] duplicate experiments at three monomer ratios all intersecting in a very small region, in excellent confirmation of the copolymerization scheme. Similar results have been obtained with a large number of other monomer pairs, the chief source of uncertainty in the results lying in errors in polymer analysis. This technique of determining r's may also be applied to higher-conversion experiments using the integrated copolymerization equation, conveniently in the form of eq. 7. The properties of the resulting function have been discussed in detail by Mayo and Walling.[1]

A third method for selecting r's which is particularly applicable to series of low-conversion experiments at different feeds is that of Fineman and Ross.[24] In their method, eq. 4 is rearranged in linear form

$$(\rho - 1)/R = r_1 - (\rho/R^2)r_2 \qquad (12)$$

with $\rho = d[M_1]/d[M_2]$, $R = [M_1]/[M_2]\cdot$. The left-hand side of eq. 12 and the quantity in parenthesis on the right-hand side may

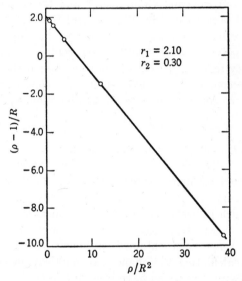

FIG. 4·6   Fineman-Ross method for determining monomer reactivity ratios.[24] System, ethyl methacrylate (M_1) with vinylidene chloride (M_2) at 68° (data of Alfrey et al.).[25]

be calculated for the experimental data of each experiment. The former is then plotted against the latter and the best straight line drawn through the resulting points by the method of least squares. The intercept and slope of this line are then equal to r_1 and $-r_2$ respectively, and well-established statistical methods are available for estimating their reliability. Figure 4·6 shows such a plot using data of Alfrey et al.[25] on the copolymerization of ethyl methacrylate–

[24] M. Fineman and S. D. Ross, *J. Polymer Sci.*, **5**, 259 (1950); a nomograph for solving the copolymerization equation has also been described, J. M. Whelan, *ibid.*, **14**, 409 (1954).

[25] P. Agron, T. Alfrey, Jr., J. Bohrer, H. Haas, and H. Wechsler, *ibid.*, **3**, 157 (1948).

vinylidene chloride at 68°. These authors originally estimated $r_1 = 2.2$, $r_2 = 0.35$ by the curve-fitting method, whereas an $r_1 - r_2$ plot indicates $r_1 = 2.04 \pm 0.12$, $r_2 = 0.28 \pm 0.08$. This gives a good comparison of the three techniques and illustrates the difficulties in choosing the best fit to a non-linear feed-copolymer composition diagram.

4·1e   Copolymerization in More Complex Systems

The procedure used in deriving eq. 4 may be extended to systems containing more than two components. The three-component case was solved by Alfrey and Goldfinger,[26] and the general case of n monomers has been treated by Walling and Briggs.[27] The resulting expressions are too complex to give here, but they give the composition of the copolymer in terms of the feed composition and the monomer reactivity ratios involved. They thus present the possibility of predicting the composition of multicomponent copolymers from data obtained on two component systems. Verification of this treatment was first obtained by Walling and Briggs [27] for various combinations of styrene, methyl methacrylate, acrylonitrile, and vinylidene chloride (Table 4·1) and has subsequently been extended to other systems as well.[28] The good agreement obtained between theory and experiment provides further verification of the correctness of copolymerization theory, as well as an interesting example of the complex systems in which radical reactions are still amenable to quantitative treatment. Integrated expressions for such polycomponent systems, however, have not been obtained, although series and numerical methods for calculating the changes in multicomponent copolymer compositions with conversion have been developed.[22, 27]

We have seen that eq. 4 provides an accurate description of the feed-copolymer composition relation for the great majority of monomer pairs. However, Fordyce and Ham,[29] and more specifically Barb,[30] have recently pointed out that appreciable discrepancies appear in certain strongly alternating systems, pointing to an effect of at least the preceding unit in the monomer chain. The copolymer composition relation for such a situation had previously been worked

[26] T. Alfrey, Jr., and G. Goldfinger, *J. Chem. Phys.*, **12**, 332 (1944).

[27] C. Walling and E. R. Briggs, *J. Am. Chem. Soc.*, **67**, 1774 (1945).

[28] (a) E. C. Chapin, G. E. Ham, and R. G. Fordyce, *ibid.*, **70**, 538 (1948); (b) S. L. Aggarwal and F. A. Long, *J. Polymer Sci.*, **11**, 127 (1953).

[29] R. G. Fordyce and G. E. Ham, *J. Am. Chem. Soc.*, **73**, 1186 (1951).

[30] W. G. Barb, *J. Polymer Sci.*, **11**, 117 (1953). A criticism of the treatment by R. M. Joshi, *ibid.*, seems to have been effectively answered, W. G. Barb, *ibid.*, **18**, 310 (1955).

TABLE 4·1   THREE- AND FOUR-COMPONENT POLYMERIZATIONS OF STYRENE (S.), METHYL METHACRYLATE (M.), ACRYLONITRILE (A.), AND VINYLIDENE CHLORIDE (V.) AT 60°C [27]

		Feed		Polymer	
	Mole %	Mono- mers	Found, mole %	Calculated, mole %
1.	31.24	S.	43.4	44.3
	31.12	M.	39.4	41.2
	37.64	V.	17.2	14.5
2.	35.10	M.	50.8	54.3
	28.24	A.	28.3	29.7
	36.66	V.	20.9	16.0
3.	34.03	S.	52.8	52.4
	34.49	A.	36.7	40.5
	31.48	V.	10.5	7.1
4.	35.92	S.	44.7	43.6
	36.03	M.	26.1	29.2
	28.05	A.	29.2	27.2
5.	53.23	S.	52.6	52.9
	26.51	M.	20.2	23.2
	20.26	A.	27.2	23.9
6.	28.32	S.	38.4	41.4
	28.24	M.	23.0	22.7
	43.44	A.	38.6	35.9
7.	27.76	S.	36.4	36.8
	52.06	M.	40.6	43.8
	20.18	A.	23.0	19.4
8.	25.21	S.	40.7	41.0
	25.48	M.	25.5	27.3
	23.91	V.	8.0	6.9
	25.40	A.	25.8	24.8

out by Merz, Alfrey, and Goldfinger.[31]   Here the reactions determining monomer consumption are

$$-d[M_1]/dt = k_{11}[M_1][M_1M_1 \cdot] + k'_{11}[M_1][M_2M_1 \cdot]$$
$$+ k_{21}[M_1][M_2M_2 \cdot] + k'_{21}[M_1][M_1M_2 \cdot]$$

$$-d[M_2]/dt = k_{12}[M_2][M_1M_1 \cdot] + k'_{12}[M_2][M_2M_1 \cdot]$$
$$+ k_{22}[M_2][M_2M_2 \cdot] + k'_{22}[M_2][M_1M_2 \cdot]$$

(13)

[31] E. Merz, T. Alfrey, and G. Goldfinger, *ibid.*, **1**, 75 (1946).

where $M_1M_1\cdot$ represents a chain ending in two consecutive M_1 units, etc. By introducing the usual steady-state approximation for each radical, they obtain:

$$\frac{d[M_1]}{d[M_2]} = \frac{1 + r'_1 \dfrac{[M_1]}{[M_2]} \dfrac{[M_2] + r_1[M_1]}{[M_2] + r'_1[M_1]}}{1 + r'_2 \dfrac{[M_2]}{[M_1]} \dfrac{r_2[M_2] + [M_1]}{[r'_2[M_2] + [M_1]]}} \tag{14}$$

with $r_1 = k_{11}/k_{21}$, $r'_1 = k'_{11}/k'_{21}$, etc.

Barb [30] has investigated the application of eq. 14 to the system of styrene (M_1)–maleic anhydride (M_2) polymerized in acetone or methyl propyl ketone. Here eq. 14 takes a somewhat simpler form

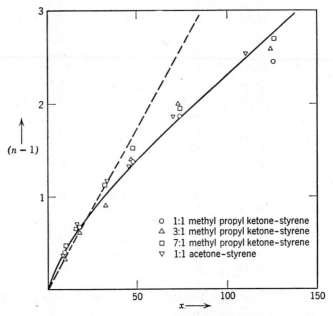

FIG. 4·7   Composition of styrene (M_1) with maleic anhydride (M_2) copolymers.[30] $n = [M_1]/[M_2]$ in polymer, $x = [M_1]/[M_2]$ in feed. Experiments run in methyl propyl ketone at different ketone-styrene ratios.

since both r_2 and r'_2 are effectively zero. Results are shown in Fig. 4·7. In Barb's notation, $n = d[M_1]/d[M_2]$ and $x = [M_1]/[M_2]$, and the solid curve is that calculated for $r'_1 = 0.063$, $r_1 = 0.017$. The dashed line indicates the best fit that can be obtained with the usual copolymerization equation. A similar application to Fordyce and Ham's data [29] on styrene (M_1)–fumaronitrile (M_2) gives a best fit with $r'_1 = 1.0$, $r_1 = 0.07$, where again the usual equation gives no consistent values. Subsequently, Ham [32] has resurveyed data on several systems, and obtained evidence for the necessity of using eq. 14 in treating the copolymerization of acrylonitrile with styrene, α-methylstyrene, and α-acetoxystyrene. On the other hand systems involving methacrylonitrile, methyl acrylate, or acrylic, methacrylic, and crotonic acids showed no such property. Detection of such an effect of the penultimate unit in a growing chain upon reactivity requires unusually precise and extensive data, and it may well be that other systems show such phenomena as well.

Another complication in the treatment of the problem of copolymer compositions arises if a significantly reversible step is introduced into the polymerization process. A number of monomer pairs, for example, styrene–maleic anhydride, form reversible, rather highly dissociated complexes in solution, with characteristic absorption spectra, often extending well into the visible region.[33, 34, 35] Although such complexes are by no means specific for polymerizable monomers (maleic anhydride forms colored complexes with anthracene, with which it undergoes a Diels-Alder reaction, and with other aromatic hydrocarbons with which it does not react at all) the possible role of such complexes in accounting for the alternating tendencies of many systems requires consideration. However, participation of such complexes in the polymerization process should introduce a dependence of monomer reactivities on concentration and solvent which has been looked for by many workers [4, 12, 13, 14] but has not been observed. Furthermore, if complex formation were the sole cause of alternation, the behavior of such systems as maleic anhydride–isobutylene (which gives an alternating copolymer but shows no evidence of complex formation) would be difficult to account for.

In contrast to this behavior of vinyl monomer systems, the "copolymerization" of sulfur dioxide and olefins, a process discussed further in Section 5·4c, shows a concentration dependence both in its overall kinetics and in the composition of the products, which strongly suggests the presence of a reversible step. In fact, since ordinary

[32] G. E. Ham, *ibid.*, **14**, 87 (1954).

[33] P. D. Bartlett and K. Nozaki, *J. Am. Chem. Soc.*, **68**, 1495 (1946).

[34] C. Walling, E. R. Briggs, K. B. Wolfstirn, and F. R. Mayo, *ibid.*, **70**, 1537 (1948).

[35] W. G. Barb, *Trans. Faraday Soc.*, **49**, 143 (1953).

Free Radicals in Solution

Table 4·2 Summary of Recent Copolymerization Data

r_1	M_2	r_2	Temperature, °C	Footnote
		M_1 = Styrene		
0.23 ± 0.1	β-Bromovinyl ethyl ether	0.02 ± 0.02	80	46
0.65	Butadiene	1.83	45 [a]	39
0.64		1.38	5 [a]	40
0.38		1.37	−18 [a]	41
0.4 ± 0.1	6-Chloro-2-vinylnaphthalene	1.5 ± 0.2	60	42
0.85 ± 0.1	4-Chloro-1-vinylnaphthalene	0.8 ± 0.1	60	42
0.33	1,1-Dihydroperfluorobutyl acrylate	0.07	50	44
0.42 ± 0.02	2,3-Dimethylbutadiene	0.92 ± 0.02	−18 [a]	36
23.5 ± 0.1	Ethyl β-ethoxyacrylate	~0	80	46
0.50 ± 0.10	2-Fluorobutadiene	1.55 ± 0.10	50	45
0.16 ± 0.08		1.61 ± 0.24	5 [a]	45
0.23 ± 0.1	Fumaronitrile	0.01	...	53
0.04	Fumaryl chloride	0.0	70	37
0.48 ± 0.01	Isoprene	1.30 ± 0.02	−18 [a]	36
4.5	Methyl vinyl sulfide	0.15	60	43
3.3	Methyl vinyl sulfone	0.01 ± 0.01	60	43
4.2 ± 0.2	Methyl vinyl sulfoxide	0.01 ± 0.01	60	38
0.66	α,β,β-Trifluorostyrene	0.07	50 [a]	56c
1.10 ± 0.01	Trimethyl aconitate	<0.01	60	56b
0.005	Vinylidene cyanide	0.001	45	56
0.5 ± 0.1	β-Vinylnaphthalene	1.4 ± 0.1	60	42
		M_1 = Butadiene		
0.28	Acrylonitrile	0.02	5 [a]	47
0.78 ± 0.12	Benzalacetophenone	<0.03	60	48
0.35	1,1-Dihydroperfluorobutyl acrylate	0.07	50 [a]	44
0.85	2,3-Dimethylbutadiene	0.63	5 [a]	40
0.75	Isoprene	0.85	5 [a]	40
1.07 ± 0.12	Methyl 2-chlorocinnamate	<0.03	60	48
1.20 ± 0.12		<0.02	80	48
2.7 ± 0.3	Methyl 4-chlorocinnamate	<0.05	80	48
0.35 ± 0.01	Methyl thiolacrylate	0.20 ± 0.05	70	48a
0.75	Methyl methacrylate	0.31	...	49
0.76	Nonyl methacrylate	0.32	...	49
0.40 ± 0.03	Trimethyl aconitate	<0.015	60	56b
		M_1 = Methyl Methacrylate		
0.45 ± 0.05	6-Chloro-2-vinylnaphthalene	1.6 ± 0.2	60	42
0.7 ± 0.2	4-Chloro-1-vinylnaphthalene	0.7 ± 0.02	60	42
1.4	1,1-Dihydroperfluorobutyl acrylate	0.25	50	44
3.5 ± 0.5	Fumaronitrile	0.01 ± 0.01	...	53
3.5	Maleic anhydride	0.03	60	56a
20 ± 10	Methyl vinyl sulfoxide	~0	60	38
0.046	Vinylidene cyanide	0.031	50	56
0.4 ± 0.05	β-Vinylnaphthalene	1.0 ± 0.15	60	42
Large	Vinyl sulfonic acid	~0	70	37
		M_1 = Acrylonitrile		
0	1-Acetoxybutadiene	0.7	70	37
0.875	Acrylamide	1.357	...	50
3.96 ± 0.53	Allyl alcohol	0.11 ± 0.10	...	56d
1.003 ± 0.012	Butyl acrylate	1.005 ± 0.005	...	51
10.5 ± 1.5	Ethyl β-ethoxyacrylate	0.02 ± 0.02	80	46
0.7 ± 0.2	Ethyl vinyl ether	0.03 ± 0.02	80	46
0.07 ± 0.03	2-Fluorobutadiene	0.59 ± 0.10	50	45
0.06	Methacrolein	2.0	70	37
5.50 ± 0.5	Trimethyl aconitate	~0	60	56b
4.3	Vinyl stearate	0.03	70	37a
6.0	Vinyl trimethoxysilane	~0	...	54
		M_1 = Methyl Acrylate		
31.5 ± 2.5	β-Bromovinyl ethyl ether	~0	80	46
0.40	Methyl vinyl sulfide	0.05	60	43
0.10 ± 0.03	2-Vinylphenanthrene	2.0 ± 0.2	60	42
0.80 ± 0.05	3-Vinylphenanthrene	1.75 ± 0.25	60	42
5.8	Vinyl stearate	0.03	70	37a
		M_1 = Vinyl Acetate		
0	1-Acetoxybutadiene	Very large	70	37
...	Fumaryl chloride	0.0	70	37
0.076 ± 0.04	Maleic anhydride	0.01	...	55
0.05	Methyl vinyl ketone	7.0	70	37
0.28	Methyl vinyl sulfone	0.35	60	43
0.522	Monomethylmaleate	0.035	56	52
0.0054	Vinylidene cyanide	0.11	45	56
0.90	Vinyl stearate	0.73	70	37a
0.6	Vinyl trifluoroacetate	0.32	60	56e

TABLE 4·2   SUMMARY OF RECENT COPOLYMERIZATION DATA (*Continued*)

r_1	M_2	r_2	Temperature, °C	Footnote
	M₁ = Vinylidene Cyanide			
0.29 ± 0.08	Acrylic acid	0.26 ± 0.06	50	56
0.0017	2-Chlorobutadiene	0.010	40	56
0.20 ± .06	2-Chloropropene	~0	40	56
30	*cis*-Dichloroethylene	~0	40	56
30	*trans*-Dichloroethylene	~0	40	56
0.0092	2,5-Dichlorostyrene	0.031	40	56
45	Maleic anhydride	~0	50	56
0.091 ± 0.05	Methyl α-chloroacrylate	0.41 ± 0.14	50	56
0.10	Vinyl benzoate	0.002	43	56
0.13 ± 0.05	Vinyl chloroacetate	<0.004	40	56
0.54 ± 0.2	Vinyl chloride	0.017 ± 0.01	50	56
0.049	Vinylidene chloride	0.012	22	56
	M₁ = 2-Fluorobutadiene			
2.05 ± 0.19	Isoprene	0.19 ± 0.10	50	45
1.54 ± 0.08	α-Methylstyrene	0.64 ± 0.08	50	45
	M₁ = 2,5-Dichlorostyrene			
1.55	2,5-Dimethylstyrene	0.27	70	37
	M₁ = Vinyl chloride			
0.15 ± 0.10	Trimethyl aconitate	>0.5	60	56b

a In emulsion.

[36] R. J. Orr and H. L. Williams, *Can. J. Chem.*,**30,** 108 (1952).
[37] H. C. Haas and M. S. Simon, *J. Polymer Sci.*, **9**, 309 (1952).
[37a] L. P. Witnauer, N. Watkins, and W. S. Port, *ibid.*, **20**, 213 (1956).
[38] C. C. Price and R. D. Gilbert, *J. Am. Chem. Soc.*, **74**, 2073 (1952).
[39] J. M. Mitchell and H. L. Williams, *Can. J. Res.*, **275**, 35 (1949).
[40] R. D. Gilbert and H. L. Williams, *J. Am. Chem. Soc.*, **74**, 4144 (1952).
[41] R. J. Orr and H. L. Williams, *Can. J. Chem.*, **29**, 270 (1951).
[42] C. C. Price, B. D. Halpern, and S. T. Yoong, *J. Polymer Sci.*, **11**, 575 (1953).
[43] C. C. Price and H. Morita, *J. Am. Chem. Soc.*, **75**, 4747 (1953).
[44] C. L. Sandberg and F. A. Bovey, *J. Polymer Sci.*, **15**, 553 (1955).
[45] R. J. Orr and H. L. Williams, *Can. J. Chem.*, **33**, 1328 (1955).
[46] C. C. Price and T. C. Schwan, *J. Polymer Sci.*, **16**, 577 (1955).
[47] W. H. Embree, J. M. Mitchell, and H. L. Williams, *Can. J. Chem.*, **29**, 253 (1951).
[48] G. P. Scott, *J. Org. Chem.*, **20**, 736 (1955).
[48a] C. S. Marvel, S. L. Jacobs, W. K. Taft, and B. G. Labbe, *J. Polymer Sci.*, **19**, 59 (1956).
[49] M. F. Margaritova and V. A. Raiskaya, *Trudy Moskov. Inst. Tonkoi Khim. Tekhnol,* **1953**, 37; *Chem. Abstr.*, **49**, 14,372 (1955).
[50] A. Hungar and H. Reichert, *Faserforshung Textiltech.*, **5**, 204 (1954).
[51] J. Muller, *Chem. Listy*, **48**, 1593 (1954).
[52] S. N. Ushakov, S. P. Mitsengendler, and B. M. Polyatskma, *Chem. Abstr.*, **47**, 7820 (1953).
[53] C. C. Price and R. D. Gilbert, *J. Polymer Sci.*, **9**, 577 (1952).
[54] B. R. Thompson, *J. Polymer Sci.*, **19**, 373 (1956). Data on copolymerization of a number of other silicon derivatives are also given in this paper; cf. also R. M. Pike and D. L. Bailey, *ibid.*, **22**, 55 (1956).
[55] E. Imoto and H. Horiuchi, *Chem. High Polymers Japan*, **8**, 463 (1951).
[56] H. Gilbert, S. J. Averill, E. J. Carlson, V. L. Folt, H. J. Heller, F. F. Miller, F. D. Stewart, R. F. Schmidt, and H. L. Trumbull, *J. Am. Chem. Soc.*, **78**, 1669 (1956).
[56a] D. C. Blackley and H. W. Melville, *Makromol. Chem.*, **18/19**, 16 (1956).
[56b] C. S. Marvel, J. W. Johnson, Jr., J. Economy, and G. P. Scott, *J. Polymer Sci.*, **20**, 437 (1956); this paper also gives data on triethyl aconitate.
[56c] D. I. Livingston, P. M. Klamath, and R. S. Corley, *ibid.*, **20**, 485 (1956).
[56d] G. Oster and Y. Mizutani, *ibid.*, **22**, 173 (1956).
[56e] H. C. Haas, E. S. Emerson, and N. W. Schuler, *ibid.*, **22**, 291 (1956).

vinyl polymerizations become significantly reversible at higher temperatures, it might be expected that, in the neighborhood of perhaps 200°, r values in ordinary copolymerizations will become notably temperature and concentration dependent.

4·1f   Structure and Reactivity; Radical Stabilization

We may now turn to actual data on monomer reactivity ratios, the raw material for beginning our discussion of the relation between

TABLE 4·3 RELATIVE REACTIVITIES OF MONOMERS WITH POLYMER RADICALS
(Temperature ~60°)

Monomer	Butadiene[a]	2-Vinyl pyridine	Styrene	Isopropenyl Acetate	Vinyl Acetate	Allyl Acetate	Allyl Chloride	Vinyl Chloride	Chloroprene	2,5-Dichloro-styrene	Methyl Methacrylate	Vinylidene Chloride	Methyl Acrylate	β-Chloroethyl Acrylate	Methacrylo-nitrile	Acrylonitrile	Methacrylic Acid	Diethyl Fumarate	Vinylidene Cyanide	Maleic Anhydride
Chloroprene	16		19						1.0		12		12			22		40	590	
1,1-Diphenylethylene									0.32	1.0	2.3		10			36				
2,5-Dichlorostyrene	2.2	1.6	5								2.5					5			110	
2-Vinylpyridine	1.0		1.8	60	100					9	2.5		7		25	5	1.7			
Butadiene[a]	1.0		1.3								4.0	>20	5						1000	
α-Methylstyrene		0.88	1.0						0.3	2.2	2.0		20		17	20				
Styrene	0.7				>50	>50	>30	30	0.12	1.3	2.2	12	5.5	12	6	17	1.4	14		>100
Phenylacetylene		5	1.9		70	>50							1.6							
Methyl methacrylate	1.3	1.2	3.5		20				0.16	0.44	1.0	10			1.5	20			32	50
Methyl vinyl ketone			4									4				5.5				
Methacrylonitrile	2.8		6.7		>50						1.5				1.0	1.6				
Methacrylic acid		0.65										6.7								
Acrylonitrile	3		2.4		18		20	>15	0.19	14	0.74	2.7				1.0				
β-Chloroethyl acrylate			1.7			>50							1.1	1.0		1.0				

118

Monomer																
Methyl acrylate	0.5	1.3	1.3	.5	4	12		0.3	0.4	1.0	1.2			1.1	0.33	22 / 20 / 50
Vinylidene chloride	0.5	0.5	0.54			5	0.09		0.07	1.0	1.0					
Methyl vinyl sulfone			0.4	>30												
Methyl vinyl sulfide			0.2	>50							1.2		3			
Methallyl chloride			0.05	8		3			0.14	0.9 / 0.4			0.18	0.30		
Isobutylene			0.014						0.1	0.7						
Methallyl acetate			0.05						0.07	0.5			0.11	0.33		
Vinyl chloride			0.03	3.5	1.0				0.02	0.26			0.11	0.2	2.1 / 1.9	120
Allyl chloride			0.02	1.4					0.05	0.25		0.25				
Vinyl acetate			0.01	1.0		1.0			0.04	0.17	0.2		0.2	0.2 / 0.33	2.3 / 9.1	300
Allyl acetate			0.01	1.7		0.5			0.03	0.3		0.18				500
Isopropenyl acetate						0.9										
Vinyl ethyl ether			0.01	0.3		0.45				0.3			0.3	0.2		
3,3,3-Trichloropropene			0.14	5.3		0.5[b]				0.36				0.082	0.90	1.00
Maleic anhydride			>20	18		3.5	0.15		0.15	0.1	0.08		0.3	0.16		
Diethyl fumarate			3.3	90		8			0.05	0.08 / 0.025				0.12	1.0	
Diethyl maleate			0.17	6		1.3				0.03				0.08		
Crotonic acid			0.05	3					0.01	0.03				0.05		
Trichloroethylene			0.06	1.5	1.5								0.03	0.015	0.02	
trans-Dichloroethylene			0.03	1.0												
cis-Dichloroethylene			0.005	0.17												
Tetrachloroethylene			0.005	0.16									0.001	0.002		

119

---

[a] Includes isoprene results which are indistinguishable from those for butadiene.

[b] Vinyl isobutyl ether.

structure and reactivity in radical addition processes. Here there is little justification in duplicating the extensive tables given in the general references cited.[1,2] Rather, significant data appearing since their publication are collected in Table 4·2.

For our purposes, it is then convenient to tabulate the relative reactivities of series of monomers towards typical reference radicals. Such series are readily derived from copolymer composition data as reciprocals of r_1's obtained by copolymerizing a series of monomers with a reference monomer (taken as M_1). Table 4·3, taken from Mayo and Walling [1] with a few subsequent additions, lists a number of such series. Any column gives the available data on the relative reactivities of thirty-six monomers with one reference radical. Twenty such series are included. However, as a different reference point (the reactivity of the reference radical with its own monomer) is taken for each column, values in different columns are not comparable. On the other hand, the ratio of values for two monomers in one column may be compared to the ratio of values for the same two monomers in another. Such a table, it may be noted, provides a very compact means of tabulating monomer reactivity ratios, which are directly the reciprocals of the numbers given; e.g., butadiene (M_1) and acrylonitrile (M_2) give $r_1 = 0.33$, $r_2 = 0.20$.

In Table 4·3 monomers have been arranged as nearly as possible in order of decreasing reactivity as the columns are descended, and it is evident that the numbers in the columns show considerable regularity. Such exceptions as occur are apparently due to the tendency of some monomer pairs to form strongly alternating copolymers. Leaving such exceptions, and also the cases of the 1,2-disubstituted ethylenes at the bottom of the table, until later, we see that the effect of substituents on the reactivity of olefins towards radical attack lies in the order $-C_6H_5 > -CH=CH_2 > -COCH_3 > -CN > -COOR > -Cl > -CH_2Y > -OCOCH_3 > -OR$, with the effect of a second 1-substituent roughly additive. Acetylenes show about the same reactivity as the corresponding olefins, although the observed reaction *rates* of systems containing acetylenes are usually slow, making them inconvenient to work with.[57]

Although reliable data on the polymerization of ethylene is lacking, it is possible to describe the effects of 1-substituents on reactivity in a rough numerical fashion summarized in Table 4·4, the observed spread in effects of a single substituent being about 100-fold.

[57] K. W. Doak, *J. Am. Chem. Soc.*, **72**, 4681 (1950).

TABLE 4·4   EFFECT OF SUBSTITUENTS UPON THE REACTIVITY OF DOUBLE
BONDS IN COPOLYMERIZATION

Substituent	Relative Reactivity	Stabilization, kcal/mole	
		Olefin	Radical
—H, —OCH$_3$	1	0	0
—OAc, —CH$_3$	1.5–5	2.5	4
—Cl	3–20	...	6
—COOR, —COOH	20–60	2.5	...
—CN, —COR	30–60	...	...
—C$_2$H$_3$, C$_5$H$_6$	50–100	3–4	25

For a good many years, such reactivity series have been discussed
in terms of the resonance stabilization of the radicals formed in the
resulting reactions, the formation of a stable radical being associated
with a relatively rapid reaction.[58, 59]   On the other hand, the presence
of conjugating groups is known to stabilize a double bond (by delocalization of its π electrons) and should accordingly decrease its
reactivity.   The relative magnitude of these two opposed effects is
indicated in Table 4·4, where the resonance stabilization of the
product radicals have been taken from the bond dissociation energy
data of Chapter 2, and the double bond stabilization from the heats
of hydrogenation measurements of Kistiakowsky, et al.[60]   Unfortunately, no data are available on the resonance stabilization of the
important group of carbonyl conjugated radicals.   The balance of
the figures, however, clearly show that, although the effects are
parallel, a given substituent is considerably more effective in stabilizing a radical than in stabilizing the olefin from which the radical is
formed.   Such a difference seems entirely reasonable and suggests
that an unpaired electron is more loosely held than one which is
engaged in forming part of a double bond, and that its orbital is more
available for overlapping with other neighboring orbitals.

The resonance structures which might be expected to contribute to
the stabilization of the radicals arising from most of the monomers
in Table 4·3 have already been discussed in Chapter 2 in connection
with bond dissociation energies.   Carbonyl-conjugated and similar
radicals are presumably stabilized by structures similar to those

[58] F. R. Mayo and C. Walling, *Chem. Revs.*, **27**, 351 (1940).

[59] G. W. Wheland, *Resonance in Organic Chemistry*, John Wiley & Sons, New
York, 1955, Chapter 8.

[60] Cf. footnote 59, Section 3·2.

contributing to the allyl radical but with the electron distributed over a heteroatom, e.g.,

$$
\begin{matrix}
& & & O & & & & & & O\cdot \\
& & & \parallel & & & & & & \diagup \\
-CH_2-\dot{C}H-C & & & & \leftrightarrow & & -CH_2-CH{=}C & & \\
& & & \diagdown & & & & & & \diagdown \\
& & & OR & & & & & & OR
\end{matrix}
\tag{15}
$$

From Table 4·4 the resulting stabilization is only slightly less.

Stabilization from alkoxy groups is apparently small, so contributions

$$
-\dot{C}H-O-R \leftrightarrow -\underset{H}{\overset{-}{C}}-\overset{+}{\underset{\cdot}{O}}-R
\tag{16}
$$

are evidently minor. The rather higher reactivity of sulfides has been attributed to the ability of sulfur to expand its valence shell beyond eight.[61]

Copolymerizations also give data on the relative reactivities of different vinyl aromatics, not shown in detail in Table 4·3. Thus 2-vinylpyridine,[1] 4-vinylpyridine,[1] 2-vinylthiophene,[1] 2-vinylnaphthalene,[42] and 4-chloro-1-vinylnaphthalene[42] are all more reactive than styrene towards the styrene radical, relative reactivities, with styrene taken as 1, being 1.8:1.6:2.9:2.0:1.2. A 1-naphthyl group is apparently considerably more effective in stabilizing the resulting radical than a 2-naphthyl group. Similarly, towards the methyl acrylate radical 2- and 3-vinylphenanthrene prove to be 1.8 and 0.225 times as reactive as styrene respectively[42] (Table 4·2), a still larger difference.

Under certain conditions, aromatic compounds may themselves enter into copolymerization with addition occurring across the aromatic nuclei. Thus anthracene copolymerizes with butadiene, ultraviolet absorption spectra of the polymer indicating addition across the 9,10-position of the anthracene.[62] From the amount of anthracene in the polymer, its reactivity is about the same as butadiene, and the copolymerization of 2-methylanthracene with styrene has also been reported.[63] Marvel has investigated a number of additional polynuclear hydrocarbons and finds that several also enter a butadiene polymer in significant amounts.[64]

[61] C. C. Price and J. Zomlefer, *J. Am. Chem. Soc.*, **72**, 14 (1950).

[62] C. S. Marvel and W. S. Anderson, *ibid.*, **75**, 4600 (1953).

[63] M. Magat and R. Bonême, *Compt. rend.*, **232**, 1657 (1951).

[64] C. S. Marvel and W. S. Anderson, *J. Am. Chem. Soc.*, **76**, 5484 (1954).

Simpler aromatic nuclei such as benzene and naphthalene are not readily attacked by butadiene radicals,[64] but the more reactive vinyl acetate even copolymerizes with benzene to a limited extent. Using C^{14}-labeled benzene (11 moles per mole of vinyl acetate) Stockmayer finds that the polymer contains about 3% benzene, indicating a relative reactivity compared with vinyl acetate of about 0.0026.[65] Later this question of radical attack on aromatic nuclei will be discussed in more detail (Section 10·2).

Although Table 4·3 gives us no information about the effect of substituents upon the relative reactivities of different *radicals*, such information may be obtained by combining copolymerization data with the chain propagation rate constants discussed in the last chapter, since $k_{11} = r_1 k_{12}$, and $k_{11} = k_p$. A list of the resulting rate constants for various radical-monomer combinations appears in Table 4·5, and more can easily be calculated from Table 4·3. As we might

TABLE 4·5   RATE CONSTANTS FOR RADICAL-OLEFIN ADDITIONS AT 60°

(From Tables 3·3, 4·2, and 4·3)

	Radical					
Olefin	Buta-diene	Sty-rene	Methyl Methac-rylate	Methyl Acrylate	Vinyl Chloride	Vinyl Acetate
Butadiene	100	190	2820	42,000	...	...
Styrene	70	145	1520	11,500	(370,000)	>100,000
Methyl methacrylate	130	278	705	...	...	>100,000
Methyl acrylate	130	194	...	2,090	(150,000)	11,500
Vinyl chloride	...	7	49	230	(12,300)	8,000
Vinyl acetate	...	3	35	230	6,150	2,300

expect, substituents which increase the reactivity of double bonds greatly *decrease* the reactivity of the resulting (stabilized) radicals. In fact, the latter effect is considerably the larger. Thus, although vinyl acetate is only about one-fiftieth as reactive as styrene towards a given radical, the vinyl acetate radical is about a thousand times as reactive as the styrene radical towards any given monomer. If we compare the chain propagation process in styrene and vinyl acetate individually, these effects largely compensate each other, leaving the propagation rate for vinyl acetate only about sixteen times that for styrene. This compensating phenomenon appears to be quite common in radical chain processes, and we will often find radical chain reactions with similar overall characteristics, even though the chain-carrying species may vary notably in energy.

[65] W. H. Stockmayer and L. H. Peebles, Jr., *ibid.*, **75**, 2278 (1953).

Values in the middle of Table 4·5 are somewhat distorted because of the tendency of some of the monomer pairs to alternate, and, as we have noted, the high reported value for the self-propagation constant of vinyl chloride seems somewhat anomalous.

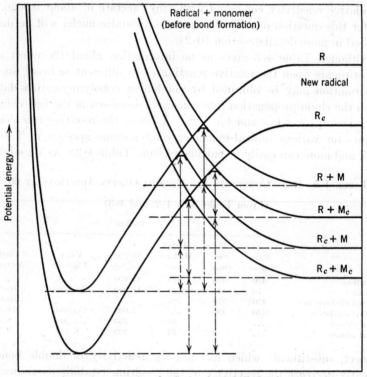

Fig. 4·8 Potential energy of system, monomer plus radical, as a function of separation of radical and unsaturated carbon atom. Subscript c indicates conjugation in monomer (M) or radical (R). Arrows with solid lines indicate energies of activation; broken lines heats of reaction.

A more detailed discussion of the effect of resonance stabilization of radicals, monomers, and transition states has been given by Evans in terms of potential energy diagrams.[66, 67] His treatment is based upon a model illustrated in Fig. 4·8. Here the potential energy changes accompanying attack of a free radical on a double bond

[66] M. G. Evans, *Discussions Faraday Soc.*, **2**, 271 (1947).
[67] M. G. Evans, J. Gergely, and E. C. Seaman, *J. Polymer Sci.*, **3**, 866 (1948).

are plotted as a function of the separation of the carbon atoms between which a new bond will be formed, the other atoms in the system being assumed to take positions of minimum energy. The two sets of curves in the figure represent repulsion between the approaching unbonded carbon atoms and the extension energy of the bond finally formed. At the intersection of the curves the bonded and unbonded states have equal energies, and the actual transition from one to the other may be facilitated by resonance contributions to the activated complex, which would round off the intersections and lower the required energy for reaction. However, in Evans's treatment, this "rounding off" is treated as equal in all cases.

As the reaction occurs, the unbonded reactants in their normal states are converted to the new normal bonded state with the evolution of the heat of reaction. The heat of polymerization or of copolymerization of a substituted olefin differs from that of ethylene (taken as standard) because of loss of the resonance energies of the initial radical (R_a) and the monomer (R_m), and gain of the resonance energy of the radical formed (R_f). Changes in the activation energy (E) accompanying changes in the heat of reaction (H) are then given by

$$\Delta E = \alpha \, \Delta H = \alpha(R_a + R_m - R_f) \qquad (17)$$

where the largest amount of heat liberated accompanies the lowest activation energy, and α is a factor less than unity with an exact value depending upon the shape of the potential energy curves.

In order to confine attention to resonance effects, in Fig. 4·8 each set of curves has arbitrarily been drawn parallel, and resonance stabilization of a monomer (if any) taken as half that of the resulting radical. From this and eq. 17 it follows that, of the initial *radicals,* those with the most resonance stabilization have the highest activation energy and the slowest rate of reaction, because they lose their resonance energy when they react; of the initial *monomers,* the conjugated have the lowest activation energy because they gain some resonance energy (less the smaller resonance energy of the monomer R_m) in conversion to a radical. However, because of this loss of R_m, the overall effect is smaller. These results are quite consistent with the data of Table 4·5.

In addition to advancing these qualitative arguments, Evans, Gergely, and Seaman [67] have attempted to put this treatment on a quantitative basis by assuming a constant value of 0.4 for α in eq. 17 and assigning plausible values for the resonance stabilization of monomers and radicals. On this basis, they have calculated changes in heats of activation for various reactions of ethylene, butadiene, and styrene. Unfortunately, their choice of values for R_a appear low, and for R_m high. Taking values from Table 4·4, the ethylene radical should be about 10^7 times as reactive as the styrene radical towards a given monomer, whereas styrene should be about 3×10^5 times as reactive as ethylene towards a given radical. The actual properties of ethylene are not known, but, since the acetoxy group contributes little to radical stability, the polyethylene radical is probably only slightly more reactive than the vinyl acetate radical; so the actual differences in reactivity are smaller by several powers of ten. Unfortunately for any further test of this theory, very few monomers are known for which we have accurate values of R_a, R_m, and k_p, so it cannot be said whether some smaller value of α will give consistent results. Further, as we will see, a number of other factors besides resonance stabilization contribute to reactivity in copolymerization.

Both the qualitative and quantitative discussions of radical and olefin reactivities given above assume, at least tacitly, that differences in reaction rate arise from differences in activation energy for the processes involved. However, as we have seen, differences in k_p between monomers arise in part from variations in PZ in the rate expression as well as from E_a. The question whether significant differences in PZ occur for different reactions of the same radical is difficult to answer, since it involves determining the temperature coefficient of monomer reactivity ratios, which are themselves subject to considerable experimental error. The copolymerization of styrene with methyl methacrylate, methyl acrylate, p-chlorostyrene, diethyl maleate, and diethyl fumarate has been subject to very careful measurement at 60° and 131°.[68] The results indicate that, for the first three pairs, differences in reactivity arise solely from differences in activation energy (within a rather large experimental error). In the latter two pairs, where, as we will see in the next section, steric hindrance is of importance, differences in PZ factor also contribute to the observed values of r's. Qualitatively, r's approach unity with rising temperature for a number of other monomer pairs as would be expected if reactivity differences were caused primarily by differences in activation energy. However, some exceptions have been

[68] F. M. Lewis, C. Walling, W. Cummings, E. R. Briggs, and F. R. Mayo, J. Am. Chem. Soc., **70**, 1519 (1948).

reported by Goldfinger and Steidlitz,[69] and additional precise measurements are needed to clarify the whole problem.

4·1g   Steric Effects

The most clear-cut examples in which steric hindrance influences reactivity in copolymerization are found when 1-substituted olefins are compared with olefins carrying an additional substituent in the 2-position. The most extensive data are on the chloroölefins,[70, 71] summarized in Table 4·6 where, in every case, the reactivity of vinyl chloride has been taken as unity.

TABLE 4·6   RELATIVE REACTIVITY OF HALOÖLEFINS TO RADICALS AT 60°

| Olefin | Radical | | |
	Acrylonitrile	Vinyl Acetate	Styrene
Vinyl chloride	1.0	1.0	1.0
Vinylidene chloride	3.6	>10	9.2
cis-1,2-Dichloroethylene	...	0.05	0.08
trans-1,2-Dichloroethylene	...	0.3	0.46
Trichloroethylene	0.05	0.45	1.0
Tetrachloroethylene	0.007	0.04	0.09

As might be expected, introduction of an additional chlorine atom in the 1-position increases reactivity 3- to 10-fold. On the other hand, 2-substitution *reduces* reactivity by a rather larger factor (2- to 20-fold). Such reduction is by no means a peculiarity of haloolefins, but is brought about by other substituents as well.[1] Thus, vinylidene chloride radicals add 12 times as readily to methyl acrylate as to ethyl fumarate, whereas with styrene radicals the difference is 2.5-fold. Similarly, styrene reacts 13 times as fast with acrylic acid as with crotonic acid, and about twice as fast with acrylonitrile as with fumaronitrile.

On a more qualitative basis, Marvel and his students have noted that cinnamic acid derivatives,[72] dibenzoylethylene,[73] and methyl β-benzoylacrylates,[74] copolymerize with styrene and butadiene, but

[69] G. Goldfinger and M. Steidlitz, *J. Polymer Sci.*, **3**, 786 (1948).

[70] T. Alfrey, Jr., and S. Greenberg, *ibid.*, **3**, 297 (1948).

[71] K. W. Doak, *J. Am. Chem. Soc.*, **70**, 1525 (1948).

[72] C. S. Marvel, G. H. McCain, M. Passer, W. K. Taft, and B. G. Labbe, *Ind. Eng. Chem.*, **45**, 2311 (1955).

[73] C. S. Marvel and A. B. Galvin, *J. Polymer Sci.*, **16**, 251 (1955).

[74] C. S. Marvel and A. B. Galvin, *J. Org. Chem.*, **20**, 587 (1955).

that they appear to be somewhat less reactive than simple acrylate derivatives. It is difficult to see how such results can be accounted for by anything other than steric hindrance at the site of radical attack by a bulky substituent in the 2-position.

An interesting aspect of the reactivities of 1,2-disubstituted olefins is the difference between *cis* and *trans* isomers, originally noted by Marvel and Schertz.[75] These differences were first studied systematically by Lewis and Mayo [76] with results summarized in Table 4·7.

TABLE 4·7　COMPARISON OF *cis* AND *trans* ISOMERS IN COPOLYMERIZATION

Reference Radical	Isomer Pair R in RHC=CHR	More Reactive Isomer [a]	Less Stable Isomer	Planar *cis* Form Hindered
Styrene	—COOC$_2$H$_5$	*trans* (21)	*cis*	+
Styrene	—COOCH$_3$	*trans* (20–40)	*cis*	+
Styrene	—COOC$_2$H$_5$, —COOH [b]	No significant difference	*cis*	−
Styrene	—CN	No significant difference	*cis*	−
Styrene	—Cl	*trans* (6)	*trans*	−
Vinyl chloride	—COOC$_2$H$_5$	*trans* (6.5)	*cis*	+
Vinyl acetate	—COOC$_2$H$_5$	*trans* (15)	*cis*	+
Vinyl acetate	—Cl	*trans* (6.5)	*trans*	−
Maleic anhydride	—C$_6$H$_5$	*trans* (1.5–2.0) [c]	*cis*	+

[a] Ratio of activities of two isomers toward reference radical.
[b] Half-esters of maleic and fumaric acids.
[c] From rates of polymerization.

As they point out, if it is assumed that a free radical has either a planar or an easily reversible pyramidal configuration (cf. Section 1·4), the addition of a reference radical to either geometric isomer of a pair should lead eventually to the same free radical. Evidence that this is actually the case has been obtained by Mayo and Wilzbach,[77] who have shown that vinyl acetate–1,2-dichloroethylene copolymers made from both isomers of the latter apparently have the same steric configuration since they liberate I$_2$ from KI solutions at identical rates. Since most of the energy difference between *cis* and *trans* isomers arises from steric repulsion, in the resulting radical (whether planar and able to rotate around the C—C bond, or pyramidal) some of this strain is relieved. Accordingly, to the extent that the transition state resembles this radical, our previous discussion suggests that the less stable, energy-rich isomer of a pair should be

[75] C. S. Marvel and G. L. Schertz, *ibid.*, **65**, 2054 (1943); **66**, 2135 (1944).

[76] F. M. Lewis and F. R. Mayo, *ibid.*, **70**, 1533 (1948).

[77] F. R. Mayo and K. E. Wilzbach, *ibid.*, **71**, 1124 (1949). Other examples appear in later chapters.

the more reactive. For the dichloroethylenes (of which the *cis* isomer is the more stable) such a difference is actually observed. Quite different results, however, are obtained with the dialkyl fumarates and maleates, where the more stable fumarates turn out to be 6- to 40-fold the more reactive. This surprising result has been ascribed to steric inhibition of resonance by Mayo and Lewis, who have pointed out that, when a radical R· adds to these monomers, the transition state can be stabilized by resonance forms such as

$$
\begin{array}{cc}
\overset{\displaystyle OEt}{\underset{\displaystyle O=C}{\diagup}}
\quad
\overset{\displaystyle OEt}{\underset{\displaystyle O=C}{\diagup}}
\end{array}
\tag{18}
$$

only if the carbonyl oxygen lies in the same plane as the atoms attached to the doubly bonded carbon atoms. Consideration of models of maleic esters shows that both ester groups cannot be coplanar simultaneously, and, in fact, considerable steric hindrance is involved if only one assumes a coplanar configuration. In the fumarate esters, on the other hand, no such interference exists; so it is reasonable that resonance stabilization of the transition state should be more effective in reducing the activation energy of radical addition to these molecules than to the maleates.

Compared with the full esters, the half-esters show little difference in reactivity, although the differences in energy content are probably similar. Here there is less interference between groups, and a planar configuration in the half-maleates may actually be favored by hydrogen bonding. Incidently, we may note that maleic anhydride, with a strictly planar molecule, shows a relatively high reactivity in copolymerization, although primarily because of polar effects discussed in the next section.

The stilbenes behave similarly to the dialkyl esters. In the *cis* isomer, only one phenyl group at a time may lie in the plane of the double bond, and in Table 4.7 it is shown to be only half as reactive as the *trans* isomer. Similar qualitative results are also noted with *cis*- and *trans*-dibenzoylethylenes.[73]

Just as substituents in the 2-position decrease the reactivity of olefins, additional substituents in the 1-position might be expected to reduce the reactivity of polymer radicals by increasing the repulsive forces present as they attack a double bond. Here, however, the situation is much less clear-cut, since any such steric contribution tends to become confused with the radical-stabilizing contribution of the substituent. On the one hand, the approximate additivity of effect of an additional 1-substituent indicates no specific effect of a second group; on the other, methyl methacrylate, the only 1,1-disubstituted olefin for which k_p is known with any accuracy, shows a particularly small PZ factor for the addition reaction. Further, there is no doubt that the heat of polymerization of 1,1-disubstituted olefins is the order of 10 kcal/mole smaller than that of ethylene (Section 5·4a). In short, it seems very evident that such steric effects are present, but, at the moment, we have no reliable way of determining the magnitude of their effect upon the propagation rate constants in polymerization. Actually, such effects may be manifested in a particularly complicated manner. If one attempts to construct a 1,1-disubstituted polymer from molecular models, little hindrance is encountered until two or more 1,1-disubstituted units are assembled in sequence. Accordingly, steric effects might well be manifested as changes in r's with the nature of the penultimate unit in the growing chain. Such effects have been discussed, but, as we have seen, are difficult to detect. However, they may account for changes in reaction properties of very short chains, discussed in Chapters 6 and 7. Significantly, in line with this same argument, a number of monomers substituted with several bulky groups, e.g., α-methylstyrene and 1,1-diphenylethylene fail to polymerize alone in the presence of radical sources, although they enter readily enough into copolymers. Similarly, 2,6-disubstituted styrenes polymerize poorly and are even relatively unreactive in copolymerization,[78] presumably because steric hindrance prevents conjugation with the aromatic ring in the transition state, and, although diethyl fumarate polymerizes satisfactorily, the less reactive maleate yields only low molecular weight products containing largely only one or two monomer units.[79]

Polyfluoroölefins provide an interesting borderline case of steric hindrance. Tetrafluoroethylene polymerizes readily and, from copolymerization data, is slightly more reactive than ethylene.[80] A

[78] T. Alfrey, Jr., and W. H. Ebelke, ibid., **71,** 3235 (1949); V. V. Korshak and N. G. Matveeva, Doklady Akad. Nauk S.S.S.R., **78,** 1145 (1951).

[79] C. S. Marvel, E. J. Prill, and D. F. DeTar, J. Am. Chem. Soc., **69,** 52 (1947).

[80] Imperial Chemical Industries, Ltd., Brit. Pat. 594,249 (1947), cf. p. 222 of reference cited in footnote 1.

number of other perfluoroölefins are also reactive in copolymerization with monomers such as vinyl acetate; [81] so it appears that fluorine atoms are sufficiently small so that even a number do not introduce much interference to radical addition to the double bond. An idea of the small amount of hindrance is given by the observation that 1,1-dichloro-2,2-difluoroethylene is actually reported to be about 1.6 as reactive as vinylidene chloride towards the vinyl acetate radical.[82]

The effect of introducing bulky groups into monomers at a greater distance from the site of reaction is certainly small and perhaps not significant. A number of cases are discussed in the earlier references.[1, 2]

At this point, our evaluation of copolymerization data permits a re-examination of the basis for the head-to-tail arrangement of monomer units in an addition polymer. It is evident that such an arrangement is favored by both resonance stabilization of the product radical and by steric factors. For a monomer like vinyl acetate, with little resonance stabilization, the magnitude of the two factors might be 2- to 5-fold and 10- to 50-fold respectively, leading to the expectation of random head-to-head arrangements every 20–250 units along the chain, with the steric factor being the most important in enforcing chain regularity. As we have seen, the measurements of Flory and Leutner [83] show an irregularity every 50–100 units, in good accord with our estimate. Their temperature coefficient measurements show that the usual orientation is favored by a 10-fold larger PZ factor and 1300 cal less activation energy over radical addition to the hindered end of the vinyl acetate double bond. As one goes to more reactive monomers, the steric factor should remain about the same, but the preference for a head-to-tail structure due to resonance stabilization of one structure over another should increase, so that with a monomer like styrene or methyl methacrylate, head-to-head structures should occur very rarely indeed, certainly not more than once every 1000 units or so. Quite similar arguments apply to the addition reactions leading to non-polymeric products discussed in Chapters 6 and 7.

[81] R. M. Adams and F. A. Bovey, *J. Polymer Sci.*, **9**, 481 (1952).

[82] T. Alfrey, Jr., J. Bohrer, H. Haas, and C. Lewis, *ibid.*, **5**, 719 (1950). Better quantitative data on the fluoroölefins would be of real value. In particular, although there is some activating effect of a fluorine atom on a double bond, cf. Section 10·2c, the negligible resonance energy of the CF_3 group from bond dissociation energy data suggest that it is certainly smaller than that of chlorine.

[83] P. J. Flory and F. S. Leutner, *ibid.*, **3**, 880 (1948); **5**, 267 (1950).

4·1h The Alternating Effect; the Role of Polar Phenomena in Radical Reactions

We now come to what is probably the most interesting aspect of the relation between structure and reactivity that is observed in the study of copolymer compositions: the property of many monomer pairs of forming copolymers in which the monomer units tend to alternate along the polymer chain. As we have seen, this tendency may be measured by the magnitude of the r_1r_2 product. If these products are examined for a large number of monomer pairs, again a striking regularity is observed, and we find that monomers may be arranged in an order such that increasing separation of two monomers in the series parallels a decreasing r_1r_2 product and an increasing tendency to alternate in copolymerization. This relation is shown in Table 4·8 taken from Mayo and Walling [1] which indicates the validity of this generalization. Inspection of Table 4·8 suggests a relation which was early noted by workers in the field of copolymerization,[84, 85, 86] namely, that there is an obvious relation between alternation and the *polar* properties of the monomers involved. In fact, the order of monomers is essentially a *polarity* series arranged in order of the electron-withdrawing and electron-supplying properties of the substituents attached to the double bond, with electron-supplying groups (phenyl, vinyl, alkyl, and acetoxy) at the left and electron-withdrawing groups (ester and nitrile) at the right.

The manner in which such polar effects bring about changes in the rates of radical addition reactions has received a good deal of discussion which parallels closely similar consideration of the detailed mechanism by which electron supply and withdrawal influences the rates of strictly polar reactions. The simplest picture, which has been much used by Price,[85, 87, 88, 89] in his treatment of the problem, is that electron-withdrawing and electron-supplying groups set up permanent charge distributions in monomer and radical which may increase or decrease the energy required to bring the two species together in the transition state. Obviously, when one species possesses an excess and the other a deficiency of electrons at the site of re-

[84] F. M. Lewis, F. R. Mayo, and W. F. Hulse, *J. Am. Chem. Soc.*, **67**, 1701 (1945).

[85] C. C. Price, *J. Polymer Sci.*, **1**, 83 (1946).

[86] P. D. Bartlett and K. Nozaki, *J. Am. Chem. Soc.*, **69**, 2299 (1947).

[87] T. Alfrey, Jr., and C. C. Price, *J. Polymer Sci.*, **2**, 101 (1947).

[88] C. C. Price, *Discussions Faraday Soc.*, **2**, 304 (1947).

[89] C. C. Price, *J. Polymer Sci.*, **3**, 772 (1948).

TABLE 4·8 PRODUCTS OF MONOMER REACTIVITY RATIOS IN COPOLYMERIZATION AT 50-80°C [a]

	Styrene (−0.8)	Isopropenyl acetate	Vinyl acetate (−0.3)	Vinyl chloride (0.2)	2-Chlorobutadiene	2,5-Dichlorostyrene	Methyl methacrylate (0.4)	Vinylidene chloride (0.6)	Methyl acrylate (0.6)	Methyl vinyl ketone (0.7)	β-Chloroethyl acrylate (0.9)	Methacrylonitrile (1.0)	Acrylonitrile (1.1)	Diethyl fumarate (1.5)	Maleic anhydride
α-Methylstyrene (−0.6)	1.0												0.07		0.006
Butadiene (−0.8)			0.2	0.2			0.19	<0.1	0.04			0.006	0.014	0.02	0.006
Styrene (−0.8)			0.34	0.4	0.16		0.24	0.16	0.14	0.10	0.06	0.06	0.02	0.02	0.00006
Isopropenyl acetate			1.0	0.55											
Vinyl acetate (−0.3)				0.63			0.5		<0.12						
Vinyl chloride (0.2)					0.07		0.7	0.9	0.75		<0.24	<0.25	0.004	0.0002	
2-Chlorobutadiene											<0.13	0.06	0.002		
2,5-Dichlorostyrene															
Methyl methacrylate (0.4)								0.61	0.5						
Vinylidene chloride (0.6)									0.8						
Methyl acrylate (0.6)										0.9					
Methyl vinyl ketone (0.7)											0.43	0.24	0.015	0.13	
β-Chloroethyl acrylate (0.9)												0.24	0.17		
Methacrylonitrile (1.0)													0.34	0.56	
Acrylonitrile (1.1)														1.1	0.6
Diethyl fumarate (1.5)															0.13

[a] The numbers in parentheses after some monomers are the e values for these monomers, as estimated by Price; cf. Section 4·1i.

action, the result will be a lowering of the required energy and an increase in the reaction rate.

Reliance on this treatment alone (which amounts to invoking the *polarization* effects alone in the Ingold treatment of the theory of polar reactions) has been criticized [90] on the basis that it would predict a pronounced dependence of monomer reactivity ratios upon the dielectric constant of the medium which, as we have seen, is not observed. A way around this difficulty is to assume a mutual polarization of radical and olefin as they approach the transition state (corresponding now to *polarizibility* effects in the Ingold treatment) that becomes important only as the separation of the reactants becomes very small, so that few lines of force radiate into the surrounding medium.

Finally, it has been suggested [34] that, at least in strongly alternating systems, the energy of the transition state may be lowered by the participation of resonance structures in which electron transfer has occurred between radical and olefin. For the attack of a styrene radical on maleic anhydride (a good example of such a strongly alternating pair) such structures might be

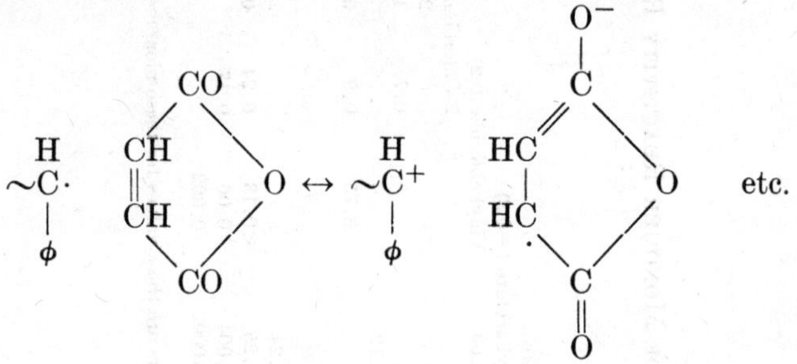

$$\text{etc.} \quad (19)$$

and, for the conjugate reaction, in which a maleic anhydride radical adds to styrene,

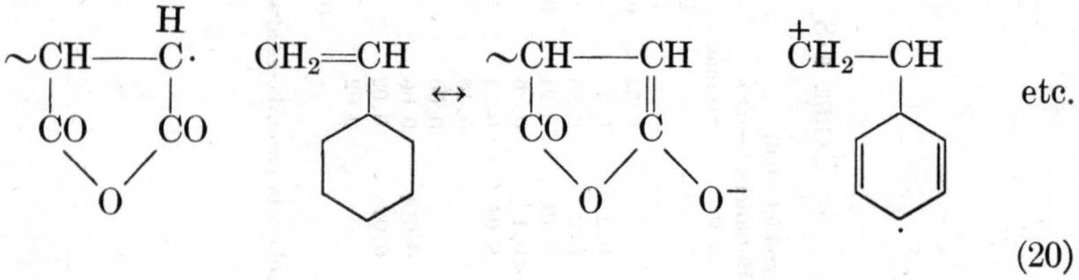

$$\text{etc.}$$

$$(20)$$

---

[90] C. Walling and F. R. Mayo, *ibid.*, **3**, 895 (1948); however, the results of calculations intended to check this sort of treatment depend somewhat upon the model of the transition state employed.[14]

The plausibility of such structures is enhanced by the fact that they contain essentially benzyl carbonium ion and enolate anion structures, which play frequent roles in polar reactions. Further, in reaction 19, it will be noted that both carbonyl functions are able to participate in the electron distribution, thus helping to account for the relatively strong alternating tendencies of monomers substituted with strongly polar groups in both the 1- and 2-positions. With the idea of the participation of such structures in mind, styrene might be referred to as an (electron) *donor* radical or substrate and maleic anhydride as an (electron) *acceptor*. We will frequently use this terminology, first employed by Bartlett and Nozaki,[86] in discussing polar effects in radical reactions.

The basis of this suggestion of electron transfer, and probably the best evidence for it, is a study of the effects of meta and para substituents on the reactivity of styrene (and α-methylstyrene) towards a series of reference radicals of differing polarity, carried out by Walling, Briggs, Wolfstirn,[34] and Mayo, and Walling, Seymour and Wolfstirn,[91] and summarized in Table 4·9. The reason for the choice

TABLE 4·9   RELATIVE REACTIVITIES OF SUBSTITUTED STYRENES TOWARDS
INDICATED RADICALS

Relative Reactivity [a]

Substituent	Styrene	Methyl Methacrylate	Maleic Anhydride [b]
p-OCH$_3$	0.86 $\pm$ 0.08 (0.95) [a]	1.59 $\pm$ 0.16 (0.093) [a]	18.5 $\pm$ 0.4
p-N(CH$_3$)$_2$	0.98 $\pm$ 0.06 (0.85)	2.24 $\pm$ 0.22 (0.023)	~300
p-CH$_3$		1.14 $\pm$ 0.06 (0.178)	1.72 $\pm$ 0.12
m-CH$_3$		0.87 $\pm$ 0.04 (0.26)	
None	1.00 (1.00)	1.00 (0.24)	1.00
p-F			0.72 $\pm$ 0.10
p-Cl	1.35 $\pm$ 0.06 (0.76)	1.11 $\pm$ 0.05 (0.37)	0.79 $\pm$ 0.02
p-Br	1.44 $\pm$ 0.04 (0.69)	1.16 $\pm$ 0.05 (0.44)	0.73 $\pm$ 0.15
p-I	1.61 $\pm$ 0.13 (0.76)	1.28 $\pm$ 0.10 (0.34)	
m-Cl	1.56 $\pm$ 0.13 (0.70)	0.98 $\pm$ 0.15 (0.43)	
m-Br	1.82 $\pm$ 0.10 (0.58)	0.96 $\pm$ 0.04 (0.56)	0.96 $\pm$ 0.14
m-NO$_2$	2.22 $\pm$ 0.25 (0.38)	1.3 $\pm$ 0.2 (0.30)	
p-CN	3.57 $\pm$ 0.35 (0.325)	2.09 $\pm$ 0.20 (0.31)	0.96 $\pm$ 0.57
p-NO$_2$	5.26 $\pm$ 0.5 (0.218)		

[a] Quantities given in parentheses following relative reactivities are monomer reactivity ratio products.

[b] Relative reactivities for substituted α-methylstyrenes against α-methylstyrene.

[91] C. Walling, D. Seymour, and K. B. Wolfstirn, *J. Am. Chem. Soc.*, **70**, 1544 (1948).

of such a system for study was, first, that the introduction of such substituents does not, in general, alter the entropy of activation of side-chain reactions of benzene derivatives (or else produces changes which are proportional to the heat of activation) and, second, that the theory of such side-chain reactions, in the case of polar reactions, is particularly well understood. In fact, they provide the basis of one of the broadest and most successful correlations of organic chemistry, the Hammett equation,[92]

$$\log k/k_0 = \rho\sigma \qquad (21)$$

which states that, for a given reaction, the ratio of the rate or equilibrium constant for a substituted benzene derivative to that of the unsubstituted derivative is given as the product of two parameters, rho, which is specific for the reaction, and sigma, specific for the substituent. Originally advanced by Hammett in 1937 to correlate data on some 52 reactions and 44 substituents, its application and subsequent extensions have recently been reviewed by Jaffe.[93]

In order to examine this relationship for a radical reaction, in Fig. 4·9 the logarithms of the relative reactivities listed in Table 4·9 are plotted against the Hammett sigma constants of the substituents present. The results present what is at first a striking paradox. For data involving the styrene radical, an excellent linear relationship is observed corresponding to a rho value of 0.5. However, for strongly alternating systems, where polar effects might be expected to predominate, the Hammett relationship breaks down, and styrenes with electron-supplying groups show abnormally enhanced reactivities, and this tendency increases with the acceptor properties of the attacking radical. Similar anomalies occur among polar reactions. Hammett[92] noted the necessity of assigning two sigma values to the p-nitro group, one for reactions involving amines and phenols, and another for all other reactions, and suggested a similar necessity for other electron-withdrawing unsaturated groups in the para position, a point further discussed by Jaffe.[93] More recently, Bordwell[94] and Hünig et al.[95] have suggested the necessity for two values for para electron-supplying groups as well. In all cases, a heightened effect of a substituent (i.e., the need for an additional,

[92] L. P. Hammett, *ibid.*, **59**, 96 (1937); L. P. Hammett, *Physical Organic Chemistry*, McGraw-Hill Book Co., New York, 1940, Chapter 7.

[93] H. H. Jaffe, *Chem. Revs.*, **53**, 191 (1953).

[94] F. G. Bordwell, quoted by Jaffe, *ibid.*, p. 228.

[95] S. Hünig, H. Lehmann, and G. Grimmer, *Ann.*, **579**, 87 (1953).

larger sigma value) has been related to specific interaction between the substituent and the reaction site, or, in other words, resonance interaction between the two positions. Of particular interest to us here is the anomalously large effect of electron-releasing groups on reactions in which transition states have the properties of carbonium ions. Figure 4·10, taken from Mayo and Walling,[1] shows a typical Hammett plot for the solvolyses of benzhydryl and triphenylmethyl

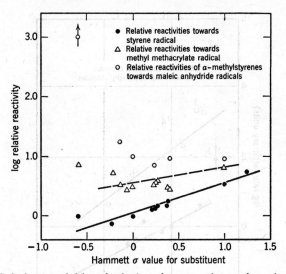

FIG. 4·9 Relative reactivities of substituted styrenes in copolymerization versus Hammett σ values of substituents.[34, 91] Positions of series on vertical scale are arbitrary.

chlorides. For the latter, the point 1 representing the p-OCH$_3$ result lies well above the best line for the remainder of the data. For the former, points 2, -p-OCH$_3$, the group of points 3, various p-alkyl substituents, and 4, -p-C$_6$H$_5$, all lie above the line through the remainder of the data. Consideration of the resonance forms involved in reactions 19 and 20 show that they also involve benzyl carbonium ion structures, to which electron-supplying groups in the para position might contribute forms such as

$$ \text{etc.} \tag{22} $$

Thus the heightened reactivity of such styrenes towards acceptor radicals suggests a similarity between the transition states in the carbonium ion and radical reactions, and supplies probably our best evidence for the participation of electron transfer structures in the transition states of the latter.

If we now return to the series involving the styrene radical itself, the relatively good fit to a Hammett plot which is observed suggests

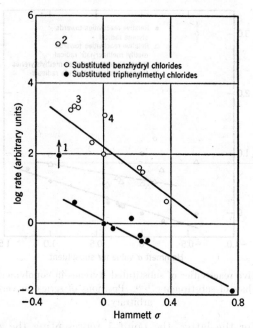

FIG. 4·10 Log relative rates of solvolysis versus Hammett σ values.

that the chief source of any polar effect here may be simply mutual polarization, although it may be noted that sigma values chosen for p-CN and p-NO$_2$ are the larger ones appropriate for reactions with phenols and amines. This in turn suggests that some electron transfer may be taking place from the styrene radical to the olefin. A similar conclusion, at least as to the direction of polarization in the transition state, is reached by comparing the slope of the lines in Hammett plots (i.e., rho values) for different substituted styrene radicals, Fig. 4·11. It will be noted that the slopes decrease as electron-withdrawing groups are introduced into the styrene radical.

Finally, a word needs to be said about the role of radical stabilization of the product radical in such series. Electron-supplying groups in general contribute little to radical stability, although radical stabilization by electron-withdrawing groups roughly parallels their electron-withdrawing ability in the para position.   Thus, radical stabilization may contribute something to the slopes of all of the plots in Figs. 4·9 and 4·11, and may also account for the fact that, in the styrene radical case, the point for unsubstituted styrene lies significantly below the best line through the remainder of the data.

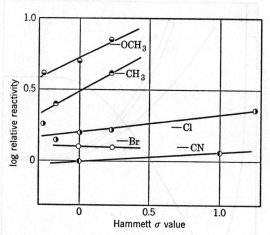

FIG. 4·11   Relative reactivities of substituted styrenes versus Hammett σ values for substituents in reaction with indicated substituted styrene radicals.[34]   Positions of series on vertical scale are arbitrary.

However, such effects appear to be small, and it is noteworthy that Szwarc, in a measurement of the bond dissociation energies of a series of substituted benzyl bromides, has detected only small, and rather erratic, differences, amounting at the most to 2–3 kcal/mole.[96]

The manner in which polar effects influence the behavior of monomers in copolymerization can also be discussed in terms of potential energy diagrams (Fig. 4·12).   If the potential energy curves for the reaction of radical and monomer in the absence of polar effects are represented by a_1 and b, any electrostatic attraction between fixed charges or dipoles on the two species will lower the repulsion curve by an amount increasing as the species approach the transition state to some new value a_2.   Mutual polarization, increasing as radical approaches monomer, will result in a further energy reduction to a_3, and actual participation of structures in which electron transfer has

[96] M. Szwarc, C. H. Leigh, and A. H. Sehon, *J. Chem. Phys.*, **19**, 657 (1951).

taken place will round off the curve in the region of the transition state to a final value a_4. Such a picture, although purely qualitative, perhaps aids in visualizing the processes involved and indicates the difficulties in separating one effect from another. It also suggests the difficulties of applying the energy diagrams of Fig. 4·8 to actual systems.

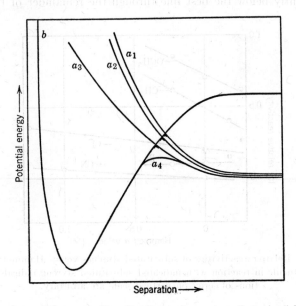

Fig. 4·12 Potential energy diagram illustrating polar effects in "alternating" copolymerization.[1]

4·1i   The Alfrey-Price Treatment of Monomer Reactivity Ratios

An interesting attempt to place the concepts of radical stabilization and polar effects on a quantitative basis has been made by Alfrey and Price [87] and has attracted considerable attention. According to these authors, the monomer reactivity ratios for a monomer pair may be expressed by the equations

$$r_1 = (Q_1/Q_2)e^{-e_1(e_1-e_2)} \tag{23a}$$

$$r_2 = (Q_2/Q_1)e^{-e_2(e_2-e_1)} \tag{23b}$$

where Q_1 and Q_2 are measures of the general reactivities of monomer M_1 and M_2 respectively, and e_1 and e_2 describe their polar properties.

The basis of the derivation of eq. 23 is Price's earlier suggestion: [85]

that the alternating tendency in copolymerization arises solely from the electrostatic interaction of permanent charges arising from polarization of radicals and double bonds, and thus parallels closely the treatment of aromatic nitration developed by Ri and Eyring.[97]   In the Alfrey-Price treatment, the rate constant for reaction of an $M_1 \cdot$ radical with M_2 is taken as a function of four independent terms

$$k_{12} = P_1 Q_2 e^{-e_1 e_2} \tag{24}$$

where P_1 is related to the reactivity of $M_1 \cdot$, Q_2 to the reactivity of M_2 and e_1 and e_2 are quantities related to the charges on $M_1 \cdot$ and M_2 respectively by the relation

$$e_1 = C_1 (rDkT)^{-1/2} \tag{25}$$

where C_1 is the actual charge on $M_1 \cdot$, r the separation of the charges in the transition state, D the "effective" dielectric constant, k the Boltzmann constant, and T the absolute temperature. If it is further assumed that the charge on a monomer and on the radical derived from it are identical, the rate constant for reaction of $M_1 \cdot$ with M_1 becomes

$$k_{11} = P_1 Q_1 e^{-e_1^2} \tag{26}$$

and division of eq. 26 by eq. 24 gives eq. 23a.

The validity of this derivation has been criticized on two grounds. The first is the picture of an alternating effect arising solely from electrostatic interaction between fixed charges, which further must be taken as equal for monomer and derived radical. The difficulties here, in regard to the independence of r's of the dielectric constant of the medium, and the behavior of substituted styrenes in strongly alternating systems, have already been mentioned. The second is that eqs. 23 do not uniquely define Q and e for any monomer. Rather, they must be arbitrarily chosen for one monomer and the remainder of the system built up on this base. Originally, Q and e were chosen for styrene as 1 and -1, respectively. Subsequently, Price [89] has changed this base to 1.0 and -0.8 as giving a series of Q values for monomers in better accord with his expectations. We may note that the effect of changing base in this way is to change the magnitude of the e values for different monomers, although the differences between them remain constant. On the other hand, both the values and order

[97] T. Ri and H. Eyring, *ibid.*, **8**, 433 (1940).

of Q values may be altered. A detailed discussion of the effect of such changes has been given by Alfrey.[98]

Since these criticisms have been largely accepted by Alfrey,[98] they will not be considered further. Rather, it is convenient to consider the Alfrey-Price equation as an essentially empirical expression. From this point of view, it has considerable utility for correlating data and predicting monomer reactivity ratios for monomer pairs where data are not available, as it amounts, basically, to a mathematical formulation of the ideas which we have developed in the preceding sections, namely, that monomer reactivities depend upon three factors: resonance stabilization of the resulting radical, steric effects (the two here lumped in the quantity Q), and a polar effect determined by the separation of monomer and radical in a polarity series ($e_1 - e_2$).

An idea of this empirical validity is given by Table 4·10, taken from Price[89] and listing Q and e values for some 31 monomers. Whenever possible, values have been calculated from several combinations, and the spread of values gives an idea of the fit of this scheme to actual data. Actually, the greatest difficulty in testing such a system lies in the experimental errors in reported r's. This is particularly true when r's lie near zero, for here the values reported are often essentially arbitrary, a particularly important case being styrene–vinyl acetate. Although this is a pair upon which many arguments are based, the actual value of r_2 is only known as having a value <0.02, and Price has assumed a value of 0.01. A better determination would certainly be in order. On the other hand, the same factors which make r's (and the derived values of Q and e) very sensitive to the exact nature of the copolymer-feed relationship (the basic measurement involved) make the value of this relationship relatively insensitive to the exact value of r's. Accordingly, even a rough estimate of r's (or only approximate validity of the Alfrey-Price equation to a particular system) may give a good estimate of a copolymer composition. Again, this whole question of experimental error has been treated in detail by Alfrey[98] and will not be considered here. Q and e values for a number of further monomers listed in Table 4·2 have been calculated and are given in the references cited.

The Q and e concept may be extended to polycomponent systems, and the resulting expressions have been developed by Fordyce,

[98] Chapters 3 and 4 of reference cited in footnote 2.

TABLE 4·10   MONOMER REACTIVITY FACTORS

Monomer$_1$	e_1	Q_1	Monomer$_2$
1. α-Methylstyrene	−1.2	0.70	Methyl methacrylate
	−1.1	0.55	Acrylonitrile
	−0.8	0.50	Methacrylonitrile
2. p-Dimethylaminostyrene	−1.2	1.35	Styrene
	−1.55	1.66	Methyl methacrylate
3. Isobutylene	−1.1	0.2	Vinyl chloride
4. p-Methoxystyrene	−1.0	1.0	Styrene
	−1.1	1.22	Methyl methacrylate
	−1.1	1.23	p-Chlorostyrene
5. p-Methylstyrene	−0.9	1.05	Methyl methacrylate
	−0.9	0.92	p-Chlorostyrene
6. m-Methylstyrene	−0.8	0.95	Methyl methacrylate
7. α-Vinylthiophene	−0.8	3.0	Styrene
8. Styrene	(−0.8)	(1.0)	
9. Butadiene	−0.8	1.33	Styrene
10. p-Chlorostyrene	−0.3	0.88	Styrene
p-Chlorostyrene	−0.6	1.20	Methyl methacrylate
11. p-Iodostyrene	−0.3	1.08	Styrene
	−0.6	1.28	Methyl methacrylate
12. m-Chlorostyrene	−0.2	0.96	Styrene
	−0.5	1.05	Methyl methacrylate
13. o-Chlorostyrene	−0.5	1.41	Styrene
	−0.2	1.15	Methyl methacrylate
14. p-Bromostyrene	−0.2	0.88	Styrene
	−0.5	1.27	Methyl methacrylate
15. m-Bromostyrene	−0.1	0.98	Styrene
	−0.4	1.20	Methyl methacrylate
16. α-Vinylpyridine	−0.1	1.07	Styrene
	−0.6	1.09	Methyl methacrylate
17. Vinyl acetate	−0.1	0.022	Vinylidene chloride
Vinyl acetate	−0.3	0.028	Methyl acrylate
	−0.4	0.026	Methyl methacrylate
	−0.3	0.047	Allyl chloride
	−0.5	0.010	Vinyl chloride
	−0.8	0.015	Vinyl chloride
	−0.9	0.022	Vinylidene chloride
18. Vinyl bromide	0.1	0.1	Vinyl acetate
19. Vinyl chloride	0.2	0.024	Styrene
	0.0	0.035	Methyl acrylate
	0.4	0.074	Methyl methacrylate
20. p-Cyanostyrene	0.3	1.61	Styrene
	−0.7	2.26	Methyl methacrylate
21. p-Nitrostyrene	0.4	1.86	Styrene
	0.4	1.06	p-Chlorostyrene
22. 2,5-Dichlorostyrene	0.4	1.67	Methyl methacrylate
23. Methyl methacrylate	0.4	0.74	Styrene
24. Vinylidene chloride	0.6	0.2	Styrene
25. Allyl chloride	0.6	0.052	Vinylidene chloride
26. Methyl acrylate	0.6	0.42	Styrene
27. Methyl vinyl ketone	0.7	1.0	Styrene
28. β-Chloroethyl acrylate	0.9	0.46	Styrene
29. Methacrylonitrile	1.0	0.46	Styrene
	0.9	1.15	Styrene
	0.9	1.06	Vinyl acetate
	1.3	1.5	Methyl methacrylate
30. Acrylonitrile	0.9	0.68	Methyl vinyl ketone
Acrylonitrile	0.9	0.37	Vinyl acetate
Acrylonitrile	1.0	0.67	Vinyl acetate
	1.2	0.44	Styrene
	1.3	0.37	Vinyl chloride
	1.6	0.9	Vinylidene chloride
	1.6	0.75	Vinyl chloride
31. Diethyl fumarate	1.2	0.77	Styrene
	1.4	0.028	Vinylidene chloride
	1.9	0.28	Vinyl chloride

Chapin, and Ham,[99] who have shown that they give good agreement with experiment. The application of a similar treatment to other radical reactions, where, as we will see, polar effects are also significant, is also possible, and examples are cited in Section 4·2.

4·1j Overall Kinetics of Copolymerization Reactions

Interpretation of the overall rate of a copolymerization reaction presents a complex problem, for it involves not only the four rate constants for chain propagation which determine copolymer compositions but also rate constants for chain initiation and chain termination as well. Nevertheless, the results are important for our understanding of more complicated radical chain processes, and the expressions obtained are general ones for radical chain processes involving more than one type of chain carrier.

Basically, the problem involved is that of reducing a multiplicity of rate constants to a smaller number of ratios of rate constants which can be separately determined. This simplification was first achieved by Melville, Noble, and Watson,[8] although the derivation given here is in a somewhat shorter form.[100] Since we are dealing with a long-chain radical process, we may assume chain termination by radical interaction, as in the case of a single monomer. Under these conditions we may use the same overall rate expressions (eqs. 2) employed in the derivation of the copolymerization equation, and the steady-state expression (eq. 3), and add the steady-state equation for overall radical formation and disappearance

$$R_i = 2k_{t11}[M_1\cdot]^2 + 2k_{t12}[M_1\cdot][M_2\cdot] + 2k_{t22}[M_2\cdot]^2 \qquad (27)$$

where R_i is the overall rate of chain initiation, k_{t11} the rate constant for chain termination by interaction of two chains ending in $M_1\cdot$, etc. Eliminating radical concentrations among eq. 3, eq. 27, and the sum of 2a and 2b gives as the overall rate expression

$$-\frac{d([M_1] + [M_2])}{dt}$$
$$= \frac{(k_{21}k_{11}[M_1]^2 + 2k_{12}k_{21}[M_1][M_2] + k_{22}k_{12}[M_2]^2)(R_i)^{1/2}}{(2k_{t11}k_{21}{}^2[M_1]^2 + 2k_{t12}k_{t21}[M_1][M_2] + 2k_{t22}k_{12}{}^2[M_2]^2)^{1/2}} \qquad (28)$$

[99] R. G. Fordyce, E. C. Chapin, and G. E. Ham, *J. Am. Chem. Soc.*, **70**, 2489 (1948).

[100] C. Walling, *ibid.*, **71**, 1930 (1949). In keeping with the present nomenclature, a factor of 2 is here employed with k_{t11} and k_{t22}.

earlier obtained by Simha and Branson.[101] Conversion of the rate constants into usable ratios involves the substitutions $r_1 = k_{11}/k_{12}$, $r_2 = k_{22}/k_{21}$, $\delta_1{}^2 = 2k_{t11}/k_{11}{}^2$, $\delta_2{}^2 = 2k_{t22}/k_{22}{}^2$, $\phi = k_{t12}/2(k_{t11}k_{t22})^{1/2}$ and leads to the final expression

$$-\frac{d([M_1] + [M_2])}{dt} = \frac{(r_1[M_1]^2 + 2[M_1][M_2] + r_2[M_2]^2)(R_i)^{1/2}}{(r_1{}^2\delta_1{}^2[M_1]^2 + 2\phi r_1 r_2 \delta_1 \delta_2 [M_1][M_2] + r_2{}^2\delta_2{}^2[M_2]^2)^{1/2}}$$

(29)

Similar equations for other termination mechanisms have also been obtained by Melville, Noble, and Watson,[8] but, since polymerizations

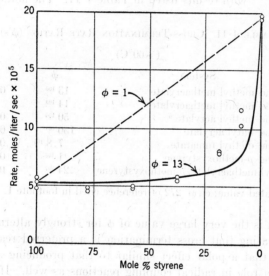

FIG. 4·13 Rates of copolymerization of styrene–methyl methacrylate at 60°. Initiator: 1 gram/liter azobisisobutyronitrile.[100]

in homogeneous media to yield high molecular weight polymers generally appear to involve bimolecular termination, they will not be considered further here.

In eq. 29 the seven rate constants for chain growth and termination have been reduced to five ratios. Thus, r's may be determined from copolymer composition studies, and δ's from rate measurements on individual monomers, leaving only ϕ, which will be seen to be a

[101] R. Simha and H. Branson, J. Chem. Phys., 12, 253 (1944); cf. R. Simha and L. A. Wall, J. Research Nat. Bur. Standards, 41, 521 (1948).

measure of the ratio of the cross-termination rate constant to the geometric mean of the rate constants for symmetric termination.[102]

Since R_i can be determined, or rendered essentially constant by using an initiator such as azobisisobutyronitrile, eq. 29 is susceptible to experimental test. Results on the styrene–methyl methacrylate system are shown in Fig. 4·13, together with the calculated rate curves for $\phi = 1$ and $\phi = 13$, the choice of ϕ giving the best fit. The failure of the curve to fit the $\phi = 1$ curve is plain. The agreement with the other value is reasonable, all points lying within the range $6 < \phi < 19$.

Subsequently, a number of other systems have been investigated [100, 103–107] with results listed in Table 4·11. The notable feature

TABLE 4·11   CROSS-TERMINATION RATE RATIOS (ϕ's)

($\sim$60°C)

System	ϕ	r_1r_2
Styrene–methyl methacrylate	13 [100]	0.24
Styrene–methyl methacrylate	14 [103]	
Styrene–methyl acrylate [a]	50 [100]	0.14
Styrene–butyl acrylate	150 [104]	0.07
Styrene–diethyl fumarate	7.8 [105]	0.021
Styrene–p-methoxystyrene	1 [106]	0.95
Methyl methacrylate–p-methoxystyrene	24 [107]	0.09

[a] Recalculated value; cf. p. 272 of reference cited in footnote 1.

of the data is the very large value of ϕ for strongly alternating systems, indicating that cross termination is a preferred reaction, and suggesting that a polar effect similar to that producing alternation may play a role in radical coupling reactions as well. If the arguments of preceding sections are correct, such increased reactivity could arise from contributions to the transition state of forms such as

[102] The factor of ½ is included in ϕ since, statistically, at equal radical concentrations collisions between unlike species are twice as probable as those between either like species.

[103] H. W. Melville and L. Valentine, *Proc. Roy. Soc. London,* **A200,** 337, 358 (1952).

[104] E. J. Arlman and H. W. Melville, *ibid.,* **A203,** 301 (1950).

[105] C. Walling and E. A. McElhill, *J. Am. Chem. Soc.,* **73,** 2819 (1951).

[106] E. P. Bonsall, L. Valentine, and H. W. Melville, *J. Polymer Sci.,* **7,** 39 (1951).

[107] E. P. Bonsall, L. Valentine, and H. W. Melville, *Trans. Faraday Soc.,* **48,** 763 (1952).

$$\underset{\phi}{\overset{H}{\sim}}C.^{\delta-}\ldots.^{\delta+}.\underset{COOR}{\overset{CH_3}{C}}\sim \qquad (30)$$

As we shall see, such preferred interaction between unlike radicals may be a rather common affair, and kinetic treatments which assume a value of $\phi = 1$ (with a resulting simplification of the kinetic expressions) are in general open to question. From the relative magnitudes of ϕ and $1/r_1r_2$ [or, more properly, $(1/r_1r_2)^{1/2}$] it appears that cross termination is more sensitive to polar effects than is the radical addition reaction, a reasonable result since radicals should be more polarizable than olefins. Further, experimental values of ϕ for any system vary appreciably with monomer feed ratios. Barb [30] has made the reasonable suggestion that this is because of polar effects of the penultimate monomer units in the terminating chains. The possibility of determining the different values of ϕ depending upon the penultimate unit has also been discussed by Arlman with tentative results for the styrene–butyl acrylate system.[104]

The opposing effects of a small r_1r_2 product and a large value of ϕ makes it difficult to make predictions about the shape of the overall rate-composition curve for strongly alternating copolymerizations. A very interesting result, however, is observed in approximately "ideal" systems in which the monomers differ markedly in reactivity. Here (with r_2 assumed small) eq. 29 may be approximated by the expression

$$-\frac{d([M_1] + [M_2])}{dt} = ([M_1] + 2[M_2]/r_1)R_i^{1/2}/\delta_1 \qquad (31)$$

Styrene–vinyl acetate represents such a system, experimental data on which are shown in Fig. 4·14.[100] Although eq. 31 necessarily breaks down as the system approaches pure vinyl acetate, it is evident from Fig. 4·14 that the addition of a small amount of styrene to vinyl acetate produces an enormous drop in polymerization rate. The explanation of this effect is very simple and is even more evident from an inspection of the actual rate constants involved (Table 4·5). Because of the high reactivity of both the vinyl acetate *radical* and the styrene *monomer*, in the presence of only a trace of styrene, vinyl acetate radicals are rapidly transformed to styrene radicals. These can find little styrene to react with and can react only very slowly with vinyl acetate. The result is a virtual stoppage of the polymerization process.   In short, styrene acts as an *inhibitor* for vinyl acetate polymerization.

The process which we have described clearly shows two important properties of the inhibition process.   First, it involves conversion of a chain-carrying radical into one which is too unreactive to carry on the chain.   Second, it may be quite specific for the particular process

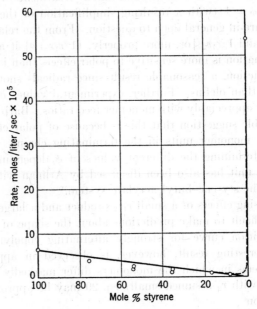

FIG. 4·14   Copolymerization of styrene–vinyl acetate at 60°.   Initiator: 1 gram/liter azobisisobutyronitrile.

involved (styrene, after all, polymerizes rapidly alone, or in the presence of more reactive monomers).   In Section 4·3 we will look at some of these inhibition processes in more detail.

4 · 2   Chain Transfer

The development of polymerization kinetics given in Chapter 3 led to a simple inverse relationship for any one monomer system between the polymer molecular weight (or degree of polymerization, $\bar{P}$) and polymerization rate.   However, we noted that in many actual systems $\bar{P}$ is found to be notably less than would be predicted by this simple theory, because of the intervention of a radical displacement reaction in the kinetic chain.   In polymer chemistry this process is known as

chain transfer, a term first introduced by Flory.[108]   A typical example
is provided by the polymerization of styrene (and many other monomers) in the presence of carbon tetrachloride, in which the reaction
involved is as follows, shown specifically and in an abbreviated form

$$\underset{\phi}{\sim}\!C\cdot \;+\; Cl\!-\!CCl_3 \;\rightarrow\; \underset{\phi}{\sim}\!C\!-\!Cl \;+\; \cdot CCl_3 \qquad (32a)$$

$$M\cdot \;+\; S \;\xrightarrow{k_{tr}}\; S\cdot \qquad (32b)$$

$$\cdot CCl_3 \;+\; CH_2\!\!=\!\!CH\phi \;\rightarrow\; Cl_3C\!-\!CH_2\!\!-\!\!\underset{\phi}{\overset{H}{C}}\!\cdot \qquad (33a)$$

$$S\cdot \;+\; M \;\xrightarrow{k_a}\; M\cdot \qquad (33b)$$

This chain transfer process is seen to be a matter of two steps, in
which first a growing polymer chain attacks some molecule in the
system to yield a stable polymer molecule and a new (small) radical,
and then this radical adds to a monomer molecule to start a new
polymer chain.   If the rate of reaction 33 is comparable to that of
ordinary chain growth, intervention of the sequence will have no
effect upon the overall polymerization kinetics,[109] but it obviously
results in a lowering of polymer molecular weight since it causes a
single *kinetic* chain to produce a *number* of polymer molecules.   The
number produced depends upon the competition between reactions 32
and the ordinary process of chain propagation.   Our primary interest
here will be in this competition and the information it gives on the
ease of various radical displacement reactions.   In the event that the
rate of reaction 32 is comparable to, or greater than, the polymerization propagation step, the resulting product will not be a polymer at
all, but rather a collection of small molecules in which the fragments
of the transfer agent have been, as it were, added across the double
bond of the olefin.   Chain transfer thus provides a bridge from the
study of radical polymerizations to the study of radical addition
processes leading to small molecules (Chapters 6 and 7); however,
here we will only consider systems in which chain transfer is essentially a perturbation of the polymerization process.

[108] P. J. Flory, *J. Am. Chem. Soc.,* **59,** 241 (1937).

[109] If reactions 33 are slow, the result is retardation or inhibition of the polymerization, and chain transfer represents one of the paths by which inhibitors
may act on radical chain reactions; cf. Section 4·3.

In principle, any molecule in a polymerizing system may undergo chain transfer with a growing polymer chain. However, the process was first identified in connection with ordinary organic solvents [110,111,112] added as presumably inert diluents in order to study the effect of monomer concentration upon polymerization kinetics. We shall discuss the reaction under these conditions first, since the results give particularly useful information on the relation between structure and reactivity in radical displacement reactions.

4·2a   Chain Transfer with Solvent

Since the most noteworthy effect of chain transfer is upon polymer molecular weight, it is reasonable that molecular weight measurements should be used to evaluate the competition between transfer and chain propagation processes. In any system the reciprocal of the degree of polymerization is given by the ratio of the rate of all chain-ending processes to the rate of polymerization, and, if we add to chain termination by radical coupling chain transfer via reaction 32, we may write

$$1/\overline{P} = (k_t[\text{M}\cdot]^2 + k_{tr}[\text{M}\cdot][\text{S}])/k_p[\text{M}\cdot][\text{M}] \tag{34}$$

By using the relationships of Chapter 3, and introducing as a new parameter the *transfer constant* $C = k_{tr}/k_p$, eq. 34 may be rewritten as

$$1/\overline{P} - k_t R_p/(k_p[\text{M}])^2 = C[\text{S}]/[\text{M}] \tag{35a}$$

or

$$1/\overline{P} - (k_t R_i/2)^{1/2}/k_p[\text{M}] = C[\text{S}]/[\text{M}] \tag{35b}$$

Since $1/\overline{P}$ is measurable, and since the other quantities on the left-hand side of eqs. 35 may be determined by the methods discussed in Chapter 3, eqs. 35 provide a means of evaluating the transfer constant for a given monomer-solvent system, for example, by plotting the left-hand side of eqs. 35 against [S]/[M] for a series of experiments, the slope of the resulting line being C.[113]

A particularly simple form of eqs. 35 occurs in the study of chain transfer in styrene polymerization when the reaction is carried out in

---

[110] F. R. Mayo, *J. Am. Chem. Soc.*, **65**, 2324 (1948).

[111] H. M. Hulburt, R. A. Harman, A. V. Tobolsky, and H. Eyring, *Ann. N. Y. Acad. Sci.*, **44**, 371 (1943).

[112] S. S. Medvedev, O. Koritskaya, and E. Alekseeka, *J. Phys. Chem. U.S.S.R.*, **17**, 391 (1943).

[113] In the event that chain termination is by disproportionation, the same treatment applies, except that the term corresponding to the formation of chain ends by radical-radical interaction is changed by a factor of 2.

the absence of added initiators. Under these conditions chains are initiated by a thermal process which is discussed in more detail in the next chapter but in which R_i is closely proportional to $[M]^2$ over a considerable concentration range. As a consequence, the second

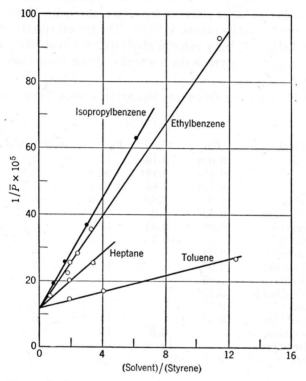

FIG. 4·15   Determination of transfer constants for styrene with various solvents via eq. 36.[114]

term on the left-hand side of eq. 35b is a constant, and the equation becomes

$$1/\bar{P} = 1/\bar{P}_0 + C[S]/[M] \tag{36}$$

where $\bar{P}_0$ represents the degree of polymerization which would be observed in the absence of transfer. From eq. 36, C may be determined from a simple plot of $1/\bar{P}$ versus [S]/[M].[110] Some examples of such plots are shown in Fig. 4·15, taken from the work of Gregg and Mayo.[114] It is evident that the data correspond well to the form of eq. 36, results

[114] R. A. Gregg and F. R. Mayo, *Discussions Faraday Soc.*, **2**, 328 (1947).

for each solvent giving a good linear plot, and all extrapolating to the same value of $\bar{P}_0$.

Partly because of this simplification, the majority of determinations of transfer constants have been for styrene polymerizations, obtained in this way. Table 4·12 lists some typical results, and values for a number of other solvents have been given by Mayo and his group [114, 115, 116] and by others.[117, 118, 119] The largest transfer constant listed in Table 4·12 has a value of about 0.02 (CCl₄ at 100°), indicating that a growing styrene chain attacks carbon tetrachloride about

TABLE 4·12   TRANSFER CONSTANTS FOR STYRENE WITH TYPICAL SOLVENTS

(All × 10⁴)

Solvent	C_{60}	C_{100}	$E_{tr} - E_p$	$\log (PZ_{tr}/PZ_p)$	Footnote
Cyclohexane	0.024	0.16	13.4	3.1	114
Benzene	0.018	0.184	14.8	3.9	114
Toluene	0.125	0.65	10.1	1.7	114
Ethylbenzene	0.67	1.62	5.5	−0.55	114
Isopropylbenzene	0.82	2.0	5.5	−0.47	114
t-Butylbenzene	0.06	0.55	13.7	3.8	114
Chlorobenzene		∼0.5	...		110
n-Butyl chloride	0.04		14	4	116
n-Butyl bromide	0.06		11	2	116
n-Butyl iodide	1.85		7	1	116
Methylene chloride	0.15				116
Chloroform	0.5				116
Ethylene dichloride	0.32		15	5	117
Ethylene dibromide		6.6	10	2.5	117
Tetrachloroethane		18			117
Carbon tetrachloride	90	180	5	1	115

one-fiftieth as readily as it adds another monomer unit to the chain. However, other substances are known which are much more reactive, and some examples are listed in Table 4·13. Since even traces of such materials profoundly affect polymer molecular weight, they are commonly known as (polymerization) regulators or modifiers and find considerable technical use for this purpose. An important example of this use is in the manufacture of synthetic rubber, where

[115] R. A. Gregg and F. R. Mayo, *J. Am. Chem. Soc.*, **70**, 2373 (1948).

[116] R. A. Gregg and F. R. Mayo, *ibid.*, **75**, 3530 (1953).

[117] C. H. Bamford and M. J. S. Dewar, *Discussions Faraday Soc.*, **2**, 314 (1947).

[118] J. A. Gannon, E. M. Fettes, and A. V. Tobolsky, *J. Am. Chem. Soc.*, **74**, 1854 (1952).

[119] S. L. Kapur, *J. Polymer Sci.*, **11**, 399 (1953).

TABLE 4·13   TRANSFER CONSTANTS IN STYRENE POLYMERIZATION OF SOME
REACTIVE TRANSFER AGENTS (POLYMERIZATION REGULATORS)

Transfer Agent	C_{60}	$E_{tr} - E_p$	Foot-note
Pentaphenylethane	2		114
Carbon tetrachloride	0.009	5	115
Carbon tetrabromide	1.36		116
t-Butyl mercaptan	3.6	−0.7	120
n-Butyl mercaptan	22		121
n-Dodecyl mercaptan	19		120
Ethyl thioglycolate	58		120
Dibutyl disulfide	(0.0125)		122

[120] R. A. Gregg, D. M. Alderman, and F. R. Mayo, *J. Am. Chem. Soc.*, **70**, 3740 (1948).
[121] C. Walling, *ibid.*, **70**, 2561 (1948).
[122] A. V. Tobolsky and B. Baysal, *ibid.*, **75**, 1757 (1953).

thiols are commonly included in the polymerization formulas in order to control polymer molecular weight.[123]

In systems containing polymerization regulators an alternative method exists for determining transfer constants, which can also be used (although less conveniently) with less reactive solvents. From our definition of the transfer process a simple relation exists between the rates of consumption of monomer and transfer agent equi-

$$d[M]/d[S] = 1 + [M]/C[S] \cong [M]/C[S] \qquad (37)$$

valent to the copolymerization equation (eq. 4) with one of the r's equal to zero. The 1 on the right-hand side of eq. 37 appears because the transfer sequence results in the consumption of one molecule of monomer through reaction 33. However, if the reaction yields high polymer, $[M]/C[S] \gg 1$, and the simpler form of the equation is valid. The quantity $d[S]$ may be determined by measuring either the rate of disappearance of the regulator, or its rate of inclusion in the polymer, and a good check with the molecular weight technique provides confirmation for the transfer scheme as written. With thiols, remaining regulator may be simply determined by titration,[120] and inclusion in polymer has been followed by using S^{35}-labeled material.[121]

Our chief interest in the data of Tables 4·12 and 4·13 is in the

[123] Transfer constants for thiols with butadiene are apparently almost identical with those with styrene; cf. E. J. Meehan, I. M. Kolthoff, and P. R. Sinha, *J. Polymer Sci.*, **16**, 471 (1955).

information that they give about the relation between structure and reactivity in radical displacement reactions, and it must be admitted that such information is largely inferential. Thus, transfer constants for benzene, toluene, isopropylbenzene, and t-butylbenzene increase in that order for the first three members of the series, but the value for t-butylbenzene is again only a little more than that of benzene. Such a series would result if transfer with toluene and isopropylbenzene occurred chiefly through attack upon benzyl hydrogen, and our discussion of bond dissociation energies suggests that the benzyl—H bond is certainly the weakest in such molecules.[124] In contrast, purely saturated aliphatic hydrocarbons such as cyclohexane with strong C—H bonds show very small transfer constants; so in the radical addition reactions of copolymerization we again see a parallel between the resonance stabilization of the radical product and reaction rate. Chain transfer of a styrene radical with ethylbenzene should be an energetically neutral process, since reactant and product radicals have essentially the same structure, and its activation energy is of some interest. Combining the data of Table 4·12 with E_p (from Table 3·4) gives a value of 12.8 kcal for E_{tr}. This is almost 20% of the energy of the bond being broken and formed, in contrast to the 5.5% predicted by the Hirshfelder "rule" (Section 2·2b) for reactions of this sort. Activation energies for the other hydrocarbons in Table 4·12 decrease with increasing substitution, but it is evident that there are also large variations in the temperature-independent component of k_{tr} between different solvents. For the hydrocarbons listed, Gregg and Mayo [114] have pointed out that a reasonably good linear relationship exists between log PZ_{tr} and E_{tr}, and have suggested that substituents which decrease the activation energy for transfer also decrease the entropy of activation through steric hindrance. However, with other solvents no obvious relation between E_{tr} and PZ_{tr} exists, and the whole table illustrates some of the difficulties in relating rates and activation energies in such reactions.

Transfer constants for halogen-containing compounds are of considerable interest. Of these, carbon tetrachloride has been particularly well studied.[115,125] Polystyrenes prepared at a wide range of

---

[124] Attack on benzyl C—H bonds of p-chlorotoluene by polymerizing vinylpyridine has been recently indicated by a study of the oxidation products of the resulting polymer; R. L. Dannley, J. A. Schufle, I. Cohen, and J. R. Chambers, *ibid.*, **19**, 285 (1956).

[125] F. R. Mayo, *J. Am. Chem. Soc.*, **70**, 3689 (1948).

[S]/[M] ratios actually contain four chlorine atoms per molecule, and, although the structure of low molecular weight products obtained in the presence of large amounts of carbon tetrachloride have not been conclusively established, the analogous 1:1 product from CBr_4 is known to have the structure indicated by eqs. 32 and 33, as have the 1:1 addition products of CCl_4 to a number of other olefins (Section 6·2). Chain transfer by radical displacement on a chlorine atom is thus well established. The effect of polymer chain length on C has also been investigated over a particularly wide range with this system and remains constant down to chains of about four styrene units. Below this chain length it decreases to 70, 25, and 6 (or less) $\times 10^4$ for chains of 3, 2, and 1 units respectively, apparently because of a corresponding decrease in k_{tr}.[125]

The high reactivity of carbon tetrachloride is somewhat surprising. In part it must arise from the resonance stabilization of the $\cdot CCl_3$ radical produced in the transfer process (12 kcal/mole from bond dissociation data) [126] and the fact that C—Cl bonds are in general weaker than C—H bonds; so less activation energy is required for processes in which they are broken and formed. It may also be helped by the additional strength of the benzyl C—Cl bond formed due to overlap between the orbitals of the Cl and the benzene ring, and by the contributions of a polar effect (see below). Similar arguments must apply to the still higher reactivity of carbon tetrabromide, Table 4·12.

Simple alkyl chlorides have transfer constants close to those of aliphatic hydrocarbons, and, by analogy to the processes discussed in Chapter 6, the transfer very probably occurs at C—H rather than C—Cl bonds. The relatively large transfer constants of bromo and particularly iodo compounds indicate that displacement here is on the halogen atom, a conclusion again supported by results on systems yielding lower molecular weight products.

Purely aromatic compounds show very little tendency to undergo transfer, in keeping with the high strength of aromatic C—H and C—X bonds, and the actual transfer process involved is somewhat complex and obscure. Mayo has recently investigated the polymerization of styrene in bromobenzene solution in some detail at 156°.[127] The molecular weight of the polymer obeys eq. 36 with $C = 3 \times 10^{-4}$.

---

[126] Since this value is obtained from $D(CCl_3—H)$ the $CCl_3—Cl$ bond may be still further weakened through repulsion between the four bulky groups attached to carbon.

[127] F. R. Mayo, *J. Am. Chem. Soc.*, **75**, 6133 (1953).

However, the polymer contains far less halogen than would be anticipated, nor is halogen lost as hydrogen bromide from the reaction
system. As we have seen, polymerization radicals are sometimes able
to add to aromatic systems, and Mayo has suggested that the apparent transfer process actually involves radical addition (reaction
38), followed by transfer of a hydrogen from the intermediate to

$$
\sim CH_2{-}\underset{\phi}{\overset{H}{C}}\cdot + \langle \text{ring} \rangle{-}Br \rightarrow \sim CH_2{-}\underset{\phi}{\overset{H}{C}}{-}\langle \text{ring} \rangle{-}Br \quad (38)
$$

another styrene molecule with regeneration of the bromobenzene
(reaction 39). How general such a process may be is not known,

$$
\sim \underset{H}{\overset{H}{C}}{-}\underset{\phi}{\overset{H}{C}}{-}\langle \text{ring} \rangle{-}Br + CH_2{=}\underset{\phi}{\overset{H}{C}} \rightarrow
$$

$$
\sim \underset{\phi}{\overset{H}{C}}{=}\overset{H}{C}\cdot + \langle \text{ring} \rangle Br + CH_3{-}\underset{\phi}{\overset{H}{C}}\cdot \quad (39)
$$

but the result points to a complexity of radical reactions with aromatic systems which will become increasingly evident in subsequent
chapters.

Amines and alcohols yield transfer constants similar to those of
hydrocarbons,[116] paralleling known high dissociation energies of N—H
and O—H bonds. In fact, as we shall see in Chapter 6, when transfer
does occur with such molecules, displacement actually takes place
at neighboring C—H bonds. On the other hand, thiols are particularly reactive, with transfer constants greater than unity. The reaction involved is certainly S—H bond cleavage, for the easily obtained 1:1 products are β-phenylethyl alkyl sulfides, and thiol-regu-
lated polymers in general contain one sulfur atom per molecule, present as organic sulfide. Such high reactivity is characteristic of many
sulfur compounds and is discussed in more detail in Chapter 7. The
transfer reaction of dibutyl disulfide is thought to involve displacement on sulfur, with cleavage of the S—S bond, i.e., the sequence

$$
M\cdot + RS{-}SR \rightarrow M{-}SR + RS\cdot \quad (40a)
$$

$$
RS\cdot + M \rightarrow RS{-}M\cdot \quad (40b)
$$

As evidence, it has been found that styrene polymerized in the presence of a cyclic disulfide, 1-oxa-4,5-dithiacycloheptane, shows little

decrease in molecular weight, but the polymer contains up to 17 sulfur atoms per molecule.[122] Similar results have been obtained with vinyl acetate,[128] and the products may be thought of as a sort of copolymer formed by a chain transfer process, with a structure

$$-M_n-S-R-S-M_n-S-R-S- \qquad (40c)$$

If this reaction is correctly formulated, it represents one of the few known examples of radical displacement on a polyvalent atom, rather than on univalent hydrogen or halogen.

A limited amount of information is available on transfer constants with solvents of other monomers than styrene, and the results add considerably to our picture. A comparison of rather scattered data on four monomers is given in Table 4·14. As in our discussion of

TABLE 4·14 COMPARISON OF TRANSFER CONSTANTS FOR DIFFERENT MONOMER-SOLVENT SYSTEMS AT 60°

(All $\times 10^4$)

Solvent	Styrene [a]	Methyl Methacry- late [129]	Acrylo- nitrile [130]	Methyl Acrylate (80°) [130a]	Vinyl Acetate [131]
Benzene	0.018	0.075	2.46	0.045	3
Toluene	0.125	0.525	5.83	2.7	21
Ethylbenzene	0.67	1.35	35.7	...	55
CCl$_4$	90	2.4	0.85	1.25	>10^4
CBr$_4$	13,600	3300 [132]	...	4100 [132]	>39×10^4 [132]
n-C$_4$H$_9$SH	22×10^4	0.67×10^4 [121]	...	1.69×10^4 [21]	>48×10^4 [b]

[a] For references, cf. Tables 4·12 and 4·13.
[b] The value cited (see reference cited in footnote 121) is undoubtedly low.

[129] S. Basu, J. N. Sen, and S. R. Palit, Proc. Roy. Soc. London, **A202,** 485 (1950).
[130] S. K. Das, S. R. Chattergee, and S. R. Palit, ibid., **A227,** 252 (1955).
[130a] S. D. Gadkary and S. L. Kapur, Makromol. Chem., **16,** 29 (1955).
[131] S. Palit and S. K. Das, Proc. Roy. Soc. London, **A226,** 82 (1954); cf. also S. L. Kapur and R. M. Joshi, J. Polymer Sci., **14,** 489 (1954). References cited in footnotes 129–131 also give data on a variety of other solvents.
[132] N. Fuhrman and R. B. Mesrobian, J. Am. Chem. Soc., **76,** 3281 (1954).

copolymerization results, it will be seen that the order of reactivity of various solvents is roughly the same regardless of the nature of the attacking radical. However, transfer constants for any one solvent increase in the order styrene < methacrylate < acrylonitrile, acrylate < vinyl acetate. When it is recalled that k_p for methacrylate acrylate and vinyl acetate are 5, 14.4 and 16 times k_p for styrene, it is evident that the actual values of k_{tr} increase very strik-

[128] W. H. Stockmayer, R. O. Howard, and J. T. Clarke, J. Am. Chem. Soc., **75,** 1756 (1953).

ingly as we go from unreactive resonance stabilized radicals to re-active, unstabilized ones, the relative values for styrene, methacrylate, acrylate, and vinyl acetate towards toluene (a typical example) being about $1:21:310:2700$ (the value of k_p for acrylonitrile is unknown).

Certain anomalies in Table 4·14 point to a polar effect in the radical displacement reaction of chain transfer comparable in importance to that which we have already discussed in connection with copolymerization. These are the unexpectedly low reactivities of CX_4 and thiols towards the acceptor-type radicals derived from methyl methacrylate, methyl acrylate, and acrylonitrile. The plausible explanation is in terms of a polar effect in which thiols and the polyhalomethanes have the properties of electron acceptors. If so, attack by *donor* radicals should be facilitated by contributions to the transition state such as

$$\underset{\phi}{\overset{H}{\sim C}}\cdot \; Cl\!-\!CCl_3 \; \leftrightarrow \; \underset{\phi}{\overset{H}{\sim C^+}}\cdots \cdot \dot{C}l \cdots \cdot {}^-CCl_3 \qquad (41)$$

and

$$\underset{\phi}{\overset{H}{\sim C}}\cdot \; H\!-\!SR \; \leftrightarrow \; \underset{\phi}{\overset{H}{\sim C^+}}\cdots \cdot \dot{H} \cdots \cdot {}^-SR \qquad (42)$$

which should be of little importance in the case of radicals derived from monomers such as methyl methacrylate. In the above formulations driving force is supplied by participation of the structures RS^- and $CCl_3{}^-$, the former the stable thiyl anion, and the latter the relatively stable species known to be involved in the facile proton exchange of chloroform, and also in its hydrolysis. Accordingly, the situation thus parallels the enolate ion contributions which increase the acceptor properties of carbonyl conjugated monomers. Interpretation of such a polar effect in terms of simple fixed dipoles or mutual polarization seems much more difficult, since the direction of the dipoles in the S—H and C—Cl bonds most certainly lies in opposite directions.

In our consideration of radical addition reactions yielding low molecular weight products we will see many more examples of such polar effects in radical displacement reactions, and also in the conjugate reactions in which non-carbon radicals add to double bonds. Later, a similar picture will aid us in interpreting radical halogenation and autoxidation processes. The possibility of correlating transfer constants for different systems on the basis of the Alfrey-Price equation (Section 4·1i) has been suggested by Fuhrman and Mesrobian,[132] and a number of "Q" and "e" values for solvents have been calculated by Katagiri, Uno, and Okamura.[133] However, too little data are available at present to evaluate the utility of the scheme in any detail.

4·2b Chain Transfer with Initiator, Monomer, and Polymer

Even in the absence of added solvents or polymerization regulators, chain transfer is possible with the species normally present in a polymerizing system, and in some systems is of considerable importance. Equation 34 may be generalized as

$$1/\overline{P} = (k_t[\text{M}\cdot^2] + k_{tr,\text{S}}[\text{M}\cdot][\text{S}] + k_{tr,\text{I}}[\text{M}\cdot][\text{I}]$$
$$+ k_{tr,\text{M}}[\text{M}\cdot][\text{M}] + k_{tr,\text{P}}[\text{M}\cdot][\text{P}])/k_p[\text{M}\cdot][\text{M}] \quad (43)$$

where $k_{tr,\text{S}}$, $k_{tr,\text{I}}$, $k_{tr,\text{M}}$, and $k_{tr,\text{P}}$ are the rate constants for chain transfer with solvent, initiator, monomer, and polymer, respectively (the concentration of the last conveniently taken in moles of monomer units per unit volume). From eq. 43 we obtain, analogous to eqs. 35

$$1/\overline{P} = C_\text{M} + C_\text{S}[\text{S}]/[\text{M}] + k_t R_p/(k_p[\text{M}])^2$$
$$+ C_\text{I}(k_t/k_p{}^2 R_i)R_p{}^2/[\text{M}]^3 + C_\text{P}[\text{P}]/[\text{M}] \quad (44)$$

where the C's are transfer constants, defined as before. By omitting added solvent, the second term may be eliminated, and at the beginning of reaction the last term (transfer with polymer) is generally unimportant; various methods are available for sorting out the remaining terms.[134] Figure 4·16 shows an analysis [135] of the sources of chain ends in the benzoyl peroxide-initiated polymerization of styrene, in which it is evident that transfer with monomer is a constant quantity ($C_\text{M} = 6 \times 10^{-5}$), and transfer with initiator becomes increasingly important as the initiator concentration increases. Values of C_M for a number of monomers are listed in Table 4·15. The actual point of attack is in some doubt, but, as we might expect, the amount of transfer increases with radical reactivity; so in a monomer like vinyl acetate it essentially determines polymer molecular weight, which remains practically constant when polymerization

[133] K. Katagiri, K. Uno, and S. Okamura, J. Polymer Sci., 17, 142 (1955).

[134] A recent discussion is given by S. R. Palit, U. S. Nandi, and N. G. Saha, J. Polymer Sci., 14, 295 (1954); cf. P. J. Flory, Principles of Polymer Chemistry, Cornell University Press, Ithaca, N. Y., 1953, pp. 138–141.

[135] F. R. Mayo, R. A. Gregg, and M. S. Matheson, J. Am. Chem. Soc., 73, 1691 (1951).

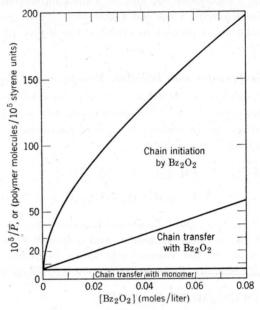

FIG. 4·16 Source of chain ends in the polymerization of styrene at 60° as a function of benzoyl peroxide concentration; Mayo, Gregg, and Matheson.[135]

TABLE 4·15 SELF-TRANSFER CONSTANTS (C_M) OF VARIOUS MONOMERS

Monomer	Temperature, °C	$C_M \times 10^4$
Styrene	60°	0.60 [135]
Methyl acrylate	60°	0.07–0.4 [140a]
Methyl methacrylate	60°	0.1,[136] 0.5,[137] 0.07 [141]
Vinyl chloride	60°	0.2 [140]
Vinyl acetate	60°	20 [138]
Allyl chloride	80°	1600 [139]
Allyl acetate	80°	700 [139]

[136] B. Baysal and A. V. Tobolsky, *J. Polymer Sci.*, **8**, 529 (1952).

[137] M. S. Matheson, E. E. Auer, E. B. Bevilacqua, and E. J. Hart, *J. Am. Chem. Soc.*, **71**, 497 (1949).

[138] M. S. Matheson, E. E. Auer, E. B. Bevilacqua, and E. J. Hart, *ibid.*, **71**, 2610 (1949).

[139] P. D. Bartlett and R. Altshul, *ibid.*, **67**, 812, 816 (1945).

[140] J. W. Breitenbach, *Makromol. Chem.*, **8**, 147 (1952).

[140a] V. Mahadevan and M. Santhappa, *ibid.*, **16**, 119 (1955).

[141] J. L. O'Brien and F. Gornick, *J. Am. Chem. Soc.*, **77**, 4757 (1955).

rate is varied over a wide range. Allyl acetate (and other allyl derivatives) represent a special case discussed in more detail below.

Chain transfer with initiator (which amounts to an induced initiator decomposition) has been mentioned previously as an important complication in the interpretation of polymerization kinetics, and varies widely with the particular initiator-monomer system, the azonitriles being one of the few classes of initiators with which it is not observed. The process has been studied in most detail with peroxides and is considered further in Chapter 10. We may note here that the transfer constant for benzoyl peroxide with styrene is 0.055 at 60°,[135] and the only reason that initiators do not, in general, have large effects on $\bar{P}$ is that they are normally used in very small quantities. Chain transfer with polymer is taken up in Chapter 5.

4·3   Polymerization Terminators, Inhibitors, and Retarders

4·3a   General Considerations

In our discussion of polymerization we have had several occasions to mention the phenomenon of inhibition of radical chain processes. We have seen how inhibitors may be used to determine the rates of radical chain-initiating processes. In copolymerization, we have seen how the addition of a small amount of one monomer may effectively inhibit the polymerization of another, pointing up the fact that the occurrence of inhibition may depend very much upon the particular system involved. In this section we will take up in more detail the mode of action of inhibitors, in particular the classes of substance which are generally effective for this purpose; we will also see how certain types of olefin, notably those with allylic C—H bonds, are often autoinhibiting and bring about the speedy termination of their own polymerization chains.

Substances which may terminate radical chains in polymerization are often classified on the basis of their effectiveness into *inhibitors*, which effectively stop every chain until they are consumed, and *retarders*, which are less effective and merely slow, rather than stop, the polymerization process. The difference in effect of the two classes upon the polymerization rate is illustrated in Fig. 4·17, taken from Schulz's study of the polymerization of styrene in the absence of added initiator.[142] In the presence of 0.1% benzoquinone (curve II), a typical inhibitor, an inhibition period is followed by polymerization

[142] G. V. Schulz, *Chem. Ber.*, **80**, 232 (1947).

at essentially the same rate as in pure styrene. In the presence of 0.5% nitrobenzene (curve III), a good example of a retarder, no inhibition period is observed, but the reaction is slowed to approximately one-third of its normal rate during the entire period of measurement. Nitrosobenzene (curve IV) shows a more complicated, but fairly common, behavior. It is an inhibitor, but, even after the inhibition period, polymerization is still slow. Apparently the reaction

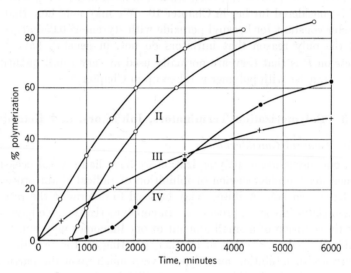

FIG. 4·17 Thermal polymerization of styrene at 100° in the presence of: I, no additive; II, 0.1% benzoquinone; III, 0.5% nitrobenzene; IV, 0.2% nitroso-benzene.[142]

products of the initial termination reaction are still able to react further and are themselves retarders. Such a classification of radical chain terminators, it should be emphasized, although convenient, is essentially of degree rather than kind and implies no difference in termination mechanism. Large quantities of retarders may bring about an apparent complete halt to polymerization, whereas, as we shall see, more sensitive methods of measurement may still detect polymerization proceeding during an apparent induction period.

4·3b   Stable Radicals

In principle, the simplest class of chain terminator would be a stable free radical which, because of its stability, or for some other reason, is unable to initiate chains, but which still reacts rapidly and stoichiometrically with the chain-propagating species. Diphenyl-picrylhydrazyl has been considered such an ideal reagent, and, in vinyl acetate and styrene polymerization, its use to "count" radicals gives results in good agreement with other methods (Section 3·3c). However, recent work of Hammond on its rate of reaction with the free radical from the decomposition of azobisisobutyronitrile in inert solvents, has indicated that the reaction in this case may be both non-stoichiometric and oxygen sensitive.[143] The nature of its reaction with radicals has only been established in a few cases, but with triphenylmethyl the overall process is: [144]

$$\phi_3 C\cdot \; + \; \phi_2 N\text{---}\overset{\cdot}{N}\text{---}\langle\text{NO}_2\rangle\text{---NO}_2 \;\rightarrow$$

with NO$_2$ groups on the ring.

$$\phi_3 C\text{---}\langle\ \rangle\text{---}N\text{---}\underset{\phi}{\overset{H}{N}}\text{---}\langle\ \rangle\text{---NO}_2 \qquad (45)$$

With polymethylmethacrylate radicals the hydrazyl becomes attached to the polymer chain, giving products with an absorption spectrum corresponding to a simliar hydrazine which can be reoxidized to a violet polymer radical.[145] Conceivably, the initial reaction with radicals could be a simple (reversible) coupling, with the formation of products such as indicated in reaction 45 arising from a slower irreversible rearrangement, a path which could account for some of Hammond's observation, e.g., the reappearance of color on exposure of a hydrazyl–azobisisobutyronitrile reaction mixture to air.

Alternatively, as suggested by Hammond, the initial reaction product between the hydrazyl and a free radical could be, not a true co-valent compound at all, but rather a "π complex" which subsequently reacts further, with or without destruction of the hydrazyl. Evidence for such radical-inhibitor complexes will be discussed further in Chapter 9.

[143] G. S. Hammond, J. N. Sen, and C. E. Boozer, *J. Am. Chem. Soc.*, **77**, 3244 (1955).
[144] S. Goldschmidt and K. Renn, *Ber.*, **55**, 628 (1922).
[145] A. Henglein, *Makromol. Chem.*, **15**, 188 (1955).

In view of these uncertainties, there seem to be definite limitations on the use of diphenylpicrylhydrazyl for quantitative radical counting in the study of free radical kinetics, and its application for the purpose in any particular system should certainly have some sort of independent confirmation.

The use of other relatively stable free radicals as inhibitors is usually complicated by their ability to initiate kinetic chains as well. The case of triphenylmethyl has been studied by Mayo and Gregg,[146] who have shown that it inhibits the polymerization of styrene at 100°, but that the inhibition period is shorter than would be anticipated from the known rate of radical production in the system. In fact calculation shows that as many as 77 triphenylmethyl radicals disappear for every polymer chain which would have been started in their absence. With larger quantities of triphenylmethyl and similar radicals, low molecular weight products have been obtained with a variety of olefins, including styrene, substituted styrenes, vinyl acetate, butadiene, and maleic anhydride. These products consist of a molecule of olefin and two triphenylmethyl residues, and have the structures which would be expected for radical addition products in

$$\phi_3 C - \overset{\overset{\displaystyle H}{|}}{\underset{\underset{\displaystyle R_1}{|}}{C}} - \overset{\overset{\displaystyle H}{|}}{\underset{\underset{\displaystyle R_2}{|}}{C}} - C\phi_3 \qquad (46)$$

which triaryl radicals both started and immediately stopped chains.

Basically, the question whether a given radical behaves as a chain initiator or terminator in a system depends upon its reactivity and concentration, and, at a low enough concentration, even triphenylmethyl would be expected to only start chains. Such a situation is approached with a number of tetraalkyldiphenylethanes and dimethyltetraphenylethane, which dissociate only very slowly into radicals and bring about the polymerization of acrylonitrile and methyl methacrylate to polymer of very high molecular weight. These materials thus approach the ordinary initiators in properties, and their use for this purpose is considered further in Section 10·4c.

The chain terminating properties of inorganic ions which can destroy radicals by single-electron transfer processes have recently been pointed out by Bamford,[146a] who has shown that hydrated ferric

[146] F. R. Mayo and R. A. Gregg, *J. Am. Chem. Soc.,* **70**, 1284 (1948).

[146a] C. H. Bamford, A. D. Jenkins, and R. Johnson, *Nature,* **177**, 992 (1956); *Proc. Roy. Soc. London,* **A239**, 214 (1957); cf. also E. Collinson and F. S. Dainton, *Nature,* **177**, 1224 (1956).

chloride in dimethylformamide or methyl ethyl ketone solution acts as an effective inhibitor of styrene polymerization and retards the polymerization of acrylonitrile. The overall reaction involved is apparently

$$\sim M\cdot + FeCl_3 \rightarrow \sim MCl + FeCl_2 \tag{47}$$

Accordingly the method can be used to determine rates of radical production by titration of the $FeCl_2$ produced. In azobisisobutyronitrile-initiated systems it gives good results, and should see much future use. Processes of this sort are considered further in Sections $10\cdot 3c$ and $11\cdot 3$.

$4\cdot 3c$ Non-Radical Chain Terminators

The much commoner class of inhibitors are substances which are not themselves radicals, but which react with the chain-propagating species by addition or transfer to yield radicals which are too unreactive to carry on the chain. Quinones are good examples of this class, and their use as radical "counters" has already been mentioned. However, a more detailed consideration of quinone inhibition experiments shows just how much and how little is actually known about the nature of their reactions with free radicals. Benzoquinone and duroquinone give sharp induction periods in the initiated polymerization of vinyl acetate, after which the reaction proceeds at its uninhibited rate.[147,148] In both cases the length of inhibition appears to correspond to a stoichiometry in which one quinone molecule terminates one kinetic chain. The benzoquinone–styrene–benzoyl peroxide system has been investigated by Cohen,[149] who has found that approximately one quinone molecule disappears for every molecule of initiator decomposed. On this basis he has concluded that one quinone terminates two kinetic chains, but, since chain initiation is not completely efficient, and some induced decomposition of peroxide can occur in such systems, his result may also correspond to a $1:1$ stoichiometry. On the other hand, chloranil, which is an efficient inhibitor of vinyl acetate, apparently copolymerizes with styrene,[150] although with a pronounced retardation of the overall polymerization rate. Quite different results are obtained in the quinone inhibition

[147] P. D. Bartlett, G. S. Hammond, and H. Kwart, *Discussions Faraday Soc.*, **2**, 342 (1947).

[148] P. D. Bartlett and H. Kwart, *J. Am. Chem. Soc.*, **72**, 1051 (1950).

[149] S. G. Cohen, *ibid.*, **67**, 17 (1945); **69**, 1057 (1947).

[150] J. W. Breitenbach and A. J. Renner, *Can. J. Research*, **28B**, 509 (1950).

of the *thermal* polymerization of styrene, in that both chloranil and benzoquinone are inhibitors but disappear at very high rates, a situation considered further in Section 5·1. Finally, quinones appear to be relatively inefficient terminators of methyl methacrylate,[151–152] and methyl acrylate,[153] polymerization, producing retardation rather than a well-defined inhibition period.

When one considers the variety of reactions which quinones may undergo with free radicals, it is not hard to see how such a diversity of results may arise. At least four initial reactions (reactions 48a-d) are possible, and have been proposed by various workers. Any of the

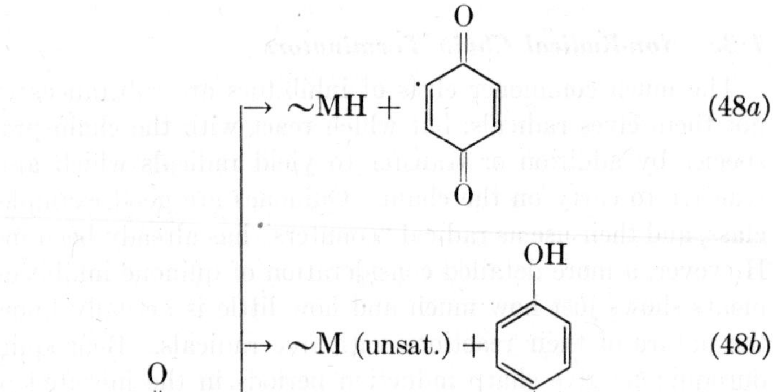

$$\rightarrow \text{~MH} + \qquad\qquad\qquad (48a)$$

$$\rightarrow \text{~M (unsat.)} + \qquad\qquad (48b)$$

$$\text{~M·} + \qquad \longrightarrow$$

$$\rightarrow \qquad \overset{?}{\rightarrow} \qquad\qquad (48c)$$

$$\rightarrow \qquad\qquad\qquad (48d)$$

---

[151] H. W. Melville and W. F. Watson, *Trans. Faraday Soc.*, **44,** 886 (1948); E. Bonsall, L. Valentine, and H. W. Melville, *ibid.*, **49,** 686 (1953).

[152] J. L. Kice, *J. Am. Chem. Soc.*, **76,** 6274 (1954).

[153] J. L. Kice, *J. Polymer Sci.*, **19,** 123 (1956).

resulting radicals may dimerize, react with another growing chain, or in the case of reactions 48b and 48c disproportionate. Dimerization gives a 1:1 stoichiometry providing the products are unreactive, whereas the other reactions predict that one quinone will terminate two chains. In addition, any of the intermediate radicals may be sufficiently reactive to occasionally add to monomer and thus restart chains with a resulting drop in efficiency.

Experimentally, there is little evidence for reaction 48a being important in the inhibition mechanism, but all the other reactions may occur under suitable conditions. The isolation of hydroquinone from the benzoquinone-inhibited polymerization of styrene, initiated either thermally at 120° [154] or with benzoyl peroxide at 80°,[151] suggests reaction 48b followed by disproportionation of semiquinone radicals. Investigation of the ultraviolet spectra of the products obtained from the benzoquinone–allyl acetate–benzoyl peroxide system indicates both C- and O-alkylation products.[147] More recent work suggests that reaction 48d is probably the commonest and most important path of radical attack on quinones. The styrene–chloranil copolymer has been shown by Breitenbach [150] to have the structure

$$(-O-\underset{Cl\ Cl}{\overset{Cl\ Cl}{\bigcirc}}-O-CH_2-CH\phi-)_n \qquad (49)$$

by cleavage to tetrachlorohydroquinone and ethylbenzene with hydriodic acid. Additional examples of addition of smaller radicals to quinones (chiefly to give hydroquinone ethers) appear in Section 6·3c.

Bevington, Ghanem, and Melville have investigated the benzoquinone-inhibited polymerization of methyl methacrylate [155] and styrene [156] using C^{14}-labeled quinone and azobisisobutyronitrile as initiator. In the first case, between one and two quinone residues are incorporated in each polymer chain, a result which they interpret as coupling between a chain ending in a quinone radical and a growing chain, together with a little copolymerization. With styrene, again,

[154] J. W. Breitenbach, A. Springer, and K. Horeischy, Ber., **71**, 1438 (1938); ibid., **74**, 1386 (1941).

[155] J. C. Bevington, N. A. Ghanem, and H. W. Melville, Trans. Faraday Soc., **51**, 946 (1955).

[156] J. C. Bevington, N. A. Ghanem, and H. W. Melville, J. Chem. Soc., **1955**, 2822.

most of the quinone is incorporated in the chain, the number of units per chain varying from 0.53 to 1.85.

Finally we may note that, although hydroquinone is ineffective as a polymerization inhibitor for styrene [154] or methyl methacrylate [157] in the absence of air, in its presence (particularly under alkaline aqueous conditions as in emulsion polymerization) it is oxidized to quinone, and, in addition, semiquinones, which may be even more effective inhibitors, can also be produced. The reactions of butadiene in such systems have been studied by Kharasch who finds that the major products are C-alkylated hydroquinones and quinones.[158]

All of these observations point to the complexity of actual quinone-radical reactions and indicate that the occurrence of a clean induction period proportional to quinone concentration is no guarantee of any simple path or stoichiometry of the reaction. Nevertheless, they do fall in line with some of the generalizations about radical reactions developed in the preceding sections of this chapter. Thus, the polymerization of unreactive vinyl acetate, with its reactive radical, is very efficiently inhibited by a number of quinones. In contrast, the inhibition of styrene is less efficient, and, with some quinones at least, the resulting radicals are still able to add to a styrene double bond. Finally, the relatively low inhibitory efficiency of quinones with methyl methacrylate and methyl acrylate suggests that a polar effect may be important in these processes, with quinones having the (expected) properties of electron acceptors. The analogy, in fact, between quinones and maleic anhydride is close and has been pointed out by Bartlett and Nozaki.[33] Both species react particularly readily with donor radicals, but the resulting quinone radicals prove to be relatively sluggish towards further reaction. To this we may now add the generalization that, although most evidence points to radical *addition* to quinones, O- or C-addition apparently may occur, depending upon the particular system involved.

A second important class of chain terminators are the aromatic di- and trinitro compounds, which show a similar pattern of behavior to the quinones, but which are rather less easily attacked by radicals as they inhibit vinyl acetate polymerization,[147,148] only retard styrene,[142,159] and have little effect on methyl methacrylate [152] or acry-

[157] C. Walling and E. R. Briggs, *J. Am. Chem. Soc.*, **68**, 1141 (1946).

[158] M. S. Kharasch, F. Kawahara, and W. Nudenberg, *J. Org. Chem.*, **19**, 1977 (1954).

[159] C. C. Price and P. A. Durham, *J. Am. Chem. Soc.*, **65**, 757 (1943); C. C. Price, *ibid.*, **65**, 2380 (1943).

late.[153] A more quantitative discussion of their relative rates of reaction is given in the next section. Again, the exact nature of the inhibition process is uncertain, and the stoichiometry of the reaction indicates that a compound such as di- or trinitrobenzene may be attacked by several radicals, becoming successively less reactive.[148] Price [159] has proposed that the initial step in the inhibition process is radical addition to the aromatic nucleus, and it is well established

$$\sim M \cdot + \underset{}{\overset{NO_2}{\bigcirc}} \rightarrow \sim M - \underset{H}{\overset{}{\bigcirc}} - NO_2 \qquad (50)$$

that ring-substituted products are obtained when nitrobenzene is attacked by methyl or phenyl radicals (Section 10·2). On the other hand, Bartlett et al.[147,148] have concluded that attack on the NO_2 group may also occur. The possibility that, in styrene polymerization, the intermediate radicals may occasionally continue the chain by transfer (or copolymerization) has been pointed out by Price and Read, who found that in a m-dinitrobenzene–styrene–p-bromobenzoyl peroxide system several dinitrobenzene residues appear in the polymer for every initiator fragment.[160]

A large number of other substances are known which inhibit or retard polymerization chains, and it should be evident from our discussion of copolymerization kinetics that such behavior should be expected in any system where radicals are produced with lower reactivities than the usual chain-carrying species. Data on such inhibitors have been assembled in several places,[142,161,162] but only two need further mention here, oxygen and sulfur.

Molecular oxygen is a particularly ubiquitous example, since it is present in any system from which it has not been specifically excluded and accounts for the induction period commonly observed when a polymerization is carried out in the presence of air.[162,163] Carbon radicals in general react very readily with oxygen to yield a peroxy radical:

$$\sim M \cdot + O_2 \rightarrow \sim M - O - O \cdot \qquad (51)$$

[160] C. C. Price and D. H. Read, J. Polymer Sci., 1, 44 (1946).
[161] S. G. Foord, J. Chem. Soc., 1940, 48.
[162] I. M. Kolthoff and F. A. Bovey, Chem. Revs., 42, 491 (1948).
[163] P. W. Allen, J. Polymer Sci., 17, 142 (1955).

Such processes are discussed at greater length in Chapter 9, but we may note here that, in styrene polymerization, reaction 51 occurs approximately 2.5×10^5 times as rapidly as chain propagation. The resulting radical is relatively unreactive, and its exact fate depends upon the particular system involved. With styrene an apparent copolymer is formed, having as a limiting composition the structure

$$(-O-O-CH_2-CH\phi-)_n \tag{52}$$

but lower molecular weight products are also formed. Similar oxygen copolymers have also been observed with many other olefins. Since the resulting products are peroxides, capable of thermal cleavage into radicals, it has often been observed that monomers, first exposed to oxygen and then placed in an oxygen-free environment, may polymerize with great rapidity and unexpected violence.

Sulfur inhibition also presents a complicated picture, since initial inhibition is followed by a progressively diminishing retardation of reaction. Bartlett and Kwart [148] have studied the inhibition of vinyl acetate and, recalling that sulfur molecules consist of eight-membered rings, have suggested the following sequence:

$$\sim M\cdot + S_8 \xrightarrow{k_a} \sim M-S_8\cdot \tag{53}$$

$$\sim M-S_8\cdot + \sim M\cdot \xrightarrow{Fast} \sim M-S_8-M\sim \tag{54}$$

$$\sim M-S_8-M\sim + \sim M\cdot \xrightarrow{k_b} \sim M-S_2-M\sim + \sim M-S_6\cdot \tag{55}$$

$$\sim M-S_6\cdot + \sim M\cdot \xrightarrow{Fast} \sim M-S_6-M\sim \tag{56}$$

etc.

with $k_a > k_b > \cdots$, etc. The choice of breaking of sulfur atoms two at a time is made on the basis that disulfides are relatively stable species, although they too undergo fairly ready chain transfer with vinyl acetate, a reaction accompanied by some retardation. For vinyl acetate at 45°, k_a is approximately 470 times k_p; so that sulfur molecules are notably less reactive than oxygen towards radical attack, a result in keeping with the diradical nature of the latter.

4·3d   The Kinetics of Inhibited or Retarded Polymerization

The overall kinetics of a retarded polymerization are given by the general copolymerization rate equation 28 provided that it follows the general scheme which has been outlined, and regardless of whether addition or transfer steps are involved in the process. In most cases the expression will be somewhat simplified, since some of the rate constants approach zero, and such modified equations have been considered by a number of investigators.[145, 153, 164]   The discussion given below follows that of Flory and serves to put several of the qualitative conclusions regarding inhibition on a firmer basis.

The fate of inhibitor molecules in a strongly retarded polymerization involves three general reactions:

$$M \cdot \; + \; Z \; \xrightarrow{k_{mz}} \; Z \cdot \tag{57}$$

$$Z \cdot \; + \; M \; \xrightarrow{k_{zm}} \; M \cdot \tag{58}$$

$$2Z \cdot \; \xrightarrow{k_{zt}} \; \text{Non-radical products} \tag{59}$$

where Z represents the inhibitor molecule and $Z \cdot$ the intermediate radical.   Reactions 57 and 58 may involve either addition or transfer.   If reaction 59 represents radical coupling, each occurrence will terminate two chains and involve two inhibitor molecules.   If it represents a disproportionation with regeneration of a molecule of inhibitor, two chains will end but only one inhibitor residue will be consumed.   In addition to reactions 57–59, a cross-termination process

$$Z \cdot \; + \; M \cdot \; \rightarrow \; \text{Non-radical products} \tag{60}$$

is possible and, since it represents reaction between unlike radicals, often with a large difference in polar properties, may have a relatively large rate constant.   However, in view of the concentration sequence $[M \cdot] \ll [Z \cdot] \ll [Z]$ which should obtain in a strongly retarded system, it may there be considered relatively unimportant. Likewise the normal termination involving two $M \cdot$ molecules can be neglected.

Under these conditions, at a constant initiation rate R_i, we have the steady-state conditions

$$d[M \cdot]/dt = R_i - k_{mz}[M \cdot][Z] + k_{zm}[Z \cdot][M] = 0 \tag{61}$$

$$d[Z \cdot]/dt = k_{mz}[M \cdot][Z] - k_{zm}[Z \cdot][M] - 2k_{zt}[Z \cdot]^2 = 0 \tag{62}$$

which may be solved for the concentrations of $[M \cdot]$ and $[Z \cdot]$.   The rate of consumption of inhibitor is

$$-d[Z]/dt = k_{mz}[M \cdot][Z] - y k_{zt}[Z \cdot]^2 \tag{63}$$

[164] P. W. Allen, F. M. Merrett, and J. Scanlan, *Trans. Faraday Soc.*, **51**, 95 (1955).

where $y = 0$ if $Z \cdot$ radicals disappear by coupling, but has a value of unity if disproportion with regeneration of inhibitor is involved. Eliminating radical concentrations between eqs. 61–63 gives

$$-d[Z]/dt = (1 - y/2)R_i + k_{zm}(R_i/2k_{zt})^{1/2}[M] \qquad (64)$$

From eq. 64 the rate of consumption of inhibitor is of zero order in inhibitor, in accordance with the well-founded observation that, at constant rates of chain initiation, the length of induction periods are proportional to inhibitor concentrations, and this is seen to apply regardless of the stoichiometry of the reaction, or the ability of inhibitor residues to occasionally restart chains (reaction 59). On the other hand, the dependence of $d[Z]/dt$ (and hence the inhibition period) upon R_i (and hence upon initiator concentration) does depend upon the frequency of such chain regeneration. If no regeneration occurs, the length of inhibition is proportional to R_i but approaches a half-order relation if regeneration is important. This relation thus supplies a test for the importance of the chain-regeneration process. Finally, the zero-order nature of inhibitor disappearance provides a demonstration of the unimportance of cross termination during most of the inhibition period, for its occurrence would introduce a term containing [Z] into eq. 64.

Even in a strongly inhibited reaction some monomer is being consumed via the usual propagation process and reaction 59. We may obtain a (rather complicated) expression for $d[M]/dt$ similar to eq. 64. However, for our purposes it is adequate to take the simpler case of $y = 0$ and $k_{zm} = 0$. Here, introducing as a new parameter an "inhibition constant," $z = k_{mz}/k_p$

$$d[Z]/d[M] = z[Z]/[M] \qquad (65)$$

or, on integrating,

$$\log([Z]/[Z]_0) = z \log([M]/[M]_0) \qquad (66)$$

It is evident that, for a good inhibitor with $z \gg 1$, the inhibitor will be almost completely consumed before appreciable monomer has polymerized. As the last inhibitor disappears, the polymerization turns to its normal course, and eq. 66 thus implies the type of inhibition curves with rather abrupt "elbows," which are actually observed.

The problem of actually determining z for a particular system required the measurement of polymerization rates during the inhibition period, which, for a good inhibitor, requires very sensitive

techniques.   Bartlett and Kwart [148] have investigated benzoyl peroxide–vinyl acetate–inhibitor systems using a very sensitive dilatometer for following the polymerization, a typical result appearing

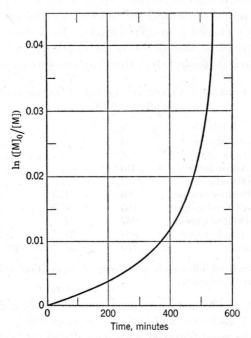

FIG. 4·18   Polymerization of vinyl acetate at 45° in the presence of 9.3×10^{-4}
M duroquinone and 0.2 M benzoyl peroxide (after Bartlett, Hammond, and
Kwart).[147]

in Fig. 4·18.   It is evident that measurements to 0.01% reaction are
required.   Under the assumptions involved in eq. 65, $- d[Z]/dt = R_i$,
whence

$$-\frac{d \ln [M]}{dt} = R_i/z([Z]_0 - R_i t) \qquad (67)$$

or, on integration,

$$z \ln [M]/[M]_0 = \ln \frac{[Z]_0 - R_i t}{[Z_0]} \qquad (68)$$

Knowing R_i, z may be determined from the initial slope of a figure
such as 4·18, or from the slopes of lines obtained by plotting against
each other the experimentally measurable portions of eqs. 67 or 68.
The vinyl acetate–duroquinone system gives good agreement with

this kinetic scheme, with $z = 90$ at 45°. The non-occurrence of chain regeneration was also shown in this system, and the relation demonstrated that one inhibitor molecule stops one chain. However, as has been mentioned, a series of polynitro compounds and sulfur gave more complicated results, indicating that an initial inhibition (with a 2:1 stoichiometry) yielded a weaker retarder. By a more complicated analysis it proved possible to isolate the successive steps, and results are summarized in Table 4·16. Here z_1 represents an initial inhibi-

TABLE 4·16 INHIBITION CONSTANTS IN THE POLYMERIZATION OF VINYL ACETATE AT 45° [148]

Inhibitor	z_1	z_2 [a]	z_3 [a]
Duroquinone	90	...	...
Nitrobenzene	38 [a]	...	...
p-Nitrotoluene	40 [a]	...	...
Dinitrodurene	2.5 [a]	...	...
o-Dinitrobenzene	96	1.5	...
m-Dinitrobenzene	105	6.5	...
p-Dinitrobenzene	267	4	...
Trinitrobenzene	890	31	5.5
Sulfur	470	57	20

[a] Assuming each inhibitor ends two chains, a supposition which cannot be checked with weak retarders.

tion constant, and z_2 and z_3 constants for inhibitors which have already reacted with one and two chains respectively. Still more complex results were observed with iodine, and the method is also limited in that, with diphenylpicrylhydrazyl and the more reactive quinones, too little polymerization occurs during the induction period for accurate measurement even by such refined techniques.

Subsequently Kice [152] has carried out similar experiments with methyl methacrylate but using a somewhat different scheme for analysis of his data. His results appear in Table 4·17 and show

TABLE 4·17 INHIBITOR CONSTANTS FOR METHYL METHACRYLATE AT 44° [152]

Inhibitor	z
Benzoquinone	5.5
Chloranil	0.26
Furfurylidene malono- nitrile	1.2
Sulfur	(0.075)
Trinitrobenzene	0.05
m-Dinitrobenzene	0.0048
p-Nitrotoluene	Immeasurably small
Diphenylamine	Immeasurably small

clearly (as has been qualitatively indicated above) that here inhibition constants are much smaller. Also, Kice finds that with chloranil and the nitro compounds the restarting of chains by inhibitor radicals (eq. 62) is significantly important. A similar study with methyl acrylate [153] gave still smaller values of z.

4·3e   The Polymerization of Allylic Monomers; Autoinhibition

In Section 3·3a we noted that, with a few exceptions, olefins containing allylic C—H bonds show little tendency to polymerize by radical processes, giving poor yields of low molecular weight products. Allyl acetate is a typical example of such a monomer, and its study by Bartlett and Altschul [139] provides the key to the problem. Kinetically the polymerization differs from that of monomers such as styrene not only in the shortness of the kinetic chains but in that R_p is proportional to initiator concentration, and that $\bar{P}$ is independent of polymerization rate and has a value (about 14 at 80°) about equal to the kinetic chain length. All these results may be rationalized on the basis that ready chain transfer occurs with monomer molecules to yield allylic radicals which are too unreactive to propagate a chain; i.e., a competition exists between the processes

$$\sim\!M\cdot\,+\,CH_2\!\!=\!\!CH\!\!-\!\!CH_2OAc\quad\begin{array}{c}\overset{k_p}{\nearrow}\quad \sim\!M\!\!-\!\!CH_2\!\!-\!\!\overset{\cdot}{C}H\!\!-\!\!CH_2OAc \\[2mm] \underset{k_{tr}}{\searrow}\quad \sim\!MH\,+\,CH_2\!\!=\!\!CH\!\!-\!\!\overset{\cdot}{C}H\!\!-\!\!OAc \\ \qquad\qquad\qquad \updownarrow \\ \qquad\qquad\overset{\cdot}{C}H_2\!\!-\!\!CH\!\!=\!\!CHOAc\end{array}$$

$$(69)$$

with $k_p/k_{tr} = 14$. Bartlett and Altschul have termed such a process "degradative chain transfer" ("allylic termination" is an alternative designation sometimes used). It provides a good example of autoinhibition, or a substance undergoing a side reaction which serves to terminate its own kinetic chains. The kinetics of such a process can be worked out as in the previous section and gives the results cited.[165]

If one considers the analogy between allyl acetate and vinyl acetate on the one hand, and allyl and benzyl radicals on the other, such

[165] As might be anticipated from the short chains involved, inhibitors have less effect on allyl acetate polymerization than is the case with vinyl acetate; cf. G. S. Hammond and P. D. Bartlett, *J. Polymer Sci.*, **6**, 617 (1951).

a result is very plausible. The transfer constant for vinyl acetate with toluene is appreciable and, as we have seen, benzyl-type radicals from styrene add to vinyl acetate only with difficulty.

The actual fate of the allyl radicals from allyl acetate is not known, since their reaction products have not been isolated. However, strong confirmatory evidence that allylic C—H bond cleavage is involved in the chain-interrupting step comes from a study of the polymerization of deuterated allyl acetate, CH_2=CH—CD_2OAc.[166] In the presence of the same amount of benzoyl peroxide, it polymerizes 1.9–2.9 times as fast as normal allyl acetate, to yield a product with $\bar{P}$ 2.4 times as high.

Since this is the first example of an *isotope effect* which we have encountered, its significance merits a brief discussion. In general, bond dissociation energies involving different isotopes vary slightly due to differences in zero-point energy of bond stretching, these zero-point energies, in turn, being a consequence of the quantization of vibrational energy. For a simple dissociation process, the situation is straightforward and is indicated in Fig. 4·19. The difference in zero-point energy (and, accordingly, in dissociation energy) depends upon the square root of the ratio of the masses of the isotopes and the force constants for stretching of the particular bond involved. As indicated, the heavy isotope has the lower zero-point energy and the larger dissociation energy, the magnitude of the difference increasing with the ratio of isotope masses and the stiffness of the bond involved. For hydrogen and deuterium bonded to carbon in a heavy molecule, the difference corresponds to approximately a 7-fold difference in R—H and R—D dissociation rates at room temperature. The quantitative extension of this picture to more complicated processes such as a radical displacement is rather uncertain,[167] but, on the basis that the hydrogen and deuterium are certainly less firmly bound in the transition state than in the reactants, an isotope effect would be anticipated in any reaction in which bonds to the isotopic atom are being formed or broken in the transition state and would be difficult to account for if such processes were not involved. Experimentally, in reactions in which R—H and R—D cleavages are unequivocal, rate ratios varying from about 10 down to almost unity are observed, and the existence of an isotope effect is generally taken

[166] P. D. Bartlett and F. A. Tate, *J. Am. Chem. Soc.*, **75**, 91 (1953).

[167] An excellent recent discussion of the whole problem is given by K. B. Wiberg, *Chem. Revs.*, **55**, 713 (1955); cf. also G. S. Hammond, *J. Am. Chem. Soc.*, **77**, 334 (1955).

as conclusive evidence of such participation of the isotope-bonding electrons in the transition state. Actually, this proves to be a very valuable tool in elucidating reaction mechanisms, and we will see additional examples in this book.

Isopropenyl acetate [168] and allyl chloride [139] show kinetics similar to those of allyl acetate, as do a number of other allyl esters,[169] and

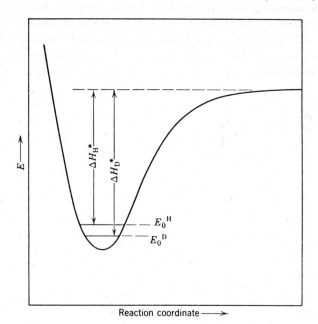

FIG. 4·19   Energy relations leading to isotope effect in the dissociation of R—H and R—D bonds: $E_0{}^H$, zero-point energy of R—H; $E_0{}^D$, zero-point energy of R—D; $\Delta H_H{}^*$, heat of activation of R—H dissociation; $\Delta H_D{}^*$, heat of activation for R—D.

also yield low molecular weight products. In the case of allyl chloride, the resulting radical is frequently able to regenerate a chain, since approximately three polymer molecules, containing approximately six monomer units apiece, are produced for every molecule of benzoyl peroxide decomposed. The conclusion seems inescapable that the failure of most other olefins containing allylic hydrogen to

[168] R. Hart and G. Smets, *J. Polymer Sci.*, **5**, 55 (1950); N. G. Gaylord and F. R. Eirich, *ibid.*, **5**, 743 (1950).

[169] N. G. Gaylord and F. R. Eirich, *J. Am. Chem. Soc.*, **74**, 334, 337 (1952); N. G. Gaylord and F. M. Kujawa, *J. Polymer Sci.*, **21**, 327, 329 (1956); N. G. Gaylord, *ibid.*, **22**, 71 (1956).

polymerize satisfactorily by a radical mechanism arises from a similar autoinhibition. The few examples which do yield high polymers, e.g., methyl methacrylate and methacrylonitrile, are characterized by unreactive chain-carrying radicals, so that they have very low self-transfer constants, and also possess double bonds which should add the few allyl radicals actually produced, both because of their reactivity and their polar properties. Finally, we may note that such allylic attack by radicals is by no means limited to polymerizations but is an important complication in many other radical addition processes as well. In fact, in processes such as autoxidation and certain halogenations, it often represents the dominant path of reaction.

CHAPTER 5

Some Further Characteristics

of Radical Polymerizations

In Chapter 3 we discussed polymerization as our best-understood example of a radical chain process in solution, employing it as a model for the development of radical chain kinetics and the determination of individual rate constants. In Chapter 4 we considered the information that polymerization experiments give on the relation between structure and reactivity in radical addition and radical displacement reactions. We may now turn to some other aspects of radical polymerizations which are of perhaps less general applicability, but which illustrate some peculiarities of radical reactions involving large molecules.

5 · 1 Thermal Initiation of Polymerization

5·1a The Occurrence of Thermal Initiation

As we have remarked in previous sections, certain monomers undergo a spontaneous thermal polymerization by a radical process even in the absence of any specific added initiators. Styrene is the best-known example, and, with only reasonable precautions (chiefly exclusion of air) or most rigorous purification, yields reproducible polymerization rates,[1-5] convincing evidence that the initiation process involves only styrene molecules and not some adventitious initiator. Experimentally, in pure styrene the rate of the thermal polymerization amounts to about 0.1% per hour at 60°, increasing to 14% per hour at 127° corresponding to an overall activation energy of 21 kcal/mole. Various substituted styrenes show comparable thermal polymerization, although the processes have not been studied in detail.

  [1] H. Dostal and W. Jorde, Z. physik. Chem., **179A**, 23 (1937).

  [2] H. Suess, K. Pilch, and H. Rudorfer, ibid., **179A**, 361 (1937).

  [3] G. V. Schulz and E. Husemann, ibid., **36B**, 184 (1937).

  [4] C. Walling, E. R. Briggs, and F. R. Mayo, J. Am. Chem. Soc., **68**, 1145 (1946).

  [5] G. Goldfinger and K. Lauterbach, J. Polymer Sci., **3**, 145 (1945).

Methyl methacrylate also undergoes purely thermal polymerization, although the actual rate is less certain. By the use of rather elaborate precautions, Walling and Briggs [6] obtained reproducible rates at 100–150°, about 1% of those observed with styrene. Rigorous exclusion of light and air was required, and the best results were obtained in the presence of 0.01–0.1% of hydroquinone or similar antioxidant. Since the amount of the particular antioxidant employed had no effect upon the rate, it was assumed that it was not involved in the chain process. This low rate has been attributed by Bamford and Dewar [7] to the spontaneous formation of an inhibitor during methacrylate polymerization, and they have reported a relatively high rate for the thermal reaction at lower temperatures. However, other workers have failed to confirm their result.[8]

In contrast to this behavior, carefully purified vinyl acetate,[9, 10] methyl acrylate,[9] and vinyl chloride [11] show no measurable polymerization at 100°, and certain other polymerizable olefins including methyl vinyl ketone,[12] acrylonitrile,[13] and tetrafluoroethylene [14] give only dimeric Diels-Alder type products at temperatures in the neighborhood of 200°. Thus, empirically, facile thermal initiation of polymerization appears to be a peculiarity of certain specific monomers characterized by relatively reactive double bonds.

5·1b   Order and Mechanism of Thermal Initiation; Biradicals

Initial rates of the thermal polymerization of styrene in solvents are approximately second order in styrene over a considerable range of concentration and essentially independent of the solvent employed, providing the system remains homogeneous.[15–17] Such a result is

[6] C. Walling and E. R. Briggs, J. Am. Chem. Soc., **68,** 1141 (1946).

[7] C. H. Bamford and M. J. S. Dewar, Proc. Roy. Soc. London, **A197,** 356 (1949).

[8] M. H. Mackay and H. W. Melville, Trans. Faraday Soc., **45,** 323 (1949); **46,** 63 (1950).

[9] J. W. Breitenbach and R. Raff, Ber., **69,** 1107 (1936).

[10] C. Cuthbertson, G. Gee, and E. K. Rideal, Nature, **140,** 889 (1937).

[11] J. W. Breitenbach and W. Thury, Experientia, **3,** 281 (1947).

[12] K. Alder, H. Offermanns, and E. Ruden, Ber., **B74,** 905 (1941).

[13] E. C. Coyner and W. S. Hillman, J. Am. Chem. Soc., **71,** 324 (1949).

[14] D. D. Coffman, P. L. Barrick, R. D. Cramer, and M. S. Raasch, ibid., **71,** 490 (1949).

[15] H. Suess and A. Springer, Z. physik. Chem., **A181,** 81 (1937).

[16] G. V. Schulz, A. Dinglinger, and E. Husemann, ibid., **B43,** 385 (1939).

[17] R. A. Gregg and F. R. Mayo, Discussions Faraday Soc., **2,** 328 (1947).

consistent with a bimolecular initiation process,[18] and the one which has been frequently proposed is the formation of a diradical. Re-

$$2CH_2{=}CHR \rightarrow R\overset{H}{\underset{}{C}}{-}CH_2{-}CH_2{-}\overset{H}{\underset{}{C}}R \qquad (1)$$

action 1 has been formulated as a tail-to-tail process in order to yield the most stable product, and, as pointed out by Flory,[19] is energetically feasible since the energy required to open two double bonds is largely compensated for by the new bond formation.[20]

Attractive as reaction 1 may appear energetically, it suffers from the consequence that the resulting growing chain will be a diradical. Accordingly, short chains should be very subject to cyclization reactions, the situation corresponding to the production of radicals in pairs discussed in Section 3·3c, with the added constraint that the radicals are physically *unable* to diffuse apart. Statistical calculations indicate that the probability of growing long chains under such conditions is vanishingly small.[21, 22] Further, if such cyclization does occur, termination becomes a first-order process, leading to termolecular kinetics.

Recently, additional evidence has become available that diradicals, when actually produced, are singularly ineffective in initiating polymerization reactions, presumably for exactly this reason. Thus photochemical polymerization of styrene sensitized by disulfides occurs readily and is considered to involve the process

$$R{-}S{-}S{-}R \xrightarrow{h\nu} 2RS\cdot \qquad (2a)$$

$$RS\cdot + CH_2{=}CHR \longrightarrow R{-}S{-}CH_2{-}\overset{\cdot}{C}HR \qquad (2b)$$

[18] Since the overall rate of polymerization is given by $k_p[M](R_i/2k_t)^{1/2}$, substitution of $k_i[M]^2$ for R_i gives a second-order expression, the only assumption being that chain propagation and termination are identical in the thermal and initiated processes.

[19] P. J. Flory, *J. Am. Chem. Soc.*, **59**, 241 (1937).

[20] A value of 20–30 kcal has frequently been quoted as ΔH for reaction 1. From the bond dissociation energies of Chapter 2, this would be about the value for two ethylene molecules (36 kcal). However, for styrene this needs to be corrected for the resonance energy of the exocyclic double bond of styrene (2×1.5 kcal, taken from heats of hydrogenation) and the resonance energy of the benzyl radicals produced (-2×24.5 kcal), giving $\Delta H = -10$ kcal, and indicating that the process might actually be exothermic. In contrast, diradical formation from a single styrene molecule, calculated similarly, would require about 58 kcal/mole.

[21] R. N. Hayward, *Trans. Faraday Soc.*, **46**, 204 (1950).

[22] B. H. Zimm and J. K. Bragg, *J. Polymer Sci.*, **9**, 476 (1952).

When cyclic disulfides are employed, the quantum yield is greatly reduced.[23] Similarly, Overberger finds that cyclic azo compounds are notably inefficient initiators.[24] The direct photochemical polymerization of styrene (which has often been formulated as excitation to a diradical, triplet state) has been shown by Tobolsky to give an R_p versus $\bar{P}$ relation indicating a monoradical initiation process.[25]

This body of evidence seems sufficient to rule out the growth of biradical chains in thermal polymerization. The possibility of initial biradical formation, followed by chain transfer, is also unlikely, since the rate of self-transfer of styrene is only about 10^{-5} that of chain propagation. However, what actually does occur remains obscure. Mayo has recently made a very careful study of the thermal polymerization of styrene in bromobenzene,[26] going down to 0.05 molar monomer concentration. Over the whole range, the reaction is more nearly 5/2 order than second order, and he points out that a third-order initiation process producing monoradicals, e.g.,

$$3CH_2{=}CH\phi \rightarrow CH_3{-}\overset{H}{\underset{\phi}{C}}\cdot \,+\, CH_3{-}\overset{H}{\underset{\phi}{C}}{=}C{-}\overset{H}{\underset{\phi}{C}}\cdot \qquad (3)$$

is energetically feasible. However, considerable transfer with solvent is occurring (by a complicated process; cf. Section 4·2a) which could produce the observed results by a mild retardation. Actually, a termolecular process may not be necessary for the formation of monoradicals. The process

$$2CH_2{=}CH\phi \rightarrow CH_3\overset{H}{\underset{\phi}{C}}\cdot \,+\, CH_2{=}\overset{\cdot}{C}{-}\phi \qquad (4)$$

gives a low enough value of ΔH (<20 kcal) if D(vinyl—H) is taken as 104 kcal, and the α-phenylvinyl radical is assumed to have a resonance energy of >18.5 kcal/mole.

It is evident that the feasibility of all the processes which we have considered depend on the high resonance stabilization of the radicals produced; so it is probably significant that the only monomers which may produce such highly stabilized radicals, styrene and methyl methacrylate, show unequivocal thermal initiations. Interestingly,

[23] K. E. Russell and A. V. Tobolsky, *J. Am. Chem. Soc.*, **76**, 345 (1954).
[24] C. G. Overberger and M. Lapkin, *ibid.*, **77**, 4651 (1955).
[25] D. H. Johnson and A. V. Tobolsky, *ibid.*, **74**, 938 (1952). The use of this test for thermal polymerization is obscured by chain transfer with monomer.
[26] F. R. Mayo, *ibid.*, **75**, 6133 (1953).

a comparison of the activation energies and rates of initiation processes show that thermal initiation, whatever its exact mechanism,
is an extremely improbable process, with a large negative value of
$\Delta S^{\ddagger}$. For styrene the PZ factor is only about 4×10^4, whereas for
methacrylate from Walling and Briggs's data,[6] if we treat the reaction
as bimolecular, it has the very low value of 0.4.[27] There are very few
reported cases of reactions with PZ factors of this order of magnitude, perhaps because they require the enormous multiplication of
effect brought about by initiating a long-chain process in order to
make them detectable.

5·1c Cross Initiation; Thermal Initiation and the Diels-Alder Reaction

Since thermal initiation is evidently a polymolecular process, the
possibility of a cross-initiation process involving unlike monomers exists in systems in which two or more monomers are present, and may
be investigated by studying copolymerization rates in the absence
of initiators. In Section 4·1j the overall kinetics of copolymerization were developed, and, from eq. 29 of Chapter 4, it is evident
that if r's, δ's, and ϕ are known for a system, R_i can be determined
from the overall copolymerization rate. If R_i is now corrected for
thermal initiation due to each of the monomers individually, any
residual initiation may be ascribed to a cross-initiation process. Such
an effect has been detected with styrene–methyl methacrylate at 60°,
the value of the calculated rate constant for bimolecular cross initiation being 2.8 times that for styrene alone, or almost 100 times the
geometric mean of the initiation constants of the two individual
monomers.[28] The relatively large value may well be a further example of a polar effect increasing the rate of a radical reaction, but,
in view of the uncertainty as to the nature of the initiation process,
it is difficult to discuss it in detail.

The generality of such cross initiations is unknown, but, in the
only other case which has been investigated quantitatively, styrene–
diethyl fumarate, no cross initiation was detected, and, in fact, R_i
proved to be only about 30% of the value calculated for thermal
initiation via styrene alone,[29] an observation for which there is no

[27] The activation energy for the initiation process is apparently lower than
that for styrene, 22 versus 29 kcal, despite its lower rate (0.35×10^{-15} versus
4.2×10^{-11} liter/mole/sec at 100°).

[28] C. Walling, *J. Am. Chem. Soc.*, **71**, 1930 (1949).

[29] C. Walling and E. A. McElhill, *ibid.*, **73**, 2819 (1951).

obvious explanation. On the other hand, the rapid, apparently spontaneous, copolymerization which is often observed in strongly alternating systems such as styrene–maleic anhydride may well arise from such a cross-initiation process.

Some observations on inhibition of the thermal polymerization of styrene are pertinent in connection with cross initiation. Inhibitors such as quinones and polynitro compounds produce the expected induction periods (cf. Fig. 4·17) at least roughly proportional in length to the amount of inhibitor initially present, and a large number of such materials have been surveyed by Foord [30] and Breitenbach.[31] However, when the length of the induction period for a given quantity of quinone is compared with the known rate of thermal chain starting due to styrene, many quinone molecules (approximately 60 and 17–21 for benzoquinone at 60 and 100°) [32, 33] disappear for every chain started. Some of this loss may be due to copolymerization, as in the initiated styrene–chloranil system,[34] but it seems likely that some additional direct reaction between quinone and styrene is involved. The products formed in the benzoquinone-inhibited reaction have been investigated by Kern [35] and by Melville,[36] and include hydroquinone (about 15%) and a mixture of partially phenolic materials of unknown structure, including a fraction corresponding roughly to a two styrene to one quinone condensation product. A similar 2:1 product has also been isolated from the thermal, chloranil-inhibited, reaction.[37]

The hydroquinone could arise from the normal inhibition process (cf. Section 4·3b), but it may be significant that many quinones, notably chloranil, are good dehydrogenating agents at the temperatures at which thermal polymerizations are often studied, 120–150°, converting ethylbenzene to styrene and dibenzyl to stilbene [38] via reactions such as:

[30] S. G. Foord, J. Chem. Soc., **1940**, 48.

[31] J. W. Breitenbach and H. L. Breitenbach, Z. physik. Chem., **A190**, 361 (1942).

[32] F. R. Mayo and R. A. Gregg, J. Am. Chem. Soc., **70**, 1284 (1948).

[33] K. E. Russell and A. V. Tobolsky, ibid., **75**, 5082 (1953).

[34] J. W. Breitenbach and A. J. Renner, Can. J. Research, **28B**, 509 (1950).

[35] W. Kern and K. Feuerstein, J. prakt. Chem., **158**, 186 (1941).

[36] H. W. Melville and W. F. Watson, Trans. Faraday Soc., **44**, 886 (1948).

[37] J. H. Breitenbach and H. Schneider, Ber., **76**, 1088 (1943).

[38] N. Dost and K. van Nes, Rec. trav. chim., **70**, 403 (1951); N. Dost, ibid., **71**, 857 (1952); E. A. Braude, L. M. Jackman, and R. P. Linstead, J. Chem. Soc., **1954**, 3548, 3564. Such dehydrogenations occur readily only with hydro-

$$+ \text{CH}_3\text{—CH}_2\phi \rightarrow \qquad + \text{CH}_2\text{=CH}\phi \quad (5)$$

Although attempts to detect phenylacetylene in the styrene-benzo-quinone reaction have been unsuccessful,[37] dehydrogenation of low molecular weight polystyrene, formed during the inhibition period, is a possibility and would still further complicate the mixture of products obtained.

The origin of the low molecular weight products mentioned is puzzling. Since they are formed in systems containing only a fraction of a mole % quinone, they can only represent products of the normal inhibition process if the quinone has a very large inhibition constant, which is not indicated by data on initiated polymerizations.[36] A more likely possibility is that they arise from some quite independent process, perhaps analogous to the Diels-Alder reaction.

The possible connection between the Diels-Alder reaction and thermal initiation processes has been pointed out by several investigators.[36, 39] Although this has been on the basis of a diradical initiation step (a concept which we have here abandoned) the relationship is still worth discussion.

Typically, the Diels-Alder reaction involves a condensation between a diene and an olefin (dienophile) in which the double bond is conjugated with electron-supplying groups, e.g.,

$$(6)$$

However, the reaction has many extensions.[40] Simple olefins such as ethylene also condense with dienes at elevated temperatures, and

---

carbons possessing benzyl or allyl hydrogen, are clearly bimolecular, and, from Linstead's work, appear to be *non-radical* processes involving hydride ion transfer.

[39] F. R. Mayo and C. Walling, *Chem. Revs.*, **46**, 274 (1950).

[40] A good review is given by K. Alder in *Newer Methods in Preparative Organic Chemistry*, Interscience Publishers, New York, 1948 (translated and

some carbonyl-conjugated olefins are able to act as dienes as in the reaction [41]

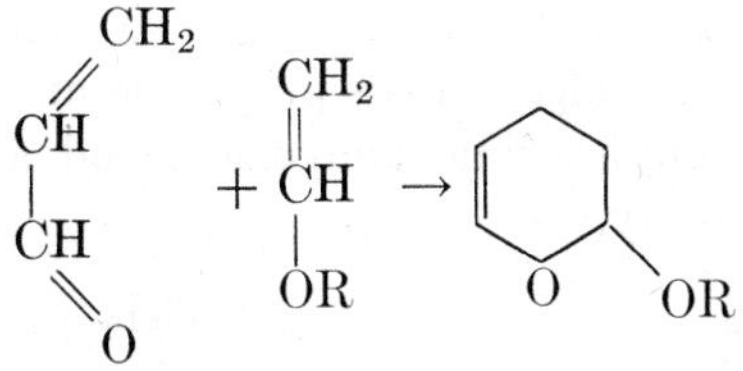

$$
\begin{array}{c}
\text{CH}_2 \\
\parallel \\
\text{CH} \\
\mid \\
\text{CH} \\
\diagdown \\
\text{O}
\end{array}
\quad + \quad
\begin{array}{c}
\text{CH}_2 \\
\parallel \\
\text{CH} \\
\mid \\
\text{OR}
\end{array}
\quad \rightarrow \quad
\text{(ring with O and OR)}
\tag{7}
$$

Simple olefins may also dimerize to yield cyclobutane derivatives,[13, 14, 42] a notable example being tetrafluoroethylene, which not only undergoes the reaction with particular ease but condenses similarly with other olefins as well: [14]

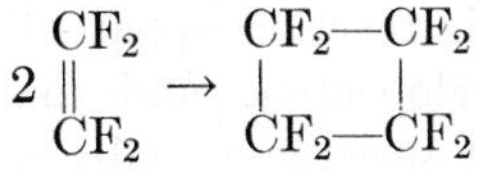

$$
2 \;
\begin{array}{c}
\text{CF}_2 \\
\parallel \\
\text{CF}_2
\end{array}
\; \rightarrow \;
\begin{array}{c}
\text{CF}_2\text{—CF}_2 \\
\mid \qquad \mid \\
\text{CF}_2\text{—CF}_2
\end{array}
\tag{8}
$$

At least one example of what seems to be a termolecular Diels-Alder reaction is also known.[43]

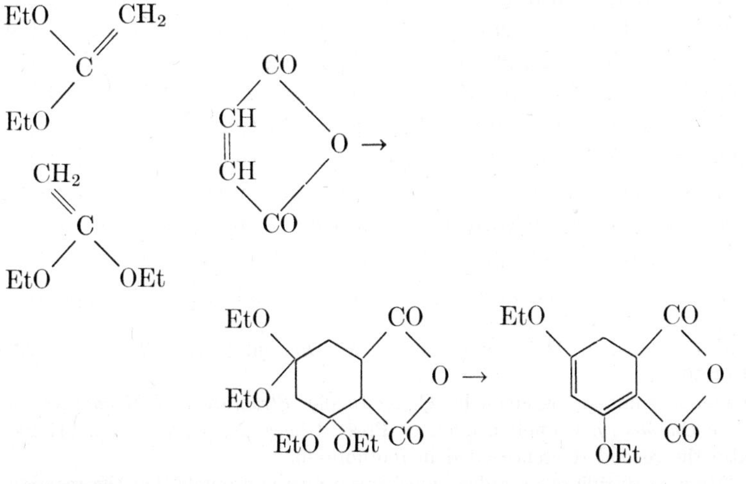

$$
\tag{9}
$$

---

revised by C. V. Wilson and J. A. Van Allen). A more recent brief account is given by C. Walling, Chapter 47, Volume III, *The Chemistry of Petroleum Hydrocarbons,* B. T. Brooks, editor; Reinhold Publishing Corp., New York (1955).

[41] C. W. Smith, D. G. Norton, and S. A. Ballard, *J. Am. Chem. Soc.,* **73,** 5267 et seq. (1951).

[42] Evidence for such products have even been obtained by Mayo [26] in his study of the thermal polymerization of styrene at high dilutions.

[43] S. M. McElvain and H. Cohen, *ibid.,* **64,** 260 (1942).

A final variant, which seems to fall in the same class, occurs between strong dienophiles and olefins with allylic hydrogen when they are heated together under conditions so that the usual radical copolymerization is avoided. Thus propylene and maleic anhydride at 180–250° yield allylsuccinic anhydride, and a number of other olefins behave similarly.[44]

$$\qquad (10)$$

It is significant that this reaction apparently involves double bond migration, methylenecyclopentene and maleic anhydride yielding (1-cyclopentenylmethyl) succinic anhydride.[45]

Insofar as they have been studied, all of these reactions seem to be clearly bimolecular and proceed at about the same rate in a variety of solvents and even in the vapor phase. They also show little sensitivity to acid or base catalysis. Their mechanism has received a good deal of discussion,[46] the present consensus being that they are "molecular" reactions in which the conformation of the transition state closely resembles that of the final product, and the bond-breaking and bond-forming steps all occur either simultaneously or in very rapid succession. The question still remains open, however, as to whether the transition state is a diradical or simply some polarized species. Although the question is difficult to test,[47] it has meaning

[44] E. H. Farmer, *Trans. Faraday Soc.*, **38**, 340 (1942); K. Alder, F. Pascher, and A. Schmitz, *Ber.*, **76**, 27 (1943).

[45] R. T. Arnold, R. W. Amidon, and R. M. Dodson, *J. Am. Chem. Soc.*, **72**, 2871 (1950).

[46] A good summary is given by C. K. Ingold, *Structure and Mechanism in Organic Chemistry*, Cornell University Press, Ithaca, N. Y., 1953, pp. 711–21; cf. also the second reference cited in footnote 40.

[47] Attempts to rule out a radical mechanism on the grounds that the reaction is not accelerated by radical sources or that the products correspond to those expected from a polar reaction are actually invalid, since initiators cannot produce the required diradical, and the strong influence of polar effects in known radical reactions indicates that the same polarizations which direct polar processes can also determine the direction of a radical reaction. On the other hand, the low *PZ* factor which characterizes typical Diels-Alder reactions is not unequivocal evidence of an (improbable) electron unpairing process, but may also arise from the loss of degrees of freedom in a highly circumscribed transition state.

since, in any molecule, electrons exist in either paired or unpaired states.[48]

If Diels-Alder condensations are radical processes, the mechanistic similarity to thermal initiation processes is plain: they simply represent special cases in which, somewhere near the transition state, certain olefin pairs prefer to fall apart into two monoradicals rather than proceeding to a cyclic product, and even if the cyclizations do not involve diradical intermediates there may still be a close relation between the two processes. However, it is worth keeping in mind that, thanks to the very short time cycle necessarily involved, the possibility of diverting what we might call a diradical on its way to becoming a Diels-Alder product by reaction with some outside reagent should be very small.

5·2   Effects of Polymer on the Polymerization Process

5·2a   Autoacceleration; the Gel Effect

An important property of many free radical polymerizations is that they show a striking autoacceleration as the reaction proceeds. In large systems this, combined with the increasing viscosity of the polymerizing mass, can lead to an impressive heat buildup and disastrous results, since the reaction becomes almost explosive. However, even in isothermal systems the acceleration persists.

The amount of autoacceleration observed varies notably with monomer and experimental conditions. With undiluted methyl methacrylate at 60° and below, the polymerization rate begins to increase at about 25% reaction, and Fig. 5·1 shows a typical plot of both reaction rate and conversion versus time for a benzoyl peroxide-initiated reaction.[49] At 130°, on the other hand, no increase in rate is observed at least up to 40% reaction.[6] Dilution with an inert solvent which is also a good solvent for polymer also first delays and then eliminates the acceleration, Fig. 5·2.[50] Methyl acrylate shows a particularly pronounced autoacceleration, detectable at

---

[48] Ingold's suggestion [46] that the reaction is "largely homolytic" cannot be taken literally, since it implies a transition state which is a resonance hybrid of structures containing different numbers of unpaired electrons, a quantum-mechanical impossibility. A better statement would be that implied in footnote 47: if it is homolytic (involving a diradical) polar factors still play a large role.

[49] E. Trommsdorff, H. Köhle, and P. Lagally, *Makromol. Chem.*, **1**, 169 (1948).

[50] G. V. Schulz and G. Haborth, *ibid.*, **1**, 106 (1948).

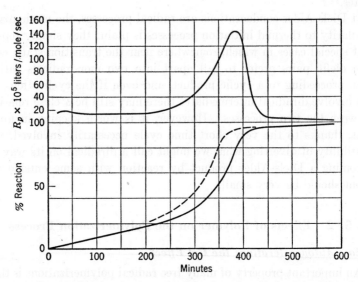

FIG. 5·1 Autoacceleration in the polymerization of methyl methacrylate initiated by benzoyl peroxide at 60°; Trommsdorff, Köhle, and Lagally.[49]

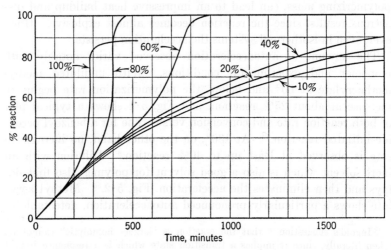

FIG. 5·2 Effect of dilution on the rate of polymerization of methyl methacrylate in benzene at 50° in the presence of 10 grams/liter benzoyl peroxide.[50]

as little as 1% reaction.[51]   On the other hand, styrene and vinyl acetate are less affected.

Since rates of chain initiation could hardly be expected to increase with conversion, autoacceleration must either arise from an increase in k_p or a decrease in k_t in the polymerization process (or both), and either would also account for the marked increase in polymer molecular weight which generally accompanies the autoacceleration.   The later was first proposed by Norrish and Smith,[52] a suggestion amplified by Trommsdorff [49,53] and Schulz,[50] on the basis that, as polymerization proceeds, chain termination becomes diffusion controlled in the increasingly viscous medium.   The idea is certainly plausible, since chain termination is a very rapid process with k_t's in the neighborhood of 10^7 liters/mole/sec, and the entangling of polymer chains as reaction proceeds leads to a marked drop in the rate of polymer molecule diffusion and should also interfere with the movement of growing polymer chains.   Chain propagation, in contrast, is slower ($k_p = 10^2$–10^3 liters/mole/sec), and small monomer molecules are still able to find their way through the tangled polymer chains.

Quantitative confirmation of the decrease in k_t has been obtained from rotating sector experiments carried out at high conversions. Table 5·1 summarizes data of Matheson et al.,[51] and indicates that

TABLE 5·1   VARIATION OF k_p AND k_t WITH CONVERSION [51]

Monomer	Tempera-ture, °C	Transition Point [a]	$k(35\%)/k(0\%)$		$\bar{P}$ Initial
			k_p	k_t	
Vinyl acetate	25	>40	...	...	2,400
Styrene	50	30	0.67	0.075	4,000
Methyl methacrylate	30	15	1.12	0.0066	5,000
Methyl acrylate	30	0	...	...	>10,000

[a] Per cent conversion at which autoacceleration becomes detectable.

for methyl methacrylate at 35% reaction k_t has decreased to less than 1% of its initial value, whereas k_p has remained sensibly constant.   No quantitative data are available for metyl acrylate, but the polymerization rate has been observed to increase as much as 20% at 30° by the time 5% reaction has occurred.

[51] M. S. Matheson, E. E. Bevilacqua, and E. J. Hart, *J. Am. Chem. Soc.,* **73,** 5395 (1951).

[52] R. G. W. Norrish and R. R. Smith, *Nature,* **150,** 336 (1942).

[53] E. Trommsdorff, *Colloquium on High Polymers* (Freiburg, 1944).

Recently Bengough and Melville[54] have extended measurements with vinyl acetate as far as 73% conversion, using their thermocouple method for following the reactions in the highly viscous system involved. At 0° a 2-fold increase in rate occurs at 50% reaction, but the autoacceleration becomes appreciable at higher temperatures. Radical lifetimes increase about 10-fold, and from measurements in the temperature range of 0–60° the authors conclude that E_t begins to increase at about 30% conversion, finally reaching a value of over 15 kcal/mole at 73%. A similar increase in E_p sets in at about 50% reaction, with the net result that the overall activation energy for photopolymerization, $E_p - E_t/2$, decreases from an initial value of 4.2 kcal to a minimum of about 1.9 kcal at 46% and then rises again to over 7 kcal.

A quantitative interpretation of the point at which k_t begins to decrease would be of considerable interest but would require knowledge both of the diffusion rates of growing polymer molecules and the effective "collision diameter" of the growing ends of polymer chains. This quantity would be related to the volume which the radical is able to sweep out rapidly by twisting and turning in spite of the slow movement of growing polymer molecule as a whole.[55] Qualitatively, though, the results of Table 5·1 appear reasonable since susceptibility to autoacceleration increases with the initial values of $\overline{P}$ listed (k_t's are roughly the same for all four monomers, Table 3·3). Further, the amount of autoacceleration of methyl acrylate decreases in the presence of a transfer agent, butyl mercaptan, which decreases $\overline{P}$ and presumably permits a higher diffusion rate for polymer molecules.[51] If so, the assumption of constancy of k_p's and k_t's with chain length used in usual kinetic developments becomes invalid as we reach the autoacceleration stage of polymerization.[56]

As k_t decreases, radical lifetimes and concentrations at a given rate of initiation necessarily increase, and, as polymerization ap-

[54] W. I. Bengough and H. W. Melville, *Proc. Roy. Soc. London,* **A230,** 429 (1955).

[55] A recent treatment of this problem, M. F. Vaughan, *Trans. Faraday Soc.,* **48,** 576 (1952), does not appear convincing since it fails to take into account peculiar diffusion properties of polymer solutions due to the long-chain nature of polymer molecules.

[56] A similar effect of thiols on the lifetime of radicals in partially polymerized methyl methacrylate is reported by S. Fujii, S. Tanaka, and S. Sutani, *J. Polymer Sci.,* **20,** 584 (1956). Also the autoacceleration of styrene may account for the low kinetic order of the thermal polymerization, carried to high conversion in the absence of diluent; cf. reference in footnote 4. The demonstration of variation in k_t should invalidate some of the arguments given there.

proaches completion, both may reach large values. Many years ago Melville observed that methyl methacrylate films, deposited by gas-phase photopolymerization, were able to absorb and polymerize monomer in the dark, even days after illumination was stopped,[57] and recently high concentrations of radicals have been detected by paramagnetic resonance absorption spectra measurements in highly polymerized methyl methacrylate.[58] Such phenomena involving "trapped" or "embalmed" radicals become particularly striking in highly cross-linked systems (Section 5·2d) and are also observed in other solid or glassy media (Section 11·1).

5·2b   Chain Transfer with Polymer; Graft Copolymers

In Section 4·2 we saw that chain transfer via a radical displacement reaction between growing polymer chains and solvent, monomer, or initiator molecules was often an important complication in the polymerization process. Once a polymerization has begun, the possibility of chain transfer with polymer also arises and obviously becomes increasingly important as reaction proceeds. The consequence of such transfer is the formation of branched polymer molecules, Fig. 5·3, and, if chain termination is by coupling, the polymer structure may be still further complicated by the linking together of two or more such Christmas-tree-like molecules.[59]

The importance of chain branching as a reaction can be inferred from transfer constants cited in Section 4·2b. Polystyrene has a structure similar to isopropyl benzene; so at 50% reaction one branch should be formed for about every 10^4 propagation steps, and at 90% reaction one for every 10^3.

Various methods are available for detecting chain transfer to polymer. With vinyl acetate most of the transfer involves C—H bonds on the acetate side chains, so molecular weight determination before and after hydrolysis followed by reacetylation is an indication of the amount of branching.[60] Sometimes methods of end-group

---

[57] H. W. Melville, *Proc. Roy. Soc. London,* **A163,** 511 (1937).

[58] G. K. Fraenkel, J. M. Hirshon, and C. Walling, *J. Am. Chem. Soc.,* **76,** 3606 (1954).

[59] If chain transfer with monomer is important, additional branches may be introduced by the incorporation of such monomer molecules (each with its own chain of attached monomer units) into a subsequent growing chain, cf. references in footnote 60.

[60] O. L. Wheeler, S. L. Ernst, and R. N. Crozier, *J. Polymer Sci.,* **8,** 409 (1952); O. L. Wheeler, E. Lavin, and R. N. Crozier, *ibid.,* **9,** 157 (1952); O. L. Wheeler, *Ann. N. Y. Acad. Sci.,* **57,** 360 (1953).

analysis are applicable,[61, 62] and, in principle, branching could be determined by a comparison of weight- and number-average molecular weights (cf. Section 3·1) since the molecular weight distribution as a function of branching has been worked out.[63]

An ingenious method of determining transfer to polymer was developed by Bevington, Guzman, and Melville,[64] who polymerize a monomer under conditions where the polymer will have some pre-

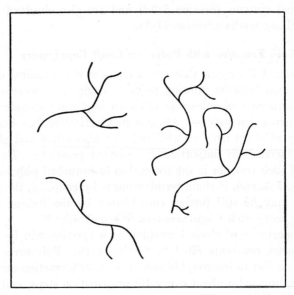

FIG. 5·3   Effect of chain branching on structure of addition polymers.

determined (average) molecular weight in the presence of polymer of a very different molecular weight, which has been labeled with a radioactive isotope. When the resulting mixed polymer is fractionated and the radioactivity of the fractions assayed, the extent of transfer may be estimated. With styrene, as might be expected from the discussion just given, the amount of branching is very small. In a typical polymerization at 75% conversion only one chain in ten

[61] J. J. Fox and A. E. Martin, *Proc. Roy. Soc. London,* **A175,** 226 (1940).

[62] J. D. Cotman, Jr., *Ann. N. Y. Acad. Sci.,* **57,** 417 (1953).

[63] C. H. Bamford and H. Tompa, *J. Polymer Sci.,* **10,** 345 (1953); J. K. Beasley, *J. Am. Chem. Soc.,* **75,** 6123 (1953).

[64] J. C. Bevington, G. M. Guzman, and H. W. Melville, *Nature,* **170,** 1026 (1952).

contains a branch.[65] On the other hand, vinyl acetate has a transfer constant with polymer of 0.003 (per acetate unit) at 40°, and appreciable branching occurs even at low conversion.[66]

The most striking example of chain transfer with polymer occurs in the technical polymerization of ethylene, carried out at very high pressures in the neighborhood of 200°C. The product is highly branched [61] to an extent which profoundly affects the physical properties of the polymer,[67, 68, 69] high molecular weight products showing one methyl group per 20–71 carbon atoms by infrared analysis.[67] Two branching processes may be distinguished.[70] One is radical attack on already formed polymer molecules such as discussed above. This increases with conversion and produces branches of many monomer units. The other is an intramolecular attack of the growing polymer molecule on its own chain,

$$
\begin{array}{ccccc}
-CH_2 & \cdot CH_2 & & -\dot{C}H & CH_3 \\
| & | & \rightarrow & | & | \\
CH_2 & CH_2 & & CH_2 & CH_2 \\
\diagdown & \diagup & & \diagdown & \diagup \\
& CH_2 & & & CH_2 \\
\end{array}
\qquad (11)
$$

which occurs at a constant rate during the polymerization and produces short branches of only a few methylene units. Similar intramolecular transfers (which we may think of as a rather indiscriminate sort of radical rearrangement) may well occur to a lesser extent in other polymerization reactions but have hitherto been undetected.

A novel modification of the reaction of chain transfer with polymer may sometimes be observed by polymerizing a monomer in the presence of a polymer of different composition. The product consists of a branched structure with a backbone made up of one type of monomer unit but with side chains of another. Such materials are called *graft copolymers* and were first prepared by Carlin and Shakespeare by polymerizing *p*-chlorostyrene in the presence of polymethyl acry-

[65] J. C. Bevington, G. M. Guzman, H. W. Melville, *Proc. Roy. Soc. London,* **A221,** 453 (1954).

[66] J. C. Bevington, G. M. Guzman, and H. W. Melville, *ibid.,* **A221,** 437 (1954).

[67] W. M. D. Bryant, *J. Polymer Sci.,* **2,** 547 (1947).

[68] C. A. Sperati, W. A. Franta, and H. W. Starkweather, Jr., *J. Am. Chem. Soc.,* **75,** 6127 (1953).

[69] F. M. Rugg, J. J. Smith, and L. H. Wartman, *Ann. N. Y. Acad. Sci.,* **57,** 398 (1953).

[70] M. J. Roedel, *J. Am. Chem. Soc.,* **75,** 6110 (1953); W. M. D. Bryant and R. C. Voter, *ibid.,* 6113; F. W. Billmeyer, Jr., *ibid.,* 6118.

late in an experiment which also provided the first demonstration of chain transfer with a polymer molecule.[71]

Subsequently a considerable number of such graft copolymers have been prepared, and, as we might expect, the reaction is most successful when a monomer which gives very reactive radicals is used for the second polymerization.[72, 73, 74] Thus both vinyl acetate and vinyl chloride may be "grafted" onto polymethyl methacrylate, but the reverse process gives only the two separate polymers.[72] Ethylene may be readily grafted onto polyvinyl acetate, and the product gives some information about the point of radical attack on this polymer.[73] Radical attack on the C—H bonds of the side-chain acetoxy groups leads, on hydrolysis, to the formation of mixtures of long-chain fatty acids. The amount of such products isolated indicates that, at low ethylene pressures, attack occurs at this point about three times as readily as at the C—H bonds along the polymer backbone, but the results are puzzling since this ratio is said to decrease at higher pressures. Natural rubber and its simpler analogs such as dihydromyrcene are also readily attacked by the radicals of growing polymer chains by transfer and perhaps also by addition to double bonds, and a number of products prepared in this manner have been investigated.[75]

The nature of the chain transfer processes which occur with polymethyl methacrylate has recently been studied by Schulz [76] by polymerizing styrene and methyl methacrylate in the presence of low molecular weight polymer. He believes that he has been able to distinguish two transfer processes, one with polymer *ends*, $C_E = 3.5 \times 10^{-2}$ and 11×10^{-2} for methacrylate and styrene radicals, and the other with hydrogens along the chain, $C_M = 1.5 \times 10^{-4}$ and 0.3×10^{-4} respectively, although the exact nature of the first process in particular is unknown.

The problem of preparing polymers containing long sequences of different monomer units (in contrast to the usual copolymers discussed in Chapter 4) is currently of much interest, and other in-

[71] R. B. Carlin and N. E. Shakespeare, *ibid.*, **68**, 876 (1946).

[72] G. Smets and M. Claesen, *J. Polymer Sci.*, **8**, 289 (1951).

[73] R. J. Rolland and L. M. Richards, *ibid.*, **9**, 61 (1952).

[74] R. A. Hayes, *ibid.*, **11**, 535 (1953).

[75] G. F. Bloomfield, F. M. Merrett, F. J. Popham, and P. McL. Swift, *Rubber World*, **131**, 358, 418 (1954); J. Scanlan, *Trans. Faraday Soc.*, **50**, 756 (1954); F. M. Merrett, *ibid.*, **50**, 759 (1954).

[76] G. V. Schulz, G. Henrici, and S. Olive, *J. Polymer Sci.*, **17**, 45 (1955).

genious techniques leading to graft copolymers are available.[77]   It is also possible to prepare *block* copolymers in which sequences of different monomers are distributed along a single chain.[78]

5·2c   Cross Linking and Gelation Processes

Polymerization of a diene leads initially to a linear unsaturated polymer with vinyl groups dependent from the polymer chain, or, in the case of 1,4 addition to a conjugated diene, with unsaturation along the polymer backbone itself, e.g.,

$$
\sim CH=CH\sim \underset{\underset{\underset{CH_2}{\parallel}}{\underset{CH}{|}}}{C}\sim \overset{\overset{CH=CH_2}{|}}{C}\sim \tag{12}
$$

Such a polymer may undergo copolymerization with subsequent growing polymer chains, to produce a *three-dimensional cross-linked* structure of great complexity, Fig. 5·4.

Since each act of cross linking reduces the number of polymer *molecules* which would otherwise be formed, cross-linked polymers may have very high molecular weights, and, in fact, a sufficiently cross-linked sample may be essentially a single giant molecule.   As a result, cross-linked polymers tend to be non-thermoplastic and are merely swollen, rather than dissolved, by solvents.[79, 80]   The transition from an initial linear polymer to a cross-linked structure may occur quite dramatically in the course of a polymerization.   Thus, ethylene dimethacrylate, polymerized at 60° in the presence of 0.1 gram of benzoyl peroxide per mole of monomer, changes abruptly from a fluid to a firm gel in a minute or two at approximately 2–3% reaction.   Similar sudden transformations are also observed in methyl methacrylate–ethylene dimethacrylate mixtures containing as little as 0.2 mole % of the latter.[81]   Such a *gel point*, the appearance of

[77] H. H. Jones, H. W. Melville, and W. G. P. Pearson, *Nature,* **174,** 78 (1954); D. J. Metz and R. B. Mesrobian, *J. Polymer Sci.,* **16,** 345 (1955).

[78] J. G. Hicks and H. W. Melville, *Nature,* **171,** 300 (1953); *J. Polymer Sci.,* **12,** 461 (1954); J. E. Guillet and R. W. G. Norrish, *Nature,* **173,** 625 (1954); A. E. Woodward and G. Smets, *J. Polymer Sci.,* **17,** 51 (1955).

[79] W. H. Carothers, *Chem. Revs.,* **8,** 402 (1931).

[80] H. Staudinger and W. Hever, *Ber.,* **67,** 1164 (1935); H. Staudinger and E. Husemann, *ibid.,* **68,** 1618 (1935).

[81] C. Walling, *J. Am. Chem. Soc.,* **67,** 441 (1945).

visible gelation in a polymerizing system, is considered to correspond to the point at which indefinitely large networks (on a molecular scale) are first formed. Flory has shown statistically the conditions under which such networks may exist.[82] For our case, it is the point where each chain is cross-linked on the average to two or more other chains.

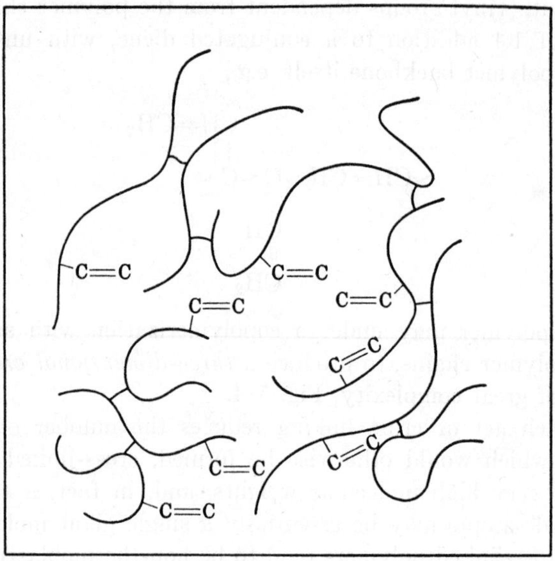

FIG. 5·4   Effect of cross linking on the structure of an addition polymer containing diene units.

The qualitative consequences of this condition upon the gel point of diolefin-containing systems are fairly obvious. Gelation will occur earlier the greater the length of the primary polymer chains, the more diolefin is present, and the greater its tendency both to enter polymer chains and to undergo the subsequent cross-linking reaction.

Quantitative treatment of gel points and molecular weight distributions in cross-linked systems in general are beyond the scope of this book but are treated in detail by Flory.[82] For the simplest case, that in which all double bonds have identical reactivities, the predicted gel point is given by

$$\theta_c = 1/X_0 \overline{P}_w \tag{13}$$

[82] P. J. Flory, *Principles of Polymer Chemistry*, Cornell University Press, Ithaca, N. Y., 1953, Chapter IX.

where θ_c is the predicted gel point, measured as the fraction of all double bonds in the system which have reacted. X_0 is the fraction of total double bonds initially present as diolefin, and $\bar{P}_w$ is the weight average degree of polymerization of the primary polymer chains.[83] An investigation [81] of gelation in methyl methacrylate–ethylene dimethacrylate and vinyl acetate–divinyl adipate systems (which should approximate the assumption of equal reactivity) indicates rough agreement with eq. 13 providing $\theta_c > 0.10$. However, the very early gel points predicted in the presence of much diolefin (for $X_0 = 0.1$, $\bar{P}_w = 10^4$, $\theta_c = 10^{-3}$) are not observed, presumably because in such dilute polymer solutions most of the cross-linking reactions occur between a growing radical and vinyl groups dependent from its own chain. Such cyclic reactions, which have been termed "incestuous" polymerization by Gordon,[84] are wasted as far as network building is concerned and are not allowed for in the statistical treatment. Their importance in the polymerization of allyl esters of polybasic acids has been studied by Simpson and Holt and varies appreciably from system to system.[85]

Practically, the most important cross-linking process is that which takes place in the polymerization of butadiene and other conjugated dienes. Thus, in the manufacture of GR-S and other synthetic rubbers, the amount of gel formed has important effects on physical properties and is usually controlled by adding thiols as chain transfer agents and by stopping polymerization short of complete conversion.[86] Here eq. 13 obviously no longer applies since the polymerization of butadiene leaves behind simple mono- and disubstituted ethylene residues which should differ greatly in reactivity from butadiene itself. The necessary modifications in the theory have, however, been worked out,[82] and by determining the point at which gel appears in emulsion-polymerized butadiene under carefully controlled conditions Morton [87] has deduced that the ratio of rate constants for attack on chain unsaturation and chain propagation, k_{pP}/k_p, is 1.02×10^{-4} at 40° and 1.98×10^{-4} at 60°, whence $E_{pP} - E_p = 7.5$ kcal/mole. Necessarily, this represents an average value

[83] W. H. Stockmayer, *J. Chem. Phys.*, **12**, 125 (1944).

[84] M. Gordon, *ibid.*, **22**, 610 (1954).

[85] W. Simpson and T. Holt, *J. Polymer Sci.*, **18**, 335 (1955); extensive additional data have been reported by M. Gordon and R. J. Roe, *ibid.*, **21**, 27, 39, 57, 75 (1956).

[86] *Synthetic Rubber*, G. S. Whitby, editor-in-chief, John Wiley & Sons, New York, 1954.

[87] M. Morton and P. P. Salatiello, *J. Polymer Sci.*, **6**, 225 (1951); M. Morton, P. P. Salatiello, and H. Landfield, *ibid.*, **8**, 215 (1952).

including attack on *cis*- and *trans*-CH=CH— and also -CH=CH$_2$ groups. Isoprene shows less tendency to cross-link, with $k_{pP}/k_p = 0.43 \times 10^{-4}$ at $70°$,[88] although the activation energy difference, $E_{pP} - E_p$, is only 5 kcal.

Some other examples of gelation during polymerization are worth mention. Vinyl benzoate yields a cross-linked product,[89] presumably by radical attack on the aromatic nucleus comparable to the copolymerization of benzene and vinyl acetate (cf. Section 4·1*f*).

An interesting group óf plastics is prepared by impregnating glass cloth or similar materials with a mixture of styrene and a polyunsaturated ester, such as ethylene polymaleate, and polymerizing the mass. Here cross-linking is obviously highly favored, and the products have sufficient strength and toughness for the manufacture of automobile bodies, boat hulls, and a variety of other structural forms.[90]

Finally, a number of monomers, notably methyl acrylate, yield cross-linked, gelled polymers, even though the polymer chains contain no ethylenic unsaturation. Presumably here networks are built up by a combination of chain transfer with polymer (and perhaps monomer) to yield branched structures which are subsequently tied together by radical combination processes. The conditions under which this process may lead to infinite network structures have been discussed by Fox and Gratch.[91] Actually, chain transfer may add somewhat to the complexity of structure of polybutadiene, although the contribution is probably small compared to the cross-linking reaction.[92]

5·2d   The Effect of Gelation on Polymerization Rates; Popcorn Polymer

In Section 5·2*a* above we saw that, as a system is converted from monomer to a mixture of linear polymer molecules, k_t may decrease since growing polymer chains are prevented from diffusing together by mutual entanglement and the increasing viscosity of the medium. If large cross-linked networks are present, the effect may be greatly

[88] M. Morton, *Ann. N. Y. Acad. Sci.*, **57**, 432 (1953); M. Morton, J. A. Cala, and I. Piirma, *J. Polymer Sci.*, **15**, 167 (1955).

[89] G. E. Ham and E. L. Ringwald, *J. Polymer Sci.*, **8**, 91 (1952); G. Smets and A. Hertoghe, *Makromol. Chem.*, **17**, 189 (1956).

[90] P. Morgan, *Glass Reinforced Plastics*, The Philosophical Library, New York, 1954.

[91] T. G. Fox and S. Gratch, *Ann. N. Y. Acad. Sci.*, **57**, 367 (1953).

[92] J. J. Drysdale and C. S. Marvel, *J. Polymer Sci.*, **13**, 513 (1954).

enhanced, since the radicals then become effectively fixed in space. The initial effect of this decrease in k_t is an increase in polymerization rate, but in a diolefinic system unreacted vinyl groups also become attached to the network and anchored in space so that polymerization may stop well short of complete utilization of all double bonds. Such cross-linked systems have been studied in some detail by Loshaek and Fox, who find that in ethylene dimethacrylate, polymerized at 60°, some 30% of the vinyl groups remain unreacted.[93]

Even though they contain residual unsaturation, such cross-linked polymers may contain relatively high concentrations of embalmed radicals which may be preserved more or less indefinitely. As long ago as 1943, Medvedev observed that polymerized chloroprene would react with iodine,[94] and gelled samples of polybutadiene rather readily absorb oxygen or other reagents which react readily with free radicals. Similarly, gelled ethylene dimethacrylate exhibits a paramagnetic resonance spectrum which corresponds to a radical concentration of 10^{-4}–10^{-5} molar, and which shows little change even after weeks of storage of the sample in the absence of air.[58]

An important phenomenon, undoubtedly arising from the presence of such long-lived radicals, is that of "popcorn polymerization." Many samples of gelled polybutadiene, exposed to either liquid or gaseous butadiene, "grow" enormously to popcorn-like masses of polymer and thus act as "seeds" for additional polymerization.[95,96,97] They are also able to induce polymerization of styrene and other monomers,[95,98,99] and other gelled systems may exhibit similar properties.[96] Seeds may be deactivated by heating, NO_2, or prolonged exposure to oxygen, but it is significant that polymer growth is often logarithmic, proceeding at a rate proportional to the amount of polymer already formed, and may be continued through many generations of seed;[99] cf. Fig. 5·5.

[93] S. Loshaek and T. G. Fox, *J. Am. Chem. Soc.*, **75**, 3544 (1953); cf. also H. W. Starkweather, Jr., and F. R. Eirich, *Ind. Eng. Chem.*, **47**, 2452 (1955).

[94] S. S. Medvedev, O. Koritskaya, and E. Alekseeva, *J. Phys. Chem. U.S.S.R.*, **17**, 391 (1943).

[95] L. M. Welch, M. W. Swaney, A. H. Gleason, and R. K. Beckwith, *Ind. Eng. Chem.*, **39**, 826 (1947).

[96] M. S. Kharasch, W. Nudenberg, E. V. Jensen, D. E. Fischer, and D. L. Mayfield, *ibid.*, **39**, 830 (1947).

[97] E. H. Immergut, *Makromol. Chem.*, **10**, 93 (1953).

[98] J. C. Devins and C. A. Winkler, *Can. J. Research*, **B26**, 357 (1948).

[99] G. H. Miller, R. L. Alumbaugh, and R. J. Brotherton, *J. Polymer Sci.*, **9**, 453 (1952); G. H. Miller, *ibid.*, **11**, 269 (1953); G. H. Miller and G. F. Perizzolo, *ibid.*, **18**, 411 (1955).

Many of the aspects of the process are easily accounted for. A gelled polymer absorbs monomer and is swollen by osmotic pressure. If the monomer polymerizes in turn, the process may continue more or less indefinitely, and the forces involved are sufficient to burst steel fractionating towers which have become contaminated with polymer seed.[95]   More puzzling is the logarithmic growth phenomenon, which

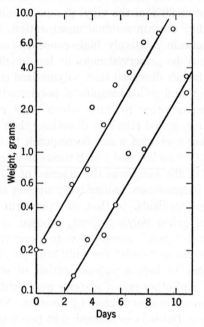

FIG. 5·5   Growth of butadiene "popcorn" polymer at 60° (after Miller, Alumbaugh, and Brotherton [99]).

implies that the number of free radicals producing polymerization is constantly increasing.

It has been suggested that the new radicals arise from the decomposition of hydroperoxides formed by autoxidation of polymer during seed formation,[96] but the facts that the whole process may be carried out in the absence of air,[99] that the rate of growth is independent of peroxide content, and that seed may be stored more or less indefinitely indicate that this is at best a partial explanation. More likely, new centers are continually formed by actual rupture of C—C bonds by the osmotic forces by which the polymer swells.[100]   Such a process

[100] P. D. Bartlett, *Scientific American*, **189**, 76 (1953).

would lead to the logarithmic rate curve actually observed, and it is frequently observed that osmotic swelling leads to the physical bursting and disintegration (but not solution) of cross-linked polymers. Finally, butadiene seeds in styrene undergo an initial growth, which, however, soon falls off in rate as the density of cross linking in the polymer being formed decreases so that the product can swell without restraint, and the growing chains become freer to undergo mutual termination.

5·3 Polymerization in Heterogeneous Systems

Our discussion of the behavior of free radical polymerizations have so far been restricted to homogeneous systems, although we have noted that relative reactivities of monomers in copolymerization are usually little affected when reactions are carried out under heterogeneous conditions. However, polymerizations in which monomers are dispersed in a non-solvent medium, or in which polymer separates from the system as it is formed, are of great practical importance and have interesting features which relate to the whole problem of the time cycle of radical chain processes, and reactions in highly viscous media, and thus merit separate discussion.

5·3a Emulsion Polymerization

Many vinyl monomers may be polymerized by dispersing them in water with the aid of an emulsifying agent such as soap in the presence of a water-soluble initiator.[101]

Such polymerizations were apparently first attempted with the idea that the reaction would simulate the process by which natural rubber might be formed in the living plant by the linking together of isoprene units.[102] Although it is now recognized that isoprene itself is not involved in the biosynthesis of rubber, the technique of emulsion polymerization has proved highly successful and is of enormous technical importance, notably in synthetic rubber manufacture. In fact, it provides the only practical means of effecting the radical polymerization to high polymers of conjugated dienes such as butadiene, either alone or as high-diene copolymers.

---

[101] For a comprehensive recent treatment of this entire topic, cf. F. A. Bovey, I. M. Kolthoff, A. I. Medalia, and E. J. Meehan, *Emulsion Polymerization*, Interscience Publishers, New York, 1955.

[102] A good historical account is given by W. P. Hohenstein and H. Mark, *J. Polymer Sci.*, **1**, 127 (1946).

Emulsion polymerizations have the obvious practical advantages that the products are obtained as aqueous dispersions rather than as single polymer masses. Also, the fluid nature of the reaction mixtures and the large amount of water present make temperature control relatively easy.

They also have two additional properties which are much less readily anticipated: very high polymerization rates may be achieved, and often the usual inverse relation between polymerization rate and polymer molecular weight, characteristic of homogeneous polymerizations (in the absence of excessive chain transfer), is not observed. Accordingly high degrees of polymerization can be combined with rapid polymerization rates. As we will see, the ability to account for this fact is one of the most important features of our present picture of the reaction path in such systems.

A very satisfactory qualitative picture of emulsion polymerization has been worked out, largely by Harkins, as part of the research carried out in conjunction with the synthetic rubber program during World War II.[103] Typically, a reaction mixture for emulsion polymerization may consist of 100 parts of water-insoluble monomer (e.g., styrene or butadiene), 180 parts of water, 2–10 parts of fatty acid soap or other surface active agent, and 0.1–0.5 parts of initiator such as potassium persulfate. At such concentrations, the bulk of the soap is in colloidal solution, clumped together into *micelles* of 50–100 molecules with their hydrocarbon tails towards the center and the charged carboxylate groups to the outside. The net negative charge of each micelle is largely neutralized by a cloud of *gegen-ions*, cations held nearby by electrostatic forces. In this sort of system, the monomer is distributed between three loci. A very small portion (depending upon its solubility) is in simple solution in the water. A larger quantity is held within the hydrocarbon cores of the soap micelles. Such *solubilization* of hydrocarbons is a well-recognized phenomenon in colloid chemistry,[103, 104] a 2–5% solution of potassium palmitate solubilizing about one mole of ethyl benzene per mole of soap present in micellar form. The bulk of the monomer, however, is dispersed as an emulsified second (or third) phase, in the form of droplets a micron or so in diameter. These droplets are covered with an adsorbed monolayer of soap molecules, again with their tails in the hydrocarbon phase and their charged ends exposed to the water. This charged layer tends to stabilize the emulsion and prevent the

[103] W. D. Harkins, *J. Am. Chem. Soc.*, **69**, 1428 (1947).

[104] H. B. Klevens, *Chem. Revs.*, **47**, 1 (1950).

coalescence of the droplets. A schematic diagram of the system at this point appears in Fig. 5·6.

The point at which polymerization occurs in such a complex system is of great importance in considering the path of reaction. The monomer droplets can be ruled out on several grounds. First, reac-

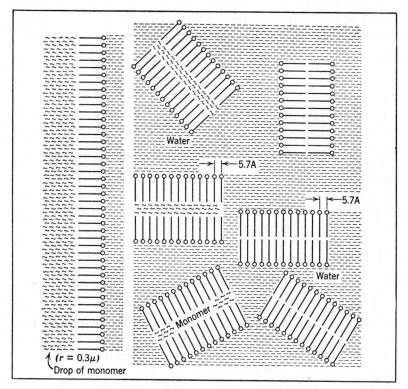

Fig. 5·6   Diagram showing structure of an emulsion of monomer prior to polymerization (after Harkins [103]).

tion can be interrupted and the monomer phase separated, when it will be found to be essentially free of dissolved polymer. Second, emulsion polymerizations can be carried out without a separate oil phase by exposing soap solutions containing initiator to monomer vapors.

Since the initiators used in emulsion polymerization are primarily water-soluble, it seems likely that radicals are initially produced in the aqueous phase. Whether they then diffuse into the interior of the micelles or feed upon dissolved monomer is not entirely clear and may well vary from system to system. However, there is no doubt that, once polymerization is underway, a notable change in the system takes place and the polymer molecules both dissolve monomer and adsorb soap onto their surfaces, taking the form of little spheres initially 100–200 A in diameter. At an early stage in the polymerization (2–15% conversion) essentially all of the soap has been adsorbed on the polymer particles, the micelles are consumed, the surface tension of the system rises, and the monomer dispersion may tend to coalesce unless well agitated.

From this point on, the chief locus of reaction becomes the polymer particles themselves, and they steadily grow in size to a diameter of 500–1500 A but do not increase in number. During this same period the separate monomer phase decreases in volume, finally vanishing at 50–80% conversion, when all of the unreacted monomer is dissolved within the polymer particles.

Figure 5·7 shows some typical time-conversion plots for emulsion polymerizations which accord well with the picture given. Polymerization rates in general increase with soap concentration, and individual reactions show an initial acceleration as particles are being formed, a steady rate during their growth period, and a final tapering off as monomer is exhausted.

The foregoing qualitative picture of emulsion polymerization is made more convincing by a quantitative treatment, developed by Smith and Ewart [105] and subsequently by Haward,[106] which combines it with some of the known quantitative properties of radical chain reactions. The argument is most easily developed by considering the steady-rate portion of the polymerization process after micelles have disappeared and the number of polymer particles has become constant. In typical emulsion polymerization systems, this number amounts to 10^{13}–10^{15} particles per cubic centimeter, and we may take 10^{14} as an average value.

The rate of radical production in the system depends upon the temperature and amount and nature of initiator employed, but again 10^{13}/cc/sec is a typical value.

Once produced, a radical diffuses to, and enters, a polymer particle, each particle receiving a new radical about once every 10 sec under the conditions cited. Once in the particle, the radical proceeds to grow by adding monomer units at a rate determined by k_p and the extent of "equilibrium swelling" of the particle by dissolved

[105] W. V. Smith and R. W. Ewart, *J. Chem. Phys.*, **16**, 592 (1948).

[106] R. Haward, *J. Polymer Sci.*, **4**, 273 (1949).

monomer (with styrene and butadiene the particles contain about 60% monomer at equilibrium). We may now consider what happens when a radical enters a particle in which another radical is already growing. Even in a particle with a diameter of 1000 A, the result is a tiny homogeneous system with a radical concentration of about

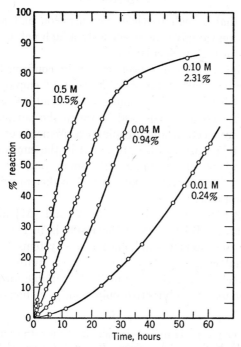

FIG. 5·7 Emulsion polymerization of isoprene at 50° in the presence of varying amounts of potassium laurate. Curve on right is below the critical micelle concentration and does not show the typical emulsion behavior (after Harkins [103]).

3×10^{-6} molar, in which the expected lifetime of the radicals would be of the order of 0.003 sec $(2k_t \simeq 10^8)$. Comparison of this time with the rate of arrival of radicals indicates that, at any instant, approximately *half of the particles will contain one radical, and the other half none*. This deduction leads immediately to the conclusion that the overall rate of polymerization per unit volume of solution is given by

$$R_p = (N/2)k_p[\text{M}] \qquad (14)$$

where N is the number of particles per unit volume, and [M] is the monomer concentration within the particles. Thus the rate is proportional to the number of particles and independent of the rate of chain initiation. (Some initiation must, of course, take place.) [107] On the other hand, ignoring chain transfer, $\bar{P}$ depends simply upon the rate of arrival of new radicals at a particle and (for coupling) would be given by

$$\bar{P} = Nk_p[M]/R_i \tag{15}$$

It is evident that a high particle concentration and a low rate of radical formation can give simultaneously a high polymerization rate and a product of high molecular weight.[108]

The foregoing picture has been elegantly confirmed for styrene systems by Smith [109, 110] and also by Morton,[111a] employing "seeded" systems in which fresh initiator and styrene is added to a preformed latex, containing no free soap, and in which the particle concentration is known by electron microscopic measurements or other means. The expected relationships also are found in the emulsion polymerization of butadiene and isoprene with some, but not all, initiator systems,[111a] but are apparently not obeyed in the emulsion polymerization of chloroprene.[111b]

From eq. 13 it is evident that, if R_p, N, and $[M]$ are known, k_p can be calculated. With styrene the result is in reasonable agreement with the measurements in homogeneous systems [109–111a] and provides additional confirmation of the scheme. With butadiene and isoprene this technique is the only method available for measuring k_p since these monomers polymerize only poorly in homogeneous systems.[112]

[107] For initiators producing radicals in pairs in the usual manner, radical production should be in the *aqueous phase*. It is well recognized that oil-soluble initiators such as benzoyl peroxide are generally poor choices for emulsion polymerizations.

[108] Actually, the above treatment involves two additional assumptions: that water-born radicals diffuse to the particles without combining in the water phase, and that polymer particles absorb monomer rapidly enough to remain swollen to equilibrium size. A simple consideration of diffusion rates of small molecules shows both assumptions to be well justified; cf. pp. 208–212 of reference cited in footnote 82, also M. Morton, S. Kaizerman, and M. W. Altier, *J. Colloid Sci.*, **9**, 300 (1954).

[109] W. V. Smith, *J. Am. Chem. Soc.*, **70**, 3695 (1948).

[110] W. V. Smith, *ibid.*, **71**, 4077 (1949).

[111a] M. Morton, P. P. Salatiello, and H. Landfield, *J. Polymer Sci.*, **8**, 111, 215, 279 (1952).

[111b] M. Morton, J. A. Cala, and M. W. Altier, *J. Polymer Sci.*, **19**, 547 (1956).

[112] The reason for this is not clear but, since k_p's for these monomers are only a little smaller than that for styrene, one suspects that k_t must have an abnor-

A complete treatment of emulsion polymerization should also predict the number of particles formed in a given system since this, in the next stage, determines the polymerization rate. This problem, too, has been treated by Smith and Ewart [105] who obtain the relationship

$$N = k(R_i/\mu)^{2/5}(a_s S)^{3/5} \qquad (16)$$

where N is the final number of particles per cubic centimeter, k is a constant between 0.37 and 0.53, R_i is the rate of formation of radicals, μ is the rate of growth of a particle (obtainable from k_p), S, the soap concentration, and a_s the surface area occupied by a molecule of soap, all in cgs units. Equation 15 appears to be valid for the styrene-soap-persulfate system,[109, 110] although minor discrepancies have been detected,[113] and seems to be obeyed, at least qualitatively, by many emulsion systems, in which overall rates increase with both emulsifier and initiator concentrations.

Although the Smith-Ewart treatment represents a particularly brilliant synthesis of colloid chemistry and reaction kinetics, its quantitative application has actually been made to very few systems and cases are known where eq. 14 is not strictly obeyed. In fact the "recipes" employed in emulsion systems are generally arrived at empirically and are often of baffling complexity.[101] However, from eq. 16 the *ultimate* rate of an emulsion polymerization depends largely upon the *initial* rate of radical production. Thus, many of the elaborate redox systems employed in initiating low temperature synthetic rubber polymerizations may owe their success to a very rapid initial radical production, and it is known that the resulting lattices are often characterized by very high numbers of small polymer particles. Finally, we may note that the technique of isolating individual radicals in individual emulsion particles presupposes their inability to diffuse through the solution from particle to particle. Thus this isolation is a peculiarity of polymerizing systems and has never been successfully observed in radical chain processes yielding low molecular weight products.

If the amount of dispersing agent in an aqueous system is reduced to a sufficiently low level, emulsions are no longer produced, and polymer is obtained in the form of little globules up to several millimeters in diameter. Such *suspension, pearl,* or *bead* polymerizations

---

mally large value, perhaps because the allylic radicals involved can interact at a number of points.

[113] Cf. Chapter 6 of reference cited in footnote 101.

retain the advantages of easy temperature control and convenient product form (with the added advantage of less contamination by the dispersing agent). However, the reaction path and kinetics become identical with ordinary homogeneous polymerization and need no further discussion here.

5·3b Polymerization with Phase Separation

Several olefins, e.g., vinyl chloride, vinylidene chloride, and acrylonitrile, yield monomer-insoluble polymers which separate out as a second phase as reaction progresses. A similar separation may be observed by polymerizing any monomer in a solvent in which the polymer is insoluble, e.g., styrene in methanol, or methyl methacrylate in hexane. Such phase separation is often accompanied by a marked rise in polymerization rate,[52] which is definitely related to the presence of the second phase, since it is brought about by adding polymer to the system (vinyl chloride) [114] and is not detected at the same point in a reaction system in which the polymer is soluble.

The situation in such systems is apparently intermediate between that in a normal homogeneous polymerization and the emulsion systems discussed in the preceding section. The polymer phase varies in consistency from a highly swollen gel (in some monomer-solvent systems) to a fine dispersion of polymer particles which are almost monomer-free (acrylonitrile and the vinyl halides). In the loose gels the acceleration may arise simply because a portion of the reaction is occurring in a viscous medium in which normal termination has become diffusion controlled and is thereby retarded (Section 5·2a). In the fine dispersions, radicals may be effectively isolated as in the emulsion systems and disappear only as new radicals diffuse to them. Because of these complications, attempts to determine absolute rate constants in such systems by rotating sector and similar methods yield results which may well be meaningless,[115, 116] and even overall kinetics are difficult to interpret. Bengough and Norrish [114] have reported that the rate of polymerization of vinyl chloride is proportional to the square root of the initiator concentration (benzoyl peroxide), indicating that bimolecular termination is still important in the kinetics, and to the surface area of the polymer formed. They

[114] W. I. Bengough and R. G. W. Norrish, *Proc. Roy. Soc. London*, **A216**, 515 (1953).

[115] G. M. Burnett and H. W. Melville, *Trans. Faraday Soc.*, **46**, 976 (1950).

[116] C. H. Bamford and A. D. Jenkins, *Proc. Roy. Soc. London*, **A216**, 515 (1953).

attribute the increase in rate with conversion to the formation of immobilized radicals by chain transfer with polymer particles (although with little direct evidence). Subsequently they have reported similar results with vinylidene chloride [117] and vinyl chloride–vinylidene chloride copolymers.[118]

Such polymerizations often show S-shaped rate curves, and Magat [119] has considered their kinetics as non-steady-state processes in which radicals have long lives, and radical concentrations increase with time, obtaining a good fit of his equations to published data. However, his interpretation has been criticized by Breitenbach and Schindler [120] who note that the autocatalytic nature of the reaction disappears in the presence of chain transfer agents such as CBr_4.

Acrylonitrile polymerization has been studied by Bamford and Jenkins,[116] who find marked autoacceleration which they attribute to occlusion of radicals in the polymer particles. Mild occlusion leads to a reduction of the rate of chain termination, but more complete burial may also interfere with chain growth. In this system the interference with normal termination leads to a higher than half-order dependence of rate on initiator concentration. Further, the presence of buried radicals of long life may be demonstrated (1) by introducing polymer, produced by low-temperature photopolymerization, into monomer at a higher temperature in the dark, where it brings about rapid further reaction; (2) by reaction of polymer with diphenylpicrylhydrazyl; [121] and (3) by the observation of paramagnetic resonance spectra.[122] The actual fraction of radicals trapped in this way amount to 1–2%, yielding concentrations of the order of 10^{-4} molar in the systems investigated.

Thomas and Pellon [123] have observed a similar catalyst dependence and note that the initial acceleration is followed by a steady polymerization rate from about 1–60% conversion. They have developed a kinetic scheme involving chain termination by both bimolecular interaction and radical burial, which has, however, been

[117] W. I. Bengough and R. G. W. Norrish, *ibid.*, **A218**, 143 (1953).

[118] W. I. Bengough and R. G. W. Norrish, *ibid.*, **A218**, 155 (1953).

[119] M. Magat, *J. Polymer Sci.*, **16**, 491 (1955).

[120] J. W. Breitenbach and A. Schindler, *ibid.*, **18**, 435 (1955).

[121] C. H. Bamford and A. D. Jenkins, *Proc. Roy. Soc. London*, **A228**, 220 (1955).

[122] C. H. Bamford, A. D. Jenkins, D. J. E. Ingram, and M. C. R. Symons, *Nature*, **175**, 894 (1955).

[123] W. M. Thomas and J. J. Pellon, *J. Polymer Sci.*, **13**, 329 (1954).

criticized by Bamford [124] on the basis that the actual number of radicals trapped is too small to account for the results. Thomas and Pellon have also examined the polymer particles by electron microscopy and find they consist of aggregates approximately 6000 A in diameter but with a fine structure suggesting closely packed spheres which nitrogen absorption measurements indicate to have average diameters of 420 A. Each little sphere thus contains about 50 polymer molecules, and the large aggregates contain about a million.

From the foregoing, it is evident that our picture of polymerization reactions in which phase separation occurs (and this would include gas-phase polymerizations [125] which are not here considered explicitly) is still largely qualitative. Although such systems are certainly of practical importance, from the point of view of understanding radical reactions phase separation represents essentially an experimental complication which yields little new information and is to be avoided if possible in the planning of experiments.

5·4 The Thermodynamics and Reversibility of Polymerization

5·4a The Energetics of Polymerization

As we have noted, Chapter 3, polymerization is an exothermic process, ΔH_p for the conversion of ethylene to polyethylene being approximately -22 kcal/mole (of monomer).[126] Although this value refers to the somewhat hypothetical reaction in the gas phase, ΔH_p should have very nearly the same value for the polymerization with both reactants and product in the condensed state, since molar heats of vaporization of hydrocarbons are approximately proportional to their molecular weights. Heats of polymerization of a number of monomers in the liquid phase have been measured, with results which have been summarized by Flory,[127] Table 5·2.

The most common technique of measurement is direct calorimetry, and a convenient apparatus has been described by Tong and Kenyon.[128] Values range from -9 to -21.3 kcal/mole, appreciably

[124] C. H. Bamford and A. D. Jenkins, *ibid.*, **14**, 511 (1954).

[125] Gas-phase polymerizations are reviewed in detail by G. M. Burnett, *Mechanism of Polymer Reactions*, Interscience Publishers, New York, 1954.

[126] F. S. Dainton and K. J. Ivin, *Trans. Faraday Soc.*, **46**, 331 (1950).

[127] Cf. pp. 246–56 of reference cited in footnote 82, which gives a more complete discussion of this topic.

[128] L. K. J. Tong and W. O. Kenyon, *J. Am. Chem. Soc.*, **67**, 1278 (1945).

TABLE 5·2   HEATS OF POLYMERIZATION OF VARIOUS MONOMERS [127]

Monomer	$-\Delta H_p$, kcal/mole
Styrene	16.1 ± 0.2
Vinyl acetate	21.3 ± 0.2
Acrylonitrile	17.3 ± 0.5
Methyl acrylate	18.7 ± 0.2
Acrylic acid	18.5 ± 0.3
Isobutylene	12.3 ± 0.2
Methyl methacrylate	13.0 ± 0.2
Phenyl methacrylate	12.3 ± 0.2
Methacrylic acid	15.8 ± 0.2
α-Methylstyrene	9.0 ± 0.2
Vinylidene chloride	14.4 ± 0.5
Isoprene [a]	17.9 ± 1.5
Butadiene	17.3 ± 0.2

[a] cis-1,4-polymer (natural rubber).

less heat being evolved with most monomers than in the case of ethylene. The difference apparently arises from two sources. First, particularly in the case of conjugated olefins, there is the loss in resonance energy associated with the disappearance of double bonds. This may be estimated from the differences in heats of hydrogenation of these olefins and ethylene, and amounts to as much as 4 kcal/mole in the case of butadiene and styrene. Second, strong steric interactions exist between substituents in successive monomer units in the polymers of polysubstituted olefins. These interactions are readily noticeable when Stuart models of polymer chains are assembled and are particularly important in 1,1-disubstituted compounds. They apparently account for the large reduction in heat evolved (up to 10 kcal/mole) in the polymerization of isobutylene and vinylidene chloride. In α-methylstyrene where both effects are combined, ΔH_p has the smallest absolute value of all, only -9 kcal/mole.

Since the formation of a polymer molecule involves a single act of initiation and of termination, and a large number of propagation steps, it is evident that ΔH_p as measured is essentially ΔH for the reaction of chain propagation, an assumption borne out by the observation of Tong and Kenyon [128] that ΔH_p for methyl methacrylate is independent of catalyst concentration and the presence of a transfer agent, carbon tetrachloride (and also of temperature over a considerable range).

This moderately exothermic nature of the chain propagation step in radical polymerization permits it to have the low activation energy and high rate actually observed but indicates that, at higher temperatures, it may become appreciably reversible. In fact, such depolymerizations are well known, and the thermal cracking of hydrocarbons to low molecular weight olefins, which involves such a process, was one of the first radical reactions to be recognized.[129]

The conditions under which the equilibrium

$$\sim M\cdot_n + M \underset{k_{-p}}{\overset{k_p}{\rightleftharpoons}} \sim M\cdot_{n+1} \qquad (17)$$

becomes important have been considered in detail by Dainton and Ivin in terms of a *ceiling temperature* for polymerization processes.[126, 130] The equilibrium constant $K_p = k_p/k_{-p}$ in eq. 17 may be written as

$$-RT \ln K_p = \Delta F_p^\circ = \Delta H_p^\circ - T\,\Delta S_p^\circ \qquad (18)$$

where the thermodynamic quantities refer to monomer in a standard state of pure liquid, and polymer chains in dilute solution in monomer, and K is assumed independent of chain length. In such a system, chains will fail to grow at a ceiling temperature T_c where $\Delta F_p^\circ = 0$, T_c being given by

$$T_c = \Delta H_p^\circ/\Delta S_p^\circ \qquad (19)$$

Values of ΔH_p° may be obtained from Table 5·2, but entropies of polymerization are more difficult to determine. From low temperature heat capacity measurements on styrene and polystyrene, Dainton and Ivin have estimated ΔS_p° as about -27 E.U./mole, decreasing slightly with temperature. They have also estimated entropies of polymerization for other monomers by various means, the values falling in the range -26 to -37 E.U./mole. Recently, Small has determined the actual monomer-polymer equilibrium for methyl methacrylate at 100–160°[131] (cf. Section 5·4b) and calculated ΔS_p° as -25.2 E.U./mole at 25°, and decreasing to -28.2 E.U./mole at 130°. From these data, and neglecting the small changes in ΔH_p° and ΔS_p° with temperature, the ceiling temperatures for styrene and methyl methacrylate should be 327° and 190° respectively. Dainton's estimates of ΔS_p° for other monomers indicate that their ceiling tem-

[129] F. O. Rice and K. K. Rice, *The Aliphatic Free Radicals,* The Johns Hopkins Press, Baltimore, 1935.

[130] F. S. Dainton and K. J. Ivin, *Nature,* **162,** 705 (1948).

[131] P. A. Small, *Trans. Faraday Soc.,* **49,** 441 (1953); cf. S. Bywater, *ibid.,* **51,** 1267 (1955).

peratures probably lie in the same range. Since the rate of the forward reaction in eq. 17 depends upon monomer concentration, it is evident that, even below these ceiling temperatures, polymerization will effectively cease somewhere short of complete conversion (hence the basis of Small's measurement) or on dilution of the system with an inert solvent. A particularly striking case of the ceiling temperature phenomenon occurs in olefin $-SO_2$ systems discussed in Section 5·4d below.

5·4b   The Kinetics of Depolymerization

As depolymerization becomes important, the overall rate expression for monomer disappearance takes the form

$$R_p = (k_p[M] - k_{-p})[M \cdot] \tag{20a}$$

or, introducing the usual assumption of bimolecular termination,

$$R_p = (k_p[M] - k_{-p})(R_i/2k_t)^{\frac{1}{2}} \tag{20b}$$

Similarly, the expression for $\bar{P}$ (for termination by radical combination) becomes

$$\bar{P} = (k_p[M] - k_{-p})/(k_t R_i)^{\frac{1}{2}} \tag{21}$$

The manner in which R_p and $\bar{P}$ might be expected to change with temperature in the neighborhood of the ceiling temperature has been calculated by Dainton,[132] and typical plots are shown in Fig. 5·8.

The situation above the ceiling temperature, where depolymerization is the dominant reaction, is much more complex and obscure and has recently been reviewed in detail by Jellinek.[133] Accordingly only a rather brief account will be given here.

The products obtained on the pyrolysis of vinyl polymers at 200–400° have been studied by many workers. In fact, depolymerization of polystyrene was first reported by Blyth and Hoffman in 1845.[134] The products include dimers and trimers, as well as styrene monomer, and the structures of these have been used by Staudinger [135] as arguments for the head-to-tail structure of polystyrene (cf. Section 3·1). The reaction has been studied by Madorsky et al. by heating styrene in vacuo and analyzing the evolved gases by mass spectrom-

[132] F. S. Dainton, *Can. Chem. Process Inds.*, **35**, 36 (1951).

[133] H. H. G. Jellinek, *Degradation of Vinyl Polymers*, Academic Press, New York, 1955.

[134] J. Blyth and A. W. Hoffman, *Ann.*, **53**, 314 (1845).

[135] H. Staudinger and A. Steinhofer, *ibid.*, **517**, 35 (1935).

etry.[136,137,138] The yield of monomer was approximately 42%. The method has also been used by Zemany.[139] Substituted styrenes give similar results,[140] and Bachman has investigated the preparation of halostyrenes by halogenating and then pyrolyzing polystyrene, the method giving yields of 20–40%.[141]

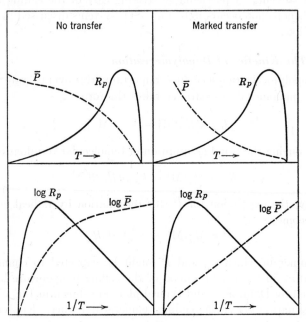

Fig. 5·8   Predicted variation in R_p and $\bar{P}$ in the region of the ceiling temperature of a reversible polymerization (after Dainton [132]).

Polymethyl methacrylate degrades more smoothly,[140] and monomer may be recovered in 90% yield by simply heating the polymer in a vessel over a free flame.[142]

Most polymers, however, degrade to monomer in only low yield.

[136] S. L. Madorsky and S. Straus, *J. Research Nat. Bur. Standards,* **40,** 417 (1948).

[137] S. L. Madorsky, S. Straus, D. Thompson, and L. Williamson, *ibid.,* **42,** 499 (1949).

[138] S. L. Madorsky, *J. Polymer Sci.,* **9,** 133 (1952); L. A. Wall, D. W. Brown, and V. E. Hart, *ibid.,* **15,** 157 (1955).

[139] P. D. Zemany, *Nature,* **171,** 391 (1953).

[140] S. L. Madorsky, *J. Polymer Sci.,* **11,** 491 (1953).

[141] G. B. Bachman, et al., *J. Org. Chem.,* **12,** 1 (1947).

[142] D. E. Strain, U.S. Pat. 2,030,901 (Feb. 18, 1936).

Polyisoprene gives 2–20% monomer on pyrolysis, and polybutadiene only 1–2%.[137] Polyacrylates [140] and polyethylene [138, 143] also give only traces of monomer, the latter breaking up chiefly into larger fragments with an average molecular weight of about 700.

Although there is little doubt that these degradations (like other pyrolytic reactions of hydrocarbons) are free radical processes, their quantitative treatment is so far less successful than that of the polymerization reaction. In the first place, there is the problem of radical production—the nature of the initial chain scission which must somehow take place. This may occur at random along a chain, at the chain ends, or at "weak links" (some sort of imperfection in the polymer chain). Once a chain is broken, depolymerization should occur by "unzipping" of the chain (i.e., the successive loss of monomer by β elimination), the reverse of the usual polymerization, although chain transfer may be an important complication. In addition the rate of diffusion of monomer out of the polymer may affect the rate, and the existence of chain branches, particularly in the case of polyethylene, may also influence the process. Kinetic schemes involving these various processes have been worked out by Simha et al.[144] and Jellinek.[145] Simha concludes that the depolymerization of methacrylate (and, to a lesser extent, styrene) are essentially long-chain processes with many monomer molecules "unzipping" from each radical formed, but that other reactions, e.g., transfer, are more important in the pyrolysis of polyethylene so that there is little chain decomposition to monomer.

The most convincing picture of the depolymerization process has been obtained by Grassie and Melville [146] employing polymethyl methacrylate at 220–280°. They heated very small samples of material (30–40 mg) as powder or film in a molecular still, designed to give accurate temperature control and under conditions where they could show that diffusion of monomer out of the polymer was not a rate-controlling process. Depolymerization was followed by the rate of evolution of methyl methacrylate vapor, and the change in molecular weight of the remaining polymer was also determined.

[143] L. A. Wall, S. L. Madorsky, D. W. Brown, S. Straus, and R. Simha, *J. Am. Chem. Soc.*, **76**, 3430 (1954).

[144] R. Simha, L. A. Wall, and P. J. Blatz, *J. Polymer Sci.*, **5**, 615 (1950); R. Simha, *ibid.*, **10**, 499 (1953).

[145] H. H. G. Jellinek, *ibid.*, **9**, 369 (1952); **10**, 457 (1952).

[146] N. Grassie and H. W. Melville, *Proc. Roy. Soc. London*, **199**, 1, 14, 24, 39 (1949).

For polymer of $\bar{P} < 500$ the rate of depolymerization was independent of molecular weight, and no degradation of residual polymer to lower molecular weight was observed. For higher molecular weight samples degradation was found, and rates of monomer evolution decreased with increasing polymer molecular weight. From these results they conclude that depolymerization is a chain process, an average of 500 monomer units being lost from each radical formed, and that the initial radical is formed at the *end* of the chain. The chain nature of the reaction was further substantiated by the observation that the rate of depolymerization was decreased about 12-fold by 0.1 mole % (on monomer) of the non-volatile inhibitor 1,4-diaminoanthraquinone. Although the path by which radicals are initially formed remains obscure, it is significant that depolymerization rates varied with the manner of polymer preparation. Compared with benzoyl peroxide-initiated polymer (used in most of the work), photopolymerized material decomposed 50% more rapidly, whereas polymer initiated with tetraphenylsuccinonitrile was much more stable, decomposing only $\frac{1}{20}$ as fast. Overall activation energies for depolymerization also varied from 31–47 kcal, depending upon the polymer source.

Experiments on some methacrylate copolymers showed that cross linking with ethylene dimethacrylate had no effect on the depolymerization. On the other hand, copolymers containing 0.4–4% acrylonitrile showed a complicated behavior interpreted as a more rapid radical production, but a blocking of the depolymerization process by the acrylonitrile units.

The degradation of polymethyl methacrylate can be accomplished at temperatures as low as 130° by irradiating polymer films in vacuo with 2537 A light.[147] The rate is approximately proportional to the square root of the light intensity, and, with polymer of $\bar{P} < 1250$, residual polymer shows no decrease in molecular weight. Since the depolymerization rate decreases with time, it is thought that only certain end groups, not present in all molecules, are involved in the initiation process. By using intermittent illumination k_{-p} has been estimated as 580 sec^{-1} and $2k_t = 4 \times 10^4$ at 167°.[148] Simha has criticized the calculation, obtaining 720 and 1.8×10^4 respectively.[149] Although these values are not as well established as those for the propagation reaction (Section 3·4) they appear reasonable, and the

[147] P. R. E. J. Cowley and H. W. Melville, *ibid.*, **A210**, 461 (1952).

[148] P. R. E. J. Cowley and H. W. Melville, *ibid.*, **A211**, 320 (1952).

[149] R. Simha, *J. Polymer Sci.*, **9**, 465 (1952).

small value of k_t indicates that chain termination in the polymer mass is essentially a diffusion-controlled reaction.

In contrast to these experiments in which polymerization is eliminated by continuous removal of monomer, Small[131] has investigated the equilibrium between methyl methacrylate and its polymer in the presence of free radicals produced by the photodissociation of benzoin. He finds that the system contains 0.3% monomer at 100° and 2.87% at 160°, from which the free energy and entropy of polymerization may be calculated.

The kinetics of styrene depolymerization in vacuo at 300–400° and also the molecular weight changes accompanying degradation have been studied by Jellinek.[150] He has interpreted his results in terms of the presence of "weak links" in the polymer chain [151] and has also studied the degradation in naphthalene solution in sealed tubes.[152] However, as we have seen, the degradation products are complex, and some of his experimental results have been questioned,[153] but there seems no doubt that a chain depolymerization is involved. It is interesting that the carbonaceous residues left on pyrolysis of polyvinylidene chloride and oxidized cross-linked polystyrene contain appreciable concentrations of unpaired electrons and show paramagnetic resonance spectra. The properties of such systems have been reviewed by Winslow, Baker, and Yager.[154]

5·4c Degradation at Lower Temperatures

As we might expect, at lower temperatures, radical attack on vinyl polymers does not lead to appreciable chain depolymerization, but chain scission may take place, presumably by paths such as

$$R\cdot + \sim CH_2-\underset{X}{\overset{H}{C}}-CH_2-\underset{X}{\overset{H}{C}}\sim \rightarrow RH + \sim CH_2-\underset{X}{\overset{H}{\dot{C}}}-CH_2-\underset{X}{\overset{H}{C}}- \tag{22}$$

$$\sim CH_2-\underset{X}{\overset{H}{\dot{C}}}-CH_2-\underset{X}{\overset{H}{C}}\sim \rightarrow \sim CH_2-\underset{X}{C}{=}CH_2 + \cdot \underset{X}{\overset{H}{C}}\sim \tag{23}$$

[150] H. H. G. Jellinek, *J. Polymer Sci.*, **3**, 850 (1948); **4**, 1, 39 (1949).

[151] H. H. G. Jellinek, *Trans. Faraday Soc.*, **40**, 266 (1944); **44**, 345 (1948).

[152] H. H. G. Jellinek and L. B. Spencer, *J. Polymer Sci.*, **8**, 573 (1951); H. H. G. Jellinek and K. J. Turner, *ibid.*, **11**, 353 (1953).

[153] E. Atherton, *ibid.*, **5**, 378 (1950).

[154] F. H. Winslow, W. O. Baker, and W. A. Yager, *J. Am. Chem. Soc.*, **55**, 4751 (1955).

Either of the resulting chain radicals may abstract hydrogen from another molecule, add to a double bond (if the polymer contains unsaturation), disproportionate, or couple. The overall effect may thus be either a decrease or an increase in polymer molecular weight, the latter perhaps accompanied by the formation of insoluble network structures. With styrene, degradation is the major reaction, whereas diene polymers and acrylates tend to cross-link and gel on exposure to radical sources.

Conflicting data exist on the details of polystyrene degradation. Some time ago, Mesrobian and Tobolsky reported that toluene solutions of polystyrene, irradiated at 100° [155] or heated with benzoyl peroxide,[156] all showed eventually the same viscosity and thus, presumably, the same average degree of polymerization, implying a facile equilibrium between polymerization and depolymerization processes. Subsequent workers,[157] however, have failed to confirm either these results or this conclusion, and the whole topic is discussed in detail by Jellinek.[133]

An interesting way of producing radicals within solid polymer samples is by irradiation with γ rays or high-energy particles, and the behavior of plastics under such conditions is of much practical importance. Since these are conditions under which trapped radicals of long life are formed, relatively high concentrations may be obtained and their presence verified by paramagnetic resonance spectroscopy. As examples, such spectra have been observed in X-ray-irradiated polymethyl methacrylate and polystyrene,[158] and in polytetrafluoroethylene,[159] polystyrene, and polyethylene irradiated in a pile under cadmium.[160] The methacrylate spectrum is apparently identical with that observed in the polymerizing system.[58] The effect of irradiation by 800 kv electrons on a number of polymers has been surveyed by Lawton, et al., who find that polyacrylates, polystyrene, polyethylene, diene polymers, polyesters, and nylon are all primarily

[155] R. Mesrobian and A. Tobolsky, *ibid.*, **67**, 785 (1945).

[156] H. W. Spodheim, W. J. Badgley, and R. Mesrobian, *J. Polymer Sci.*, **3**, 410 (1948); cf. also G. Tasset and G. Smets, *ibid.*, **12**, 517 (1954).

[157] D. S. Montgomery and C. A. Winkler, *Can. J. Research*, **B28**, 407, 416, 429 (1950); J. O. Thompson, *J. Phys. Colloid Chem.*, **54**, 338 (1950).

[158] E. E. Schneider, M. J. Day, and G. Stein, *Nature*, **168**, 645 (1951). These authors, however, described their spectra as due to trapped electrons, an interpretation which now seems unlikely.

[159] E. E. Schneider, *J. Chem. Phys.*, **23**, 978 (1955).

[160] J. Combrisson and J. Uebersfeld, *Compt. rend.*, **238**, 1397 (1954).

cross-linked, whereas polymethyl methacrylate, polyisobutylene, and various polyhaloölefins are degraded.[161]

The behavior of polyethylene is of particular importance, since exposure to any type of high-energy particle or radiation leads to a cross-linked product of improved temperature resistance. The effect of pile irradiation has been studied by Charlesby [162] and more recently by Lawton [163] and by Dole,[164] who gives a good review of previous work. The reaction involves both cross linking and the production of unsaturation together with hydrogen. Since it is certainly very complex, it will not be discussed further here, although some of the aspects of radical production by high-energy particles is considered further in Section 11·2.

Polymers can often be degraded by purely mechanical means, presumably since their entangled long-chain structure permits a sufficient concentration of forces to produce the scission of a bond in the chain into free radicals. An example of this has already been seen in the case of the popcorn polymer phenomenon, Section 5·2d.

The effect of ultrasonic energy on polymer solutions has been studied by a number of workers, the first detailed work being by Schmid and Rommel on polystyrene.[165] Since the rate of degradation is decreased either at high pressures [165] or in evacuated systems,[166] it is considered that chain scisson occurs largely through cavitation phenomena involving the large forces produced by the collapse of tiny bubbles, although there is also some degradation in the absence of cavitation due to shearing forces in the rapidly oscillating solvent. Melville has obtained evidence that the freshly cleaved polymer molecules are actually radicals capable of initiating polymerization in additional monomer,[166] although aqueous solutions of acrylonitrile polymerize alone, apparently by dissociation of the water.[167] Radicals can also be detected by their reaction with diphenylpicrylhy-

161 E. J. Lawton, A. M. Bueche, and J. S. Balwit, *Nature*, **172**, 76 (1953); A. A. Miller, E. J. Lawton, and J. S. Balwit, *J. Polymer Sci.*, **14**, 503 (1954).

162 A. Charlesby, *Proc. Roy. Soc. London*, **A215**, 187 (1952).

163 E. J. Lawton, J. S. Balwit, and A. M. Bueche, *Ind. Eng. Chem.*, **46**, 1703 (1954).

164 M. Dole, C. D. Keeling, and D. G. Rose, *J. Am. Chem. Soc.*, **76**, 4304 (1954).

165 G. Schmid and O. Rommel, *Z. Elektrochem.*, **45**, 659 (1939); *Z. physik. Chem.*, **A185**, 97 (1939).

166 H. W. Melville and G. J. R. Murray, *Trans. Faraday Soc.*, **46**, 996 (1950).

167 O. Lindstrom and O. Lamm, *J. Phys. Colloid Chem.*, **55**, 1139 (1951).

drazyl.[168] Such degradations have also been studied by Jellinek,[169] who has discussed the resulting molecular weight distributions and has reviewed the subject giving references to other work.[133]

Polymer solutions can also be degraded by vigorous stirring in a Waring Blendor,[170] pumping with turbulent flow through a small orifice,[171] or stirring more gently in the presence of small glass or quartz particles.[172]

The very vigorous shearing forces arising on milling or masticating a polymer on a rubber mill should produce a rapid scission of covalent bonds, although the process is usually complicated by the rapid reaction of the resulting radicals with oxygen. Thus, rubber itself breaks down to lower molecular weight polymer much more rapidly on mastication in air than under nitrogen, and, as long ago as 1940, Kauzmann and Eyring [173] suggested that the difference arises by reaction of the radicals produced with oxygen so as to prevent their recombination.[174]

Our picture of this sort of breakdown has been extended by Watson and his colleagues at the British Rubber Producers Research Laboratories, who have shown that the breakdown of rubber under nitrogen is facilitated by a variety of substances, e.g., thiophenol, benzoquinone, trinitrobenzene, and iodine, which should react with the primary radicals.[175] In an elegant series of experiments employing highly purified rubber and rigorous exclusion of air, it was further shown that the rate of reaction of rubber with diphenylpicrylhydrazyl or S^{35}-labeled α-naphthyldisulfide during mastication agrees well with the measured drop in molecular weight.[176] When rubber and Neoprene are milled together, interpolymers are produced,[177] as might be anticipated, and Watson proposes that, when rubber is milled with

[168] R. Schulz and A. Henglein, Z. Naturforsch., **8B**, 160 (1953).

[169] H. H. G. Jellinek and G. White, J. Polymer Sci., **6**, 745, 757 (1951); **7**, 21, 33 (1951); H. W. W. Brett and H. H. G. Jellinek, ibid., **13**, 441 (1954).

[170] P. Alexander and M. Fox, ibid., **12**, 533 (1954).

[171] H. Staudinger and E. Dreher, Ber., **69**, 1091 (1936).

[172] F. Sonntag and E. Jenckel, Kolloid Z., **135**, 1 (1954).

[173] W. Kauzmann and H. Eyring, J. Am. Chem. Soc., **62**, 3113 (1940).

[174] Actually the processes are more complex, since autoxidation of rubber, on the one hand, may lead to further chain scission [for a recent discussion, cf. E. M. Bevilacqua, ibid., **77**, 5394, 5396 (1955)] and radicals may not only recombine, but also may attack double bonds and lead to cross-linking reactions.

[175] M. Pike and W. F. Watson, J. Polymer Sci., **9**, 229 (1952).

[176] G. Ayrey, C. G. Moore, and W. F. Watson, ibid., **19**, 1 (1956).

[177] D. F. Angier and W. F. Watson, ibid., **18**, 129 (1955).

carbon black, the radicals react to form actual chemical bonds to the carbon [178] (which indeed becomes irreversibly bound to the rubber). The notable property of carbon black of "reinforcing" rubbers (increasing their tensile strength and abrasion resistance) may be largely due to this sort of process.

5·4d   The Copolymerization of Olefins and Sulfur Dioxide

Many olefins react with sulfur dioxide to form linear polymers with the structure of polysulfones, arranged with the olefin units in a head-to-tail fashion.[179]   The radical nature of the reaction is indicated by its initiation by peroxides and other radical sources, oxidizing agents, and ultraviolet light, and the chain propagation process can be formulated as involving the alternating steps:

$$
-CH_2-\underset{R}{\overset{H}{C}}\cdot \;+\; SO_2 \;\rightarrow\; -CH_2-\underset{R}{\overset{H}{C}}-\underset{O}{\overset{O}{S}}\cdot \qquad (24)
$$

$$
-CH_2-\underset{R}{\overset{H}{C}}-\underset{O}{\overset{O}{S}}\cdot \;+\; CH_2{=}CHR \;\rightarrow\; -CH_2-\underset{R}{\overset{H}{C}}\cdot \qquad (25)
$$

The most interesting feature of the reaction is that it shows a sharp ceiling temperature in the neighborhood of room temperature,[180] and for this reason our discussion has been deferred to this point.   However, before taking up this phenomenon, we may look at some other properties of the reaction.

The simple olefins, ethylene, propylene, the butenes, etc., all readily form 1:1 copolymers with SO_2 from a range of feed compositions,[181,182,183] as do such materials as allyl ethers and allylacetic acid.[182]   In contrast, ethyl crotonate, crotonaldehyde and methyl

---

[178] W. F. Watson, *Ind. Eng. Chem.*, **47**, 1281 (1955). The suggestion has been made elsewhere as well.

[179] C. S. Marvel and E. D. Weil, *J. Am. Chem. Soc.*, **76**, 61 (1954). This paper revises certain earlier conclusions.

[180] R. D. Snow and F. E. Frey, *ibid.*, **65**, 2417 (1943).

[181] W. Solonina, *J. Russ. Phys. Chem. Soc.*, **30**, 826 (1898).

[182] L. I. Ryden, F. J. Glavis and C. S. Marvel, *J. Am. Chem. Soc.*, **59**, 1014 (1937).

[183] R. D. Snow and F. E. Frey, *Ind. Eng. Chem.*, **30**, 176 (1938).

acrylate do not react,[181, 182, 184] which suggests that a polar effect is involved in the production of the alternating copolymer, the SO_2 showing electron-accepting properties, with contributions

$$
\begin{array}{ccc}
& \text{O} & & & \text{O} \\
\text{H} & | & & & | & \text{H H} \\
-\text{C}^+ & \cdot\text{S:} & \text{and} & & -\text{S}^- & \cdot\text{C—C}^+ \quad \text{etc.} \qquad (26) \\
\text{R} & | & & & | & \text{H R} \\
& \text{O}_- & & & \text{O}
\end{array}
$$

to the transition states involved. In support of this idea, the only two monomers reported to give a copolymer with more than one monomer unit per SO_2 are vinyl chloride,[185] with little tendency to donate an electron, and styrene,[186] with a particularly reactive double bond. Dienes such as butadiene, incidentally, also yield copolymers, but the process is competitive with a Diels-Alder-type condensation to give a cyclic sulfone.[187]

Now turning our attention to the ceiling temperature phenomena, Snow and Frey observed that SO_2-isobutene mixtures containing a suitable initiator polymerize at temperatures below 4°C, but the reaction stops on warming to 6°, to start again on cooling, and this cycle may be repeated at will.[180] Propylene and 1- and 2-butenes showed similar ceilings at 87–89°, 63–66°, and 43–45° respectively. The reaction has been studied in more detail by Dainton and Ivin, using 1-butene,[188] who obtain a ceiling temperature of 63.5°C for an olefin-SO_2 mixture containing 9.1 mole % 1-butene, independent of the initiator system employed (since ceiling temperatures depend upon the competition of first- and second-order processes, they are necessarily concentration dependent). By calorimetry they have also determined $-\Delta H_p = 22 \pm 0.7$ kcal per base mole of polymer, from which $-\Delta S° = 71.9$ E.U. The much larger entropy loss compared with vinyl polymerization thus accounts for the low ceiling temperature, although its origin in turn is obscure. Additional evidence that above the ceiling temperature chain propagation becomes less important than depropagation has been gained by studying the simultaneous copolymerization and isomerization of cis-2-butene.[189] As

[184] H. Staudinger and B. Ritzenthaler, Ber., **68**, 455 (1935).

[185] C. S. Marvel and L. H. Dunlap, J. Am. Chem. Soc., **61**, 2709 (1939).

[186] H. D. Noether and E. P. Irany, U.S. 2,572,185 October 23, 1951.

[187] R. L. Frank and R. P. Seven, Organic Syntheses, **29**, 59 (1949).

[188] F. S. Dainton and K. J. Ivin, Proc. Roy. Soc. London, **A212**, 96, 202 (1952).

[189] F. S. Dainton and G. M. Bristow, Nature, **172**, 804 (1953); Proc. Roy. Soc. London, **A229**, 509, 525 (1955).

the ceiling temperature is approached, isomerization to *trans*-2-butene becomes increasingly rapid, whereas above the ceiling temperature only isomerization is observed, and this requires the presence of both SO_2 and initiator. The ceiling temperatures for *cis*- and *trans*-2-butene are measurably different, 35.7° and 32.5° respectively at 9.1 mole % olefin. These observations indicate that the highly reversible step is probably reaction 25, attack of the polysulfone radical on olefin.

ΔH_p for the copolymerization of *cis*- and *trans*-2-butene were reported [189] as -19.3 kcal and -20.1 kcal respectively, and, since the heats of formation of *cis*- and *trans*-2-butene differ by 3.1 kcal, this implies that the two copolymers have different heat contents and hence, presumably, different stereochemical structures.

This conclusion, however, has been seriously questioned by Skell, Woodworth, and McNamara,[189a] who have made a careful comparison of the infrared spectra of SO_2 copolymers from *cis*- and *trans*-2-butene and find no significant differences. These workers also obtained further evidence for the identity of the products arising from attack of $RSO_2\cdot$ radicals on 2-butenes by studying the addition of benzenesulfonyl iodide to *cis*- and *trans*-2-butene (cf. Chapters 6 and 7). Radicals from the butenes abstract iodine from this molecule, and the resulting $\phi SO_2\cdot$ radical then adds to the butene double bond. In competitive experiments, benzenesulfonyl iodide reacts with butene more rapidly than does SO_2, so in such systems the radicals from 2-butene have shorter lives than in the presence of SO_2 alone. Nevertheless, the resulting products from *cis*- and *trans*-2-butene (2-benzenesulfonyl-3-iodobutanes) consist of identical diastereomeric mixtures. In view of these findings, Dainton's conclusion about the SO_2 copolymers appears to be incorrect.

Dainton and Ivin have also looked at the kinetics of the copolymerization reaction of 1-butene well below the ceiling temperature,[188] and they postulate participation of an olefin-SO_2 complex, although their results can be accounted for equally well as arising from the reversibility of one of the propagation steps, even at this temperature (see below).

At higher temperatures, over 200°, olefin-SO_2 polymers pyrolyze rather smoothly, the propylene-SO_2 copolymer giving back SO_2 and propylene in 85% yield.[190]

[189a] P. S. Skell, R. C. Woodworth, and J. H. McNamara, *J. Am. Chem. Soc.*, **79**, 1253 (1957).

[190] M. A. Naylor and A. W. Anderson, *J. Am. Chem. Soc.*, **76**, 3962 (1954).

The styrene-SO_2 reaction is of particular interest, for here the reaction incorporating SO_2 in the polymer competes with the normal
chain propagation process to yield polystyrene, and a phenomenon
analogous to the ceiling temperature is found in that the amount of
SO_2 entering the copolymer decreases markedly with temperature.[186]
The system has been studied in detail by Barb,[191, 192] and, as in
other copolymerizations, the determination of the effect of variables
on copolymer compositions illuminates the roles of the competitive
processes involved.

Copolymer compositions vary not only with temperature and the
styrene-SO_2 ratio but also with concentration when solvents are
employed. Barb has given an interpretation involving reversible
propagation steps and inclusion of SO_2 in the polymer only by reaction of a growing chain with a 1:1 styrene-SO_2 complex, which,
indeed, can be shown to be present spectroscopically. However, an
entirely equivalent scheme can be derived without invoking complex
participation,[193] and the latter is given here. (For other comments
on complex participation in radical reactions, cf. Section 4·1e.) The
reactions required are:

$$M\cdot + M \xrightarrow{k_{11}} M\cdot \qquad (27)$$

$$M\cdot + S \underset{k_{-12}}{\overset{k_{12}}{\rightleftharpoons}} S\cdot \qquad (28)$$

$$S\cdot + M \underset{k_{-21}}{\overset{k_{21}}{\rightleftharpoons}} M\cdot' \qquad (29)$$

$$M\cdot' + M \xrightarrow{k_{31}} M\cdot \qquad (30)$$

$$M\cdot' + S \underset{k_{-32}}{\overset{k_{32}}{\rightleftharpoons}} S\cdot' \qquad (31)$$

$$S\cdot' + M \xrightarrow{k_{21}} M\cdot' \qquad (32)$$

where M and S represent styrene and SO_2 respectively, $M\cdot$ is a growing chain ending in the sequence $-M-M\cdot$, and $M\cdot'$ one with
the sequence $-S-M\cdot$. Similarly, $S\cdot$ represents the sequence
$-M-M-S\cdot$, and $S\cdot'$ represents $-S-M-S\cdot$. Equations 27–32 are
thus an extension of the usual copolymerization equations to include
not only reversibility of some of the steps but also an effect of the

191 W. G. Barb, *Proc. Roy. Soc. London,* **A212,** 66 (1952).

192 W. G. Barb, *J. Polymer Sci.,* **10,** 49 (1953).

193 C. Walling, *ibid.,* **16,** 315 (1955).

penultimate monomer unit in the polymer chain on its reaction properties. At temperatures of 20° and higher, $M \cdot'$ radicals show a
negligible tendency to react with SO_2, so the copolymer composition
is determined by eqs. 27–30. Further, $k_{-12} \gg k_{21}$, i.e., SO_2 addition
is a highly reversible process. Under these conditions, the copolymer
composition is given by

$$n - 2 = (r_1 p_1 / [S])(1 + p_2 / [M]) \qquad (33)$$

where $n = d[M]/d[S]$, $r_1 = k_{11}/k_{12}$, $p_1 = k_{-12}/k_{21}$, $p_{-2} = k_{-21}/k_{31}$.
The quantity r_1 is a normal monomer reactivity ratio and the p's are

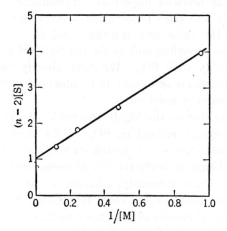

FIG. 5·9   Determination of $p_1 r_1$ and p_2 in the copolymerization of styrene-
sulfur dioxide at 60°.[193]

measures of the relative tendencies of $S \cdot$ and $M \cdot'$ chains to add M or
lose end units. $r_1 p_1$ and p_2 may be evaluated by plotting $(n - 2)[S]$
versus $1/[M]$, Fig. 5·9. At 60°, $r_1 p_1 = 1.0$ moles/liter, and $p_2 = 3.1$
moles/liter. Both decrease rapidly with decreasing temperature, as
the reactions become less reversible. At 20° $r_1 p_1 = 0.084$, $p_2 = 0.9$.
The good linear plot of Fig. 5.9 indicates that r_1 must be very small,
<0.01 at 60°. Some of the individual activation energies can also be
estimated from the data, $E_{-21} = 13.5$ kcal, $4 < E_{-12} < 14$ kcal.

At lower temperatures eqs. 31 and 32 become important so that
values of $n < 2$ are observed. Here eqs. 29 and 32 are essentially
irreversible, and the copolymer composition is given to a good approximation by

$$n - 1 = r_3 p_3 / (r_3 p_3 + [S]) \qquad (34)$$

with $r_3 = k_{31}/k_{32}$, $p_3 = k_{-32}/k_{21}$. At $0°$ $r_3 p_3 = 11$ liters/mole compared with $r_1 p_1 = 0.02$ liters/mole, but whether the difference arises from differences in r's or p's is not indicated by the data.

Barb has also investigated the overall kinetics of the styrene-SO_2 copolymerization [194] with results again consistent both with reversible propagation steps and possible complex participation. Chains end by the usual bimolecular path, $M\cdot$ and $M\cdot'$ being the chief species involved at $20°$, with some termination involving $S\cdot$ entering at $60°$. The small involvement of $S\cdot$ radicals in termination follows since the large value of p_1 keeps their concentration low until the reverse of eq. 29 becomes important. Terminations involving two $M\cdot$'s, two $M\cdot'$'s, and cross termination between the two species apparently have the same rate constant, and $k_{31} \simeq k_{11}$. Thus, the only effect of the preceding unit on the reactivity of a styrene radical is on its reactivity with SO_2. We have already noted that such penultimate unit effects seem only to be observed in reactions where a strong polar effect is involved.

In the styrene system, the highly reversible step is that involving attack of the styrene radical on SO_2. With unconjugated olefins the situation must change with attack on SO_2 becoming less reversible, since it no longer involves the loss of resonance energy of a conjugated radical. Simultaneously, addition of the $S\cdot$ radical to the unreactive olefin must become more reversible. We have already concluded, in our discussion of Dainton's work, that attack on olefin is highly reversible in the SO_2-butene systems.

Another "copolymerization" in which product compositions are concentration sensitive is the reaction of ethylene with carbon monoxide to yield polyketone polymers. The explanation is probably the same, and the reaction is discussed in Section $6\cdot3b$.

$5\cdot5$　Some Characteristics of 1,3-Diene Polymerization

In Section $5\cdot2c$ above, we noted that, in the polymerization of 1,3-dienes such as butadiene, 1,2 or 1,4 addition may occur, and, in the latter case, either *cis* or *trans* products may result (*cis-trans* isomers are also possible from 1,2 addition to a 1,4-disubstituted butadiene, but such species are less reactive in radical processes and have had little study). The same situation arises in any radical addition to a 1,3-diene, and it is convenient to discuss the matter here in more

[194] W. G. Barb, *Proc. Roy. Soc. London*, **A212**, 177 (1952).

detail.   The processes giving rise to the three products may be plausibly diagrammed as (for butadiene)

$$
\begin{array}{c}
\text{H}\quad\quad\text{H} \\
\text{C}=\text{C} \quad\text{(IV)} \\
\text{MCH}_2 \quad \text{CH}_2\!-\!\text{M}\cdot \\
\overset{k_5}{\nearrow}\text{M}
\end{array}
$$

$$
\begin{array}{ccc}
\text{H}\quad\text{H} & & \text{H}\quad\text{H} \\
\text{C}=\text{C} & \leftrightarrow & \dot{\text{C}}\!-\!\text{C} \quad\text{(I)} \\
-\text{MCH}_2 \quad \text{CH}_2\!\cdot & & -\text{MCH}_2 \quad \text{CH}_2
\end{array}
$$

$$
-\text{M}\cdot + \text{C}_4\text{H}_6 \quad \overset{k_1}{\underset{k_2}{\rightleftarrows}} \quad \Big\Updownarrow K
$$

$$
\begin{array}{ccc}
-\text{MCH}_2 \quad \text{H} & & -\text{MCH}_2 \quad \text{H} \\
\text{C}=\text{C} & \leftrightarrow & \dot{\text{C}}\!-\!\text{C} \quad\text{(II)} \\
\text{H} \quad \text{CH}_2\!\cdot & & \text{H} \quad \text{CH}_2
\end{array}
$$

$$
\overset{k_3}{\searrow}\text{M} \quad
\begin{array}{c}
\text{H} \\
-\text{MCH}_2\!-\!\overset{|}{\text{C}}\!-\!\text{M}\cdot \quad\text{(III)} \\
\text{CH}=\text{CH}_2
\end{array}
$$

$$
\underset{k_6}{\searrow}\text{M} \quad
\begin{array}{c}
-\text{MCH}_2 \quad \text{H} \\
\text{C}=\text{C} \quad\text{(V)} \\
\text{H} \quad \text{CH}_2\!-\!\text{M}\cdot
\end{array}
$$

$$(35)$$

Attack of a growing chain on butadiene gives rise to a resonance-stabilized allylic radical which presumably has an essentially planar structure.   However, since it is most unlikely that such a radical is *linear*, it should have two isomeric structures: I, *cis*, and II, *trans*. Either can presumably react further to give a 1,2 product (III), but, in 1,4 addition I would certainly be expected to yield the *cis* product (IV), and II the *trans* isomer (V).   In this picture the relative yields of III, IV, and V will depend both upon the relative concentrations of I and II, which may or may not be in equilibrium, and upon the relative values of k_3, k_4, k_5, and k_6.   At present there is no way of determining these quantities (or even demonstrating directly the validity of this scheme), but, in the case of polybutadienes, the relative amounts of 1,2, *cis*-1,4, and *trans*-1,4 structure has received much study, chiefly via infrared spectra of the products, although chemical methods are also available.   Condon [194a] has reviewed the work of a number of groups with results shown in Fig. 5·10, and has concluded that the following energy relationships apply:

$$\Delta H^{\ddagger}_{cis} - \Delta H^{\ddagger}_{trans} = 2800 \pm 200 \text{ cal}$$

$$\Delta S^{\ddagger}_{cis} - \Delta S^{\ddagger}_{trans} = 6.8 \pm 0.9 \text{ E.U.}$$

$$\Delta H^{\ddagger}_{vinyl} - \Delta H^{\ddagger}_{trans} = 870 \pm 110 \text{ cal}$$

$$\Delta S^{\ddagger}_{vinyl} - \Delta S^{\ddagger}_{trans} = 0.46 \pm 0.47 \text{ E.U.}$$

[194a] F. E. Condon, *J. Polymer Sci.*, **11**, 139 (1953).

The curves in Fig. 5·10 have been drawn on this basis. These differences in $\Delta H^{\ddagger}$ and $\Delta S^{\ddagger}$, from our discussion, must represent com-

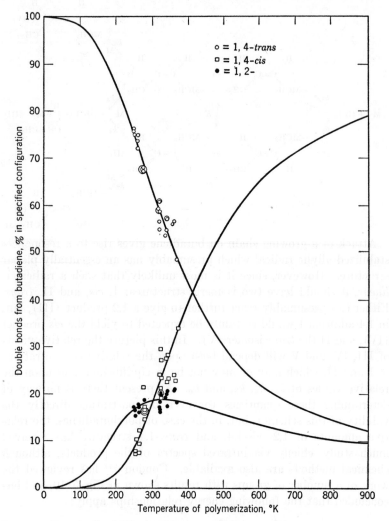

Fig. 5·10 Distribution of double bonds in polybutadiene as a function of polymerization temperature (after Condon [194a]).

posite quantities, and their origin cannot be accurately assigned. However, one plausible interpretation would be that k_5 and k_6 are comparable, but that I and III are in equilibrium, with the *trans* isomer having the lower heat content, thus accounting for the rise in yield of 1,4-*trans* product at lower temperatures. Regardless of its cause, this increase is of great practical importance, the superior properties of "cold rubber," GR-S prepared near 0°C, apparently arising largely from its 1,4-*trans* structure.[195, 196]

The relative amounts of 1,2 and 1,4 structures formed in butadiene copolymers varies, as we might expect, with the olefin to which the butadiene radical adds [i.e., the ratio of $(k_5 + k_6)/(k_3 + k_4)$ depends upon the structure of M]. Thus Foster and Binder[197] report that addition of a number of common monomers including styrene, acrylonitrile, and methyl vinyl ketone to butadiene polymerizations all significantly increase the fraction of butadiene appearing as *trans*-1,4 units. Most of the increase is at the expense of 1,2 structure, but *cis*-1,4 structures also decrease, a 4:1 styrene-butadiene copolymer prepared at 50° containing 75% *trans*-1,4, 14% *cis*-1,4, and 11% 1,2 structure (compare Fig. 5·10).

Other radical additions to butadiene discussed in subsequent chapters also give predominantly 1,4 addition, although the stereochemistry of the products has generally been ignored.

Substitution in the 2- or 2,3-positions of butadiene increases the fraction of 1,4 addition, which amounts to 88% in polyisoprene[198] (both *cis* and *trans*) and 97% in chloroprene.[199] In the case of isoprene, initial radical addition occurs to either end of the molecule since 1,2 addition yields both vinyl and propenyl sidechains in about equal quantity.

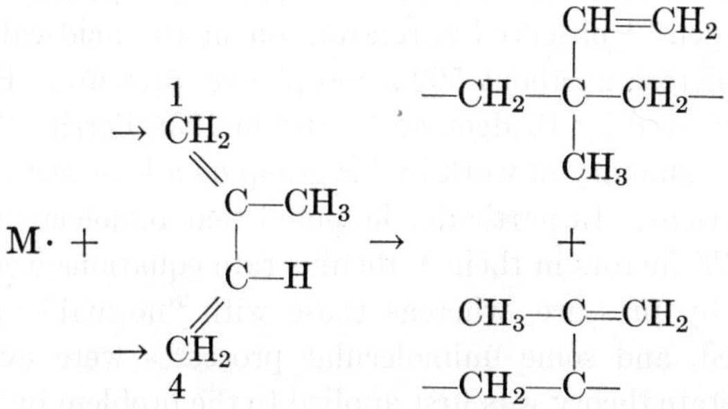

$$
M\cdot + \quad
\begin{matrix}
1 \\
\xrightarrow{\quad} CH_2 \\
\diagdown \\
C-CH_3 \\
| \\
C-H \\
\diagup \\
\xrightarrow{\quad} CH_2 \\
4
\end{matrix}
\quad \rightarrow \quad
\begin{matrix}
CH{=}CH_2 \\
| \\
-CH_2-C-CH_2- \\
| \\
CH_3 \\
\\
+ \\
\\
CH_3-C{=}CH_2 \\
| \\
-CH_2-C-
\end{matrix}
\qquad (36)
$$

[195] K. E. Beu, W. B. Reynolds, C. F. Fryling, and H. L. McMurry, *ibid.*, **3**, 466 (1948).

[196] E. J. Hart and A. W. Meyer, *J. Am. Chem. Soc.*, **71**, 1980 (1949).

[197] F. C. Foster and J. L. Binder, *ibid.*, **75**, 2910 (1953).

[198] W. S. Richardson and A. Sacher, *J. Polymer Sci.*, **10**, 353 (1953); I. M. Kolthoff and T. S. Lee, *ibid.*, **2**, 206 (1947); I. M. Kolthoff, T. S. Lee, and M. A. Mairs, *ibid.*, **2**, 220 (1947).

[199] A. Klebanskii and K. Cherychalova, *J. Gen. Chem. U.S.S.R.*, **17**, 941 (1947).

Since the majority of product has the 1,4 structure, which can arise from either point of attack, the actual amounts of addition at carbons 1 and 4 cannot be determined, although resonance stabilization arguments suggest that attack at carbon 1 should be preferred.

Finally, we may point out that, although experimental conditions (other than temperature) apparently have little effect on the ratio of 1,2, *cis*-1,4, and *trans*-1,4 products formed on a particular *radical* addition to a diene, change of mechanism to polar and heterogeneous processes permits these ratios to be varied widely, and recent reports [200] indicate that, in some cases, chains with essentially only a single type of unit may be produced.

5 · 6   Radical Polymerizations under High Pressures

5·6a   The Effect of High Pressures on Chemical Reactions

The effect of moderate pressures (1000 atmospheres and less) on gas-phase reactions are well known to chemists, and arise from simple mass law effects resulting from changes in reagent concentrations. Many examples of the effect of such pressures on radical reactions involving a gaseous reactant such as ethylene appear in this book. Pressure also has an effect on purely liquid-phase reactions, although measurable changes in rate are not usually observed until much higher pressures (2000–25,000 atmospheres) are reached.

Such phenomena have been investigated intermittently since 1892 when Roentgen [201] observed a retardation in the acid-catalyzed inversion of sucrose at about 500 atmospheres' pressure. Early work has been reviewed by Bridgeman,[202] and in 1938 Perrin [203] published an extensive summary of work by his group on a long series of typical organic reactions. In particular he noted that bimolecular processes with small *PZ* factors in their Arrhenius rate equations were strongly accelerated by pressure, whereas those with "normal" values were little affected, and some unimolecular processes were even slowed. Transition-state theory was first applied to the problem by Evans and Polanyi,[204] who derived the expression

[200] G. Natta, *Makromol. Chem.*, **16**, 213 (1955).

[201] W. C. Roentgen, *Wien. Ann.*, **45**, 98 (1892).

[202] P. W. Bridgeman, *The Physics of High Pressure*, G. Bell & Sons, London, 1949.

[203] M. W. Perrin, *Trans. Faraday Soc.*, **34**, 144 (1948).

[204] M. G. Evans and M. Polanyi, *ibid.*, **31**, 875 (1935). Actually an expression equivalent to eq. 37 was obtained by van't Hoff in 1901; cf. E. A. Moelwyn-

$$d \ln k/dP = -\Delta V^{\ddagger}/RT \qquad (37)$$

relating the effect of pressure to the change in volume, $\Delta V^{\ddagger}$, in going from reactants to transition state. We may note that the effects predicted by eq. 37 are rather small except at very high pressures, a value of $\Delta V^{\ddagger} = -10$ cc per mole corresponding to a 60-fold increase in rate at 10,000 atmospheres at room temperature. Qualitatively the relation between eq. 37 and Perrin's observations is easy to explain. Small PZ factors correspond to negative entropies of activation, and these, in turn, are commonly associated with small, compressed, and rigid transition states in which degrees of freedom associated with the reactants have been lost.

In 1941 Stearn and Eyring [205] attempted to apply eq. 37 quantitatively to published data with only moderate success. Subsequently, progress has been made, notably by Hamann [206] and Laidler,[207] who have recognized that, in reactions involving ions or ionic intermediates, $\Delta V^{\ddagger}$ is greatly influenced by electrostriction of solvent involved in ion solvation.

If we now consider radical processes, the chain propagation steps in radical chains are commonly bimolecular reactions which should have negative values of $\Delta V^{\ddagger}$ as they involve the close approach of two reactants; furthermore, they are largely free from the solvation difficulties mentioned above.

On the other hand, as we have seen, the rates of such processes are determined by combinations of rate constants, so that the interpretation of a pressure effect on an overall rate requires some sort of unsorting in order to determine to which step $\Delta V^{\ddagger}$ applies. Some progress has been made in this direction in polymerization, and we may note that the problem is of some practical importance with the development of technology for carrying out large-scale reactions at pressures of 1000–3000 atmospheres.

5·6b Polymerization under High Pressures

The effect of high pressures on what is now recognized as the radical polymerization of olefins was first reported by Conant, working with

Hughes, *The Kinetics of Reaction in Solution,* second edition, Clarendon Press, Oxford, 1947, p. 338.

[205] A. E. Stearn and H. Eyring, *Chem. Revs.,* **29**, 509 (1941).

[206] J. Buchanan and S. D. Hamann, *Trans. Faraday Soc.,* **49**, 1425 (1953); H. G. David and S. D. Hamann, *ibid.,* **50**, 1188 (1954); S. D. Hamann and W. Straus, *ibid.,* **51**, 1684 (1955).

[207] C. T. Burries and K. J. Laidler, *ibid.,* **51**, 1497 (1955).

Bridgeman's equipment,[208] who noted polymerization of styrene, vinyl acetate, isoprene, and 2,3-dimethylbutadiene at room temperature and 9000–12,000 atmospheres under conditions where negligible reaction occurs at atmospheric pressure. Subsequently, a number of workers have noted similar increases in polymerization rate in a whole variety of systems.[209-215]

The most meticulous and illuminating study is apparently that of Merrett and Norrish,[215] who investigated the benzoyl peroxide-initiated polymerization of styrene at 60° under pressures up to 5000 atmospheres. Changes in R_p and $\overline{P}$ are shown in Figs. 5·11 and 5·12. The polymerization rate rises continuously with pressure, increasing 10- to 12-fold at 5000 atmospheres, but $\overline{P}$ appears to level off after an initial increase.

Merrett and Norrish discuss their results in some detail but are still confronted with the difficulty of relating the pressure effect to specific processes mentioned above. Thus, for a system obeying typical polymerization kinetics with bimolecular chain termination (Section 3·3b), $d \ln k/dP$ is given by the expression

$$d \ln k/dP = -(\Delta V_p^{\ddagger} + \tfrac{1}{2}\Delta V_i^{\ddagger} - \tfrac{1}{2}\Delta V_t^{\ddagger})/RT \qquad (38)$$

where $\Delta V_p^{\ddagger}$, $\Delta V_t^{\ddagger}$ and $\Delta V_i^{\ddagger}$ are the volume changes associated with the transition states of chain growth, chain termination, and chain initiation respectively. Similarly, in a case where $\overline{P}$ is being determined by a chain transfer step (Section 4·2)

$$d \ln C/dP = -(\Delta V_{tr}^{\ddagger} - \Delta V_p^{\ddagger})/RT \qquad (39)$$

Qualitatively, $\Delta V_p^{\ddagger}$ and $\Delta V_{tr}^{\ddagger}$ should have negative values, as should $\Delta V_t^{\ddagger}$, although, if chain termination becomes diffusion controlled

[208] P. W. Bridgeman and J. B. Conant, *Proc. Nat. Acad. Sci.*, **15**, 680 (1929); J. B. Conant and C. O. Tonberg, *J. Am. Chem. Soc.*, **52**, 1659 (1930); J. B. Conant and W. R. Peterson, *ibid.*, **54**, 628 (1932).

[209] G. Tamman and A. Pape, *Z. anorg. Chem.*, **200**, 113 (1931).

[210] H. W. Starkweather, *J. Am. Chem. Soc.*, **56**, 1870 (1934).

[211] R. H. Shapiro, R. P. Linstead, and D. M. Newitt, *J. Chem. Soc.*, **1937**, 1784.

[212] L. F. Vereshchagin, V. Derevitskaya, and Z. Rogavin, *J. Phys. Chem. U.S.S.R.*, **21**, 233 (1947), and subsequent papers by L. F. Vereshchagin, M. G. Gonikberg, et al.

[213] P. P. Kobeko, E. V. Kuvshinskii, and A. S. Semenova, *Zhur. Fiz. Khim.*, **24**, 345, 415 (1950).

[214] R. C. Gillham, *Trans. Faraday Soc.*, **46**, 497 (1950).

[215] F. M. Merrett and R. G. W. Norrish, *Proc. Roy. Soc. London*, **A206**, 309 (1951).

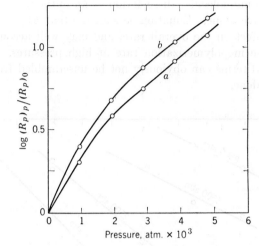

Fig. 5·11   Effect of pressure on the polymerization of styrene initiated by benzoyl peroxide at 60°; a, 0.429 mole % peroxide; b, 0.043% (after Merritt and Norrish [215]).

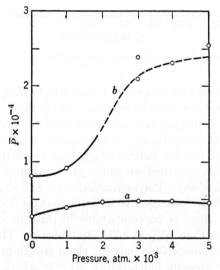

Fig. 5·12   Effect of pressure upon the degree of polymerization of polystyrene prepared at 60° in the presence of benzoyl peroxide: a, 0.429 mole %; b, 0.043 mole % (after Merritt and Norrish [215]).

under pressure, the last may change sign. However, $\Delta V_i{}^\ddagger$, if it relates to the unimolecular dissociation of an initiator, probably has a small positive value. Equation 38 suggests that $\Delta V_p{}^\ddagger$ should have the largest effect on the overall rate, and may well account for the usual increase in polymerization rate at high pressures. However, the individual terms can obviously not be unscrambled from overall rate studies alone.

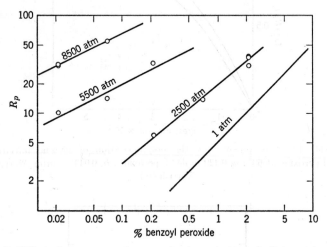

Fɪɢ. 5·13   Effect of pressure on the rate of polymerization of allyl acetate at 80°.

Some progress on this problem has recently been made at Columbia.[216-217] As we have seen in Section 4.3e, both R_p and $\bar{P}$ in the polymerization of allyl acetate are determined by degradative chain transfer, attack of the growing polymer radical on allylic C—H bonds to yield an inactive allyl radical which fails to continue the chain. When this reaction is carried out under pressure, the results shown in Fig. 5·13 are obtained. Polymerization rates are greatly increased, and the kinetic order in respect to initiator changes from 1 to ½. On the other hand, there is no comparable increase in $\bar{P}$, the increase amounting to less than 40% at 8000 atmospheres. This latter result indicates that the competition between chain growth and chain transfer is essentially pressure independent, $\Delta V_p{}^\ddagger \cong \Delta V_{tr}{}^\ddagger$. The increase in overall rate and change in kinetic order, however, show that, under

[216] C. Walling, *Am. Chem. Soc. Meeting Abstr.*, **128,** 30-O (1955).
[217] J. Pellon, thesis, Columbia University, 1957.

high pressures, allylic radicals are now able to restart chains, i.e., for the processes

$$CH_2=CH-\dot{C}HOCOCH_3 + M \rightarrow M\cdot \qquad (40)$$

$$2CH_2=\dot{C}H-CHOCOCH_3 \rightarrow \text{Non-radical products} \qquad (41)$$

reaction 40 is now favored (measurement of the decomposition rate of benzoyl peroxide in the system shows that it is initially slightly *decreased* by pressure, reinforcing our conclusion; at higher pressures a rapid induced decomposition sets in).

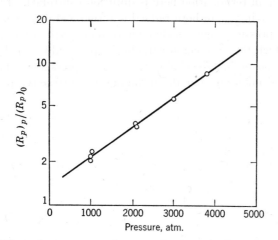

FIG. 5·14   Effect of pressure on the rate of polymerization of seeded styrene emulsions.

The relative invariance of $\bar{P}$ with pressure deserves further mention since it indicates that radical displacements should be accelerated by pressure to about the same degree as radical additions.   In confirmation, the transfer constant for the CCl_4-styrene system has been found to be essentially pressure independent, and it is interesting that the limiting values of $\bar{P}$ reported by Merrett and Norrish [215] at high pressure (Fig. 5·12) are approximately those which one calculates if chain transfer with peroxide is assumed to be the major chain-ending step, using the value of C_I (Section 4·2b) determined at atmospheric pressure.

The results on allyl acetate give no direct measure of $\Delta V_p{}^{\ddagger}$ and the quantitative effect of pressure on chain growth.   This, however, has been evaluated for styrene by comparing the rates of polymerization in seeded emulsions at atmospheric and high pressures using the Smith-Ewart theory of the emulsion polymerization process (Section 5·3a). In such systems, at identical monomer and particle concentrations, polymerization rates are directly proportional to k_p's. Results are shown in Fig. 5·14, from which k_p increases approximately 10-fold at 5000 atmospheres. Above 1000 atmospheres $\Delta V^{\ddagger} = -11.5$ cc/mole compared with the overall ΔV for styrene polymerization of -17.3 cc/mole at 40°. Combination of this value with data of Merrett and Norrish indicates that $\Delta V_t^{\ddagger}$ is probably positive, and, under pressure, chain termination here is diffusion controlled. Finally, the large increase in rate of both radical addition and displacement processes with pressure suggests that many other types of radical reactions in which they are chain-carrying steps should also show higher rates and longer kinetic chains under high pressures. These seem to have had no study, but the technique has attractive possibilities.

CHAPTER 6

Radical Addition Reactions Yielding Small Molecules

6·1 General Survey

In Chapter 4 the reaction of chain transfer was considered as a complication arising in free radical polymerization through the intervention of a radical displacement process in the midst of successive radical additions to double bonds. We may now turn to the related class of reactions in which displacement is the dominant reaction and in which substrates are, in effect, added across double bonds by the chain process:

$$B \cdot + CH_2{=}CHR \rightarrow B{-}CH_2{-}\dot{C}HR \qquad (1)$$

$$B{-}CH_2{-}\dot{C}HR + A{-}B \rightarrow B{-}CH_2{-}CAHR \qquad (2)$$

Such reactions are among the most important examples of the synthesis of small molecules via radical chains, and also provide more valuable information on the relation between structure and reactivity in radical displacement processes.

Materials which undergo radical additions to suitable olefins include halogens, hydrogen bromide, alkyl polyhalides, aldehydes, alcohols, amines, mercaptans, and other sulfur compounds, certain phosphorus and silicon compounds and a few derivatives of the less common elements. In general, the atom upon which displacement occurs, A in reaction 2, is hydrogen or halogen, although displacements on sulfur, and perhaps oxygen, are known. Interestingly, few unequivocal displacements on saturated carbon have been established, even where they might be energetically favorable. This is in notable contrast to polar reactions in which displacement on carbon is the most common process.

6·1a Energetics of Radical Addition Processes

Since combination and disproportionation processes between small radicals are at least as rapid as those between radicals in polymerizing systems, radical chain additions are confined to the same sort of rigid time schedule, in which an entire chain sequence must take place in a time of the order of a second. Accordingly, individual steps must be rapid, with low activation energies. From the arguments given in Chapter 2, such activation energies must be equal to or greater than ΔH for the step involved, and the latter can be calculated as the difference between the energies of bonds broken and formed in the individual chain steps. It is thus often possible to predict circumstances under which additions may or may not be possible. A series of such ΔH's for radical additions are listed in Table 6·1, using the bond dissociation energies of Tables 2·1–2·3, and making the assumption that

240

TABLE 6·1 ENERGETICS OF CHAIN STEPS IN RADICAL ADDITIONS TO ETHYLENE

(In kcal/mole at 25°C)

A—B	ΔH_A B· + CH$_2$=CH$_2$	ΔH_D [a] BCH$_2$CH$_2$· + A—B
H—H	−40	6
H—CH$_3$	−22	4
H—NH$_2$	−17	4
H—OH	−32	22
H—F	. . .	37
H—SiH$_3$	. . .	−14
H—PH$_2$	. . .	−13
H—SH	−16	−8
H—Cl	−26	5
H—Br	−5	−11
H—I	7	−27
Cl—OH	−32	−17
Cl—Cl	−26	−19
Br—Br	−5	−17
I—I	7	−13
Cl—SiCl$_3$	. . .	17
Cl—PCl$_2$	. . .	9
H—CH$_2\phi$	−1.5	−21
H—COCH$_3$	−16	−10
H—CCl$_3$	−14	−8
Cl—CCl$_3$	−14	−8

[a] For reactions in which A = halogen, $D(BCH_2CH_2—A)$ has been taken as $D(CH_3—A) − 4$ kcal, 4 kcal/mole being the difference between $D(CH_3—H)$ and $D(C_2H_5—H)$.

a β-substituent has a negligible effect on the resonance stabilization of the ethyl radical.

The hydrogen halides provide a good example of the use of such tables. Only in the addition of hydrogen bromide are both addition and displacement steps exothermic. With hydrogen iodide, the addition step is endothermic by 7 kcal/mole and must have an equal or higher activation energy. With hydrogen chloride and hydrogen fluoride there are 5 and 37 kcal barriers to the displacement step. Experimentally, only hydrogen bromide undergoes addition via a long chain process, although short chains have been detected with hydrogen chloride, the next most favorable case. Again, a large (22 kcal) barrier exists for the radical addition of water at the displacement step, and the barrier for additions of alcohols is only slightly lower. No radical addition of water has been detected, and with alcohols addi-

$$\overset{\text{OH}}{\underset{|}{}}$$

tion occurs by breaking at the $R\overset{|}{C}H$—H bond.

Changes in olefin structure may alter the energetic picture from that of Table 6·1. As a substituent R stabilizes the radical formed by addition in reaction 1, $-\Delta H_A$ is increased and $-\Delta H_D$ decreased. A few values for addition to styrene are given in Table 6·2. These have

TABLE 6·2 ENERGETICS OF CHAIN STEPS IN RADICAL ADDITIONS TO STYRENE

(In kcal/mole at 25°C)

A—B	ΔH_A B· + CH$_2$=CHϕ	ΔH_D B—CH$_2$ĊHϕ + A—B
H—SH	−39	16.5
H—Cl	−49	26
H—Br	−28	13.5
H—I	−16	−3.5
Cl—Cl	−49	−6 [a]
Br—Br	−28	0
I—I	−16	1
H—COCH$_3$	−39	14.5
H—CCl$_3$	−37	16.5
Cl—CCl$_3$	−37	5 [a]

[a] These values are probably low; cf. Chapter 2.

been calculated by taking the difference in resonance energies of the substituted phenylethyl radical and the ethyl radical (E_R) as 24.5 kcal (the same as the resonance energy of the benzyl radical), the resonance energy of the vinyl group of styrene (E_S) as 1.5 kcal (from data on heats of hydrogenation), and, in the cases where displacement occurs on halogen, correcting for the bond strengthening of the benzyl halogen bond (E_X) indicated by the measured bond dissociation energies of the benzyl halides. Thus

$$\Delta H_A \text{ (styrene)} = \Delta H_A \text{ (ethylene)} - E_R + E_S \qquad (3a)$$

and

$$\Delta H_D \text{ (styrene)} = \Delta H_D \text{ (ethylene)} + E_R - E_X \qquad (3b)$$

The actual situation in regard to activation energies and rates in addition reactions is, of course, more complicated than is indicated by the calculations of Tables 6·1 and 6·2, which merely indicate mini-mum possible activation energies (and are also subject to considerable uncertainty). From our discussion of polymerizations, it is evident that even exothermic addition processes may have appreciable activation energies and low PZ factors. Further, since addition processes usually involve considerable loss of entropy, unless they are strongly exothermic they may be significantly reversible, cf. Section 5·4.

The manner in which PZ factors and excess activation energy vary with structure in the displacement step is not well understood, but, in general, for displacements on univalent atoms ease of reaction increases with decreasing bond dissociation energy for the bond being broken, even when the overall energetics of the displacement step remain the same. Thus, the ease of displacement on halogen atoms attached to carbon lies in the order Cl < Br < I. The relative rates of radical attack on hydrogen and halogen are a more complicated matter discussed further below.

Another generalization that can be made is that, although even exothermic displacements involving atoms attached to carbon may have appreciable activation energies, displacements involving H—S and H—X bonds appear to have very little additional barrier of this sort.

Finally, as has been suggested in Section 4·1h, polar factors appear very important in these radical chain processes. Both in the addition and displacement steps attack of "donor" radicals on "acceptor" substrates is facilitated, and vice versa, and many examples will become evident in subsequent sections.

6·1b   Kinetics of Addition Reactions; Side Reactions

The overall kinetics of radical chain addition processes can be developed by the methods described in our discussion of polymerization. For the case of bimolecular chain termination, reactions 1 and 2 may be symbolized as

$$B\cdot + M \xrightarrow{k_a} M\cdot \tag{4a}$$

$$M\cdot + A—B \xrightarrow{k_d} P + B\cdot \tag{4b}$$

with three possible termination steps (indicated as coupling, but disproportionation gives the same kinetics):

$$2M\cdot \xrightarrow{k_{t1}} M—M \tag{5}$$

$$B\cdot + M\cdot \xrightarrow{k_{t12}} B—M \tag{6}$$

$$2B\cdot \xrightarrow{k_{t2}} B—B \tag{7}$$

Where R_i represents the rate of chain initiation, by the usual steady-state treatment we obtain:

$$-\frac{d[M]}{dt} = -\frac{d[AB]}{dt}$$

$$= \frac{k_a k_d [AB][M](R_i)^{\frac{1}{2}}}{(2k_a^2 k_{t1}[M]^2 + k_a k_d 2\phi(k_{t1}k_{t2})^{\frac{1}{2}}[AB][M] + 2k_d^2 k_{t2}[AB]^2)^{\frac{1}{2}}} \quad (8)$$

where $\phi = k_{t12}/2(k_{t1}k_{t2})^{\frac{1}{2}}$.

Equation 8 is complex, and the rate constants are not easily separated. However, by working in large excesses of olefin or addend, reactions 5 or 7 can be made respectively the sole important termination steps. In excess olefin eq. 8 becomes

$$-d[M]/dt = -d[AB]/dt = k_d[AB](R_i/2k_{t1})^{\frac{1}{2}} \quad (9)$$

with the rate determined by the competition between reactions 4b and 5. In excess addend, the competition is between eq. 4a and reaction 7, and we have

$$-d[M]/dt = -d[AB]/dt = k_a[M](R_i/2k_{t2})^{\frac{1}{2}} \quad (10)$$

The same rotating sector and other non-steady-state methods are available for determining individual rate constants in systems obeying eqs. 9 and 10 as have been discussed in connection with polymerization (Section 3·4). Although a start has been made experimentally (Sections 6·2b and 7·2) some of the kinetic complications mentioned below add to experimental difficulties.

Many of the olefins commonly employed in radical additions contain allylic hydrogen, which introduces the complication of degradative chain transfer (Section 4·3e) into the kinetics, and of allylic substitution products into the reaction products. If displacement of an allylic hydrogen leads to an inactive radical, an alternative termination step

$$B\cdot + M \xrightarrow{k'_t} X\cdot \quad \text{(allylic radical)} \quad (11)$$

is introduced. If it is the major termination process, but chains are still long, the rate expression becomes independent of both olefin and addend

$$-d[M]/dt = -d[AB]/dt = fR_i k_a/k'_t \quad (12)$$

where $1 \lesssim f \lesssim 2$, its value depending on whether $X\cdot$ reacts finally with another $X\cdot$ or with $B\cdot$ or $M\cdot$. Although such kinetics are known, it is obvious that they are obeyed only over limited concentrations of reagents, and commonly at high [M]/[AB] ratios.

A second complication arises in the intermediate situation between simple radical addition and "regulated" polymerizations, where addition of additional olefin units competes with radical attack on the addend. Under such conditions, the products are mixtures of short chain polymers $B-(CH_2-CHR)_n-A$. Such products have been named "telomers" by Hanford and his collaborators at du Pont and obviously offer very interesting synthetic possibilities.

The overall kinetics under such conditions are obviously very complicated, but the distribution of products is easily derived. At any moment, the ratio of product formed containing n units to product containing more than n units is determined by the competition

$$B-M_n \cdot \; + \; A-B \; \xrightarrow{k_{dn}} \; B-M_n-A + B\cdot \tag{13}$$

$$B-M_n \cdot \; + \; M \; \xrightarrow{k_{pn}} \; B-M\cdot_{n+1} \tag{14}$$

whence

$$\frac{d[B-M_n-A]}{\sum\limits_{n+1}^{\infty} d[B-M_i-A]} = C_n[AB]/[M] \tag{15}$$

where $C_n = k_{dn}/k_{pn}$, analogous to the transfer constant discussed in Section 4·2. Interestingly, in some systems, C's vary considerably for $n = 1, 2,$ and 3, although they appear constant for higher n's. The value of each C may be determined by fractionating the products from carefully controlled reactions, and, once known, may be used to calculate the yield of each product which will be obtained under any particular set of conditions.

The appropriate equations may be obtained by an essentially statistical procedure. For long chains, the fraction of growing chains that yield 1:1 product is given by

$$F_1 = \frac{k_{d1}[M\cdot][AB]}{k_{d2}[M\cdot][AB] + k_{p1}[M\cdot][M]} = \frac{C_1R}{C_1R + 1} \tag{16}$$

where $[AB]/[M] = R$. Similarly, the fraction of chains that continues is

$$1 - F_1 = 1/(C_1R + 1) \tag{17}$$

The fraction of total chains yielding a 2:1 telomer is, in turn, the fraction that continues but then ends

$$F_2 = C_2 R/(C_1 R + 1)(C_2 R + 1) \tag{18}$$

or, in general

$$F_n = C_n R \prod_1^n (C_i R + 1)^{-1} \tag{19}$$

Since $\Sigma F_n = 1$, F_n's also represent the mole fraction of product $F_{n(p)}$ appearing in chains of length n.

The average chain length $\bar{P}$ in turn becomes

$$\bar{P} = \sum_1^\infty n C_n R \prod_1^n (C_i R + 1)^{-1} \tag{20}$$

Since C's in general reach a constant value C at some low value of $n > m$, eq. 20 can be put in finite form, for the average length of these longer chains is simply $m + 1/CR$, whence

$$\bar{P} = \sum_1^{m-1} n C_n R \prod_1^n (C_i R + 1)^{-1} + (m + 1/CR) \prod_1^{m-1} (C_i R + 1)^{-1} \tag{21}$$

Frequently, the mole fraction of reacted monomer appearing in chains of length n, $F_{n(m)}$ is of greater interest than $F_{n(p)}$. This is given by

$$F_{n(m)} = (n C_n R/\bar{P}) \prod_1^n (1 + C_i R)^{-1} \tag{22}$$

Fortunately, C usually becomes constant at chain lengths of four or less, and one is rarely interested in the yields of higher telomers, so that the necessary expansions of eqs. 21 and 22 are relatively simple.

The F's and $\bar{P}$'s defined above are, of course, instantaneous values, whereas, in any practical synthetic reaction, R varies as the reaction progresses. An average value may often be employed with reasonable precision, or the calculation of F's and $\bar{P}$ may be made with any desired degree of precision by graphical integration, using essentially the method described in our discussion of copolymer compositions, Section 4·1c.

Finally, before going on to specific reaction systems, we may note that the addition reaction is sometimes complicated by the presence of reversible steps (chiefly involving the loss of halogen atoms), rearrangements, and the formation of significant amounts of product by attack of the chain-carrying radicals on allylic C—H bonds. Examples of all of these ramifications will appear at appropriate places below.

6 · 2   Additions of Alkyl Polyhalides

6·2a   History and Scope

The relatively low degree of polymerization of polystyrene prepared in the presence of carbon tetrachloride was noted in 1937 by Suess and co-workers [1] and their observations interpreted quantitatively in terms of a chain transfer process by Mayo [2] in 1943. The first published observation that products containing one molecule each of olefin and adduct could be obtained in this way, however, was that of Kharasch [3] in 1945, who reported that carbon tetrachloride and chloroform reacted with 1-octene in the presence of radical sources to yield 1,1,1,3-tetrachlorononane and 1,1,1-trichlorononane respectively.

$$CCl_4 + CH_2\!\!=\!\!CH\!-\!C_6H_{13} \rightarrow CCl_3\!-\!CH_2\!-\!CHCl\!-\!C_6H_{13} \quad (23)$$

$$CHCl_3 + CH_2\!\!=\!\!CH\!-\!C_6H_{13} \rightarrow CCl_3C_8H_{17} \quad\quad\quad (24)$$

Interestingly, somewhat before Kharasch's publication, the same sort of reaction had been observed independently by groups at du Pont and the United States Rubber Company. Since that time a variety of other halomethanes and related compounds have been observed to add to a large number of different olefins. A summary of published results appears in Tables 6·3–6·6, which represent a reasonably complete coverage of reactions described in the scientific literature or given as specific examples in patents. However, since reactions of this sort have received extensive evaluation in industry, much additional information undoubtedly exists.

Table 6·3 summarizes data on carbon tetrachloride–olefin systems which have been investigated quite extensively. The majority of the reactions have been run at 60–100°C in the presence of a considerable excess of carbon tetrachloride using a few per cent of benzoyl or acetyl peroxide as initiator for the reaction chains, although other initiators serve satisfactorily. With normally gaseous olefins it is desirable to carry out the addition under pressure. A number of simple and substituted olefins give excellent yields of the expected 1:1 products under these conditions, the chief complications being telomer formation, attack by $\cdot CCl_3$ radicals on allylic C—H bonds,

[1] H. Suess, K. Pilch, and H. Rudorfer, Z. physik. Chem., A179, 361 (1937); H. Suess and A. Springer, ibid., A181, 81 (1937).

[2] F. R. Mayo, J. Am. Chem. Soc., 65, 2324 (1943).

[3] M. S. Kharasch, E. V. Jensen, and W. H. Urry, Science, 102, 128 (1945).

TABLE 6·3   RADICAL ADDITIONS OF CCl_4 TO OLEFINS

Olefin	Conditions [a]	Product, % yield [b]	Footnote [c]
Ethylene	B	$ClCH_2CH_2CCl_3$, T	4–6
Propylene	B	$CCl_3CH_2CHClCH_3$	4, 7
Isobutylene	B	$CCl_3CH_2CCl(CH_3)_2$ (78)	7, 7a
t-Butylethylene	B	$CCl_3CH_2CHClC(CH_3)_3$	8
1-Heptene	B	$CCl_3CH_2CHClC_5H_{11}$ (72)	8, 8a
1-Octene	A	$CCl_3CH_2CHClC_6H_{13}$ (85)	3, 4
1-Hexadecene	B	$CCl_3CH_2CHClC_{14}H_{29}$	8
Cyclohexene	B	, other products [d]	8, 9
Biallyl	...	$C_7H_{10}Cl_4$ (26), $C_8H_{10}Cl_8$ (31)	4
Butadiene	B	$CCl_3CH_2CH=CHCH_2Cl$ (23)	11
Allyl chloride	B	$CCl_3CH_2CHClCH_2Cl$, T	7
Vinyl butyl ether	L	$CCl_3CH_2CHClOC_4H_9$	12
Allyl acetate	B	$CCl_3CH_2CHClCH_2OAc$, T	7, 10
Vinyl acetate	B	$CCl_3CH_2CH_2ClOAc$, T	13, 14
$ClCH=CHHgCl$	A, B	$CCl_3CH=CHCl$ (46)	15
$(ClCH=CH)_2Hg$	A, B	$CCl_3CH=CHCl$ (36)	15
$CH_2=CH—CH(OEt)_2$	L	$CCl_3CH_2CHClCH(OEt)_2$	18
Camphene	A		16, 17
Limonene	B	(70)	19, 22
β-Pinene	B	(97)	20, 21, 22
Butadiene sulfone	B	(low)	11, 23
		$CCl_3CH_2CH=CHCH_2Cl$ (62)	

[a] B = benzoyl peroxide, A = acetyl peroxide, L = photochemical initiation.
[b] T indicates telomeric products.
[c] When more than one reference is given, italic type describes experiments giving indicated yield.
[d] See text.

4 M. S. Kharasch, E. V. Jensen, and W. H. Urry, J. Am. Chem. Soc., **69,** 1100 (1947).
5 W. E. Hanford and R. M. Joyce, U.S. 2,440,800 (May 4, 1948).
6 J. Harmon, T. A. Ford, W. E. Hanford, and R. M. Joyce, J. Am. Chem. Soc., **72,** 2213 (1950).
7 F. M. Lewis and F. R. Mayo, J. Am. Chem. Soc., **76,** 457 (1954).
7a A. V. Topchiev, N. F. Bogomolova, and Y. Y. Goldfarb, Doklady Akad. Nauk S.S.S.R., **107,** 420 (1956).
8 E. C. Kooyman and E. Farenhorst, Rec. trav. chim., **70,** 867 (1951).
8a G. DuPont, R. Dulou, and C. Pigerol, Compt. rend., **240,** 628 (1955).
9 S. Israelashvili and J. Shabatay, J. Chem. Soc., **1951,** 3261.
10 M. S. Kharasch, O. Reinmuth, and W. H. Urry, J. Am. Chem. Soc., **69,** 1105 (1947).
11 W. R. Peterson, U.S. 2,401,099 (May 28, 1946).
12 Kh. S. Bagdasar'yan and R. I. Milyutinskaya, Zhur. Fiz. Khim., **28,** 498 (1954).
13 J. Harmon, U.S. 2,396,261 (March 12, 1946).
14 T. M. Patrick, Jr., U.S. 2,676,981 (April 27, 1954).
15 A. E. Borisov, Izvest. Akad. Nauk S.S.S.R., Otdel. Khim. Nauk, 524 (1951).
16 G. DuPont, R. Dulou, and G. Clement, Bull. soc. chim. France, **1951,** 1002.
17 G. Clement, Compt. rend., **232,** 2016 (1951).
18 R. H. Hall and D. I. H. Jacobs, J. Chem. Soc., **1954,** 2034.
19 S. Israeleshvili and E. Diamant, J. Am. Chem. Soc., **74,** 3185 (1952).
20 D. M. Oldroyd, G. S. Fisher, and L. A. Goldblatt, J. Am. Chem. Soc., **72,** 2407 (1950).
21 G. DuPont, R. Dulou, and G. Clement, Bull. soc. chim. France, **1950,** 1056, 1115.
22 G. DuPont, R. Dulou, and G. Clement, Compt. rend., **236,** 2512 (1953).
23 M. S. Kharasch, M. Freiman, and W. H. Urry, J. Org. Chem., **13,** 570 (1948).

TABLE 6·4   RADICAL ADDITIONS OF CCl_3Br TO OLEFINS

Olefin	Conditions [a]	Product, % yield	Footnote
Ethylene	A	$CCl_3CH_2CH_2Br$	10
Vinyl acetate	A	$CCl_3CH_2CHBrOAc$ (90)	10, 24
Propylene	L	$CCl_3CH_2CHBrCH_3$	10
Allyl chloride	A	$CCl_3CH_2CHBrCH_2Cl$	10, 24
Allyl bromide	L	$CCl_3CH_2CHBrCH_2CCl_3$ (37), $CH_2BrCHBrCH_2Br$ (41), $CCl_3CH_2CH{=}CH_2$	81
$CH_2{=}CHCCl_3$	B	$CCl_3CH_2CH{=}CCl_2$, $CCl_3CH_2CHClCCl_2Br$, $C_3H_3Cl_4Br$	25
$CH_2{=}CClCH_2Cl$	L	$CCl_3CH_2CClBrCH_2Cl$ (8)	24
Isopropenyl acetate	B, L	$CCl_3CH_2CBr(CH_3)OAc$ (27)	26
$CH{\equiv}CCH_2OAc$	AN	$CCl_3CH{=}CBrCH_2OAc$	27
2-Butene [b]	L	$CCl_3CH(CH_3)CHBrCH_3$	28
Isobutylene	A	$CCl_3CH_2CBr(CH_3)_2$	10
Butadiene	...	$CCl_3CH_2CH{=}CHCH_2Br$ (75), $CCl_3CH_2CHBrCH{=}CH_2$ (25)	24, 26
Butadiene sulfone	A	(62)	23
Methallyl chloride	L	$CCl_3CH_2CBr(CH_3)CH_2Cl$ (45)	24
Ethyl vinylacetate	L	$CCl_3CH_2CHBrCH_2COOEt$ (92)	24
Allyl cyanide	L	$CCl_3CH_2CHBrCH_2CN$ (65)	24
$CH_2{=}CHCH_2CCl_3$	L	$CCl_3CH_2CHBrCH_2CCl_3$	24
Dimethyl fumarate	L	$CCl_3CH{-}COOMe$ / $BrCH{-}COOMe$	29, 30
Dimethyl maleate	L	$CCl_3CH{-}COOMe$ / $BrCH{-}COOMe$	29
2-Methyl-2-butene	L	$CCl_3CH(CH_3)CBr(CH_3)_2$ (77)	24
Cyclopentene			31
Cyclopentadiene			31
2-Ethyl-1-butene		$CCl_3CH_2CBr(C_2H_5)_2$ (91)	24
Cyclohexene		(30)	24, 31
Cyclohexadiene		(68) (32)	31
Bicyclo[2.2.1]heptene [d]			31
1-Octene	L, A	$CCl_3CH_2CHBrC_6H_{13}$ (88)	10, 24
2-Octene [c]	A	$C_9H_{16}Cl_3Br$ (45)	10
1-Octyne	A	$CCl_3CH{=}CBrC_6H_{13}$ (80)	32
2-Octyne [c]	L	$C_9H_{14}Cl_3Br$ (33)	32
Phenylacetylene	...	$CCl_3CH{=}CBr\phi$ (32)	32
Styrene	A	$CCl_3CH_2CHBr\phi$ (78)	10, 24, 26
p-Chlorostyrene	L	$CCl_3CH_2CHBrC_6H_4Cl$ (74)	26
2,4-Dichlorostyrene	L	$CCl_3CH_2CHBrC_6H_3Cl_2$ (20)	24

TABLE 6·4   RADICAL ADDITIONS OF CCl_3Br TO OLEFINS (Continued)

Olefin	Conditions [a]	Product, % yield	Footnote
Bicyclo[2.2.2]octene [d]	...		31
α-Methylstyrene	L	$CCl_3CH=C(CH_3)\phi$ (40)	26
β-Methylstyrene	L	$CCl_3CH(CH_3)CHBr\phi$	24
Allylbenzene	L	$CCl_3CH_2CHBrCH_2\phi$ (44)	24
Indene	...		31
Ethyl cinnamate	A	$CCl_3CH(COOEt)CHBr\phi$ (60)	24
Dicyclopentadiene [d]	...	$C_{11}H_{12}CCl_3Br$	31

[a] AN = azobisisobutyronitrile. Cf. Table 6·3 for other symbols.
[b] Both cis and trans isomers give identical mixture of stereoisomers.
[c] Mixture of isomers.
[d] For product structure, see text.

[24] M. S. Kharasch and M. Sage, J. Org. Chem., **14**, 537 (1949).
[25] A. N. Nesmeyanov, R. Kh. Freidlina, and L. I. Zakharin, Doklady Akad. Nauk S.S.S.R., **81**, 199 (1951).
[26] M. S. Kharasch, E. Simon, and W. Nudenberg, J. Org. Chem., **18**, 328 (1953).
[27] E. C. Ladd, U.S. 2,554,533 (May 29, 1951).
[28] P. S. Skell and R. C. Woodworth, J. Am. Chem. Soc., **77**, 4638 (1955).
[29] M. S. Kharasch, U.S. 2,485,099 (October 18, 1949).
[30] M. S. Kharasch, U.S. 2,464,869 (March 22, 1949).
[31] M. S. Kharasch and H. N. Friedlander, J. Org. Chem., **14**, 239 (1949).
[32] M. S. Kharasch, J. J. Jerome, and W. H. Urry, ibid., **15**, 966 (1950).

and, rather rarely, rearrangement. In some cases, the actual material isolated represents a dehydrohalogenation product of the original adduct.

Table 6·4 lists similar data for CCl_3Br, which undergoes preferential scission of the C—Br bond to yield products of the type CCl_3CH_2CHBrR. Experimental conditions are essentially the same as with CCl_4, but the reaction occurs with particular ease. In fact, little initiator is required, and care must be used that the reaction does not become uncontrollably violent. Since CCl_3Br absorbs light almost up into the visible range, photoinitiation is feasible using near-ultraviolet light transmitted by ordinary Pyrex glass equipment. Further, traces of adventitious initiator are often adequate to bring about reaction, even in the dark or in the absence of added peroxides, etc. The ease of C—Br bond scission also decreases the complication of telomer formation, so that little excess CCl_3Br is required, and high yields of 1:1 product can be obtained with many polymerizable olefins, even including styrene. Addition also occurs with acetylenes where the CCl_4 reaction fails.[32]

Reactions in which either olefin or substrate (or both) contain several fluorine atoms are of particular interest as routes to highly fluorinated products and thus make up a special group, collected in

TABLE 6·5 ALKYL POLYHALIDE ADDITIONS YIELDING FLUORINATED
PRODUCTS

Halide	Olefin	Conditions[a]	Product, % yield	Footnote
CCl_3Br	$CF_2{=}CFCl$	...	$CCl_3CF_2CFClBr$	33
	$CH_2{=}CHCF_3$	...	$CCl_3CH_2CHBrCF_3$	34
	$CF_2{=}CHCH_3$	L	$CCl_3CH(CH_3)CF_2Br$	35
CCl_3I	$CH_2{=}CHCF_3$	L, T	$CCl_3CH_2CHICF_3$ (57)	51
	$CH{\equiv}CCF_3$	L	$CCl_3CH{=}CICF_3$ (74)	51
CF_3I	Ethylene	L, T	$CF_3CH_2CH_2I$ (82), T	36
	$CH_2{=}CHF$	L	CF_3CH_2CHFI (65)	39
	$CH_2{=}CHCl$	L	CF_3CH_2CHClI (47)	39
	$CH_2{=}CF_2$	L	$CF_3CH_2CF_2I$	40
	$CF_2{=}CFCl$	...	CF_3CF_2CFClI, T	33, 38
	$CF_2{=}CF_2$	L	$CF_3CF_2CF_2I$, T	36, 37
	Acetylene	L, T	$CF_3CH{=}CHI$ (78)	41, 42
	Propylene	L	$CF_3CH_2CHICH_3$ (50)	39
	$CH_2{=}CHCF_3$	L, T	$CF_3CH_2CHICF_3$ (68)	34, 43
	$CF_2{=}CHCH_3$	L	$CF_3CH(CH_3)CF_2I$ (77)	35
	$CF_3CH{=}CF_2$	L	$(CF_3)_2CHCF_2I$ (80)	44
	$CF_2{=}CFCF_3$	L	$CF_3CF_2CFICF_3$, T	45
	$CH{\equiv}CCH_3$	L	$CF_3CH{=}CICH_3$ (91)	46, 47
	$CH{\equiv}CCF_3$	L	$CF_3CH{=}CICF_3$	47
	Acrylonitrile	L	CF_3CH_2CHICN (72), T	48
	Methyl acrylate	L	$CF_3CH_2CHICOOMe$ (38)	39
	$CH_2{=}C(CF_3)_2$	L	$CF_3CH_2CI(CF_3)_2$ (71)	35
	$CH_2{=}C(CF_3)CF_2Cl$	L	$CF_3CH_2CI(CF_3)CF_2Cl$ (69)	35
	$CH{\equiv}CC_2F_5$	L	$CF_3CH{=}CIC_2H_5$	47
CF_2Br_2	Ethylene	B	$CF_2BrCH_2CH_2Br$, T	49
	$CH_2{=}CHF$	B	CF_2BrCH_2CHFBr (34), T	50
	$CH_2{=}CF_2$	B	$CF_2BrCH_2CF_2Br$ (28), T	50
	$CHF{=}CF_2$	B	$CF_2BrCHFCF_2Br$ (9), T	50
	Propylene	B	$CF_2BrCH_2CHBrCH_3$	49
	$CHF{=}CHCH_3$	B	$CF_2BrCHFCHBrCH_3$ (55)	50
	2-Butene	B	$CF_2BrCH(CH_3)CHBrCH_3$	49
	$CH_3CH{=}CFCH_3$	B	$CF_2BrCH(CH_3)CFBrCH_3$	50
$CF_2BrCFClBr$	Ethylene	B	$CF_2BrCFClCH_2CH_2Br$ (58)	52
	$CH_2{=}CHF$	B	$CF_2BrCFClCH_2CHFBr$ (74)	53
	$CH_2{=}CF_2$	B	$CF_2BrCFClCH_2CF_2Br$ (44), T	53
	$CHF{=}CF_2$	B	$CF_2BrCFClCHFCF_2Br$ (16), T	53
	Propylene	B	$CF_2BrCFClCH_2CHBrCH_3$ (83)	52
	Allyl chloride	B	$CF_2BrCFClCH_2CHBrCH_2Cl$ (45)	52
	Isobutylene	B	$CF_2BrCFClCH_2CBr(CH_3)_2$ (43)	52
	2-Butene	B	$CF_2BrCFClCH(CH_3)CHBrCH_3$ (35)	52
	1-Octene	B	$CF_2BrCFClCH_2CHBrC_6H_{13}$ (34)	52
$CF_2ClCFClI$	$CH_2{=}CFCl$	B	$CF_2ClCFClCH_2CFClI$ (45)	53
	$CHF{=}CF_2$	B	$CF_2ClCFClCHFCF_2I$ (79)	53
	$CH_2{=}CHCF_3$	B	$CF_2ClCFClCH_2CHICF_3$ (95)	53
	$CF_2{=}CHCH_3$	B	$CF_2ClCFClCH(CH_3)CF_2I$ (89)	53
	$CH_2{=}C(CH_3)CF_3$	B	$CF_2ClCFClCH_2CI(CH_3)CF_3$ (87)	53
$CF_3CF_2CF_2I$	Acetylene	T	$C_3F_7CH{=}CHI$ (90)	37
$CF_3CF_2CFICF_3$	Acetylene	T	$C_2F_5CF(CF_3)CH{=}CHI$ (83)	45
$CF_2{=}CFI$	Ethylene	L	$CF_2{=}CFCH_2CH_2I$ (67)	53a
	$CH_2{=}CHF$	L	$CF_2{=}CFCH_2CHFI$ (50)	53a
	$CH_2{=}CF_2$	L	$CF_2{=}CFCH_2CF_2I$ (24)	53a
	$CF_2{=}CFI$	L	$CF_2{=}CFCF_2CFI_2$ (50)	53a
	$CF_2{=}CHCl$	L	$CF_2{=}CFCHClCF_2I$ (4)	53a

[a] T = Thermal reaction at approximately 200°. For other symbols, see Tables 6·3 and 6·4.

33 A. L. Henne and D. W. Kraus, J. Am. Chem. Soc., **76**, 1175 (1954).
34 A. L. Henne and M. Nager, ibid., **73**, 5527 (1951).
35 R. N. Haszeldine, J. Chem. Soc., **1953**, 3565.
36 R. N. Haszeldine, ibid., **1949**, 2856.
37 R. N. Haszeldine, ibid., **1950**, 3037.
38 R. N. Haszeldine and B. R. Steele, ibid., **1953**, 1562.
39 R. N. Haszeldine, ibid., **1953**, 1199.
40 R. N. Haszeldine and B. R. Steele, ibid., **1954**, 923.
41 R. N. Haszeldine, ibid., **1950**, 3037.
42 R. N. Haszeldine, ibid., **1951**, 588.
43 R. N. Haszeldine, ibid., **1952**, 2504.
44 R. N. Haszeldine and B. R. Steele, ibid., **1955**, 3005.
45 R. N. Haszeldine, ibid., **1953**, 3559.
46 R. N. Haszeldine and K. Leedham, ibid., **1954**, 1261.
47 K. Leedham and R. N. Haszeldine, ibid., **1954**, 1634.
48 R. N. Haszeldine, ibid., **1952**, 3490.
49 P. Tarrant and A. M. Lovelace, J. Am. Chem. Soc., **76**, 3466 (1954).
50 P. Tarrant, A. M. Lovelace, and M. R. Lilyquist, ibid., **77**, 2783 (1955).
51 R. N. Haszeldine, J. Chem. Soc., **1953**, 922.
52 P. Tarrant and E. G. Gillman, J. Am. Chem. Soc., **76**, 5423 (1954).
53 P. Tarrant and M. R. Lilyquist, ibid., **77**, 3640 (1955).
53a J. D. Park, R. J. Seffl, and J. R. Lacher, ibid., **78**, 59 (1956).

TABLE 6·6   ADDITION OF MISCELLANEOUS ALKYL POLYHALIDES TO OLEFINS

Halide	Olefin	Conditions [a]	Product, % yield	Footnote
CH_2ClI	Ethylene	...	$CH_2ClCH_2CH_2I$, T	5
$CHCl_3$	Ethylene	...	$CCl_3CH_2CH_3$, T	5
	Propylene	B	$CCl_3CH_2CH_2CH_3$, T	10
	1-Octene	B	$CCl_3CH_2CH_2C_6H_{13}$ (22)	4
	Biallyl	A	$C_7H_{11}Cl_3$ (5)	4
$CHCl_2Br$	Vinyl acetate		$CHCl_2CH_2CHBrOAc$	54
	Propylene		$CHCl_2CH_2CHBrCH_3$	54
	Isobutylene		$CHCl_2CH_2CBr(CH_3)_2$	54
	1-Octene		$CHCl_2CH_2CHBrC_6H_{13}$	54
$CHBr_3$	1-Octene	A	$CHBr_2CH_2CHBrC_6H_{13}$ (31)	4
	Styrene	B	$CHBr_2CH_2CHBr\phi$ (10), T	4
CHI_3	$CH_2{=}CHCH_2OCO\phi$	A	$CHI_2CH_2CHICH_2OCO\phi$	55
	Limonene	A	(cyclohexene ring structure, CH_2CHI_2 substituent) (35)	55
CCl_2Br_2	Propylene		$CCl_2BrCH_2CHBrCH_3$	54
	Isobutylene		$CCl_2BrCH_2CBr(CH_3)_2$	54
CBr_4	Ethylene	L	$CBr_3CH_2CH_2Br$	4
	Styrene	L	$CBr_3CH_2CHBr\phi$ (96)	4
	1-Octene	L, A	$CBr_3CH_2CHBrC_6H_{13}$ (96)	4
ϕ_2CHCCl_3	Ethylene		$\phi_2CHCCl_2CH_2CH_2Cl$, T	56
$BrCH_2CN$	1-Octene	B	$NCCH_2CH_2CHBrC_6H_{13}$ (66)	57
$BrCH_2COOEt$	1-Octene	A	$EtOCOCH_2CH_2CHBrC_6H_{13}$ (48)	58
$CHCl_2COOMe$	1-Octene	A	$MeOCOCCl_2CH_2CH_2C_6H_{13}$ (40)	59
$CHBr_2CN$	Allyl acetate	B	$NCCHBrCH_2CHBrCH_2OAc$ (52)	57
CCl_3CN	Ethylene	B	$NCCCl_2CH_2CH_2Cl$, T	57
	1-Octene	B	$NCCCl_2CH_2CHClC_6H_{13}$ (66)	57
CCl_3COCl	1-Octene	A	$ClCOCCl_2CH_2CHClC_6H_{13}$ (81)	59
CH_2ClCCl_2CN	Allyl acetate	B	$NCCCl(CH_2Cl)CH_2CHClCH_2OAc$	57
	1-Octene	B	$NCCCl(CH_2CL)CH_2CHClC_6H_{13}$ (74)	57
$CH_3CHBrCOOEt$	1-Octene	A	$EtOCOCH(CH_3)CH_2CHBrC_6H_{13}$ (64)	58
$CH_3CHBrCOO\text{-}t\text{-}Bu$	1-Octene	A	$t\text{-}BuOCOCH(CH_3)CH_2CHBrC_6H_{13}$ (49)	58
$C_2H_5CHBrCOOEt$	1-Octene	A	$EtOCOCH(C_2H_5)CH_2CHBrC_6H_{13}$ (47)	58
$(CH_3)_2CBrCOOEt$	1-Octene	A	$EtOCOC(CH_3)_2CH_2CHBrC_6H_{13}$ (24)	58
$CHBr(COOEt)_2$	1-Octene	A	$(EtOCO)_2CHCH_2CHBrC_6H_{13}$ (58)	58
$CCl_2(COOEt)_2$	Ethylene		$(EtOCO)_2CCl_2CH_2CH_2Cl$, T	59a
CH_3COCCl_2COOEt	1-Octene	B	$EtOCOCCl(COCH_3)CH_2CHClC_6H_{13}$ (28)	59a
$\begin{array}{c}CCl_3CHCOOCH_3\\ \mid \\ BrCHCOOCH_3\end{array}$	1-Octene	...	$\begin{array}{c}CCl_3CHCOOCH_3\\ \mid \quad (80)\\ C_6H_{13}CH{=}CHCHCOOCH_3\end{array}$	30
CCl_3CHO	β-Pinene	B	(cyclohexane ring structure with CH_2CCl_2CHO and Cl substituents)	59b

[a] For significance of symbols, cf. Tables 6·3–6·5

54 M. S. Kharasch, B. M. Kuderna, and W. Urry, *J. Org. Chem.*, **13**, 895 (1948).
55 M. Weizmann, S. Israelashvili, A. Halevy, and F. Bergmann, *J. Am. Chem. Soc.*, **69**, 2569 (1947).
56 E. C. Ladd, U.S. 2,609,402 (September 2, 1952).
57 E. C. Ladd, U.S. 2,615,915 (October 28, 1952).
58 M. S. Kharasch, P. S. Skell, and P. Fisher, *J. Am. Chem. Soc.*, **70**, 1055 (1948).
59 M. S. Kharasch, W. H. Urry, and E. V. Jensen, *J. Am. Chem. Soc.*, **67**, 1626 (1945).
59a E. C. Ladd, U.S. 2,577,422 (December 4, 1951).
59b M. Vilkas, G. DuPont, and R. Dulou, *Bull. Soc. Chim. France*, **1955**, 799.

Table 6·5. The majority of results are due to Haszeldine and his group, who have made an extensive investigation of additions involving trifluoromethyl iodide, CF_3I. The occasional formation of telomers noted in the table suggests that the ease of radical attack on CF_3I lies between that of CCl_4 and CCl_3Br, the lower apparent resonance stabilization of the $\cdot CF_3$ radical compared with $\cdot CCl_3$ being partially balanced by the lower strength of the C—I bond.

In general, the fluorocarbon products of Table 6·5 are those anticipated, but the addition of CF_3I to $CF_3CH{=}CF_2$ is noteworthy, in that addition of the $\cdot CF_3$ radical occurs to the non-terminal carbon.[44] Resonance stabilization of the resulting $-\overset{\cdot}{C}F_2$ radical is suggested by Haszeldine as the determining factor, but it is interesting that, in the apparent radical addition of HBr, addition is in the reverse direction.[44]

Table 6·6 summarizes data on a variety of other halides which are reactive enough to yield 1:1 adducts under suitable conditions, and contains a number of points of interest.

Carbon tetrabromide and CCl_2Br_2 appear to behave much like CCl_3Br. Bromoform, iodoform, and $CHCl_2Br$ react to give 1:1 products of the general structure CX_2CH_2CHXR and, with addition of CH_2ClI, scission of the C—I bond also occurs.

Chloroform is in interesting contrast in that here the C—H bond is broken to give products of the type $CCl_3-CH_2CH_2R$. This might appear as a useful way of introducing the CCl_3 group, but Cl_3C-H bond cleavage appears to be a relatively slow reaction, occurring readily only with very reactive radicals, and, even here, telomer formation is an important complication.

A number of α-haloesters and other α-haloacid derivatives also undergo addition involving C—X bond scission. Although this suggests a number of synthetic possibilities, the reaction is again limited to relatively reactive radicals and may not have the scope of, say, the CCl_3Br addition.

Finally, Table 6·6 contains results on a number of miscellaneous halo compounds, which do not merit individual comment but give an idea of possible variants of synthetic utility.

6·2b   Relative Reactivity in Addition Reactions; Telomer Formation

Turning now to a more detailed examination of the relation between structure and reactivity, as in the case of polymerization, information can often be obtained most simply by a consideration of competitive reactions. Relative reactivities of various olefins towards $\cdot CCl_3$ radicals have been investigated by Kharasch and his group [24, 26, 31] by reacting mixtures of two olefins with a limited amount of CCl_3Br and examining the composition of the product, determined by the competition.

$$\cdot CCl_3 \begin{cases} \overset{CH_2=CHR_1}{\nearrow}{}^{k_{a1}} CCl_3CH\dot{C}HR_1 \xrightarrow{CCl_3Br} CCl_3CH_2CHBrR_1 \\ \underset{CH_2=CHR_2}{\searrow}{}_{k_{a2}} CCl_3CH_2\dot{C}HR_2 \xrightarrow{CCl_3Br} CCl_3CH_2CHBrR_2 \end{cases} \tag{25}$$

Data, representing the relative value of k_a's are summarized in Table 6·7.

TABLE 6·7   RELATIVE REACTIVITIES OF OLEFINS TOWARDS THE $\cdot CCl_3$ RADICAL [24, 26, 31]

(1-Octene taken as unity unless indicated)

Olefin	Relative Reactivity	Olefin	Relative Reactivity
Styrene	100	Ethyl cinnamate	0.80
Butadiene	18	Cyclopentene	0.80
Cyclopentadiene	4.5	Vinyl acetate	0.8
Cyclohexadiene	4.0	Ethylvinyl acetate	0.7
Indene	3.0		
Methallyl chloride	1.6	Allyl benzene	0.7
2-Ethyl-1-butene	1.4	Allyl chloride	0.5
	1.2	Allyl cyanide	0.3
β-Methylstyrene	1.1	4,4,4-trichloro-1-butene	0.3
Dicyclopentadiene	1.05	Cyclohexene	0.24
1-Octene	1.0		0.11
2-Methyl-1-butene	0.9	Butadiene sulfone	0.06
Styrene [a]	1.0	Butadiene [a]	2.0
p-Chlorostyrene [a]	1.0	α-Methylstyrene [a]	4.2

[a] Styrene as reference olefin.

Results are in good qualitative agreement with the more extensive data on olefin reactivities obtained in copolymerization studies (Chapter 4).

Styrene and butadiene, which yield resonance-stabilized radicals, are notably more reactive than simple terminal olefins. The data at the bottom of Table 6·7, in which reactivities of these monomers are directly compared, are probably most reliable, and, taking into account the fact that that butadiene has two possible sites of attack, indicate that vinyl and phenyl groups again have about the same activating effect on the double bond. The lowered reactivity of 1,2-disubstituted olefins, β-methylstyrene and ethyl cinnamate versus styrene, and most of the cyclic olefins versus 1-octene, shows that steric hindrance is important in these additions. Our discussions in Chapter 4 suggest that $\cdot CCl_3$ should be an "acceptor-type" radical, preferentially attacking double bonds with electron-donating groups, and this, in turn, is borne out by the lowered reactivity of allyl cyanide, butadiene sulfone, and the chloroölefins.

Quantitative data on relative reactivities in the displacement step of radical additions, i.e., the relative rates of attack of a given hydrocarbon upon different halomethanes, are available from two sources: competitive reactions in which an olefin is exposed to a radical source in the presence of a mixture of substrates, and measurement of initial transfer constants as described in Section 6·1b.

The order of reactivity is certainly $I > Br > Cl$, since CF_3I is the only trifluoromethyl halide which undergoes ready radical addition to any olefin, and CCl_4 may be used as a convenient solvent for CCl_3Br additions.[10]   A more quantitative measurement is not available for radicals from simple olefins, but transfer constants (Table 4·13) show that CBr_4 is 150 times as reactive as CCl_4 toward radicals from polymerizing styrene.

Increasing reactivity thus parallels decreasing strength of the C—X bond involved in the displacement, even though the overall energy change should be essentially the same. We may also note that all displacement steps between radicals from simple olefins and trichloromethyl and tribromomethyl halides are somewhat exothermic, since the $\cdot CCl_3$ and $\cdot CBr_3$ radicals are stabilized by some 12 kcal of resonance energy (cf. Table 2·3).

The reactivity and behavior of chloroform is particularly interesting, since here displacement occurs preferentially at the C—H bond, the greater resonance energy of the $\cdot CCl_3$ radical formed apparently overbalancing the greater strength of the C—H bond involved. Actually, the balance is rather close, since in additions of $CDCl_3$, where the rate of C—D bond cleavage is reduced about

11- to 12-fold due to the isotope effect, significant amounts of C—Cl cleavage occur.[60] Interesting differences also have been pointed out by Lewis and Mayo[7] in the relative reactivities of chloroform and carbon tetrachloride towards different radicals. Although carbon tetrachloride is almost exactly as reactive as chloroform towards radicals from ethylene, with propylene the $CCl_4/CHCl_3$ reactivity ratio is 5–10, with vinyl acetate 60, and with styrene 180. The origin of the difference is obscure, but several factors may be involved. First, one is changing from a system in which the displacement is exothermic to one where it is endothermic, so the strength of the bond involved in the displacement may become increasingly important. Second, carbon tetrachloride should be a better acceptor substrate, and polar factors may be involved. Finally, at least in the case of styrene, the transition state involving carbon tetrachloride could have a lowered energy because of interaction between the chlorine atom and the π electrons of the benzene ring in much the same way that benzyl halide bonds appear to be strengthened on the basis of their increased bond dissociation energies (cf. Chapter 2).

No quantitative data are available on the relative reactivities towards radicals from simple olefins of CCl_4 or CCl_3Br or of the more complicated substrates of Table 6·6 containing carbonyl or nitrile groups. However, ethyl bromoacetate and ethyl α-bromo-butyrate are reported to have approximately the same reactivity towards radicals from 1-octene, whereas ethyl α-bromoisobutyrate is at least eight times as reactive.[58] Additional quantitative information would certainly be welcome.

The addition of CH_2ClI to ethylene gives much telomer,[56] and, in fact, no successful additions to obtain 1:1 products in good yield have been reported for halomethanes containing less than three halogen atoms unless the bonds are further activated by conjugation with —CO— or —CN groups. Quantitative evidence of the low reactivity of such molecules is given by measurements of transfer constants with ethylene,[61] Table 6·8. The data are actually for reactions of rather long chains, and, as indicated further below, initial transfer constants are probably lower still. Such reactions are almost thermo-

[60] F. W. Stacey, thesis, University of Chicago, 1953. Calculation indicates that, in reaction with 1-octene, attack on C—H bonds occurs 50–60 times as readily as on C—Cl.

[61] J. R. Little, L. W. Hartzel, F. O. Guenther, and F. R. Mayo, private communication.

TABLE 6·8 TRANSFER CONSTANTS FOR HALOALKANES AND ETHYLENE [61]

(70°, chiefly at 340 atmospheres ethylene pressure, benzoyl peroxide initiator)

Alkyl halide	C	Alkyl halide	C
CH_3Cl	0.0004	CH_3CH_2Cl	0.012
CH_2Cl_2	0.07	CH_3CHCl_2	0.15
$CHCl_3$	0.8	CH_3CCl_3	0.05
CCl_4	0.7	$(CH_3)_2CHCl$	0.025
		$(CH_3)_3Cl$	0.004

neutral, regardless of whether C—H or C—Cl scission occurs, and they thus lack the driving forces of production of a highly resonance-stabilized radical and also the polar interaction between the several electron-withdrawing groups of polyhalomethanes and electron-supplying hydrocarbon radicals.

As we have noted earlier, systems in which displacement and monomer addition compete on an approximately equal basis offer interesting possibilities for telomer synthesis. Further, the manner in which transfer constants vary with chain length is of considerable interest. The rather limited available data [7,62,63] are summarized in Table 6·9, and it is evident that transfer constants increase as much

TABLE 6·9 VARIATION OF TRANSFER CONSTANTS FOR POLYHALOMETHANES WITH CHAIN LENGTH

System	C_1	C_2	C	Footnote
Ethylene–CCl_4 (70°)	0.08	1.9	3.2 [a]	62
Propylene–CCl_4 (100°)	1.3		5–10	7
Propylene–$CHCl_3$ (100°)	0.11 ± 0.01	0.55 ± 0.03	1.03 ± 0.05	7
Isobutylene–CCl_4 (100°)	1.4 ± 0.4		17 ± 3	7
Allyl chloride–CCl_4 (100°)	0.01 − 0.02	0.10 ± 0.05	0.48 ± 0.03	7
Allyl acetate–CCl_4 (100°)	0.01 ± 0.01	0.5 ± 0.2	2.0 ± 1.0	7
Styrene–CCl_4 (76°)	0.0006	0.0025	0.0115 [b]	63

[a] Actually C_3.
[b] $C_3 = 0.007$.

as 50-fold as chains reach a length of 2–4, and then become constant for chains of greater length.

Two plausible explanations exist for this variation.[7] First, the presence of a CCl_3 group not too many carbons removed from the radical end of a short chain may reduce its donor properties, and thus

[62] J. R. Little, C. H. Stiteler, F. O. Guenther, and F. R. Mayo, private communication.

[63] R. A. Gregg and F. R. Mayo, J. Am. Chem. Soc., **70**, 3689 (1948).

the value of k_d, in systems like these, subject to a strong polar effect. Second, with substituted ethylenes steric effects making addition of additional monomer units difficult increase rapidly with the addition of the first few units (Section 5·4a), so that k_p may decrease for the first few steps. It seems likely that both of these phenomena may occur in suitable systems.

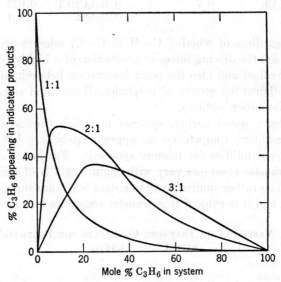

FIG. 6·1   Effect of propylene/CHCl$_3$ ratio on product distribution in the addition of CHCl$_3$ to propylene.

The variation in transfer constants with chain length, whatever its cause, has a profound effect on yields of telomers of various length. As discussed in Section 6·1b, once C's are known, product distributions can be calculated for any particular monomer-addend combination. A typical distribution curve, for propylene-chloroform, appears in Fig. 6·1. A high yield of 1:1 product is obtained only at very low propylene concentration, whereas yields of the successive low telomers go through flat maxima at successively higher propylene concentrations. Although these maxima are each somewhat higher than they would be if C's were independent of chain length, it is evident that appreciable yields of any individual telomer above about $n = 3$ cannot be expected. This, in turn, suggests at least one reason why such telomer-forming reactions have not so far proved of much practical importance.

Figure 6·1 refers to the distribution of products arising from a given feed at any instant, although, in general, in any batch process the composition of reactants will be continually changing. Accordingly, in any real process, actual distribution curves (except for the 1:1 product) will be flattened and lowered. In practice, the flattening can be partially compensated for by continually adding the component which is being most rapidly consumed. Similarly, when the 1:1 product is desired and C_1 is low, it is sometimes possible to obtain a good yield and good conversion of the addend by slowly adding olefin as it is consumed during the entire course of the reaction. Patrick [14] has described such a technique for reacting equimolecular quantities of carbon tetrachloride and vinyl acetate and getting 39% 1:1 and 44% 2:1 products, with high overall conversion even though C_1 and C_2 are probably much smaller than unity.

6·2c   Overall Rates in Halomethane Additions; Complications of Allylic Termination

The problem of overall rates in radical addition processes, although of more practical importance than mere relative reactivities of olefins and substrates, is necessarily much more complex because of the large number of rate constants involved. Such systems have received much less investigation than polymerizations, but Lewis and Mayo [7] have indicated a very promising method of attacking the problem by determining the variation in yields with substrate-olefin ratio in systems in which a fixed amount of initiator is allowed to decompose completely. Although such a technique is not a direct measure of rate, yields under these conditions are related to the actual kinetic chain lengths and are thus of theoretical as well as practical significance. Their data, for a number of systems involving carbon tetrachloride and chloroform, reacted in the presence of 0.01 mole % benzoyl peroxide at 70–100°, are summarized in Fig. 6·2, where moles of solvent reacted per mole of initiator have been plotted against mole fraction of solvent. In every case the yield goes through a pronounced maximum, although the position and height of these maxima vary from system to system. Their existence follows readily from the kinetics developed in Section 6·1b. At high mole fraction of solvent, chain termination is largely by interaction of $\cdot CCl_3$ radicals, and the reaction rate follows eq. 10, rising linearly with olefin concentration. At high olefin concentration, alkyl radicals are the dominant species, eq. 9 is followed, and the rate rises linearly with the concentration of solvent. At the

maxima, both types of chain termination occur, and the maxima
are presumably further rounded off and lowered by cross termination between $\cdot CCl_3$ and alkyl radicals. The height and position

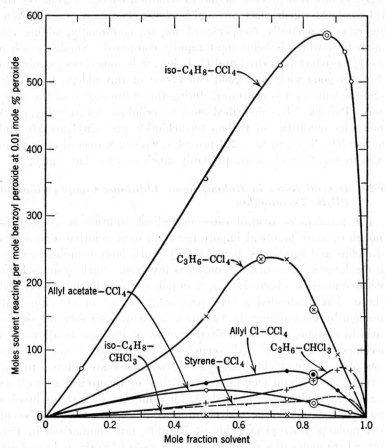

FIG. 6·2   Variation in yield with solvent–monomer ratio in radical addition of
halomethanes to olefins.[7]

of the maxima also are in keeping with our ideas of radical reactivities. Thus *t*-butyl radicals should be less reactive than isopropyl
radicals and should remain the major species in the system up to a
higher mole fraction of solvent, and the isobutylene–CCl_4 maximum
lies further to the right than that for propylene–CCl_4. The steeper
rise and higher maximum yield with isobutylene may result either
from a greater reactivity of the isobutylene double bond, or a lower

combination rate for tertiary radicals. Again, the lower maximum observed with propylene–CHCl$_3$, compared with propylene–CCl$_4$, together with its shift to the right, could follow from the lower reactivity of chloroform compared with carbon tetrachloride. Isobutylene, with a less reactive radical, is apparently unable to attack chloroform rapidly enough to maintain a satisfactory chain.

Lewis and Mayo's results also indicate the importance of degradative chain transfer in radical addition processes. From eq. 11 allylic attack by radicals to give an inactive product results in a flattening off of the yield curve which is particularly indicated by the allyl chloride–CCl$_4$ and allyl acetate–CCl$_4$ systems. Better evidence may be obtained by varying the initiator concentration at a fixed monomer-solvent ratio since bimolecular termination predicts a yield proportional to the square root of initiator concentration, whereas allylic termination gives a first-order relation (cf. Section 4·3e). This has been done at the points indicated by large circles, and leads to the conclusion that considerable allylic termination is involved in isobutylene–CCl$_4$ and also propylene–CCl$_4$ and –CHCl$_3$.

Conclusive evidence of allylic attack by ·CCl$_3$ radicals has been obtained by Israelashvili and Shabatay,[9] who have shown that 3-chlorocyclohexene is a product in the reaction of CCl$_4$ with cyclohexene. The matter has been investigated in greater detail by Kooyman and Farenhorst,[8] who have made a complete study of the products obtained on decomposing benzoyl peroxide in cyclohexene-carbon tetrachloride mixtures. Results are listed in Table 6·10. From the data it is evident that most chains are initiated by addition of benzoate radicals to cyclohexene, and the resulting radicals are able to attack carbon tetrachloride. However, the ·CCl$_3$ radicals evidently abstract allylic hydrogen to yield chloroform about as readily as they add to the cyclohexene bond, and the cyclohexenyl radicals which result chiefly dimerize. Chains are thus very short.

With 1-heptene and propylene,[8] chains are longer, 23 and 11.5 respectively under the experimental conditions employed, but again in each case chloroform was isolated in 65% yield, based upon the initial radicals formed from the benzoyl peroxide. In contrast, t-butylethylene, with no allylic hydrogens, gave very long chains and no chloroform, the only product from ·CCl$_3$ radicals, in addition to the normal addition product, being traces of C$_2$Cl$_6$.[8, 64] The importance of similar degradative chain transfer with cetene was

[64] E. C. Kooyman, *Rec. trav. chim.*, **69**, 492 (1950).

TABLE 6·10 PRODUCTS OBTAINED ON DECOMPOSING BENZOYL PEROXIDE
IN CYCLOHEXENE–CCl₄ [8]

(Yield in moles/mole ϕCOO· radicals produced)

(cyclohexyl benzoate structure, OCOφ / Cl) 0.55	CHCl₃	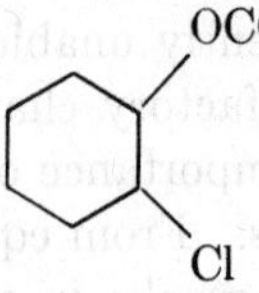 0.95
Benzene, 0.08	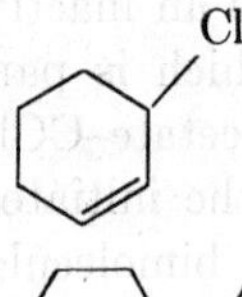 (3-chlorocyclohexene structure, Cl)	0.11
Chlorobenzene, 0.10	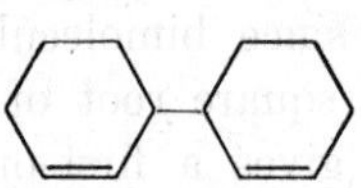 (bicyclohexenyl structure)	0.60
Benzoic acid, 0.12 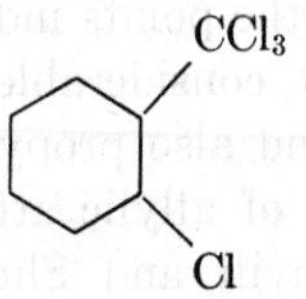	(trichloromethylcyclohexane structure, CCl₃ / Cl)	0.89
CO₂, 0.11		

also indicated by kinetic measurement, which showed a reaction rate proportional to the peroxide concentration.[65] The various reactions involved in such systems have been diagrammed in an illuminating manner by Kooyman, as shown in Fig. 6·3.

In contrast to carbon tetrachloride, CCl₃Br adds readily to cyclohexene by a long-chain process,[24, 31] and kinetic measurements indicate a square-root dependence on initiator concentration.[66] Since the same ·CCl₃ radicals are involved in the chain, considerable attack on allylic hydrogens must take place, but presumably the resulting cyclohexenyl radicals are able to attack the more reactive CCl₃Br and carry on the chain:

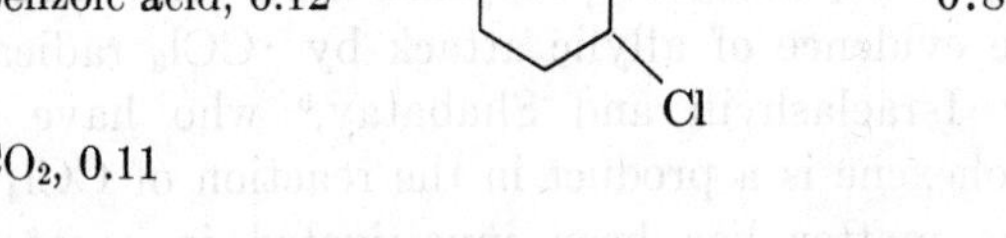

$$\text{(cyclohexene)} + \text{BrCCl}_3 \rightarrow \text{(3-bromocyclohexene)} + \cdot\text{CCl}_3 \qquad (26)$$

The expected 3-bromocyclohexene has never been identified among the addition products, but it is interesting that Kharasch [24] obtained

[65] E. C. Kooyman, *Discussions Faraday Soc.*, **10**, 163 (1951).
[66] H. W. Melville, J. C. Robb, and R. C. Tutton, *ibid.*, **14**, 150 (1953).

considerable quantities of low-boiling material from his additions with about the right physical properties for this substance.

The ability of $\cdot CCl_3$ radicals to abstract hydrogen rather than add to olefinic double bonds has been studied at greater length by

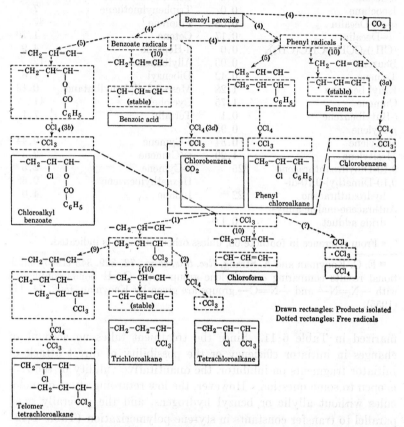

Fig. 6·3   Major reaction paths and products in the reaction of benzoyl peroxide, CCl_4, and olefins (after Kooyman and Farenhorst [8]).

Kooyman by determining the retarding effect of various substances on the CCl_4-cetene reaction.[65] The kinetics of such systems are essentially the same as those of inhibited polymerizations, cf. Section 4·3d, and Kooyman's analysis gives a quantity K_r, proportional to the rate constant for attack of the $\cdot CCl_3$ radical on inhibitor, divided by the rate constant for addition to cetene.[67] Results are sum-

---

[67] If all peroxide fragments were effective in starting chains, K_r would be actually one-half of this ratio.

TABLE 6·11　RETARDATION CONSTANTS, K_r, FOR VARIOUS SUBSTANCES ON
THE CCl_4-CETENE REACTION [a]

Substance	$K_r \times 10^2$	Substance	$K_r \times 10^2$
n-decane	0.0	Diphenylmethane	3.35
Isooctane	0.0	Triphenylmethane	7
trans-Decalin	0.08	Fluorene	47
cis-Decalin	0.17	Cetene	1.79
$(CH_3)_3CCH=CHC(CH_3)_3$	0.0	3-Heptene	4.9
Benzene	0.03	Allylbenzene	12
Toluene	0.42	Dibenzyl	1.3
Ethyl benzene	1.28	Meso-2,3-diphenylbutane	0.13
Cumene	1.75	Cyclohexene	11
t-Butylbenzene	0.1	Tetralin	7.1
p-Xylene	0.95		
m-Xylene	0.84	o-Cymene	0.44 [68]
Mesitylene	1.29	m-Cymene	2.3 [68]
9,10-Dihydroanthracene	325	p-Cymene	2.5 [68]
9,10-Dimethyl-9,10-di-		Hexaethylbenzene	0.68 [68]
hydroanthracene	22 [68]	Indane	4.0
Anthracene-maleic anhy-			
dride adduct	0.1 [68]		

[a] From reference in footnote 65, unless other reference is indicated.

[68] E. C. Kooyman and A. Strang, Rec. trav. chim., 72, 329, 343 (1953); additional results comparing α-methylene groups with C—H bonds conjugated with —N=N— and —N=C— groups are given by Kooyman, ibid., 74, 117 (1955).

marized in Table 6·11. Since the treatment takes no account of changes in initiator efficiency or the possibility of direct attack of initiator fragments on inhibitor, the quantitative validity of the K_r's is open to some question. However, the low retarding effect of molecules without allylic or benzyl hydrogens, and the generally good parallel to transfer constants in styrene polymerization (Table 4·12) suggests that Kooyman's analysis is essentially correct, although, if any of the retarder radicals are able to restart chains, actual K_r values will be larger than those given. Table 6·11 has several interesting features. Six-membered cyclic compounds, e.g., tetralin and cyclohexene, have relatively high reactivities compared with the analogous ethylbenzene and 3-hexene, even after statistical correction in the first case. o-Cymene, hexaethylbenzene, and 9,10-dimethyl-9,10-dihydroanthracene have unexpectedly low reactivities, a result ascribed by Kooyman to steric hindrance, which prevents the resulting benzyl-type radicals from realizing their full resonance stabilization. The very low reactivity of the anthracene–maleic anhydride adduct is presumably a more extreme example, since this dihydroanthracene molecule cannot give a planar radical.

Although benzene is apparently unreactive towards ·CCl₃ radicals, several polynuclear hydrocarbons are powerful retarders, even for the addition of CCl₃Br to styrene.[69] The most striking examples are 1,2-benzanthracene, anthracene, naphthacene, and 3,4-benzopyrene, the last being about 10^4 times as effective as benzene. Presumably addition occurs to the aromatic system, although products have not been isolated,[70] and Kooyman [69, 71] has pointed out an interesting correlation between reactivity and the "free valence number" of the most reactive positions calculated by Coulson.[72]

As a final extension of his technique, Kooyman has compared the retarding effects of p-cyanotoluene and p-toluic acid with toluene itself,[73] finding that all three have essentially the same K_f values $(\pm 6\%)$. Although this suggests that the ·CCl₃ has essentially no polar properties, contrary to the conclusions developed earlier, the very limited data are compatible with a situation where the contribution of resonance stabilization of the resulting p-cyano- and p-carboxybenzyl radicals to the transition state counterbalances their unfavorable polar properties in reaction with a moderately strong acceptor radical.

6·2d Rate Constants in Halomethane Additions

It should be possible to apply the same non-steady-state techniques discussed in Chapter 3 to radical addition reactions and thus determine values for the individual rate constants involved in the chain process. An attempt to do so has been described by Melville, Robb and Tutton,[66] using the rotating sector method with CCl₃Br–vinyl acetate and CCl₃Br–cyclohexene, with results summarized in Table 6·12.

The agreement between the values of k_{t2} (recombination of ·CCl₃ radicals) in the two systems is good, but, as Mayo points out,[74] in

[69] E. C. Kooyman and E. Farenhorst, *Trans. Faraday Soc.*, **49**, 58 (1953).

[70] Irradiation of anthracene in CCl₄ suppresses the normal dimerization and apparently yields products with ·CCl₃ groups substituted in the 9,10-positions; cf. Section 11·1c.

[71] E. C. Kooyman and E. Farenhorst, *Nature*, **169**, 153 (1952).

[72] C. A. Coulson, *J. chim. phys.*, **45**, 243 (1948).

[73] E. C. Kooyman, R. Van Helden, and A. F. Bickel, *Proc. Koninkl. Nederland. Akad. Wetenschap.*, **B56**, 75 (1953).

[74] F. R. Mayo, *Discussions Faraday Soc.*, **14**, 231 (1953).

TABLE 6·12   ABSOLUTE RATE CONSTANTS FOR CCl_3Br ADDITION AT $30°$ [66]

Process	Cyclohexene	Vinyl acetate
$CCl_3 \cdot + M \xrightarrow{k_a}$	256	1120
$M \cdot + CCl_3Br \xrightarrow{k_d}$	63.8	2740
$2CCl_3 \cdot \xrightarrow{2k_{t2}}$	5×10^7	5×10^7
$M \cdot + CCl_3 \cdot \xrightarrow{k_{t12}}$	28×10^7	19×10^7
$2M \cdot \xrightarrow{2k_{t1}}$	2×10^7	2.84×10^7
ϕ (av.)	6.36	35.3
E_a [a]	3.4	6.1
E_d [b]	4.5	7.5

[a] Overall activation energy at high CCl_3Br concentrations, kcal/mole.
[b] Overall activation energy at high monomer concentrations, kcal/mole.

the vinyl acetate system at high vinyl acetate–CCl_3Br ratios, where k_d and k_{t1} are determined, appreciable telomer formation must be taking place, so k_d may be too high, and k_{t1} and k_{t2} are in doubt. A still more serious difficulty arises in the cyclohexene system, where, as we have seen, allylic attack by CCl_3 radicals is approximately as important as addition, so that to just what processes k_a, k_d, k_{t1}, and k_{t12} refer is in doubt. Nevertheless, it is encouraging to see that non-steady-state methods give reproducible results in addition reactions, and a further example involving mercaptan additions is taken up in Section 7·2.

6·2e   Stereochemistry of Halomethane Additions; Rearrangements

As we have seen in our previous discussion, Section 1·4, the properties of carbon radicals indicate that they either have a planar structure or, more probably, a pyramidal structure which is easily inverted. Nevertheless, addition of a radical to one end of a disubstituted olefin, $R_1CH{=}CHR_2$, yields an asymmetric radical which may react preferentially, to yield as a product predominantly one of the two possible pairs of diastereomers. Such cases are well established for the mercaptan and hydrogen bromide addition products discussed in Chapter 7, but are more doubtful in halomethane additions. The photochemical addition of CCl_3Br to both cis- and trans-2-butene at $0–10°$ yields the same mixture of diastereomers, under conditions where unreacted olefin undergoes no isomerization, indicating that the intermediate $CCl_3CH(CH_3)\dot{C}HCH_3$ radicals are either identical or non-selective.[28] On the other hand, Kharasch and Friedlander [31] have reported that CCl_3Br addition to [2.2.1]bicyclo-

2-heptene (norbornylene), [2.2.2]bicyclo-2-octene, and dicyclopentadiene yield single products.

Since all of these products from bicyclic olefins are inert towards treatment with alcoholic KOH, Fawcett [75] has suggested that all are formed by *trans* additions which may be formulated as shown, assuming that initial attack is on the less-hindered exo side of the double bonds, and that HBr cannot be eliminated, because the only hydrogen which could be lost without producing a bridgehead olefin lies *cis* to the bromine (reaction 27). However, investigations by

$$+ \ \cdot CCl_3 \longrightarrow \quad \xrightarrow{CCl_3Br} \qquad (27)$$

Cristol make this sort of generalization doubtful in the case of bridged-ring compounds,[76] and Weinstock has recently concluded that the analogous addition of ethyl bromoacetate actually yields the exo-*cis* derivative.[77]

$$+ \ \cdot CH_2COOEt \longrightarrow \quad \xrightarrow{CH_2BrCOOEt} \qquad (28)$$

It accordingly seems probable that Kharasch's products have a similar configuration.   It is of interest to compare these radical additions with polar reactions which lead to rearranged products,[78] i.e.,

$$+ \ A^+ \longrightarrow \quad \xrightarrow{B^-} \qquad (29)$$

It seems a safe generalization that radical rearrangements are less common than those of the corresponding carbonium ions.   However,

[75] E. S. Fawcett, *Chem. Revs.*, **47**, 219 (1950).

[76] S. J. Cristol and N. L. Hause, *J. Am. Chem. Soc.*, **74**, 2193 (1952).

[77] J. Weinstock, *Am. Chemical Soc. Meeting Abstr.*, **128**, 19-O (1955).

[78] Cf. for example, C. K. Ingold, *Structure and Mechanism in Organic Chemistry*, Cornell University Press, Ithaca, New York, 1953, Chapter IX.

an interesting example of rearrangement occurs in the addition of CCl_4 to β-pinene. This reaction occurs with great ease in the presence of benzoyl peroxide to give an almost quantitative yield of a single crystalline product which has been unequivocally identified.[20,21] The reaction path appears to be as follows:

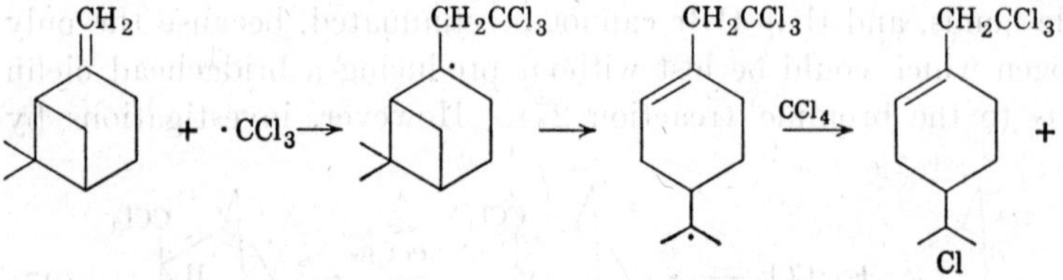
CH2
+ ·CCl3
CH2CCl3
CH2CCl3
CCl4
CH2CCl3
+ ·CCl3
Cl

(30)

Analogous products have been identified in the addition of chloroform and ethyl bromoacetate,[79] and addition is also observed (without product identification) with ethyl dichloroacetate and bromoform.[21] The driving force in such a rearrangement must be the relief of strain due to the four-membered ring in the parent pinene skeleton.

As well as these examples of rearrangement of the carbon skeleton of molecules during free radical additions, a few cases are known in which either shift or loss of a neighboring halogen atom takes place. Addition of CCl_3Br to 3,3,3-trichloropropene is reported to give, instead of the expected 1,1,1,4,4,4-hexachloro-2-bromobutane, a mixture of 1,1,1,3,4,4-hexachloro-4-bromobutane I, 1,1,4,4,4-pentachloro-1-butene II, and product $C_3H_3Cl_4Br$ III of otherwise unknown structure.[25] These products can be rationalized by the following scheme:

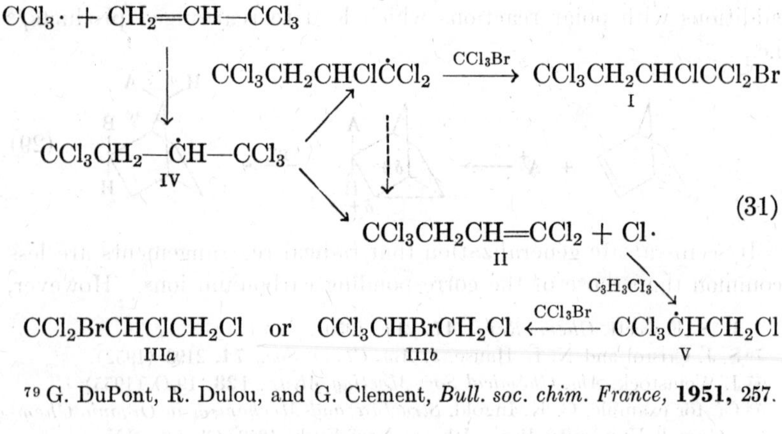
CCl3· + CH2=CH—CCl3
CCl3CH2CHClĊCl2
CCl3Br
CCl3CH2CHClCCl2Br
I
CCl3CH2—ĊH—CCl3
IV
CCl3CH2CH=CCl2 + Cl·
II
C3H3Cl3
CCl2BrCHClCH2Cl or CCl3CHBrCH2Cl
IIIa
IIIb
CCl3Br
CCl3ĊHCH2Cl
V

(31)

[79] G. DuPont, R. Dulou, and G. Clement, *Bull. soc. chim. France,* **1951,** 257.

in which the intermediate radical IV rearranges before attacking CCl_3Br to yield I. Alternatively, either before or after rearrangement, IV loses a chlorine atom to give II.[80] The chlorine atom subsequently attacks another olefin molecule to finally yield III, which may have one of two structures, depending upon whether the intermediate radical V also rearranges in turn.

Kharasch and Sage have observed unexpected products in the addition of CCl_3Br to allyl bromide, which could also be explained on the basis of β elimination of a halogen atom from an intermediate radical.[81] Irradiation of a 4:1 CCl_3Br–allyl bromide mixture at 25° gave two products, 1,2,3-tribromopropane VI and 1,1,1,5,5,5-hexachloro-3-bromopentane VII, formed possibly as follows:

$$CCl_3 \cdot + CH_2{=}CH{-}CH_2Br \rightarrow CCl_3CH_2{-}\overset{\cdot}{C}H{-}CH_2Br$$

$$\underset{\text{VII}}{CCl_3CH_2CHBrCH_2CCl_3} \xleftarrow{CCl_3Br} CCl_3CH_2\overset{\cdot}{C}HCH_2CCl_3 \xleftarrow{\cdot CCl_3} \underset{\text{VIII}}{CCl_3CH_2Cl{=}CH_2} \quad (32)$$

$$CH_2BrCHBrCH_2Br \xleftarrow{CCl_3Br} CH_2Br\overset{\cdot}{C}HCH_2Br \xleftarrow{C_3H_5Br} Br \cdot$$

When the reaction is run in excess allyl bromide, the intermediate 4,4,4-trichloro-1-butene VIII is isolated in place of VII.

Loss of halogen atoms from intermediate radicals may also account for the structure of dimers isolated from the attempted polymerization of certain haloölefins, reactions which bear a close enough resemblance to halomethane additions to be discussed at this point. However, in all of these processes the possibility of a halogen atom transfer exists as an alternative hypothesis.

Irradiation of methallyl chloride at 80° in the presence of about 0.5% tetraethyl lead as photosensitizer gives a 79% yield of dimer plus 5% higher polymers. The dimer has been unequivocally identified as 2-methyl-4,4-bischloromethyl-1-pentene by Wilzbach, Mayo, and Van Meter,[82] and the reaction chain shown in reaction 33 appears plausible, although these authors originally proposed the alter-

$$Cl \cdot + CH_2{=}\underset{\underset{CH_2Cl}{|}}{\overset{\overset{CH_3}{|}}{C}} \rightarrow Cl{-}CH_2{-}\underset{\underset{CH_2Cl}{|}}{\overset{\overset{CH_3}{|}}{C}} \cdot \xrightarrow{C_4H_7Cl} Cl{-}CH_2{-}\underset{\underset{CH_2Cl}{|}}{\overset{\overset{CH_3}{|}}{C}}{-}CH_2{-}\underset{\underset{CH_2Cl}{|}}{\overset{\overset{CH_3}{|}}{C}} \cdot \rightarrow CH_3{-}\underset{\underset{CH_2Cl}{|}}{\overset{\overset{CH_2Cl}{|}}{C}}{-}CH_2{-}\underset{}{\overset{\overset{CH_3}{|}}{C}}{=}CH_2 + Cl \cdot \quad (33)$$

[80] Although chlorine or bromine atom addition to a double bond is an exothermic process, it is accompanied by considerable entropy loss, and is readily reversible, cf. Ch. 7.

[81] M. S. Kharasch and M. Sage, *J. Org. Chem.*, **14**, 537 (1949).

[82] K. E. Wilzbach, F. R. Mayo, and R. Van Meter, *J. Am. Chem. Soc.*, **70**, 4069 (1948).

native direct transfer of halogen from the intermediate radical to methallyl chloride. The good yield of dimer in all probability arises because of the steric difficulties of stringing more than two isobutylene units together in a chain. Accordingly, dimer radicals have a long enough life for halogen loss to occur.

Allyl bromide yields a similar dimer, $CH_2Br\text{—}CH(CH_2Br)CH\text{=}CH_2$ in the presence of acetyl peroxide,[83] but allyl chloride gives essentially only polymer at temperatures below 100°. However, at 165°, the yield of dimer (although of unknown structure) is approximately 25% of all the polymeric products formed.[84] If halogen loss from an intermediate radical actually occurs, both the easier loss when bromine is involved and the increased yield with temperature are to be expected. sym-Dichloroethylene dimerizes similarly in the presence of benzoyl peroxide to give $CHCl_2\text{—}CHCl\text{—}CH\text{=}CHCl$.[85] Interestingly, at high pressures only high polymer is obtained.[86] Trichloroethylene also gives a dimer,[87] the structure of which has been investigated by Henne and Ruh,[88] who concluded it was a mixture of allylic isomers.

$$CHCl_2\text{—}CCl_2\text{—}CH\text{=}CCl_2 \qquad CHCl_2\text{—}CCl\text{=}CH\text{—}CCl_3$$
$$\text{IX} \qquad\qquad\qquad\qquad\qquad \text{X}$$

$$CHCl\text{=}CCl\text{—}CHCl\text{—}CCl_3 \qquad\qquad (34)$$
$$\text{XI}$$

However, their reasoning, based on its behavior on chlorination and fluorination, does not eliminate the possibility that it is IX alone, formed by the path shown in reaction 35.

$$Cl\cdot + CHCl\text{=}CCl_2 \rightarrow CHCl_2\text{—}\dot{C}Cl_2 \xrightarrow{C_2HCl_3}$$
$$CHCl_2\text{—}CCl_2\text{—}CHCl\text{—}\dot{C}Cl_2 \rightarrow XIII + Cl\cdot \qquad (35)$$

An interesting modification of the radical-olefin addition reaction in which free halogen atoms have been postulated has been described

[83] M. S. Kharasch and G. Büchi, J. Org. Chem., 14, 84 (1949).

[84] C. E. Frank and A. V. Blackham, J. Am. Chem. Soc., 72, 3283 (1950).

[85] W. Bauer, U.S. Pat. 2,267,712 (December 30, 1941).

[86] K. W. Weale, J. Chem. Soc., 1952, 2223. This is good evidence that actual dissociation occurs in this case; cf. Section 5·6.

[87] M. Mugden and J. Wimmer, U.S. Pat. 2,161,078 (June 6, 1939).

[88] A. L. Henne and R. P. Ruh, J. Am. Chem. Soc., 69, 279 (1947).

by Schmerling and West,[89] who have treated chloroölefins with di-t-butyl peroxide at 130–140° in the presence of saturated hydrocarbons.   Thus cyclopentane gives two products with *sym*-dichloro-ethylene by a reaction which they formulate as follows, R = cyclo-C_5H_9:

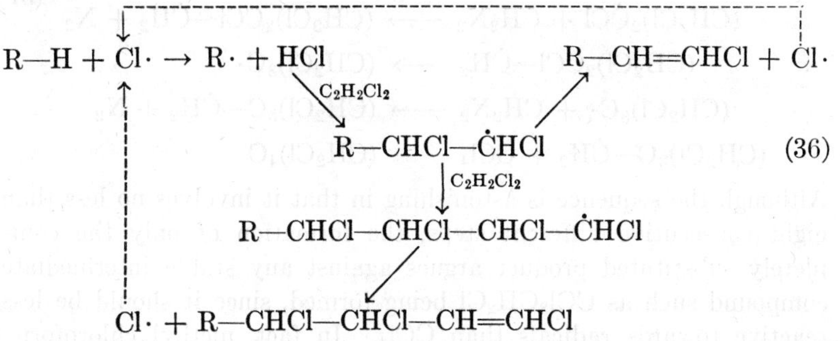

$$R-H + \dot{C}l \cdot \rightarrow R \cdot + HCl \qquad\qquad R-CH{=}CHCl + \dot{C}l \cdot$$

$$\xrightarrow{C_2H_2Cl_2}$$

$$R-CHCl-\dot{C}HCl \qquad\qquad (36)$$

$$\downarrow C_2H_2Cl_2$$

$$R-CHCl-CHCl-CHCl-\dot{C}HCl$$

$$\dot{C}l \cdot + R-CHCl-CHCl-CH{=}CHCl$$

A number of other examples are given using *sym*-dichloroethylene, trichloroethylene, and tetrachloroethylene and various paraffins. However, in general only the 1:1 products (obtained in 7–50% yields) were investigated in detail.   Relatively large quantities of initiator were required, so kinetic chains are short, generally 1–6. Similar reactions also occur with alkyl benzenes.[90]

Returning now to the reaction in which the intermediate radical undergoes a halogen shift, rather than halogen loss, this too might be formulated as dissociation, followed by readdition of the halogen atoms to the other end of the double bond.   However, recent work by Urry strongly supports a true intramolecular rearrangement, at least in the systems which he has investigated.[91]   Urry has irradiated diazomethane in excess carbon tetrachloride, obtaining as the sole halogenated product pentaerythritol tetrachloride in 60% yield. Since the reaction is very slow in the dark, rapid in moderate illumination (with a quantum yield of ~300), and inhibited by diphenyl-amine, it has the characteristics of a radical chain process, and Urry has proposed a mechanism involving initial radical production by photodissociation of the diazomethane and the following propagation sequence:

[89] L. P. Schmerling and J. P. West, *ibid.*, **71**, 2015 (1949).
[90] L. P. Schmerling and J. P. West, *ibid.*, **75**, 6216 (1953).
[91] W. H. Urry and J. R. Eiszner, *ibid.*, **74**, 5822 (1952).

$$\cdot CCl_3 + CH_2N_2 \longrightarrow CCl_3\dot{C}H_2 + N_2$$
$$CCl_3\dot{C}H_2 \longrightarrow CH_2Cl-\dot{C}Cl_2$$
$$CH_2Cl-\dot{C}Cl_2 + CH_2N_2 \longrightarrow CH_2Cl-CCl_2-\dot{C}H_2 + N_2$$
$$CH_2Cl-CCl_2-\dot{C}H_2 \longrightarrow (CH_2Cl)_2\dot{C}Cl$$
$$(CH_2Cl)_2\dot{C}Cl + CH_2N_2 \longrightarrow (CH_2Cl)_2CCl-\dot{C}H_2 + N_2 \qquad (37)$$
$$(CH_2Cl)_2CCl-\dot{C}H_2 \longrightarrow (CH_2Cl)_3C\cdot$$
$$(CH_2Cl)_3C\cdot + CH_2N_2 \longrightarrow (CH_2Cl)_3C-\dot{C}H_2 + N_2$$
$$(CH_2Cl)_3C-\dot{C}H_2 + CCl_4 \longrightarrow (CH_2Cl)_4C$$

Although the sequence is astonishing in that it involves no less than eight consecutive different steps, the formation of only the completely substituted product argues against any stable intermediate compound such as CCl_3CH_2Cl being formed, since it should be less reactive towards radicals than CCl_4. In fact, methyl chloroform, CCl_3CH_3, and CH_2ClCCl_3 both prove to be unreactive towards diazomethane.

A number of other halomethanes which undergo ready double-bond addition react similarly (Table 6·13). Urry suggests that a number

TABLE 6·13   HALOMETHANE–DIAZOMETHANE REACTIONS [91]

Halomethane	Product	Yield, %
CCl_4	$C(CH_2Cl)_4$	60
CCl_3Br	$BrCH_2C(CH_2Cl)_3$	40
$CHCl_3$	$CH_3C(CH_2Cl)_3$	45
CCl_3COOCH_3	$(CH_2Cl)_3CCOOCH_3$	60
$CH_3CHBrCOOCH_3$	$CH_3CH(CH_2Br)COOCH_3$	20
$CH_2BrCOOCH_3$	$BrCH_2CH_2COOCH_3$	...

of other reactions of diazomethane follow radical paths. Methyl diazoacetate also reacts with chloroform, carbon tetrachloride, and CCl_3Br as follows: [92]

$$CHN_2COOCH_3 + CHCl_3 \rightarrow CH_2ClCOOCH_3$$
$$+ CHCl_2-CHCl-COOCH_3$$
$$CHN_2COOCH_3 + CCl_3Br \rightarrow CCl_2Br-CHCl-COOCH_3$$
$$+ CCl_2{=}CCl-COOCH_3 \qquad (38)$$
$$CHN_2COOCH_3 + CCl_4 \rightarrow CCl_2{=}CCl-COOCH_3$$

Here, however, overall yields and quantum yields are both low and it is doubtful that radical chains are involved.

[92] W. H. Urry and J. W. Wilt, *ibid.*, **76**, 2594 (1954).

6·3   Radical Chain Processes Involving Carbonyl Compounds

6·3a   The Radical Addition of Aldehydes to Olefins

A second important group of radical addition processes are those involving aldehydes and olefins, in which addition involves the sequence

$$RC\overset{O}{{\Large\diagup}}{}\cdot + CH_2{=}CHR' \xrightarrow{k_a} R{-}C\overset{O}{{\Large\diagup}}{-}CH_2{-}\dot{C}HR' \qquad (39a)$$

$$R{-}C\overset{O}{{\Large\diagup}}{-}CH_2{-}\dot{C}HR' + H{-}CO{-}R \xrightarrow{k_d}$$

$$R{-}CO{-}CH_2CH_2R' + R{-}C\overset{O}{{\Large\diagup}}{}\cdot \qquad (39b)$$

with an acyl radical, $R{-}C\overset{O}{{\Large\diagup}}{}\cdot$ as one of the chain-carrying species.

Although the kinetics of these additions have not been elucidated, the rate constant for the simplest analog of reaction 39b in the gas phase has been determined by Dodd [93] from a study of the high-temperature photolysis of acetaldehyde, cf. Section 6·3b.

$$CH_3\cdot + HCOCH_3 \rightarrow CH_4 + CH_3C\overset{O}{{\Large\diagup}}{}\cdot \qquad (40)$$
$$k_d = 10^{12.8}(T)^{1/2}e^{-10,700/RT}$$

To the extent that this measurement can be transferred to the liquid phase, we find a somewhat higher activation energy than those for typical polymerizations (in spite of the exothermic nature of the reaction) offset to some extent by a favorable PZ factor.

The observation that the presence of acetaldehyde during the polymerization of vinyl acetate lowers the molecular weight of the product appears in a 1929 patent,[94] but the first published account of the radical addition of aldehydes to olefins to yield identifiable 1:1 products is that of Kharasch, Urry, and Kuderna in 1949.[95] Since that time, with the exception of two papers by Patrick,[96] the majority

---

[93] R. E. Dodd, *Trans. Faraday Soc.*, **47**, 56 (1951).

[94] H. W. Matheson and F. W. Skirrow, U.S. Pat. 1,725,362 (August 20, 1929).

[95] M. S. Kharasch, W. H. Urry, and B. M. Kuderna, *J. Org. Chem.*, **14**, 248 (1949).

[96] (a) T. M. Patrick, Jr., *ibid.*, **17**, 1009 (1952); (b) T. M. Patrick, Jr., *ibid.*, **17**, 1269 (1952).

TABLE 6·14 RADICAL ADDITIONS OF ALDEHYDES TO OLEFINS

(Ac$_2$O$_2$ or Bz$_2$O$_2$ initiator unless indicated)

Aldehyde	Olefin	Product	Per Cent Yield	Foot-note
Acetaldehyde	Ethylene	CH$_3$COC$_2$H$_5$ + telomer	...	97, 98
n-Butyraldehyde	Ethylene	C$_3$H$_7$COC$_2$H$_5$ + telomer	...	97
Acetaldehyde	Acetylene	CH$_2$=CHCOCH$_3$ + CH$_3$COCH$_2$CH$_2$COCH$_3$	...	105a
Acetaldehyde	Propylene	CH$_3$COCH$_2$CH$_2$CH$_3$	11	99
n-Butyraldehyde	Isobutylene	C$_3$H$_7$COCH$_2$CH(CH$_3$)$_2$	30	99
n-Butyraldehyde	1-Hexene	C$_3$H$_7$CO(CH$_2$)$_5$CH$_3$	41	95
n-Butyraldehyde	1-Octene	C$_3$H$_7$CO(CH$_2$)$_7$CH$_3$	57	95
n-Heptaldehyde	1-Octene	C$_6$H$_{13}$CO(CH$_2$)$_7$CH$_3$	75	95
Acetaldehyde	1-Octene	CH$_3$CO(CH$_2$)$_7$CH$_3$	36	99
Isobutyraldehyde	1-Octene	(CH$_3$)$_2$CHCO(CH$_2$)$_7$CH$_3$	Low	99
Acetaldehyde	1-Decene	CH$_3$CO(CH$_2$)$_9$CH$_3$	36	99
Acetaldehyde	1-Dodecene	CH$_3$CO(CH$_2$)$_{11}$CH$_3$	23	98,^{c} 99
n-Butyraldehyde	1-Dodecene	C$_3$H$_7$CO(CH$_2$)$_{11}$CH$_3$	...	98
n-Butyraldehyde	Cyclohexene	[cyclohexane ring with COC$_3$H$_7$ substituent]	Low	99
n-Heptaldehyde	Cyclohexene	[cyclohexane ring with COC$_6$H$_{13}$ substituent]	Low	95
n-Heptaldehyde	Vinylcyclohexene	[cyclohexene ring with CH$_2$CH$_2$COC$_3$H$_7$ substituent]	21	99
Acetaldehyde	1,5-Hexadiene	CH$_3$CO(CH$_2$)$_4$CH=CH$_2$	15	99
Acetaldehyde	Allyl acetate	CH$_3$COCH$_2$CH$_2$CH$_2$OAc	63	100
n-Butyraldehyde	Allyl acetate	C$_3$H$_7$CO(CH$_2$)$_3$OAc	41	100
Acetaldehyde	Acrolein diethyl acetal	CH$_3$COCH$_2$CH$_2$CH(OEt)$_2$	48	104
n-Butyraldehyde	Acrolein diethyl acetal	C$_3$H$_7$COCH$_2$CH$_2$CH(OEt)$_2$	28	100

Acetaldehyde	Diethyl maleate	CH$_3$COCH—COOEt
		      |
		     CH$_2$—COOEt
			78^a	96a

n-Butyraldehyde	Diethyl maleate	C$_3$H$_7$COCH—COOEt
		      |
		     CH$_2$—COOEt
			76$^{a,\,b}$	96a, 101

n-Heptaldehyde	Diethyl maleate	C$_6$H$_{13}$COCH—COOEt
		      |
		     CH$_2$—COOEt
			76^a	96a

α-n-Propyl-n-butyraldehyde	Diethyl maleate	(C$_3$H$_7$)$_2$CHCOCH—COOEt
		        |
		       CH$_2$—COOEt
			59^a	96a

Benzaldehyde	Diethyl maleate	C$_6$H$_5$COCH—COOEt
		      |
		     CH$_2$—COOEt
			5^a	96a

β-Methoxypropionaldehyde	Diethyl maleate	CH$_3$OCH$_2$CH$_2$COCH—COOEt
		          |
		        CH$_2$—COOEt
			55^a	96a

Glutaraldehyde	Diethyl maleate	CH$_2$=$\left(\begin{array}{c}\text{CH}_2\text{COCH—COOEt}\\ \text{\|}\\ \text{CH}_2\text{—COOEt}\end{array}\right)_2$	100^a	96a

TABLE 6·14 RADICAL ADDITIONS OF ALDEHYDES TO OLEFINS (*Continued*)

Aldehyde	Olefin	Product	Per Cent Yield	Foot-note

n-Butyraldehyde	Diethyl fumarate	C$_3$H$_7$COCH—COOEt
		
		         |
		    CH$_2$—COOEt
			26 [a]	96a, 101

n-Butyraldehyde	Methyl acrylate	CH$_3$COCH$_2$CH$_2$COOCH$_3$	11 [d]	101
Acetaldehyde	Methyl undecylenate	CH$_3$CO(CH$_2$)$_{10}$COOCH$_3$	30	101
Acetaldehyde	Mesityl oxide	CH$_3$COC(CH$_3$)$_2$CH$_2$COCH$_3$	31 [a]	96b
n-Butyraldehyde	Mesityl oxide	C$_3$H$_5$COC(CH$_3$)$_2$CH$_2$COCH$_3$	60–100 [a, e]	96b
n-Heptaldehyde	Mesityl oxide	C$_6$H$_{13}$C(CH$_3$)$_2$CH$_2$COCH$_3$	61 [a]	96b
n-Butyraldehyde	Phorone	C$_3$H$_7$C(CH$_3$)$_2$CH$_2$COCH=C(CH$_3$)$_2$	80 [a]	96b
n-Butyraldehyde	3-Penten-2-one	C$_3$H$_7$COCH(CH$_3$)CH$_2$COCH$_3$	64 [a]	96b
n-Butyraldehyde	3-Decen-2-one	C$_3$H$_7$COCH(C$_6$H$_{13}$)CH$_2$COCH$_3$	42 [a]	96b
n-Butyraldehyde	Crotonophenone	C$_3$H$_7$COCH(CH$_3$)CH$_2$COC$_6$H$_5$	24 [a]	96b
n-Butyraldehyde	Methyl isopropenyl ketone	C$_3$H$_7$COCH$_2$CH(CH$_3$)COCH$_3$	...	102
n-Butyraldehyde	5-Hexen-2-one	C$_3$H$_7$CO(CH$_2$)$_4$COCH$_3$	71	102
Acetaldehyde	Perfluoropropylene	CH$_3$COCF$_2$CFHCF$_3$	76	105
n-Butyraldehyde	Perfluoro-1-butene	C$_3$H$_7$COCF$_2$CFHC$_2$F$_5$	70	105

[a] Yield based on actual olefin reacted.
[b] Comparable yields obtained with several other maleate esters.
[c] Additional examples of addition of aldehydes to long-chain terminal olefins are given by Rust and Vaughan.[103]
[d] By dropwise addition of methyl acrylate to excess butyraldehyde to minimize telomer formation.
[e] Product contains about 10% isomeric 3-isopropyl-2,4-heptadione; see text.

[97] C. H. Stiteler and J. R. Little, U.S. Pat. 2,517,732 (August 8, 1950).
[98] K. Ziegler, *Brennstoff Chemie*, 30, 181 (1949).
[99] E. C. Ladd, U.S. Pat. 2,517,684 (August 8, 1950).
[100] E. C. Ladd, U.S. Pat. 2,533,944 (December 12, 1950).
[101] E. C. Ladd, U.S. Pat. 2,577,133 (December 4, 1951).
[102] E. C. Ladd, U.S. Pat. 2,621,212 (December 9, 1952).
[103] F. F. Rust and W. E. Vaughan, U.S. Pat. 2,650,253 (August 25, 1953).
[104] A. Mondon, *Angew. Chem.*, 64, 224 (1952).
[105] J. D. La Zerte and R. J. Koshar, *J. Am. Chem. Soc.*, 77, 910 (1955).
[105a] H. H. Schlubach, V. Franzen, and E. Dahl, *Ann.*, 587, 124 (1954).

of examples appear in the patent literature. Published results are summarized as far as possible in Table 6·14. Experimental conditions are not given in detail, but the majority of experiments have been carried out at 60–100°, using excess aldehyde to minimize telomer formation, and 1–5 mole % of benzoyl or acetyl peroxide as initiator. In some cases the reaction has been initiated photochemically at room temperature, but, with the exception of Kharasch's [95] and Patrick's [96] papers, there is little information on the effect of variables or the conditions for optimum yields.

From Table 6·14, the addition reaction appears to proceed well with straight-chain aldehydes and terminal olefins. Non-terminal olefins such as cyclohexene do not give good yields, and most attempted photochemical additions give quite different products, discussed in Section 11·1c. With reactive olefins such as styrene, transfer constants are too low to obtain 1:1 products.

Significantly, dialkyl maleates give good yields of 1:1 products,[96a] although with the more reactive fumarates yields are poorer, and a 1:1 product is obtained from methyl acrylate only under special conditions where the aldehyde/olefin ratio is kept high.

A number of α,β-unsaturated ketones also give good yields.[96b] In the n-butyraldehyde–mesityl oxide reaction, which Patrick has investigated in detail, it turns out that about 10% of the addition occurs at the carbonyl end of the double bond.

$$
\begin{array}{c}
\text{CH}_3 \\
| \\
\text{R—CO—C—}\overset{\cdot}{\text{C}}\text{H—COCH}_3 \\
| \\
\text{CH}_3
\end{array}
\xrightarrow{\text{RCHO}}
\begin{array}{c}
\text{CH}_3 \\
| \\
\text{R—CO}\overset{}{\text{C}}\text{—CH}_2\text{COCH}_3 \\
| \\
\text{CH}_3
\end{array}
$$

$$
\begin{array}{c}
\text{O} \\
\parallel \\
\text{R—C}\cdot
\end{array}
\quad + \quad
\begin{array}{c}
\text{CH}_3 \\
\diagdown \\
\text{C}=\text{CH—COCH}_3 \\
\diagup \\
\text{CH}_3
\end{array}
\qquad\qquad (41)
$$

90% ↗ (from the lower reactant to the top product)

10% ↘

$$
\begin{array}{c}
\text{CH}_3 \quad \text{COR} \\
\diagdown\;\;\diagup \\
\cdot\text{C—CH—COCH}_3 \\
| \\
\text{CH}_3
\end{array}
\xrightarrow{\text{RCHO}}
\begin{array}{c}
\text{CH}_3 \quad \text{COR} \\
|\;\;\;\;\diagup \\
\text{HC—CH} \\
| \quad\quad \diagdown \\
\text{CH}_3 \quad \text{COCH}_3
\end{array}
$$

Apparently, steric hindrance is enough to overcome partially the tendency of the reaction to go only through the carbonyl-conjugated radical, which is not only more stable but is favored by polarity (see below).

It is likely that a similar side reaction occurs in analogous systems, and in this regard Pitts, Tolberg, and Martin have made the interesting observation [106] that, when methyl radicals attack *trans*-3-penten-2-one, significant quantities of CO and 2-butene are produced by a path which can best be formulated as

$$
\begin{array}{c}
\text{CH}_3 \quad\quad \text{H} \\
\diagdown \quad\quad \diagup \\
\text{C}=\text{C} \\
\diagup \quad\quad \diagdown \\
\text{H} \quad\quad \text{COCH}_3
\end{array}
+ \cdot\text{CH}_3 \rightarrow
\begin{array}{c}
\text{CH}_3 \quad\quad \text{CH}_3 \\
\diagdown \quad\quad | \\
\overset{\cdot}{\text{C}}\text{—C—H} \\
\diagup \quad\quad \diagdown \\
\text{H} \quad\quad \text{COCH}_3
\end{array}
\rightarrow
$$

$$
\text{CH}_3\text{CH}=\text{CHCH}_3 + \text{CH}_3\text{CO}\cdot \qquad (42)
$$

$$
\text{CH}_3\cdot + \text{CO}
$$

[106] J. N. Pitts, Jr., R. S. Tolberg, and T. W. Martin, *J. Am. Chem. Soc.*, **76**, 2843 (1954).

i.e., some addition in the "unexpected" direction, followed by the reverse of the carbonyl addition reaction. Since their reactions were carried out in the vapor phase at 150–275°, conditions are favorable for such a dissociation.

This ready reaction of aldehydes with carbonyl-conjugated olefins is paralleled by a high yield of 1:1 products with perfluoroölefins [105] and merits attention, particularly in view of the high activation energy of the $\cdot CH_3$ reaction with aldehydes. The plausible explanation is that it is another example of a polar effect, the aldehyde and acyl radical acting as electron donors, and the transition states of both addition and displacement steps receiving stabilization through structures such as

$$R-C \overset{O}{\underset{\cdot}{\big\Vert}} \quad CH_2{=}CH{-}CO{-} \;\leftrightarrow\; R-C \overset{O}{\underset{+}{\big\Vert}} \quad \dot{C}H_2{-}CH{=}C \overset{O^-}{\diagup} {-} \tag{43}$$

and

$$-CO-\overset{|}{\underset{|}{C}}\cdot \quad H-C\overset{O}{\underset{}{\big\Vert}}-R \;\leftrightarrow\; -C\overset{O^{(-)}}{\underset{}{=}}\overset{|}{\underset{|}{C}} \quad H\cdot \quad {}^{+}C\overset{O}{\underset{}{\big\Vert}}-R \tag{44}$$

The participating acyl carbonium ion structure is one of considerable stability, apparently playing a role in Friedel-Crafts acylations [107] and even existing as a stable entity in sulfuric acid solutions of highly hindered acids.[108]

Another significant side reaction in aldehyde additions to simple olefins is breakdown of the acyl radical with CO evolution:

$$R-C\overset{O}{\underset{}{\big\Vert}}\cdot \;\rightarrow\; R\cdot + CO \tag{45}$$

This reaction is discussed further below but undoubtedly accounts for the low yields of ketones from α-substituted aldehydes. In fact, with trimethylacetaldehyde, CO evolution is complete, and the reaction takes the path:

$$(CH_3)_3C-C\overset{O}{\underset{}{\big\Vert}}\cdot + (CH_3)_3C\cdot \overset{+}{\overset{CO}{}} \xrightarrow{RCH=CH_2}$$

$$(CH_3)_3CCH_2\dot{C}HR \xrightarrow{(CH_3)_3CCHO} (CH_3)_3CCH_2CH_2R \tag{46}$$

$$+ \;\;(CH_3)_3C-C\overset{O}{\underset{}{\big\Vert}}\cdot$$

[107] Cf. pp. 295–297 of reference in footnote 78.
[108] H. P. Treffers and L. P. Hammett, *J. Am. Chem. Soc.*, **59**, 1708 (1937)

From 1-octene and excess aldehyde 2,2-dimethyloctane is obtained in 41% yield.[109]

The addition reaction also gives low yields with aromatic aldehydes such as benzaldehyde. The explanation here is not as easy, but apparently the ϕCO—H bond is stronger than might be anticipated. Thus, benzaldehyde is also relatively unreactive in competitive autoxidation reactions (Section 9·2d).

Examples of successful additions of formaldehyde are also lacking (as might be expected, since the product is itself an aldehyde), although methyl formate, which gives rise to a substituted acyl radical, adds to various terminal olefins (cf. Section 6·4).

Telomer formation is a significant complication in aldehyde additions to simple olefins. In the case of ethylene, sufficient data [97] are available to calculate that the transfer constant is approximately 0.8, independent of chain length from 1–3 units. This value is comparable to the transfer constant of CCl_4 with long ethylene chains, and the notable difference in reactivity of these two substrates towards carbonyl-conjugated radicals again points up the importance of polar effects in additions of this sort. Qualitative inspection of data in the patent literature for additions to other olefins suggests that transfer constants in these systems are also generally independent of chain lengths, as might be anticipated from one of the arguments developed in Section 6·2b, namely, that such variations are largely polar in origin, arising when a radical alters the polar properties of an olefin to which it adds.

6·3b Some Radical Chains Involving Carbon Monoxide

The dissociation of acyl radicals into CO and alkyl radicals has been mentioned as a side reaction in aldehyde additions, and, in the absence of olefins, provides a path for the chain decomposition of aldehydes themselves.

$$RC \overset{O}{\overset{\|}{\cdot}} \;\rightarrow\; R\cdot \,+\, CO \tag{47}$$

$$R\cdot \,+\, RCHO \;\rightarrow\; RH + R—C \overset{O}{\overset{\|}{\cdot}} \tag{48}$$

The rapid photochemical decomposition of trimethylacetaldehyde and α,α-dimethylbutyraldehyde at room temperature to CO and isobutane or isopentane was described by Conant in 1929, who also

[109] E. C. Ladd, U.S. Pat. 2,552,980 (May 15, 1951).

noted that the reaction was inhibited by hydroquinone.[110]   Less highly branched aldehydes require higher temperatures, since both steps require appreciable energy and the reaction is best run above 100° and requires relatively reactive initiating radicals.   Thus methyl azobisisobutyrate is almost ineffective in starting chains.[111]

The higher temperature and photochemical reactions have also been investigated extensively in the vapor phase, and are discussed in detail by Steacie.[112]

In liquid-phase reactions, reaction sequence 47 and 48 is chiefly of interest as a means of producing alkyl radicals of a known structure, and noting their properties, particularly their tendencies to rearrange.   Thus, Winstein and Seubold [113] heated β-phenylisovaleraldehyde for 5 hours at 130° in the presence of about 10 mole % di-t-butyl peroxide, obtaining 90% of the theoretical yield of CO and a 70% yield of a 1:1 mixture of t-butyl- and isobutylbenzenes, a result that they interpreted as a rearrangement of the intermediate "neophyl" radical.

$$\phi\mathrm{-CH_2-CH(CH_3)_2} \quad (49)$$

Subsequently Seubold [114] has shown that decarbonylation and rearrangement are successive steps and that the neophyl radical has an independent existence, since the ratio of isobutylbenzene to t-butylbenzene increases from 1.3 to 4.0 as the medium is changed from pure aldehyde (6.4 molar) to a 1 molar solution in chlorobenzene. The amount of rearrangement is essentially temperature independent from 130° to 170°, indicating it has about the same activation energy as the radical attack on aldehyde.   Curtin and Hurwitz have investigated the decomposition of several other β-aryl aldehydes in the presence of di-t-butyl peroxide with the following results.[115]

[110] J. B. Conant, C. N. Webb, and W. C. Mendum, *J. Am. Chem. Soc.,* **51,** 1246 (1929).

[111] E. F. P. Harris and W. A. Waters, *J. Chem. Soc.,* **1952,** 3108.

[112] E. W. R. Steacie, *Atomic and Free Radical Reactions,* second edition, Reinhold Publishing Corp., New York, 1954, pp. 205–219, 275–317.

[113] S. Winstein and F. H. Seubold, Jr., *J. Am. Chem. Soc.,* **69,** 2916 (1947).

[114] F. H. Seubold, Jr., *ibid.,* **75,** 2532 (1953).

[115] D. Y. Curtin and M. J. Hurwitz, *ibid.,* **74,** 5381 (1952).

$$\phi_3CCH_2CHO \rightarrow \phi_2CHCH_2\phi + CO$$

$$\phi_3CCH(CH_3)CHO \rightarrow \phi_2CHCH(CH_3)\phi$$

$$+ \phi_2C{=}C(CH_3)\phi \quad (50)$$

$$\phi_2CHCH_2CHO \rightarrow \text{No rearrangement}$$

$$CH_3O-\hexagon-CH\phi-CH_2CHO \rightarrow \text{No rearrangement}$$

On the other hand Seubold has found no rearrangement in the decomposition of β,β-dimethylvaleraldehyde, cyclopentylacetaldehyde, and cyclohexanecarboxaldehyde.[116] Again, rearrangements of the carbon skeletons of radicals at moderate temperatures appear to be rather rare (and certainly have higher activation energies than those involving carbonium ions). The only present examples involve the migration of aryl groups, and some additional examples appear in Chapter 10.

The reverse of the decarbonylation reaction, radical attack on carbon monoxide, apparently is unimportant at ordinary pressures in the gas or liquid phase.[117] However, if the carbon monoxide concentration is increased by going to higher pressures, reaction 45 may be reversed, i.e.,

$$R\cdot + CO \rightarrow R-C\overset{\displaystyle O}{\underset{\displaystyle \cdot}{\big/\!\!\big/}} \quad (51)$$

The best example is the copolymerization of ethylene and carbon monoxide, investigated by Brubaker, Coffman, and Hoehn.[118] At 135° in cyclohexane solution in the presence of di-t-butyl peroxide and a pressure of 133 atmospheres, these substances copolymerize smoothly to give a high molecular weight product with the properties of a linear polyketone, $-CO-(C_2H_4)_n-CO-$. The number of carbonyl groups in the product increases with the CO/ethylene ratio, and, since a feed containing 36 mole % CO apparently represents an azeotropic composition (cf. Chapter 4), an ethylene radical must add carbon monoxide 2.3 times as readily as it does ethylene under these conditions (assuming equal solubilities of the two gases in the reacting phase).

[116] F. H. Seubold, Jr., *ibid.*, **76**, 3732 (1954).

[117] G. B. Porter and S. W. Benson, *ibid.*, **75**, 2773 (1953).

[118] M. M. Brubaker, D. D. Coffman, and H. H. Hoehn, *ibid.*, **74**, 1509 (1952); D. D. Coffman, P. S. Pinkney, F. T. Wall, W. H. Wood, and H. S. Young, *ibid.*, 3391.

The copolymer composition varies somewhat with the solvent, more CO entering the product in benzene than in cyclohexane, perhaps because of differences in solubility.   More interestingly, however, copolymer compositions vary markedly both with temperature and total pressure.   Thus a 42 mole % CO feed gives a polymer containing 22.8% CO at 120°, and only 9.1% at 165°.   Again, at 135° with the same feed, raising the total pressure from 13.3 atmospheres to 1000 atmospheres increases the CO content of the copolymer from 12.6% to 44.9%.

Barb has suggested that these variations arise from the reversible formation of a carbon monoxide–ethylene complex, and that this complex is involved in the reaction by which CO is incorporated in the polymer.[119]   However, it seems more likely [120] that we are observing simply the reversibility of the CO addition step, and the copolymer composition is determined by the reactions (using the usual polymerization symbols)

$$\text{M} \cdot + \text{M} \xrightarrow{\; k_{11} \;} \text{M} \cdot \tag{52}$$

$$\text{M} \cdot + \text{CO} \underset{k_{-12}}{\overset{k_{12}}{\rightleftharpoons}} -\overset{\displaystyle O}{\underset{\displaystyle }{C}} \cdot \tag{53}$$

$$-\overset{\displaystyle O}{\underset{\displaystyle }{C}} \cdot + \text{M} \xrightarrow{\; k_{21} \;} \text{M} \cdot \tag{54}$$

If we use the same treatment as for SO_2 copolymerization with reversible steps (Section 5·4d), this set of equations yields, for the copolymer composition,

$$d[\text{M}]/d[\text{CO}] - 1 = (r_1 p_1 + r_1[\text{M}])/[\text{CO}] \tag{55}$$

where $r_1 = k_{11}/k_{12}$, and $p_1 = k_{-12}/k_{21}$.   Barb has shown that the data agree with eq. 55 if p_1 is large,[119] and the variation of copolymer composition with temperature indicates that $E_{11} - E_{12} + E_{-12} \cong 9$ kcal.[120]   Since all the quantities but E_{-12} are probably small, the activation energy for CO dissociation must be 10–14 kcal, in reasonable agreement with results from other sources.[112]   The reason that the dissociation, with its relatively high activation energy, competes so successfully with the low activation energy chain growth processes must again be that dissociation processes involve little entropy change

[119] W. G. Barb, *ibid.*, **75**, 224 (1953).
[120] C. Walling, *J. Polymer Sci.*, **16**, 315 (1955).

in going to the transition state, whereas radical additions usually have appreciable negative entropies of activation.

Copolymerization of carbon monoxide with other olefins should be more difficult since CO addition should be increasingly reversible when substituted radicals are involved, and we would expect that it should only be observed at very high carbon monoxide pressures.

6·3c   *Other Chain Processes Involving the Carbonyl Function*

Although treatment of aldehydes with radical sources at elevated temperatures leads chiefly to decarbonylation, at lower temperatures in carbon tetrachloride solution a chain reaction with solvent has been observed, leading to the formation of acid chlorides and chloroform.[113] The steps involved are apparently

$$R\!-\!\overset{\displaystyle O}{\overset{\|}{C}}\!\cdot \;+\; CCl_4 \;\rightarrow\; RC\overset{\displaystyle O}{\underset{\displaystyle Cl}{\overset{\|}{\diagdown}}} \;+\; \cdot CCl_3 \tag{56}$$

$$\cdot CCl_3 \;+\; RCHO \;\rightarrow\; R\!-\!\overset{\displaystyle O}{\overset{\|}{C}}\!\cdot \;+\; CHCl_3 \tag{57}$$

However, chains are rather short, and the reaction has received little investigation.

In our discussion of polymerization inhibitors we saw that radicals are capable of adding to the carbonyl function of molecules like chloranil to yield products which are ethers of the corresponding hydroquinones. A number of similar reactions involving simpler radicals are known, although the majority are not chain processes. The decomposition of azobisisobutyronitrile in the presence of chloranil yields the di-α-cyanoisopropyl ether of tetrachlorohydroquinone,[98, 121] and Waters has obtained similar mono- and diethers from azobisisobutyronitrile and a variety of other quinones, only 1,4-naphthoquinone giving appreciable nuclear substitution.[122]

An interesting reaction sequence occurs when di-*t*-butyl peroxide is decomposed in the presence of benzaldehyde.[123] The products are *t*-butyl alcohol and *meso*-dihydrobenzoin dibenzoate, presumably formed by the path

[121] K. Ziegler, W. Deparade, and W. Meye, *Ann.*, **567**, 141 (1950).

[122] F. J. Lopez Aparicio and W. A. Waters, *J. Chem. Soc.*, **1952**, 4666.

[123] F. F. Rust, F. H. Seubold and W. E. Vaughan, *J. Am. Chem. Soc.*, **70**, 3258 (1948).

$$C_4H_9O—OC_4H_9 \rightarrow 2C_4H_9O\cdot$$

$$C_4H_9O\cdot + \phi CHO \rightarrow C_4H_9OH + \phi—\overset{\displaystyle O}{\underset{\displaystyle }{C\cdot}}$$

$$\phi—\overset{\displaystyle O}{\underset{\displaystyle \bullet}{C\cdot}} + \phi CHO \rightarrow \phi—\overset{\displaystyle OCO\phi}{\underset{\displaystyle H}{C\cdot}} \qquad (58)$$

$$2\phi—\overset{\displaystyle OCO\phi}{\underset{\displaystyle H}{C\cdot}} \rightarrow \phi—COO—\overset{\displaystyle H}{\underset{\displaystyle \phi}{C}}—\overset{\displaystyle H}{\underset{\displaystyle \phi}{C}}—OCO\phi \quad (85\%)$$

This sequence, involving hydrogen abstraction from benzaldehyde, followed by addition of a benzoyl radical to the carbonyl group of benzaldehyde and dimerization of the ensuing radical, is supported by the fact that the same product results from decomposing benzoyl peroxide in benzaldehyde, or di-t-butyl peroxide in benzyl benzoate (which gives the third radical in the sequence directly).

Another reaction which must involve addition of a carbonyl radical to a carbonyl double bond occurs when benzaldehyde is irradiated in the presence of phenanthraquinone, yielding the hydroquinone mono-benzoate.[124]   Although its mechanism is unknown, a chain process can be formulated

$$(59)$$

Similar reactions occur with anisaldehyde and phenanthraquinone, and with benzaldehyde and chloranil.

Two rather obscure reactions which seem to be related to the above have recently been described by Kharasch.   In one, benzaldehyde and azobenzene, heated with di-t-butyl peroxide, yield benzanilide and 1-benzoyl-1,2-diphenylhydrazine.[125]   Here the benzoyl radical has

[124] R. F. Moore and W. A. Waters, *J. Chem. Soc.*, **1953**, 238.   Other examples are given by A. Schonberg and A. Mustafa, *Chem. Revs.*, **40**, 181 (1947).

[125] M. S. Kharasch, M. Zimmermann, W. Zimmt, and W. Nudenberg, *J. Org. Chem.*, **18**, 1045 (1953).

apparently added to the N,N double bond, followed by hydrogen abstraction or decomposition of the resulting radical.

In the second, benzaldehyde and pyridine, heated with di-t-butyl peroxide, give a mixture of products including the molecule [126]

$$\phi-\underset{\underset{\displaystyle \text{(pyridyl)}}{|}}{\overset{\overset{\displaystyle H}{|}}{C}}-O-CO\phi \tag{60}$$

which could conceivably arise from addition of the same dimer radical as in reaction 58 to the pyridine nucleus, followed by oxidation of the resulting radical.

Another example of what must be radical addition to a carbonyl group occurs in early work by Conant on the high-pressure polymerization of aldehydes.[127] At 12,000 atmospheres n-butyraldehyde polymerizes to a solid, high molecular weight material which is evidently a polyacetal

$$\underset{O}{\overset{\overset{\displaystyle R}{\overset{\displaystyle CH}{}}}{}}\quad\underset{O}{\overset{\overset{\displaystyle R}{\overset{\displaystyle CH}{}}}{}}\quad\underset{O}{\overset{\overset{\displaystyle R}{\overset{\displaystyle CH}{}}}{}}\quad\underset{O}{\overset{\overset{\displaystyle R}{\overset{\displaystyle CH}{}}}{}}\quad\underset{O}{} \tag{61}$$

since it readily depolymerizes to aldehyde in the presence of acid, or more slowly on standing. Since carefully purified aldehyde shows no polymerization in 28 hours at room temperature at this pressure, whereas aldehyde which has been exposed to air, or which contains benzoyl peroxide, polymerizes rapidly, a radical chain polymerization is evident, but one which is highly reversible and accordingly not observed at ordinary pressures. It may be noted that pressure, which accelerates the polymerization reaction (cf. Section 5·6), should also decrease the rate of the usual aldehyde chain decomposition by reversing the step in which carbon monoxide is lost.

Finally, radical attack on the C—H bonds of ketones is also possible, and Kharasch [128] has reported the addition of cyclohexanone to

[126] M. S. Kharasch, D. Schwartz, M. Zimmermann, and W. Nudenberg, *ibid.*, **18**, 1051 (1953).

[127] J. B. Conant and C. O. Tongberg, *J. Am. Chem. Soc.*, **52**, 1659 (1930); J. B. Conant and W. R. Peterson, *ibid.*, **54**, 628 (1932).

[128] M. S. Kharasch, J. Kuderna, and W. Nudenberg, *J. Org. Chem.*, **18**, 1225 (1953).

1-octene, to give, on irradiation, 20–25% each of 1:1 and 2:1 products,

$$C_6H_{13}CH{=}CH_2 + \text{(cyclohexanone)} \rightarrow \text{(2-substituted cyclohexanone, } C_8H_{17}\text{)} \qquad (62)$$

However, most photochemical olefin-ketone reactions seem to take a different non-chain course (Section 11·1c).

6·4   Addition Reactions Involving Alcohols, Amines, Etc.

Although early work indicated that alcohols and ethylene react to give chiefly telomers, Urry et al.[129,130] have shown that, by using a large excess of alcohol, a number of alcohol-olefin combinations yield 1:1 products via the overall reaction

$$\overset{\text{OH}}{\underset{|}{}}$$
$$RCH_2OH + CH_2{=}CHR \rightarrow R{-}CH{-}CH_2CH_2R \qquad (63)$$

in which the chain process must be

$$\overset{\text{OH}}{\underset{|}{}}$$
$$R{-}\overset{\cdot}{C}HOH + CH_2{=}CHR \rightarrow R{-}CH{-}CH_2{-}\overset{\cdot}{C}HR \qquad (64)$$

$$\overset{\text{OH}}{\underset{|}{}}$$
$$R{-}CH{-}CH_2{-}\overset{\cdot}{C}HR + RCH_2OH \rightarrow$$
$$\overset{\text{OH}}{\underset{|}{}}$$
$$R{-}CH{-}CH_2CH_2R + R\overset{\cdot}{C}HOH \qquad (65)$$

Displacement must be on a hydrogen attached to the carbon bearing the —OH, so the reaction is limited to primary and secondary alcohols.

Urry has measured the first transfer constant for a number of systems,[130] Table 6·15, and the small values indicate that the reaction is rather marginal as a synthetic process. Rather special conditions are also necessary to produce appreciable chains, best results

129 W. H. Urry, F. W. Stacey, O. O. Juveland, and C. H. McDonnell, *J. Am. Chem. Soc.*, **75**, 250 (1954).

130 W. H. Urry, F. W. Stacey, E. S. Huyser, and O. O. Juveland, *ibid.*, **76**, 450 (1954).

TABLE 6·15 TRANSFER CONSTANTS FOR ALCOHOL ADDITIONS [130]

Olefin	Alcohol	C_1	Olefin	Alcohol	C_1
1-Octene	Methyl	0.011	1-Hexene	Cyclohexyl	0.039
1-Octene	Ethyl	0.017	Ethylene	Ethyl	0.019
1-Octene	Isopropyl	0.052–0.063	Ethylene	Isopropyl	0.057
1-Octene	n-Butyl	0.027			
1-Octene	sec-Butyl	0.052			

being obtained at 115–130° using di-t-butyl peroxide as initiator. However, even here, with ethanol-octene only about 2.4 moles of 2-decanol are obtained per mole of initiator employed.[129] Alternatively, the reaction can be induced photochemically, but benzoyl peroxide or azobisisobutyronitrile are reported to be ineffective, the former presumably because of its induced decomposition in the presence of alcohols (cf. Section 10·2b).

Alcohols and their resulting α-hydroxyalkyl radicals should behave as electron donors in radical processes, since the corresponding carbonium ion

$$\begin{array}{ccc} \overset{+}{O}H & & OH \\ \overset{\parallel}{-C-} & \leftrightarrow & \overset{\diagup}{-C-} \\ & & + \end{array}$$

(the conjugate acid of a carbonyl compound) is relatively stable. Thus we find that a number of alcohol-perfluoroölefin combinations give good yields of 1:1 products.[105] Here the reaction would seem to have considerable utility. With methanol -C_2F_4, both 1:1 product and telomers can be produced,[131] giving a route to substances of the structure $H(C_2F_4)_nCH_2OH$. Several other reactions are known involving

$$\overset{OH}{\underset{|}{}}$$

radical attack on C—H bonds, such attack representing one of the paths by which alcohols are oxidized (Sections 10·2 and 11·3).

A very remarkable reaction between ethylene, carbon monoxide, and methanol has recently been described by Cairns et al.[132] At 130° in the presence of di-t-butyl peroxide at 1000–8000 atmospheres polymeric products are produced, which, as the pressure is increased, approach the composition one C_2H_4 to two CO to one CH_3OH, and have the structure

[131] W. E. Hanford and J. R. Roland, U.S. Pat. 2,402,157 (June 18, 1946); R. M. Joyce, U.S. Pat. 2,559,628 (July 10, 1951).

[132] T. L. Cairns, D. D. Coffman, R. Cramer, A. W. Larchar, and B. C. McKusick, J. Am. Chem. Soc., 76, 3024 (1954).

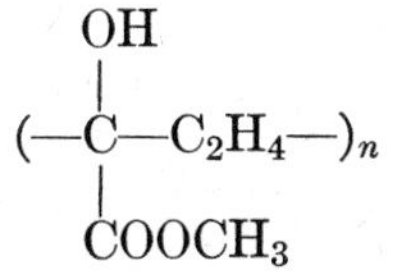

$$
\begin{array}{c}
OH \\
| \\
(-C-C_2H_4-)_n \\
| \\
COOCH_3
\end{array}
$$

Since added ketones do not enter into the reaction, it does not involve a subsequent addition to the ethylene–CO copolymer (Section 6·3b), and the authors suggest the path

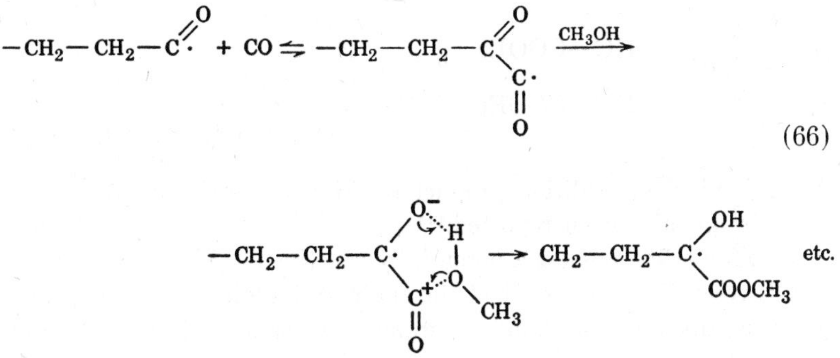

(66)

Ethyl, isopropyl, benzyl, and t-butyl alcohols are similarly incorporated in the polymer, and propylene and some additional olefins undergo the same reaction. If this formulation is correct, we see another radical process in which a polar transition state plays an important role.

Polar properties and C—H bond dissociation energies of ethers should be much the same as those of alcohols, and some 1:1 products have been described in reactions employing olefins with electron-withdrawing groups. Tetrafluorethylene is claimed by Hanford to give a 1:1 product (plus telomer) with dioxane,[133] and reactions with other ethers are also described.

Methylal, in which a C—H bond is activated by two ether groups, reacts with maleic anhydride in the presence of various initiators or ultraviolet light to give as high as a 36% yield of 1:1 product,[134] the overall reaction being presumably

[133] W. E. Hanford, U.S. Pat. 2,433,844 (January 6, 1948). Interestingly, ethylene oxide is reported to give a *copolymer* with perfluoropropylene or perfluorovinyl chloride at 135° in the presence of di-t-butyl peroxide; M. Haupschein and J. M. Lesser, *J. Am. Chem. Soc.*, **78**, 676 (1956).

[134] T. M. Patrick, Jr., U.S. Pat. 2,628,238 (February 10, 1953); cf. also T. M. Patrick, Jr., U.S. Pat. 2,716,600 (August 30, 1955).

$$CH_2(OCH_3)_2 + \begin{matrix} CO \\ CH \\ \| \\ CH \\ CO \end{matrix} \Big> O \to (CH_3O)_2CH-CH-CO \quad \begin{matrix} | \\ CH_2-CO \end{matrix} \Big> O \quad (67)$$

A similar reaction occurs between 1,3-dioxanes or dioxolanes and α-β-unsaturated esters,[135] e.g.,

$$\begin{matrix} O \\ CH_2 \\ O \end{matrix} + \begin{matrix} HC-COOEt \\ \| \\ HC-COOEt \end{matrix} \xrightarrow[80-100°]{Bz_2O_2} \begin{matrix} O \\ C-CH-COOEt \\ O \quad CH_2-COOEt \end{matrix} \quad (68)$$

A small yield of addition product of ethyl orthoformate to diethyl maleate has also been reported.[136]

Formate esters possess a potentially reactive C—H bond, and Urry and Huyser [137] have described the successful addition of methyl formate to ethylene. Six hundred grams of ester heated at 130° under 22–29 atmospheres' ethylene pressure in the presence of di-t-butyl peroxide gave 70–80 grams of product consisting of about equal quantities of methyl esters of odd-numbered acids from C_3–C_{13}. Transfer constants cannot be calculated from the data, but the product distribution suggests that they are essentially independent of chain length. Addition was also successful to 1-hexene, but higher esters of formic acid give complex mixtures of products.

Urry has also observed the addition of amines with the structure N—C—H to terminal olefins.[138] Piperidine at 120° in the presence of di-t-butyl peroxide adds to 1-octene and propylene to give 2-octylpiperidine and d,l-coniine (2-propylpiperidine)

$$\begin{matrix} \\ N \\ H \end{matrix} + CH_2=CHR \to \begin{matrix} \\ N \quad CH_2CH_2R \\ H \end{matrix} \quad (69)$$

[135] T. M. Patrick, Jr., U.S. Pat. 2,684,873 (July 20, 1954).

[136] A. Nagasaka, R. Oda, and S. Nukina, *J. Chem. Soc. Japan Ind. Chem Sect.*, **57**, 169 (1954); *ibid.*, **58**, 46 (1955); A. Nagasaka, S. Nakamura and R. Oda, *ibid.*, **58**, 460 (1955).

[137] W. H. Urry and E. S. Huyser, *J. Am. Chem. Soc.*, **75**, 4876 (1953).

[138] W. H. Urry, O. O. Juveland, and F. W. Stacey, *ibid.*, **74**, 6155 (1952).

respectively.   Here again attack is on the C—H bond, and experimental conditions appear to be important, since many initiators such as benzoyl peroxide react rapidly with amines (Section 11·5a).

Amines, like alcohols, should be donor radicals, and the scope of this reaction is worth further study.   Urry and his students [138a] have made an interesting comparison of transfer constants of amines. With 1-octene, C's for piperidine, N-methylpiperidine, n-butylamine, isopropylamine, and cyclohexylamine are 0.26, 0.053, 0.062, 0.095, and 0.081, piperidine being significantly the most reactive.   For comparison, C_1 for methyl formate is 0.014; cf. also the alcohol values in Table 6·15.

As a further process related to all of these additions we may note the rearrangement of α-alkoxystyrenes which was observed by Claisen [139] to occur thermally at around 200°

$$\phi-\overset{\overset{\textstyle OR}{\diagup}}{C}=CH_2 \rightarrow \phi-\overset{\overset{\textstyle O}{\diagup\!\!\!\diagup}}{C}-CH_2R \qquad (70)$$

The reaction of α-methoxystyrene was investigated in more detail by Lauer and Spielman,[140] who observed 1,2-dibenzoyl propane and methane as additional products.   More recently, Wiberg and Rowland [141] have obtained strong evidence that, at least under some circumstances, a radical chain process is involved since, at 135°, the reaction is strongly catalyzed by di-t-butyl peroxide.   A plausible path would be

$$R\cdot \, + \, CH_2{=}\overset{\overset{\textstyle OR}{|}}{C}{-}\phi \rightarrow R{-}CH_2{-}\overset{\overset{\textstyle OR}{|}}{C}{-}\phi \qquad (71)$$

$$R{-}CH_2{-}\overset{\overset{\textstyle OR}{|}}{C}{-}\phi \rightarrow R{-}CH_2{-}CO\phi \, + \, R\cdot \qquad (72)$$

The by-products noted by Lauer are certainly consistent with such a chain, as is the observation [141] that the optically active sec-butyl ether yields inactive ketone.

[138a] E. Huyser, private communication.

[139] L. Claisen, Ber., 29, 2931 (1896).

[140] E. H. MacDougall, W. M. Lauer, and M. A. Spielman, J. Am. Chem. Soc., 55, 4089 (1933); W. M. Lauer and M. A. Spielman, ibid., 55, 4923 (1933); M. A. Spielman and C. W. Mortenson, ibid., 61, 666 (1939); 62, 1609 (1940).

[141] K. B. Wiberg and B. I. Rowland, ibid., 77, 1159 (1955).

CHAPTER 7

Radical Addition Reactions

Involving Atoms Other than Carbon

In this chapter we will continue our discussion of addition reactions to olefins, taking up reactions involving non-carbon radicals. It will also be convenient to discuss a few related reactions, notably those of sulfur radicals.

7 · 1   Additions Involving Halogen Atoms

Numerous radical chain processes are known which have as a step the addition of halogen atoms to double bonds. The most important are those involving the halogen acids and halogens themselves, but the chlorination of olefins by sulfuryl chloride also belongs in this class, and so do certain olefin dimerization reactions (Section 6·2d). The halogen acid and halogen addition processes are complicated by the competing polar addition reactions (which may or may not yield identical products), and the separation of these two reaction paths represents an important step in the development of the electronic theory of organic reactions. Halogen atom additions also sometimes compete with displacement reactions involving allylic hydrogen and are thus related to the halogen substitution reactions discussed in Chapter 8.

7·1a   The Radical Addition of Hydrogen Bromide to Olefins

This process is of considerable historical interest as one of the first cases in which polar and radical chain processes were differentiated, and the story is worth relating. During the 1920's, the then-developing electronic theory of organic chemistry required a theoretical explanation for the addition of unsymmetric reagents to olefins according to Markownikoff's rule. Most of the available data involved the addition of hydrogen bromide, largely through the experimental chance that halogen acid additions may be carried out simply, the products are well known, and hydrogen bromide is particularly convenient since it reacts more rapidly than hydrogen chloride and is easier than hydrogen iodide to prepare and handle. With the majority of olefins the data were consistent, but, with a few, the reported products varied with the investigator and experimental conditions leading to a choice of ingeneous formulations of the reaction. Two notable cases were 2-pentene, where different workers reported various ratios of 2- and 3-bromopentane as the addition product, and allyl bromide, where both 1,2- and 1,3-dibromopropane were observed.

The allyl bromide reaction was studied with great care by Mayo and Kharasch, who, with increasing experimental refinements, and after following up several of the inevitable false leads, finally established that scrupulously purified hydrogen bromide and allyl bromide in the dark and in the absence of all added reagents reacted slowly to give 1,2-dibromopropane, the expected "Markownikoff" product, but, in the presence of air or added peroxides, the reaction is faster and the product may be entirely 1,3-dibromopropane.[1,2]

The reaction leading to 1,2-dibromopropane was termed *normal* addition since it was that predicted by Markownikoff's rule, and since it corresponded to that observed with other halogen acids. The reaction leading to 1,3-dibromopropane was termed *abnormal* addition, and the reversal of the direction of addition became known as the *peroxide effect.*

Kharasch and his students began a thorough study of the peroxide effect, showing it to be a general phenomenon with a variety of olefins,[3] and in 1937 he [4] (and Hey and Waters independently but in less detail [5]) proposed that abnormal addition was a radical chain process proceeding through the steps

$$Br\cdot + CH_2{=}CHR \rightarrow BrCH_2{-}\dot{C}HR \qquad (1)$$

$$BrCH_2{-}\dot{C}HR + H{-}Br \rightarrow BrCH_2CH_2R + Br\cdot \qquad (2)$$

Although there was much controversy at the time, the mechanism seems now to be universally accepted. Its kinetics have not been investigated in detail, but it has the characteristics now well identified with radical chain processes: acceleration by light and peroxides, inhibition by hydroquinone and diphenylamine, and independence of the polar nature of the solvent. The energetics of the propagation steps are favorable (Section $6\cdot 1b$), ΔH for reactions 1 and 2 being -5 and -11 kcal respectively for ethylene. With substituted olefins ΔH decreases for reaction 1 and increases for reaction 2, becoming positive for styrene, but the radical process still proceeds satisfactorily.[6] The direction of addition is that expected if a bromine atom

---

[1] M. S. Kharasch and F. R. Mayo, *J. Am. Chem. Soc.*, **55**, 2468 (1933).

[2] The 2-pentene case subsequently proved to be trivial, both the *cis-* and *trans-*isomers yielding essentially a 50:50 mixture of 2- and 3-halopentanes under all conditions, previous observations to the contrary apparently arising from the use of impure starting materials or from errors in product analysis; cf. M. S. Kharasch, C. Walling, and F. R. Mayo, *ibid.*, **61**, 1559 (1939).

[3] F. R. Mayo and C. Walling, *Chem. Revs.*, **27**, 351 (1940).

[4] M. S. Kharasch, H. Engelmann, and F. R. Mayo, *J. Org. Chem.*, **2**, 288 (1937).

[5] D. H. Hey and W. A. Waters, *Chem. Revs.*, **21**, 169 (1937).

[6] C. Walling, M. S. Kharasch, and F. R. Mayo, *J. Am. Chem. Soc.*, **61**, 2693 (1939).

were the chain carrier, being favored both sterically and through resonance stabilization of the resulting radical (with R = alkyl, the steric effect is probably the most important factor; cf. Section 4·1g). Indeed, the alternative process,

$$H \cdot + CH_2{=}CHR \rightarrow \dot{C}H_2{-}CH_2R \qquad \Delta H = -40 \text{ kcal} \qquad (3)$$

$$\cdot CH_2{-}CH_2R + HBr \rightarrow CH_2Br{-}CH_2R + H \cdot \quad \Delta H = 24 \text{ kcal} \quad (4)$$

which has occasionally been suggested, can be ruled out on energetic grounds, as indicated by the values of ΔH.

Since most of the work on the radical addition of hydrogen bromide was carried out prior to 1940 and has been thoroughly reviewed,[3] systems which have been investigated will not be tabulated in detail. The reaction has been demonstrated with a large number of terminal olefins, and a few unsymmetric compounds like trimethylethylene. It also occurs with acetylenes and haloethylenes, and thus has been used to prepare CD_2BrCD_2Br from C_2D_2 and DBr,[7] and 1-bromo-3,3,3-trifluoropropene from 3,3,3-trifluoropropyne.[8] Radical chain addition of hydrogen bromide to α,β-unsaturated acids and other carbonyl-conjugated olefins has not been established, very possibly merely because most workers have only examined the structures of the products, rather than examining reaction rates, and here both radical and polar processes usually yield the same product. However, Shimamura and Takahashi[9] have reported that, whereas cinnamic acid gives $\phi{-}CHBrCH_2COOH$ by the non-radical reaction, in the cold in the presence of oxygen the products include $\phi CHBr{-}CHBrCOOH$ and $\phi COCH_2Br$ and suggest the following partial reaction path:

$$\phi CH{=}CH{-}COOH + Br \cdot \rightarrow \phi{-}\dot{C}H{-}CHBr{-}COOH \qquad (5)$$

$$CO_2 + \phi COCHBr \leftarrow \phi{-}\underset{\underset{O}{\|}}{C}{-}CHBr\overset{O_2}{\diagup}\overset{Br_2}{\diagdown}COOH \quad \phi CHBrCHBrCOOH$$

The bromine presumably arises from oxidation of HBr, and the oxygen reaction may involve an intermediate hydroperoxide (Chapter 9).

An important problem in actually carrying out hydrogen bromide additions is choosing conditions to favor either the polar or radical

[7] L. C. Leitch and A. T. Morse, *Can. J. Chem.*, **30**, 924 (1952).

[8] R. N. Haszeldine, *J. Chem. Soc.*, **1952**, 3490.

[9] O. Simamura and M. Takahashi, *Bull. Chem. Soc. Japan*, **22**, 60 (1949); cf. also H. Kashiwagi, *ibid.*, **26**, 355 (1953).

process.[10] The former is favored by weakly basic, polar solvents or, if it is carried out in a non-polar solvent, is apparently of very high order in halogen acid,[11] so that high halogen acid concentrations are desirable. Further, it is a wise precaution to hinder the radical process by avoiding the presence of air, using peroxide-free reagents, and adding an inhibitor. Hydroquinone, catechol, diphenylamine, and thiophenol have often been employed, and they probably act largely by suppressing the formation of peroxide by the HBr catalyzed autoxidation process (Section $9\cdot3c$). Although the radical addition appears to go in any solvent which does not actually interfere with the radical chain, non-polar solvents are probably advantageous for the radical process since they decrease the competition of normal addition. In early work adventitious peroxides, ascaridole, or molecular oxygen were generally used as initiators. The last has been suggested [4] as acting via the process

$$O_2 + HBr \rightarrow Br\cdot + HOO\cdot \qquad (6)$$

as little as 0.03 mole $\%$ being effective to give 96$\%$ abnormal addition to allyl bromide.[12] However, in view of experience with other radical processes, more dependable radical sources such as benzoyl peroxide or the azonitriles are probably preferable. The reaction can also be initiated photochemically in either the liquid or gas phase, alone, or, better, in the presence of photosensitizers such as carbonyl compounds and metal alkyls.[3,13] Large amounts of oxygen inhibit the photochemical addition,[14] just as it inhibits many other chain processes, by forming relatively unreactive peroxy radicals (Chapter 9),

$$BrCH_2\dot{C}HR + O_2 \rightarrow BrCH_2{-}\overset{\overset{\displaystyle OO\cdot}{\diagup}}{C}HR \qquad (7)$$

A number of other initiators have also been described, including α-haloketones,[14] and finely divided metals such as iron, cobalt, and nickel,[3] which presumably produce radicals by some sort of redox

[10] A third "molecular" mechanism, the reverse of the unimolecular decomposition of alkyl halides (see below) must also exist but has not been unequivocally observed. Presumably it could occur at high pressures in the gas phase or in non-polar solvents.

[11] F. R. Mayo and J. J. Katz, *J. Am. Chem. Soc.*, **69**, 1339 (1947); F. R. Mayo and M. G. Savoy, *ibid.*, 1348.

[12] Y. Urushibara and M. Takebayashi, *Bull. Chem. Soc. Japan*, **12**, 138 (1937).

[13] W. E. Vaughan, F. F. Rust, and T. W. Evans, *J. Org. Chem.*, **7**, 477 (1942).

[14] F. F. Rust and W. E. Vaughan, *ibid.*, **7**, 491 (1942).

reaction with hydrogen bromide. In the gas phase, the reaction may also be initiated by a silent electric discharge.[15]

The stereochemistry of the radical addition is of some interest. In 1939 it was noted that radical addition of two moles of hydrogen bromide to 2-butyne gave solely racemic 2,3-dibromobutane, a product which could be the result of two successive *trans* (or *cis*) additions.[16]   The problem has been investigated in more detail by Goering,[17] who found that both 1-methyl- and 1-bromocyclohexene [17a] gave exclusively *trans* addition, yielding *cis*-1-bromo-2-methylcyclohexane and *cis*-1,2-dibromocyclohexane respectively under conditions where the products are stable towards rearrangement. They suggested initially that the intermediate radical may have a bridged structure, i.e.,

$$(8)$$

which determines the stereochemistry of the product. However, such a formulation involves an expansion in the valence shell of bromine, among other difficulties.

Later, as a result of more extensive work,[17b] in which the stereospecificity of the reaction of 1-chloro- and 1-bromocyclohexane was demonstrated under a variety of conditions, they have concluded that the observed stereochemistry arises from radical attack on the cyclohexene from an *axial* direction to yield an intermediate radical of conformation I, which again reacts with HBr at an *axial* position to give the *trans* addition and a *cis* product (III). The displacement step

$$(9)$$

[15] N. V. de Bataafsche Petroleum Maatschappij, Brit. Pat., 668,159 (March 12, 1952).

[16] C. Walling, M. S. Kharasch, and F. R. Mayo, *J. Am. Chem. Soc.*, **61,** 1711 (1939). More recent work by H. L. Goering and D. W. Larsen, *ibid.*, **79,** 2653 (1957), now shows that both stereoisomeric 2-bromo-2-butenes undergo stereospecific *trans* addition of HBr at −80°.

[17] (a) H. L. Goering, P. I. Abell, and B. F. Aycock, *ibid.*, **74,** 3588 (1952); (b) H. L. Goering and L. L. Sims, *ibid.*, **77,** 3465 (1955).

must be very rapid since it occurs before isomerization to conformation II which should give the *trans* product (IV). Other addends, notably thiols (Section 7·2a), show a similar, although sometimes less specific, stereochemistry of addition in these systems, in contrast to the apparent *cis* addition to bridged rings noted in Section 6·2e, and give further support to this picture.

Finally a case of what may be radical rearrangement is known in these reactions. The addition of hydrogen bromide to 3,3,3-trichloropropene was studied by Kharasch,[18] who found no reaction could be obtained under radical-free conditions, but that irradiation in the presence of benzoyl peroxide and air gave up to 50% of a product different from the then known 1,1,1-trichloro-2-bromopropane, which he considered to be 1,1,1-trichloro-3-bromopropane. Subsequently this material has been prepared by another route, and Nesmayanov et al. have shown that the addition product is a third substance.[19] By analogy to the rearranged products described in Section 6·2e it is probably 1,1,2-trichloro-3-bromopropane, formed via the sequence

$$CH_2{=}CH{-}CCl_3 + Br\cdot \longrightarrow BrCH_2\dot{C}HCCl_3 \xrightarrow{} BrCH_2CHCl\dot{C}Cl_2$$

$$\underset{\displaystyle BrCH_2CHCl\dot{C}HCl_2 + Br\cdot}{\overset{\displaystyle HBr}{\Big\diagdown}} \qquad (10)$$

7·1b   *Addition of Other Halogen Acids*

Hydrogen fluoride and olefins make a very poor combination for a radical chain process, because of the very high strength of the H—F bond (cf. Table 6·1). With hydrogen chloride–ethylene the energetics are as indicated. Reaction 11b must overcome an appreciable

$$Cl\cdot + CH_2{=}CH_2 \rightarrow ClCH_2{-}\dot{C}H_2 \qquad \Delta H = -26 \text{ kcal} \qquad (11a)$$

$$ClCH_2{-}\dot{C}H_2 + HCl \rightarrow ClCH_2CH_3 + Cl\cdot \qquad \Delta H = +5 \text{ kcal} \qquad (11b)$$

energy barrier, but, in 1948, Raley, Rust, and Vaughan showed that the radical addition of hydrogen chloride to ethylene in the vapor phase could be induced by either ultraviolet light or the thermal decomposition of di-*t*-butyl peroxide at 140–185°.[20] In keeping with the radical chain nature of the addition, it is inhibited by oxygen and a number of other substances.

[18] M. S. Kharasch, E. H. Rossin, and E. K. Fields, *ibid.*, **63**, 2558 (1941).

[19] A. N. Nesmayanov, R. K. Freidlina and V. I. Firstov, *Izvest. Akad. Nauk S.S.S.R. Otdel. Khim Nauk,* **1951**, 505.

[20] J. H. Raley, F. F. Rust, and W. E. Vaughan, *J. Am. Chem. Soc.,* **70**, 2767 (1948).

Substitution in the ethylene molecule should increase ΔH for reaction 11b. Only a very slow analogous reaction was observed with propylene, and isobutylene proved to be an effective inhibitor for the ethylene addition, presumably by trapping the chain-carrying radicals, either by addition or by attack on allylic C—H bonds. In the liquid phase, however, in the presence of benzoyl peroxide, hydrogen chloride adds to excess t-butyethylene to give up to 24% primary alkyl chloride,[21] radical and polar processes apparently competing, but chains are short, and it is not difficult to see why earlier workers [3] failed to detect the radical addition of this halogen acid.

At higher pressures telomer formation competes in the addition of ethylene, and Ford et al.[22] have obtained a whole series of even-numbered n-alkyl chlorides (identified through $C_{20}H_{41}Cl$) by heating ethylene at 100–1000 atmospheres with aqueous hydrochloric acid at 100° in the presence of benzoyl peroxide. Here the situation is further complicated by the fact that most of the hydrogen chloride must have been present in ionic form.

They also reported low telomers with allyl chloride and styrene, and these reactions have been investigated in more detail by Mayo.[23] Allyl chloride, polymerized in the presence of either aqueous or anhydrous HCl, gives a polymer of reduced molecular weight. In the absence of water, 1,3-dichloropropane can be isolated (together with a large amount of the normal addition product), the first and second transfer constants being 1.8 and 5.4. A small amount of n-propyl chloride was also obtained from propylene-HCl in hexane solution in the presence of benzoyl peroxide at 70°. On the other hand, the "telomer" formation with styrene is apparently the result of simultaneous radical polymerization to give high molecular weight polymer and an acid-catalyzed polymerization giving low molecular weight, chlorine-containing polymer.

The energetics for the radical addition of hydrogen iodide to olefins indicates that here the slow step should be iodine atom attack on the double bond, particularly since radical addition processes commonly

$$I\cdot + CH_2{=}CH_2 \rightarrow ICH_2{-}\dot{C}H_2 \qquad \Delta H = 7 \text{ kcal} \qquad (12)$$

$$ICH_2{-}\dot{C}H_2 + HI \rightarrow ICH_2CH_3 + I\cdot \qquad \Delta H = -27 \text{ kcal} \qquad (13)$$

[21] G. G. Ecke, N. C. Cook, and F. C. Whitmore, ibid., 72, 1511 (1950).

[22] T. A. Ford, W. E. Hanford, J. Harmon, and R. D. Lipscomb, ibid., 74, 4323 (1952).

[23] F. R. Mayo, ibid., 76, 5392 (1954).

have large negative entropies of activation. Accordingly, it is not surprising that this reaction has not been observed with simple olefins,[24] particularly since the normal addition is rapid and iodine catalyzed. On the other hand, with a molecule like styrene, from Table 6·2, ΔH for reaction 12 is lowered to about -15 kcal by the resonance energy of the benzyl radical, whereas ΔH for reaction 13 becomes -2 kcal. It would be interesting to see if this chain reaction could be carried out in the gas phase or in a suitable non-polar solvent.

7·1c   Halogen Additions to Olefins

By far the majority of studies on radical additions of halogens to olefins have been on the photochemical reaction in the gas phase. Since such reactions lie outside the proper scope of this book, and the results have been reviewed by Schumacher,[25] and recently in more detail by Steacie,[26] the subject will be treated rather briefly, even though predictions concerning radical reactions based on gas-phase data can apparently be extended to liquid-phase reactions with little change. In the case of liquid-phase halogen additions, however, an important complication arises in the competition with the polar addition process, which is very rapid with simple olefins, particularly in polar solvents (cf. for example the familiar bromine test for unsaturation). As a consequence, observations on liquid-phase radical additions of halogens are largely restricted to non-polar solvents and to olefins with electron-withdrawing substituents, circumstances where the polar process is greatly repressed.[27] Heats of reaction for the addition and displacement steps in the chlorination of ethylene are both -26 kcal, and the gas-phase photoinduced reaction to yield ethylene dichloride [28, 29] has the usual characteristics of a radical chain process, with a quantum yield as high as 3×10^6.[29] The reaction is strongly oxygen inhibited, and follows the rate law

[24] M. S. Kharasch, J. A. Norton, and F. R. Mayo, *ibid.*, **62**, 81 (1940).

[25] H. J. Schumacher, *Angew. Chem.*, **53**, 501 (1940).

[26] E. W. R. Steacie, *Atomic and Free Radical Reactions*, second edition, Reinhold Publishing Corp., New York, 1954.

[27] Cf. C. K. Ingold, *Structure and Mechanism in Organic Chemistry*, Cornell University Press, Ithaca, N. Y., 1953, Chapter 12. Reactions of fluorine appear to be entirely radical processes, and only a few cases of simple addition to double bonds are known, as the reaction is usually uncontrollably violent (cf. Section 8·2).

[28] T. D. Stewart and M. H. Hanson, *J. Am. Chem. Soc.*, **53**, 1121 (1931); T. D. Stewart and B. Weidenbaum, *ibid.*, **57**, 2036 (1935).

[29] H. Schmitz, H. J. Schumacher, and A. Jäger, *Z. physik. Chem.*, **B51**, 281 (1942).

$$d[C_2H_4Cl_2]/dt = kI_{abs}^{1/2}[Cl_2][C_2H_4]^{1/2} \qquad (14)$$

for which the consistent sequence

$$Cl_2 + h\nu \rightarrow 2Cl\cdot \qquad (15)$$

$$Cl\cdot + C_2H_4 \rightleftharpoons \cdot C_2H_4Cl \qquad (16)$$

$$\cdot C_2H_4Cl + Cl_2 \rightarrow C_2H_4Cl_2 + Cl\cdot \qquad (17)$$

$$\cdot C_2H_4Cl + Cl\cdot \rightarrow C_2H_4 + Cl_2 \qquad (18)$$

has been proposed.[29] Formation of ethylene dichloride in reaction 18 would yield the same result, and the reversibility of reaction 16 is considered further in Section 7·1d. The overall activation energy is very low, consistent with the necessary rapidity of the chain steps. At higher temperatures, ethylene apparently undergoes a thermal chlorine addition reaction to give ethylene dichloride, although other products are formed as well.[30]

The chloroethylenes including vinyl chloride,[31] cis- and trans-dichloroethylene,[32] trichloroethylene,[32] and tetrachloroethylene [33] show similar photochemical chain reactions, but a rate law

$$-d[Cl_2]/dt = kI_{abs}^{1/2}[Cl_2] \qquad (19)$$

indicating that the reaction analogous to reaction 16 was not reversible under the conditions studied and that chain termination involves two chloroalkyl radicals (cf. Section 6·1b). Both results are in keeping with the expected greater stability and lower reactivity of the intermediate polychloro radicals, as is the decreasing quantum yield with increased substitution, that suggests a retardation of reaction 17. The tetrachloroethylene reaction has also been studied in carbon tetrachloride solution,[34] yielding similar kinetics with long chains, and oxygen inhibition of the addition.

A few measurements have also been made on longer chain olefins. At low temperatures addition occurs, but at elevated temperatures chlorine atom addition becomes increasingly reversible and is replaced as a chain-carrying step by hydrogen abstraction, propylene, for example, yielding primarily allyl chloride [30] (Section 8·3).

[30] F. F. Rust and W. E. Vaughan, J. Org. Chem., 5, 472 (1940).

[31] H. Schmitz and H. J. Schumacher, Z. physik. Chem., B52, 72 (1942).

[32] K. L. Müller and H. J. Schumacher, ibid., B35, 285, 455 (1937); Z. Elektrochem., 43, 807 (1937).

[33] R. G. Dickinson and J. L. Carrico, J. Am. Chem. Soc., 56, 1473 (1934); C. Schott and H. J. Schumacher, Z. physik. Chem., B49, 107 (1941).

[34] J. A. Leermakers and R. G. Dickinson, J. Am. Chem. Soc., 54, 4648 (1932).

Radical additions of bromine follow a similar course, except that the steps are increasingly reversible, since the heats of reaction of the addition and displacement steps with ethylene are now -5 and -1 kcal respectively.

Acetylene [35] and ethylene [29] in the gas phase both undergo photo-bromination via long chains, although the quantum yield with ethylene is lower than in the photochlorination. The kinetics also show that chain termination is chiefly via bromine atoms, so that the step involving bromine atom addition must be slower compared with the attack of the alkyl radical on a bromine molecule. Photochemical addition has been studied with vinyl chloride [31] and *trans*-dichloroethylene.[36] The latter reaction has also been investigated in the liquid phase by Ketelaar et al.[37] Since much of the work is concerned with the reversibility of the reaction, it is considered further in the next section. With tetrachloroethylene, the reversibility of addition reaches the point [38] at which the equilibrium

$$C_2Cl_4 + Br_2 \rightleftharpoons C_2Cl_4Br_2 \tag{20}$$

lies far to the left in the gas phase at temperatures as low as $100°$. In the liquid phase at room temperature, however, the photochemical addition proceeds reasonably satisfactorily.[38, 39]

Radical addition of bromine to more complicated olefins is apparently also observable, providing it is not obscured by the polar addition process. Thus the addition of bromine to cinnamic acid is light catalyzed with a good quantum yield, and shows strong oxygen inhibition.[40]

In contrast to the situation with chlorine and bromine, radical addition of iodine to olefins is at best a marginal proposition, ΔH for the addition and displacement steps with ethylene being 7 and -15 kcal, respectively. In fact the overall equilibrium is unfavorable at ordinary temperatures. However, by working at $-55°$ in chloroform solution, Forbes and Nelson [41] have actually observed the photochemical addition to ethylene, propylene, and the four butylenes,

[35] K. L. Müller and H. J. Schumacher, Z. physik. Chem., **B39**, 352 (1938); **B40**, 318 (1938).

[36] K. L. Müller and H. J. Schumacher, ibid., **B42**, 327 (1939).

[37] J. A. A. Ketelaar, P. F. VanVelden, G. H. J. Broers, and H. R. Gersmann, J. Phys. Colloid Chem., **55**, 987 (1951).

[38] J. L. Carrico and R. G. Dickinson, J. Am. Chem. Soc., **57**, 1343 (1935).

[39] J. Willard and F. Daniels, ibid., **57**, 2240 (1935).

[40] W. H. Bauer and F. Daniels, ibid., **56**, 378, 2014 (1934).

[41] G. S. Forbes and A. F. Nelson, ibid., **59**, 693 (1937).

obtaining essentially quantitative yields (but quantum yields of 2.81 or below). The reversible additions of iodine atoms at higher temperatures are considered in detail in the next section.

Little attention has been paid to the stereochemistry of radical halogen additions, and in fact most of the work has been on systems where no stereochemistry could be observed. However, an interesting example of what appears to be *cis* addition via a radical chain was noted by Berson in the bromination of exo-*cis*-3,6-endoöxo-Δ^4-tetrahydrophthalic anhydride [42] and the corresponding endomethylene compound.[43] In the dark, both give *trans*-dibromide, but, on irradiation, the product is a mixture of *trans*- and exo-*cis*-dibromides, e.g.,

$$(21)$$

The result is striking, since the *cis*-dibromide is probably not the most stable product, and Berson suggests that the intermediate radical may be a mesomeric species.

$$(22)$$

However, we note that the stereochemistry is apparently the same as in radical additions to norbornylene (Section 6·2e).

A final reaction which actually appears to involve halogen atom addition is the reaction of sulfuryl chloride with olefins

$$CH_2{=}CHR + SO_2Cl_2 \rightarrow CH_2Cl{-}CHClR + SO_2 \qquad (23)$$

However, since intermediate sulfur-containing radicals are apparently involved, it is discussed in Section 7·3b.

[42] J. A. Berson and R. Swidler, *ibid.*, **75**, 4366 (1953).
[43] J. A. Berson, *ibid.*, **76**, 5748 (1954).

7·1d Reversibility of Halogen Atom Additions

As we have seen, the heat evolved in halogen atom additions decreases in the order Cl > Br > I, being small with bromine and negative with iodine and simple olefins. We have noted that reversibility complicates the kinetics of many of the gas-phase additions involving these atoms and, in Section 6·2e, saw that halogen atom loss sometimes leads to unexpected products in addition to allylic halides which also produce radicals with halogens on an adjacent carbon. We now examine some other consequences of this reversibility.

It has long been known that traces of bromine or iodine lead to *cis-trans* isomerization of such substances as dimethyl maleate and stilbene, and early work has been reviewed by Mayo and Walling.[3] Many observations indicate that the isomerization can be a radical chain process; thus, the isomerization of dimethyl maleate to dimethyl fumarate by bromine in carbon tetrachloride is induced by light of a wave length which dissociates bromine, and a quantum yield of 600 has been observed.[44a] Alternatively, the bromine atoms may be generated via redox systems, for example, using ferrous bromide and bromine; [44a, b] again up to 10^4 isomerizations occur per mole of bromine.[44a]

It seems plausible that such isomerizations arise via the reversible addition of bromine atoms.

$$\text{(24)}$$

Since the intermediate radical easily undergoes both inversion and rotation about the C—C bond, halogen atom loss can lead to either isomer, and elimination to yield the more stable form might be expected to be favored. The same intermediate radical is involved as

[44] (a) F. Wachholtz, Z. physik. Chem., **125**, 1 (1927); (b) D. H. Derbyshire and W. A. Waters, Trans. Faraday Soc., **45**, 749 (1949).

in the addition reaction, so addition and isomerization necessarily compete. This competition with the dichloroethylenes in the liquid phase at 25° in the presence of 0.05 molar Br_2 has been investigated in detail by Ketelaar et al.,[37] who have shown that a constant relation between isomerization and addition is maintained at different light intensities and in the presence and absence of traces of oxygen, the oxygen reducing the quantum yield from about 10^5 to about 10^3. They also conclude that bromine atoms add at identical rates ($\pm 50\%$) to both *cis* and *trans* dichloroethylene, but consider that bromine atom loss is a bimolecular transfer reaction to another olefin. molecule, rather than dissociation to a free bromine atom. Although the latter interpretation is preferred here, cf. Section 6·2e, the two paths in their system are experimentally indistinguishable. In the gas phase Müller and Schumacher [36] estimate that the activation energy for reaction 24 is 6.2 kcal higher than for attack of the intermediate radical on Br_2. (On the other hand, the latter probably has a smaller *PZ* factor.) Obviously, isomerization is favored by higher temperatures and also by low halogen concentration.

The bromine-catalyzed isomerization of *cis*-dibromoethylene has been investigated at 39–59° in CCl_4 solution by Steinmetz and Noyes,[45] using radioactive bromine and relying upon the thermal dissociation of Br_2 to initiate chains. If we picture the isomerization as arising from rotation about the C—C bond, the reaction involved may be diagrammed as

By measuring the relative rates of exchange and isomerization, they conclude that the rate constant for dissociation, process A, is about

[45] H. Steinmetz and R. M. Noyes, *J. Am. Chem. Soc.*, **74**, 4141 (1952).

twice that for the rotation, process B, but that the two have almost identical activation energies of something greater than 3 kcal. Bromine atoms generated from hydrogen bromide can also lead to isomerization. In the absence of light and air, the isomerization of stilbene by HCl or HBr is slow, requiring several days in benzene solution. The hydrogen bromide reaction, however, is greatly accelerated by air, light, or peroxides, and the acceleration, in turn, inhibited by diphenylamine.[46] Dichlorostilbene is said to be isomerized by HBr only in the presence of oxygen.[47] With other olefins, for example maleic acid and its derivatives, the radical isomerization does not compete with the acid-catalyzed polar process.[46, 48]

Iodine atom-catalyzed isomerizations have also been investigated, chiefly with the dihaloethylenes. The most detailed picture is obtained with diiodoethylene in decalin solution, using radioactive iodine and producing iodine atoms both photochemically and thermally.[49] The formulation is the same as in eq. 25, the activation energies for exchange and isomerization being 8 and 12 kcal, respectively. The difference should be the barrier to rotation in the intermediate radical, and leads to the result that exchange is about 100 times as rapid as isomerization under the experimental conditions employed. The 8-kcal activation energy for exchange is also in good agreement with the endothermicity of the iodine atom addition reaction.

The iodine-atom-catalyzed isomerizations of dibromo-[50] and dichloroethylene[51] have also been studied, the activation energy for the overall photochemical process with the latter being 11.9 kcal.

Radical addition to an allylic halide presents the possibility of halogen atom loss. If the radical is a similar halogen atom, the overall process is an allylic rearrangement. Sibbett and Noyes[52] have investigated the rapid photochemical exchange between radioactive I_2 and allyl iodide in hexane, concluding that such a process is involved. The overall kinetics are very complex but have been worked

[46] M. S. Kharasch, J. V. Mansfield, and F. R. Mayo, *ibid.*, **59**, 1155 (1937); Y. Urushibara and O. Sinamura, *Bull. Chem. Soc. Japan,* **13**, 566 (1938).

[47] T. W. J. Taylor and A. R. Murray, *J. Chem. Soc.,* **1938**, 2078.

[48] O. Sinamura, *Bull. Chem. Soc. Japan,* **14**, 22 (1939), other examples are given in the reference in footnote 3.

[49] R. M. Noyes, R. G. Dickinson, and V. Schomaker, *J. Am. Chem. Soc.,* **67**, 1319 (1945).

[50] R. M. Noyes and R. G. Dickinson, *ibid.*, **65**, 1427 (1943).

[51] R. E. Wood and R. G. Dickinson, *ibid.*, **61**, 3259 (1939); R. G. Dickinson, R. F. Wallis, and R. E. Wood, *ibid.*, **71**, 1238 (1949).

[52] D. J. Sibbett and R. M. Noyes, *ibid.*, **75**, 763 (1953).

out and shown to be consistent with other iodine atom reactions in the same solvent. At 25° the rate constant for iodine atom addition is 5×10^6 liter/mole/sec, about 2000 times that for addition to di-iodoethylene. In the dark, a slower, non-radical exchange also takes place.[53]

A similar path probably accounts for many of the very facile rearrangements of allylic bromides, and the fact that hydrogen bromide or bromine addition to conjugated dienes commonly leads to the equilibrium mixture of possible products. Thus, 1-bromo-2-butene and 3-bromo-1-butene are rapidly equilibrated by hydrogen bromide and peroxides, even at $-12°$.[54]

The rearrangement of α-bromoacetoacetic esters to the γ-isomers which occurs rapidly in the presence of hydrogen bromide plus radical sources,[55] but more slowly in their absence, is more obscure but may involve bromine atom addition to trace quantities of the appropriate enol.

$$\underset{\displaystyle \overset{OH}{|}}{Br\cdot + CH_2{=}C{-}CHBrCOOR} \rightarrow \underset{\displaystyle \overset{OH}{|}}{CH_2Br{-}C{-}CHBrCOOR} \rightarrow$$

$$\underset{\displaystyle \overset{OH}{|}}{CH_2Br{-}C{=}CH{-}COOR} \quad (26)$$

At higher temperatures radical chain processes are known by which the overall reaction of halogen acid and halogen addition is reversed, so that alkyl halides and dihalides break down into olefins. Alkyl halide pyrolyses have been comprehensively investigated by D. H. R. Barton, who has shown that, in addition to heterogeneous decompositions, two distinct homogeneous gas-phase reactions exist, a simple unimolecular decomposition into olefin and hydrogen halide, and a radical chain which is the reverse of "abnormal addition." A good example of the latter process occurs when ethylene dichloride is pyrolyzed at 350–500°.[56] The reaction is first order and has an overall activation energy of 47 kcal but is greatly accelerated by traces of oxygen, chlorine, or bromine (iodine is ineffective) and inhibited by propylene, saturated hydrocarbons, and alcohols. Chain

[53] D. J. Sibbett and R. M. Noyes, ibid., **75**, 761 (1953).

[54] M. S. Kharasch, E. T. Margolis and F. R. Mayo, J. Org. Chem., **1**, 393 (1936); W. G. Young and K. Nuzak, J. Am. Chem. Soc., **62**, 311 (1940).

[55] M. S. Kharasch, E. Sternfeld and F. R. Mayo, ibid., **59**, 1655 (1937).

[56] D. H. R. Barton, J. Chem. Soc., **1949**, 148, 155.

lengths are estimated as about 10^5 and the chain propagation steps must be

$$Cl\cdot + CH_2Cl—CH_2Cl \rightarrow CH_2Cl—\dot{C}HCl + HCl \qquad (27)$$

$$CH_2Cl—\dot{C}HCl \rightarrow CH_2{=}CHCl + Cl\cdot \qquad (28)$$

vinyl chloride and HCl being essentially the sole products. The actual initiation process in the absence of added materials is not entirely clear, and Barton suggests the unimolecular process

$$CH_2Cl—CH_2Cl \rightarrow C_2H_4 + Cl_2 \qquad \Delta H = 44\ \text{kcal} \qquad (29)$$

followed by dissociation of Cl_2 into atoms, since it is less endothermic than the process

$$CH_2Cl—CH_2Cl \rightarrow CH_2Cl—CH_2\cdot + Cl\cdot \qquad \Delta H = 80\ \text{kcal} \qquad (30)$$

However, judging from Barton's own data on the unimolecular decomposition of alkyl halides, reactions such as 28 and 29 generally have activation energies well in excess of their endothermicity (Barton has taken E_{act} for 29 as 72 kcal), and the energetics of 30 are still feasible since the rate constant for initiation enters into the overall rate expression to the one-half power. Reaction 27, involving radical displacement on hydrogen by a halogen atom, is a critical step in radical halogen substitutions and will be of great importance in the next chapter. Since the corresponding reactions with bromine and iodine atoms are appreciably endothermic, similar chain decompositions are not observed with bromides and iodides. The inhibitors mentioned must act by undergoing displacement reactions with the chain carriers to yield alkyl radicals incapable of carrying on the chain.

Similar chain decompositions occur with trichloroethane [56] and both sym- [56,57] and unsym-tetrachloroethane,[57] β,β-dichloroethyl ether decomposes by a short-chain process at higher temperatures (to yield a mixture of products),[58] and 1,1,1-trichloroethane decomposes to vinylidene chloride by concurrent radical and unimolecular paths.[59] On the other hand, the decomposition of ethyl chloride, 1,1-dichloroethane, and propyl and butyl chlorides [60] are unimolecular, non-radi-

[57] D. H. R. Barton and K. E. Howlett, *ibid.*, **1951**, 2033.

[58] D. H. R. Barton, A. J. Head, and R. J. Williams, *ibid.*, **1951**, 2039.

[59] D. H. R. Barton, *J. Am. Chem. Soc.*, **72**, 988 (1950).

[60] D. H. R. Barton, *J. Chem. Soc.*, **1949**, 165; D. H. R. Barton and P. F. Onyon, *Trans. Faraday Soc.*, **45**, 725 (1949); D. H. R. Barton and A. J. Head, *ibid.*, **46**, 114 (1950).

cal processes, essentially because radical attack at any point in the molecule not β to a halogen atom (which must occur at least occasionally) terminates the kinetic chain and permits the unimolecular mechanism to compete.

Turning now to the reverse of halogen additions, such reactions are best observed with the diiodides since the overall equilibria are favorable even in solution at ordinary temperatures, and there is no competition by hydrogen abstraction, the analog of reaction 29. A good example is the iodine-sensitized photolysis of ethylene diiodide in CCl_4 solution, studied by Schumacher [61] and others.[62] The rate expression is

$$-d[C_2H_4I_2]/dt = kI_{abs}{}^{1/2}[C_2H_4I_2] \tag{31}$$

consistent with the sequence

$$I_2 \rightarrow 2I \cdot \tag{32a}$$

$$I \cdot + C_2H_4I_2 \rightarrow CH_2I{-}\dot{C}H_2 + I_2 \tag{32b}$$

$$CH_2I{-}\dot{C}H_2 \rightarrow C_2H_4 + I \cdot \tag{32c}$$

$$2I \cdot \rightarrow I_2 \tag{32d}$$

Kinetics chains are short (<25), and the overall activation energy, 11.8 kcal, must be close to that of reaction 32b. At shorter wave lengths (3030–3130 A) initiation by photolysis of the diiodide also occurs.[62] The reverse of bromination has also been observed but chiefly at higher temperatures in the gas phase, for example with $CHBrClCHBrCl^{36}$ and $CBrCl_2CBrCl_2{}^{38}$. The processes by which displacement of halogen occur, reaction 32b, are again considered further in Chapter 8.

A somewhat different sort of decomposition of an intermediate radical has been observed by Rondestvedt [63] in the halogenation of β-styryl sulfonyl chloride. The reaction with bromine is light catalyzed and oxygen inhibited, and results in SO_2 elimination.

$$\phi{-}CH{=}CHSO_2Cl \xrightarrow{Br_2} \phi{-}CHBrCHBrCl + \phi CHBrCHBr_2 + SO_2 \tag{33}$$

[61] H. J. Schumacher and E. O. Wiig, *Z. physik. Chem.*, **B11**, 45 (1931); H. J. Schumacher and G. Stieger, *ibid.*, **B12**, 348 (1931).

[62] R. E. DeRight and E. O. Wiig, *J. Am. Chem. Soc.*, **57**, 2411 (1935).

[63] C. S. Rondestvedt, Jr., R. L. Grimsley, and C. D. Ver Nooy, *J. Org. Chem.*, **21**, 206 (1956).

Chlorine similarly produces 1-phenyl-1,2,2-trichloroethane, and Rondestvedt suggests the chain

$$\cdot Cl + \phi CH{=}CHSO_2Cl \rightarrow \phi{-}\overset{\cdot}{C}H{-}CHClSO_2Cl \rightarrow$$

$$\phi CH{=}CHCl + SO_2 + \cdot Cl$$
$$\downarrow Cl_2 \qquad\qquad (34)$$
$$\phi CHClCHCl_2$$

7·1e Halogen Additions to Aromatic Systems

Halogen additions to aromatic systems represent an interesting group of reactions of which the most important, practically, is the addition of chlorine to benzene. This reaction was first described by Faraday in 1825, and now carried out on a large scale, since the ultimate product, benzene hexachloride (BHC), is an important insecticide. Actually BHC is a mixture of five stereoisomeric 1,2,3,4,5,6-hexachlorocyclohexanes, of which only one, the γ-isomer obtained in 12–18% yield, has important insecticidal properties.

The addition reaction of chlorine to benzene, in contrast to the substitution reaction giving chlorobenzene, has the characteristics of a radical chain process, and in the technical process is usually initiated with 3600–4000 A light.[64] The light-initiated reaction is further accelerated by traces of iodine [65] (although the radical nature of the reaction under these conditions is not established), and the reaction can also be initiated by peroxides or similar radical sources. The photochemical reaction in the vapor phase has been studied by Noyes and his students,[66] who found quantum yields of 20 or more,[67] and a rate expression

$$-d[Cl_2]/dt = kI_{abs}{}^n[Cl_2][C_6H_6] \qquad\qquad (35)$$

with $0.5 < n < 1.0$. Because of this result, they suggested that radical attack on benzene is a termolecular process.

$$Cl\cdot + Cl_2 + C_6H_6 \rightarrow C_6H_6Cl_2 + Cl\cdot \qquad\qquad (36)$$

[64] J. J. Jacobs in R. E. Kirk and D. F. Othmer, *Encyclopedia of Chemical Technology*, Vol. 3, Interscience Encyclopedia, New York, 1949, p. 808.

[65] H. Müller, *J. Chem. Soc.*, **15**, 41 (1862).

[66] C. E. Lane and W. A. Noyes, Jr., *J. Am. Chem. Soc.*, **54**, 161 (1932); H. P. Smith, W. A. Noyes, Jr., and E. J. Hart, *ibid.*, **55**, 4444 (1933).

[67] In the liquid phase, with higher concentrations of reagents, quantum yields are larger, ~2500. Cf. K. Schwabe and P. P. Rammelt, *Z. physik. Chem.*, **204**, 310 (1955).

But a reversible addition yields the same kinetics

$$\text{Cl}\cdot \;+\; \bigcirc \;\rightleftharpoons\; \overset{\text{H}}{\underset{\cdot}{\text{Cl}}}\bigcirc \;\xrightarrow{\text{Cl}_2}\; \overset{\text{Cl}}{\underset{\text{Cl}}{\text{H}-\text{H}-}}\bigcirc \;+\; \text{Cl}\cdot \qquad (37)$$

and is plausible because of the high resonance energy of the aromatic system being attacked. Qualitative evidence in liquid-phase reactions supports this view; see below. Some chlorobenzene is also formed in the photochemical reaction, perhaps by direct hydrogen abstraction, although the path is not clear, and, at elevated temperatures in the vapor phase, halogens appear to substitute benzene by a radical process.[68]

The product from reaction 37 has never been isolated but is assumed to add further chlorine by a similar path. Recently, the next product, benzene tetrachloride, has been obtained (unfortunately from the rather equivocal iodine-sensitized reaction) [69] and identified as a mixture of four stereoisomers of the expected 3,4,5,6-tetrachloro-cyclohexene.[70]

The final step has been shown to be definitely a radical chain, since the isomers are stable to chlorine in the dark but react rapidly on illumination. Each yields two or three of the stereoisomeric hexachlorocyclohexanes; so radical addition occurs on either side of the double bond, and the final reaction with chlorine may be either *cis* or *trans*. Bromine also adds photochemically to benzene, but the reaction has a larger temperature coefficient,[71] as might be anticipated, because of the lower strength of the C—Br bond formed in the initial addition.

When benzene and maleic anhydride are chlorinated together in the presence of light or peroxide, a remarkable reaction occurs leading to phenylchlorosuccinic anhydride in up to 45% yield, together with some

[68] J. P. Wibaut, L. M. E. Van de Laude, and G. Wallach, *Rec. trav. chim.*, **52**, 794 (1933).

[69] G. Calingaert, M. E. Griffing, E. R. Kerr, A. J. Kolka, and H. D. Orloff, *J. Am. Chem. Soc.*, **73**, 5224 (1951).

[70] H. D. Orloff, A. J. Kolka, G. Calingaert, M. E. Griffing, and E. R. Kerr, *ibid.*, **75**, 4243 (1953).

[71] W. Meidinger, *Z. physik. Chem.*, **B5**, 29 (1929); E. Rabinowitch, *ibid.*, **B19**, 190 (1932).

pentachlorocyclohexylchlorosuccinic anhydride,[72] apparently via a sequence such as

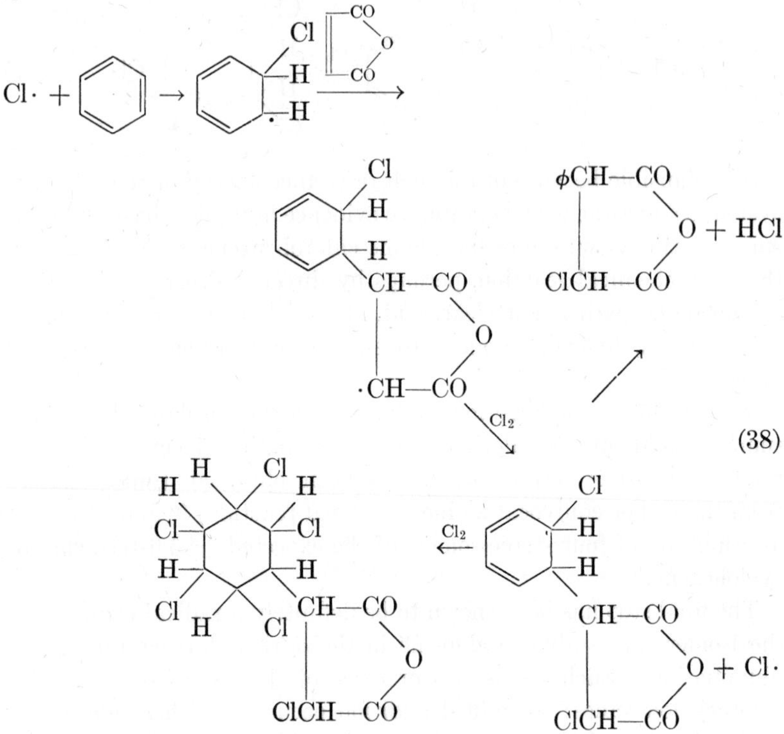

$$Cl\cdot + \bigcirc \rightarrow \cdots \longrightarrow$$

$$(38)$$

The most striking feature of the reaction is the necessarily very rapid attack of the chlorocyclohexadienyl radical on maleic anhydride which is able to compete with attack on Cl_2 (significantly, yields in reaction 38 are best when Cl_2 is added very slowly to the mixture of benzene and maleic anhydride) and recalls the maleic anhydride–styrene copolymerization discussed in Chapter 4.

A number of substituted benzenes also undergo radical addition of chlorine and bromine, and, in the chlorine addition to chlorobenzene and o-dichlorobenzene, the corresponding polychlorocyclohexenes (each mixture of four isomers) have been isolated.[73] With toluene, the radical addition of both chlorine and bromine competes with the radical side-chain substitution (Chapter 8). The chlorine addition is

[72] G. G. Ecke, L. R. Buzbee, and A. J. Kolka, *J. Am. Chem. Soc.*, **78**, 79 (1956).

[73] A. J. Kolka, H. D. Orloff, and M. E. Griffing, *ibid.*, **76**, 1244 (1954).

favored by low temperatures and high chlorine concentration,[74] further suggesting that the initial step of radical addition is reversible.

Addition reactions to more elaborate aromatic systems may be complicated by a competing polar addition. The bromination of naphthalene has been studied by Mayo and Hardy.[75] In the dark in CCl_4, about 15% addition accompanies substitution, but illumination gives over 80% addition. When the photochemical reaction is carried out in toluene, addition competes with side-chain bromination of the solvent, and again the initial step appears to be reversible since reaction with naphthalene rather than with toluene is favored by high bromine concentration.

Rather similarly, phenanthrene can react with bromine by a polar reaction to yield 9-bromophenanthrene and 9,10-dibromo-9,10-dihydrophenanthrene,[76] but the addition in CCl_4 solution is greatly accelerated by light, air, or peroxides and under these circumstances has characteristics of a radical chain reaction.[77]

A little-known reaction which must be related to halogen addition is the exchange between halogen molecules and aromatic halides. When bromobenzene is treated with chlorine at room temperature in the absence of halogen carriers (e.g., $FeCl_3$), chlorobenzene and bromine are produced by a reaction (39) first noted by Eibner,[78] who

$$Cl_2 + 2 \underset{}{\bigcirc}^{Br} \rightarrow Br_2 + 2 \underset{}{\bigcirc}^{Cl} \qquad (39)$$

reported that the reaction is catalyzed by light or traces of moisture. The reaction has been investigated more recently by Miller and Walling,[79] who confirmed the light catalysis and noted a similar peroxide-catalyzed reaction between bromobenzene and sulfuryl chloride, giving chlorobenzene (in rather low yield), bromine, and sulfur dioxide. Further evidence that a radical chain process involving chlorine atoms is involved was obtained by treating a mixture of bromobenzene and toluene with chlorine in the light and dark. The ratio of side-chain chlorination to exchange remained constant at approxi-

[74] M. S. Kharasch and M. G. Berkman, *J. Org. Chem.*, **6**, 810 (1941).

[75] F. R. Mayo and W. B. Hardy, *J. Am. Chem. Soc.*, **74**, 911 (1952).

[76] C. C. Price, *Chem. Revs.*, **29**, 37 (1941).

[77] M. S. Kharasch, P. C. White, and F. R. Mayo, *J. Org. Chem.*, **2**, 574 (1938).

[78] A. Eibner, *Ber.*, **36**, 1229 (1903).

[79] B. Miller, thesis, Columbia University, 1955.

mately 4–5, in spite of the necessarily great difference in overall rate and chlorine atom concentration.

A number of halogen-substituted bromobenzenes exchange similarly,[80] and the formation of chloro-substituted benzyl halides is generally a complication when o-, m-, or p-bromotoluenes are chlorinated with either chlorine [81] or sulfuryl chloride [82] under radical-forming conditions. The relative ease of exchange of substituted bromobenzenes has been measured by competitive experiments with bromobenzene,[79] relative reactivities versus bromobenzene being p-Cl, 0.9; m-COOH, 0.26; o-COOH, 0.23; p-SO$_2$Cl, <0.12; with reactivity clearly retarded by electron withdrawal.

Although all of these data point of an exchange via chlorine atoms, the exact formulation is puzzling, since a path

$$+ \; Cl \cdot \; \rightarrow \qquad \rightarrow \qquad + \; Br \cdot \qquad (40)$$

seems improbable, requiring addition of the chlorine atom at the most unlikely spot in the aromatic system. Direct displacement, too, seems unlikely, and an alternative might be an intermediate

$$+ \; Cl \cdot \; \longrightarrow \qquad \longleftrightarrow \qquad \rightarrow \qquad + \; Br$$

$$(41)$$

analogous to the "π complexes," discussed in regard to electrophilic substitution,[83] in which the chlorine atom is not specifically bonded to any carbon but is associated with, and undergoes electron transfer from, the whole π electron system. The same sort of step would then presumably be involved in the halogen additions already discussed. Similar interactions have been suggested in radical reactions involved in the inhibition of autoxidation (Section 9·2g), and this formulation is in keeping with the decreased reactivity of bromobenzenes with electron-withdrawing groups.

[80] W. Voegtli, H. Muhr and P. Läuger, *Helv. Chim. Acta.*, **37**, 1627 (1954).
[81] F. Asinger, *Monatschr.*, **64**, 153 (1934).
[82] G. L. Goerner and R. C. Nametz, *J. Am. Chem. Soc.*, **73**, 2940 (1951).
[83] H. C. Brown and D. J. Brady, *ibid.*, **74**, 3570 (1952).

If radioactive bromine is used, a similar light-catalyzed exchange between bromobenzene and radioactive bromine can also be observed,[79] but iodobenzene exchanges with iodine only at very high temperatures, and then by both radical and non-radical paths.[84] When iodobenzene is treated with chlorine, the only product is iodobenzene dichloride.[85]

Interestingly, chlorine atoms are able to displace SO_2 from diphenylsulfone and benzenesulfonyl chloride,[79] e.g.,

$$+ \; Cl \cdot \; \rightarrow \qquad + \; SO_2 + Cl_2 \qquad (42)$$

In the latter case, chlorine is regenerated, so only small amounts of reagent are required. A variety of other groups, however, are not displaced, and bromine is ineffective.

7 · 2 Additions of Thiols and Hydrogen Sulfide to Olefins

The addition of thiols to olefins is known to occur under a variety of conditions, and at least three mechanisms for the process are recognizable. The first is an acid-catalyzed reaction, which follows Markownikoff's rule and should be mechanistically similar to olefin hydration. Thus, in the presence of sulfuric acid, isobutylene and thiophenol yield the tertiary thioether [86]

$$+ \; CH_2 = C(CH_3)_2 \; \rightarrow \qquad \qquad (43)$$

A second is the base-catalyzed addition of thiols to α,β-unsaturated carbonyl compounds and other olefins with strongly electron-withdrawing groups, in which attack is by the thiyl anion, paralleling the addition of other nucleophilic species to such systems, e.g.,

$$RSH + CH_2{=}CH{-}CN \xrightarrow{\;OH^-\;} R{-}S{-}CH_2CH_2{-}CN \qquad (44)$$

[84] S. Levine, thesis, Columbia University, 1955.

[85] C. Willgerodt, *J. prakt. Chem.*, **2**, 33, 154 (1886).

[86] V. N. Ipatieff, N. Pines, and B. S. Friedman, *J. Am. Chem. Soc.*, **60**, 2731 (1938). At present a similar reaction using H_2S and C_{12} olefins is employed on a large scale to prepare tertiary thiols for use as synthetic rubber modifiers.

The third is the radical chain reaction with which we are here concerned. It has already been mentioned briefly in connection with chain transfer processes in polymerization (Section 4·2a) and is of great practical importance in controlling the molecular weight of synthetic rubber and other polymers. It is also of some synthetic utility, since the addition is "abnormal" (contrary to Markownikoff's rule), and the ease of the reverse reaction, dehydrogenation by thiyl radicals (Section 7·2c), has interesting features which will become apparent below.

7·2a   General Properties of Thiol Additions

Characteristic marks of a radical chain process, an effect of air and acceleration by light, were noted by Ashworth and Burkhardt [87] in the addition of thiophenol to styrene as long ago as 1928, and initiation by a variety of radical sources has subsequently been observed in a great number of systems. This, together with the "abnormal" direction of addition, has provided the bulk of the evidence that a radical chain is involved. In addition to the kinetic investigations discussed below, the extensive work on chain transfer with thiols in polymerization reactions (Section 4·2c and 7·2b below) serve effectively to relate the addition to other radical processes. The likelihood that free radicals were involved in the addition was first suggested by Burkhardt in 1934,[88] and the presently accepted chain mechanism (here shown for methyl mercaptan–ethylene) by Kharasch in 1938.[89]

$$CH_3\text{---}S\cdot \ + \ CH_2\text{=}CH_2 \ \xrightarrow{k_a}$$

$$CH_3\text{---}S\text{---}CH_2\dot{C}H_2 \qquad \Delta H \ = \ -14 \ \text{kcal} \qquad (45a)$$

$$CH_3\text{---}S\text{---}CH_2\dot{C}H_2 \ + \ H\text{---}SCH_3 \ \xrightarrow{k_d}$$

$$CH_3SCH_2CH_3 \ + \ CH_3S\cdot \ \Delta H \ = \ -12 \ \text{kcal} \qquad (45b)$$

Both addition and displacement are appreciably exothermic, making a rapid chain reaction possible. In fact, as we will see, there appears to be very little extra energy requirement for these reactions, and, in many systems, they derive extra driving force from the polar nature of the reactants.

[87] F. Ashworth and G. N. Burkhardt, *J. Chem. Soc.*, **1928**, 1791.

[88] G. N. Burkhardt, *Trans. Faraday Soc.*, **30**, 18 (1934).

[89] M. S. Kharasch, A. T. Read, and F. R. Mayo, *Chemistry & Industry*, **57**, 752 (1938).

Work on radical additions of thiols prior to 1940 has been summarized by Mayo and Walling,[3] and here we shall not attempt to tabulate all subsequent reactions but merely note the more significant developments. More quantitative relations between structure and reactivity are considered in the next section (7·2b).

. Peroxides have been commonly employed to initiate thiol additions to olefins, first by Jones and Reid.[90] In addition to acting via their thermal dissociation, in some systems (but certainly not invariably) they may also initiate chains by redox reaction with the thiol (Chapter 11). Although the details of the process in such cases are not clear, other examples of redox initiation, e.g., with peroxides and ferrous ion [91] are also known. The reaction may be initiated photochemically in the absence of oxygen or peroxides even at 0°C.[92] Light of wave length 3000 A is required, but, in the presence of photosensitizers such as acetone, the longer wave lengths transmitted by Pyrex are effective. Actually, many olefin samples contain enough peroxide that added initiators are unnecessary, even for rapid reaction. Traces of oxygen generally accelerate addition, but larger quantities lead to more complex autoxidations (Chapter 9). The oxygen- or peroxide-initiated addition is suppressed by antioxidants such as hydroquinone and usual radical inhibitors like trinitrobenzene. Sulfur appears to inhibit the radical process and catalyze "normal" addition to simple olefins.[90]

The radical addition can apparently be carried out with virtually any olefin not containing obviously inhibiting functional groups, and, even in the case of α,β-unsaturated carbonyl compounds like methyl acrylate where polar and radical reactions lead to addition in the same direction, the two processes can be distinguished and carried out independently.[93] The very high rate of reaction (reactions 45) incidently is apparent from the fact that ethylene gives appreciable quantities of telomer only at very high ethylene pressures (>500 atm.).[94]

Hydrogen sulfide may be added to olefins in the same manner as a thiol, but, unless an appreciable excess is present, the thiol product

[90] S. O. Jones and E. E. Reid, J. Am. Chem. Soc., 60, 2452 (1938).

[91] J. M. Hoeffelmann and R. Berkenbosch, U.S. Pat. 2,352,435 (June 27, 1944); J. T. Hackmann and R. Berkenbosch, Rec. trav. Chim., 68, 745 (1949).

[92] W. E. Vaughan and F. F. Rust, J. Org. Chem., 7, 472 (1942); U.S. Pats. 2,392,294-5 (1946).

[93] M. S. Kharasch and C. F. Fuchs, J. Org. Chem., 13, 97 (1948).

[94] J. Harmon, U.S. Pat. 2,390,099 (December 4, 1945).

reacts further to yield a dialkyl sulfide.[92,95] Thus, vinyl chloride yields mustard gas (β,β'-dichlorodiethyl sulfide). Similar additions are observed with thiol acids, $RC\overset{O}{\underset{SH}{\diagdown}}$,[96] and, in fact, go with extreme ease.[97] Since the product can be hydrolyzed to the corresponding thiol, the reaction could have synthetic use, e.g.,

$$R—CH{=}CH_2 + CH_3COSH \rightarrow$$

$$R—CH_2—CH_2SCOCH_3 \rightarrow RCH_2CH_2SH \quad (46)$$

The analogous reaction with acetylenes can be conducted to add either one or two moles of thiol acid [98]

$$RC{\equiv}CH + CH_3COSH \rightarrow R—CH{=}CHSCOCH_3 \rightarrow$$

$$\overset{\displaystyle SCOCH_3}{\underset{\displaystyle R—CH—CH_2SCOCH_3}{|}} \quad (47)$$

to give, on hydrolysis, either the aldehyde or dithiol. Similar addition of simple thiols to acetylenes apparently also occurs, thio-p-cresol and phenylacetylene giving a mixture of approximately equal quantities of *cis* and *trans* products.[99]

Hydrogen sulfide and diolefins such as diallyl ether as might be anticipated give polymeric products,[100] and the polymers from olefins and dithiols, formed, e.g., by the reaction

$$HS(CH_2)_6SH + CH_2{=}CH—(CH_2)_2—CH{=}CH_2 \rightarrow$$

$$(—S—(CH_2)_6—S(CH_2)_6—)_n \quad (48)$$

[95] F. F. Rust and W. E. Vaughan, U.S. Pat. 2,396,479–80 (April 16, 1946); M. F. Shostakofskii, E. N. Prilezhaeva, and E. S. Shapiro, *Izvest. Akad. Nauk S.S.S.R. Otdel. Khim. Nauk*, **1954**, 292.

[96] B. Holberg, *Arkiv Kemi Min. Geol.*, **12B**, No. 47 (1938); B. Holmberg and E. Schjanberg, *ibid.*, **14A**, No. 7 (1940); V. N. Ipatieff and B. S. Friedmann, *J. Am. Chem. Soc.*, **61**, 71 (1939); E. Schjanberg, *Ber.*, **74**, 64 (1941); R. Brown, W. E. Jones, and A. R. Pinder, *J. Chem. Soc.*, **1951**, 2123.

[97] J. I. Cunneen, *J. Chem. Soc.*, **1947**, 134.

[98] H. Bader, L. C. Cross, I. Heilbron, and E. H. R. Jones, *ibid.*, **1949**, 619.

[99] E. P. Kohler and H. Potter, *J. Am. Chem. Soc.*, **57**, 1316 (1935).

[100] W. E. Vaughan and F. F. Rust, U.S. Pat. 2,522,589 (September 19, 1950). 1,5-Dienes such as dihydromyrcene similarly yield cyclic sulfides, R. F. Naylor, *J. Polymer Soc.*, **1**, 305 (1946); *J. Chem. Soc.*, **1947**, 1532.

have been studied in some detail by Marvel and his students,[101] molecular weights as high as 60,000 being achieved.

Where it is possible to distinguish the products, thiol additions show the same sort of stereospecificity which we have noted in other additions. The products of addition of hydrogen sulfide, thiophenol, and thioacetic acid to 1-chlorocyclohexene are reported to be $>75\%$, $>94\%$, and $>66\%$ cis-1,2-disubstituted cyclohexane respectively, predominantly *trans* addition taking place.[102] Very interestingly, the amount of *trans* addition increases at high thiol/olefin ratios (i.e., under conditions when the intermediate radical has a short life), in keeping with the formulation of the HBr addition given in eq. 9. This suggests in turn that the rate of reaction of the intermediate radical with thiols is somewhat slower than with HBr. Addition of thiophenol to norbornylene gives solely the *exo*-thioether,[103] but a partial rearrangement has been observed with the corresponding diene, bicyclo[2.2.1.]heptadiene-2,5 as indicated.[104]

$$+ \; \phi SH \longrightarrow \qquad + \qquad \qquad (49)$$

40%   60%

When olefins, CO, and thiols are heated together at high pressures in the presence of radical sources, Foster, Lachar, Lipscomb, and McKusick [104a] find that β-alkylthioaldehydes are produced, apparently via the reaction sequence

$$RS\cdot + CH_2{=}CHR' \rightarrow RSCH_2\dot{C}HR' \xrightarrow{CO} RSCH_2\overset{H}{\underset{R'}{C}}{-}\dot{C}{=}O$$

$$\xrightarrow[RSH]{} \quad (49a)$$

$$\text{------------------------------} RS\cdot + RSCH_2CHR'CHO$$

[101] C. S. Marvel, et al., *J. Am. Chem. Soc.*, **70**, 993 (1948); **72**, 1978, 5026 (1950); **73**, 1064, 1097 (1951); *J. Polymer Sci.*, **6**, 127, 711, 717 (1951); **8**, 313 (1952); **9**, 53 (1952).

[102] H. L. Goering, D. I. Relyea, and D. W. Larsen, *J. Am. Chem. Soc.*, **78**, 348 (1956).

[103] S. J. Cristol and G. D. Brindell, *ibid.*, **76**, 5699 (1954).

[104] S. J. Cristol and G. D. Brindell, *Am. Chem. Soc. Meeting Abstr.*, **128**, 35N (1955).

[104a] R. E. Foster, A. W. Larchar, R. D. Lipscomb, and B. C. McKusick, *J. Am. Chem. Soc.*, **78**, 5606 (1956).

The reaction is reversible at lower pressures (cf. Section 7·2c) since, on heating with di-t-butyl peroxide, β-ethylthioisobutyraldehyde decomposes into CO, propylene, and ethyl mercaptan. The same authors have also described a number of other three-component telomers from olefins, CO, and such reagents as CCl_4, ketones, alcohols, etc.

A similar sequence of reactions has been observed by Kharasch and Friedlander [104b] when 1-octene is irradiated in the presence of CCl_3Br and SO_2

$$C_8H_{16} + SO_2 + CCl_3Br \rightarrow$$

$$CCl_3CH_2CHBrC_6H_{13} + CCl_3CH_2CH(C_6H_{13}) \qquad (49b)$$
$$\underset{SO_2CH_2CHBrC_6H_{13}}{|}$$

7·2b   Structure and Reactivity

As in chain reactions, the best information on the relation between structure and reactivity in thiol additions comes from studies of competitive reactions using the sort of kinetic treatment developed for copolymerization and chain transfer (Chapter 4). Compelling evidence that the thiyl radical is a strong electron acceptor, attacking points of high electron availability, comes from a study of the competitive addition of thioglycolic acid, $HSCH_2COOH$.[105] Results, compared with similar data on relative reactivities towards the maleic anhydride radical (polymer chains ending in maleic anhydride units), another strong acceptor, appear in Table 7·1.

TABLE 7·1 RELATIVE REACTIVITIES OF α-METHYLSTYRENES TOWARDS THIYL AND MALEIC ANHYDRIDE RADICALS (60°) [105]

Substituent	HOOC—CH₂—S·	Maleic Anhydride
p-OCH₃	100	18.5
p-CH₃	2.28	1.72
None	1.00	1.00
p-F	0.51	0.72
p-Br	0.90	0.73
m-Br	0.96	0.96

Although the accuracy of the measurements is not high, the great accelerating effect of electron-supplying groups is plain, and may be correlated, in the picture of these reactions which we have developed, with polar contributions to the transition state, such as

104b M. S. Kharasch and H. N. Friedlander, J. Org. Chem., 13, 882 (1948).

105 C. Walling, D. Seymour, and K. B. Wolfstirn, J. Am. Chem. Soc., 70, 2559 (1948).

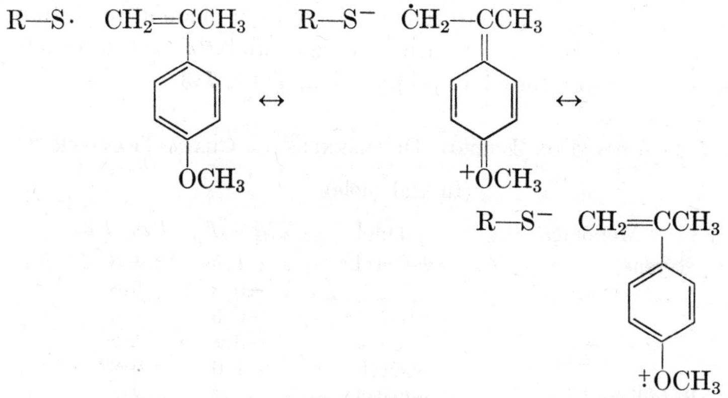

$R—S·$ $CH_2=CCH_3$ $R—S^-$ $\dot{C}H_2—CCH_3$

(structures with benzene rings and OCH_3, $^+OCH_3$ groups) $\leftrightarrow$

$R—S^-$ $CH_2=CCH_3$

(50)

$^+OCH_3$

In our scheme, electron-withdrawing groups in the thiyl radical should also increase reactivity, but here direct evidence is lacking. In the conjugate displacement reaction (45b), data on the effects of structure on both reactants are available, chiefly from transfer constants in polymerization reactions, and were considered briefly in Section 4·2a. Table 7·2 summarizes significant results.

TABLE 7·2   TRANSFER CONSTANTS OF THIOLS

(At 60° unless otherwise indicated)

Thiol	Styrene	Butadiene	Methyl Methacrylate	Methyl Acrylate
n-Butyl	22 [106]		0.67 [106]	1.69 [106]
n-Amyl	17.8 [107]			
n-Octyl	19 (50°) [109]	16 (50°) [109]		
n-Dodecyl	19.7 [108]			
t-Butyl	3.6 [108]			
t-Octyl	4.3 (50°) [109]	3.7 (50°) [109]		
α-Naphthylmethyl	18.3 (50°) [110]			
β-Ethoxypropyl	21 [108]			
Ethyl thioglycolate	58 [108]			
β-Thiylpropionic acid	6.0 (50°) [110]			
Thiophenol	Very high [108]			
2-Mercaptobenzothiazole	0.03 (50°) [110]			

[106] C. Walling, ibid., **70**, 2561 (1948).

[107] W. V. Smith, ibid., **68**, 2059, 2064 (1946).

[108] R. A. Gregg, D. M. Alderman, and F. R. Mayo, ibid., **70**, 3740 (1948).

[109] E. J. Meehan, I. M. Kolthoff, and P. R. Sinha, J. Polymer Sci., **16**, 471 (1955). This paper gives a number of additional values.

[110] R. M. Pierson, A. J. Costanza, and A. H. Weinstein, J. Polymer Sci., **17**, 221 (1955).

In a number of cases, measurements have been made at more than one temperature, so that activation energies and PZ factors can be compared with those for chain propagation, Table 7·3.

TABLE 7·3   ACTIVATION ENERGY DIFFERENCES IN CHAIN TRANSFER [109]

(In kcal/mole)

Monomer	Thiol	$E_{tr} - E_p$	PZ_{tr}/PZ_p
Styrene	n-Octyl [a]	-1.5	1.8
		-0.8	5.8
	t-Butyl [a]	-0.9	1.0
		-0.7	1.2
	t-Octyl	-1.0	0.93
Butadiene	n-Octyl	-1.2	2.3
	t-Octyl	-1.4	0.4
Methyl methacrylate	n-Amyl	1.2	4.2
Methyl acrylate	n-Butyl	0.6	4.5

[a] Calculated from two sets of data.

From Table 7·2 we see that there is little difference between normal thiols, but electron-supplying groups in the thiol decrease reactivity with hydrocarbon radicals, whereas an electron-withdrawing group increases reactivity. Conversely, the low transfer constants of acrylate and methacrylate show that electron-withdrawing groups on the carbon radical decrease the rate of attack on thiol. The low reactivity of 2-mercaptobenzothiazole can be accounted for because it exists chiefly as the tautomeric thione, but the low reactivity of β-thiylpropionic acid is surprising. The activation energy differences are small, and, since the E_p is only 6–8 kcal in these systems, indicate the low activation energy of these displacement reactions. In keeping with these low activation energies, transfer constants with styrene show only a moderate isotope effect, k_H/k_D for n-butyl mercaptan being 4.0 at 60°.[111]

This increased rate of the chain propagation steps between olefins with electron-supplying groups and thiols with electron-withdrawing ones suggests that particularly high overall rates of addition should be observed in such systems. Qualitative but convincing evidence of this has been reported by Cunneen,[96, 112] who noted that the olefins cyclohexene, dihydromyrcene, squalene, and natural rubber show reactivity with thiols in decreasing order, whereas for a series of thiols

[111] L. A. Wall and D. W. Brown, *ibid.*, **14**, 513 (1954).
[112] J. I. Cunneen, *J. Chem. Soc.*, **1947**, 36.

the order is isoamyl mercaptan < thioglycolic acid < thiophenol < thioacetic acid. Only the last reacted appreciably with rubber, but increasingly fast rates were found in the further series CH_3COSH < $CH_2ClCOSH$ < $CHCl_2COSH$ < CCl_3COSH. The order of thiol reactivities parallels electron withdrawal except for thiophenol (see below). The order of reactivity of the olefins is less obvious.

There is less evidence of the role of steric hindrance or resonance stabilization in thiol additions, but the high reactivity of thiophenol (which gives the thio analog of a benzyl radical) may be noted, and the high reactivity of thioacids may be aided by the resonance stabilization of the R—C⟨$^O_{S\cdot}$⟩ radical. In the case of thiophenol addition to benzothiophene dioxide, radical and polar additions give different products,[113] presumably because of the greater resonance stabilization of the benzyl radical determines the direction of the radical addition.

$$\text{(51)}$$

Aliphatic thiols give the 3-sulfide under all conditions, perhaps because, with these more reactive thiyl radicals, resonance stabilization in the intermediate radical is less important.

This picture of thiol additions has recently been clarified by kinetic studies carried out by Sivertz and his students, chiefly on the photochemical addition of n-butyl mercaptan to various olefins, using azobisisobutyronitrile as photosensitizer. At approximately 1:1 thiol:olefin ratios, systems follow the rate law,[114]

$$-d[\text{RSH}]/dt = k_d[\text{RSH}](R_i/2k_t)^{1/2} \tag{52}$$

[113] F. G. Bordwell, R. D. Chapman, and W. H. McKellin, *J. Am. Chem. Soc.*, **76**, 3637 (1954).

[114] R. Back, G. Trick, C. McDonald, and C. Sivertz, *Can. J. Chem.*, **32**, 1078 (1954).

indicating chain termination by interaction of R· rather than RS· radicals. This in turn suggests that $[R·] \gg [RS·]$ and $k_a \gg k_d$; cf. eqs. 45. Determination of individual rate constants by the rotating sector technique confirms this view (Table 7·4).

TABLE 7·4   RATE CONSTANTS FOR n-BUTYL MERCAPTAN ADDITIONS (25°) [a]

Olefin	k_a	k_d	$k_t \times 10^{-8}$ [b]	$E_{overall}$
1-Pentene	7,000,000 [115]	1,400,000 [115]	6000	2.4 kcal
Styrene	(8×10^8) [116]	2,600	5	6.2 kcal
Isoprene	...	93	1.4	...

[a] Reference in footnote 114 unless otherwise indicated.
[b] For interaction of 2R· radicals.

[115] M. Onyszchuk and C. Sivertz, *ibid.*, **33**, 1034 (1955).
[116] C. Sivertz, private communication.

The most striking features of the work are the very high values of k_a and k_d for simple olefins. In Table 7·4 we observe the expected increase in k_a and decrease in k_d as we go from pentene to styrene, and Sivertz has extended his investigations to a number of other systems with similar results.[116] For example, again, with thiophenol with a weaker S—H bond and a less reactive RS· radical, k_a's decrease and k_d's become larger.

7·2c   Reversibility of Thiol Additions; Dehydrogenation by Thiyl Radicals

The energetics of the steps in thiol additions, reactions 45, show that both are significantly exothermic in simple olefin-thiol systems. However, addition reactions frequently have appreciably negative entropies of activation, and the high values of k_a indicate little additional energy barrier to either the forward or reverse process.

$$RS· + CH_2\!\!=\!\!CHR' \rightleftharpoons RSCH_2\dot{C}HR' \qquad (53)$$

Accordingly, significant reversibility might be anticipated particularly for processes involving resonance-stabilized thiyl radicals such as $\phi S·$ or $RC\!\!\overset{O}{\diagup}\!\!S·$. Sivertz [117] has recently concluded that this actually occurs in the gas phase (where it is favored by low concentrations of reactants) since photochemical additions of methyl mercaptan to isobutylene, propylene, and ethylene show *negative* overall activation

[117] C. Sivertz, W. Andrews, W. Elsdon, and K. Graham, *J. Polymer Sci.*, **19**, 587 (1956).

energies of -8.9, -8.8, and -7.9 kcal, respectively, corresponding to the expected higher activation energy for the back process.

If such reversibility also occurs in solution, in spite of the presence of the higher thiol concentrations present, it should produce such phenomena as the *cis-trans* isomerization of olefins during thiol additions. Such isomerization actually occurs rapidly at 60° during the addition of methyl mercaptan to *cis*-2-butene,[117a] and, as a result, the rate constants in Table 7·4 may be open to question.

Considering the displacement step, a simple calculation based on the chain transfer reaction of styrene leads to a very interesting and similar conclusion. The activation energy for transfer with a normal aliphatic mercaptan, from Table 7·3 and $E_p = 7.3$ kcal (Chapter 3), gives the activation energy for the displacement reaction as $\sim$6.5 kcal. The RS—H dissociation energy of *n*-alkyl mercaptans, from electron-impact data,[118] is close to 86 kcal, and, if we take the C—H bond dissociation energy of the substituted phenylethyl radical to be the same as in toluene (77.5 kcal), we obtain, for the displacement, $\Delta H = 8.5$ kcal. Within the appreciable experimental error of bond dissociation energies (at least ± 2 kcal), these numbers are identical, and we conclude that, when polar and steric factors are favorable, reactions of the type

$$R{—}S{\cdot} + H{—}R' \rightarrow R{—}SH + {\cdot}R' \qquad (54)$$

will have negligible activation energies in excess of those required by the energetics of the overall displacement. Since S—H bond dissociation energies appear to be about 10 kcal less than the corresponding values for C—H bonds, this suggests that hydrogen abstraction by R—S$\cdot$ radicals should occur readily in many cases when the resulting carbon radicals are somewhat resonance stabilized.

Many scattered observations in the literature support this view, although in most cases the reactions involved do not seem to be chains and their details are obscure. In 1937, Ritter and Sharpe reported that tetralin, refluxed with isoamyl disulfide, yielded naphthalene in 70% yield, together with isoamyl mercaptan, and that the reaction appeared to go more rapidly with old (peroxide-containing) samples of tetralin.[119] This sort of reaction was reinvestigated by Nakasaki,[120] who found a similar dehydrogenation of tetralin, 9,10-

[117a] W. Helmreich and C. Walling, unpublished work.

[118] J. L. Franklin and H. E. Lumpkin, *J. Am. Chem. Soc.*, **74**, 1023 (1952).

[119] J. J. Ritter and E. D. Sharpe, *ibid.*, **59**, 2351 (1937).

[120] M. Nakasaki, *J. Chem. Soc. Japan, Pure Chem. Sect.*, **74**, 403, 518 (1953).

dihydroanthracene, phenylcyclohexane, and several other materials by diphenyl disulfide at around 260°, and also by 2-benzothiazyl disulfide. With cyclohexene and diphenyl disulfide dehydrogenation occurs at 140°. Presumably at these temperatures some dissociation of the disulfides into radicals occurs (Section 10·4a), and the idea that a radical reaction is involved is supported by the observation that similar reactions may be induced photochemically at room temperature.[121] Thus, ultraviolet irradiation of benzothiazoylyl disulfide dehydrogenates tetralin, cyclohexene, and squalene, and exposure of a petroleum ether solution of diphenyl disulfide and benzhydrol to sunlight yields benzopinacol plus thiol. Similarly, benzyl alcohol is oxidized to benzaldehyde. In 1948 Lyons reported that photolysis of di-o-tolyl and di-p-tolyl disulfides gives rise to thiols but with low quantum yield (0.046).[122] Unpublished work at Columbia [123] shows that room temperature irradiation of di-n-butyl disulfide in isopropylbenzene with 2537 A light leads to quite rapid formation of thiol. Another major product is 2,3-dimethyl-2,3-diphenylbutane, so the reaction can be formulated in part as

$$R\text{—}S\text{—}S\text{—}R \xrightarrow{h\nu} 2R\text{—}S\cdot$$

$$RS\cdot + \phi\text{—}\underset{\underset{CH_3}{|}}{\overset{\overset{CH_3}{|}}{C}}H \longrightarrow RSH + \phi\text{—}\underset{\underset{CH_3}{|}}{\overset{\overset{CH_3}{|}}{C}}\cdot \qquad (55)$$

$$2\phi\text{—}\underset{\underset{CH_3}{|}}{\overset{\overset{CH_3}{|}}{C}}\cdot \longrightarrow \phi\text{—}\underset{\underset{CH_3}{|}}{\overset{\overset{CH_3}{|}}{C}}\text{——}\underset{\underset{CH_3}{|}}{\overset{\overset{CH_3}{|}}{C}}\text{—}\phi$$

Thiol is also produced in ethylbenzene solution, and more slowly in toluene, but becomes negligible in isoöctane and cyclohexane, the expected order.

Some examples of apparent chain processes involving dehydrogenation are also known. Bickel and Kooyman [124] find that thermal decomposition of α-phenylazoethane at 125° gives nitrogen and mixed *meso* and racemic 2,3-diphenylbutanes

[121] M. Nakasaki, *ibid.,* **74,** 405 (1953).

[122] W. E. Lyons, *Nature,* **162,** 1004 (1948).

[123] C. Walling, R. Rabinowitz, and R. Natoli, unpublished work.

[124] A. F. Bickel and E. C. Kooyman, *Nature,* **170,** 211 (1952).

$$\phi - \underset{\underset{H}{|}}{\overset{\overset{CH_3}{|}}{C}} - N{=}N - \underset{\underset{H}{|}}{\overset{\overset{CH_3}{|}}{C}} - \phi \xrightarrow{125°} 2\phi - \underset{\underset{H}{|}}{\overset{\overset{CH_3}{|}}{C}} \cdot + N_2 \rightarrow \phi - \underset{}{\overset{\overset{CH_3}{|}}{CH}} - \underset{}{\overset{\overset{CH_3}{|}}{CH}} - \phi \quad (56)$$

In the presence of n-octyl mercaptan, acetophenoneazine, and ethyl-benzene are formed as well, perhaps through steps:

$$\phi - \overset{\overset{CH_3}{|}}{CH} + RSH \rightarrow \phi - CH_2CH_3 + RS\cdot \qquad (57)$$

$$RS\cdot + \phi - \underset{\underset{H}{|}}{\overset{\overset{CH_3}{|}}{C}} - N{=}N - \underset{\underset{H}{|}}{\overset{\overset{CH_3}{|}}{C}} - \phi \rightarrow \phi - \underset{}{\overset{\overset{CH_3}{|}}{C}} - N{=}N - \underset{\underset{H}{|}}{\overset{\overset{CH_3}{|}}{C}} - \phi + RSH \quad \text{etc.} \qquad (58)$$

In the further presence of 9,10-dihydroanthracene, its dimer is produced plus ethylbenzene and a quantitative yield of nitrogen. Here reaction 57 is apparently followed by

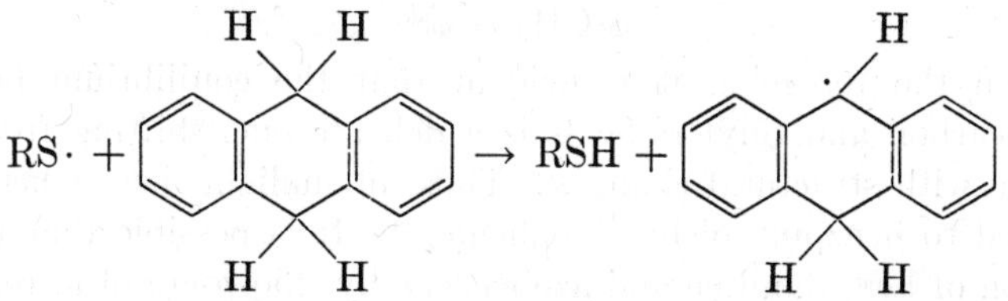

$$RS\cdot + \quad \rightarrow RSH + \qquad (59)$$

with the dihydroanthracene radicals dimerizing and the mercaptan being recycled, since four moles of ethylbenzene are produced per mole of mercaptan consumed.

A similar chain seems to be involved in the thiol-catalyzed decarbonylation of aldehydes described by Waters.[124a] Decomposition of methyl α-azobisisobutyrate in the presence of α-branched aldehydes produces only small amounts of carbon monoxide. In the presence of 0.5 mole % benzyl mercaptan, 80–90% of the aldehyde decomposes. Straight-chain aldehydes decompose to a smaller extent, whereas benzaldehyde is stable. Azobisisobutyronitrile may also be used to initiate the process. Thioglycolic acid is a less effective catalyst, and thio-p-cresol and mercaptobenzothiazole are ineffective. The proposed chain would be:

[124a] E. F. P. Harris and W. A. Waters, *ibid.*, **170**, 211 (1952); K. E. J. Barrett and W. A. Waters, *Discussions Faraday Soc.*, **14**, 221 (1953).

$$R\text{—}S\cdot + R'CHO \rightarrow RSH + R'\text{—}\overset{\displaystyle O}{\overset{\|}{C}}\cdot$$

$$R'\text{—}\overset{\displaystyle O}{\overset{\|}{C}}\cdot \ \rightarrow R'\cdot + CO \tag{60}$$

$$R'\cdot + RSH \rightarrow R'H + RS\cdot$$

Again, the thiol catalysis of exchange between diphenylmethyl radicals and diphenylmethane has been demonstrated by Cohen and Wang [125] by decomposing diphenylazomethane in C^{14}-labeled diphenylmethane. The overall process is

$$\phi_2CH\text{—}N\text{=}N\text{—}CH\phi_2 \rightarrow N_2 + 2\phi_2\overset{\cdot}{C}H \rightarrow \phi_2CHCH\phi_2 \tag{61}$$

In the absence of thiols the tetraphenylethane has only 1.1% of the activity of the solvent, but, in the presence of a small amount of thiophenol, the activity increases to 17%. The postulated reactions are

$$\phi_2\overset{\cdot}{C}H + \phi_2CH_2{}^* \underset{\text{Slow}}{\overset{\text{Slow}}{\rightleftharpoons}} \phi_2CH_2 + \phi_2\overset{\cdot}{C}H^* \ (+\phi SH)$$

$$\underset{\phi SH}{\searrow_{\text{Fast}}} \qquad\qquad \overset{\text{Fast}}{\nearrow_{\phi_2CH_2{}^*}} \tag{62}$$

$$\phi_2CH_2 + \phi S\cdot$$

From the foregoing it is evident that the equilibrium between hydrocarbon and thiyl radicals is a delicate one, shifting from side to side with structural changes. Thus, in sunlight, benzophenone is reduced to benzpinacol by thiophenol.[120] It is possible that the reduction of benzalaniline and azobenzene by thio-p-cresol in refluxing xylene [126] is a similar process. It is an interesting speculation whether many biochemical oxidations and reductions (in which the enzyme systems generally contain thiol-disulfide systems) do not go through similar paths. In this regard we may note that the oxidation of thiols to disulfides can be achieved by many ionic oxidants, so thiyl radical dehydrogenations may provide a path by which ionic oxidation-reduction systems are able to attack organic molecules at points where the ionic system alone is ineffective.

7·3   Addition Reactions Involving Other Sulfur Radicals

7·3a   The Addition of Bisulfite to Olefins

The addition of bisulfite to carbonyl-conjugated and similar olefins is a well-known reaction with kinetics and a pH dependence in accord

[125] S. G. Cohen and C. H. Wang, *J. Am. Chem. Soc.*, **77**, 4435 (1955).
[126] H. Gilman, J. L. Towle, and R. K. Ingham, *ibid.*, **76**, 2920 (1954).

with a simple Michael addition of sulfite ion to the conjugated system, e.g.,[127]

$$SO_3^= + CH_2{=}CH{-}COOCH_3 \xrightarrow{\text{Slow}}$$

$$SO_3^-{-}CH_2{-}\overline{C}H{-}COOCH_3 \xrightarrow[\text{Fast}]{H_2O} SO_3^-CH_2CH_2COOCH_3 \quad (63)$$

The addition to a simpler system, allyl alcohol, was reported by Mueller in 1873,[128] and similar reactions with other olefins have been carried out sporadically by other investigators with varying success. Mueller did not unequivocally determine the structure of his product beyond showing it was a salt of a hydroxysulfonic acid, but the reaction was reinvestigated by Kharasch, May, and Mayo,[129] who established the product as a salt of 3-hydroxypropanesulfonic acid. They also showed that this and similar reactions occur only in the presence of oxygen or other oxidizing agents, and that the reaction is inhibited by hydroquinone and similar antioxidants. From these observations (reaction conditions and the "abnormal" direction of addition), they concluded that bisulfite addition to simple olefins occurs only by a radical chain process, and proposed the chain-carrying steps

$$SO_3 \cdot^- + CH_2{=}CHR \rightarrow {}^-SO_3{-}CH_2{-}\dot{C}HR \quad (64)$$

$${}^-SO_3{-}CH_2{-}\dot{C}HR + HSO_3^- \rightarrow {}^-SO_3{-}CH_2{-}CH_2{-}R + SO_3 \cdot^-$$
$$(65)$$

The exact nature of the chain-carrying sulfite radical is not actually known, since a similar chain involving $HSO_3 \cdot$ can be written, and both species have been proposed [130] for the autoxidation of bisulfite and sulfite ions by oxygen (Chapter 11). The radical nature of the addition was also shown with ethylene, propylene, isobutylene, styrene, and cinnamyl alcohol,[129] and a number of additional olefins.[3] In the case of carbonyl-conjugated olefins, however, it was found impossible to make the radical reaction compete with the polar Michael addition, oxygen having no effect on the rate.[3]

Oxygen was employed as an initiator in most of Kharasch's work, but it leads to the complication that the resulting alkyl sulfonate may

[127] M. Morton and H. Landfield, ibid., **74**, 3523 (1952).

[128] M. Mueller, Ber., **6**, 1441 (1873).

[129] M. S. Kharasch, E. M. May, and F. R. Mayo, J. Org. Chem., **3**, 175 (1938). Earlier references are given in this paper, and also in the reference in footnote 3.

[130] H. L. J. Backstrom, Z. physik. Chem., **B25**, 122 (1934).

be contaminated with other products.[131] Thus, in the case of styrene, the following mixture was actually obtained:

$$NaHSO_3 + \phi CH=CH_2 \rightarrow \phi-CH_2CH_2SO_3Na$$
$$25\%$$

$$+ \phi CH=CHSO_3Na + \phi\overset{\overset{\displaystyle OH}{|}}{CH}-CH_2SO_3Na \quad (66)$$
$$10\% \qquad\qquad 65\%$$

Presumably the additional products arise by competing autoxidation, i.e., reaction of the intermediate radicals with oxygen. The initiation process in the presence of oxygen has been suggested [129] as

$$HSO_3^- + O_2 \rightarrow SO_3\cdot^- + HO_2\cdot \qquad (67)$$

and it is relevant that oxygen plus bisulfite is a known polymerization initiator, its effect being greatly increased by traces of heavy metal ions (Chapter 11). Alternatively, nitrite or nitrate ion may be used to initiate reaction in the absence of oxygen,[129] and peroxides are also effective.[132] Since Kharasch's investigation, the radical addition of bisulfite has had little attention. However, the addition to vinyl chloride has been described (although, puzzlingly, the product is given as 1-chloroethanesulfonic acid),[133] and good yields of long-chain sulfonic acids have been obtained by using solvent systems in which both olefin and bisulfite are somewhat soluble.[132] Thus ammonium n-octylsulfonate is obtained in 96.8% yield by heating 1-octene and excess ammonium bisulfate in methanol at 120° for two hours in the presence of 2,2-bis-(t-butylperoxy)-butane as initiator. Pyridine, ethanol, and hexanolamine are also suitable solvents, and other peroxides are effective.

Although ethylene at close to atmospheric pressure gives salts of ethanesulfonic acid, telomers are formed from both it and propylene in the presence of aqueous bisulfite at high pressures.[134] One-to-one products are also obtained from a variety of perfluoroölefins.[135]

[131] M. S. Kharasch, R. T. Schenk, and F. R. Mayo, *J. Am. Chem. Soc.*, **61**, 3092 (1939).

[132] D. Harman, U.S. Pat. 2,504,411 (April 18, 1950).

[133] J. E. Wicklatz, U.S. Pat. 2,600,287 (June 10, 1952).

[134] W. E. Hanford, U.S. Pat. 2,398,426 (April 16, 1946); *Imperial Chemical Industries, Ltd.*, Brit. Pat. 583,118 (December 8, 1946).

[135] R. J. Koshar, P. W. Trott, and J. D. LaZerte, *J. Am. Chem. Soc.*, **75**, 4595 (1953).

7·3b   Other Sulfur-Containing Radicals

A number of other chain reactions are known in which the chain carriers bear sulfur atoms with an odd number of electrons. One, in which the sulfur-containing radical is rather ephemeral and usually does not appear in the final product, is the peroxide-initiated chlorination of olefins using sulfuryl chlorine described by Kharasch and Brown.[136]   Although *sym*-dichloroethylene can be refluxed with sulfuryl chloride for hours without appreciable reaction, addition of 1 mole % of benzoyl peroxide gives an 85% yield of tetrachloroethane (plus sulfur dioxide) in two hours. Similar reactions occur with tetrachloroethylene, cyclohexene, stilbene, and other olefins, and, in fact, unless special precautions are taken to eliminate adventitious peroxides, the reactions often occur spontaneously. The chain involved is suggested [136] as

$$Cl\cdot + CHCl{=}CHCl \rightarrow CHCl_2{-}\dot{C}HCl \qquad (68)$$

$$CHCl_2{-}\dot{C}HCl + SO_2Cl_2 \rightarrow CHCl_2CHCl_2 + \cdot SO_2Cl \qquad (69)$$

$$\cdot SO_2Cl \rightarrow SO_2 + Cl\cdot \qquad (70)$$

Since sulfuryl chloride is often more convenient to measure and handle than is gaseous chlorine, the reaction has considerable synthetic value. However, in additions to 1-olefins such as 1-octene, an interesting side reaction occurs leading to 10–30% of a by-product, originally believed to be a sulfonyl chloride [137] but subsequently identified as a β-chloro-n-alkyl sulfone, $(R{-}CHClCH_2)_2SO_2$ by dehydrohalogenation, followed by hydrogenation to the known n-alkyl sulfone.[138]   Kharasch and Zavist [138] propose that this side reaction involves reaction of the intermediate (unstable) chlorosulfonyl radical, followed by rearrangement

$$\cdot SO_2Cl + CH_2{=}CHR \rightarrow Cl{-}SO_2{-}CH_2{-}\dot{C}HR$$

$$\xrightarrow{\quad o \quad} \cdot SO_2{-}CH_2CHClR \qquad (71)$$

$$\cdot SO_2{-}CH_2CHClR + CH_2{=}CHR \rightarrow$$

$$RCHClCH_2{-}SO_2{-}CH_2\dot{C}HR \qquad \text{etc.} \qquad (72)$$

Although in halogen substitution reactions involving sulfuryl chloride there is only rather equivocal evidence for the existence of the $\cdot SO_2Cl$

[136] M. S. Kharasch and H. C. Brown, *ibid.*, **61**, 3432 (1939).

[137] M. S. Kharasch and A. F. Zavist, *ibid.*, **70**, 3526 (1948).

[138] M. S. Kharasch and A. F. Zavist, *ibid.*, **73**, 964 (1951).

radical (Section 8·6c) the yield of sulfone is apparently decreased by sweeping out the reaction mixture with nitrogen, which should displace any equilibrium as

$$Cl\cdot + SO_2 \rightleftharpoons \cdot SO_2Cl \qquad (73)$$

However, the reaction still remains somewhat mysterious.

Reaction between sulfuryl chloride (containing traces of S_2Cl_2) and ethylene, vinyl chloride, and propylene carried out at room temperature are reported to give small amounts (up to 15%) of β-chloroalkylchlorosulfite.[139] With propylene, the product is ClSO—OCH$_2$CHClCH$_3$, which Kharasch [138] suggests as arising from the reaction

$$\cdot SO_2Cl + CH_2{=}CHR \rightarrow Cl{-}SO{-}O{-}CH_2{-}\overset{\cdot}{C}HR \qquad (74)$$

However, this would be surprising in view of the known structures of the polysulfones (Section 5·4c) and the radical additions discussed below.

Several other radical chain processes involving sulfonyl radicals,

$$R{-}\overset{\displaystyle O}{\underset{\displaystyle O}{\overset{\nearrow}{\underset{\searrow}{S}}}}\cdot$$

, are known, although data are rather spotty. The compound N-chlorosulfonylphthalimide reacts with olefins such as 1-octene to give β-chlorosulfonamide derivatives as indicated.[140]

$$(75)$$

[139] A. Y. Yakubovich and Y. M. Zinovev, *J. Gen. Chem. U.S.S.R.*, **17**, 2028 (1947).

[140] M. S. Kharasch and R. A. Mosher, *J. Org. Chem.*, **17**, 453 (1952).

The chain-carrying steps are presumably

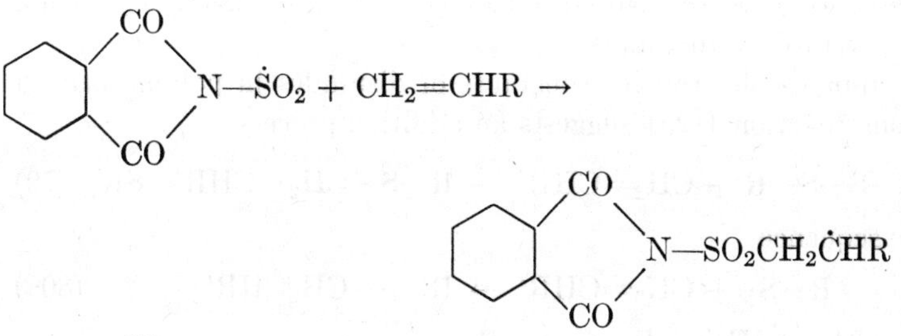

$$N-\dot{S}O_2 + CH_2{=}CHR \rightarrow$$

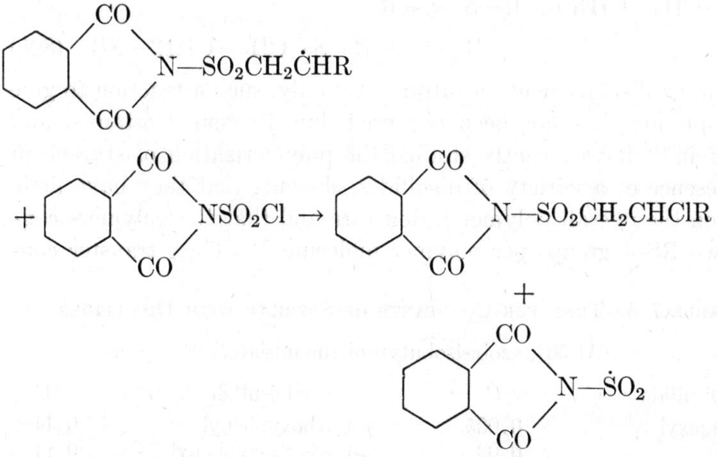

$$N-SO_2CH_2\dot{C}HR \quad (76)$$

$$N-SO_2CH_2\dot{C}HR$$

$$+ \quad NSO_2Cl \rightarrow \quad N-SO_2CH_2CHClR \quad (77)$$

$$+$$

$$N-\dot{S}O_2$$

A similar addition is reported by Ladd using p-chlorobenzenesulfonyl chloride and allyl acetate [141] or isobutylene.[142] With ethylene at 100 atmospheres both 1:1 product and telomers are obtained.[142] Rather remarkably other aryl sulfonyl chlorides are reported to be less reactive,[141-142] and alkylsulfonyl chlorides apparently do not undergo chain additions.[138] With trichloromethylsulfonyl chloride, sulfur dioxide is lost, and the products are the same as in the addition of carbon tetrachloride.[143]

$$CCl_3SO_2Cl + CH_2{=}CHR \rightarrow CCl_3CH_2CHClR + SO_2 \quad (78)$$

The sulfonyl chloride is apparently more readily attacked than CCl_4, since 1:1 products are obtained, even with styrene. Few data

[141] E. C. Ladd, U.S. Pat. 2,521,068 (September 5, 1950).

[142] E. C. Ladd, U.S. Pat. 2,573,580 (October 30, 1951).

[143] U.S. Rubber Co., Brit. Pat. 649,555 (January 31, 1951); E. C. Ladd and L. Y. Kiley, U.S. Pat. 2,606,213 (August 5, 1952).

have been reported on other sulfonyl halides, but recently Skell [143a] has noted that benzenesulfonyl iodide, with a weaker S—X bond, adds very rapidly to simple olefins.

The appreciable transfer constants of disulfides in polymerization reactions (Section 4·2a) suggests an addition process

$$R—S—S—R + CH_2\!\!=\!\!CHR' \rightarrow R—S—CH_2—CHR'—SR \quad (79)$$

via the sequence

$$R—S\cdot + CH_2\!\!=\!\!CHR' \rightarrow R—S—CH_2\dot{C}HR' \quad\quad (80a)$$

$$R—S—CH_2—\dot{C}HR' + R—S—S—R \rightarrow$$

$$R—S\cdot + R—S—CH_2—CHR'—SR \quad (80b)$$

involving a displacement on sulfur. Actually, such a reaction to give a 1:1 product has not been observed, but Pierson, Costanza, and Weinstein [110] have recently studied the polymerization of styrene in the presence of a variety of disulfides, showing that they have little effect on the overall polymerization rate and that the polymers contain two RS— groups per polymer molecule.[144] Their transfer con-

TABLE 7·5   TRANSFER CONSTANTS OF STYRENE WITH DISULFIDES

(At 50°, azobisisobutyronitrile initiator) [110]

Disulfide	C	Disulfide	C
2-Ethylhexyl	0.005	p-Carboxyphenyl	0.11 [a]
Benzyl	0.03	p-Carbethoxyphenyl	0.11
p-Chlorobenzyl	0.005	p-Hydroxymethylphenyl	0.09
β-(2-Pyridyl)-ethyl	0.03	o-Chloromethylphenyl	1.3
β-Chloroethyl	0.01	o-Bromomethylphenyl	1.0
β-Hydroxyethyl	0.005	o-Aminophenyl	3.0
Phenyl	0.06	β-Naphthyl	0.19 [a]
o-Tolyl	0.23	2-Benzothiazyl	2.1 [a]
p-Tolyl	0.11	Isopropylxanthogen	5.3
2,6-Dimethylphenyl	0.69	N-Morpholyl	0.005
2,3,5,6-Tetramethyl-			
phenyl	0.73		

[a] Presence of 2RS— end groups per polymer molecule shown by end-group analysis.

stants are summarized in Table 7·5 and indicate that the preparation of 1:1 adducts to styrene should be feasible with many of the more

[143a] P. S. Skell, R. C. Woodworth, and J. H. McNamara, *J. Am. Chem. Soc.*, **79**, 1253 (1957).

[144] Many additional examples (and also thiol transfer constants) are given by V. A. Dinaburg and A. G. Vansheidt, *Zhur. Obshchei Khim.*, **24**, 840 (1954).

reactive disulfides. With olefins yielding more reactive radicals, 1:1 products should be formed even more readily, the transfer constant of dibutyl disulfide with vinyl acetate being about 1.5.[145] However, the polymerization is appreciably retarded, and more complicated reactions may be involved.

The general features of the variations of disulfide reactivity with structure in Table 7·5 appear reasonable, the higher reactivity of diaryl disulfide correlating with the greater resonance energy and stability of the RS· radicals formed in the displacement. The increased reactivity due to o-substitution is noteworthy, and somewhat surprising, and it must be admitted that the increase in reactivity of aryl disulfides with electron-supplying groups and decrease with electron-withdrawing ones is contrary to the behavior of the thiols, and puzzling since electron withdrawal should increase the acceptor properties of the disulfide.[146]

Esters of dithiophosphoric acids, e.g.,

$$(EtO)_2P \overset{\displaystyle S}{\underset{\displaystyle SH}{<}}$$

add to olefins by both radical and non-radical paths which have been distinguished by Bacon and LeSuer.[147] Crude ester reacts with olefins to give a normal product.

$$(EtO)_2 - P \overset{\displaystyle S}{\underset{\displaystyle SH}{<}} \ + \ CH_2 = CHR \qquad (EtO)_2 - P \overset{\displaystyle S}{\underset{\displaystyle S - \overset{|}{C}HR}{<}} CH_2 \qquad (81)$$

With purified ester, particularly in the presence of peroxides, "abnormal" products are obtained from both styrene and 1-octene:

$$(EtO)_2P \overset{\displaystyle S}{\underset{\displaystyle SH}{<}} \ + \ CH_2 = CHR \ \rightarrow \ (EtO)_2P \overset{\displaystyle S}{\underset{\displaystyle SCH_2 - CH_2R}{<}} \qquad (82)$$

[145] W. H. Stockmayer, R. O. Howard, and J. T. Clarke, *J. Am. Chem. Soc.*, **75**, 1756 (1953).

[146] A similar phenomenon is observed in the thermal dissociation of substituted benzoyl peroxides (Section 10·2b) and here could conceivably arise from a weakening of the S—S bond by increasing the R → S dipole.

[147] W. E. Bacon and W. M. LeSuer, *ibid.*, **76**, 670 (1954).

presumably by a chain involving $(EtO)_2P \overset{\displaystyle S}{\underset{\displaystyle S\cdot}{<}}$ radicals. A number of similar additions have been described by Russian investigators,[148] both to simple olefins and to vinyl and allyl silanes.

Finally, a possible radical addition of thiocyanic acid has been reported by Kharasch, May, and Mayo,[149] but a mixture of products is obtained, and the reaction does not seem to have been investigated further.

7·3c   *Elemental Sulfur*

Any consideration of the addition of sulfur radicals would be incomplete without mention of the reactions of elemental sulfur, even though the detailed chemistry of this important substance is at present so obscure that discussion can be little more than suggestive. Accordingly, here we will do no more than point out the few facts which appear unequivocally established and indicate the evidence for radical participation in the important reactions of vulcanization, sulfur dehydrogenation, etc.

From room temperature to somewhat above its melting point, the stable form of sulfur, both molten and in solution, is S_8, an eight-membered, puckered ring, although metastable forms consisting of S_6 (a six-membered ring) and linear chains are also known. As the temperature of liquid sulfur is raised, the initially mobile liquid darkens and increases rapidly in viscosity, reaching a maximum at around 180°. From there to the boiling point the viscosity again decreases. These properties have been correlated by Powell and Eyring,[150] and more recently by Gee,[151] with an equilibrium between S_8 rings and long chains, which reach a maximum length at the point of highest viscosity. From an analysis of specific heat data, Fairbrother, Gee, and Merrall [152] estimate that the heat of polymerization, i.e., ΔH for $nS_8 \rightarrow S_{8n}$ is 3180 cal/mole of S_8. A more detailed

[148] N. N. Mel'nikov and K. D. Shvetsova-Shilovskaya, *Doklady. Akad. Nauk S.S.S.R.,* **86,** 543 (1952); A. D. Petrov, V. F. Mironov, and V. G. Glukhovtsev, *ibid.,* **93,** 499 (1953).

[149] M. S. Kharasch, E. M. May, and F. R. Mayo, *J. Am. Chem. Soc.,* **59,** 1580 (1937).

[150] R. E. Powell and H. Eyring, *ibid.,* **65,** 648 (1943).

[151] G. Gee, *Trans. Faraday Soc.,* **48,** 515 (1952).

[152] F. Fairbrother, G. Gee, and G. T. Merrall, *J. Polymer Sci.,* **16,** 459 (1955).

picture of the state of liquid sulfur is obtained from its paramagnetic resonance spectra (Section 1·2b).[153] Radicals are detected at elevated temperatures, reaching a concentration of about 6×10^{-3} moles/liter at 300°C, indicating that the chains are diradicals $\cdot S-(S)_n-S\cdot$, perhaps together with large rings (the possibility of branched chains cannot be excluded but seems unlikely). From the variation of radical concentration with temperature $D(-S-S-)$ is calculated to be 33.4 kcal/mole (in good agreement with the value from specific heat data [152]). Further, in addition to the process of random scission of S—S bonds and recombination of —S· radicals, the variation in absorption band width with temperature indicates a very rapid displacement reaction between radicals and chains with

$$-S\cdot + -S-S- \rightarrow -S-S- + \cdot S- \qquad (83)$$

an activation energy of 3.1 kcal/mole and a PZ factor of 2.8×10^8. Thus there can be little doubt that sulfur at elevated temperatures contains a high concentration of potentially reactive radical species. Further, the low S—S bond dissociation energy (compared with 70–73 kcal for dialkyl disulfides) [118] indicates a great deal of resonance stabilization in polysulfide radicals, and their easy formation and equilibration are matters of importance in the reactions discussed below.

The most direct evidence of the participation of elemental sulfur in reactions of organic free radicals is in its effectiveness as an inhibitor in vinyl polymerization. This inhibition was discussed in some detail in Section 4·3, and we may recall that not only do vinyl acetate radicals attack sulfur some 470 times as rapidly as they add monomer, but that the resulting products (presumably polysulfies $R-S_8-R$, $R-S_6-R$, etc.) are in turn inhibitors, being attacked only slightly less readily.[154]

Technically, the most important reaction of sulfur with organic molecules is certainly the vulcanization of natural and synthetic rubbers. However, a more intractable system for study could hardly be imagined, not only because of the polymeric nature of the products but because the reaction is normally carried out in the presence of a whole array of accelerators, compounding agents, antioxidants, and reinforcing materials, most of which have some effect on the vulcanization process. As a consequence, much that has been writ-

[153] D. M. Gardner and G. K. Fraenkel, *J. Am. Chem. Soc.,* **75,** 5891 (1954); *ibid.,* **78,** 3479 (1956).

[154] P. D. Bartlett and H. Kwart, *J. Am. Chem. Soc.,* **74,** 3969 (1952).

ten on the mechanism of the vulcanization reaction is speculation, and we will consider here some of the reactions of simple olefins with sulfur and take up the extension of such reactions to unsaturated polymers only briefly.

Farmer and Shipley [155] have investigated the reaction of simple olefins with sulfur in some detail and find that cyclohexene reacts slowly at 140° with negligible evolution of H_2S to give a mixture of polysulfides $C_{12}H_{20}S_x$ which, on molecular distillation, can be separated into mono-, di-, tri-, and higher polysulfide fractions. These they consider to have the structure A, although the presence of

$$(84)$$

A   B   C

mixtures of B and C cannot be excluded. 1-Methylcyclohexene gives similar products but reacts more rapidly, and sulfides believed to be $(CH_3)_2CHCH_2—S_x—CH_2C(CH_3)\!=\!CH_2$ are obtained from isobutylene. With dihydromyrcene, $CH_3C(CH_3)\!=\!CHCH_2CH_2C(CH_3)\!=\!CHCH_3$, a cyclic monosulfide is also obtained. The detailed reaction path is certainly not known, but a scheme (essentially theirs) such as

$$(85)$$

or some equivalent is plausible, taking into account the rapid equilibria between different S_x chains and the ability of RS· radicals to

[155] E. H. Farmer and F. W. Shipley, *J. Polymer Sci.*, **1**, 293 (1946); *J. Chem. Soc.*, **1947**, 1519.

dehydrogenate hydrocarbons (Section 7·2c). Farmer, Ford, and Lyons [156] have reported a similar formation of allylic polysulfides at 0–83° on treatment of olefins with SO_2 and H_2S, the latter reagents interacting to produce sulfur in what is apparently a highly reactive metastable state.

The reaction of trimethylethylene (and several other olefins) at 120–140° has been studied by Armstrong, Little, and Doak,[157] who found that, although sulfur alone gave chiefly polymers and polysulfides, sulfur plus 2-mercaptobenzothiazole, zinc oxide, and zinc propionate (a typical accelerated vulcanization formulation) gave almost entirely allylic mono- and disulfides with the following distribution of structures:

$$
\underset{60-70\%}{-S-CH_2-\overset{\overset{\displaystyle CH_3}{|}}{C}=CH-CH_3} \quad \underset{20-30\%}{-S-CH_2-CH=\overset{\overset{\displaystyle CH_3}{|}}{\underset{\underset{\displaystyle CH_3}{|}}{C}}} \quad \underset{10\%}{-S-\overset{\overset{\displaystyle CH_3}{|}}{CH}-\overset{\overset{\displaystyle CH_3}{|}}{C}=CH_2}
$$

(86)

Little conclusive can be said as to the reason for the change in products, but the structures again correspond to those which might arise from radical abstraction of allylic hydrogen. The hydrogen lost must eventually appear in water or propionic acid, since corresponding amounts of zinc sulfide are also formed. The disappearance of polysulfides could be related to a more effective equilibration of $-S_n-$ chains and strikingly parallels the fact that such formulations lead to a greatly increased efficiency in the rubber vulcanization process over the use of sulfur alone and was the reason for its choice in the investigation.

The products formed when styrene is heated at 80° in the presence of sulfur have been investigated by Bartlett and Trifan,[157a] who find that the thermal polymerization is strongly inhibited (cf. Section 4·3) and that the initial product is evidently a low molecular weight copolymer containing approximately eight sulfur atoms per styrene unit. On further heating the amount of sulfur in the polymer decreases, probably by chain transfer with the polysulfide groups present. The initial rates of disappearance of sulfur and styrene also

[156] E. H. Farmer, J. F. Ford, and J. A. Lyons, *J. Appl. Chem.*, **4**, 554 (1954).

[157] R. T. Armstrong, J. R. Little, and K. W. Doak, *Ind. Eng. Chem.*, **36**, 628 (1944).

[157a] P. D. Bartlett and D. S. Trifan, *J. Polymer Sci.*, **20**, 457 (1956).

indicate some sort of reaction between these two species in addition to the usual polymolecular radical production which occurs in styrene alone (Section 5·1a).

At temperatures a little above 140°, the polysulfides formed in sulfur-olefin reactions begin to decompose, H_2S is evolved, and more complex products result.[155,158] Redistribution becomes rapid between polysulfides, and further additions and hydrogen abstractions occur. Thus, cyclohexene and diethyl tetrasulfide give a mixture of products including ethyl cyclohexyl sulfide, and cyclohexene and 2-benzothiazyl disulfide give 2-mercaptobenzothiazole.[151] It is likely that both radical and polar reactions are involved, since diphenyl tetrasulfide and 1-methylcyclohexene gives phenyl 1-methylcyclohexyl sulfide,[158] a *normal* addition product, perhaps from the sulfur-catalyzed[90] addition of thiophenol.

The reaction of sulfur with trimethylethylene at 160–170° now gives, in addition to the polysulfides $C_{10}H_{20}S_x$ found at lower temperatures, the remarkable product 4,5-dimethyl-1,2-dithiole-3-thione:[159]

$$CH_3-\underset{\underset{\displaystyle S}{\parallel}}{\underset{|4}{C}}=\!=\!=\underset{\underset{\displaystyle S}{5|}}{\underset{5|}{C}}-CH_3$$

Such dithiolethiones appear to be products of many sulfur-olefin reactions in the neighborhood of 200°[160–163] involving olefins with structures $\diagdown$C=CH—CH₃ or $\diagdown$CH—C=CH₂. Yields are often surprisingly high, α-methylstyrene giving the 4-phenyl compound in 42% yield, and 1,2-diphenyl-1-propene the 4,5-diphenyl analog in 80% yield.[162] The path of these reactions is certainly not known, but it has been suggested that they involve a thioacrylic acid derivative

[158] G. F. Bloomfield, *J. Chem. Soc.*, **1947**, 1547.

[159] A. S. Broun, M. G. Voronkov, and K. P. Katkova, *Zhur. Obshchei Khim.*, **20**, 726 (1950). Various numbering systems have been used for such compounds, and that used here is indicated.

[160] B. Bottcher and A. Luttringhaus, *Ann.*, **557**, 89 (1947).

[161] N. Lozac'h, *Compt. rend.*, **225**, 686 (1947).

[162] M. G. Voronkov, A. S. Broun, and G. B. Karpenko, *Zhur. Obshchei Khim.*, **19**, 1927 (1949).

[163] E. K. Fields, *J. Am. Chem. Soc.*, **77**, 4255 (1955). This paper reports base catalysis of the reaction.

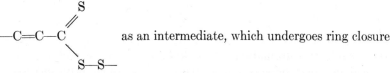

as an intermediate, which undergoes ring closure

and subsequent dehydrogenation.[162]   Other olefins often give thiophenes under these conditions,[164] and thiophene itself is even obtained from butane in good yield at about 600° in the vapor phase.[165]

Toluene reacts with sulfur at above 200° to give a variety of products including 2,2-dimethylbiphenyl, bibenzyl, stilbene, 1,2,3,4-tetraphenylbutane, and 2-phenylthianaphthene.   The reaction has been discussed by Horton,[166] who points out that all the products can be accounted for in terms of radical hydrogen abstractions and couplings, together with some plausible hydrogen shifts.   Similarly, 4,4'- and 3,3'-stilbene dicarboxylic acids are obtained by heating p- and m-toluic acids respectively with sulfur at about 270°.[167]   Two further reactions of simple molecules with sulfur need mention; these again indicate the increasing hydrogen abstracting ability of sulfur (and presumably sulfur radicals) at higher temperatures.   The first is the well-known sulfur dehydrogenation of compounds containing saturated six-membered rings to aromatics,[168] commonly carried out at 200–220°, and the second the Willgerodt reaction.[169]   Typically in the latter an alkyl phenyl ketone is heated at 140–200° with ammonium polysulfide (or more conveniently with sulfur and an amine such as morpholine) to yield the amide or substituted thioamide of the corresponding ω-phenyl carboxylic acid.

$$\phi CO(CH_2)_n CH_3 \xrightarrow{NH_4S_x} \phi(CH_2)_n CONH_2 \qquad (87)$$

[164] A. S. Broun and M. G. Voronkov, *J. Gen. Chem. U.S.S.R.*, **17**, 1162 (1947); M. G. Voronkov and A. S. Broun, *ibid.*, **18**, 70 (1948); M. G. Voronkov, A. S. Broun, G. B. Karpenko, and B. L. Gol'shtein, *Zhur. Obshchei Khim.*, **19**, 1356 (1949); M. G. Voronkov and B. L. Gol'shtein, *ibid.*, **20**, 1218 (1950).

[165] H. E. Rasmussen, R. C. Hansford, and A. H. Sachanen, *Ind. Eng. Chem.*, **38**, 376 (1946).

[166] A. W. Horton, *J. Org. Chem.*, **14**, 761 (1948).

[167] W. G. Toland, Jr., J. R. Wilkes, and F. J. Brutschy, *J. Am. Chem. Soc.*, **75**, 2263 (1953).

[168] For a recent review, cf. P. A. Plattner and E. C. Armstrong in *Newer Methods of Preparative Organic Chemistry*, Interscience Publishers, New York, 1948.

[169] Reviewed by M. Carmack and M. A. Spielman, *Organic Reactions*, Volume III, John Wiley & Sons, New York, 1946.

The reaction also occurs with dialkyl ketones, alcohols, thiols, and some unsaturated molecules, e.g., styrene gives derivatives of phenylacetic acid in yields up to 64%. Again, the detailed path of this remarkable transformation is not known, nor the extent to which radical or polar processes are involved, but apparently successive dehydrogenations and hydrogenations occur along the chain until the methyl group is reached, at which point oxidation becomes irreversible.[170] In confirmation of this picture, the reaction is blocked by a quarternary carbon in the chain, and the deuterium in C_6H_5-$COCH_2CD_2CH_3$ is almost completely exchanged with solvent during reaction.[171] Further, when a methyl n-alkyl ketone is employed, by the use of a C^{14} label it has been shown that migration to the CH_3 is preferred (60% with 2-butanone, 86% with 2-heptanone) but is not the sole reaction.[171] The role of the amine is certainly not clear, but we may note the analogy between the structure of the final product and the dithiole thiones obtained from olefins and sulfur alone.

Returning now to the vulcanization process, the complexities arising in simple olefin reactions certainly rule out any simple interpretation. In fact, it is likely that many reaction paths are available under different conditions. However, a few points are worth noting. First, vulcanization is normally carried out at temperatures of 140° or below,[172] which rule out some of the complex transformations described. Second, there is little doubt that the physical process involved is one of chemically linking polymer chains together to produce a simple giant network (Section 5·2c). In fact, the number of cross links can be estimated from the physical properties of the vulcanizate.[173] Third, sulfur becomes chemically bound to rubber during the process, and, from analogy to the simple olefin reactions, the cross links are presumably mono- and polysulfide chains. Here, direct evidence for diallylic monosulfide linkages comes from the observation that vulcanized rubber, with methyl iodide, yields tri-

[170] J. A. King and F. H. McMillan, *J. Am. Chem. Soc.*, **68**, 525, 1369 (1946); M. Carmack and D. F. DeTar, *ibid.*, 2029.

[171] E. Cerwonka, R. C. Anderson, and E. V. Brown, *ibid.*, **75**, 28, 30 (1953).

[172] In fact vulcanization can be carried out at room temperature using S_2Cl_2. For a recent discussion, cf. J. Glazer and J. H. Sculman, *J. Polymer Sci.*, **14**, 169, 225 (1954).

[173] P. J. Flory, *Principles of Polymer Chemistry*, Cornell University Press, Ithaca, N. Y., 1953, Chapter 11.

methylsulfonium iodide, a reaction thought peculiar to sulfides of this structure,[174] and careful measurements with butyl rubber (which contains very little unsaturation) indicate (in a particular vulcanization formula) very close to two atoms of sulfur incorporated in the rubber per cross link formed.[175] On the other hand, in rubber itself considerable sulfur may be involved in cyclic, rather than cross-linked structures, judging by the behavior of dihydromyrcene.[176] Finally, although the practical effect of accelerators (2-mercapto-benzothiazole, tetramethylthiuram disulfide, and many others) is to increase vulcanization rate and also the efficiency of cross-linking, i.e., a "tighter" cure for a given amount of sulfur, very little can be said definitely about how they accomplish this end. The kinetics of accelerated vulcanization has been discussed by Gordon,[177] and a possible mode of action of tetramethylthiuram disulfide has been considered by Craig et al.[178] Additional references are given in a recent review by VanAlphen,[179] for the reader who wishes to pursue the matter further.

7·4   Radical Chain Additions Involving Other Elements

7·4a   Phosphorus

Radical processes are known in which addition of a phosphorus atom to the double bond is coupled with cleavage of either P—H or P—Cl bonds. Since the dissociation energies of P—C bonds are not accurately known, we can say little about the energetics of the addition step. However, from Table 6·1, displacements involving P—H bonds (ΔH for attack on PH_3 = −13 kcal/mole) should occur more readily than displacements involving P—Cl bonds ($\Delta H = 9$ kcal for PCl_3).

[174] M. L. Selker and A. R. Kemp, *Ind. Eng. Chem.*, **36**, 20 (1944).

[175] R. L. Zapp, R. H. Decker, M. S. Dyroff, and H. A. Rayner, *J. Polymer Sci.*, **6**, 331 (1951).

[176] Cf. reference in footnote 155; squalene, another rubber analog behaves similarly; G. F. Bloomfield, *J. Polymer Sci.*, **1**, 312 (1946); *J. Chem. Soc.*, **1947**, 1546.

[177] M. Gordon, *J. Polymer Sci.*, **7**, 485 (1951).

[178] D. Craig, A. E. Juve, W. L. Davidson, W. L. Semon, and D. C. Hay, *ibid.*, **8**, 321 (1952), and previous papers.

[179] J. VanAlphen, *Angew. Chem.*, **66**, 193 (1954).

Actually, radical addition of a phosphorus compound was first observed with phosphorus trichloride and 1-octene by Kharasch, Jensen, and Urry using acetyl peroxide as initiator.[180] The overall reaction is

$$PCl_3 + CH_2=CHC_6H_{13} \rightarrow PCl_2-CH_2-CHCl-C_6H_{13} \quad (88)$$

and the chain carrier presumed to be the $\cdot PCl_2$ radical. A few similar additions to olefins which produce reactive radicals are known, but yields are generally low and chains short, as might be anticipated from the endothermic nature of the displacement step.[181]

The addition of phenyldichlorophosphine seems to proceed more readily,[182] since the $\phi-\dot{P}-Cl$ radical should be stabilized by resonance with the benzene ring and, accordingly, the P—Cl bond weakened. Telomers are obtained with acrylonitrile, methyl methacrylate, and styrene, but 1:1 products with both allyl ethyl ether and isoprene are reported.

The addition of phosphine to olefins occurs readily either at elevated temperatures in the presence of di-t-butyl peroxide or on irradiation at room temperature, alone or in the presence of a photosensitizer such as acetone.[183] A 1:1 mixture of phosphine and 1-butene gives a mixture of 38% mono-, 10% di-, and 2% tri-n-butyl phosphine (plus 36% unreacted PH_3), from which it is evident that mono- and dialkyl phosphines also react, although somewhat less readily. A 3:1 phosphine-olefin mixture gives 70% tributylphosphine and other examples of such additions are known.[183–184]

The overall reactions are

$$PH_3 + CH_2=CHR \rightarrow PH_2-CH_2CH_2R \xrightarrow{\quad CH_2=CHR \quad}$$

$$PH(CH_2CH_2R)_2 \xrightarrow{\quad CH_2=CHR \quad} P(CH_2CH_2R)_3 \quad (89)$$

and the chain carriers evidently $\cdot PH_2$, $\cdot PHR$, and $\cdot PR_2$ radicals.

---

[180] M. S. Kharasch, E. V. Jensen, and W. H. Urry, *J. Am. Chem. Soc.*, **67**, 1864 (1945).

[181] Polar additions of PCl_3 to carbonyl-conjugated olefins are also known, and the addition of PCl_5 to olefins is also apparently a polar reaction.

[182] W. B. McCormack, U.S. Pats. 2,671,077 and 2,671,079 (March 3, 1954).

[183] A. R. Stiles, F. F. Rust, and W. E. Vaughan, *J. Am. Chem. Soc.*, **74**, 3282 (1952).

[184] N. V. de Bataafsche Petroleum Maatschappij, Brit. Pat. 673,451 (June 4, 1952); H. C. Brown, U.S. Pat. 2,584,112 (February 5, 1952).

Dialkyl phosphites have the structure $H\overset{O}{\overset{\nearrow}{P}}(OR)_2$ and readily undergo radical additions to olefins.[185-188] The reaction should be of importance,

$$H\overset{O}{\overset{\nearrow}{P}}(OR)_2 + CH_2=CHR' \rightarrow R'CH_2CH_2-\overset{O}{\overset{\nearrow}{P}}(OR)_2 \qquad (90)$$

since the starting materials are easily obtained and the resulting dialkyl phosphonates are of some interest. With ethylene, both 1:1 and telomeric products are formed and similar results are obtained with tetrafluoroethylene.[186] Additions occur with a variety of other olefins,[187-188] and apparently sodium hypophosphite, alkyl hypophosphite, $ROPOH_2$, and ethyl phenylphosphinate, $\phi POHOEt$, behave similarly.[188] Unfortunately this type of reaction is only described in a few patents, and it should be kept in mind that carbonyl-conjugated olefins also undergo polar (base-catalyzed) additions with these classes of reagents.[189]

7·4b Silicon

The energetics of the displacement step in silicon hydride and halide additions resemble those of phosphorus (ΔH for Si—H = −14 kcal, ΔH for Si—Cl = +12 kcal), except that the R· + Cl—Si displacement is even more endothermic. In fact, radical addition of $SiCl_4$ or $SiBr_4$ to olefins has not been accomplished except to give high molecular weight telomers with ethylene.[190] With trichlorosilane, $SiHCl_3$, displacement occurs at the Si—H bond, and 1-octene gives a 99% yield of n-octyltrichlorosilane in the presence of acetyl peroxide.[191] Many analogous additions have been carried out with

$$SiHCl_3 + CH_2=CHR \rightarrow SiCl_3CH_2CH_2R \qquad (91)$$

185 W. E. Hanford and R. M. Joyce, U.S. Pat. 2,478,390 (August 9, 1949).

186 J. A. Bittles, Jr., and R. M. Joyce, U.S. Pat. 2,559,754 (July 10, 1951).

187 E. C. Ladd and M. P. Harvey, U.S. Pat. 2,664,438 (December 29, 1953).

188 N. V. de Bataafsche Petroleum Maatschappij, Brit. Pat. 660,918 (November 14, 1951); A. R. Stiles and F. F. Rust, U.S. Pat. 2,724,718 (November 22, 1955).

189 A. N. Pudovic, Zhur. Obshchei Khim., 21, 382, 1837 (1951); 22, 462, 467, 473, 1143 (1952); B. Bochwic and J. Michalski, Nature, 167, 1035 (1951).

190 S. L. Scott, U.S. Pat. 2,407,171 (September 3, 1946).

191 L. H. Sommer, E. W. Pietrusza, and F. C. Whitmore, J. Am. Chem. Soc., 69, 188 (1947).

other olefins, interesting examples being vinyl- and allyltrichlorosilane, which yield $SiCl_3(CH_2)_2SiCl_3$ and $SiCl_3(CH_2)_3SiCl_3$ respectively.[192]   With styrene a telomer is obtained,[192] the transfer constant for $SiHCl_3$ being about 0.026, much larger than that for chloroform.   Reaction conditions have involved either peroxide initiators [192] or high temperatures and pressures in the absence of added materials.[193]   Acetylene adds either one or two moles of $SiHCl_3$,[194] giving $CH_2\!=\!CHSiCl_3$ and $SiCl_3(CH_2)_2SiCl_3$, and $SiH(OC_2H_5)_3$ adds similarly.

Additions of other silicon hydrides are known,[195] silane, SiH_4, reacts with ethylene either thermally or on irradiation to give a 1:1 product plus telomer, and also polyalkyl silanes by further addition.[195a]   Additions of $SiHBr_3$, alkyldichlorosilanes, $RSiHCl_2$, and dialkylchlorosilanes R_2SiHCl also occur,[192–193] but methyldiisopropylsilane is reported to give very little reaction.[192]

7·4c   Other Elements

Relatively few radical chain additions are known in which the odd electron of the chain carrier is associated with elements other than those already discussed.   Among the higher row elements, apparently the only hydride addition involves trichlorogermane, which, on refluxing with 1-hexene in the presence of 3% benzoyl peroxide,[196] undergoes the expected reaction.

$$GeHCl_3 + CH_2\!=\!CH\!-\!C_4H_9 \rightarrow GeCl_3CH_2C_5H_{11} \qquad (22\%) \quad (92)$$

Analogous reactions might be anticipated with hydrides of neighboring elements but have not been reported at this time.

The higher row elements which form stable carbon bonds generally form too stable bonds to halogens for feasible radical additions of their halides.   A possible exception is mercury.   Although no radical additions of mercury halides have been established (polar additions are well known), Russian workers have made several in-

[192] C. A. Burkhard and R. H. Krieble, *ibid.*, **69**, 2687 (1947).

[193] A. J. Barry, L. DePree, J. W. Gilkey, and D. E. Hook, *ibid.*, **69**, 2916 (1947).

[194] G. H. Wagner, U.S. Pat. 2,637,738 (May 5, 1953).

[195] (a) D. G. White and E. G. Rochow, *J. Am. Chem. Soc.*, **76**, 3897 (1954); (b) J. L. Speier, R. Zimmerman, and J. Webster, *ibid.*, **78**, 2278 (1956); (c) D. Seyforth and E. G. Rochow, *J. Org. Chem.*, **20**, 250 (1955); (d) J. W. Curry, *J. Am. Chem. Soc.*, **78**, 1686 (1956).

[196] A. K. Fischer, R. C. West, and E. G. Rochow, *J. Am. Chem. Soc.*, **76**, 5878 (1954).

vestigations of other radical reactions of organic mercury compounds (Section 10·2b). A difficulty in any addition might arise from the very low dissociation energy of R—Hg bonds, 6–7 kcal compared with 51 kcal for $D(CH_3Hg—CH_3)$,[197] so any intermediate radical RHg· might be expected to decompose with loss of mercury.

Returning to the remaining likely first row elements, oxygen and nitrogen, the strong bonds which they form to hydrogen make radical attack on their hydrides energetically unfavorable, and also favor hydrogen abstraction by RO· and $R_2N·$ radicals rather than double-bond addition (Chapter 10). Nevertheless, a few examples of apparent radical chain additions exist.

Benzoyl peroxide has a significant transfer constant with styrene ($C = 0.055$, Section 4·2b), and when 1,2-diethoxyethylene is treated with an equivalent of benzoyl peroxide in benzene, 1,2-diethoxy-1,2-dibenzoyloxyethane is obtained.[198] A similar rapid reaction between vinyl butyl ether and benzoyl peroxide has been investigated by Shostakovskii et al.[199] and apparently involves the chain

$$\phi COO· + CH_2{=}CHOR \rightarrow \phi COOCH_2—\dot{C}HOR \qquad (93)$$
$$\phi COOCH_2—\dot{C}HOR + Bz_2O_2 \rightarrow \phi COOCH_2CH(OR)OCO\phi + \phi COO· \qquad (94)$$

If so, these reactions may receive considerable driving force from the extreme donor and acceptor properties of the reactants, and the process may, in part, account for the poor yields of polymer obtained in peroxide-initiated polymerizations of vinyl ethers. Additional examples of reactions analogous to reaction 94 appear in Section 10·2b.

Transfer constants of hydroperoxides are of similar magnitude (Section 10·2d), and here attack is apparently on the ROO—H bond which is sufficiently weakened by the resonance stabilization of the $RO_2·$ radical (Chapter 9). However, no 1:1 products have actually been isolated.

With nitrogen, the only cases showing any evidence for radical chain additions involve nitryl chloride, NO_2Cl, and possibly N_2O_4. The addition of these materials to methyl acrylate has been studied

[197] J. C. Polanyi, *Discussions Faraday Soc.*, **14**, 115 (1953).

[198] S. M. McElvain and C. H. Stammer, *J. Am. Chem. Soc.*, **75**, 2154 (1953).

[199] M. F. Shostakovskii, N. A. Gershtein, and V. A. Neterman, *Doklady Akad. Nauk S.S.S.R.*, **103**, 265 (1955).

by Shechter,[200] who suggests that they are radical process in which initial attack is by the $\cdot NO_2$ radical, e.g.:

$$NO_2 \cdot + CH_2{=}CHR \rightarrow NO_2{-}CH_2{-}\dot{C}HR \tag{95}$$

$$NO_2CH_2\dot{C}HR + ClNO_2 \rightarrow NO_2CH_2CHClR + NO_2 \tag{96}$$

[200] H. Shechter, F. Conrad, A. L. Daulton, and R. S. Kaplan, *J. Am. Chem. Soc.*, **74**, 3052 (1952); H. Shechter and F. Conrad, *ibid.*, **75**, 5610 (1953).

CHAPTER 8

Halogen Substitution Reactions

8·1   Introduction

In this chapter we will take up a number of radical chain processes in which a hydrogen atom in an organic molecule is replaced by halogen through reactions which can be written in general terms as

$$A—X + H—R \rightarrow A—H + X—R \tag{1}$$

and which occur via the chain

$$A\cdot + H—R \rightarrow A—H + \cdot R \tag{2}$$

$$R\cdot + X—A \rightarrow R—X + A\cdot \tag{3}$$

In the commonest examples, A—X is simply a halogen molecule and halogen atoms provide the chain carrier $A\cdot$. However, other halogen carriers exist, N-bromosuccinimide being a good example. Such reactions are extremely important, since, by changing the nature of $A\cdot$, the selectivity of the reagent may be altered and controlled.

Radical halogenations occur, not only with saturated hydrocarbons where they are perhaps best known, but also with molecules containing a variety of substituent groups which have important effects upon reaction rates and the point of radical attack. However, it is, of course, well known that polar mechanisms of halogen substitution also exist, notably in the acid- and base-catalyzed halogenation of ketones (and other enolizable species) where the halogen enters α to the activating group, and in aromatic substitution at ordinary temperatures, and it is necessary to be sure which process is being observed.

We have already encountered reaction 3 as a step in halogen addition processes (Section 7·1c), and reaction 2 in the pyrolytic decomposition of certain alkyl halides (Section 7·1d). Their energetics are considered in more detail below, but for the molecular halogens ΔH increases in the order F < Cl < Br < I. As a consequence, the tendency to undergo radical chain halogenation decreases in the same order.

8·2 Molecular Fluorine

Elemental fluorine reacts with organic compounds with great violence, and, as a consequence, the fluorine atom is generally introduced into such molecules by indirect means.[1] However, by carrying out the reaction with suitable care, in many cases a series of identifiable products can be obtained, and such reactions have been reviewed by Bigelow.[2] In general, hydrogen is replaced by fluorine, although fragmentation of molecules also occurs, carbon tetrafluoride being a common product from almost any starting material. Reactions have been carried out in the gas phase, best diluted with nitrogen and in the presence of metal packing to help dissipate the liberated heat, and also in the liquid phase alone or in the presence of diluents such as CF_2Cl_2 and CCl_3CF_3 (CCl_4 has been used but is appreciably attacked). Thus, the vapor-phase fluorination of methane yields all of the fluoromethanes plus C_2F_6 and C_3F_8,[3] whereas ethane (suitably diluted) gives a mixture of products including CF_4, CHF_2CH_2F, CHF_2CHF_2, CH_3CH_2F, and C_2F_6.[4]

Although fluorinations have not been investigated in the same detail as other halogenations, they are considered [3] to be radical chain processes, and the expected chain propagation steps are certainly

$$F\cdot + CH_4 \rightarrow HF + \cdot CH_3 \qquad \Delta H = -33\,kcal \qquad (4)$$

$$\cdot CH_3 + F\!-\!F \rightarrow CH_3F + F\cdot \qquad \Delta H = -60\,kcal \qquad (5)$$

strongly exothermic.[5] The fragmentation reaction in which CF_4 is produced from higher alkanes is obscure but may involve a direct displacement on carbon by fluorine atoms.

[1] *Fluorine Chemistry*, J. H. Simons, editor, Academic Press, New York, 1950.

[2] L. A. Bigelow, *Chem. Revs.*, **40**, 51 (1947); cf. also Chapter 11 of reference cited in footnote 1.

[3] E. H. Hadley and L. A. Bigelow, *J. Am. Chem. Soc.*, **62**, 3302 (1940).

[4] D. S. Young, N. Fukuhara, and L. A. Bigelow, *ibid.*, **62**, 1172 (1940). A jet fluorination reaction has recently been described which gives C_2F_6 and C_2HF_5 in 92% yield; E. A. Tyczkowski and L. A. Bigelow, *ibid.*, **77**, 3007 (1955).

[5] The value of $D(CH_3\!-\!F)$ is not accurately known; that used to calculate ΔH is based on a recent estimate of N. W. Luft, *J. Chem. Phys.*, **23**, 973 (1955).

The reactions occur in the dark in the absence of usual radical initiators, and the initiation step has been written as

$$F_2 \rightarrow 2F \cdot \qquad \Delta H = 37 \text{ kcal} \qquad (6)$$

However, since fluorination occurs spontaneously at temperatures as low as $-80°$, chains would have to be extraordinarily long, a situation belied by the frequent formation of dimeric products (see below). Accordingly, it seems likely that other initiation processes are possible, and we may note that the bimolecular reaction is only slightly

$$F_2 + CH_4 \rightarrow HF + F \cdot + \cdot CH_3 \qquad \Delta H = 2 \text{ kcal} \qquad (7a)$$

endothermic, and becomes exothermic for hydrocarbons with weaker C—H bonds. A similar radical forming process with olefins would be

$$F_2 + C_2H_4 \rightarrow FCH_2\dot{C}H_2 + F \cdot \qquad \Delta H = \sim - 2 \text{ kcal} \qquad (7b)$$

and such processes have been suggested by Miller and co-workers [6b] to account for the initiation of a number of radical chlorinations and autoxidations by traces of fluorine.[6] Among fluorinations which have been studied, of particular interest for our purposes are a series of liquid-phase fluorinations of chlorinated hydrocarbons described by Miller,[7] carried out simply by passing carefully purified fluorine over the substances (alone at 0–90°C or dissolved in CF_3CCl_3). His results are summarized in Table 8·1.

The most complete data are on pentachloroethane and tetrachloroethylene. From the former, it is plain that olefin is formed in addition to the expected substitution, perhaps by chlorine atom dissociation from the intermediate $C_2Cl_5 \cdot$ radical (Section 7·1d), and chlorine and fluorine addition to C_2Cl_4 could account for the remaining products.

With tetrachloroethylene, the expected addition occurs, but the very large amount of dimer, presumably formed by radical coupling

$$2CFCl_2\dot{C}Cl_2 \rightarrow CFCl_2CCl_2CCl_2CFCl_2 \qquad (8)$$

is very significant, indicating very short kinetic chains and (since the reaction is certainly fast) high radical concentrations, and pointing to a very rapid chain initiation. The alternative of telomeric

[6] (a) W. T. Miller, Jr., and A. L. Dittman, *J. Am. Chem. Soc.*, **78**, 2793 (1956); (b) W. T. Miller, Jr., S. D. Koch, Jr., and F. W. McLafferty, *ibid.*, **78**, 4992 (1956). An earlier observation of fluorine-induced chlorination was apparently made by McBee; cf. p. 376 of reference cited in footnote 1.

[7] W. T. Miller, *J. Am. Chem. Soc.*, **62**, 341 (1940).

TABLE 8·1 REACTIONS OF CHLORINATED HYDROCARBONS WITH FLUORINE [7]

Starting Material	Temperature	Products	Yield, %
$CHCl_3$	0°	$CFCl_3$	
		C_2Cl_6	
CCl_3CHCl_2	90°	$CFCl_2CFCl_2$	2
		$CCl_2=CCl_2$	7
		CCl_3CFCl_2	30
		C_2Cl_6	9
		C_4Cl_{10}	Trace
$CHCl_2CHCl_2$	50°	$CCl_2=CHCl$	...
		$CFCl_2CFCl_2$	...
		$CHCl_2CFCl_2$	35
		$CHCl_2CCl_3$	5
$CCl_2=CCl_2$	0°	$CFCl_2CFCl_2$	12, 58 [a]
		CCl_3CFCl_2	11, 12 [a]
		$CFCl_2CCl_2CCl_2CFCl_2$	18, 68 [a]
$CHCl=CCl_2$	0°	$CHCl=CFCl$	...
		$CHFClCFCl_2$	...
		$CFCl=CCl_2$	...
		$CHFClCCl_3$	...
		$CHCl_2CFCl_2$	...
		$C_4H_4Cl_3$	...
		$C_4H_2Cl_8$	...

[a] Second figure in CCl_3CF_3 solution. Evidently some solvent reaction products are included.

addition of fluorine with the 1,4-difluorooctachlorobutane as the 2:1 product certainly seems unlikely in view of the exothermic nature of reaction 3, and, in any case, would not account for the dimeric products formed in fluorination of saturated molecules.

Two other fluorinations, from those summarized by Bigelow, may be mentioned. One is of benzene (vapor phase),[8] which yields a variety of products including CF_4, C_2F_6, C_3F_8, C_4F_{10}, C_5F_{10}, C_6F_{12}, C_6HF_{11}, and $C_{12}F_{22}$, and indicates that addition, substitution, and fragmentation are all taking place. The second is the Bockemuller's fluorination of n- and isobutyric acids in solvents at low temperatures.[9] The products are β- and γ-fluorobutyric acids and α-methyl-β-fluoropropionic acid respectively, showing that even the highly re-

[8] N. Fukuhara and L. A. Bigelow, *ibid.*, **63**, 2792 (1941).
[9] W. Bockemuller, *Ann.*, **506**, 20 (1933).

active fluorine atom shows the same significant selectivity as chlorine atoms discussed in Section 8·3c below.

8 · 3   Molecular Chlorine

8·3a   General Properties of Radical Chain Substitution by Chlorine

The free radical chlorination of hydrocarbons occurs in the vapor phase at high temperatures, or at lower temperatures photochemically or in the presence of radical sources such as tetramethyllead or azomethane.[10] Similarly, in the liquid phase the reaction may be initiated by triphenylmethyl radicals [10] or more usual radical sources like benzoyl peroxide. However, since chlorine is dissociated by short wave length visible light, the photochemical reaction is most commonly employed.[11]

The energetics of the chain propagation steps for methane are as indicated, and for other molecules reaction 9 must become increas-

$$Cl\cdot + CH_4 \rightarrow HCl + \cdot CH_3 \qquad \Delta H = -1\,kcal \qquad (9)$$

$$\cdot CH_3 + Cl_2 \rightarrow CH_3Cl + Cl\cdot \qquad \Delta H = -24\,kcal \qquad (10)$$

ingly exothermic. Chains are commonly very long, and quantum yields high, as might be anticipated. A notable feature of chlorinations is that they are strongly oxygen inhibited, presumably by replacement of reaction 10 by

$$R\cdot + O_2 \rightarrow RO_2\cdot \qquad (11)$$

In fact, in the presence of large amounts of oxygen, chlorination may be entirely replaced by a chlorine-catalyzed oxidation of the organic molecule (Section 9·3c). In addition to reaction 11, however, chlorine atoms have recently been shown to react with oxygen to give the transient species ClO, which subsequently decomposes bimolecularly to chlorine and oxygen,[12] and this reaction could also play a role in the inhibition. Other inhibitors have not received much study, but it is significant that the radical side-chain chlorination of nitrotoluenes proceeds relatively slowly, and, in fact, nitroaromatics are poor media for radical chlorinations in general.

[10] W. E. Vaughan and F. F. Rust, J. Org. Chem., 5, 449 (1940).

[11] For a survey of technical chlorination procedures, cf. E. T. McBee and H. E. Ungnade, The Chemistry of Petroleum Hydrocarbons, Volume III, B. T. Brooks et al., editors, Reinhold Publishing Co., New York, 1955.

[12] G. Porter and K. J. Wright, Discussions Faraday Soc., 14, 23 (1953).

The effect of several variables on liquid phase chlorinations have been discussed by Kharasch and Berkman.[13] Cyclohexane in air-free systems chlorinates within a minute at 0° under strong visible light; the reaction is only 25% complete in 24 hours in the dark but is greatly accelerated by 1% ascaridole. The chlorination is oxygen inhibited, and heptane, butyl chloride, and cyclohexyl chloride behave similarly. With toluene under the same conditions (5 molar excess of toluene) similar phenomena are noted, but there is strong competition by radical addition to the nucleus. About 45% addition occurs in both the light and dark reaction, indicating the same radical chain carrier, $Cl\cdot$, in both processes. The yield of side-chain substitution is increased by slow chlorine addition, in line with the reversibility of the addition process (Section 7·1e). m-Xylene, interestingly, undergoes solely addition at −55°, but the product decomposes on warming. At elevated temperatures under radical-forming conditions both toluene and xylene give almost entirely side-chain substitution.

A good demonstration that alkyl radicals are actually involved in the chain has been provided by Brown, Kharasch, and Chao,[14] who chlorinated optically active 1-chloro-2-methylbutane and showed that the 1,2-dichloro-2-methylbutane fraction of the product was optically inactive as would be anticipated if it were formed through the corresponding radical.

$$CH_2Cl-\underset{\underset{H}{|}}{\overset{\overset{CH_3}{|}}{C}}-C_2H_5 \xrightarrow{Cl\cdot} \underset{Racemized}{CH_2Cl-\overset{\overset{CH_3}{|}}{C}-C_2H_5} \xrightarrow{Cl_2} CH_2Cl-\overset{\overset{CH_3}{|}}{C}Cl-C_2H_5$$

$$(12)$$

8·3b Kinetics of Radical Chain Chlorinations

As in the case of halogen additions, most of the data on the kinetics of chlorine substitution reactions have been obtained in the vapor phase and are reviewed by Steacie.[15] However, we will discuss the more significant results, assuming as before that liquid- and vapor-phase processes are closely parallel. The chlorination of methane yields methyl chloride plus higher chlorinated products, and

[13] M. S. Kharasch and M. G. Berkman, *J. Org. Chem.*, **6**, 810 (1941).

[14] H. C. Brown, M. S. Kharasch, and T. H. Chao, *J. Am. Chem. Soc.*, **62**, 3435 (1940).

[15] E. W. R. Steacie, *Atomic and Free Radical Reactions*, second edition, Reinhold Publishing Corp., New York, 1954 (cf. especially Chapter X).

the thermal reaction was investigated as long ago as 1931 by Pease and Walz,[16] who found formally bimolecular kinetics but a very pronounced inhibition by traces of oxygen, and proposed initiation by dissociation of chlorine and two possible chain processes, reactions 9 and 10 and the alternative, now energetically implausible, process involving a hydrogen atom as chain carrier.

$$Cl\cdot + CH_4 \rightarrow CH_3Cl + H\cdot \qquad \Delta H = 20 \text{ kcal} \qquad (13)$$

$$H\cdot + Cl_2 \rightarrow HCl + Cl\cdot \qquad \Delta H = -45 \text{ kcal} \qquad (14)$$

The kinetic chains under their conditions were very long, of the order of 10^7.

The photoinduced reaction has been studied by several groups, most recently by Ritchie and Winning.[17] Again strong oxygen inhibition is observed (2% oxygen based on chlorine about cuts the rate in half), and quantum yields are of the order of 2000–20,000. The actual overall kinetics proved to be complex, the rate expression changing from $k[CH_4](I_{abs})^{1/2}$ at low methane pressures and light intensities to $k'(I_{abs})$ at high pressures and intensities. At the least, more than one chain termination step must be involved.

Recently Pritchard, Pyke, and Trotman-Dickenson have succeeded in determining the actual rate constant for reaction 9 by competitive chlorination of methane and hydrogen.[18] Hydrogen also reacts with chlorine via a chain, and the rate constant for reaction 15 has been

$$Cl\cdot + H_2 \rightarrow HCl + H\cdot \qquad (15)$$

$$H\cdot + Cl_2 \rightarrow HCl + Cl\cdot \qquad (16)$$

measured between 0 and 777°C and has the value 7.9×10^{10} exp $(-5500/RT)$ liters per mole per sec.[19] In the presence of both hydrogen and methane, reactions 9 and 15 are competitive reactions and

$$d[H_2]/d[CH_4] = k_{15}[H_2]/k_9[CH_4] \qquad (17)$$

Accordingly, by measuring the relative rates of disappearance of hydrogen and methane illuminated together in the presence of chlorine,

[16] R. N. Pease and F. Walz, *J. Am. Chem. Soc.*, **53**, 3728 (1931).

[17] M. Ritchie and W. I. H. Winning, *J. Chem. Soc.*, **1950**, 3583; this paper reviews earlier work.

[18] H. O. Pritchard, J. B. Pyke, and A. F. Trotman-Dickenson, *J. Am. Chem. Soc.*, **77**, 2629 (1955); an earlier note appears in *ibid.*, **76**, 1201 (1954).

[19] P. G. Ashmore and J. Chanmugain, *Trans. Faraday Soc.*, **49**, 254 (1953).

the rate constant for reaction 9 may be calculated. Fortunately for accurate determination of k_9, the rates of the two processes lie close together (methane reacts 2.5–3.0 times as rapidly as hydrogen at 100°), and $k_9 = 2.6 \times 10^{10}$ exp $(-3850/RT)$. At 100°, $k_9 = 1.44 \times 10^8$ liters/mole sec, and it is plain that chlorine atom attack on methane is an extremely rapid process. No evidence was obtained for significant interference by the back reaction although the process

$$CH_3 \cdot + H—Cl \rightarrow CH_4 + Cl \cdot \qquad (18)$$

has been detected with methyl radicals produced by photolysis of acetone,[20] and analogous reactions must occur in the radical addition of HCl to olefins (Section 7·1b). From E_9 and known bond strengths, $E_{18} = 4.5$ kcal [16] and must be higher for other alkyl radicals forming weaker C—H bonds.

By competitive chlorinations of methane and other hydrocarbons, rate constants for chlorine atom attack on other molecules RH were also obtained (Table 8·2). Although values of PZ and E are cer-

TABLE 8·2   RATE CONSTANTS FOR CHLORINE ATOM ATTACK ON R—H [18]

RH	$PZ \times 10^{-10}$	E, kcal/mole	k (100°) $\times 10^{-8}$
CH_4	2.6	3.85	1.82
CH_3Cl	5.7	3.36	6.0
C_2H_6	12.0	1.00	310
C_2H_5Cl	4.6	1.49	61.3
C_3H_8	17.6	0.67	710
Iso-C_4H_{10}	19.6	0.86	613
Neo-C_5H_{12}	12.3	0.70	477
Cyclo-C_5H_{1c}	29.3	0.58	1340

tainly not known to the precision indicated, relative k's calculated from them (i.e., the direct experimental ratios) should be reliable. The significance of these relative values (which of course include attack at more than one point in the more complex molecules) are discussed further in the next section.

Kinetic data are available on a number of other gas-phase chlorinations, and all point to long kinetic chains which are strongly O_2-inhibited and beyond doubt proceed via chains analogous to reactions 9 and 10. However, since overall kinetics differ considerably, termination mechanisms (if not concentrations of trace impurities) must vary from system to system.

Relatively few kinetic studies have been made in the liquid phase.

[20] R. J. Cvetanovic and E. W. R. Steacie, *Can. J. Chem.*, **31**, 518 (1953).

One of the first is of the photochemical chlorination of chloroform in carbon tetrachloride by Schwab and Heyde,[21] who postulated the usual chain, with termination by combination of chlorine atoms, but considered the step

$$Cl \cdot + HCCl_3 \leftrightarrows HCl + \cdot CCl_3 \qquad (19)$$

to be reversible to accommodate their results.

The photochlorinations of n-heptane and n-hexadecane [22,23] have been investigated in carbon tetrachloride solution, and both give rate expressions

$$-d[RH]/dt = k[Cl_2]I_{abs} \qquad (20)$$

consistent with chain termination by unimolecular disappearance of alkyl radicals. The result is puzzling and suggests the presence of a trace of inhibitor (chains are very long, approaching 10^4, so little would be required). At higher chlorine concentrations, the kinetics with hexadecane change to

$$-d[RH]/dt = k'[Cl_2]^{1/2}[RH]^{1/2}(I_{abs})^{1/2} \qquad (21)$$

corresponding to the termination process

$$R \cdot + Cl \cdot \rightarrow RCl \qquad (22)$$

The apparent activation energy is 9 ± 2 kcal, from which the activation energy for hydrogen abstraction is estimated as 6 kcal, which is certainly high in view of the data in Table $8 \cdot 2$.

$8 \cdot 3c$ *Structure and Reactivity in Chlorine Atom Reactions*

Important as kinetics are in establishing the existence and nature of the chain reaction involved in chlorination, the problem of the relation between structure and reactivity is of more general interest since, in complicated molecules with a variety of C—H bonds, it determines the actual structure of the products obtained. Further, in long-chain processes it should be evident that just how chains are started and stopped (and, in most cases, where we are not concerned with reversible steps, the actual rates and relative concentrations of hydrocarbon and chlorine) has nothing to do with the composition of the initial product, which is determined solely by the relative rates

[21] G. M. Schwab and U. Heyde, *Z. physik. Chem.*, **B8**, 147 (1930).

[22] J. Stauff and H. J. Schumacher, *Z. Elektrochem.*, **48**, 271 (1942).

[23] J. Stauff, *ibid.*, **48**, 550 (1942).

of attack of halogen atoms on different C—H bonds (of course, if large amounts of chlorine are employed, the problem is further complicated by the formation of polyhalogenated products).

To commence with the saturated aliphatic hydrocarbons, Hass, McBee, and Weber in 1935 [24] reviewed older data, and in 1936 [25] added more precise measurements of their own on propane, isobutane, butane, n-pentane, and isopentane from which they formulated a series of important chlorination rules, the first five of which are (somewhat abbreviated):

(1) *Carbon skeleton rearrangements do not occur during photochemical or thermal chlorinations below pyrolysis temperatures, but every possible monochloride is always formed.*

(2) *The hydrogen atoms are always substituted at rates which are in the order primary < secondary < tertiary.*

(3) *At increasing temperatures these relative rates approach 1:1:1.*

(4) *Liquid-phase chlorination gives relative rates comparable to those obtained at much higher temperatures in the vapor phase.*

(5) *Moisture, carbon surfaces, and light have no effect upon these ratios.*

To discuss these useful and valid rules in the light of the chain mechanism of chlorination, rule 5 is certainly in keeping with what has been said above about the nature of the products in chain processes, rule 3 indicates that differences in reactivity here depend chiefly on activation energies, and rule 1 is in keeping with our picture of the chain process. Rule 2 is plausible since reactivity increases with decreasing C—H bond strength and increasing resonance stabilization of the alkyl radical produced. However, as we will see, the problem is actually much more complicated. Rule 4 is interesting, as it indicates significant differences in the selective properties of chlorine atoms in gas and liquid phase and needs further discussion. Quantitatively, the differences in reactivity of primary, secondary, and tertiary hydrogens are listed in Table 8·3 and plotted as a function of temperature in Fig. 8·1. The values in Table 8·3 are read off the smoothed curves including data on all five hydrocarbons and differ slightly from those originally reported. Figure 8·1 shows that there is considerable scatter among the data, but the temperature variation of relative reactivities in the gas phase indicates that the activation energies for attack on secondary and

[24] H. B. Hass, E. T. McBee, and P. Weber, *Ind. Eng. Chem.,* **27,** 1190 (1935).
[25] H. B. Hass, E. T. McBee, and P. Weber, *ibid.,* **28,** 333 (1936).

TABLE 8.3   RELATIVE REACTIVITIES OF C—H BONDS IN SATURATED HYDRO-
CARBONS TOWARDS CHLORINE ATOMS [25]

(Figures in parentheses for liquid-phase reaction)

Temperature	Primary	Secondary	Tertiary
600°	1	2.1	2.6
500°	1	2.4	3.2
400°	1	2.7	3.8
300°	1	3.2	4.4
200°	1	3.7	5.4
100°	1	4.3 (2.0)	7.0 (3.0)
50°	1	4.8 (2.9)	(4.5)
0°	1	(4.5)	(7.0)
−50°	1	(7.2)	(11.8)

tertiary C—H bonds are some 650 and 800 cal/mole lower than for
primary C—H, in good agreement with the sort of variation found
in Table 8·3.

Activation energy differences are greater in solution, and a possible explanation together with the lower selectivity lies in the very
high rates of the chlorine atoms reaction (Table 8·2), e.g., for
isobutane, $k = 6.13 \times 10^{10}$ at 100°, which is comparable to the rate

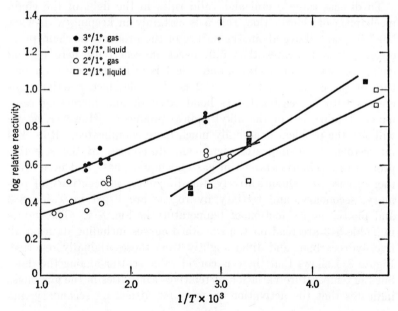

FIG. 8·1   Relative reactivities of C—H bonds in alkane chlorination from data
of Hass.[25]

of diffusion of chlorine atoms. Accordingly, a chlorine atom colliding with any portion of a hydrocarbon molecule will be constrained in contact by surrounding solvent long enough so that there is a good chance for reaction, even if more reactive sites are available elsewhere. Oddly, however, the two sets of data appear to cross at higher temperatures.

The data of Hass et al. were obtained simply by chlorinating hydrocarbons to low conversions and determining the distribution of isomeric monochlorides from which relative reactivities of each type of hydrogen were then calculated. Thus, at 300°C 2-methylbutane actually gives 33.5% 1-chloro-, 22% 2-chloro-, 28% 3-chloro-, and 16.5% 4-chloro-2-methylbutane. The calculated values are 30, 22, 33, and 15% from Table 8·3.

In any practical chlorination of a complex molecule with a variety of aliphatic C—H bonds, monochlorides are further chlorinated (the effect of chlorine substitution on reactivity is discussed below). Thus a technical reaction product of, say, stearic acid or a kerosene fraction with one mole of chlorine is not only a mixture of isomeric monochlorides but also of polychlorides and unchlorinated material as well, a fact which it is well to keep in mind if one works with such products.

Turning now to more complicated hydrocarbons, in unsaturated molecules the competing radical addition of chlorine atoms to the double bond is introduced, so little can be said quantitatively about the reactivity of an allylic C—H bond. However, by raising the temperature to 600°, the *addition* is almost completely reversed, and propylene and isobutylene give allyl and methallyl chloride in good yields.[26] Ethylene itself initially gives almost entirely addition except perhaps at very high temperatures.[10]

The side chain of toluene is readily attacked by chlorine atoms, but a very interesting comparison has been carried out by Brown and Russell,[27] who conducted the competitive chlorination of toluene and cyclohexane, finding that, at 80° in the liquid phase, cyclohexane reacts 11.2 times as rapidly as the toluene. Correcting for the number of hydrogens involved, this corresponds to a relative reactivity per C—H bond of 2.8:1 in favor of cyclohexane.[28] The striking

[26] H. P. A. Groll and G. Hearne, *ibid.*, **31**, 1530 (1939).

[27] (*a*) H. C. Brown and G. A. Russell, *J. Am. Chem. Soc.*, **74**, 3996 (1952); (*b*) G. A. Russell and H. C. Brown, *ibid.*, **77**, 4578 (1955).

[28] Essentially the same ratio (2:1) is found in the vapor phase; C. Walling and B. Miller, unpublished work.

feature of this result is that the high resonance energy of the resulting benzyl radical does very little to facilitate hydrogen removal in the strongly exothermic displacement step. Indeed, from Table 8·2, reactions of this sort have very little activation energy to reduce, and, to anticipate slightly the argument to be developed in connection with more polar substituents, reactivity is determined largely by electron supply and withdrawal and the strong electron-acceptor properties of the chlorine atom.

The data on relative reactivities of simple hydrocarbons can be put in somewhat better form by combining the isomer distributions of Hass et al.[25] with the absolute rate data of Table 8·2 and further data of Russell's.[27]   Table 8·4 summarizes the results, indicat-

TABLE 8.4   RELATIVE REACTIVITIES OF C—H BONDS TOWARDS CHLORINE ATOMS

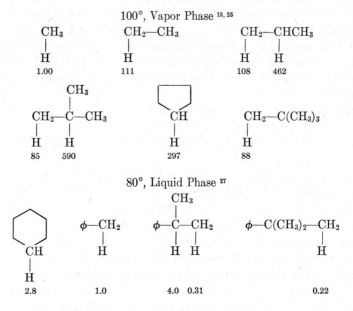

ing that primary hydrogens on all simple alkanes are approximately 100 times as reactive as those on methane, and secondary and tertiary hydrogens (as we already knew) 4.3 and 7 times still more so.[29]

[29] If we take the C—H bonds of neopentane and t-butylbenzene as equivalent and ignore differences between liquid- and vapor-phase results, the C—H bonds of toluene appear 400 times as reactive as those of methane. However, G. A. Russell, J. Am. Chem. Soc., **79**, 2977 (1957), has recently reported significant

The much larger difference between C—H bonds in methane and ordinary primary C—H bonds than between primary and secondary C—H's is striking, but it may arise simply because as usual primary C—H bonds are reached activation energies are almost zero and cannot be further decreased. Also some steric effects could be involved, collision with a primary or secondary C—H being more probable than with a tertiary one which is largely buried in the molecule (cf. the apparently rather low reactivity of double bonds in polymeric molecules like rubber, Section 7·2b).[30]

Considering next the haloalkanes, from Table 8·2 a C—H bond in methyl chloride is attacked 4.4 times as fast as in methane. However, with ethyl chloride the situation reverses, and, since the chlorination yields about 80% 1,1-dichloroethane,[31] relative reactivities compared with a single —H of *ethane* are $\alpha \sim 0.47$, $\beta \sim 0.08$. Isomer distributions and relative reactivities for a series of longer-chain halides are listed in Table 8·5. All refer to liquid-phase reactions, but some of the data were obtained using sulfuryl chloride rather than chlorine. Since this reaction also usually appears to proceed through a chlorine atom chain (Section 8·6c), they can be used with little reservation.

The notable feature of Table 8·5 is the marked *decrease* in reactivity of hydrogens on carbons α (or β) to halogen. This result is certainly contrary to our anticipation on the basis of bond strengths (Section 2·3c) and resonance of the resulting alkyl radicals. A plausible explanation will be given after we take up the even more striking effect of carbonyl and similar groups.

First, however, we should again note that the product distributions of Table 8·5 are those of ordinary temperature chlorinations. At higher temperature, polyhalides and olefins are also produced by essentially the dehydrohalogenation chains discussed in Section 7·1d together with substitution and addition processes. Thus, for example, at 415°, ethyl chloride gives both ethylene (41.7%) and vinyl chloride (6.8%), whereas ethyl bromide gives 40% ethylene even at

changes in selectivity of chlorine atoms in aromatic media, apparently due to complexing with solvent.

[30] There is also some variation (although in no very systematic manner) in PZ factor among the compounds listed in Table 8·2, calculated either per molecule or per C—H bond when all are equivalent; cf. reference listed in footnote 17.

[31] W. E. Vaughan and F. F. Rust, *J. Org. Chem.*, **6**, 479 (1941). These data are at 208°; however, in liquid ethyl chloride near the boiling point the product is also at least 70% 1,1-dichloroethane; J. D'ans and J. Kautzach, *J. prak. Chem.*, **2**, 80, 305 (1909).

TABLE 8.5   PRODUCT COMPOSITIONS AND RELATIVE REACTIVITIES OF C—H BONDS IN CHLORINATION OF HALOALKANES

(Relative reactivities in parentheses)

Compound	Conditions	Footnote

% 20   80
    C——C——Cl
   (1)   (6)
	208°, gas phase	31

% 24   47   22   7
    C——C——C——C——Cl
   (1) (2.9) (1.4) (0.44)
	SO$_2$Cl$_2$, 70°	32

% 37   49   12   2
    C——C——C——CCl$_2$
   (1) (2.0) (0.53) (0.16)
	SO$_2$Cl$_2$, 70°	32

% 50   42   8
    C——C——C——CCl$_3$
   (1) (1.26) (0.24)
	SO$_2$Cl$_2$, 70°	32

% 40   60
    C——C——C——Cl
   (1) (2.25) (0)
	SO$_2$Cl$_2$, 70°	33

% 38   62   0
    C——C——C——Br
   (1) (2.4) (0)
	SO$_2$Cl$_2$, 70°	33

% 60   40   0
    C——C——CF$_2$——C
   (1)   (1)   (0)
	Cl$_2$, light, room temperature	34

% 55   45   0
    C——C——C——CF$_3$
   (1) (1.25)
	Cl$_2$, light, room temperature	34

[32] (a) A. B. Ash and H. C. Brown, *Record of Chemical Progress*, **9**, 81 (1948); (b) H. C. Brown and A. B. Ash, *J. Am. Chem. Soc.*, **77**, 4019 (1955).
[33] M. S. Kharasch and H. C. Brown, *ibid.*, **61**, 2142 (1939).
[34] A. L. Henne and F. B. Hinkamp, *ibid.*, **67**, 1194, 1197 (1945).

278°.[10] Additional recent examples are given by Hearne et al.[35] More strikingly, at about 470° polychlorobutanes give hexachlorobutadiene, and polychloropentanes give hexachlorocyclopentadiene, both in good yield.[11]

Similar decompositions must account for the "vicinal effect" described by Vaughan and Rust,[36] in which the yield of vicinal dichlorides from haloalkanes decreases with temperature, whereas the yields of other products change very little. Data for *n*-propyl chloride are given in Table 8·6. Evidently chlorine attack on a β-C—H

[35] G. W. Hearne, T. W. Evans, H. L. Yale, and M. C. Hoff, *J. Am. Chem. Soc.*, **75**, 1392 (1953).
[36] W. E. Vaughan and F. F. Rust, *J. Org. Chem.*, **6**, 479 (1941).

TABLE 8·6 EFFECT OF TEMPERATURE ON ISOMER DISTRIBUTION IN CHLO-
RINATION OF n-PROPYL CHLORIDE [36]

(Figures in parentheses are apparent relative reactivities of C—H bonds,
based on dichloride yields)

Temperature	158°	260°	340°	380°
1,1-dichloride	22% (1.1)	27% (1.5)	35% (1.2)	49% (1.4)
1,2-dichloride	46% (2.2)	46% (2.6)	22% (0.8)	0 (0)
1,3-dichloride	32% (1)	27% (1)	43% (1)	51% (1)

bond is increasingly followed by chlorine atom loss, and the resulting

$$Cl \cdot + CH_3{-}CH_2{-}CH_2Cl \rightarrow CH_3{-}\dot{C}H{-}CH_2Cl$$
$$\rightarrow CH_3{-}CH{=}CH_2 + Cl \cdot \quad (23)$$

propylene does not add chlorine at these temperatures. Other alkyl
halides behave similarly.

Returning to substituent effects, Table 8·7 presents data on product distribution in the chlorination of a series of carboxylic acids
and related compounds chiefly from the investigations of Bruylants
et al.[37,38] The work appears reliable, and two generalizations can
safely be made from the somewhat confusing results. First, acids,
acid chlorides, and nitriles all show very similar product distributions. Second, the C—H bonds α to carbonyl and similar groups are
strongly deactivated, and β—C—H bonds are somewhat activated
compared with other secondary C—H bonds in the molecules. In regard to the deactivation of the α—C—H bonds, it is significant that
acetic acid,[37] acetyl chloride,[37] and acetonitrile [38] all fail to undergo
vapor-phase photochemical chlorination under conditions where the
other members of the series react readily. Acetyl chloride also fails
to chlorinate with SO_2Cl_2,[32] and acetate esters are attacked in the
alcohol portion of the molecule (Table 8·10).[39]

These results are even more at variance with our ideas of bond
strengths and the role of resonance stabilization than are the data
on the alkyl halides, for, although the resonance stabilization of carbonyl-conjugated radicals is not known, copolymerization results

[37] A. Bruylants, M. Tits, and R. Danby, *Bull. soc. chim. Belges,* **58,** 210 (1949).
[38] A. Bruylants, M. Tits, C. Dieu, and R. Gauthier, *ibid.,* **61,** 266 (1952).

[39] Unfortunately, no comparable data on purely radical chlorination of ketones
is available. However, from the results on acid halogenations, one suspects that
the device of shortening the induction period in ketone chlorination by irradiating the reaction system succeeds because more or less random chlorination produces HCl, which, in turn, catalyzes enolization and brings on the polar reaction.

TABLE 8.7   PRODUCT COMPOSITIONS AND RELATIVE REACTIVITIES OF C—H BONDS IN CHLORINATION OF CARBONYL AND SIMILAR COMPOUNDS [d]

(Relative reactivities in parentheses referred to terminal carbon)

Structure	Foot-note	Structure	Foot-note
% 65 35 C—C—COOH (1) (0.81)	a, 40	C C—C—C—COCl % 8 60 32 (1) (45) (12)	b, 38
% 70 30 C—C—COOH (1) (0.64)	b, 38	% 0 30 65 5 C—C—C—C—COCl (0) (1) (2.2) (0.17)	c, 37
% 31 64 5 C—C—C—COOH (1) (3.1) (0.24)	b, 38	% 75 25 C—C—CN (1) (0.5)	b, 38
C C—C—COOH % 67 33 (1) (3)	b, 38	% 31 69 C—C—C—CN (1) (3.3) (0)	b, 38
C C—C—COOH % 85 15 (1) (1.06)	a, 40	% 25 75 C—C—C—C—CN (0) (1) (3) (0)	b, 37
C C—C—C—COOH % 5 69 26 (1) (83) (15.6)	b, 38	% 66 34 C—C—COOCH₃ (1) (0.77)	c, 37
% 60 40 C—C—C—COCl (1) (1) (0)	a, 40	% 30 70 C—C—C—COOCH₃ (1) (3.5) (0)	c, 37
% 30 65 5 C—C—C—COCl (1) (3.25) (0.25)	c, 37	% 29 71 C—C—C—C—COOCH₃ (0) (1) (2.5) (0)	c, 37
C C—C—COCl % 80 20 (1) (1.5)	a, 40	C C—C—C—COOCH₃ % 2 49 49 (1) (150) (75)	c, 38
C C—C—COCl % 69 31 (1) (2.7)	c, 37	% 100 0 C—C—SO₂Cl (or F)	41

[a] SO₂Cl₂, peroxide.
[b] Cl₂, light (liquid).
[c] Cl₂, light (vapor phase).
[d] Additional values for some of these compounds appear in reference cited in footnote 32.

[40] M. S. Kharasch and H. C. Brown, *ibid.*, **62**, 925 (1940).
[41] O. Scherer and H. Petrie, German Pat. 907,775 (March 29, 1954).

(Chapter 4) indicate that they approach the stability of benzyl and allyl radicals.

On the other hand, deactivation of the α position accords very well with the idea that the chlorine atom is a strong acceptor radical, preferentially attacking points of high electron density, and the polar properties of neighboring groups are primarily responsible for determining which C—H bond in a molecule is attacked. In fact, the primary $<$ secondary $<$ tertiary order observed in alkanes can be explained in this manner, their role in resonance stabilization of the transition state being through polar structures symbolized as:

$$Cl\cdot \quad H—CH_2—CH_3 \leftrightarrow Cl^- \quad H\cdot \quad \overset{H^+}{CH_2=CH_2}$$

$$\leftrightarrow Cl^- \quad H^+ \quad \overset{H\cdot}{CH_2=CH_2} \qquad (24)$$

In support of this idea [42] preferential deactivation of C—H bonds by carbonyl groups is not observed in all radical reactions. Thus, by decomposing acetyl peroxide in deuterium-labeled isobutyryl chloride and determining the composition of the methane evolved, Price and Morita [43] have shown that methyl radicals (which are not electron acceptors) attack a C—H bond in the α position 12.4 times as rapidly as in the β position, the reaction involved being:

$$(CH_3COO)_2 \rightarrow 2CO_2 + 2\cdot CH_3 \qquad (25)$$

$$\cdot CH_3 + \rightarrow D\overset{\overset{CH_3\leftarrow}{|}}{\underset{|}{C}}—COCl \rightarrow CH_4 + CH_3D \qquad (26)$$

$$\underset{CH_3}{}$$

Other examples of this sort appear in Section 10·2c.[44] The increased reactivity of β—C—H bonds is harder to account for, except in terms of some sort of alternating polarity.

A somewhat more quantitative idea of the magnitude of the polar effect in radical chlorinations may be gained by carrying out competi-

---

[42] Actually, the situation in regard to overall rates may be more complicated than we have made out, for, although acetic acid is not chlorinated, presence is reported [38] to reduce the quantum yield in pentane chlorination from 10^5–10^6 to 1500. Additional data on quantum yields in the photochlorination of acids are given by F. de Pauw and J. C. Jungers, *Bull. soc. chim. Belges,* **60,** 385 (1951).

[43] C. C. Price and H. Morita, *J. Am. Chem. Soc.,* **75,** 3683 (1953).

[44] The suggestion that such differences in reactivity result from radical rearrangements [32a] seems to be ruled out by tracer experiments [27a] using deuterium to determine the actual point of Cl· attack in several molecules.

tive chlorinations of substituted toluenes, in the same manner as the effect was investigated in copolymerization and mercaptan additions (Sections 4·1h, 7·2b). This has been done by Van Helden and Kooyman,[45] using sulfuryl chloride as a chlorine atom source, and by Miller,[46] using chlorine and light. Both sets of data are listed in Table 8·8, and Miller's data are plotted in Fig. 8·2 against Hammett

TABLE 8·8   COMPETITIVE CHLORINATION OF SUBSTITUTED TOLUENES

(Relative reactivities compared with toluene)

Substituent	Kooyman [45]	Miller [46]
p-CH$_3$	. . .	1.62
p-C$_6$H$_5$	. . .	1.59
p-t-C$_4$H$_9$	1.44	. . .
m-CH$_3$	. . .	1.33
m-C$_6$H$_5$	. . .	1.12
H	1.00	1.00
p-Cl	0.35	0.72
m-Cl	. . .	0.54
m-CN	0.16	0.36
p-CN	. . .	0.38
p-COOH	0.30	. . .
p-SO$_2$CH$_3$	0.12	. . .
p-NO$_2$	0.06	. . .

σ values for the substituents, using the values recently compiled by Jaffe.[47]

The two sets of measurements are in qualitative agreement, but the data of Miller, with more points and a more reproducible analytical technique, appear preferable. With the exception of the phenyl substituents, they yield a good linear relation with $\rho = -0.76 \pm .03$.[48] There is obviously no relation to the anticipated resonance stabilization of the benzyl radicals produced, and in fact such differences are apparently very small.[49] Miller used a deuterium tracer technique for analysis, and also determined k_H/k_D for chlorine atom attack on toluene as 2.1 (2.0 in CCl$_4$), a low value, consistent with the low activation energy of the process.

[45] R. Van Helden and E. C. Kooyman, *Rec. trav. chim.*, **73**, 269 (1954).

[46] B. Miller, thesis, Columbia University, 1955.

[47] H. Jaffe, *Chem. Revs.*, **53**, 191 (1953).

[48] This value is less negative than that reported by Kooyman (−1.5).[45] The reasons for excluding the phenyl points and a more detailed comparison of the two determinations are given in the reference cited in footnote 46. There is some evidence that ρ varies slightly with solvent, cf. footnote 29.

[49] M. Szwarc, C. H. Leigh, and A. H. Sehon, *J. Chem. Phys.*, **19**, 657 (1951).

The magnitude of the polar effect is comparable to that in the addition of thiyl radicals to α-methylstyrene (Section 7·2b) and impressively large for a process with almost negligible activation energy.

In addition to their measurements on toluenes, Van Helden and Kooyman [45] ran competitive chlorinations (using SO_2Cl_2) on a series

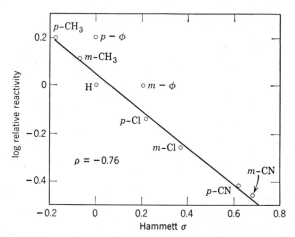

Fig. 8·2   Relative reactivities of substituted toluenes towards chlorine atoms versus Hammett σ values of substituents.[46]

of compounds $X—C(CH_3)_3$, and noted further evidence for the importance of polarity in the form of a good correlation between reactivity and the ionization constants of the corresponding acids, $X—CH_2—COOH$ (Table 8·9).

TABLE 8·9   RELATIVE REACTIVITIES TOWARD CHLORINE ATOMS OF C—H BONDS IN $X—C(CH_3)_3$ [45]

Substituent X	Relative Reactivity	ΔK_a [a]
Phenyl	1.00	0
t-Butyl	1.2 ± 0.1	0.7
p-Nitrophenyl	0.5 ± 0.1	-0.4
Phenyl—CO—	0.4 ± 0.1	-0.8
—COCl	0.19 ± 0.03	-1.5 [b]
—CN	0.17 ± 0.03	-1.7

[a] Difference in acid ionization constant of acid $X—CH_2—COOH$ and $\phi—CH_2—COOH$.
[b] For $HOOC—CH_2—COOH$.

Directive effects of other groups are of practical interest and, in general, accord with chlorine atom attack at points of high electron

TABLE 8·10   PRODUCT DISTRIBUTION IN CHLORINATION OF ESTERS

Ester	Foot-note	Ester	Foot-note

%   CH₃CO—O—C—C
         65   35
	a, 37	% CH₃CO—O—C—C
		                 51 49
			a, 37

%   CH₃CO—O—C—C—C
         25   40   29
	b, 32	% CH₃CO—O—C—C—C
		                    66
			a, 37

%   CH₃CO—O—C—C—C
                 69   31
	a, 37	% CCl₃CO—O—C—C—C
		                3 50 47
			b, 50

%   CH₃CO—O—C—C
         50   50
	a, 37	% CCl₃CO—O—C—C—C—C—C
		                        63 37
			b, 51

%   CH₃CO—O—C—C—C—C
                 4   71   25
	a, 37	% CCl₃CO—O—C—C—C
		                    47 53
			b, 51

%   CH₃CO—O—C
                 100
	a, 38	% CCl₃CO—O—C—C—C—C
		                    53 47
			b, 51

ᵃ Cl₂, light (vapor phase).
ᵇ Cl₂, light, liquid, 80–120°.

⁵⁰ H. M. Waddle and H. Adkins, J. Am. Chem. Soc., **61,** 3361 (1939).
⁵¹ C. W. Gayler and H. M. Waddle, ibid., **63,** 3358 (1941).

availability.   In acetate or chloroacetate esters, the alcohol moiety is attacked (Table 8·10), and we see that, in the trichloroacetates, substitution is shifted to the far end of the chain.   Similarly, in partially fluorinated ethers, attack is initially on the non-fluorinated side of the oxygen,[52] e.g.,

$$CH_3—O—CF_2CHFCl \xrightarrow[\substack{\text{Light}\\ \text{Liquid phase}}]{3Cl_3} CCl_3—O—CF_2CHFCl \xrightarrow{Cl_2}$$

$$CCl_3OCF_2CFCl_2 \quad (27)$$

Results in the chlorination of alkyl silanes are interesting.   Neighboring silicon appears to have much the same effect as neighboring carbon, Speier [53] finding that trimethylchlorosilane and t-butyl chloride chlorinate photochemically at 55–60° at about the same rate in competition.   Introduction of further chlorine decreases reactivity, trimethyl chlorosilane reacting nine times as fast in competition as dimethyldichlorosilane.   Again, methyltrichlorosilane is reported not to react with sulfuryl chloride, although other alkyl silanes are chlorinated.[54]   Further data on isomer distribution are given in Table 8·11.

Results are about what might be anticipated, except in the second

⁵² J. D. Park, B. Striklin, and J. R. Lacher, ibid., **76,** 1387 (1954).
⁵³ J. L. Speier, ibid., **73,** 824 (1951).
⁵⁴ L. H. Sommer and F. C. Whitmore, ibid., **68,** 485 (1946).

TABLE 8·11 PRODUCT DISTRIBUTION AND RELATIVE REACTIVITIES OF C—H BONDS IN CHLORINATION OF SILANES

$$C-C-C-SiCl_3 \quad 55,\ a$$
% 41 46 13

$$C-Si-C-Cl \quad 53$$
with C (top) and Cl (below Si)
% 17 Cl 83

$$C-C-SiCl_3 \quad 53,\ a$$
% 71 29

$$C-Si-C-Cl \quad 53$$
with C (top) and C (below Si)
% 80 C 20

$$C-C-SiCl_2C_2H_5 \quad 56,\ a$$
% 62 38

$$C-C-SiCl_3 \quad 56,\ a$$
with Cl on first C
% 51 49

$$C-C-Si(C_2H_5)_3 \quad 57,\ a$$
% 0 100

$$C-C-SiCl_3 \quad 56,\ a$$
with Cl on first C
% >72

^{a} SO₂Cl₂ chlorinations.

[55] L. H. Sommer, E. Dorfman, G. M. Goldberg, and F. C. Whitmore, *ibid.*, **68**, 448 (1946).

[56] L. H. Sommer, F. C. Whitmore, et al., **76**, 1613 (1954).

[57] L. H. Sommer, D. L. Bailey, W. A. Strong, and F. C. Whitmore, *ibid.*, **68**, 1881 (1946).

column, where a marked tendency towards polychlorination on a single carbon atom is noted.

In general the chlorinations of aldehydes and alcohols become involved in polar reactions. However, photochemical chlorination of benzaldehyde gives benzoyl chloride, and the photochemical chlorination of fluorinated alcohols in CCl₄ solution described by McBee [58]

$$CF_3CF_2CF_2CH_2OH \xrightarrow[\text{Light}]{Cl_2} CF_3CF_2CF_2CHO \quad 2HCl \qquad (28)$$

certainly sounds like a radical process:

$$Cl\cdot + RCH_2OH \rightarrow R-\overset{\cdot}{C}H-OH + HCl \qquad (29)$$

$$R-\overset{\cdot}{C}HOH + Cl_2 \rightarrow R-\overset{Cl}{\underset{|}{C}H}-OH \quad (+Cl\cdot) \rightarrow R-CHO + HCl \qquad (30)$$

8 · 4   Molecular Bromine

8·4a   General Characteristics of Radical Brominations: Comparison with Chlorination

Since we have just discussed radical chlorinations in detail, we can best introduce the topic of radical bromination by comparing the

[58] E. T. McBee, O. R. Pierce, and W. F. Marzluff, *ibid.*, **75**, 1609 (1953).

energetics of the two processes. This is done in Fig. 8·3, where the major difference is immediately apparent. Chlorine atom attack on C—H bonds is a strongly exothermic, low activation energy process, whereas bromine atom attack is endothermic except for the very weakest C—H bonds. The difference, of course, arises from the 16

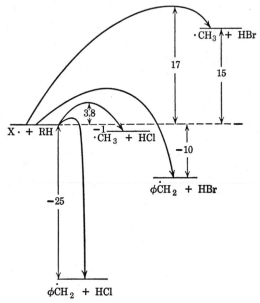

Fɪɢ. 8·3   Energetics of Cl· and Br· reactions: ΔH's and E_{act}'s in kcal/mole.

kcal lower bond strength of H—Br compared with H—Cl. The other step in any radical chain bromination is exothermic in all cases

$$R\cdot + Br—Br \rightarrow R—Br + Br\cdot \tag{31}$$

($\Delta H = -21$ kcal for $\cdot CH_3$, -4 kcal for $\phi CH_2\cdot$). It presents no energy barrier to the chain and apparently occurs extremely rapidly (see below).

Even though, as is established, reactions of the type

$$Br\cdot + H—R \rightarrow H—Br + R\cdot \tag{32}$$

require little activation energy over that demanded by the energetics of the overall process, it is evident from Fig. 8·3 that radical chain brominations can be expected only in the case of hydrocarbons yielding relatively stable radicals, and, in fact, study of the non-chain reaction of bromine atoms with methane (Section 2·3b) provides one of the most reliable measurements of the (CH_3—H) dissociation energy.

We can immediately draw four important conclusions from Fig. 8·3.

(1) Except for reactions producing very stable radicals, kinetic chains will be short, particularly in liquid-phase, low-temperature reactions.

(2) Resonance stabilization of the resulting radical will be very important in determining the point of attack of bromine atoms.

(3) Compared with chlorine, bromine atoms will be highly selective.

(4) In most cases the reverse action

$$R\cdot + H\text{—}Br \rightarrow R\text{—}H + Br\cdot \tag{33}$$

will be detectable and important.

All of these predictions are confirmed by experiment. The vapor-phase photochemical bromination of cyclohexane, studied by Jost [59] gives quantum yields of about 2 at room temperature and 12–37 at 100°, compared with typical values of 10^4 in chlorine reactions. The bromination of n-pentane proceeds rather slowly in the vapor phase at 80° to give a mixture of amyl bromides [60] which are presumably almost entirely secondary. Kharasch [61] reports that neopentane fails to react with bromine in the liquid phase at room temperature and is only slowly brominated photochemically (or in the presence of traces of oxygen) at higher temperatures. Similarly, t-butylbenzene fails to undergo side-chain bromination under any conditions (the bromine is consumed by the competing polar ring substitution) and trimethylacetic acid only reacts at 150° where it apparently decomposes to give brominated hydrocarbons and a little (9%) trimethylacetoxytrimethyl acetic acid. Again, the vapor-phase bromination of isobutane gives exclusively t-butyl bromide,[62] and, in iso-

---

[59] W. Jost, Z. physik. Chem., Bodenstein Festband, 291 (1931).

[60] M. S. Kharasch, W. Zimmt and W. Nudenberg, J. Chem. Phys., 20, 1659 (1952). These workers were unable to confirm the fragmentation of the molecule reported by R. R. Williams, Jr., and W. H. Hamill, J. Am. Chem. Soc., 72, 1857 (1950).

[61] M. S. Kharasch and M. Z. Fineman, J. Am. Chem. Soc., 63, 2776 (1941).

[62] M. S. Kharasch, W. Hered, and F. R. Mayo, J. Org. Chem., 6, 818 (1941); B. H. Eckstein, H. A. Scheraga, and F. E. Van Artsdalen, J. Chem. Phys., 22, 28 (1954).

pentane, the t-C—H bond is reported to react 30–40 times as readily as sec-C—H.[63]

With toluene, however, the chain reaction can be very rapid, and bromine added slowly to 10-fold excess toluene in CCl$_4$ at 20° under an incandescent lamp is instantaneously decolorized, giving benzyl bromide in about 98% yield [64] (larger quantities of bromine begin to produce benzal bromide as well). The effect of experimental variables on the side-chain bromination of toluene have been investigated in some detail by Kharasch, White, and Mayo,[65] whose data helped to confirm the radical chain process. Optimum conditions are the slow addition of bromine to excess toluene in the presence of light and oxygen at a somewhat elevated temperature, since larger bromine concentrations actually seem to slow down the reaction, as well as favoring radical addition to the ring (Section 7·1e) and polar ring substitution. The competition with the polar ring reaction is less favorable in acetic acid or nitrobenzene, and the radical reaction is markedly inhibited by traces of alcohol, NO$_2$, or nitrobenzene.

The frequent catalytic effect of oxygen on brominations must be related to peroxide formation by bromine-atom-induced autoxidation (Section 9·3c), and Kharasch indeed detected a peroxidic substance in his reactions in the presence of oxygen and light.[65] The contrast with chlorinations, where oxygen seems to be invariably an inhibitor, may be rather heuristically related to the facts that in the bromine reaction chains are shorter (and so less subject to inhibition) and that, since hydrogen abstraction is the slow step, bromine atoms, which are oxygen inert, are the chief species present, rather than alkyl radicals.

As further examples of the difference in selectivity of chlorine and bromine atoms, bromination of cumene yields solely t-bromide,[63] and, in competitive bromination of toluene and cyclohexane, C—H bonds in the former are the more reactive by a factor of 230.[27b] Again, on halogenation 2,3,4,5,6-pentachloroethylbenzene gives the β-phenylethyl chloride, but it gives the α-phenylethyl bromide.[66]

Demonstration of the reversibility of hydrogen abstraction, i.e., attack of alkyl radicals on HBr, reaction 33, comes chiefly from

[63] G. A. Russell and H. C. Brown, *J. Am. Chem. Soc.*, **77**, 4025 (1955).

[64] F. R. Mayo and W. B. Hardy, *J. Am. Chem. Soc.*, **74**, 911 (1952).

[65] M. S. Kharasch, P. C. White, and F. R. Mayo, *J. Org. Chem.*, **3**, 33 (1938).

[66] S. D. Ross, M. Markarian, and M. Nazzewski, *J. Am. Chem. Soc.*, **69**, 1914, 2468 (1947).

kinetic studies, although 33 is one of the steps in the well-established free radical addition of HBr. However, Wiberg [67] has recently shown that HBr exchanges readily with α-deuterotoluene in a reaction which is inhibited by thiocresol (which removes bromine atoms). Accordingly, HBr concentrations must be kept low in any determination of the isotope effect in toluene bromination. The value of k_H/k_D turns out to be 4.6–4.9 at 77°,[67] appreciably higher than that for chlorination, as might be anticipated for a process of higher activation energy.

Finally, we may note that bromination of more complicated hydrocarbons frequently gives polybromides by an apparent polar process which has been discussed by Russell and Brown.[63] Thus, from 2,3-dimethylbutane, even small amounts of bromine may yield chiefly 2,3-dibromo-2,3-dimethylbutane.[63, 68] Additional products, obtained in the vapor phase, include 1,4-dibromo-2,3-dimethyl-2-butene, and are described by Kharasch,[69b] who also reports a rearrangement occurring in the bromination of 2,2,4,4-tetramethylpentane to give 4-bromo-2,2,3,4-tetramethylpentane.[69] However, the product identification does not seem to the writer to preclude a polar rearrangement of the expected initial unrearranged product, 3-bromo-2,2,4,4-tetramethylpentane.

8·4b Kinetics of Bromination Reactions

As the reader must already anticipate, no conclusive kinetic studies of liquid-phase bromine substitution reactions are available. However, vapor-phase investigations give valuable information and confirm the radical chain nature of the process.

Sullivan and Davidson [70] have made an elegant investigation of the kinetics of the thermally induced bromination of chloroform at 147–180°C and find that the results are consistent with the process

$$Br_2 \rightleftharpoons 2Br \cdot \tag{34}$$

$$Br \cdot + HCCl_3 \underset{k_{-35}}{\overset{k_{35}}{\rightleftharpoons}} HBr + \cdot CCl_3 \tag{35}$$

$$\cdot CCl_3 + Br_2 \underset{k_{-36}}{\overset{k_{36}}{\rightleftharpoons}} CCl_3Br + Br \cdot \tag{36}$$

[67] K. B. Wiberg, private communication.

[68] A. V. Gross and V. N. Ipatieff, *J. Org. Chem.*, **8**, 438 (1943).

[69] (a) M. S. Kharasch, Y. C. Liu, and W. Nudenberg, *ibid.*, **19**, 1150 (1954); (b) *ibid.*, **20**, 680 (1955).

[70] J. H. Sullivan and N. Davidson, *J. Chem. Phys.*, **19**, 143 (1951).

in which all steps in the usual chain are reversible, and, in fact, the overall equilibrium constant,

$$K = [HBr][CCl_3Br]/[Br_2][CHCl_3] \cong 2 \qquad (37)$$

The individual rate constants have been evaluated as $k_{35} = 2.3 \times 10^9 \exp (-9300/RT)$ and $k_{-36} = 8.1 \times 10^{10} \exp (-10,200/RT)$, with $k_{36}/k_{-35} = 25$, i.e., the $\cdot CCl_3$ radical reacts with bromine only 25 times as readily as with HBr. It is interesting to compare the calculated value of k_{35} at $100°$, 8×10^3, with typical values of over 10^9 in chlorine reactions, giving a good quantitative idea of the difference between the two reactions. Further, if we take $D(CCl_3—Br) = 48$ kcal,[71] from thermochemical data $E_{36} = 7–8$ kcal, our first data on the activation energy for alkyl radical attack on a halogen molecule, and substantiating a rapid process (with $CH_3 \cdot$, E is substantially zero). The back reaction of reaction 36, a displacement on bromine, can also be checked by measurements of exchange between radioactive bromine and CCl_3Br, which give the same value,[72] and establishes the latter as the chain process

$$Br \cdot + CCl_3Br \rightleftharpoons Br_2 + \cdot CCl_3 \qquad (38)$$

We have already mentioned the determination of $D(CH_3—H)$ through study of the non-chain radical bromination of methane. Similar investigations have been made on ethane,[73] neopentane,[74] and isobutylene,[62] in which bromination becomes an increasingly long-chain process. Results are in good agreement with other methods, although some peculiarities in the data are discussed by Steacie.[15] In the case of toluene,[75] the method gives $D(\phi CH_2—H) = 89.6$ kcal, some 12 kcal/mole higher than the value which we have used here and which comes from pyrolysis and electron impact data (Section $2\cdot3$). Basically, the technique of determining $D(R—H)$ in such systems is as follows. Since a third body, M, is required for bromine atom recombination in the gas phase, the reactions considered are:

[71] M. Szwarc and A. H. Sehon, *ibid.*, **18**, 1685 (1950).

[72] N. Davidson and J. H. Sullivan, *ibid.*, **17**, 176 (1949); A. A. Miller and J. E. Willard, *ibid.*, **17**, 168 (1949).

[73] H. C. Andersen and F. R. Van Artsdalen, *ibid.*, **12**, 479 (1944).

[74] E. I. Hormats and E. R. Van Artsdalen, *ibid.*, **19**, 778 (1951).

[75] H. R. Anderson, H. A. Sherega, and E. R. Van Artsdalen, *ibid.*, **21**, 1258 (1952).

$$Br_2 \xrightarrow{h\nu} 2Br\cdot \tag{39}$$

$$Br\cdot + \phi CH_3 \underset{k_{-40}}{\overset{k_{40}}{\rightleftharpoons}} \phi CH_2\cdot + HBr \tag{40}$$

$$\phi CH_2\cdot + Br_2 \xrightarrow{k_{41}} \phi CH_2Br + Br\cdot \tag{41}$$

$$M + 2Br\cdot \xrightarrow{k_{42}} Br_2 \tag{42}$$

Without going into the detailed kinetics, the initial rate (no HBr) is given by

$$-d[Br_2]/dt = k_{40}[\phi CH_3]I_{abs}{}^{1/2}(k_{42}[M])^{-1/2} \tag{43}$$

and, since the activation energy of reaction 42 is taken as zero, the overall activation energy, 7.2 kcal, should be E_{40}. By measuring the rate in the presence of various ratios of HBr and Br_2 at different temperatures, $E_{-40}-E_{41}$ is obtained as 5.0 kcal. Setting $E_{41} = 0$, $E_{-40} = 5$ kcal, and ΔH for the equilibrium, 40, = 2.2 kcal, whence, from $D(H—Br) = 87.4$, $D(\phi CH_2—H) = 89.6$ kcal. Although in this case the data fit the kinetic equations well, the actual numerical values of k_{41}/k_{-40} pass through unity in the temperature range measured, in spite of the 5 kcal difference in activation energy, and it is difficult to see how the activationless reaction with bromine would have a very small PZ factor. Further, since the activation energy for reaction of $CCl_3\cdot$ radicals with Br_2 appears to be 6–7 kcal, the assumption $E_{41} = 0$ is probably faulty. In short, these facts, together with the discrepancy with other measurements, makes the whole result seem doubtful.

8·4c Polar Effects in Bromine Atom Reactions

In Section 8·4a we found that bond strengths and resonance energies were important in determining the point of attack of bromine atoms. We may now see that these species also show their expected acceptor properties. Kooyman, Van Helden, and Bickel [76] have investigated the competitive bromination of toluenes in the manner described for chlorination with results shown in Fig. 8·4. The tendency to attack a point of high electron availability appears even more pronounced than with chlorine, the slope of the best line through the plot giving a Hammett ρ value of -1.05. The effect of substituents appears purely polar, and the higher activation energy compared with chlorine probably accounts for the greater selectivity. Never-

[76] E. C. Kooyman, R. Van Helden, and A. F. Bickel, *Koninkl. Ned. Akad. Wetenshappen Proc.*, **B56**, 75 (1953).

theless, we should note that this is one of the few molecules in which hydrogen abstraction is an exothermic process. With less reactive hydrocarbons, polar effects should be increasingly obscured by changes in C—H bond strengths, in keeping with recent results reported by Kharasch, Zimmt, and Nudenberg.[77] These workers studied the bromination of a series of alkyl halides in the vapor phase at 100°, finding, as examples, that n-propyl chloride gave a 90%

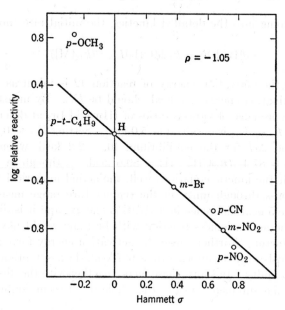

Fig. 8·4   Relative reactivities of substituted toluenes towards bromine atoms versus Hammett σ values for substituents (after Kooyman, Van Helden, and Bickel [76]).

yield of dihalide, 50% 1,1- and 50% 1,2-, and n-butyl chloride gave a 92% yield of dihalide with a composition of 25% 1,1-, 25% 1,2-, and 50% 1,3-.   Comparing these results with chlorinations listed in Table 8·5, we see an increased tendency of bromine atoms to attack —CCl—H bonds.

8 · 5   Molecular Iodine

The prospects of chain iodination by iodine atoms are unpromising, since ΔH for the displacement step with the iodine atom is 30.5 kcal for methane, and 6.0 kcal for toluene, and such reactions

[77] M. S. Kharasch, W. S. Zimmt, and W. Nudenberg, J. Org. Chem., **20**, 1430 (1955).

have seemingly not been observed. In fact, the equilibria are also unfavorable, hydrogen iodide reducing alkyl iodides to hydrocarbon plus molecular iodine. However, alkyl iodides undergo a series of exchange reactions with iodine atoms which have been studied by Noyes and are of considerable interest.[78] The most complete story is available with benzyl iodide, which undergoes exchange with radioactive iodine in hexachlorobutadiene (an exotic but extremely unreactive solvent) at a convenient rate thermally at 60–90° or photochemically at room temperature.[79] The reaction was studied under an unusual range of experimental conditions (a 10^6-fold range of benzyl iodide–iodine ratios), and the data accounted for by the following series of reaction steps:

$$\phi CH_2 I \rightarrow \phi CH_2 \cdot + I \cdot \tag{44}$$

$$I_2 \rightarrow 2I_2 \cdot \tag{45}$$

$$I \cdot + \phi CH_2 I \rightarrow \phi CH_2 \cdot + I_2 \tag{46}$$

$$\phi CH_2 \cdot + I_2 \rightarrow \phi CH_2 I + I \cdot \tag{47}$$

$$2I \cdot \rightarrow I_2 \tag{48}$$

$$\phi CH_2 \cdot + I \cdot \rightarrow \phi CH_2 I \tag{49}$$

$$2\phi CH_2 \cdot \rightarrow \phi CH_2 CH_2 \phi \tag{50}$$

reactions 44 and 45 representing initiation processes, 46 and 47 the exchange chain, and 48–50 chain termination. The overall rate expression is extremely complex and closely resembles those for overall rates in copolymerization (Section $4 \cdot 1j$), in fact being derived in essentially the same manner. Rather overwhelmingly, it has proved possible to evaluate the six of the seven rate constants, the seventh, k_{49}, was taken as twice k_{48}, i.e., assuming that an iodine atom reacts with a benzyl radical at the same rate as with another iodine. They have the following values at 36°C in moles, liters, and seconds.

$$
\begin{aligned}
k_{44} &= 6.0 \times 10^{-14} & k_{48} &= 7.0 \times 10^{9} \\
k_{45} &= 1.4 \times 10^{-12} & k_{49} &= 1.4 \times 10^{10} \qquad (51) \\
k_{46} &= 7.1 \times 10^{4} & k_{50} &= 1.6 \times 10^{9} \\
k_{47} &= 3.3 \times 10^{6} &
\end{aligned}
$$

[78] For a general discussion and summary of earlier work, cf. R. M. Noyes and D. J. Sibbett, *J. Am. Chem. Soc.*, **75**, 767 (1953). Exchange reactions of unsaturated iodides were discussed in Section $7 \cdot 1d$.

[79] M. Gazith and R. M. Noyes, *ibid.*, **77**, 6091 (1955).

The large values of k_{46} and k_{47} show that the process can be a very long-chain one with rapid steps, but k_{47} is still small enough to indicate another reaction involving exothermic radical attack on a halogen molecule with an appreciable activation energy (Section 8·4b). The exchange proves to be strongly oxygen inhibited, and since the inhibition is much more marked at high $\phi CH_2I/I_2$ ratios, it appears that (as we anticipate) oxygen reacts with benzyl radicals but not with iodine atoms.

In addition to the type of chain occurring with benzyl iodide, and with CCl_3Br (Section 8·4b), exchange might also occur via displacement on carbon as in the mechanism of iodide ion exchange in solution,[80] i.e.:

$$I\cdot + R{-}I \rightarrow I{-}R + I\cdot \tag{52}$$

Again in analogy to the ionic reaction, such a reaction should involve inversion of configuration at the carbon atom attacked, and the most likely case would be a primary or secondary carbon when there is little hindrance to back-side approach, and where the C—I bond is relatively strong to slow the competing chain involving attack on iodine. The radical exchange of radioactive I_2 and optically active sec-butyl iodide has very recently been studied by Herrmann and Noyes,[81] who, by comparing the rates of exchange and racemization, conclude that exchange is taking place by both paths.[82]

The data discussed in connection with benzyl iodide and CCl_3Br indicate a halogen exchange reaction which competes in rate very favorably with the usual displacement reaction on hydrogen leading to halogen substitution. Normally, in halogenations such exchanges are not detected, but we should keep in mind that they are probably going on, that they can conceivably complicate kinetics and even influence reaction products, and so should not be ignored.

[80] E. D. Hughes, et al., *J. Chem. Soc.*, **1935**, 1525; **1936**, 1173; **1938**, 209.

[81] R. A. Herrmann and R. M. Noyes, *J. Am. Chem. Soc.*, **78**, 5764 (1956).

[82] Another example of what is quite definitely radical displacement on carbon occurs in radical attack on mercury dialkyls, e.g.:

$$\cdot CH_3 + CH_3HgCH_3 \rightarrow C_2H_6 + Hg + \cdot CH_3$$

$$H\cdot + CH_3Hg\phi \rightarrow CH_4 + Hg + \cdot\phi$$

cf. A. T. Blades and E. W. R. Steacie, *Can. J. Chem.*, **32**, 1142 (1954); H. G. Oswin, R. Rebbert, and E. W. R. Steacie, *ibid.*, **33**, 472 (1955).

8 · 6   Other Halogen Chain Carriers

8·6a   Introduction

From what has gone before, it should be clear that, once a halogen is selected and a chain process initiated, little further can be done to alter the nature of the products in radical halogenations. Further, the more reactive halogens are discouragingly undiscriminating in their attack on C—H bonds in complex molecules. We will now see how the utility of radical chain halogenation can be greatly increased by the use of other more complex halogen carriers than the halogen molecules themselves, which in many cases lead to quite different products.

8·6b   Chlorine-Bromine Mixtures

A very intriguing reaction which in all probability involves chlorine bromide as a halogenating agent was described in 1951 by Speier,[83] who noted that, although trimethylchlorosilane failed to react with bromine in light at the reflux point, when chlorine was passed into the solution, bromomethyldimethylchlorosilane was obtained in 61% yield, together with polybrominated products, i.e.:

$$(CH_3)_3SiCl + \tfrac{1}{2}Br_2 + \tfrac{1}{2}Cl_2 \rightarrow CH_2BrSi(CH_3)_2Cl + HCl \quad (53)$$

By a similar procedure, toluene gave 71% benzyl bromide, and cyclohexane 45% cyclohexyl bromide plus 38% dibromides. The obvious rationalization of the reaction is

$$Cl\cdot + RH \rightarrow R\cdot + HCl \quad (54)$$

$$R\cdot + Br—Cl \rightarrow RBr + Cl\cdot \quad (55)$$

If this is correct, the reaction gives a procedure for introducing bromine into a molecule at the point where chlorine normally appears in chlorinations, and for evading the energy barrier which prevents direct bromination. The reaction also occurs thermally in the vapor phase, for Ruh and Davis report the bromination of CH_2F_2 and CHF_3 with chlorine-bromine mixtures at 200–500°.[84]

A somewhat surprising feature of the reaction is that in reaction 55 the alkyl radical attacks the bromine rather than the chlorine end of Br—Cl, since attack at the chlorine end leads to a reaction

[83] J. L. Speier, *J. Am. Chem. Soc.*, **73**, 826 (1951).
[84] R. P. Ruh and R. A. Davis, U.S. Pat. 2,658,086 (November 3, 1953).

which is more exothermic by 14 kcal. However, Br—Cl is rather egg shaped with Br occupying most of its surface, and, if one likes polar effects in reactions of this sort, the carbon radical has a high electron density, with the dipole of Cl—Br certainly lying in the direction Cl $\leftrightarrow$ Br.

8·6c Sulfuryl Chloride

The use of SO_2Cl_2 as a convenient chlorinating agent was eluci- dated by Kharasch and Brown in 1939,[33] and has already been an- ticipated here in Section 7·3b and 8·3c. These investigators found that, although SO_2Cl_2 could be refluxed for a long period in cyclo- hexane without reaction, either alone or in the presence of air, CuCl, sulfur, iodine, HCl, O_2, or numerous other materials, addition of a little benzoyl peroxide led to a rapid reaction, the overall course of which was

$$SO_2Cl_2 + C_6H_{12} \rightarrow C_6H_{11}Cl + HCl + SO_2 \qquad (56)$$

Since the reaction is peroxide initiated (other radical sources are also effective) it is evidently a radical chain and is generally formulated as

$$Cl\cdot + RH \rightarrow R\cdot + HCl \qquad (57)$$

$$R\cdot + SO_2Cl_2 \rightarrow RCl + \cdot SO_2Cl \qquad (58)$$

$$SO_2Cl\cdot \rightarrow SO_2 + Cl\cdot \qquad (59)$$

A very wide variety of other hydrocarbons and more complex mole- cules are similarly chlorinated (cf. Tables 8·5, 8·7, and 8·11), and there is much evidence that attack on the C—H bonds is actually by chlorine atoms. Thus, the isomer distribution in the tables just mentioned agree well with those observed with chlorine, and there is reasonable agreement between Kooyman's [45] and Miller and Wall- ing's [46] competitive experiments on side-chain chlorinations of toluene (Section 8·3c). Further, the isotope effects [46] on toluene chlorination are in good agreement, k_H/k_D for $SO_2Cl_2 = 2.11$, for $Cl_2 = 2.09$. On the other hand, Kharasch and Brown report that chloroform and benzal chloride (which can certainly be chlorinated) are not attacked by SO_2Cl_2 under their conditions, and, more recently, Russell and Brown [85] have noted significant differences in the ratio of primary and tertiary chlorides formed on chlorination of hydrocarbons by Cl_2 and SO_2Cl_2. Typically, they find that, with triptane, (2,3,4-tri-

[85] G. A. Russell and H. C. Brown, J. Am. Chem. Soc., 77, 4031 (1955).

methylpentane) at 80° a tertiary C—H bond is attacked 7.33 times as readily as a primary C—H bond by SO_2Cl_2, compared with 3.2 for Cl_2. It may be that an actual equilibrium between SO_2, Cl·, and ·SO_2Cl exists in these systems (i.e., that reaction 59 is rapidly reversible), and also that the reaction may be complicated by reaction between SO_2 and the hydrocarbon radical (cf. Sections 5·4d and 7·3b). In any case, the problem needs further study before the formulation given in reaction sequence 57–59 can be accepted as generally applicable to all systems.

8·6d N-Bromosuccinimide and Related Compounds

The reaction of N-bromoacetamide with olefins such as 2,3-dimethyl-2-butene to yield allylic bromides was first described by Wohl in 1919,[86] but reactions of this sort received little attention, until Ziegler et al. in 1942 [87] published the results of an intensive investigation with a variety of N-haloamides, selecting N-bromosuccinimide as a particularly convenient and effective reagent. Since the introduction of halogen into an allylic position is a highly desirable operation in many fields of organic chemistry, the reaction has been avidly seized upon by practicing organic chemists, and a large literature has accumulated. The earlier portion has been reviewed by Djerassi,[88] and we will restrict ourselves here to the relatively little that applies to reaction mechanism.

The suggestion that N-bromosuccinimide (NBS) reacts via a radical chain mechanism was made in 1944 by Bloomfield [89] and by Hey [90] and is generally accepted,[91] the chain-carrying steps being written

$$\text{N·} + \text{H—R} \rightarrow \text{NH} + \text{R·} \qquad (60)$$

[86] A. Wohl, *Ber.*, **52**, 51 (1919).

[87] K. Ziegler, A. Spaeta, E. Schaaf, W. Schumann, and E. Winkelmann, *Ann.*, **551**, 80 (1942).

[88] C. Djerassi, *Chem. Revs.*, **43**, 271 (1948).

[89] G. F. Bloomfield, *J. Chem. Soc.*, **1944**, 14.

[90] D. H. Hey, *Ann. Rpts. Chem. Soc.*, **41**, 184 (1944).

[91] Such a mechanism applies only to reactions in non-hydroxylic solvents. In polar media such as water, NBS reacts in a polar manner, behaving as a carrier of electrophilic halogen; cf. reference in footnote 88, also I. Salamon and T. Reichstein, *Helv. Chim. Acta*, **30**, 1616 (1947).

$$R\cdot + Br-N\underset{CO}{\overset{CO}{\diagdown}} \rightarrow RBr + \underset{CO}{\overset{CO}{\diagdown}} N\cdot \qquad (61)$$

Initially, the point of bromine substitution provided the chief argument for such a chain process, but in 1946 Schmid and Karrer [92] showed that the reaction was accelerated by benzoyl peroxide, and many other radical sources including visible light have been found to be effective. Dauben and McCoy [93] have made a detailed survey of the effect of numerous variables on the reaction of NBS with cyclohexene in CCl_4, which throws a good deal of light on inconsistencies in former work and adds further substantiation to the radical chain hypothesis. Very pure reagents were found to react only very slowly in the dark, but the reaction was speeded by traces of peroxide in the olefin, impurities in the NBS, and water, amines, bromine, thiophenol (perhaps by a redox initiation process), and several other substances. On the other hand, hydroquinone, dinitrobenzene, bromanil, and iodine were inhibitors. They conclude, contrary to previous suggestions,[89] that there is no thermal initiation process via NBS dissociation.

Oxygen also has a complicated effect on the reaction,[94] appreciable quantities inhibiting bromination, but traces helping to initiate chains, particularly at low concentrations of initiator. A study of the kinetics of the NBS–cyclohexene reaction in benzene solution has been made by Dauben and Youngman,[94] working in carefully degassed systems at 20–40° and using azobisisobutyronitrile, and cumene hydroperoxides as initiators. With the azonitrile, the rate law is

$$-d[\text{NBS}]/dt = k[\text{cyclohexene}][\text{initiator}]^{1/2} \qquad (62)$$

typical chain kinetics for termination by interaction of two NBS radicals. Chains were of the order of 10^3. With the hydroperoxide (which commonly gives peculiar results, Section $10\cdot2d$), the order in respect to initiator was lower, 0.22–0.25.

Turning now to the types of compounds brominated by NBS, at the time of Djerassi's review [88] the reaction was considered reasonably general for C—H bonds α to simple or conjugated olefins, aromatic

[92] H. Schmid and P. Karrer, Helv. Chim. Acta, **29**, 573 (1946).
[93] H. J. Dauben, Jr., and L. L. McCoy, private communication.
[94] H. J. Dauben, Jr., and E. A. Youngman, private communication.

(or often heterocyclic) nuclei, and for carbonyl compounds (where, in the steroid series, it is widely employed). Subsequently, other types of compounds have been found to react, e.g., cyclohexane is brominated in the presence of azobisisobutyronitrile,[95] or benzoyl peroxide,[96] and N-chlorosuccinimide effects a similar chlorination. Similarly,[96] a variety of esters, including methyl laurate, are reported to brominate or chlorinate selectively in the β position, a rather astonishing observation but similar peculiar results are reported with nitriles.[97] The result with N-chlorosuccinimide is notable because this substance was originally reported to be unreactive.[86] However, in 1949, Hebbelynck and Martin [98] showed that it readily converts toluene to benzyl chloride in the presence of benzoyl peroxide or actinic light, and also oxidizes benzyl alcohol and benzhydrol to benzaldehyde and benzophenone respectively, cf. Section 8·3a. Accordingly, many of the earlier statements [88] concerning reactivities, or relative properties of NBS analogs, are to be accepted with reserve and are not repeated here.

An interesting and important point in connection with NBS is the question why, according to the mechanism formulated, are olefins attacked at the allylic position rather than undergoing addition to give a β-bromoalkylsuccinimide (reactions of this sort are sometimes observed [87] but may represent a polar process). A consideration of bond strengths gives a clue. For the $NH_2\cdot$ radical energetics are as follows:

$$NH_3 + \dot{C}H_2\text{---}CH{=}CH_2 \quad \Delta H = -25 \text{ kcal}$$

$$NH_2\cdot + CH_3\text{---}CH{=}CH_2 \nearrow \searrow \tag{63}$$

$$CH_3\text{---}\dot{C}H\text{---}CH_2NH_2 \quad \Delta H = -17 \text{ kcal}$$

The resonance energy of the NBS radical is not known, but, if we estimate that it is over 17 kcal,[99] the addition step becomes endothermic, whereas for hydrogen abstraction ΔH is still negative. In

[95] M. C. Ford and W. A. Waters, *J. Chem. Soc.*, **1952**, 2240.

[96] Ng. Ph. Buu-Hoi and P. Demerseman, *J. Org. Chem.*, **18**, 649 (1953).

[97] P. Couvreur and A. Bruylants, *ibid.*, **18**, 501 (1953).

[98] M. F. Hebbelynck and R. H. Martin, *Experientia*, **5**, 69 (1949); *Bull. soc. chim. Belges*, **59**, 193 (1950).

[99] The sketchy basis of this estimate is that two RCO groups substituted into H_2O_2 reduce the O—O bond strength by 22 kcal (Section 10·2b), and that two H's are somewhat similarly replaced in NBS.

any case, the high strength of the resulting N—H bond should favor the displacement process.[100]

Taking up now what is known reliably about structure and reactivity in NBS bromination, the presumed chain carrier, the succinimide radical, should have electron-acceptor properties (succini-

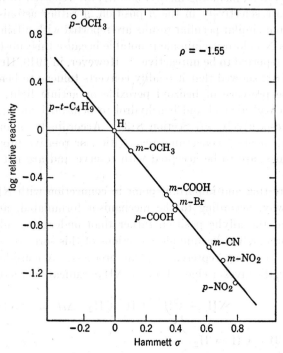

FIG. 8·5 Relative reactivities of substituted toluenes towards NBS versus Hammett σ values for substituents (after Kooyman, Van Helden, and Bickel[76]).

mide itself is a weak acid) and preferentially attack points of high electron availability. This expectation has been confirmed by Kooyman, Van Helden, and Bickel,[76] who have carried out competitive brominations of substituted toluenes with NBS. Their results give a good plot against Hammett σ values, with $\rho = -1.55$ (Fig. 8·5), the succinimide radical being more selective than either Br· or Cl·.

In allylic brominations, the situation is complicated because a

[100] The suggestion, J. Adam, P. A. Gosselain, and P. Goldfinger, *Nature,* **171,** 704 (1953), that NBS reacts by producing trace concentrations of Br_2 which abstract hydrogen in preference to undergoing reversible addition appears untenable in view of the kinetics cited, as well as other reasons.

number of products are possible, there often not only being more than one point of possible attack but also (if our formulation is correct) two possible products from each intermediate allylic radical, e.g., for a non-terminal olefin:

$$R_1-CH=CH-\dot{C}H-CH_2R_2 \quad R_1CH=CH-CHBrCH_2R_2$$
$$\updownarrow \qquad\qquad \rightarrow \qquad +$$
$$R_1-\dot{C}H-CH=CH-CH_2R_2 \quad R_1CHBrCH=CH-CH_2R_2$$

$$R_1-CH_2-CH=CH-CH_2-R_2 \tag{64}$$

$$R_1CH_2-CH=CH-\dot{C}HR_2 \quad R_1CH_2-CH=CHCHBrR_2$$
$$\updownarrow \qquad\qquad \rightarrow \qquad +$$
$$R_1CH_2-\dot{C}H-CH=CHR_2 \quad R_1CH_2CHBrCH=CHR_2$$

As a further complication, the resulting allylic bromides are extremely sensitive to allylic rearrangement (Section 7·1d).

Data on what actually occurs in allylic brominations with NBS are confused and contradictory. Bateman and Cunneen [101] investigated the benzoyl peroxide-initiated reaction of 1-octene, and reported that the product consisted of 17% 3-bromo-1-octene, 39% *cis*-1-bromo-2-octene, and 44% *trans*-1-bromo-2-octene. Similarly,[102] 1,5-hexadiene gave 90% 1-bromo-2,5-hexadiene and 10% 3-bromo-1,5-hexadiene, contrary to Karrer and Schneider's finding that the latter was the major product.[103] Another example of the formation of both products from an allylic radical is in the bromination of methylenecyclobutane to give 2-bromomethylenecyclobutane and 1-bromomethylcyclobutene in a ratio of 15:1.[104] On the other hand, Greenwood and Kellert [105] state that 2-heptene gives essentially pure 4-bromo-2-heptene since the product yields 95% acetic acid on ozonization. This is a surprising result if a free allylic radical is actually involved since it is hard to see why it would be so selective.

Again, with α,β and β,γ unsaturated acids and derivatives, NBS bromination should go through the same intermediate radical. *cis*- and *trans*-crotononitrile yield the same *cis-trans* mixture of γ-bromocrotononitriles, whereas allyl cyanide gives 25% of the same mixture

[101] L. Bateman and J. I. Cunneen, *J. Chem. Soc.*, **1950**, 941.
[102] L. Bateman, J. I. Cunneen, J. M. Fabian, and H. P. Koch, *ibid.*, **1950**, 936.
[103] P. Karrer and P. Schneider, *Helv. Chim. Acta*, **31**, 395 (1948).
[104] E. R. Buchman and D. R. Howton, *J. Am. Chem. Soc.*, **70**, 2517 (1948).
[105] F. L. Greenwood and M. D. Kellert, *ibid.*, **75**, 4842 (1953).

plus 75% β,γ-dibromobutyronitrile,[106] suggesting that the succinimide radical attacks the α position only with difficulty so (perhaps polar) addition occurs instead. Corey, using the corresponding methyl esters, obtained methyl γ-bromocrotonate from methyl crotonate, but observed only a very slow reaction with its allylic isomer to give methyl β,γ-dibromobutyrate,[107] and interpreted his results as above.

Where two allylic positions are open to attack, secondary C—H appears to be attacked more readily than primary (cf. 2-heptene above). Although Ziegler[87] reported that tertiary C—H is not attacked (steric hindrance), ethyl 4-methyl-2-pentenoate has been brominated to ethyl 4-bromo-4-methyl pentenoate,[92] so this generalization is in doubt. Perhaps the best summary of the preceding paragraph is to state that the reactions of NBS and related materials are of such interest that they deserve further careful mechanistic studies, and that it is not feasible to interpret the various observations in further detail at this time.

8·6e t-Butyl Hypochlorite and Other Hypohalites

t-Butyl hypochlorite is a moderately stable yellow liquid[108,109] which, in solvents such as water, alcohols, and acetic acid, readily attacks olefins by an electrophilic process to yield halohydrins and their derivatives.[110,111] Aromatics with activating groups such as —OH similarly undergo ring chlorination.[112-114] On the other hand, there are reports in the literature which indicate that this reagent can also behave as a radical chlorinating agent. In 1931 Clarke noted briefly that t-butyl hypochlorite converts toluene to benzyl chloride,[112] and in 1939 Harford disclosed in a patent that it produces allylic chlorides from isobutylene and trimethylethylene.[115] Again, in 1945 Kenner[116] stated rather cryptically that cyclohexene yields 3-chloro-

106 P. Couvreur and A. Bruylants, *Bull. soc. chim. Belges,* **61,** 253 (1952); cf. W. J. Bailey and J. Bello, *J. Org. Chem.,* **20,** 525 (1955).

107 E. J. Corey, *J. Am. Chem. Soc.,* **75,** 2251 (1953).

108 F. D. Chattaway and O. G. Backeberg, *J. Chem. Soc.,* **1923,** 2999.

109 H. M. Teeter and E. W. Bell, *Organic Syntheses,* **32,** 20 (1952).

110 C. F. Irwin and G. F. Hennion, *J. Am. Chem. Soc.,* **63,** 858 (1941); B. L. Emling, R. R. Vogt, and G. F. Hennion, *ibid.,* 1624.

111 M. Anbar and D. Ginsberg, *Chem. Revs.,* **54,** 925 (1954). This paper gives a comprehensive review of hypohalite chemistry.

112 B. F. Clarke, Jr., *Chem. News,* **1931,** 265.

113 D. Ginsberg, *J. Am. Chem. Soc.,* **73,** 702 (1951).

114 D. Ginsberg, *ibid.,* 2723.

115 C. G. Harford, U.S. Pat. 2,179,787 (November 14, 1939).

116 J. Kenner, *Nature,* **156,** 370 (1945).

cyclohexene "under Ziegler conditions," that in the presence of benzoyl peroxide cyclohexane gives cyclohexyl chloride, and that toluene, ethyl benzene, p-bromotoluene, and even p-nitrotoluene undergo side-chain chlorination.   Benzaldehyde is converted to benzoyl chloride,[112,113] as are its methyl and chloro homologs.   Nitro and carboxyl groups suppress the reaction, whereas hydroxyl and similar activating groups lead to ring substitution.[113]   The most detailed study seems to have been made by Teeter,[117] whose chief concern has been the t-butyl hypochlorite chlorination of soybean oil and similar materials as a step toward converting them to drying oils.[117,118]   The reactions occur readily at 40–60° (generally after an induction period), are light catalyzed, and much of the chlorine enters the molecule in the allylic positions.   Further, with 1,4-dienes (esters of linoleic acid, etc.) the double bonds tend to become conjugated in the product.

All of these results suggest (as Teeter implies) a radical chain process, which we might formulate most simply as

$$(CH_3)_3CO\cdot + H\!-\!R \rightarrow (CH_3)_3C\!-\!OH + R\cdot \tag{65}$$

$$R\cdot + Cl\!-\!O\!-\!C(CH_3)_3 \rightarrow RCl + (CH_3)_3C\!-\!O\cdot \tag{66}$$

However, it is well established that t-butoxy radicals are unstable (Section 10.2a), and the chain

$$(CH_3)_3C\!-\!O\cdot \rightarrow CH_3COCH_3 + \cdot CH_3 \tag{67a}$$

$$\cdot CH_3 + H\!-\!R \rightarrow CH_4 + R\cdot \tag{67b}$$

could be alternative to reaction 65.   Recent work at Columbia [119] on the reaction of t-butyl hypochlorite with toluene has shown the halogenation to be strongly accelerated by light or azobisisobutyronitrile and inhibited by oxygen or hydroquinone, thus substantiating a radical chain.   Here the sequence involved is evidently reactions 65 and 66, since t-butyl alcohol is the sole oxygenated product.   With more complex substrates (and in competitive reactions) the point of attack by t-butoxy radicals appears to be quite different from that of chlorine atoms (for further data on t-butoxy radical reactions, cf. Section 10·2a), which suggests that t-butyl hypochlorite may be of interest as providing a new type of chain carrier in halogenation.

[117] H. N. Teeter, R. C. Bachman, E. W. Bell, and J. C. Cowan, *Ind. Eng. Chem.*, **41**, 849 (1949).

[118] E. W. Bell and H. M. Teeter, *J. Am. Oil Chemists' Soc.*, **27**, 102 (1950); H. M. Teeter, E. W. Bell, and L. C. Woods, *ibid.*, **29**, 401 (1952).

[119] C. Walling and B. B. Jacknow, unpublished work.

Although t-butyl hypochlorite is reasonably stable and can be distilled without decomposition, it decomposes rapidly in bright sunlight to methyl chloride and acetone.[108] A chain process is evidently involved, and the following seems plausible:

$$(CH_3)_3COCl \xrightarrow{h\nu} (CH_3)_3C\text{---}O\cdot + Cl\cdot \qquad (68)$$

$$(CH_3)_3C\text{---}O\cdot \longrightarrow CH_3COCH_3 + \cdot CH_3 \qquad (69)$$

$$\cdot CH_3 + Cl\text{---}OC(CH_3)_3 \longrightarrow CH_3Cl + (CH_3)_3C\text{---}O\cdot \qquad (70)$$

An interesting extension of the sequence 68–70 has been reported by Cairns and Englund [120] in the decomposition of 1-methylcyclopentyl hypochlorite, which follows the course

$$(71)$$

in essentially quantitative yield and suggests a number of analogous synthetic possibilities.

In contrast to t-hypochlorites, primary and secondary hypochlorites decompose rapidly at room temperature.[108] In diffuse daylight the process is so rapid that it may lead to ignition. Here a different chain (which leads to the observed products) might be suggested which could be even more rapid since reaction 69 has an appreciable activation energy, e.g.:

$$(CH_3)_2CHOCl \xrightarrow{h\nu} (CH_3)_2CH\text{---}O\cdot + Cl\cdot \qquad (72)$$

$$Cl\cdot + (CH_3)_2CHOCl \longrightarrow (CH_3)_2\dot{C}\text{---}OCl + HCl \qquad (73)$$

$$(CH_3)_2\dot{C}\text{---}OCl \longrightarrow CH_3COCH_3 + Cl\cdot \qquad (74)$$

However, no real study has been made of the reaction.

In closing this section we may mention briefly the reaction of the silver salts of carboxylic acids with bromine and other halogens. Such reactions are generally carried out in inert solvents such as carbon tetrachloride, and under one of two sets of conditions.[121] In one, the so-called "Simonini conditions," 1 mole of molecular halogen

[120] T. L. Cairns and B. E. Englund, *J. Org. Chem.,* **21,** 140 (1956).

[121] For a review of early work, cf. J. Kleinberg, *Chem. Revs.,* **40,** 381 (1947), and also the reference cited in footnote 111.

is used for 2 moles of silver salt and an insoluble complex [122] is formed,

$$2RCOOAg + X_2 \rightarrow (RCOO)_2AgX + AgX \qquad (75)$$

which decomposes on heating, chiefly to the ester of the next lower alcohol.

$$(RCOO)_2AgX \rightarrow AgX + R—COO—R + CO_2 \qquad (76)$$

Although a radical mechanism can be formulated for the process, it is a heterogeneous reaction and necessarily difficult to treat.[123]

When 1 mole of halogen (usually bromine) is used per mole of silver salt, the chief result is the formation of alkyl halide, often in excellent (70–80%) yield (the Hunsdiecker reaction). This reaction has generally been written as

$$RCOOAg + Br_2 \rightarrow RCOOBr + AgBr \qquad (77)$$

$$RCOOBr \rightarrow RBr + CO_2 \qquad (78)$$

Indeed, if the addition is done in the cold, and the reaction mixture quickly filtered, the filtrate contains a material which has the expected oxidizing power of the acyl hypohalite, and which adds to olefins to yield halohydrin esters.[124, 125] Bockemuller and Hoffman's results are particularly interesting, because they observed that 0.1 molar acetyl hypochlorite prepared in this way had a half-life in CCl$_4$ of 255 min in the dark at 0°, but a 0.5 molar solution had a half-life at only 110 sec. Decomposition was more rapid in diffuse daylight, with an 85-min half-life for the 0.1 molar solution. Butyryl hypochlorite behaved similarly. Butyryl and benzoyl hypobromites were more stable, the later having a half-life of about 10 hours, but all decomposed rapidly in the light. Furthermore, the decomposition of acetyl hypobromite in methylene chloride produces CHCl$_2$Br as well as methyl bromide. All of these observations (particularly the extreme light sensitivity) suggest a radical chain decomposition as the path of the Hunsdiecker reaction, analogous to that for the decomposition of t-butyl hypochlorite, with chain steps

[122] The complexes from perfluoro acids are soluble in fluorinated solvents, from which they can be crystallized; G. H. Crawford and J. H. Simons, *J. Am. Chem. Soc.*, **77**, 2605 (1955).

[123] Cf. R. N. Haszeldine, *J. Chem. Soc.*, **1951**, 584; R. N. Haszeldine and A. G. Sharpe, *ibid.*, **1952**, 993, 4259.

[124] L. Birckenbach, J. Goubeau, and E. Berninger, *Ber.*, **65**, 1339 (1932).

[125] W. Bockemuller and F. W. Hoffman, *Ann.*, **519**, 165 (1935).

$$R \cdot + Br\!-\!O\!-\!COR \rightarrow RBr + \cdot O\!-\!COR \qquad (79)$$

$$RCOO \cdot \rightarrow R \cdot + CO_2 \qquad (80)$$

As another example of attack on solvent by the intermediate radical, treatment of the silver salt of apocamphane carboxylic acid, with bromine in petroleum ether, yields 50% 1-bromoapocamphane [126] (radicals, in contrast to carbonium ions, seem to form on bridgeheads without difficulty, adamantane 1,3-dicarboxylic acid behaving similarly [127]) but, in CCl_4, attack on solvent occurs as well, giving a mixture of chloro- and bromoapocamphanes.

Similarly, chlorobenzene (5.3%) and CCl_3Br (6.7%) are found among the products of reaction of silver benzoate and bromine in CCl_4.[128]

In the presence of silver bromide, the process may be more complicated than just written, and we may note that there are occasional, if not well-confirmed, reports of retention of optical activity in the bromides obtained from acids in which the α-carbon provides the center of asymmetry. Thus Arcus, Campbell, and Kenyon [129] reported an optically active bromide from α-phenylpropionic acid, but later Abbott and Arcus [130] were unable to obtain any bromide whatsoever from the reaction. They did, however, report an active bromide from 2-ethylhexanoic acid which, in turn, was not observed by Bell and Smyth.[131] Obviously in addition to the radical path, a polar decarboxylation could exist which might be observable under some conditions.

8·6f   Further Halogen Carriers and Related Reactions

The participation of CCl_4 in the bromine silver salt reaction has just been mentioned, and other cases are known where it behaves as a chlorine carrier, with $\cdot CCl_3$ serving as the carrier radical. A good

[126] P. Wilder, Jr., and A. Winston, *J. Am. Chem. Soc.*, **75**, 5370 (1953).

[127] V. Prelog and R. Seiweith, *Ber.*, **74B**, 1769 (1941).

[128] W. G. Dauben and H. Tilles, *J. Am. Chem. Soc.*, **72**, 3183 (1950).

[129] C. L. Arcus, A. Campbell, and J. Kenyon, *J. Chem. Soc.*, **1949**, 1510.

[130] D. C. Abbott and C. L. Arcus, *ibid.*, **1952**, 3195. A similar failure is reported by J. Cason, M. J. Kalm, and R. H. Mills, *J. Org. Chem.*, **18**, 1670 (1953).

[131] F. Bell and I. F. B. Smyth, *J. Chem. Soc.*, **1949**, 2372.

example is the reaction with aldehydes described by Winstein and Seubold.[132] Thus β-phenylisovaleraldehyde, refluxed with 20% excess CCl_4 and 10 mole % benzoyl peroxide, gives 56% β-phenylisovaleryl chloride and chloroform. With isovaleraldehyde itself, the yield is 60%. The overall reaction is

$$R—CHO + CCl_4 \rightarrow R—COCl + CHCl_3 \qquad (82)$$

and, since the yield is several times the amount of initiator employed, a (rather short) chain is evidently involved which we may write as

$$\cdot CCl_3 + HCOR \rightarrow CHCl_3 + R—\dot{C}{=}O \qquad (83)$$
$$R—\dot{C}{=}O + CCl_4 \rightarrow RCOCl + \cdot CCl_3 \qquad (84)$$

The overall reaction (82) is close to thermoneutral but is not reversible, isovaleryl chloride giving no reaction with chloroform. Since CCl_4 and aldehydes belong to our classification of acceptor and donor species respectively, a polar effect probably contributes to lowering the activation energies of the propagation steps.

Similar halogenations of aliphatic hydrocarbons in the presence of radical sources such as peroxides have also been described by West and Schmerling, using both CCl_4 and CBr_4,[133] and Ol'dekop has reported that toluene and CCl_4, heated together at 225–235° for 40 hours, give benzyl chloride and chloroform, together with benzotrichloride, HCl, and considerable tar.[134] An oxidation of alcohols by CCl_4 which seems to be a radical process, has also been noted by Razuvaev. Photolysis of mercury diphenyl in CCl_4–CH_3OH yields formaldehyde and $CHCl_3$,[135] whereas ethanol reacts with CCl_4 at 200° to give acetaldehyde, $CHCl_3$, ethyl chloride, and other products. Similarly irradiation in quartz gives HCl, acetaldehyde, and C_2Cl_6.[136] A somewhat better authenticated chain process occurs between isopropyl alcohol and CCl_4 in the presence of benzoyl peroxide to give acetone and chloroform.[137]

In addition to halogenation reactions in which other species than halogen atoms act as the radical chain carriers, reactions can also exist in which halogen atoms are the chain carriers but other species are introduced into the molecule. A possible example is the car-

[132] S. Winstein and F. H. Seubold, Jr., *J. Am. Chem. Soc.*, **69**, 2916 (1947).

[133] J. P. West and L. Schmerling, U.S. Pats. 2,553,799, 2,553,800 (May 22, 1951).

[134] Y. A. Ol'dekop, *Doklady Akad. Nauk S.S.S.R.*, **93**, 75 (1953).

[135] G. A. Razuvaev and N. S. Vasileiskaya, *ibid.*, **80**, 69 (1951).

[136] G. A. Razuvaev and Y. A. Sorokin, *Zhur. Obshchei Khim.*, **23**, 1519 (1953).

[137] G. A. Razuvaev, B. N. Moryganov, and A. S. Volkova, *ibid.*, **25**, 495 (1955).

boxylation reaction using oxalyl chloride, discovered by Kharasch and Brown.[138] Irradiation of 2:1 molar mixture of cyclohexane and oxalyl chloride at 30–35° with ultraviolet light leads to the evolution of HCl and CO and the formation of cyclohexane carbonyl chloride in essentially quantitative yield based on oxalyl chloride consumed (55%). Similarly a 3:2 mixture, refluxed with 2.5 mole % benzoyl peroxide (based on oxalyl chloride), gives a 65% yield of acid chloride. A number of other aliphatic hydrocarbons behave similarly, and Kharasch and Brown suggest a chain process initiated by photodissociation of the oxalyl chloride (or by the peroxide) and involving the chain steps

$$Cl\cdot + RH \rightarrow HCl + R\cdot \tag{85}$$

$$R\cdot + ClCOCOCl \rightarrow RCOCl + \cdot COCl \tag{86}$$

$$\cdot COCl \rightarrow CO + \cdot Cl \tag{87}$$

Reaction 87 is considered to be involved in the photochemical reactions of phosgene,[15] but reaction 86 is unusual, although it accounts for the products, and the C—C bond should be weak.

A comparable addition of oxalyl chloride to olefins to give β-chloro acid chlorides could not be observed,[139] but toluene and several substituted toluenes gave low yields (5–10%) of phenylacetyl chlorides in the presence of benzoyl peroxide,[140] Kharasch suggesting that the benzyl radical is too stable to attack oxalyl chloride, reaction 86.[141]

Since 1942, this interesting reaction seems to have received little attention.[142]

A final example of what may be a chain substitution involving chlorine atoms is the photochemical reaction of nitrosyl chloride and cyclohexane to give cyclohexanone oxime, best accomplished by slow

[138] M. S. Kharasch and H. C. Brown, *J. Am. Chem. Soc.*, **64**, 329 (1942); preliminary note, *ibid.*, **62**, 454 (1940).

[139] M. S. Kharasch, S. S. Kane, and H. C. Brown, *ibid.*, **64**, 333 (1942).

[140] M. S. Kharasch, S. S. Kane, and H. C. Brown, *ibid.*, **64**, 1621 (1942).

[141] The photochemical reaction gave no acid chloride with toluene, apparently because of absorption of light by the aromatic nucleus, since cyclohexane gave only low yields in benzene.

[142] However, F. Runge, *Z. Elektrochem.*, **56**, 779 (1952), has reported that cyclohexanecarbonyl chloride may be further substituted in the α position, and that similar substitution occurs with other acid chlorides. Similar observations are reported by S. Kambara, N. Yamazaki, A. Kagi, and T. Oikawa, *J. Chem. Soc. Japan, Ind. Chem. Sect.*, **57**, 652 (1954).

addition of NOCl to the hydrocarbon at $-25°$ under strong visible light.[143] The overall reaction is

$$\text{(cyclohexane)} + NOCl \rightarrow HCl + \left[\text{(cyclohexyl-NO)}\right] \rightarrow \text{(cyclohexanone oxime, =NOH)} \tag{88}$$

the last step being a well-known rearrangement of primary and secondary nitroso compounds. Naylor and Anderson [143] suggest a possible chain process

$$Cl\cdot + RH \rightarrow R\cdot + HCl \tag{89}$$

$$R\cdot + O{=}N{-}Cl \rightarrow R{-}NO + Cl\cdot \tag{90}$$

which resembles somewhat the photolysis of t-butyl nitrite to acetone and nitrosomethane,[144] for which a plausible chain should be

$$\cdot CH_3 + O{=}N{-}O{-}C(CH_3)_3 \rightarrow CH_3NO + \cdot O{-}C(CH_3)_3 \tag{91}$$

$$\cdot O{-}C(CH_3)_3 \rightarrow CH_3COCH_3 + \cdot CH_3 \tag{92}$$

A similar process involving the photochemical reaction of hydrocarbons with chlorine and nitric oxide to give nitroso- and *gem*-chloronitroso compounds as products has been reported by Müller and Metzger.[145]

8·7   The Chlorosulfonation of Alkanes

The reaction of sulfur dioxide and chlorine with paraffin hydrocarbons to yield alkane sulfonyl chlorides

$$RH + SO_2 + Cl_2 \rightarrow RSO_2Cl + HCl \tag{93}$$

(the Reed reaction) was patented by Reed in 1939 [146] and was used extensively in Germany during the last war to prepare synthetic detergents from suitable synthetic petroleum fractions by hydrolysis of the resulting sulfonyl chlorides. It was also introduced for a time in this country but is not operated at present since the products do not compete favorably in properties with synthetic detergents from other sources. Nevertheless, it is of sufficient interest to discuss in some detail.

[143] M. A. Naylor and A. W. Anderson, *J. Org. Chem.*, **18**, 115 (1953).

[144] C. S. Coe and T. F. Duomani, *J. Am. Chem. Soc.*, **70**, 1516 (1948).

[145] E. Müller and H. Metzger, *Chem. Ber.*, **87**, 1282 (1954); *ibid.*, **88**, 165 (1955).

[146] C. F. Reed, U.S. Pat. 2,174,492 (September 26, 1939).

The reaction has usually been run in the liquid phase between the boiling point of SO_2 and room temperature, by adding chlorine and something of an excess of SO_2 to the liquid hydrocarbon under strong illumination with short-wave-length visible or ultraviolet light. The products, in addition to sulfonyl chlorides, usually contain chloroalkanes and some polysulfonated material (which may account for their inferior detergent properties). However, the reaction is also initiated by other radical sources,[147] and there seems to be little doubt that it can be represented as a radical chain process via the sequence

$$Cl \cdot + RH \rightarrow R \cdot + HCl \tag{94}$$

$$R \cdot + SO_2 \rightleftharpoons RSO_2 \cdot \tag{95}$$

$$RSO_2 \cdot + Cl_2 \rightarrow RSO_2Cl + Cl \cdot \tag{96}$$

Step 95 is indicated as reversible in line with our discussion of olefin-SO_2 copolymerization (Section 5·4d), and it is significant that the reaction proceeds best at temperatures below the expected "ceiling temperatures" for SO_2–alkyl radical reactions, and also that it is apparently unsuccessful in the vapor phase.[147]

The kinetics of the photochemical sulfochlorination of n-heptane and n-hexadecane in CCl_4 solution (chiefly at 25°) has been studied by Stauff,[148] who finds that, at most concentrations of reactants, the rate law is consistent with the chain given, with reaction 95 essen-

$$d[Cl_2]/dt = k[RH](I_{abs})^{\frac{1}{2}} \tag{97}$$

tially irreversible, and chains started by photodissociation of Cl_2 and ended by recombination of chlorine atoms. At about equal initial Cl_2 and SO_2 concentrations, reaction 95 apparently competes very favorably with reaction of $R \cdot$ with Cl_2, since less than 10% chloroalkane is produced.

With high molecular weight paraffins, a mixture of products is necessarily produced. However, a few studies have been made on low molecular weight hydrocarbons and derivatives, giving the product distributions shown in Table 8·12. Most are what would be expected for a process in which the final product structure is determined by chlorine atom attack, and the disagreement between the two sets of

---

[147] F. Povenz, *Z. Elektrochem.*, **56**, 746 (1952); there is also an extensive patent literature on initiators.

[148] J. Stauff, *ibid.*, **49**, 550 (1942).

TABLE 8·12   PRODUCT DISTRIBUTIONS IN SULFOCHLORINATION REACTIONS

Compound	Footnote	Compound	Footnote
C—C—C % 55 45	149	C—C—Cl % 100	153
C—C—C—C % 33 67	150, a	C—C—C—Cl % 100	152
C | C—C—C % 100	151	C—C—C—CCl % 16 45 39	152
C—C—C—SO₂Cl % 100	149	C—C—C—CCl % 75 25	154

a A small amount of disulfonyl chlorides are also obtained consisting of 80% 1,3 and 20% 1,4 isomers.

---

[149] F. Asinger, W. Schmidt, and F. Ebeneder, *Ber.*, **75**, 34 (1942).
[150] F. Asinger, F. Ebeneder, and E. Bock, *ibid.*, **75**, 42 (1942).
[151] F. Asinger and F. Ebeneder, *ibid.*, **75**, 344 (1942).
[152] J. H. Helberger, G. Manecke, and H. M. Fischer, *Ann.*, **562**, 23 (1949).
[153] C. Walling and W. F. Pease, unpublished work.
[154] A. P. Terent'ov and A. I. Gershenovich, *Zhur. Obshchei Khim.*, **23**, 208 (1953).

results on *n*-butyl chloride may arise from analytical uncertainty.[155] However, results on isobutane and ethyl chloride are anomalous. Isobutane gives 33% *t*-butyl chloride on chlorination at the same temperature, but we are above the ceiling temperature for isobutylene–SO₂ copolymerization, so reaction 95 for *t*-butyl radicals may be substantially reversed. The ethyl chloride result is harder to explain, since chlorination gives at least 80% 1,1-dichloroethane, but the 2-chlorosulfonyl chloride is obtained in up to 35% yield, the balance being 1,1-dichloroethane. Apparently some reaction is involved not included in the simple scheme given.

Substantially the same sulfochlorination reaction has been carried out by Kharasch and Read,[156] using SO₂Cl₂ and light in the presence of substances such as pyridine, which catalyze the breakdown of SO₂Cl₂ into SO₂ and Cl₂. Thus, with cyclohexane, as much as 55% sulfonyl chloride (plus 10% cyclohexyl chloride) is obtained. Other

---

[155] The chlorosulfonyl chlorides were analyzed by heating at 200–220° for several hours, under which conditions they decompose to dihalides and SO₂, and the composition of the dihalides was determined. The decomposition is interesting and is conceivably another radical chain process; cf. A. P. Terent'ov and A. I. Gershenovich, *ibid.*, **23**, 204 (1953), and also Section 7·1*d* and *e*.

[156] M. S. Kharasch and A. T. Read, *J. Am. Chem. Soc.*, **61**, 3089 (1939).

aliphatic hydrocarbons behave similarly, as does t-butylbenzene, but toluene gives only chlorination, very likely because the stability of the benzyl radical reverses reaction 95, so reaction with Cl_2 (or SO_2Cl_2) occurs instead.

With aliphatic acids, even in the absence of pyridine, considerable chlorosulfonation occurs on irradiation.[157] Interestingly, with short chain acids (propionic, isobutyric, butyric) the product isolated is the cyclic sulfoanhydride, attack occurring (as we expect) chiefly in the β position.

$$
CH_3CH_2COOH \xrightarrow[\text{Light}]{SO_2Cl_2} \underset{\substack{| \\ SO_2Cl}}{CH_2CH_2COOH} \rightarrow \underset{\substack{\diagdown \\ CH_2 \diagup}}{\overset{\substack{O \\ \uparrow \\ O \leftarrow S \longrightarrow O \\ | \qquad\qquad | }}{CH_2 \qquad CO}} + HCl \quad (98)
$$

From a preparative point of view the direct use of SO_2 and Cl_2 in sulfochlorination appears preferable to the use of SO_2Cl_2, since competition with chlorination is more favorable because of the ease in maintaining a high SO_2 concentration and the lower temperatures at which the reaction can be run.

[157] M. S. Kharasch, T. H. Chao, and H. C. Brown, *ibid.*, **62**, 2393 (1940).

CHAPTER 9

Autoxidations

9·1   General Survey of Autoxidation Reactions

Oxygen, reacting with organic molecules through the process of respiration and combustion, both maintains animal life and provides most of our immediate available energy. In addition, it reacts with organic substances in less spectacular ways, the number and variety of which we may overlook in our search for more exotic and less ubiquitous reagents.

Since these processes may occur more or less spontaneously (or with a little judicious encouragement) under very mild conditions, they are referred to as *autoxidations*. The drying of linseed oil paint is an example of such a process, as are the various direct reactions with oxygen employed for synthetic purposes which are discussed in this chapter. Others are of importance in a negative sense in that they are processes which we wish to avoid. Here we include the deterioration of rubber and plastics, the breakdown of lubricants, the rancidification of edible oils, and numerous other processes by which organic substances are altered and lose their usefulness.

Since the oxygen molecule itself is a diradical with the electronic structure

$$\cdot \ddot{\underset{\cdot\cdot}{O}} - \ddot{\underset{\cdot\cdot}{O}} \cdot \qquad\qquad (1)$$

it is no surprise to find that the majority of these processes are free radical reactions, often involving long kinetic chains, and that organic peroxides are commonly either intermediates or end products. In spite of certain common features, these reactions may follow a variety of detailed paths, so it is well to begin this chapter with a short survey of autoxidation reactions in general and also to trace their historical development.

One of the most important and certainly the most studied type of autoxidation process is that undergone by hydrocarbons, aldehydes, and certain other oxygen- or nitrogen-containing molecules in which the first stable product is a hydroperoxide (or, in the case of alde-hydes, a peracid).

$$RH + O_2 \rightarrow ROOH \qquad (2)$$

In many cases a radical chain process is well established, with propa-gation steps which can be generalized as

$$R\cdot + O_2 \rightarrow ROO\cdot \qquad (3)$$

$$ROO\cdot + HR \rightarrow ROOH + R\cdot \qquad (4)$$

Aldehyde autoxidation provides a good example of the develop-ment of our knowledge of such processes.

The slow transformation of benzaldehyde to benzoic acid, i.e., the reaction which we now write as

$$2\phi CHO + O_2 \rightarrow 2\phi COOH \qquad (5)$$

was described by Wohler and Liebig in 1832,[1] who correctly ascribed the change to reaction with air and noted that it was accelerated by light.

Subsequently, it was found that freshly oxidized solutions of ben-zaldehyde were strong oxidizing agents, and that, in the presence of acetic anhydride, twice as much oxygen is consumed, the products being benzoylacetyl peroxide and acetic acid.[2] These observations

$$\phi CHO + O_2 + (CH_3CO)_2O \rightarrow$$

$$\phi{-}CO{-}O{-}O{-}COCH_3 + CH_3COOH \qquad (6)$$

suggest that reaction 5 is not a single-step process, and, in 1900, Baeyer and Villiger[3] proposed that the intermediate is perbenzoic acid.

$$\phi CHO + O_2 \rightarrow \phi{-}C{\overset{\displaystyle O}{\underset{\displaystyle OOH}{\big\langle}}} \qquad (7)$$

$$\phi{-}C{\overset{\displaystyle O}{\underset{\displaystyle OOH}{\big\langle}}} + \phi CHO \rightarrow 2\phi COOH \qquad (8)$$

[1] F. Wohler and J. Liebig, *Ann.*, **3**, 253 (1832).

[2] W. R. Jorissen, *Z. physik Chem.*, **22**, 34 (1897).

[3] A. Baeyer and V. Villiger, *Ber.*, **33**, 1575 (1900); however, the peracid was first actually isolated from such a system by W. P. Jorissen and P. A. A. Van der Beek, *Rec. trav. chim.*, **45**, 245 (1926).

The second step is a polar reaction, relatively rapid and catalyzed by benzoic acid [4] so that the relative concentration of products is that shown in Fig. 9·1. In the presence of acetic anhydride, the intermediate acid is acetylated and yields of diacyl peroxide (which reacts only very slowly with benzaldehyde) are essentially quantitative,[5] particularly in the presence of sodium acetate which catalyzes the acetylation.[6] The curve for oxygen consumption in Fig. 9·1

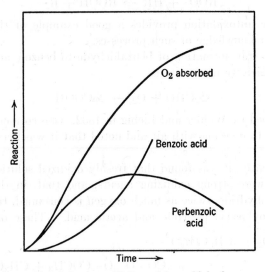

Fig. 9·1 Autoxidation of benzaldehyde.

shows an autoacceleration which is typical for many autoxidations, and which, as we shall see, arises from the buildup of peroxides which serve as chain initiators.

Kinetic investigations in the 1920's showed other properties of the autoxidation which we now identify with radical chain processes. Thus, aldehyde autoxidations are inhibited by traces of *antioxidants* such as hydroquinone, or α-naphthol, and are catalyzed by many heavy metal salts. When induced photochemically, they were shown by Bäckström to give quantum yields of 10,000–15,000.[7] Further, autoxidizing benzaldehyde contains a reactive species, capable of

[4] W. A. Waters and C. Wickham-Jones, *J. Chem. Soc.*, **1951,** 812.

[5] P. A. A. Van der Beek, *Rec. trav. chim.*, **51,** 411 (1932).

[6] C. Walling and E. A. McElhill, *J. Am. Chem. Soc.*, **73,** 2927 (1951).

[7] H. L. J. Bäckström, *ibid.*, **49,** 1460 (1927).

oxidizing anthracene [8] and even carbon tetrachloride [9] (substances which are stable towards perbenzoic acid). Although the reaction leading to peracid formation was soon identified as a chain process, for a time correct formulation was hindered by two concepts which have continued to plague the development of radical chain reactions. One was the idea of an energy chain (in which inhibitors acted by deactivating hot molecules), and the other the idea of a transient intermediate *moloxide* here suggested as

$$
\begin{array}{c}
\text{O} \\
\diagup \ \diagdown \\
\text{R—C} \qquad \text{O} \qquad\qquad (9) \\
\diagdown \ \diagup \\
\text{H} \quad \text{O}
\end{array}
$$

and considered to be the reactive species mentioned.[10] In 1934, however, Bäckström,[11] in an important and well-argued paper, proposed a radical chain process with the propagation steps

$$
\begin{array}{c}
\text{O} \qquad\qquad\qquad \text{O} \\
\diagup\!\!\!\!\diagup \qquad\qquad\qquad \diagup\!\!\!\!\diagup \\
\text{R—C·} \ + O_2 \rightarrow \text{R—C} \qquad\qquad (10) \\
\diagdown \\
\text{OO·}
\end{array}
$$

$$
\begin{array}{c}
\text{O} \qquad\qquad\qquad\qquad \text{O} \qquad\qquad\qquad \text{O} \\
\diagup\!\!\!\!\diagup \qquad\qquad\qquad \diagup\!\!\!\!\diagup \qquad\qquad\qquad \diagup\!\!\!\!\diagup \\
\text{R—C} \ + \text{RCHO} \rightarrow \text{R—C} \qquad + \text{R—C·} \quad (11) \\
\diagdown \qquad\qquad\qquad\qquad \diagdown \\
\text{OO·} \qquad\qquad\qquad\qquad \text{OOH}
\end{array}
$$

which is now generally accepted. Further details of aldehyde autoxidations are discussed in Sections 9·2b, d, and e.

The study of hydrocarbon autoxidations has followed a similar course. It has long been known that simple olefins, on prolonged exposure to air, develop the ability to liberate iodine from weakly acidic iodide solutions and show other typical peroxide reactions. In

[8] H. L. J. Bäckström and H. A. Beatty, *J. Phys. Chem.*, **35**, 2530 (1931).

[9] W. R. Jorissen and P. A. A. Van der Beek, *Rec. trav. chim.*, **46**, 43 (1927), **49**, 139 (1930).

[10] For reviews of these ideas, cf. C. Moureau and C. Dufraisse, *Chem. Revs.*, **2**, 113 (1926); N. A. Milas, *ibid.*, **10**, 295 (1932); R. P. Linstead, *Ann. Repts. Chem. Soc.*, **34**, 233 (1937). Although there now seems to be no good evidence for either energy chains in any liquid-phase reactions or moloxides as chain carriers in any autoxidations (however, cf. Section 9·4), these concepts continue to be advanced from time to time.

[11] H. L. J. Bäckström, *Z. physik. Chem.*, **B25**, 99 (1934).

1897 Bach [12] and Engler [13] proposed that the reaction involved the addition of oxygen to the double bond to form a cyclic peroxide or moloxide:

$$R—CH{=}CH—R' + O_2 \rightarrow R—\overset{\displaystyle O—O}{\overset{|\qquad|}{CH—CH}}—R' \qquad (12)$$

In 1928 Stephens [14] isolated the peroxide from cyclohexene and assigned it this cyclic structure (in spite of the fact that longer oxidation gives 3-cyclohexenone and 3-cyclohexenol), as did Hock and Schrader [15] eight years later. The correct structure, that of cyclohexene-3-hydroperoxide, was assigned by Criegee [16] and subsequently

$$(13)$$

confirmed by Hock [17] and in more detail by Farmer.[18]

Formation of such allylic hydroperoxides is typical of a wide variety of olefins, and the reactions show all of the qualitative characteristics (trace inhibition and catalysis, high quantum yields, etc.) of radical chain processes. The detailed demonstration that they indeed involve the propagation sequence of reactions 3 and 4 is largely the accomplishment of Farmer and his successors at the British Rubber Producers' Research Laboratories and is discussed further in Section 9·2 below.

Among non-olefinic hydrocarbons, species possessing benzyl C—H bonds autoxidize with particular ease, and the first important clue to the understanding of the processes involved was the identification, in 1932, of the hydroperoxide obtained in the autoxidation of tetralin.[19]

[12] A. Bach, *Compt. rend.*, **124**, 951 (1897).

[13] C. Engler, *Ber.*, **30**, 1669 (1897); **31**, 3046 (1898); **33**, 1090 (1900).

[14] H. N. Stephens, *J. Am. Chem. Soc.*, **50**, 568 (1928).

[15] H. Hock and O. Schrader, *Naturwiss.*, **24**, 159 (1936); *Angew. Chem.*, **39**, 565 (1936).

[16] R. Criegee, *Ann.*, **522**, 75 (1935); R. Criegee, H. Pilz and H. Flygare, *Ber.*, **B72**, 1799 (1939).

[17] H. Hock and K. Ganicke, *ibid.*, **B71**, 1430 (1938); **B72**, 2516 (1939).

[18] E. H. Farmer and A. Sundralingham, *J. Chem. Soc.*, **1942**, 121.

[19] M. Hartmann and M. Seiberth, *Helv. Chim. Acta*, **15**, 1390 (1932); H. Hock and W. Susemihl, *Ber.*, **66B**, 61 (1933).

$$\text{(14)}$$

The same sort of radical chain is involved in such processes, and a particularly interesting example is provided by cumene (isopropylbenzene) which gives dimethylbenzyl hydroperoxide in high yield. The hydroperoxide, in turn, rearranges in acid

$$\phi\!-\!\underset{\underset{CH_3}{|}}{\overset{\overset{CH_3}{|}}{CH}} + O_2 \rightarrow \phi\!-\!\underset{\underset{CH_3}{|}}{\overset{\overset{CH_3}{|}}{C}}\!-\!OOH \xrightarrow{\text{H}^+} \phi\!-\!OH + CH_3COCH_3 \quad \text{(15)}$$

to phenol and acetone. The overall process, described by Hock and Lang in 1944,[20] now appears to be a preferred route for phenol manufacture and should provide encouragement to anyone doubtful about the practicality of radical chain processes, or about the possibility of discovering new reactions between simple reagents.

Saturated hydrocarbons autoxidize more sluggishly, but certain oxygen- and nitrogen-containing molecules undergo analogous chain autoxidation to hydroperoxides with great ease, Sections 9·2c–e. In addition, a number of radical chain processes are known which yield products other than hydroperoxides. Among these are the copolymerization reaction of oxygen with reactive olefins, chiefly those having terminal double bonds (Section 9·3a) and the more complex autoxidation chains discussed in Sections 9·3b–d.

Turning now to non-chain processes, an interesting group of photosensitized olefin reactions are known which may yield either cyclic endoperoxides or hydroperoxides and are currently being elaborated by G. O. Schenck (Section 9·4).

Another are a group yielding hydrogen peroxide. Typical are the autoxidations of alkaline solutions of hydroquinones, and again these have a long history, the overall reaction having been apparently

$$\text{(16)}$$

[20] H. Hock and S. Lang, *Ber.*, **77B**, 257 (1944).

first suggested by Manchot in 1901.[21] The details of such reactions have been partially worked out by Weissberger and his colleagues, who have shown that they go through intermediate semiquinones (Section 9·5a).

$$\text{(structure)} + O_2 \rightarrow \text{(structure)} + O_2 \cdot^- \qquad (17)$$

Although these two classes have not received as much study as those involving hydroperoxide chains, they should be of particular interest to biochemists since the photochemical reaction may parallel an important early step in photosynthesis, and there is good reason to believe that the enzymatic reactions with oxygen involved in respiration resemble the autoxidations of hydroquinones.[22]

9·2   Autoxidations Involving Hydroperoxide Chains

9·2a   Hydrocarbons

We may now turn to a more detailed examination of reactions which in general terms involve the chain sequence of reactions 3 and 4, directing our attention first to the process as a synthetic method for the preparation of hydroperoxides (or, in the case of aldehydes, peracids).[23] As has been intimated in the previous section, hydrocarbons and aldehydes have been the commonest substrates for such reactions, although their full range has not yet been fully explored.

Table 9·1 lists examples of simple saturated hydrocarbons which have been found to autoxidize to hydroperoxides in reasonable yield. In addition to the examples given, there is an extensive patent literature, chiefly on mixed hydrocarbons.[24] Experimental conditions vary somewhat but usually involve shaking or bubbling the hydrocarbon

[21] W. Manchot, *Ann.*, **314**, 177 (1901).

[22] J. E. LuValle, *J. Am. Chem. Soc.*, **70**, 2234 (1948).

[23] For a discussion of other techniques for preparing hydroperoxides, see A. V. Tobolsky and R. B. Mesrobian, *Organic Peroxides,* Interscience Publishers, New York, 1954.

[24] For example, the conversion of kerosene to mixed hydroperoxides in yields as high as 20% by blowing with air at about 120° in the presence of MgO and CaO is described by P. D. Brewer, U.S. Pat. 2,447,494 (August 24, 1948).

TABLE 9·1   AUTOXIDATIONS OF SATURATED HYDROCARBONS

Hydrocarbon	Product	Footnote
2,5-Dimethylhexane	$CH_3-\underset{\underset{OOH}{\overset{\overset{CH_3}{\mid}}{\mid}}}{C}-CH_2CH_2-\underset{\underset{OOH}{\overset{\overset{CH_3}{\mid}}{\mid}}}{C}-CH_3$	28
n-Decane	Mixed 2° hydroperoxides	29
2,7-Dimethyloctane	$HOO\underset{\underset{CH_3}{\mid}}{\overset{\overset{CH_3}{\mid}}{C}}CH_2CH_2CH_2CH_2CH(CH_3)$	30
Cyclohexane	(cyclohexane ring with OOH)	25
Methylcyclopentane	(cyclopentane ring with CH₃ and OOH)	33
Methylcyclohexane	(cyclohexane ring with CH₃ and OOH)	26, 27
Decalin	(decalin ring system with OOH) (trans)	31
Pinane	(pinane structure with CH₃, OOH, and CH₃ groups)	32

25 A. Farkas and E. Passaglia, *J. Am. Chem. Soc.*, **72**, 3333 (1950).
26 K. I. Ivanov and V. K. Savinova, *Doklady Akad. Nauk S.S.S.R.*, **59**, 493 (1948).
27 A. Farkas and A. F. Stribley, U.S. Pats. 2,430,864–5 (November 8, 1947).
28 J. P. Wibaut and A. Strang, *Koninkl. Ned. Akad. Wetenschap. Proc.*, **5B**, 102 (1951).
29 J. L. Benton, *Nature*, **171**, 269 (1953); cf. also W. Pritzkow and K. A. Müller, *Ann.*, **597**, 12 (1956) for similar data on n-heptane.
30 K. I. Ivanov, V. K. Savinova, and V. P. Zhakhovskaya, *Doklady Akad. Nauk S.S.S.R.*, **59**, 703 (1948).
31 R. Criegee, *Ber.*, **77B**, 22 (1944); K. I. Ivanov and V. K. Savinova, *Compt. rend. Acad. Sci. U.R.S.S.*, **48**, 31 (1945).
32 G. S. Fisher, J. H. Stinson, and L. A. Goldblatt, *J. Am. Chem. Soc.*, **75**, 3675 (1953).
33 E. J. Gasson, E. G. E. Hawkins, A. F. Millidge, and D. C. Quin, *J. Chem. Soc.*, **1950**, 2798.

with air at somewhat above room temperature, and either relying on peroxide formed to initiate chains, irradiating with ultraviolet light, or adding a radical source. Since the resulting peroxides tend to decompose, particularly in the presence of radicals (Section 9·3b), good yields are generally obtained only at low conversions. It will be noted that the order of radical attack on C—H bonds is 3° > 2° >

Table 9·2　Autoxidations of Aryl-Substituted Hydrocarbons

Hydrocarbon	Hydroperoxide	Yield, %	Footnote [b]
p-Xylene	CH_3—⟨ring⟩—CH_2OOH	0.4	34, 35, *39*
Ethylbenzene	$\phi\underset{CH_3}{\overset{OOH}{C}}HCH_3$	1	34
Cumene [a]	$\phi\underset{CH_3}{\overset{CH_3}{C}}OOH$	89	19, 20, 36, 50, *51*
Cymene	CH_2OOH ⟨ring⟩ CH_3CHCH_3 (20%)　　$CH_3\overset{OOH}{C}CH_3$ ⟨ring⟩ CH_3 (80%)	60	35, 37
sec-Butylbenzene	$\phi-\underset{C_2H_5}{\overset{CH_3}{C}}OOH$	30	38, *49*
Indane	⟨indane ring with OOH⟩	5	*40*, 45
Tetralin	⟨tetralin ring with OOH⟩	44–57	18, *41*
1-Methyltetralin	⟨methyltetralin ring with CH_3 OOH⟩	17	42
2-Isopropylnaphthalene	⟨naphthalene⟩$\underset{CH_3}{\overset{CH_3}{C}}-OOH$	18	43
Diphenylmethane	$\underset{\phi}{\overset{\phi}{C}}\overset{H}{\underset{OOH}{}}$	3	20
1,1-Diphenylethane	$\underset{\phi}{\overset{\phi}{C}}\overset{OOH}{\underset{CH_3}{}}$	24	44
1,1-Diphenylpropane	$\underset{\phi}{\overset{\phi}{C}}\overset{OOH}{\underset{C_2H_5}{}}$	...	45

TABLE 9·2 AUTOXIDATIONS OF ARYL-SUBSTITUTED
HYDROCARBONS (*Continued*)

Hydrocarbon	Hydroperoxide	Yield, %	Footnote [b]
Fluorene		...	46
Octahydroanthracene		...	47
Methyl dehydroabietate	Methyl 9-hydroperoxydehydroabietate	56	52

[a] Diisopropylbenzenes similarly yield both mono- and dihydroperoxides.[48]
[b] Yield from reference in italic type.

[34] H. Hock and S. Lang, *Ber.*, **76B,** 169 (1943).
[35] G. S. Serif, C. F. Hunt, and A. N. Bourns, *Can. J. Chem.*, **31,** 1229 (1953).
[36] G. P. Armstrong, R. H. Hall, and D. C. Quin, *J. Chem. Soc.*, **1950,** 666; in addition there are several patents on this reaction.
[37] H. H. Helberger, A. Rebay, and H. Feltback, *Ber.*, **72B,** 1643 (1939).
[38] K. I. Ivanov, V. K. Savinova, and V. P. Zhakhovskaya, *Doklady Akad. Nauk S.S.S.R.*, **59,** 905 (1948).
[39] E. J. Lorand and E. I. Edwards, *J. Am. Chem. Soc.*, **77,** 4035 (1955).
[40] H. Hock and S. Lang, *Ber.*, **75B,** 1051 (1942).
[41] H. B. Knight and D. Swern, *Org. Syntheses*, **34,** 90 (1954).
[42] H. Hock, F. Depke, and G. Knavel, *Chem. Ber.*, **83,** 227 (1950).
[43] W. Webster and D. C. Quin, Brit. Pat. 654.035 (May 30, 1951).
[44] T. I. Yurzhenko, D. K. Tolopko, and V. N. Puchin, *Doklady Akad. Nauk S.S.S.R.*, **74,** 85 (1950).
[45] D. K. Tolopko and T. I. Yurzhenko, *ibid.*, **94,** 707 (1954).
[46] H. Hock, S. Lang, and G. Knavel, *Chem. Ber.*, **83,** 227 (1950).
[47] H. Hock and S. Lang, *Ber.*, **76B,** 1130 (1943).
[48] E. G. E. Hawkins, *Quart. Revs.*, **4,** 251 (1950).
[49] E. G. E. Hawkins, *J. Chem. Soc.*, **1949,** 2076.
[50] J. C. Conner, Jr., U.S. Pat. 2,632,026 (March 17, 1953).
[51] G. G. Joris, U.S. Pat. 2,681,936 (June 22, 1954).
[52] P. F. Ritchie, T. F. Sanderson, and L. F. McBurney, *J. Am. Chem. Soc.*, **75,** 2610 (1953)

1°, and best results are usually obtained on hydrocarbons containing a 3° C—H bond (pinane, for example, giving a 50% yield of the indicated hydroperoxide [32]). The chief problem in carrying out autoxidations of this sort is evidently to pick conditions of high enough temperature and radical concentration to maintain a rapid chain reaction leading to hydroperoxide formation, and yet to avoid hydroperoxide decomposition. In fact, at higher temperatures, essentially all hydrocarbons take up oxygen rapidly but yield complicated mixtures of products.

Many aromatic substituted hydrocarbons are readily converted to hydroperoxides, often in good yield, Table 9·2, and the reaction is of technical importance, both for the synthesis of hydroperoxides used as polymerization initiators (Section 10·2d) and, as mentioned above, as a step in the preparation of phenols.

Reaction conditions are similar to those employed with saturated hydrocarbons, and it is difficult to compare yields since they reflect, as much as anything, the amount of development effort devoted to the syntheses. Thus, with cumene, early experiments [20] gave yields of only about 7%, and best results are obtained at around 100° in the presence of sodium carbonate [51] or other bases [36, 50] which stabilize the hydroperoxide against decomposition into phenol, an effective inhibitor. Nevertheless, simple methyl benzenes appear to autoxidize rather slowly so that hydroperoxide formation competes poorly with decomposition. Thus no benzyl hydroperoxide has been isolated from toluene, although the hydroperoxide prepared by a different route is reasonably stable in the absence of free radicals.[53] Similarly, with p-xylene, chains are short, since autoxidation of 1000 grams at 120–130° in the presence of 200 grams of di-t-butyl peroxide gives only 40 grams of product.[39]

The lower reactivity of the simple methyl group is shown directly in p-cymene, where 80% of the radical attack occurs on the isopropyl group.[35]

Hexaarylethanes and tetraaryldialkylethanes, which dissociate spontaneously into free radicals (Section 10·4c) show a somewhat different autoxidation, which appears to be a chain process but follows the overall course

$$R_3C\!-\!CR_3 + O_2 \rightarrow R_3C\!-\!O\!-\!O\!-\!CR_3 \qquad (18)$$

perhaps via

$$R_3C\cdot + O_2 \rightarrow R_3C\!-\!OO\cdot \qquad (19)$$

$$R_3C\!-\!OO\cdot + R_3C\!-\!CR_3 \rightarrow R_3COOCR_3 + R_3C\cdot \qquad (20)$$

Hydroperoxides are only obtained in the presence of hydrogen donors such as pyrogallol, under which condition the chain process is inhibited. These reactions have been studied in some detail by Ziegler,[54] but Lichtin and Thomas have recently reported peculiarities in the stoichiometry of the reaction.[55]

Turning now to olefin oxidations, a variety of substances with allylic C—H bonds yield allylic hydroperoxides, Table 9·3. Again, techniques are similar to those of previous hydrocarbon autoxidations, but olefin oxidations have a number of peculiarities which merit discussion. First, although autoxidation initially may give hydro-

[53] C. Walling and S. A. Buckler, *J. Am. Chem. Soc.*, **77**, 6032 (1955); preliminary note, *ibid.*, **75**, 4372 (1953).

[54] K. Ziegler, *Ann.*, **551**, 127 (1942); this paper summarizes earlier work.

[55] N. N. Lichtin and G. R. Thomas, *J. Am. Chem. Soc.*, **76**, 3020 (1954).

TABLE 9·3   TYPICAL OLEFIN AUTOXIDATIONS YIELDING HYDROPEROXIDES

Olefin	Product	Yield, %	Foot-note [a]
(cyclohexene)	(3-hydroperoxy-cyclohexene, OOH)	20	16
(1-methylcyclohexene, CH₃)	(OOH, CH₃) (+ isomers)	20	14, *16*
(1,2-dimethylcyclohexene, CH₃ / CH₃)	(OOH, CH₃, CH₃) + (CH₃, CH₃, OOH)	12	56
(cyclopentene)	(OOH cyclopentene)	.	14
Methyl oleate	Mixed allylic hydroperoxides	10	*57*, 62
Methyl elaidate	Mixed allylic hydroperoxides	...	58
CH_3CHCH_3 (isopropyl-methylcyclohexene, CH₃)	CH_3CHCH_3 (OOH, CH₃)	15	59
(CH₂ bicyclic diene)	(CH₂ bicyclic diene, OOH)	40	60
Limonene	Mixed hydroperoxides	35	61
Ethyl linoleate	Chiefly —CH=CH—CH=CH—CH— (OOH)	...	63
$\phi—CH_2—CH=CH—CH_3$	$\phi—CH—CH=CH—CH_3$ (OOH)	65	64
(methyltetralin, CH₃)	(CH₃, OOH dihydronaphthalene)	...	46

[a] Yield from reference in italics when more than one is cited.

56 E. H. Farmer and D. A. Sutton, *J. Chem. Soc.*, **1946,** 10.
57 E. H. Farmer and D. A. Sutton, *ibid.*, **1943,** 119.
58 E. H. Farmer and D. A. Sutton, *ibid.*, **1944,** 242.
59 H. Hock and S. Lang, *Ber.*, **75B,** 300 (1942).
60 H. Hock and F. Depke, *Chem. Ber.*, **84,** 356 (1951).
61 H. E. Eschinazi, *Bull. Research Council Israel*, **2,** 73 (1952).
62 J. Ross, A. I. Gebhart, and J. F. Gerecht, *J. Am. Chem. Soc.*, **71,** 282 (1949).
63 J. L. Bolland and H. P. Koch, *J. Chem. Soc.*, **1945,** 445.
64 J. W. Lawrence and J. R. Shelton, *Ind. Eng. Chem.*, **42,** 136 (1950).

peroxide in high yield,[65] the hydroperoxide can subsequently attack the double bonds of other molecules by both polar and radical processes. As a result, prolonged oxidation generally yields a complex mixture of products often containing several olefin residues per molecule in addition to hydroperoxides. Such reactions are apparently the basis of the formation of insoluble films in the autoxidation of drying oils and paints. Second, the possibility of peroxide addition to the double bond, rather than hydrogen abstraction, is a potential complication, and, indeed, with polymerizable olefins may lead to the alternate copolymerization chain discussed in Section 9·3a. Finally, the intermediate allylic radical, being a resonance hybrid of two structures, may add oxygen at either end of its electronic system and lead to rearranged products. The olefins of Table 9·3 show several examples of such isomerization, which provide further evidence for the radical chain mechanism of the autoxidation process. Thus, 1,2-dimethylcyclohexene yields rearranged and unrearranged hydroperoxide in about equal amounts,[56] whereas conversion of the hydroperoxides from methyl oleate to the corresponding ketones gives all four isomeric 8-, 9-, 10-, and 11-ketostearic acids.[62] Further, *cis-trans* isomerization occurs as well, with the hydroperoxides having the more stable *trans* configuration.[66] With methyl linoleate, and other 1,4-dienes, the C—H bond α to both double bonds is most readily attacked, and, as might be expected, a conjugated system results

$$-CH=CH-CH_2-CH=CH- \xrightarrow{\text{ROO·}} \begin{array}{c} -CH=CH-CH=CH-\overset{.}{C}H- \\ \updownarrow \\ -CH=CH-\overset{.}{C}H-CH=CH- \\ \updownarrow \\ -\overset{.}{C}H-CH=CH-CH=CH- \end{array} \begin{array}{c} \overset{OO·}{\underset{|}{-CH=CH-CH=CH-\overset{|}{C}H-}} \\ \nearrow \\ \\ \searrow \\ \underset{OO·}{-CH-CH=CH-CH=CH-} \end{array} \quad (21)$$

in very nearly quantitative yield, as indicated both by ultraviolet and infrared spectra [63, 67] and hydrogenation to a mixture of 9- and 13-hydroxystearic acids. Again, infrared spectra indicate that the double bonds have a mixture of *trans-trans* and *trans-cis* configurations.[67] Another example is provided by terpinolene, which does not

[65] L. Bateman, *Quart. Revs.*, **8**, 147 (1954), reports that, at 2% reaction, several of the olefins in Table 9·3 give over 90% hydroperoxide based on oxygen absorbed.

[66] D. Swern, J. E. Coleman, M. B. Knight, C. Ricciuti, C. O. Willits, and C. R. Eddy, *J. Am. Chem. Soc.*, **75**, 3135 (1953).

[67] N. A. Khan, *J. Chem. Phys.*, **21**, 952 (1953); N. A. Khan, W. O. Lundberg, and R. T. Holman, *J. Am. Chem. Soc.*, **76**, 1779 (1954).

give an identifiable hydroperoxide but rather a mixture of triols,[68] apparently resulting from the sequence

$$(22)$$

Additional cases are discussed by Bateman.[65]

9·2b   Oxygen-Containing Compounds

Autoxidations of aldehydes occur with great ease, but the intermediate peracids are rarely isolated, although, as we have seen, they can be stabilized by conversion to diacyl peroxides. In the case of acetaldehyde, a different sort of peroxide has been detected,[69, 70] apparently arising via the reaction:

$$CH_3CHO + CH_3COO_2H \rightarrow CH_3C \overset{OH\quad O}{\underset{O—O}{\diagup\diagdown}} CCH_3 \qquad (23)$$

Although the ultimate products of aldehyde autoxidations are usually the acids, probably formed by polar rearrangement of the product of reaction 23, at low temperatures the overall reaction can take another course and provides one of the technical processes for the manufacture

$$CH_3CHO + CH_3COO_2H \rightarrow CH_3CO—O—COCH_3 + H_2O \quad (24)$$

of acetic anhydride.[71] If aldehydes are autoxidized at higher temperatures and lower oxygen concentrations, the decarbonylation chain (Section 6·3b) competes successfully with autoxidation, particularly with α-branched aldehydes. Thus, at 80° 2-methylpentanal gives up

[68] J. N. Borglin, D. A. Lister, E. J. Lorand, and J. E. Reese, ibid., 72, 4591, 4596 (1950).

[69] M. J. Kagan and G. D. Lubarsky, J. Phys. Chem., 39, 837, 847 (1935).

[70] C. E. H. Bawn and J. B. Williamson, Trans. Faraday Soc., 47, 721 (1951).

[71] G. Benson in R. E. Kirk and D. F. Othmer, Encyclopedia of Chemical Technology, Interscience Encyclopedia, New York, 1947, pp. 83–5.

to 20% n-pentane, 32% carbon monoxide, and only 10% acid when bubbled with oxygen in the presence of metal catalysts.[72]

Another group of compounds which autoxidize with marked (and often perilous) facility are many ethers. The reaction of isopropyl ether with oxygen shows the characteristic autoacceleration and susceptibility to added radical sources or inhibitors of a radical chain autoxidation.[73, 74] Although the initial product is believed to be a monohydroperoxide, the dihydroperoxide has also been isolated.[74, 75]

$$
\begin{array}{ccc}
\underset{\substack{|\\ \mathrm{CH_3}}}{\overset{\mathrm{CH_3}}{\underset{|}{\mathrm{CH}}}}\!-\!\mathrm{O}\!-\!\underset{\substack{|\\ \mathrm{CH_3}}}{\overset{\mathrm{CH_3}}{\underset{|}{\mathrm{CH}}}} & \xrightarrow{\mathrm{O_2}} & \mathrm{HOO}\underset{\substack{|\\ \mathrm{CH_3}}}{\overset{\mathrm{CH_3}}{\underset{|}{\mathrm{C}}}}\!-\!\mathrm{O}\!-\!\underset{\substack{|\\ \mathrm{CH_3}}}{\overset{\mathrm{CH_3}}{\underset{|}{\mathrm{CH}}}} & \xrightarrow{\mathrm{O_2}} & \mathrm{HOO}\underset{\substack{|\\ \mathrm{CH_3}}}{\overset{\mathrm{CH_3}}{\underset{|}{\mathrm{C}}}}\!-\!\mathrm{O}\!-\!\underset{\substack{|\\ \mathrm{CH_3}}}{\overset{\mathrm{CH_3}}{\underset{|}{\mathrm{C}}}}\mathrm{OOH}
\end{array} \quad (25)
$$

Similarly, tetrahydrofuran and derivatives yield stable α-hydroperoxides,[76] as does benzyl ether.[77] On the other hand, phthalan, on exposure to air, gives a good yield of a solid dialkyl peroxide[78] with the apparent structure

$$ (26) $$

However, as in the case of the alcohols considered below, the peroxides derived from ethers have essentially hemiacetal or acetal structures and easily rearrange and equilibrate with other peroxide structures,[79] so the initial product with phthalan may actually be the expected hydroperoxide.

Although one usually thinks of aliphatic alcohols as being stable

[72] P. Thuring and A. Perret, *Helv. Chim. Acta,* **36,** 13 (1953).

[73] V. A. Molodovskii and M. B. Neiman, *Zhur. Fiz. Khim.,* **23,** 30 (1949); cf. W. Hunter and J. Downing, *J. Soc. Chem. Ind.,* **68,** 362 (1949).

[74] K. I. Ivanov, V. K. Savinova, and G. Mikhailova, *J. Gen. Chem. U.S.S.R.,* **16,** 65, 1003, 1015 (1946).

[75] A. Rieche and K. Koch, *Ber.,* **75,** 1016 (1942).

[76] A. Robertson, *Nature,* **162,** 153 (1948); H. Rein and R. Criegee, *Angew. Chem.,* **62,** 120 (1950).

[77] L. Debiais, M. Niclause, and M. Letort, *Compt. rend.,* **239,** 539 (1954).

[78] J. Entel, C. H. Ruof and H. C. Howard, *J. Am. Chem. Soc.,* **74,** 441 (1952).

[79] Thus, the peroxides found in old samples of ethyl ether are actually a complicated mixture of products.

molecules which show little tendency to react with atmospheric oxygen, the relatively rapid autoxidation of cyclohexanol at moderately elevated temperatures has recently been described by Brown, et al.[80] At 125°, in the presence of added peroxide (from a previous oxidation) rapid oxygen uptake occurs, to give (as long as the conversion is kept low) products which are some 80% peroxidic. The initial product is undoubtedly the hydroxyhydroperoxide (I). However, as shown by Criegee,[81] this substance (which can also be prepared from cyclohexanone and H_2O_2) equilibrates with ketone, H_2O_2, and the three products II, III, and IV, of which III is here present in largest amount. Cyclopentanol undergoes a comparable oxidation,

$$H_2O_2 + \quad \overset{O}{\bigcirc} \; \rightleftharpoons \; \overset{HO \quad OOH}{\underset{I}{\bigcirc}} \; \rightleftharpoons \; \overset{HO \quad O{-}O}{\underset{II}{\bigcirc}} \; \overset{OH}{\bigcirc} \; \rightleftharpoons$$

$$\overset{HO \quad O{-}O}{\bigcirc} \; \overset{OOH}{\underset{III}{\bigcirc}} \; \rightleftharpoons \; \overset{HOO \quad OOH}{\underset{IV}{\bigcirc}} \quad\quad (27)$$

which can be carried out photochemically at 100°, using benzoin as an initiator, and yields similar products.[82]

It would be interesting to know how general are reactions of this sort, but these seem the best examples. However, the oxidation of aqueous alcohol solutions (containing air) induced by supersonic vibrations has been described,[83] and alcohol oxidation by peroxides (Section 10·2b) and Fenton's reagent (Section 11·3) involve $R{-}O\cdot$ radicals, somewhat similar to (but more reactive than) the $ROO\cdot$ radicals of autoxidation chains.

Carbonyl compounds other than aldehydes show little tendency to undergo this type of autoxidation. Di-n-propyl ketone takes up oxygen slowly at 110–120° to give chiefly butyric and propionic

[80] N. Brown, M. J. Hartig, M. J. Roedel, A. W. Anderson, and C. E. Schweitzer, J. Am. Chem. Soc., 77, 1756 (1955).

[81] R. Criegee, W. Schnorrenberg, and J. Becke, Ann., 565, 7 (1949).

[82] N. Brown, A. W. Anderson, and C. E. Schweitzer, J. Am. Chem. Soc., 77, 1760 (1955).

[83] E. M. Lapinskaya and M. A. Khenokh, Zhur. Obshchei Khim., 23, 1464 (1953).

acids.[84] An intermediate peroxide, presumably 3-hydroperoxy-4-heptanone, has been detected but not isolated. However, 2-phenyl-cyclopentanone, with a more reactive benzyl C—H bond, is reported to autoxidize rapidly at room temperature, with ring opening to γ-benzoylbutyric acid.[85] Esters not containing an activating group elsewhere in the molecule autoxidize only slowly at elevated temperatures,[86] apparently at points remote from the carbonyl group.

In contrast to carbonyl compounds, many enols autoxidize with ease,[87–89] an early example being the reaction [87a]

$$\begin{array}{c}\phi \\ \diagdown \\ \diagup \\ \phi\end{array}\!\!CH\!-\!\!\underset{\underset{\phi}{|}}{C}\!\!=\!\!\underset{}{\overset{\overset{OH}{|}}{C}}\!\!-\!\phi \xrightarrow{\;O_2\;} \begin{array}{c}\phi \\ \diagdown \\ \diagup \\ \phi\end{array}\!\!CH\!-\!\!\underset{\underset{\phi}{|}}{\overset{\overset{O\!-\!O}{|}}{C}}\!\!-\!\!\underset{\underset{OH}{|}}{C}\!\!-\!\phi \qquad (28)$$

which occurs readily in ether below 0°C. The cyclic structure of the product is inferred because such peroxides are non-acidic,[87b] but the reaction path has not been investigated. In alkaline solution, enolate anions appear to react even more rapidly, but perhaps by a hydrogen peroxide-forming mechanism, Section 9·5c.

As a final example involving oxygen-containing molecules, a rather remarkable autoxidation of triphenylglycidol has been noted by Kohler and Nygaard.[90] The overall reaction is given by

$$\phi\!-\!\!\underset{\underset{}{\overset{\overset{OH}{|}}{C}}}{}\!\!H\!-\!CH\!\!\underset{}{\overset{\overset{O}{\diagup\;\diagdown}}{}}\!\!\underset{\diagdown_{\phi}}{C} + O_2 \rightarrow \phi\!-\!\!\underset{\underset{H}{|}}{\overset{\overset{OH}{|}}{C}}\!\!-\!O\!-\!O\!-\!CH\!\!\underset{}{\overset{\overset{O}{\diagup\;\diagdown}}{}}\!\!\underset{\diagdown_{\phi}}{C} \qquad (29)$$

but, although the reaction was studied at some length, a satisfactory path has not been formulated.

9·2c   Nitrogen-Containing Compounds

Several autoxidations of organic nitrogen compounds are known which appear to be typical hydroperoxide-forming chain processes.

[84] D. B. Sharp, S. E. Whitcomb, L. W. Patton, and A. D. Moorhead, *J. Am. Chem. Soc.*, **74**, 1802 (1952).

[85] K. Mislow and A. K. Lazarus, *ibid.*, **77**, 6383 (1955).

[86] M. W. Rigg and H. Gisser, *ibid.*, **75**, 1415 (1953).

[87] (a) E. P. Kohler, *Am. Chem. J.*, **36**, 177 (1906); (b) E. P. Kohler and R. B. Thompson, *J. Am. Chem. Soc.*, **59**, 887 (1937).

[88] R. B. Woodward and E. R. Blout, *ibid.*, **65**, 562 (1943).

[89] R. C. Fuson, E. W. Maynert, and W. J. Shenk, Jr., *ibid.*, **67**, 1939 (1945)

[90] E. P. Kohler and E. M. Nygaard, *ibid.*, **55**, 310 (1933).

An interesting example was described by Busch and Dietz in 1914,[91] who noted that a benzene solution of the phenylhydrazone of benzaldehyde, shaken with oxygen at room temperature, absorbed one equivalent in 6 hours to give a yellow crystalline (but explosive) peroxide in 73% yield. A number of other hydrazones of aldehydes give similar products, but, if the reaction is carried out in alcohol, a complicated series of non-peroxidic products are obtained instead.[92] These peroxides have been subsequently investigated by Pausacker [93] and Criegee [94] and are now considered to have the structure

$$\phi-\underset{\underset{H}{|}}{\overset{\overset{OOH}{|}}{C}}-N{=}N-\phi \tag{30}$$

suggesting their explosive properties, and perhaps formed by the chain propagation steps

$$\phi-\underset{\underset{|}{\overset{|}{C}H}}{}-N{=}N-\phi + \phi-CH{=}N-NH-\phi \rightarrow$$

where the first term bears $\overset{O-O\cdot}{|}$

$$\phi-\underset{\underset{|}{\overset{OOH}{|}}}{CH}-N{=}N-\phi + \phi-CH{=}N-\dot{N}-\phi \tag{31}$$

$$O_2 + \phi-CH{=}N-\dot{N}-\phi \leftrightarrow \phi-\dot{C}H-N{=}N-\phi \rightarrow$$

$$\phi-\underset{\underset{|}{\overset{O-O\cdot}{|}}}{CH}-N{=}N-\phi \tag{32}$$

involving radical attack on the N—H bond, followed by allylic shift of the odd electron system.

A rather similar autoxidation occurs with tetrahydrocarbazole and related compounds,[95] e.g.,

[91] M. Busch and W. Dietz, *Ber.*, **47**, 2377 (1914).

[92] M. Busch and H. Kunder, *ibid.*, **49**, 2345 (1916).

[93] K. H. Pausacker, *J. Chem. Soc.*, **1950**, 3478.

[94] R. Criegee and G. Lohaus, *Chem. Ber.*, **84**, 219 (1951).

[95] R. J. S. Beer, L. McGrath, A. Robertson, and A. B. Woodier, *Nature*, **164**, 362 (1949); R. J. S. Beer, L. McGrath and A. Robertson, *J. Chem. Soc.*, **1950**, 2118; R. J. S. Beer, T. Broadhurst, and A. Robertson, *ibid.*, **1952**, 4946; R. J. S. Beer, T. Donavanik, and A. Robertson, *ibid.*, **1954**, 4139; B. Witkop, *J. Am. Chem. Soc.*, **72**, 1428 (1950); B. Witkop, J. B. Patrick, and M. Rosenblum, *ibid.*, **73**, 2641 (1951); B. Witkop and J. B. Patrick, *ibid.*, **74**, 3855 (1952).

$$\text{(structure)} + O_2 \rightarrow \text{(structure with OOH)} \qquad (33)$$

which can be formulated in essentially the same way, with allylic rearrangement of an intermediate radical. The autoxidation of di-N-substituted hydroxylamines has been described [96] and takes place in aqueous alkaline solution in the presence of copper. Products are aldehyde and the mono-N-alkylhydroxylamine, together with H_2O_2 and organic peroxide, and the reaction is suggested as being initiated by a redox reaction followed by the usual hydroperoxide chain.

$$\begin{array}{c} RCH_2 \\ \diagdown \\ N\!-\!O^- + Cu^{++} \rightarrow \\ \diagup \\ RCH_2 \end{array} \qquad \begin{array}{c} RCH_2 \\ \diagdown \\ N\!-\!O\cdot + Cu^+ \\ \diagup \\ RCH_2 \end{array} \qquad (34)$$

$$\begin{array}{c} RCH_2 \\ \diagdown \\ N\!-\!O\cdot + \\ \diagup \\ RCH_2 \end{array} \begin{array}{c} RCH_2 \\ \diagdown \\ N\!-\!OH \rightarrow \\ \diagup \\ RCH_2 \end{array} \begin{array}{c} R\dot{C}H \\ \diagdown \\ N\!-\!OH + \\ \diagup \\ RCH_2 \end{array} \begin{array}{c} RCH_2 \\ \diagdown \\ N\!-\!OH \\ \diagup \\ RCH_2 \end{array} (35)$$

Finally, the formation of osazones has recently been suggested as occurring via the autoxidation of the enol form of the intermediate hydrazone.[97]

The autoxidation of organic molecules containing other elements has received less attention. However, the behavior of allylic and saturated sulfides is important in connection with the aging of vulcanized rubber (Section 7·3c). According to Bateman,[97a] sulfides autoxidize more rapidly than the corresponding hydrocarbons, and the products are largely sulfoxides plus products in which a C—S bond has been cleaved. No peroxides were isolated, but they believe a chain reaction to be operative.

Autoxidation of organometallic compounds are discussed in Section 9·5d.

[96] D. H. Johnson, M. A. Thorold-Rogers, and G. Trappe, *Chemistry & Industry*, **1953**, 1032; H. Brown and J. Grundy, *ibid.*, **1954**, 460.

[97] V. C. Barry, *Nature*, **175**, 220 (1955).

[97a] L. Bateman and J. I. Cunneen, *J. Chem. Soc.*, **1955**, 1596; L. Bateman and F. W. Shipley, *ibid.*, **1955**, 1996.

9·2d Structure and Reactivity

The foregoing data permit some worth-while generalizations about the relation between structure and reactivity in radical chain autoxidations. Considering the general scheme indicated by reactions 3–4, it is evident that the hydrogen abstraction process (4) determines the isomer distribution and, as it is the slow step in the autoxidation chain, qualitatively the overall rates as well.

The rate of reaction 4 will, in part, be determined by C—H bond strengths, which predicts the usual observed order of reactivity of primary < secondary < tertiary C—H bonds, and also the high reactivity of allylic and benzyl C—H bonds. More quantitatively, Bateman [65] estimates from his collected data that an additional alkyl group increases reactivity about 3.3-fold, whereas an additional vinyl group has a 107-fold effect. However, with too high a concentration of substituents, reactivity may fall off somewhat.[98]

In addition to these factors of C—H bond dissociation energies and steric hindrance, the ROO· radical should have electron-acceptor properties, and, like the halogen atoms (Chapter 8), preferentially attack points of electron availability. This polar factor, in all probability, accounts for the ease of autoxidation of the oxygen- and nitrogen-substituted molecules just discussed.

With the aldehydes, both a lowered C—H bond strength and electron-donor properties must contribute to their high reactivities, and it is noteworthy that, when cyclohexene and benzaldehyde are autoxidized in mixture, the major product is the monobenzoate of trans-cyclohexene glycol,[99] undoubtedly arising from polar addition of the preferentially formed perbenzoic acid to the olefin. Similar preferential aldehyde oxidation is also noted in benzaldehyde-terpene systems.[99]

A more unequivocal and quantitative measure of the role of electron availability in autoxidation is obtained by a study of the competitive autoxidation of substituted benzaldehydes, carried out in acetic anhydride to arrest the autoxidation at the peroxide stage.[6] The competitive kinetics of such systems are identical with copolymerizations (Chapter 4) and typical results appear in Table 9·4.

[98] Preferential radical attack on the 6-position of 1-methylcyclohexene (Table 9·3) and similar molecules may seem puzzling, since attack at carbon 3 permits isomerization to a tertiary radical. Perhaps the important factor is that, in the former case, both contributing species to the resonance hybrid are trisubstituted olefins.

[99] W. Triebs and L. Schulz, Chem. Ber., **80**, 214, 217 (1947). In the original paper the glycol, m.p. 103–104°, is erroneously identified as cis.

TABLE 9·4   RELATIVE REACTIVITIES OF SUBSTITUTED BENZALDEHYDES
TOWARDS p-CHLOROPERBENZOATE RADICALS[6] (30°)

Substituent	Relative Reactivity	Substituent	Relative Reactivity
p-OCH$_3$	3.70	H	1.00
p-CH$_3$	2.29	p-Cl	0.54
p-iso-C$_3$H$_7$	1.90	p-CN	0.47
m-CH$_3$	1.61	n-Butyraldehyde	1.94

The effect of electron-supplying groups on facilitating peroxy radical attack on the RCO—H bond is evident, ρ for the p-chloroperbenzoate radical having a value of about -0.8.

The greater reactivity of n-butyraldehyde compared with aromatic aldehydes is noteworthy, suggesting that polar effects, rather than C—H bond strengths are of primary importance, and has been confirmed as well in the decanal–benzaldehyde system where relative reactivities are 5–10:1.[100] A similar comparison which also shows reactivity paralleling electron availability has recently been reported by Russell using series of toluenes and cumenes, the two series showing ρ values of -0.6 and -0.43 respectively.[101] In competitive oxidations, relative reactivities of tetralin, indane, allyl benzene, diphenylmethane, cumene, ethylbenzene, and toluene are 5.0, 2.8, 2.7, 1.2, 1.0, 0.59, and 0.075.

As in the cases of polymerization and other chain processes, the problem of *overall* rates of autoxidation of different substrates is a much more complex one than that of relative reactivities and is considered further below.

9·2e   Kinetics of Hydroperoxide Formation

In the preceding sections we have seen many qualitative indications that the autoxidative formation of hydroperoxides is a radical chain process with propagation steps corresponding to eqs. 3 and 4. Kinetic studies further support this conclusion and give crucial information as to the exact nature of chain initiation and chain termination processes. These in turn permit a more detailed discussion of the relation between structure, reactivity, and overall rates in autoxidation processes.

Application of the same sort of kinetic scheme as has been suc-

[100] T. A. Ingles and H. W. Melville, *Proc. Roy. Soc. London,* **A218,** 163 (1953).

[101] G. A. Russell, *J. Am. Chem. Soc.,* **78,** 1047 (1956).

cessful with polymerization (Chapter 3) and other radical chain processes suggests that the reactions to be considered are initiation processes with rates R_i, the propagation reactions here repeated:

$$R\cdot + O_2 \xrightarrow{k_o} R\text{—}O\text{—}O\cdot \tag{3}$$

$$R\text{—}O\text{—}O\cdot + R\text{—}H \xrightarrow{k_p} R\text{—}OOH \quad R\cdot \tag{4}$$

and three possible terminations (the products not specified)

$$2ROO\cdot \xrightarrow{k_{t1}} X \tag{36}$$

$$R\cdot + R\text{—}OO\cdot \xrightarrow{k_{t12}} Y \tag{37}$$

$$2R\cdot \xrightarrow{k_{t2}} Z \tag{38}$$

This system of equations is identical with the set involved in radical addition reactions (Section 6·1b) and, on introduction of the usual steady-state conditions, yields

$$\frac{d[O_2]}{dt} = \frac{d[ROOH]}{dt}$$

$$= \frac{k_o k_p [RH][O_2](R_i)^{\frac{1}{2}}}{(2k_o{}^2 k_{t1}[O_2]^2 + k_o k_p k_{t12}[O_2][RH] + 2k_p{}^2 k_{t2}[RH]^2)^{\frac{1}{2}}} \tag{39}$$

where k_{t12} may be replaced by $2\phi(k_{t1}k_{t2})^{\frac{1}{2}}$. Again, under certain conditions, eq. 39 takes simpler forms, the most important to us here being the situation at relatively high oxygen concentrations, where peroxy radicals are the major chain-carrying species present, and chain termination is almost exclusively via reaction 36. Here the rate expression becomes simply

$$\frac{-d[O_2]}{dt} = \frac{d[ROOH]}{dt} = k_p[RH]\left(\frac{R_i}{2k_{t1}}\right)^{\frac{1}{2}} \tag{40}$$

Reliable kinetic measurements on liquid-phase autoxidations are difficult, because of the problem of maintaining oxygen saturation in the liquid phase, an obstacle discussed in detail by Bateman.[65] Further, autoxidations commonly show complicated sigmoid rate curves, for reasons considered further below. Accordingly, rate measurements must be made at low conversions, and some means of producing a controllable (preferably constant and known) rate of radical production is required: e.g., by an added initiator or photochemically, often in the presence of a photosensitizer.

When these requirements are met, a variety of autoxidations, carried out at oxygen pressures near atmospheric, obey a rate equation in the form of eq. 40, among the first examples being the gas-phase autoxidation of acetaldehyde, studied by Bowen and Tietz in 1930,[102] and Bäckström's investigation of benzaldehyde.[11]   Other aldehyde oxidations have given similar results, including the photochemical liquid-phase autoxidation of acetaldehyde at −90 to −40° at pressures above 0.5 atmospheres,[103] the autoxidation of n-decanal,[104] and that of benzaldehyde initiated with benzoyl peroxide.[105]   On the other hand, McNesby and Davis have reported that, although the photooxidation of n-heptaldehyde obeys eq. 40 at oxygen pressures of 200–400 mm, the rate rises again at higher pressures.[106]   Hydrocarbon oxidations present a similar picture; eq. 40 is obeyed in the benzoyl peroxide-[107,108] and azobisisobutyronitrile-initiated [108] autoxidations of tetralin, the photoöxidation of cumene, photosensitized with azobisisobutyronitrile,[109] and (above certain critical pressures) in a variety of olefin autoxidations.[65,110]   Recently, the same sort of kinetics have been reported for the photochemical [77] and also the benzoyl peroxide- and azobisisobutyronitrile-initiated [111] autoxidation of benzyl ether.   The behavior of olefin autoxidations at lower oxygen pressures has been investigated by Bateman,[65,112] who points out that, the more reactive the C—H bond of an olefin, the higher the oxygen pressure below which the autoxidation rate is oxygen dependent.   By an analysis of rate data in the low-pressure region, ϕ can be evaluated in the same way as in copolymerization (Section 4·1j) and the relative contribution of each sort of chain ending calculated.   This distribution of chain-ending processes for ethyl li-

[102] E. J. Bowen and E. L. Tietz, *J. Chem. Soc.*, **1930**, 234.

[103] P. Fillet, M. Niclause, and M. Letort, *Compt. rend.*, **236**, 1489 (1953); *J. chim. phys.*, **53**, 8 (1956).

[104] H. R. Cooper and H. W. Melville, *J. Chem. Soc.*, **1951**, 1984.

[105] M. F. R. Mulcahy and I. C. Watt, *ibid.*, **1954**, 2971.

[106] J. R. McNesby and T. W. Davis, *J. Am. Chem. Soc.*, **76**, 2148 (1954); their data, however, seem somewhat irreproducible.

[107] C. H. Bamford and M. J. S. Dewar, *Proc. Roy. Soc. London*, **A198**, 252 (1949); somewhat different results were reported earlier by P. George, *ibid.*, **A185**, 337 (1946).

[108] A. E. Woodward and R. B. Mesrobian, *J. Am. Chem. Soc.*, **75**, 6189 (1953).

[109] H. W. Melville and S. Richards, *J. Chem. Soc.*, **1954**, 944.

[110] L. Bateman and G. Gee, *Proc. Roy. Soc. London*, **195A**, 376 (1948).

[111] L. Debiais, P. Horstmann, M. Niclause, and M. Letort, *Compt. rend.*, **239**, 587 (1954).

[112] L. Bateman and A. L. Morris, *Trans. Faraday Soc.*, **49**, 1026 (1953).

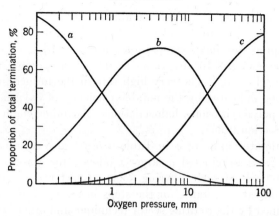

F_IG. 9·2 Relative contribution of different chain termination processes as a function of oxygen pressure in the autoxidation of ethyl linoleate at 45°: a, $R· + R·$; b, $R· + ROO·$; c, $ROO· + ROO·$ (after Bateman [65]).

noleate is shown in Fig. 9·2, and some ϕ values together with the rate constant ratios which determine autoxidation rates at high and low oxygen pressures are listed in Table 9·5.

T_ABLE 9·5 R_ATE C_ONSTANT R_ATIOS AND ϕ V_ALUES IN O_LEFIN
A_UTOXIDATIONS [65,a]

(At 45° unless indicated)

Olefin	$k_p/k_{t1}^{1/2} \times 10^3$	$k_o/k_{t2}^{1/2} \times 10^{-3}$	ϕ
Methyl oleate	1.53	0.5	0.3
Phytene	1.07	0.4	1.0
Digeranyl	3.82	0.9	3.1
Ethyl linoleate	20.7	1.6	2.5
Ethyl linolenate	41.4	1.3	3.3
2,6-Dimethyl-2,5-heptadiene	130 (25°)	1.2 (25°)	6.5

[a] Calculated assuming 100% efficiency of chain starting in benzoyl peroxide-initiated systems. As in other systems, this is not actually the case,[113] so the values are somewhat high.

[113] L. Bateman, Mrs. H. Hughes, and A. L. Morris, *Discussions Faraday Soc.*, **14**, 190 (1953).

The fact that autoxidation rates commonly become independent of oxygen pressures above 50–100 mm, at a point where the actual oxygen concentration in solution is still very low, indicates that reaction 3 must be an enormously faster process than reaction 4, since it is implausible that reaction 36 should be very greatly faster than the known rapid coupling of alkyl radicals. Table 9·5 gives numerical expression to this idea, indicating that, if the different termination processes have comparable rates, addition of oxygen to alkyl radicals occurs 10^6–10^8 times as rapidly as peroxy radical attack on C—H bonds. The very high rate of the former process has already been indicated by the notable efficiency of oxygen as an inhibitor in polymerizations, halogenations, and other chain processes (see also Section 9·3a).

The moderate values of ϕ in Table 9·5 are also of interest, since we might have anticipated a larger tendency for cross termination between radicals of such differing polar character.

Individual rate constants for the steps in autoxidation chains can be determined by the rotating sector technique and other non-steady-state methods outlined in Section 3·4, although there are formidable experimental difficulties, ably pointed out by Bateman.[65] Table 9·6

TABLE 9·6   RATE CONSTANTS IN AUTOXIDATION PROCESSES

R—H	Temperature, °C	$k_o \times 10^{-6}$	k_p	$k_{t1} \times 10^{-6}$	$k_{t12} \times 10^{-6}$	$k_{t2} \times 10^{-6}$	Footnote
Cyclohexene	10	...	0.65	0.95	...	...	114
1-Methylcyclo-hexene	10	...	1.1	0.5	...	...	114
Dihydromyrcene	10	...	0.40	0.65	...	...	114
Ethyl linoleate	10	...	5.7	0.5	...	...	114
Ethyl linoleate	25	10	50	20	50	20	65
Digeranyl	25	1	3	10	10	1	65
1-Octene	25	...	0.03	0.3	...	...	116
Tetralin	25	67.6	13.3	21.5	...	7.1	107
Cumene	50	...	0.31	0.028	...	...	109
Cumene	65	...	0.56	0.033	...	...	109
n-Decanal	5 [a]	...	720	7.5	...	...	115a
n-Decanal	5 [b]	...	2700	34	...	...	115a
Benzaldehyde	5	...	1910	210	...	...	115b

[a] No solvent.
[b] In decane solution.

[114] L. Bateman and G. Gee, *Proc. Roy. Soc. London*, **195A**, 391 (1948).
[115] (a) H. R. Cooper and H. W. Melville, *J. Chem. Soc.*, **1951**, 1994; (b) T. A. Ingles and H. W. Melville, *Proc. Roy. Soc. London*, **A218**, 175 (1952).
[116] L. Bateman and G. Gee, *Trans. Faraday Soc.*, **47**, 155 (1951).

summarizes the results which have been obtained to date. Values of k_p and k_{t1} may be reasonably reliable, but the other constants probably indicate only orders of magnitude. Also, in addition to the data cited, activation energies have been reported for many of the steps. In general, $E_p = 5$–8 kcal and $E_{t1} \leqq 2$ kcal, but it seems doubtful if the differences between different compounds are very significant.

The values of the chain propagation constants, k_p, for hydrocarbons are notably smaller than in polymerization and halogenation chains, but k_p's for aldehydes are comparable to those noted in rapid polymerizations, consistent with the long kinetic chains through which these autoxidations proceed. Among the olefins, k_p's vary roughly as might be anticipated from C—H bond dissociation energies, 1,4-dienes being relatively reactive. The most striking anomaly is between cumene and tetralin, the easy autoxidation of cumene apparently arising from a very low value of k_{t1}, rather than from a large value of k_p. This difference again points up the difficulty in relating overall rates in radical chains and relative rates of a single step.

The problem of the nature of termination step 36 is interesting since it is difficult to picture the nature of the reaction between two peroxy radicals. The process has been written as

$$2R—O—O\cdot \rightarrow R—O—O—R + O_2 \qquad (41a)$$

but has no experimental verification, and as we shall see (Section 9·3b), there is good evidence for an alternative, non-radical-destroying interaction.

$$2R—O—O\cdot \rightarrow 2R—O\cdot + O_2 \qquad (41b)$$

Conceivably, for radicals with α-hydrogens the reaction can be instead [108] a step such as

$$2R_2CH—O—O\cdot \rightarrow R_2C{=}O + R_2CHOH + O_2 \qquad (42)$$

which is available to all of the species in Table 9·6 except the peroxy radical from cumene, thus accounting for its unique stability.

Boozer [117] has recently carried out a significant series of experiments on the nature of the termination step in cumene autoxidation. When rates of autoxidation of cumene and cumene in which 23–50% of the β-hydrogens have been replaced by deuterium are compared under identical conditions, the deutero compound autoxidizes 10–15% more rapidly, suggesting that reaction 41a is not correct, and that termination involves some process such as

$$
2\phi—\underset{\underset{\textstyle CH_3}{|}}{\overset{\overset{\textstyle CH_3}{|}}{C}}—OO\cdot \rightarrow \phi—\underset{\underset{\textstyle CH_3}{|}}{\overset{\overset{\textstyle CH_3}{|}}{C}}—OOH + \phi—\underset{\underset{\textstyle CH_3}{|}}{\overset{\overset{\textstyle CH_2}{\|}}{C}} + O_2 \qquad (43)
$$

[117] C. E. Boozer, B. W. Ponder, J. C. Trisler, and C. E. Wightman, III, *J. Am. Chem. Soc.*, **78**, 1506 (1956).

Interestingly, in the presence of the retarder 2,4-dichlorophenol, which leads to an alternate more rapid chain termination (Section 9·2g), the autoxidation of the deuterocumene is some 20–25% *slower* than that of cumene itself. This, in turn, suggests (as we would anticipate) that hyperconjugation with the methyl groups is signifi-

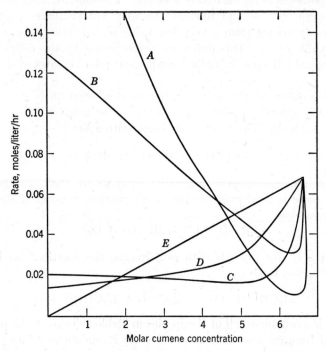

Fig. 9·3   Oxidation of mixtures of cumene and aralkyl hydrocarbons: *A*, dibenzyl ether; *B*, indan; *C*, diphenylmethane; *D*, ethylbenzene, all at 90° in presence of 0.02 *M* *t*-butyl perbenzoate. Curve *E* is calculated for an inert diluent. (After Russell.[101])

cant in the transition state of the step in which the peroxy radical attacks cumene.

Reactions such as 42 might also occur between secondary and tertiary peroxy radicals and lead to high termination rates in systems in which both types of species were present. Such an interpretation has been given by Russell to his observation [117a] that a small amount of tetralin notably retards the autoxidation of cumene, even though, under comparable conditions, tetralin alone autoxidizes approxi-

[117a] G. A. Russell, *ibid.*, **77**, 4583 (1955).

mately three times as rapidly as pure cumene. Comparable phenomena occur in a number of other systems; [101] see Fig. 9·3.

Russell's results are of particular importance since they indicate the kind of kinetic complications which may arise in more complex molecules which may undergo simultaneous autoxidation at more than one point.

With this background, we can now consider the autocatalytic nature of most autoxidations carried out in the absence of added initia-

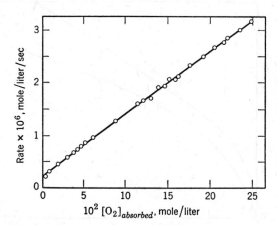

FIG. 9·4   Plot showing autocatalytic nature of autoxidation of cyclohexene at 45° and 728 mm O_2 pressure (after Bateman [65]).

tor (Fig. 9·1). Although the problem had been discussed by various workers,[118] the first successful kinetic attack on the autocatalytic nature of hydrocarbon oxidation was made by Bolland,[119] who showed that with ethyl linoleate the initial product was entirely allylic hydroperoxide, and that the autoxidation rate was a straight-line function of hydroperoxide concentration. A similar relation occurs with other olefins, cf. Fig. 9·4. From eqs. 39 and 40, since $d[O_2]/dt$ $\propto R_i^{1/2}$, this linear relation indicates initiation by bimolecular decomposition of hydroperoxide, a reaction which was suggested as

$$2ROOH \rightarrow ROO\cdot + RO\cdot + H_2O \qquad (44)$$

Although the kinetics of hydroperoxide decompositions are complex (Section 10·2d), allylic hydroperoxides do show approximately sec-

[118] See, for example, P. George, E. K. Rideal, and A. Robertson, *Proc. Roy. Soc. London,* **A185,** 288 (1946); P. George and A. Robertson, *ibid.,* 309.

[119] J. L. Bolland, *ibid.,* **A186,** 218 (1946).

ond-order decomposition rates,[120] and there is a good correlation between measured rates of oxygen uptake in several olefinic systems
and calculated rates based upon decomposition rates of the peroxides
present.[65] Thus, the increasing rate of reaction during the early
stages of autoxidation, in these cases at least, seems to be due entirely
to buildup of peroxide which, in turn, serves as initiator for new
chains. Later, of course, the rate falls off, both through exhaustion

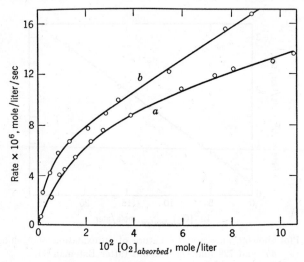

Fig. 9·5 Autocatalytic nature of autoxidation of (a) tetralin at 75°, 180 mm O_2
pressure; (b) 1-methylcyclohexene at 65°, 350 mm O_2 pressure; both at very low
extents of oxygen absorption.[65]

of substrate and because minor products of peroxide breakdown (e.g.,
alcohols and carbonyl compounds) can act as retarders of the chain
process.

   Extrapolation of Bolland's data to zero time originally indicated
a small positive intercept and raises the interesting question whether
autoxidation of hydrocarbons will begin spontaneously in the absence of any sort of initiator. Several investigators have suggested
a direct bimolecular reaction between hydrocarbon and oxygen to
produce a peroxide which subsequently initiates chains.[121] Here,
however, Bateman, Hughes, and Morris [113] have shown that the ap-

   [120] L. Bateman and Mrs. H. Hughes, *J. Chem. Soc.*, **1952**, 4594.
   [121] For a recent exposition of this viewpoint, cf. N. A. Kahn, *Can. J. Chem.*,
32, 1149 (1954); *J. Chem. Phys.*, **22**, 2090 (1954).

parent intercept arises because their hydroperoxide decompositions change from second to first order at very low concentrations. Further, the autoxidation rate of, for example, tetralin and 1-methylcyclohexene is still dependent on peroxide concentrations at levels well below 10^{-3} molar (Fig. 9·5). On the other hand, appreciable yields of cyclic, monomeric peroxides have been reported from olefins such as α-methyl styrene,[122] where there is evidence for a direct thermal initiation (Section 9·3a), conjugated dienes,[123] and also trifluorochloroethylene.[124] The *photochemical* formation of such products is discussed in Section 9·4.

The situation with aldehydes is more obscure, since, for one thing, in addition to any role of peracids, the acyl hydroxyperoxides and similar compounds formed by peracid addition to the carbonyl group may be the actual initiators of subsequent chains. Aldehyde autoxidations carried out in the dark in the absence of initiator are apparently very difficult to make reproducible. Mulcahy and Watt [125] have recently reported detecting a rather mysterious slow dark reaction which appears independent of the usual peroxide-initiated chain, but which is inhibited by β-naphthol.

9·2f Metal-Catalyzed Autoxidations

Trace amounts of salts of heavy metals, Fe, Co, Mn, Cu, etc., often have profound effects upon the rates of radical chain autoxidations, a matter of much practical importance since, on the one hand, metal impurities may lead to the rapid deterioration of autoxidizable materials and, on the other, metal salts are often added as desirable catalysts in technical autoxidations, e.g., of aldehydes to acids, or when used as "driers" to accelerate the hardening of paints.

The major path by which such salts act appears to be by reaction with the intermediate hydroperoxides to produce radicals via redox reactions which, in turn, initiate additional autoxidation chains. As a consequence, although autoxidation rates are accelerated, hydroperoxide yields are commonly reduced by the presence of metal salts.

To anticipate somewhat the material of Chapter 11, metal salt–peroxide reactions appear to involve the processes

[122] H. Hock and M. Siebert, *Chem. Ber.,* **87,** 546 (1954).

[123] A. Halpern, *J. Am. Pharm. Assoc.,* **40,** 68 (1951).

[124] R. L. Myers, *Ind. Eng. Chem.,* **45,** 1783 (1953).

[125] M. F. R. Mulcahy and I. C. Watt, *Proc. Roy. Soc. London,* **A216,** 1030 (1953).

$$M^{n+} + ROOH \rightarrow M^{(n+1)+} + RO\cdot + OH^- \qquad (45)$$

and

$$M^{(n+1)+} + ROOH \rightarrow ROO\cdot + H^+ + M^{n+} \qquad (46)$$

and thus require metal ions which can exist in two oxidation states with a suitable oxidation-reduction potential.[126] Further, with the metals usually employed, reaction 45 is much more rapid than reaction 46, so that the metal is chiefly in its more highly oxidized state and the rate of chain initiation depends upon reaction 46. Thus, for example, cobalt-containing systems show the green color of trivalent cobalt,[127] and manganese systems the brown of trivalent manganese.[67]

The kinetics of the metal-catalyzed oxidation of tetralin has been studied by Robertson, Waters, and George,[128] using iron and copper stearates and, more completely and recently, by Woodward and Mesrobian,[108] using cobalt salts. In general the catalytic effect of metal salts reaches a constant value at a low concentration, (0.02–0.5%), a phenomenon accounted for by Woodward and Mesrobian on the basis of the following reaction scheme.[108, 129] Initiation is considered to proceed via reaction of n cobalt ions with hydroperoxide

$$ROOH + nCo \xrightarrow{k_i} \text{Radicals} \qquad (47)$$

(the exact stoichiometry of reaction 47 is not critical to the argument, but presumably it involves the sequence 46, 45, producing two radicals). Subsequent oxidation follows reactions 3, 4, and 36, giving, as an overall rate expression,

$$-d[O_2]/dt = k_p(k_i/k_{t1})^{1/2}[RH][ROOH]^{1/2}[Co]^{n/2} \qquad (48)$$

As reaction proceeds, a steady-state concentration of hydroperoxide is achieved at which reactions 4 and 47 proceed at the same rate. Here

$$[ROOH] = k_p^2[RH]^2/k_ik_{t1}[Co]^n \qquad (49)$$

and

$$-d[O_2]/dt = k_p^2[RH]^2/k_{t1} \qquad (50)$$

[126] The role of metal deactivators such as ethylenediamine tetraacetic acid in such systems seems to be either to remove the metal entirely by precipitation, or else to modify the oxidation-reduction potential of the metal to the point where one of reactions 45 or 46 is suppressed.

[127] C. E. H. Bawn and J. B. Williamson, *Trans. Faraday Soc.*, **47**, 735 (1951).

[128] A. Robertson and W. A. Waters, *ibid.*, **42**, 201 (1946); P. George and A. Robertson, *ibid.*, 217.

[129] Cf. A. V. Tobolsky, D. J. Metz, and R. B. Mesrobian, *J. Am. Chem. Soc.*, **72**, 1942 (1950).

the cobalt concentration having disappeared from the rate equation.

Experimental data, chiefly on tetralin in acetic acid at 50°, agree well with these predictions. Oxidation rates become cobalt independent at about 0.002 molar and proportional to the square of the tetralin concentration. Further, the hydroperoxide concentration reaches a steady-state concentration proportional to $[RH]^2$ and $[Co]^{-2}$, indicating that $n = 2$ in reaction 47, and the whole kinetic picture is supported by measurement of the actual rates of decomposition of tetralin hydroperoxide in the presence of cobalt ion. We may note, incidently, that, at this steady state, we are no longer dealing with a chain reaction involving many repeating steps, since every decomposition of ROOH leads to the formation of only one new hydroperoxide molecule.

Finally, the usual rate expression for oxidations induced by radical sources such as benzoyl peroxide or azobisisobutyronitrile can be put in the form

$$\frac{(-d[O_2]/dt)^2}{fk_i[\text{Init.}]} = \frac{k_p{}^2[RH]^2}{k_{t1}} \tag{51}$$

where the right-hand side of eq. 51 is the same as that of eq. 50. Accordingly, from kinetic measurements on autoxidation of tetralin in the presence of initiators with known decomposition rates, $k_p{}^2[RH]^2/k_{t1}$ can be calculated and compared with eq. 50. For the initiators mentioned, values are about double those from eq. 50, indicating that f, the efficiency of chain starting, is about 0.5. On the other hand, tetralin hydroperoxide itself appears to decompose largely by paths which do not start chains.[130]

Some studies have also been made on metal-catalyzed autoxidations of aldehydes but with differing and not altogether conclusive results. With acetaldehyde the autoxidation rate is proportional to aldehyde and cobalt concentrations, but independent of $[O_2]$,[127] whereas with benzaldehyde in acetic acid the rate law is [131]

$$-d[O_2]/dt = k[RCHO]^{3/2}[Co]^{1/2} \tag{52}$$

Here, a direct initiation involving aldehyde has been suggested. As

$$Co^{+++} + RCHO \rightarrow Co^{++} + H^+ + R-\dot{C}{=}O \tag{53}$$

[130] This interpretation differs somewhat from that of Woodward and Mesrobian, who assume that reaction 46 produces single radicals, whence $f \sim 1$. Also they attribute the low efficiency of tetralin hydroperoxide to the formation of retarders in its decomposition, which may certainly contribute to the result.

[131] C. E. H. Bawn, *Discussions Faraday Soc.*, **14,** 181 (1953).

an indication of the complexity of some of these catalyst systems, a variety of solids including kieselguhr, silica, Al_2O_3, and bentonite are reported to be strong catalysts for tetralin autoxidation.[132]

9·2g   Inhibitors in Radical Chain Autoxidations

The inhibition of radical autoxidation chains is of tremendous practical importance in the preservation of all sorts of organic materials from deterioration in the presence of air. Aromatic amines and phenols are the inhibitors or autoxidants which are most commonly employed, and a large technical literature exists concerned with many kinds of systems. Our interest here, however, will be only with those papers concerning the mechanism of the inhibition. These, although few, supply some very interesting and suggestive information about radical processes.

Observations on the inhibition of autoxidation processes go back many years,[10] and Bäckström demonstrated that autoxidants act by providing an alternate reaction to the chain-propagation process[7] and are thereby oxidized.[133] However, the first investigation in the light of the present hydroperoxide chain mechanism is that of Bolland and ten Have in 1947,[134] who studied the hydroquinone inhibition of ethyl linoleate autoxidation initiated both by benzoyl peroxide and its own hydroperoxide. Since inhibition involves interruption of the hydroperoxide-forming chain, two types of interaction are possible

$$\text{R—O—O} \cdot + \text{Inhibitor} \xrightarrow{k_{in}} \text{Inactive products} \qquad (54)$$

$$\text{R} \cdot + \text{Inhibitor} \xrightarrow{k_{in'}} \text{Inactive products} \qquad (55)$$

yielding inactive products discussed further below. Reaction 54, taken as the chain-terminating step and combined with the other steps in the autoxidation (at high O_2 pressures), gives as an overall rate expression

$$-d[O_2]/dt = R_i k_p [\text{RH}]/n k_{in}[\text{Inh.}] \qquad (56)$$

where n represents the number of chains stopped by each inhibitor molecule. If R represents the inhibited rate and R_0 that under the same conditions but in the absence of inhibitor, combining eqs. 56 and 40 yields

$$R/R_0{}^2 = 2k_{t1}/n k_p k_{in}[\text{RH}][\text{Inh.}] \qquad (57)$$

[132] P. George, *Trans. Faraday Soc.*, **42**, 210 (1946).
[133] H. N. Alyea and H. L. J. Bäckström, *J. Am. Chem. Soc.*, **51**, 90 (1929).
[134] J. L. Bolland and P. ten Have, *Trans. Faraday Soc.*, **43**, 201 (1947).

A similar derivation, assuming reaction 55 as the termination process gives a parallel expression.

$$R/R_0^2 = 2k_0k_{t1}[O_2]/nk_p^2k_{in'}[\text{Inh.}][\text{RH}]^2 \qquad (58)$$

Experimentally, eq. 57 is obeyed, i.e., inhibitor efficiency is independent of oxygen pressure and inhibition occurs through reaction of peroxy radicals. This appears to be a general situation and is certainly plausible since these are the carrier radicals present in largest concentration, and since efficient autoxidants are generally quite different in structure from the inhibitors found to be effective in polymerization and similar processes involving hydrocarbon radicals (Section 4·3). However, inhibition involving the hydrocarbon rather than the peroxy radical cannot be ruled out in all cases and has apparently been detected by Waters in the 3,5,3′,5′-tetramethyl-4,4′-diphenoquinone-retarded autoxidation of benzaldehyde, both through kinetic measurements and through isolation of the dibenzoate of the corresponding hydroquinone from the reaction mixture.[134a]

Bolland and ten Have considered the inhibiting action of hydroquinone to involve the overall reaction,

$$2\text{ROO·} + \text{(hydroquinone, OH/OH)} \rightarrow 2\text{ROOH} + \text{(quinone, O/O)} \qquad (59)$$

with the initial step the abstraction of a phenolic hydrogen to yield a semiquinone radical,

$$\text{ROO·} + \text{(hydroquinone, OH/OH)} \rightarrow \text{ROOH} + \text{(semiquinone radical, O·/OH)} \qquad (60)$$

and subsequently showed that in series of hydroquinones and phenols, antioxidant efficiency (measured by the reduction in autoxidation rate at constant R_i) paralleled known oxidation-reduction potentials.[135] Recently, however, Hammond and co-workers have pub-

[134a] J. R. Dunn, W. A. Waters, and C. Wickham-Jones, *J. Chem. Soc.*, **1952**, 2427; R. F. Moore and W. A. Waters, *ibid.*, **1952**, 2432.

[135] J. L. Bolland and P. ten Have, *Discussions Faraday Soc.*, **2**, 252 (1948).

lished a very interesting series of papers which give further insight into the details (and also complexities) of antioxidant behavior.[136-139]

As a starting point,[137] the stoichiometry of reaction of a number of effective antioxidants in the autoxidation of cumene may be obtained from the length of induction periods under conditions where chains are being initiated at known rates by azobisisobutyronitrile, Table 9·7.

TABLE 9·7 CHAINS STOPPED PER MOLECULE, n, FOR VARIOUS ANTIOXIDANTS IN THE AUTOXIDATION OF CUMENE [137]

(62.5° in chlorobenzene solution)

Antioxidant	n	Antioxidant	n
Chloranil, trinitrobenzene	a	Diphenylamine	2.8
Diphenylpicrylhydrazyl	1.98	p,p^1-Dihydroxyazobenzene	2.0
2,6-Di-t-butyl-p-cresol	2.0	p-Hydroxydiphenylamine	2.1
2,5-Di-t-butylhydroquinone	0.85	2,2-Bis(4-hydroxyphenyl)-	
4-t-Butylcatechol	2.0	propane	4.1
N-Methylaniline	2.0	p-Cresol	2.2
p-Methoxydiphenylamine	3.3	o-Cresol	2.2
Diphenylpicrylhydrazine	2.6	Phenol	2.0
Tetraphenylpyrrole	1.6	N,N′-Diphenyl-p-phenyl-	
β-naphthol	2.1	enediamine	2.2

a Ineffective.

Although the majority of the substances in Table 9·7 give $n \sim 2$, it should be pointed out that most give complicated mixtures of final products and, further, that n may vary appreciably for a given antioxidant both with changes in the hydrocarbon being oxidized and with the solvent employed.[139]

Although most workers have followed Bolland and ten Have[134] in assuming that the initial attack by peroxy radicals on amine and phenol inhibitors is on the amine or phenol hydrogen, Hammond et al. come to the conclusion that this is not generally the case on the basis of several lines of evidence. First, N-deuterated N-methylaniline[136] and diphenylamine[138] (which are weak inhibitors so that the kinetics of the inhibited reaction can actually be followed) show

[136] C. E. Boozer and G. S. Hammond, *J. Am. Chem. Soc.*, **76**, 3861 (1954).

[137] C. E. Boozer, G. S. Hammond, C. E. Hamilton, and J. N. Sen, *ibid.*, **77**, 3233 (1955).

[138] C. E. Boozer, G. S. Hammond, C. E. Hamilton, and J. N. Sen, *ibid.*, 3238.

[139] C. E. Boozer, G. S. Hammond, C. E. Hamilton, and C. Peterson, *ibid.*, 3380.

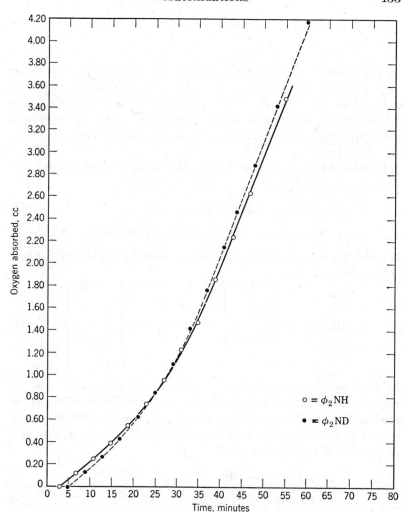

FIG. 9·6   Oxidation of tetralin in chlorobenzene inhibited with ϕ_2NH and ϕ_2ND.[138]   System contains 1×10^{-5} mole inhibitor and 6.09×10^{-4} mole azobisisobutyronitrile in 4 cc solution.

kinetics identical with those of the undeuterated materials, Fig. 9·6, with no evidence that N—H bond scission is a rate-determining step. Second,[138] cumene autoxidations in the presence of phenol and N-methylaniline follow the kinetic relation

$$-d[O_2]/dt = kR_i^{1/2}/[\text{Inh.}]^{1/2} \qquad (61)$$

rather than eq. 56, consistent only with a termination process involving an inhibitor molecule and *two* peroxy radicals. Third, on the basis of both published data and Hammond and others' own measurements,[138] a remarkably good correlation exists between Hammett σ values for substituents in classes of antioxidants and their antioxidant efficiency, Fig. 9·7, independent of steric effects which might interfere with attack on O—H or N—H bonds. As we would anticipate, antioxidant efficiency is greatly increased by electron-supplying groups, $\rho = -3.7$.

In the light of these observations, Hammond[138] suggests that the inhibition reaction involves the following step

$$\text{ROO}\cdot + \text{Inhibitor} \rightleftharpoons \text{Complex} \qquad (62)$$

$$\text{Complex} + \text{ROO}\cdot \rightarrow \text{Inactive products} \qquad (63)$$

in which the complex in reaction 62 is a loose π-complex type of species, perhaps,

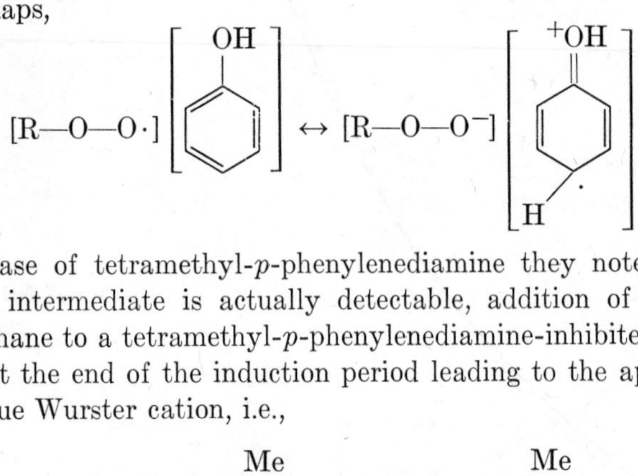

$$[\text{R—O—O}\cdot]\left[\begin{array}{c}\text{OH} \\ \bigcirc \end{array}\right] \leftrightarrow [\text{R—O—O}^-]\left[\begin{array}{c}{}^+\text{OH} \\ \bigcirc \\ \text{H} \end{array}\right] \qquad (64)$$

In the case of tetramethyl-*p*-phenylenediamine they note that an unstable intermediate is actually detectable, addition of water or nitromethane to a tetramethyl-*p*-phenylenediamine-inhibited cumene system at the end of the induction period leading to the appearance of the blue Wurster cation, i.e.,

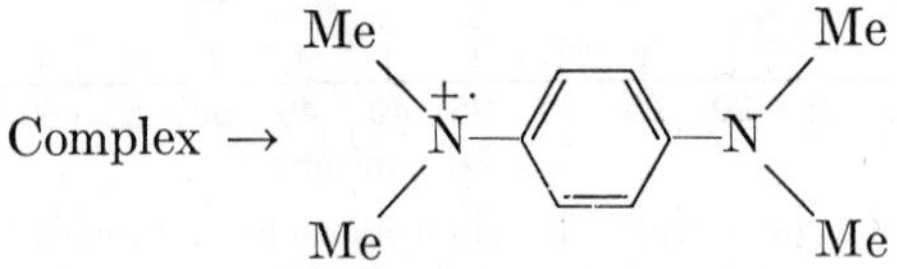

$$\text{Complex} \rightarrow \quad \begin{array}{c}\text{Me} \qquad\qquad \text{Me} \\ \diagdown\overset{+\cdot}{\text{N}}\!\!-\!\!\bigcirc\!\!-\!\!\text{N}\diagup \\ \diagup\text{Me} \qquad\qquad \diagdown\text{Me} \end{array} \qquad (65)$$

Consistent with such a scheme, a similar suggestion was made in connection with the chlorine-bromobenzene exchange (Section 7·1e) and oxygen itself apparently forms reversible complexes (detectable by ultraviolet spectra) with a variety of aromatic systems.[140] Further, such loose complexes might undergo many different types of subsequent reaction with peroxy radicals, accounting for the variety of oxidation products actually observed.

[140] D. F. Evans, *J. Chem. Soc.*, **1953**, 345.

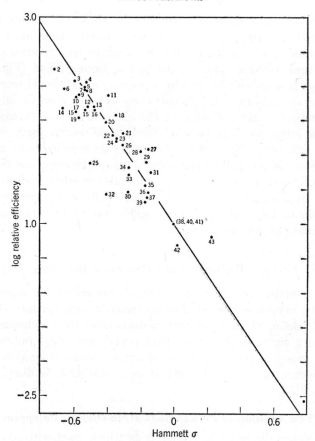

Fɪɢ. 9·7 Correlation of relative inhibitor efficiencies with the Hammett relationship.[138]

1, 1,4-naphthohydroquinone; 2, 2,3,5-trimethylhydroquinone; 3, N-[2-butyl]-4-aminophenol; 4, 3-*n*-dodecylcatechol; 5, 2,4-dimethyl-6-*t*-butylphenol; 6, 2-amino-4-phenylphenol; 7, pyrogallol; 8, 4-*t*-butylcatechol; 9, 2,6-di-*t*-butyl-4-methylphenol; 10, 2-*t*-butyl-4-methoxyphenol; 11, 2-phenylhydroquinone; 12, 2,4,6-trimethylphenol; 13, 2,4-dimethyl-6-alkylphenol; 14, 1- and 4-aminophenols; 15, 2,6-dimethoxyphenol; 16, toluohydroquinone; 17, 2,4,6-tri-*t*-butylphenol; 18, 2-*t*-butyl-4-alkylphenol; 19, 2,4-di-*t*-6-methylphenol; 20, hydroquinone; 21, 2-alkyl-4-methylphenols; 22, catechol; 23, α-naphthol; 24, 2,6- and 2,4-dimethylphenols; 25, N,N'-diphenyl-*p*-phenylenediamine; 26, 2-methyl-6-alkylphenols; 27, 2-methyl-4-alkylphenols; 28, 2-*t*-butylphenol; 29, 3-aminophenol; 30, 4-methoxydiphenylamine; 31, 2-alkylphenols; 32, 4-hydroxydiphenylamine; 33, 4-methoxyphenol; 34, 4-methoxy-N-methylaniline; 35, 2- and 4-methylphenol; 36, 4-alkylphenols; 37, β-naphthol; 38, diphenylamine; 39, 4-methyl-N-methylaniline; 40, phenol; 41, N-methylaniline; 42, resorcinol; 43, 4-bromo-N-methylaniline; 44, 4-nitro-N-methylaniline.

On the other hand, in order to give the observed kinetics, eq. 61, the equilibrium (62) must be far to the left, indicating that reaction 63 is a very rapid reaction. If it has essentially no activation energy, this in turn would account for the lack of isotope effect (Fig. 9·6). However, it is difficult to see why a peroxy radical should react with a peroxy radical-amine (or phenol) complex much more rapidly than with another peroxy radical, even though, with cumene peroxy radicals, the latter seems to be a relatively slow process for a radical-radical interaction, Table 9·6. At present there seems to be no way of judging how general are Hammond's type of kinetics, and they are apparently not observed in the hydroquinone–ethyl linoleate system.[134] It is conceivable that they occur chiefly with monofunctional antioxidants, incapable of forming stable intermediate radicals, but further data are indeed required.

9 · 3   Further Radical Chain Processes Involving Oxygen

In this section we will consider a number of radical chain processes involving oxygen or occurring simultaneously with the usual hydroperoxide chain, which either give products other than hydroperoxides or involve chain carriers other than peroxy and alkyl radicals. A further group of reactions, those of oxygen with carbanions, where the evidence of a radical chain is more doubtful, is discussed in Section 9·5d.

9·3a   The Addition of Peroxy Radicals to Olefins; Polyperoxides

The olefins discussed in Section 9·2a which react with oxygen to yield allylic hydroperoxides have double bonds which, judged from copolymerization data (Section 4·1), are relatively unreactive. With olefins which polymerize or copolymerize readily, autoxidation generally takes a different course. Here addition of peroxy radicals to the double bond takes place and chain propagation occurs largely via the sequence

$$-CH_2-\overset{\cdot}{C}HR + O_2 \rightarrow -CH_2-\overset{\overset{\displaystyle O-O\cdot}{|}}{C}HR \qquad (66)$$

$$-CH_2-\overset{\overset{\displaystyle O-O\cdot}{|}}{C}HR \ + CH_2{=}CHR \rightarrow -CH_2-\underset{\underset{\displaystyle R}{|}}{C}H-O-O-CH_2-\overset{\cdot}{C}HR$$

$$(67)$$

Autoxidations 437

i.e., the copolymerization of olefin and oxygen to yield a polyperoxide.

The olefin which has been studied in most detail is styrene, from which the polyperoxide $(C_8H_8O_2)_n$ ($n = 35$–40) was first identified by Bovey and Kolthoff,[141] who obtained it from the emulsion polymerization of styrene in the presence of air. It has also been isolated from bulk styrene and oxygen by Barnes et al.,[142] and the reaction has recently been investigated in more detail by Miller and Mayo.[143] They find[143a] that styrene at 50° saturated with oxygen at 760-mm pressure yields essentially a 1:1 copolymer, but at 5 mm the styrene/O_2 ratio increases to 1.56. From this variation with pressure (and the solubility of oxygen in styrene) they conclude that styrene radicals react with oxygen 2.5×10^5 times as rapidly as with styrene, or from k_p for styrene polymerization (Section 3·4d) k for reaction 66 is 3×10^7, a good agreement with values for other hydrocarbon-radical reactions in Table 9·5. The kinetics of the azobisisobutyronitrile-initiated reaction above 100-mm oxygen pressure follow the relation

$$-d[O_2]/dt = kR_i^{1/2}[\text{styrene}] \tag{68}$$

indicating the usual radical chain with bimolecular termination via two peroxy radicals. Since several molecules of polyperoxide (molecular weight approximately 3000) are formed for every initiating radical produced by the initiator, Miller and Mayo conclude that a chain transfer reaction (of unestablished nature) is also taking place.

At lower oxygen pressures, rates of both oxygen absorption and styrene disappearance drop, going through a minimum at about 0.5 mm pressure (cf. the inhibition of many radical processes by oxygen) and suggesting a rapid cross-termination process between styrene and peroxy radicals.

In the absence of initiator, autoxidation of styrene occurs more slowly and the process follows the kinetic expression

$$-d[O_2]/dt = k[\text{styrene}]^{1.4}[O_2]^{0.4} \tag{69a}$$

suggesting some sort of cross-initiation process involving styrene and oxygen, which, if bimolecular, should give

$$-d[O_2]/dt = k[\text{styrene}]^{3/2}[O_2]^{1/2} \tag{69b}$$

[141] F. A. Bovey and I. M. Kolthoff, *J. Am. Chem. Soc.*, **69**, 2143 (1947); the reaction had been studied by other workers, but without isolation of the polyperoxide (cf. footnote 143).

[142] C. E. Barnes, R. M. Elofson, and G. D. Jones, *ibid.*, **72**, 210 (1950).

[143] (a) A. A. Miller and F. R. Mayo, *ibid.*, **78**, 1017 (1956); (b) F. R. Mayo, private communication.

From the observed rate of oxygen uptake, at 760 mm and 50° this initiation process occurs some 38 times as rapidly as the thermal initiation process between styrene molecules observed in polymerization (Section 5·1), in spite of the low concentration of oxygen actually present.

Two interesting side reactions also occur during the autoxidation of styrene. One leads to the formation of equal quantities of benzaldehyde and formaldehyde,[144] and, since Miller and Mayo have shown that the ratio of aldehydes to polyperoxide remains constant during the course of an autoxidation (and since the polyperoxide is stable under the autoxidation conditions, being a poor initiator for either autoxidation or polymerization), these products must be formed from the growing polyperoxide chains. Further, since the ratio of polyperoxide to aldehydes decreases markedly with decreasing oxygen pressure (from 17 at 760 mm to 1 at 25 mm), the process appears to involve chains ending in styrene radicals,

$$
\underset{\phi}{-CH_2-\overset{H}{\underset{|}{C}}-O-O-CH_2-\overset{H}{\underset{|}{C}}\cdot} \rightarrow \underset{\phi}{-CH_2-\overset{H}{\underset{|}{C}}\cdot} + CH_2O + \phi CHO \tag{70a}
$$

perhaps via some sort of cyclic attack of the radical on itself. A rather small increase in aldehyde yield with temperature indicates that this process, whatever its nature, has a low activation energy in the neighborhood of 6–10 kcal.

The other side reaction produces styrene oxide, and the yield appears to go through a sharp maximum at about 1 mm oxygen pressure,[143b] an observation which certainly points up the striking changes in product composition which can accompany variations in experimental conditions in autoxidation processes. Epoxide formation as a side reaction has been detected in a number of other autoxidations (cf. the discussion of cyclohexene and of α-methylstyrene below), and appears to be particularly important in the autoxidation of olefins such as diisobutylene with the structure $R_1R_2C{=}CH_2$.[143b] A possible path for epoxide formation is the reaction (for styrene),

[144] N. A. Milas, *Proc. Natl. Acad. Sci.*, **14**, 844 (1928); S. Medvedev and P. Zeitlin, *Acta Physicochim. U.R.S.S.*, **20**, 3 (1945); H. Trenne, *Chem. Ztg.*, **74**, 692 (1950).

$$R—O—O—CH_2—\dot{C}H\phi \rightarrow R—O\cdot + \overset{\displaystyle O}{\overset{\displaystyle /\;\backslash}{CH_2—CH\phi}} \qquad (70b)$$

a process which parallels the chain decomposition of pure liquid di-t-butyl peroxide, Section 10·2b, but it is difficult to reconcile such a step with the maximum in yield observed at a particular oxygen pressure. Also, it is possible that, in some olefin autoxidations, epoxide arises from a polar reaction between hydroperoxide and olefin analogous to the well-known epoxidation by peracids.

Polyperoxides with compositions approaching 1:1 copolymers have been obtained from a number of other olefins, including 1,1-diphenylethylene,[145] dimethyl and diethylketene,[146] methyl methacrylate,[142] vinyl acetate,[142] methylacrylonitrile[147] and α-methylstyrene,[122] and indene,[148] and from conjugated polyenes, including cyclopentadiene,[149] cyclohexadiene,[149, 150] α-terpinene,[150] α-phellandrene,[150] isoprene,[150] 2,3-dimethylbutadiene,[150,151] furan,[152] and alloöcymene.[153] Polyperoxide formation is commonly attended by the same sort of carbonyl-forming side reaction as in the case of styrene, and, in other cases, including methyl acrylate,[147] acrylonitrile,[147] and chloroprene,[154] either this is the chief reaction, or the polyperoxide once formed is too unstable to isolate.

The autoxidation of indene has been studied in some detail by Russell,[148] who has shown that, as in the case of styrene, the product approaches a 1:1 copolymer but with an average chain length of less than 10. Using azobisisobutyronitrile as initiator, 40 or more molecules are produced per kinetic chain; so again chain transfer is important, perhaps via the competition

[145] H. Staudinger, *Ber.,* **58B,** 1075 (1925).

[146] H. Staudinger, *ibid.,* 1079; the corresponding products from diphenylketene and phenylmethylketene proved too unstable to isolate.

[147] K. C. Smeltz and E. Dyer, *J. Am. Chem. Soc.,* **74,** 623 (1952); S. F. Strause and E. Dyer, *ibid.,* **78,** 136 (1956).

[148] G. A. Russell, *ibid.,* **78,** 1035, 1041 (1956). This paper also reviews earlier work on this reaction.

[149] H. Hock and F. Depke, *ibid.,* **84,** 349 (1951).

[150] K. Bodendorf, *Arch. Pharm.,* **271,** 1 (1933).

[151] W. Kern and J. Stallman, *Makromol. Chem.,* **7,** 199 (1951).

[152] G. O. Schenck, *Ber.,* **77B,** 661 (1944).

[153] G. L. Dranishnikov, *Izvest. Akad. Nauk S.S.S.R., Otdel Khim Nauk,* **1953,** 470.

[154] W. Kern, H. Jockusch, and A. Wolfram, *Makromol. Chem.,* **3,** 223 (1949).

$$\text{ROO} \cdot \ + \quad \text{(71)}$$

Actually, however, infrared spectra of the polymer show a variety of functional groups in small amount; so the exact nature of the process is unknown. Reduction of the polymer yields approximately equal quantities of *cis*- and *trans*-indene glycol so that the copolymerization is apparently stereochemically non-specific.

A study of the kinetics gives results similar to those obtained with styrene, and again a bimolecular thermal initiation process is noted, and Russell estimates that the rate constant for the process is 7.6×10^{-12} atmosphere^{-1} sec^{-1}.

Mayo and Miller [155] find that the autoxidation of α-methylstyrene also qualitatively resembles that of styrene in that, at high oxygen pressures, the chief product is a 1:1 polyperoxide, whereas at 50- to 150-mm oxygen pressure about 70% acetophenone and formaldehyde are produced. At 25 mm 25% α-methylstyrene oxide appears, and a 38% yield is obtained by passing oxygen into α-methylstyrene at 170°.

Some of the other olefin reactions have also been investigated by Miller, Mayo, and Russell,[155a] who have compared overall autoxidation rates and some of the other properties of the reactions. Relative rates of oxygen uptake under fixed conditions of initiator decomposition are given in Table 9·8. If we make the considerable assumptions that initiator efficiencies and rate constants for chain termination are comparable, and kinetics correspond to those of eq. 68, these rates should be proportional to the rate of addition of peroxy radicals to the olefins. If so, the order is a plausible one for a strongly electron-accepting radical, with phenyl-conjugated olefins more re-

[155] F. R. Mayo and A. A. Miller, private communication.
[155a] A. A. Miller, F. R. Mayo, and G. A. Russell, private communication.

TABLE 9·8   AUTOXIDATION OF POLYPEROXIDE-FORMING OLEFINS [155]

(50°, 760-mm O_2 pressure in presence of 0.01 molar azobisisobutyronitrile)

Olefin	$-d[O_2]/dt$ [a]	$k_{overall} \times 10^{-4}$ [b]	Per Cent Carbonyl Products
α-Methylstyrene	0.118	158	36
Indene	0.081	97	~0
Styrene	0.060	71	5
β-Methylstyrene	0.027	37	...
1,1-Diphenylethylene	0.018	31	~2
Acrylonitrile	0.018	10	...
Allylbenzene	0.0059	7.9	~0
Methyl methacrylate	0.0063	6.7	~21
Butyl methacrylate	0.0039	6.2	...
Vinyl acetate	0.0062	5.7	...
Butyl acrylate	0.0013	1.9	...
β-Bromostyrene	<0.0001	<0.1	...

[a] Moles/liter/hour.
[b] Calculated value for O_2 uptake at 1 molar solution from reaction 67.

active than vinyl acetate and carbonyl- and nitrile-conjugated olefins showing low reactivity. This conclusion is also borne out by competitive experiments in which α-methylstyrene, styrene, and methyl methacrylate were shown to react with the methacrylate peroxy radical in the ratio 31:16:1, in good agreement with the overall rates.

Table 9·8 also includes some information on relative yields of polyperoxide and carbonyl compounds in these oxygen copolymerizations. It is noteworthy that α-methylstyrene, which gives high yields of acetophenone at 760-mm oxygen pressure, is still in a region where the autoxidation rate is O_2 dependent so that a significant concentration of alkyl radicals must be present. On the other hand, methyl methacrylate, which gives chiefly polyperoxide, autoxidizes at a constant rate down at least to 25-mm O_2 pressure. Polyperoxide analyses in the latter case, incidently, indicate that the rate constant for attack on oxygen (reaction 66) has approximately the same value as with styrene.

Comparison of the results described in this section with those given earlier indicate that the competition between addition and displacement reactions by peroxy radicals and the rates of the former are governed by much the same structural factors as in radical reactions discussed previously, and it seems likely that, even in systems giving chiefly hydroperoxides, small amounts of polyperoxides (of low molecular weight) must be formed as well. An interesting intermediate case, incidently, is supplied by certain 1,5-dienes such as squalene,[156] in which a cyclic peroxyhydroperoxide is formed via a sequence such as

$$
\xrightarrow{\text{ROO·}} \quad \xrightarrow{\text{O}_2} \quad \rightarrow
$$

$$
\xrightarrow{\text{O}_2} \quad \xrightarrow{\text{RH}} \quad (72)
$$

Here the addition reaction is facilitated by the formation of a six-membered ring, and similar reactions are probably important in the autoxidations of polyisoprenes such as rubber (cf. corresponding sulfur reactions, Section 7·3c).

9·3b   Chain Steps Yielding Other Products

When autoxidations which might be expected to give hydroperoxides are carried to high conversions or conducted at too elevated temperatures, a variety of non-peroxidic products are obtained, and we may now consider some of the processes involved. However, the

[156] J. L. Bolland and Mrs. H. Hughes, *J. Chem. Soc.*, **1949**, 492.

reader should be warned that, important as such reactions are with large molecules, such a complicated array of reaction paths are available for hydroperoxide breakdown that it is generally impossible to do more than account qualitatively for the sorts of products found.

One point of entrance into this labyrinth is via studies on t-butyl peroxide decompositions carried out by Vaughan and his colleagues at the laboratories of the Shell Development Company.[157-159]

Di-t-butyl peroxide is a moderately stable substance (it has a half-life of about 4.4 hours at 135°) which decomposes unimolecularly in the gas phase or in inert solvents by a two-step process:

$$(CH_3)_3C—O—O—C(CH_3)_3 \rightarrow 2(CH_3)_3C—O \cdot \rightarrow$$
$$2CH_3COCH_3 + 2CH_3 \cdot \quad (73)$$

If the reaction is carried out in oxygen (gas phase) at 120–160°, the products are chiefly acetone, methanol, and carbon monoxide,[157] suggested as arising via the sequence

$$CH_3 \cdot + O_2 \rightarrow CH_3OO \cdot \qquad (74)$$

$$2CH_3OO \cdot \rightarrow 2CH_3O \cdot + O_2 \qquad (75)$$

$$2CH_3O \cdot \rightarrow CH_3OH + CH_2O \qquad (76)$$

$$CH_3O \cdot + CH_2O \rightarrow CH_3OH + H\dot{C}O \qquad (77)$$

$$CH_3O \cdot + H\dot{C}O \rightarrow CH_3OH + CO \qquad (78)$$

Reaction 75 is particularly interesting and important since it appears to be required by the type of products found, and indicates an additional, non-chain-terminating reaction between peroxy radicals.

Compared with di-t-butyl peroxide, t-butyl hydroperoxide is relatively stable in the gas phase, undergoing about 10% decomposition in two minutes at 195°. However, in the presence of 5% t-butyl peroxide 27% decomposition occurs by a chain process, yielding chiefly, in addition to acetone, methanol, formaldehyde, and methane.[158] Here the further reactions suggested are

$$R \cdot + (CH_3)_3COOH \rightarrow RH + (CH_3)_3COO \cdot \qquad (79)$$
$$R = (CH_3)_3CO \cdot, \ CH_3O \cdot, \ CH_3 \cdot$$

[157] J. H. Raley, L. M. Porter, F. F. Rust, and W. E. Vaughan, *J. Am. Chem. Soc.*, **73**, 15 (1951).

[158] F. H. Seubold, Jr., F. F. Rust, and W. E. Vaughan, *ibid.*, 18.

[159] E. R. Bell, J. H. Raley, F. F. Rust, F. H. Seubold, Jr., and W. E. Vaughan, *Discussions Faraday Soc.*, **10**, 246 (1953).

$$2(CH_3)_3COO\cdot \rightarrow 2(CH_3)_3CO\cdot + O_2 \qquad (80)$$

$$(CH_3)_3COO\cdot + CH_3\cdot \rightarrow (CH_3)_2COOCH_3 \qquad (81)$$

$$(CH_3)_3COOCH_3 \rightarrow (CH_3)_3CO\cdot + CH_3O\cdot \qquad (82)$$

Again we see a non-terminating reaction between peroxy radicals and also reaction 79, radical attack upon the O—H bond of the hydroperoxide, a process confirmed by the isolation of CH_3D and CH_3OD from the decomposition of deuterated hydroperoxide, $(CH_3)_3COOD$. Reaction 81 is also established by the isolation of ethyl-t-butyl peroxide from a t-amyl peroxide-induced decomposition, this latter compound producing ethyl radicals via

$$(t\text{-}C_5H_{11}O)_2 \rightarrow 2t\text{-}C_5H_{11}O\cdot \rightarrow 2CH_3COCH_3 + 2C_2H_5\cdot \qquad (83)$$

A similar (slower) chain decomposition of t-butyl hydroperoxide is also observed in chlorobenzene solution at 140°,[159] giving t-butyl alcohol and oxygen via the plausible sequence

$$(CH_3)_3COOH \xrightarrow{\text{Slow}} (CH_3)_3CO\cdot + \cdot OH \qquad (84)$$

followed by reactions 79 and 80, which provide a repeating chain ($R = t\text{-}C_4H_9O\cdot$).

The noteworthy features of all of these observations are the reversal of the usual hydrogen abstraction step in hydroperoxide formation, reactions 75 and 80, and the several paths leading to alkoxy radicals. Vaughan, et al.,[159] have summarized these latter (Fig. 9·8) together with the known reactions which alkoxy radicals undergo (Fig. 9·9).

In addition to these sets of reactions, primary and secondary hydroperoxides should also be subject to C—H bond attack by alkyl or alkoxy radicals in reactions comparable to those of alcohols and

$$
\begin{array}{ccc}
\text{O—O—H} & & \text{O—O—H} \\
| & & | \\
-\text{C}- & + \text{R}\cdot \rightarrow & -\text{C}- & + \text{RH} \\
| & & \\
\text{H} & &
\end{array}
\qquad (85)
$$

ethers discussed in Section 10·2b.

A plausible sequence to reaction 85 in turn would be

$$
\begin{array}{ccc}
\text{O—O—H} & & \text{O} \\
| & & \parallel \\
-\text{C}- & & -\text{C}- + \cdot\text{OH} \\
\bullet & &
\end{array}
\qquad (86)
$$

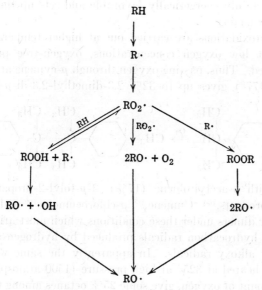

FIG. 9·8 Paths for formation of alkoxy radicals in autoxidations.[159]

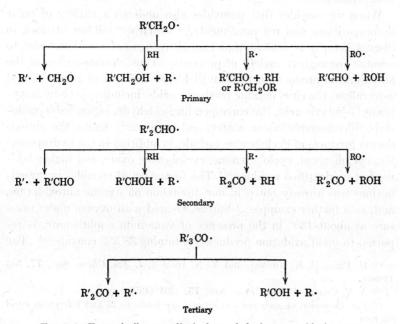

FIG. 9·9 Fate of alkoxy radicals formed during autoxidations.[159]

which is certainly energetically favorable and sets up the possibility of a further chain.

When autoxidations are carried out at higher temperatures, particularly at low oxygen concentrations, oxygen-free products are also obtained. Thus, passing oxygen through p-cymene at reflux temperature (177°) gives up to 32% 2,3-dimethyl-2,3-di-p-tolylbutane

$$(87)$$

together with p-acetyltoluene (17%), 2-p-tolyl-2-propanol (17%), and other products.[160] Cumene,[160] p-chlorocumene,[160] and p-xylene [39] give similar dimers under these conditions which must arise from the coupling of hydrocarbon radicals produced by hydrogen abstraction, perhaps by alkoxy radicals. In apparently the same way, n- and isobutanes, heated at 325° at high pressure (1500 atmospheres) with a small amount of oxygen, give some 25% octanes among their oxidation products.[161]

When we consider that peroxides also undergo a variety of polar decompositions and rearrangements,[162] which we will not attempt to discuss here, it is evident that enough recognized reactions exist to account for a great variety of products. Thus, decomposition of the autoxidation products of tetralin yields, in addition to α-tetralol and α-tetralone, the chief organic products, acids, including γ-(o-hydroxyphenyl)-butyric acid, the corresponding aldehyde, saponifiable materials, dihydronaphthalene, water, and oxygen.[163] Again, the autoxidation products of cyclohexene include, in addition to the hydroperoxide, cyclohexenol, cyclohexenone, cyclohexene oxide, and higher boiling but unidentified residues.[18] The formation of epoxides in autoxidations was already noted in our discussion of styrene autoxidation, and, as a further example, 2-butene, treated with oxygen under pressure at about 130° in the presence of vanadium naphthenate, is reported to yield oxidation products containing 38.5% epoxide.[164] The

[160] H. Pines, B. Kvetinskas, and V. N. Ipatieff, *J. Am. Chem. Soc.*, **77**, 343 (1955).

[161] A. V. Grosse, *J. Am. Chem. Soc.*, **75**, 1261 (1953).

[162] For discussion of such polar reactions, see footnote 23 and references cited therein.

[163] A. Robertson and W. A. Waters, *J. Chem. Soc.*, **1948**, 1574, 1578.

[164] A. F. Millidge and W. Webster, Brit. Pat. 708,913 (May 12, 1954).

Autoxidations 447

process by which ethylene and oxygen yield ethylene oxide at high temperatures over heterogeneous catalysts, particularly silver, may well involve a different, new radical chain mechanism.[165] Gamma-ray irradiation of aqueous ethylene-oxygen systems, incidently, yields acetaldehyde and hydrogen peroxide,[166] by what must be a radical process, but again of unknown path.

9·3c   *Autoxidation Chains Involving Halogen Atoms*

The strong oxygen inhibition of radical chain halogenations was repeatedly noted in Chapter 8. When larger quantities of oxygen are present, and the substrate is already highly halogenated, an interesting halogen-catalyzed autoxidation process may take place, with quantum yields indicating long chains. As an example, in 1932 Dickinson and Leermakers [167] reported that tetrachloroethylene and oxygen yield trichloroacetyl chloride (about 87%) plus a small amount of phosgene when illuminated with visible light in CCl_4 solution in the presence of small amounts of chlorine.

$$CCl_2{=}CCl_2 + \tfrac{1}{2}O_2 \xrightarrow[h\nu]{Cl_2} CCl_3COCl \qquad (88)$$

Similarly, pentachloroethane gives the same product and HCl,[168]

$$CCl_3CHCl_2 + \tfrac{1}{2}O_2 \xrightarrow[h\nu]{Cl_2} CCl_3COCl \quad (90\%) + HCl \qquad (89)$$

trichloroethylene gives dichloroacetyl chloride,[169]

$$CHCl{=}CCl_2 + \tfrac{1}{2}O_2 \xrightarrow[h\nu]{Cl_2} CHCl_2COCl \qquad (90)$$

and chloral is decomposed to phosgene, CO, and HCl.[170] These latter reactions have chiefly been studied in the vapor phase, although they should behave in the same manner in solution. In addition, a number of gas-phase chlorine-catalyzed autoxidations of polyhalomethanes are known, which are discussed by Steacie,[171] and yield chiefly phos-

[165] G. W. Twigg, *Proc. Roy. Soc. London,* **188A,** 92, 105, 123 (1946).

[166] E. J. Henley and J. P. Schwartz, *J. Am. Chem. Soc.,* **77,** 3167 (1955).

[167] R. A. Dickinson and J. A. Leermakers, *ibid.,* **54,** 3852 (1932).

[168] H. J. Schumacher and W. Thurauf, *Z. physik. Chem.,* **A189,** 183 (1941).

[169] K. L. Muller and H. J. Schumacher, *ibid.,* **B37,** 365 (1937).

[170] W. A. Alexander and H. J. Schumacher, *ibid.,* **B44,** 313 (1939).

[171] E. W. R. Steacie, *Atomic and Free Radical Reactions,* second edition, Reinhold Publishing Corp., New York, 1954, Chapters 10 and 11. Analogous oxidations of fluoroalkanes $C_nF_{2n+1}H$ to perfluoroacyl fluorides have been described by W. C. Francis and R. N. Haszeldine, *J. Chem. Soc.,* **1955,** 2151.

gene. Schumacher [168-170] has postulated mechanisms involving chain initiation by chlorine atoms and intermediate peroxy radicals which break down into ClO and observed products, but an alternative scheme, using only types of reactions which we have already considered, is possible. This might be, for C_2Cl_4

$$CCl_2\!=\!CCl_2 + Cl\cdot \;\rightarrow\; CCl_3\!-\!\dot{C}Cl_2 \qquad (91)$$

$$CCl_3\!-\!\dot{C}Cl_2 + O_2 \;\rightarrow\; CCl_3\!-\!\overset{\displaystyle Cl}{\underset{\displaystyle Cl}{\overset{|}{\underset{|}{C}}}}\!-\!O\!-\!O\cdot \qquad (92)$$

$$2CCl_3\!-\!\overset{\displaystyle Cl}{\underset{\displaystyle Cl}{\overset{|}{\underset{|}{C}}}}\!-\!OO\cdot \;\rightarrow\; 2CCl_3\!-\!\overset{\displaystyle Cl}{\underset{\displaystyle Cl}{\overset{|}{\underset{|}{C}}}}\!-\!O\cdot + O_2 \qquad (93)$$

$$CCl_3\!-\!\overset{\displaystyle Cl}{\underset{\displaystyle Cl}{\overset{|}{\underset{|}{C}}}}\!-\!O\cdot \;\rightarrow\; CCl_3\!-\!COCl + Cl\cdot \qquad (94)$$

where reaction 93 is again a bimolecular oxygen elimination by peroxy radicals, and 94 the analog of the known reverse of halogen atom addition to olefins.

The reaction of trichloroethylene can be formulated similarly (predicting the right product), whereas for pentachloroethane, reaction 91 would be replaced by

$$CCl_3\!-\!CHCl_2 + Cl\cdot \;\rightarrow\; CCl_3\!-\!\dot{C}Cl_2 + HCl \qquad (95)$$

Alternatively, in the case of the olefins the acid chlorides could arise from the acid-catalyzed rearrangement of intermediate epoxides, and, indeed, such epoxides have been reported from both $CHCl\!=\!CCl_2$ and $CCl_2\!=\!CCl_2$.[171a]

A second interesting group of reactions are the hydrogen bromide-sensitized autoxidations discovered by Vaughan and his co-

[171a] C. Schott and H. J. Schumacher, Z. physik. Chem., **B49**, 107 (1941); L. L. McKinney, A. H. Uhing, J. C. White, and J. C. Picken, Jr., J. Agri. and Food Chem., **3**, 413 (1955).

workers,[172-176] which, although carried out in the gas-phase, are sufficiently important for discussion. A simple and striking example is provided by isobutane.[173] Although this hydrocarbon is normally stable in oxygen to quite high temperatures, a 1:1 mixture with oxygen plus 8 mole % HBr, heated 10 minutes at 163°, gives 88% reaction and yields a mixture of products containing 70% t-butyl hydroperoxide, along with t-butyl alcohol, di-t-butyl peroxide, and traces of other materials. The major overall reaction is thus simple autoxidation, apparently occurring via the chain

$$\text{Br}\cdot + (CH_3)_3C\text{—H} \rightarrow (CH_3)_3C\cdot + \text{HBr} \qquad (96)$$

$$(CH_3)_3C\cdot + O_2 \rightarrow (CH_3)_3C\text{—O—O}\cdot \qquad (97)$$

$$(CH_3)_3C\text{—OO}\cdot + \text{HBr} \rightarrow (CH_3)_3COOH + \text{Br}\cdot \qquad (98)$$

The hydrogen bromide is regenerated and serves to lower the activation energy for hydrogen abstraction by breaking it into a two-step process (reactions 96 and 98).

When larger quantities of hydrogen bromide are employed, the yield of hydroperoxide drops and that of dialkyl peroxide and alcohol rises. The origin of these products is less evident, but the dialkyl peroxide is formed when steam, HBr, and t-butyl hydroperoxide are heated together. Isopentane and isobutyl chloride behave in the same manner as isobutane, but straight-chain hydrocarbons such as propane and n-butane give chiefly ketones (plus acid),[174] whereas ethane gives acetic acid.[175] Progressively higher temperatures are required for these reactions, and evidently the initial hydroperoxides decompose to further products. The side chains of alkyl benzenes are oxidized under these conditions, and also by oxygen and HBr in the liquid phase.[176] Toluene gives benzoic acid, and ethylbenzene acetophenone, but yields are low, and phenols are also formed, presumably by acid-catalyzed rearrangement of the initial hydroperoxides.[23]

[172] F. F. Rust and W. E. Vaughan, *Ind. Eng. Chem.*, **41**, 2595 (1949).

[173] E. R. Bell, F. H. Dickey, J. H. Raley, F. F. Rust, and W. E. Vaughan, *ibid.*, 2597; W. E. Vaughan and F. F. Rust, U.S. Pat. 2,395,522–3 (February 26, 1946).

[174] P. J. Nawrocki, J. H. Raley, F. F. Rust, and W. E. Vaughan, *ibid.*, 2604; W. E. Vaughan and F. F. Rust, U.S. Pat. 2,369,181 (February 13, 1945).

[175] E. R. Bell, G. E. Irish, J. H. Raley, F. F. Rust, and W. E. Vaughan, *ibid.*, 2609.

[176] B. Barnett, E. R. Bell, F. H. Dickey, F. F. Rust, and W. E. Vaughan, *ibid.*, 2612.

Unsaturated organic molecules also undergo HBr-sensitized autoxidations, but yield rather complex mixtures of products,[177] and, interestingly, many of the slower autoxidations are accelerated by the presence of alkyl bromides.[178]

As a final example of autoxidation in the presence of halogen acids, a number of aromatic compounds are reported to undergo oxidation to phenols in hydrogen fluoride solution at 100–150° and high oxygen pressures in the presence of silver oxide and various other carriers.[179] Presumably a reaction of quite different, but unknown, path is involved.

9·3d   Other Complex Autoxidation Chains; Formation of Sulfur and Phosphorus Compounds

Various other more complicated reactions exist involving oxygen, organic molecules (usually hydrocarbons), and additional species which appear, with differing degrees of probability, to involve radical chains.

One example, which received considerable investigation in Germany during the war and subsequently as a means of preparing synthetic surface-active agents, is the reaction of sulfur dioxide, oxygen, and

$$RH + SO_2 + \tfrac{1}{2}O_2 \rightarrow RSO_3H \tag{99}$$

saturated hydrocarbons to yield (as end products) alkyl sulfonic acids. The reaction of cyclohexane has been investigated by Graf [180] by a method which yields a good picture of the probable reaction path. When cyclohexane is irradiated with ultraviolet light in the presence of SO_2 and oxygen, a heavy oil soon separates, which is evidently the persulfonic acid, whereas, in the presence of acetic anhydride a crystalline mixed anhydride is obtained. Both the peracid and anhydride

$$\tag{100}$$

177 F. F. Rust and W. E. Vaughan, U.S. Pat. 2,369,182 (February 13, 1945); H. de V. Finch and S. A. Ballard, U.S. Pat. 2,373,240 (April 10, 1945).

178 J. H. Raley and F. F. Rust, U.S. Pat. 2,391,740 (December 25, 1945).

179 J. H. Simons and R. E. McArthur, *Ind. Eng. Chem.*, **39**, 364 (1947).

180 R. Graf, *Ann.*, **578**, 50 (1952).

are effective radical sources to induce this and other chain processes, so the reaction may have autocatalytic properties. If the autoxidation is carried out in the presence of iodine, the sulfonic acid rather than the peracid is formed, the iodine being oxidized to I_2O_5. The peracid is also rather unstable and hydrolyzes slowly in the presence of water to sulfonic acid and H_2O_2. Isolation of a peracid and the powerful oxidizing power of the reacting system strongly suggests an analogy to the autoxidation of aldehydes, and an obvious reaction chain is

$$R\cdot + SO_2 \rightarrow R\!-\!SO_2\cdot \qquad (101)$$

$$R\!-\!SO_2\cdot + O_2 \rightarrow RSO_2\!-\!OO\cdot \qquad (102)$$

$$RSO_2\!-\!OO\cdot + RH \rightarrow RSO_2OOH + R\cdot \qquad (103)$$

using steps already noted in simple autoxidations and in polysulfone formation.

Because of the potential technical utility of this "sulfoxidation" process a considerable patent literature exists on reaction conditions and initiators. As examples, azonitriles are claimed to be good initiators at 20–80°,[181] and traces of chlorine act as an initiator, either with visible light [182] or under pressure at about 45°.[183]

Another example of coöxidation of a sulfur compound and hydrocarbon has been described by Kharasch, who studied the simultaneous reaction of thiols and oxygen with olefins.[184] Styrene, shaken with n-propyl mercaptan and oxygen in heptane solution, gives an 89% yield of stereoisomeric hydroxysulfones.

$$\overset{\displaystyle OH}{\underset{\displaystyle |}{}}$$
$$\phi\!-\!CH\!=\!CH_2 + O_2 + RSH \rightarrow \phi\!-\!CH\!-\!CH_2\!-\!SO\!-\!R \quad (104)$$

1-Octene behaves similarly, and other thiols give comparable products. Although the reaction of t-butyl mercaptan is slow, it can be accelerated by adding a radical source such as the redox system cumene hydroperoxide–ferrous sulfate.

[181] W. H. Lockwood, U.S. Pat. 2,503,280 (April 11, 1950).

[182] J. Kowalsky and H. Weghofer, *Przemysl Chem.*, **9**, 138 (1953).

[183] G. T. Kennedy, Brit. Pat. 703,474 (February 3, 1954).

[184] M. S. Kharasch, W. Nudenberg, and G. J. Mantell, *J. Org. Chem.*, **16**, 524 (1951).

The scheme

$$R—S\cdot + CH_2=CH\phi \rightarrow R—S—CH_2—\dot{C}H\phi \qquad (105)$$

$$R—S—CH_2—\dot{C}H\phi + O_2 \rightarrow R—S—CH_2—\overset{\overset{\displaystyle O—O\cdot}{|}}{C}H\phi \qquad (106)$$

$$R—S—CH_2—\overset{\overset{\displaystyle O—O\cdot}{|}}{C}H\phi + RSH \rightarrow R—S—CH_2—\overset{\overset{\displaystyle OOH}{|}}{C}H\phi \qquad (107)$$

is suggested with subsequent self-oxidation-reduction of the sulfide-hydroperoxide to the observed product, or, as a possible alternative, rearrangement of the intermediate peroxy radical

$$R—S—CH_2—\overset{\overset{\displaystyle O—O\cdot}{|}}{C}H\phi \rightarrow R—SO—CH_2—\overset{\overset{\displaystyle O\cdot}{|}}{C}H\phi \qquad (108)$$

Obviously, this reaction is closely related to the autoxidation of organic sulfides studied by Bateman.[97a]

Several coöxidations are known, chiefly through the work of Soborovskii and Zinov'ev, which involve phosphorus in low oxidation states, and which may represent radical processes, but have not been elucidated in detail. Thus, oxygen passed through a mixture of cyclohexane and excess PCl_3 at 60° yields cyclohexylphosphonyl chloride plus considerable phosphorus oxychloride.[185] The reaction is not light

$$PCl_3 + \tfrac{1}{2}O_2 + RH \rightarrow R—POCl_2 + HCl \qquad (109)$$

sensitive but is inhibited by iodine,[185, 186] and a variety of other saturated hydrocarbons behave similarly, as do alkyl halides and ethers.[187] In some cases, isomer distributions have been determined,[187] propane giving 73% secondary and 27% primary phosphonyl chloride, and 2,3-dimethylbutane 92% t-phosphonyl chloride. With n-butyl chloride, the isomeric chlorophosphonyl chlorides have the distribution 1,1 (9.5%); 1,2 (20.5%); 1,3 (54%); 1,4 (16%) reminiscent of chlorination data (Section 8·3c).

Since PCl_3 does not react with saturated hydrocarbons but is read-

[185] J. O. Clayton and W. L. Jensen, *J. Am. Chem. Soc.*, **70**, 3880 (1948). A recent detailed discussion of the effect of variables on the reaction is given by A. F. Isbell and F. T. Wadsworth, *ibid.*, **78**, 6042 (1956).

[186] L. Z. Soborovskii, Y. M. Zinov'ev, and M. A. Englin, *Doklady Akad. Nauk S.S.S.R.*, **67**, 293 (1949).

[187] L. Z. Soborovskii, Y. M. Zinov'ev, and M. A. Englin, *ibid.*, **73**, 333 (1950).

ily autoxidized, Soborovskii et al.[187] propose, as an initial step in the reaction, the process

$$O_2 + PCl_3 \rightarrow \cdot O\!-\!O\!-\!\dot{P}Cl_3 \qquad (110)$$

The product may attack another PCl_3 to yield two molecules of $POCl_3$, but in the presence of hydrocarbons it can abstract hydrogen to start a chain (of so far unknown nature, although they suggest possible steps). Alkyldichlorophosphines react similarly,[188] e.g.,

$$(111)$$

With olefins, PCl_3 and oxygen give β-chloroalkyl phosphonyl chlorides [186]

$$RCH\!=\!CH_2 + PCl_3 + \tfrac{1}{2}O_2 \rightarrow RCHClCH_2POCl_2 \qquad (112)$$

and with acetylenes β-chlorovinyl phosphonyl chlorides (and with acetylene itself the diphosphonyl chloride as well) [189]

$$RC\!\equiv\!CH + PCl_3 + \tfrac{1}{2}O_2 \rightarrow RCCl\!=\!CHPOCl_2 \qquad (113)$$

Here we observe the typical "abnormal" direction of addition of the phosphorus radical, even if we are in doubt as to its structure.

Finally, Willstatter [190] has reported that white phosphorus itself reacts with cyclohexene and oxygen to give a "phosphorate" with the empirical formula $C_6H_{10}P_2O_4$ but of unestablished structure which hydrolyzes under oxidizing conditions to cyclohexene-1-phosphonic acid,

$$(114)$$

9·4   Non-Chain Photoöxidations

In addition to the chain autoxidations covered in previous sections, an intriguing group of reactions are known in which oxygen reacts

[188] L. Z. Soborovskii and Y. M. Zinov'ev, *Zhur. Obshchei Khim.*, **24**, 516 (1954).

[189] Y. M. Zinov'ev, L. I. Muler, and L. Z. Soborovskii, *ibid.*, **24**, 380 (1954).

[190] R. Willstatter and E. Sonnenfeld, *Ber.*, **47**, 2801 (1914).

photochemically to yield peroxides. Most of the examples involve cyclic dienoid systems and give transannular peroxides. The first case was discovered by Moureau, Dufraisse, and Dean, in 1926,[191] who noted that solutions of rubrene in light absorb oxygen to yield a transannular peroxide. Strikingly, the reaction is largely reversible, the

$$\text{(115)}$$

peroxide giving about 80% oxygen on heating under reduced pressure. Subsequently numbers of polynuclear hydrocarbons have been found to form similar transannular peroxides (although the reaction is frequently not reversible), one of the simplest examples being anthracene,[192] and the reaction has been reviewed by Bergmann and

$$\text{(116)}$$

McLean[193] and by Etienne.[194, 195] In general there is said to be a parallel between the ease of the photochemical oxygen addition and that of the Diels-Alder reaction, and oxygen and maleic anhydride form bridges at the same points in these polynuclear compounds.[193] There is also a pronounced variation in the rate of peroxide formation with solvent, relative rates with rubrene in CS_2, $CHCl_3$, ether, and nitrobenzene being $90:30:10:1$.

Compounds which form photoperoxides directly make up a rather limited class, so it is particularly interesting that suitable photosensi-

---

[191] C. Moureau, C. Dufraisse, and P. M. Dean, *Compt. rend.*, **182**, 1440, 1584 (1926).

[192] C. Dufraisse and M. Gerard, *ibid.*, **201**, 428 (1935); **202**, 1859 (1936).

[193] W. Bergmann and M. J. McLean, *Chem. Revs.*, **28**, 367 (1941).

[194] A. Etienne, *Traite de chimie organique*, **17**, 1299 (1944).

[195] Some anthracene derivatives give hydroperoxides with oxygen, e.g., 10-phenyl-9-anthrone yields the 10-hydroperoxide; C. Dufraisse, A. Etienne, and J. Rigaudy, *Compt. rend.*, **226**, 1773 (1948). It is conceivable that here we are observing the ordinary chain autoxidation or a case of ring-chain tautomerism.

tizers permit the reaction to be extended considerably. The first example to be noted was the eosin-sensitized autoxidation of ergosterol, observed by Windaus in his investigation of Vitamin D.[196] The reaction took some time to unravel, but it is now recognized[193] as

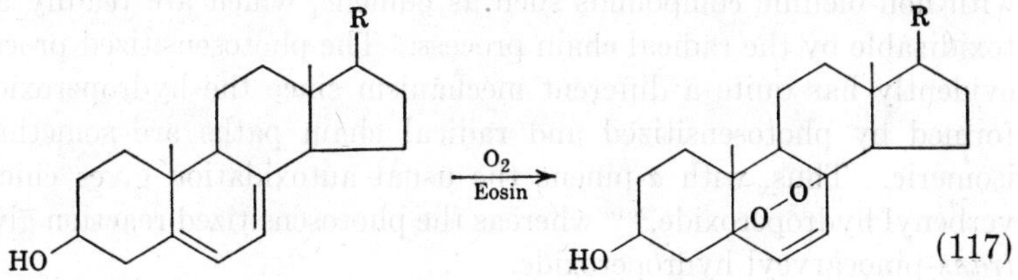

(117)

Comparable reactions are known in the sterol series involving dehydroergosterol and 2,4-cholestadiene. This sort of photosensitized process has recently been extended by Schenck to a variety of simpler molecules,[197] the first reported example being the synthesis of ascaridole from α-terpinene[198]

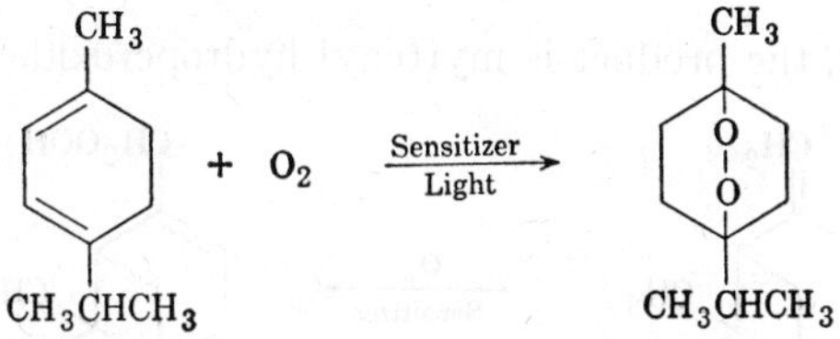

(118)

The reaction is best carried out in dilute solution, and a variety of photosensitizers including eosin, chlorophyll, and methylene blue are effective, methylene blue in isopropylalcohol giving the highest yield, 31%.[199] A number of other examples are known,[197, 199] α-phellandrene, and 1,3-cyclohexadiene giving the corresponding products I and II, whereas furanes give ozonide-like structures (III) or their rearrange-

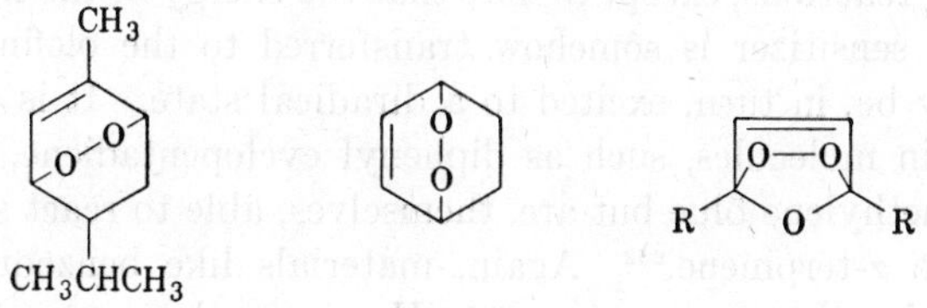

(119)

I   II   III

[196] A. Windaus and O. Linsert, *Ann.*, **465**, 157 (1928); A. Windaus, W. Bergmann, and A. Luttringhaus, *ibid.*, **472**, 195 (1929).

[197] G. O. Schenck, *Angew. Chem.*, **64**, 12 (1952). This article summarizes earlier communications.

[198] G. O. Schenck and K. Ziegler, *Naturwissenschaften*, **32**, 157 (1944).

[199] G. O. Schenck, K. G. Kinkel, and H. J. Mertens, *Ann.*, **584**, 125 (1953).

ment products.[200] Methylene blue-sensitized photoöxidations also occur in dilute alcohol solution with a whole variety of monoölefins such as cyclohexene, 1-methylcyclohexene, and various terpenes to give allylic hydroperoxides.[201] On the other hand no reaction occurs with non-olefinic compounds such as cumene, which are readily autoxidizable by the radical chain process. The photosensitized process evidently has quite a different mechanism since the hydroperoxides formed by photosensitized and radical chain paths are sometimes isomeric. Thus, with α-pinene the usual autoxidation gives chiefly verbenyl hydroperoxide,[201a] whereas the photosensitized reaction gives *trans*-pinocarveyl hydroperoxide.

$$(120)$$

With β-pinene, the product is myrtenyl hydroperoxide

$$(121)$$

Reactions 120 and 121 can obviously have no common allylic radical intermediate, and Schenck points out the analogy to maleic anhydride–olefin reactions, involving hydrogen transfer and a double bond shift.

It is difficult to say much more about the steps involved in these interesting reactions, except to note that the energy of the light picked up by the sensitizer is somehow transferred to the olefin or diene, which may be, in turn, excited to a diradical state. It is of interest that certain molecules, such as diphenyl cyclopentadiene, are sensitized by methylene blue but are, themselves, able to react slowly and to activate α-terpinene.[202] Again, materials like benzoquinone are inhibitors for the photoprocess.[203] However, these recent observa-

[200] G. O. Schenck, *ibid.*, 156.

[201] G. O. Schenck, H. Eggert, and W. Denk, *ibid.*, 177.

[201a] For further data on the chain autoxidation, cf. R. N. Moore, C. Golumbic, and G. S. Fisher, *J. Am. Chem. Soc.*, **78**, 1173 (1956).

[202] G. O. Schenck, W. Muller, and H. Pfennig, *Naturwissenschaften*, **41**, 374 (1954).

[203] G. O. Schenck and K. H. Ritter, *ibid.*, 374.

tions are reported only briefly and cannot be evaluated in much detail. Some further comments on photochemical processes appear in Section 11·1.

9·5 The Autoxidation of Organic Anions; Hydrogen Peroxide-Forming Reactions

9·5a *The Autoxidation of Hydroquinones*

Alkaline solutions of hydroquinones rapidly take up oxygen but commonly yield a complicated mixture of products. The autoxidation of durohydroquinone, examined by James and Weissberger,[204] provides the best model of the reaction, since here the products are quantitatively duroquinone and hydrogen peroxide, formed by a process which presumably represents the first steps in other hydro-

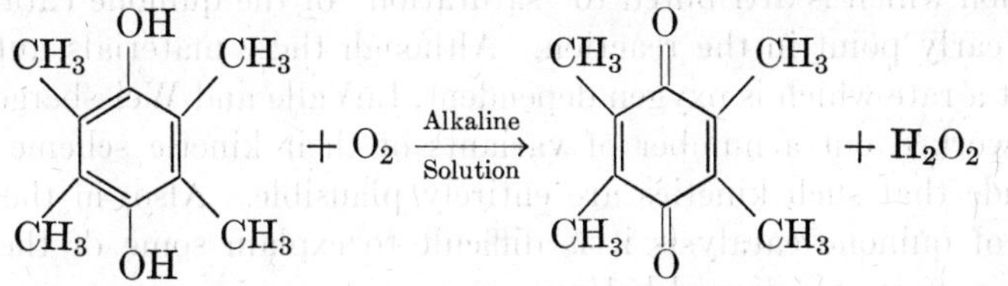

$$+ O_2 \xrightarrow[\text{Solution}]{\text{Alkaline}} \qquad + H_2O_2 \quad (122)$$

quinone autoxidations. The initial rate of reaction follows the law

$$-d[O_2]/dt = k[O_2][\text{DHQ}][\text{OH}^-]^2 \qquad (123)$$

suggesting a direct reaction between oxygen and the duroquinone dianion. However, the reaction is autocatalytic, being accelerated by duroquinone (shown by adding quinone to the initial system), and, further, the duroquinone-catalyzed process proceeds at a rate independent of oxygen pressure. All of these observations are rationalized by the following scheme:

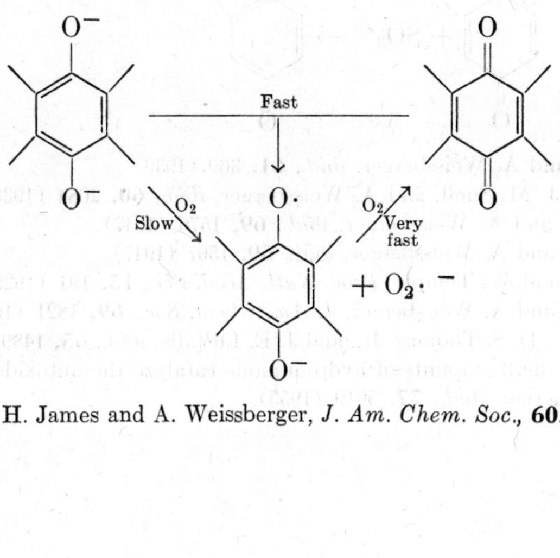

$$+ O_2 \cdot^- \quad (124)$$

$$+ O_2 \cdot^-$$

[204] T. H. James and A. Weissberger, *J. Am. Chem. Soc.*, **60**, 98 (1938).

Here, initially, oxygen and hydroquinone dianion react to yield the semiquinone radical ion (plus a peroxy radical ion). This radical anion reacts very rapidly with oxygen to yield quinone. Once quinone is formed, it reacts with more hydroquinone anion to give more semiquinone (which is rapidly oxidized further), and soon this oxygen-independent process becomes rate determining. The peroxy radicals formed in the various steps are assumed to react very rapidly with any oxidizable species in the system to give H_2O_2.

The kinetics of autoxidation of other hydroquinones are more difficult to interpret. Dilute solutions of trimethylhydroquinone behave like duroquinone, but, at higher concentrations, the kinetics become more complicated, presumably because of further reactions.[205] As methyl substitution is reduced, oxidation rates decrease and quinone acceleration of the reaction becomes harder to detect,[206, 207] a phenomenon which is attributed to "saturation" of the quinone catalysis at an early point in the reaction. Although these materials autoxidize at a rate which is oxygen dependent, LuValle and Weissberger[208] have worked out a number of variants of their kinetic scheme and conclude that such kinetics are entirely plausible. Also, in the absence of quinone catalysis it is difficult to explain some of the inhibiting effects mentioned below.

Many substances besides hydroxide ion affect the rate of hydroquinone autoxidation. A number of metal salts, including those of copper[204] and manganese[209] are catalysts, although their mechanism of action is not entirely clear.[210] On the other hand, reducing agents are generally inhibitors,[211] presumably because they reduce the quinone, which is a potential catalyst. The strong inhibition by sulfite

$$(125)$$

[205] G. Kornfeld and A. Weissberger, *ibid.*, **61**, 360 (1939).

[206] T. H. James, J. M. Snell, and A. Weissberger, *ibid.*, **60**, 2084 (1938).

[207] J. E. LuValle and A. Weissberger, *ibid.*, **69**, 1576 (1947).

[208] J. E. LuValle and A. Weissberger, *ibid.*, **69**, 1567 (1947).

[209] V. K. Lamer and W. Temple, *Proc. Natl. Acad. Sci.*, **15**, 191 (1929).

[210] J. E. LuValle and A. Weissberger, *J. Am. Chem. Soc.*, **69**, 1821 (1947).

[211] A. Weissberger, D. S. Thomas, Jr., and J. E. LuValle, *ibid.*, **65**, 1489 (1943). On the other hand, small amounts of hydroquinone catalyze the autoxidation of thiols; G. H. Meguerian, *ibid.*, **77**, 5019 (1955).

is considered to involve the Michael addition reaction as does the inhibition by thiols.[211] In both cases the potentially catalytic quinone is rapidly removed from the system.

Many quinones are unstable in the presence of air and alkali with the result that hydroquinone autoxidations commonly proceed further than the quinone stage and give a variety of products. Thus, 1,4-naphthoquinone gives 2-hydroxy-1,4-naphthoquinone in 20% yield,[212] and 4,6-di-t-butyl pyrogallol gives an intensely purple intermediate and the following stable products: [213]

$$(126)$$

Like duroquinone, anthraquinone is relatively stable, and the autoxidation of alkyl anthrahydroquinones has been developed as a technical process for the manufacture of hydrogen peroxide.[214, 215]

9·5b Semiquinones

The semiquinones involved as intermediates in hydroquinone autoxidations are such important examples of the class of stable free radicals that they deserve special mention, although, since they are discussed in detail elsewhere,[216, 217] their chemistry will not be reviewed in detail.

The existence of equilibria of the sort shown in reaction 127 is well

$$(127)$$

[211] M. Kowalski, *Ber.*, **25**, 1658 (1892).

[213] T. W. Campbell, *J. Am. Chem. Soc.*, **73**, 4190 (1951).

[214] N. A. Milas, *Encyclopedia of Chemical Technology*, Interscience Encyclopedia, Vol. 7, New York, 1951, p. 735.

[215] A. Etienne and Y. Fellion, *Compt. rend.*, **238**, 1429 (1954), note that the autoxidation in non-alkaline solution is chemiluminescent and suggest it has a different mechanism.

[216] L. Michaelis, *Chem. Revs.*, **16**, 243 (1935); *Ann. N. Y. Acad. Sci.*, **40**, 39 (1940).

[217] W. A. Waters, *The Chemistry of Free Radicals*, second edition, Oxford University Press, Oxford, 1948, pp. 73–78.

established in a number of systems and, with duroquinone-durohydro-quinone, can be demonstrated by paramagnetic susceptibility measurements, potentiometric titration, and absorption spectra, the last method [218] giving the equilibrium constant as 1.28.

With other systems the equilibrium is less favorable for the semiquinones, but it has proved possible to detect and study a variety of semiquinones, including unsubstituted semiquinone (which is not detected by other means) by paramagnetic resonance absorption spectrometry [219] (cf. Section 1·2b). The existence of semiquinones at all is undoubtedly due to the resonance stabilization possible because of their symmetric structure, and, indeed, in acid solution they are unstable, equilibria of the sort shown in reaction 128 lying immeasurably

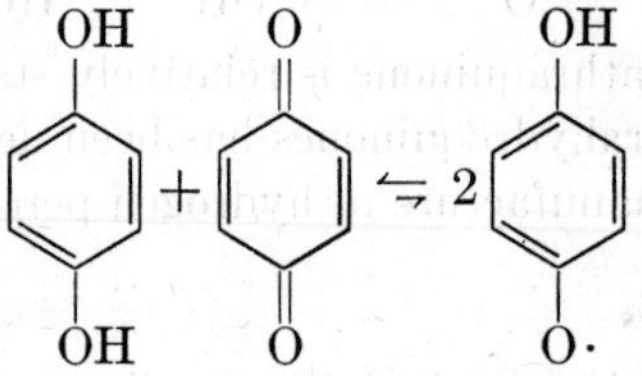

$$
\begin{array}{c}
\text{OH} \\
\bigcirc \\
\text{OH}
\end{array}
\;+\;
\begin{array}{c}
\text{O} \\
\bigcirc \\
\text{O}
\end{array}
\;\rightleftharpoons\; 2
\begin{array}{c}
\text{OH} \\
\bigcirc \\
\text{O·}
\end{array}
\tag{128}
$$

far to the left. Thus the well-known molecular complexes between quinones and hydroquinones, *quinhydrones*, are diamagnetic.

An entirely analogous series of nitrogen-containing free radicals are also known, of which the Wurster's salts

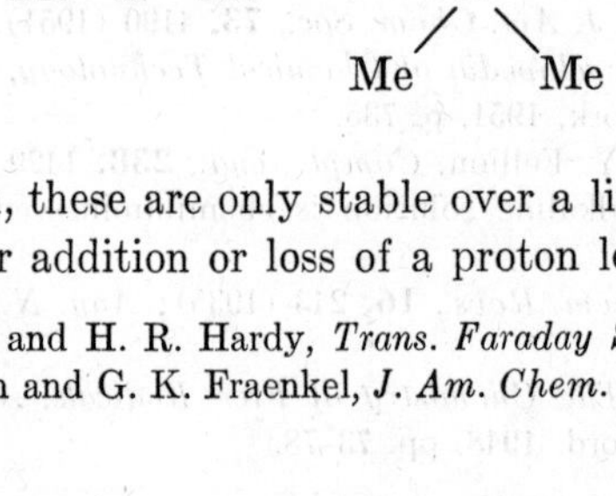

$$
\begin{array}{c}
\overset{+\,\cdot}{\text{Me—N—Me}} \\
\bigcirc \\
\text{Me—N—Me}
\end{array}
\;\leftrightarrow\;
\begin{array}{c}
\text{Me—N—Me} \\
\bigcirc \\
\underset{\text{Me}\quad\text{Me}}{\text{N}\cdot^{+}}
\end{array}
\tag{129}
$$

are typical. Again, these are only stable over a limited range of pH (3.5–6) since either addition or loss of a proton leads to an unsym-

[218] J. H. Baxendale and H. R. Hardy, *Trans. Faraday Soc.*, **49**, 1433 (1953).
[219] B. Venkataraman and G. K. Fraenkel, *J. Am. Chem. Soc.*, **77**, 2707 (1955).

metric, less stable structure. Actually, these nitrogen compounds are somewhat better known and more stable than the simple oxygen semiquinones. Many classes have been investigated, some of which are stable, crystalline materials.

Semiquinones seem to be chiefly important in the sort of reactions discussed in this section and, because of their low reactivity, probably can only rarely partake in radical chain processes.[220] However, Michaelis has suggested that they may be important in establishing the reversibility of organic oxidation-reduction systems, and they also seem to be of biochemical significance in enzyme systems.

9·5c   Other Hydrogen Peroxide-Forming Autoxidations

Several other types of systems appear to autoxidize by essentially the same path as hydroquinones. An early example is provided by benzoin. Here the overall reaction is

$$\overset{\displaystyle OH}{\underset{\displaystyle |}{\phi—CO—CH—\phi}} + O_2 \rightarrow \phi—CO—CO—\phi + H_2O_2 \qquad (130)$$

and the rate-determining step has been shown by Weissberger [221] to be the formation of the enolate anion, which then reacts rapidly with oxygen. During autoxidation, the system develops a violet color, believed to be due to the semiquinone anion, and the paramagnetic nature of the intermediate has recently been demonstrated by magnetic susceptibility measurements.[221a] Similar results are obtained with desylamine, $\phi—CO—CHNH_2\phi$, and benzoin methyl ether,[222] although the latter autoxidizes only very slowly.

The most important of these autoxidizable hydroxy ketones or enediols is probably ascorbic acid. Here the initial reaction is

[220] However, in regard to their possible importance as inhibitors in alkaline emulsion polymerization, cf. M. S. Kharasch, F. Kawahara, and W. Nudenberg, J. Org. Chem., 19, 1977 (1954).

[221] A. Weissberger, H. Mainz, and E. Strasser, Ber., 62, 1942 (1929); A. Weissberger, E. Strasser, H. Mainz, and W. Schwarze, Ann., 478, 112 (1930); A. Weissberger, W. Schwarze, and H. Mainz, ibid., 481, 68 (1930); A. Weissberger, A. Dorken, and W. Schwarze, Ber., 64, 1200 (1931); A. Weissberger and E. Dym, Ann., 502, 74 (1932).

[221a] J. L. Ihrig and R. G. Caldwell, J. Am. Chem. Soc., 78, 2097 (1956).

[222] T. H. James and A. Weissberger, ibid., 59, 2040 (1937).

$$
\begin{array}{c}
\underset{\text{HO}}{}\diagdown\underset{}{}\;\;\;\;\underset{\text{OH}}{}\diagup \\
C\!\!=\!\!C \\
O\!\!=\!\!C\;\;\;\;CHCHOHCH_2OH \\
\diagdown\;\diagup \\
O
\end{array}
\;\; + O_2 \rightarrow
$$

$$
\begin{array}{c}
O\;\;\;\;\;\;\;\;\;\;O \\
\parallel\;\;\;\;\;\;\;\;\;\;\parallel \\
C\!\!-\!\!-\!\!C \\
O\!\!=\!\!C\;\;\;\;CHCHOHCH_2OH \\
\diagdown\;\diagup \\
O
\end{array}
\;\; + H_2O_2 \;\;\; (131)
$$

Weissberger has found that oxygen reacts with both the mono- and dianion, but approximately 10^5 times as rapidly with the latter.[223] The reaction is characterized by an extraordinarily great catalysis by copper ion, and only the monoanion appears to be involved in the catalyzed reaction.[224]

The copper-catalyzed reaction has been investigated further by Nord,[225] who concludes that cupric ion is the actual oxidizing agent which reacts with the ascorbic acid anion and is in turn reoxidized by air. He has developed a detailed kinetic scheme for the reaction, which is in good accord with experiment. It is interesting that Brackman and Havinga [226] have recently described a whole series of rather similar phenol oxidations catalyzed by copper-amine systems, and a comparable oxidation of aromatic amines such as aniline occurs in the presence of copper ion and pyridine.[227]

Baxendale and Lewin [228] have investigated the extremely rapid autoxidation of leucoindophenols, finding kinetics consistent with reaction of oxygen with a monoanion, and LuValle, Glass, and Weiss-

[223] A. Weissberger, J. E. LuValle, and D. S. Thomas, Jr., *ibid.*, **65**, 1934 (1943).

[224] A. Weissberger and J. E. LuValle, *ibid.*, **66**, 700 (1944).

[225] H. Nord, *Acta Chem. Scand.*, **9**, 442 (1955).

[226] W. Brackman and E. Havinga, *Rec. trav. chim.*, **74**, 937, 1021, 1070, 1100, 1107 (1955). It is interesting that the enzymatic autoxidation of ascorbic acid also involves a copper-containing enzyme which is, in turn, enormously more effective than inorganic copper, and Brackman and Havinga point out the similarity between the action of their systems and the enzyme tyrosinase.

[227] A. P. Terentev and Y. D. Mogilyanskii, *Doklady Akad. Nauk S.S.S.R.*, **103**, 91 (1955).

[228] J. H. Baxendale and S. Lewin, *Trans. Faraday Soc.*, **12**, 126 (1946).

berger[229] find a rapid, autocatalytic autoxidation of p-phenylene-diamine and some of its derivatives suggesting again an analog of quinone catalysis. Again, hydrazobenzene autoxidizes in alkaline solution to give azobenzene and hydrogen peroxide,[230] and the re-action has been studied as a means of preparing the latter.[214]

Simple phenols in general are relatively stable towards oxygen and are only slowly converted to colored products in alkali. The course of such reactions are obscure, but we may note that some interesting examples of stable phenoxy radicals are known (although they are usually prepared by other oxidation reactions). Early supposed ex-amples are the 9-substituted-10-oxyphenanthrene radicals (I), dis-covered by Goldschmidt.[231] However, paramagnetic susceptibility measurements by Cutforth and Selwood[232] throw some doubt on Goldschmidt's conclusions since the supposed radical ($X = OC_2H_5$) exhibits paramagnetism only on irradiation.

More recently Cook and Woodworth[233] and Muller and Ley[234] have obtained an intensely blue similar radical (II), from 2,4,6-t-butylphenol which adds NO_2 and Br_2 reversibly, with oxygen, gives the peroxide (III), and is paramagnetic. A number of other 2,4,6-

I   II   III

X = —OR or —Cl   R = t—C_4H_9

(132)

[229] J. E. LuValle, D. B. Glass, and A. Weissberger, *J. Am. Chem. Soc.*, **70**, 2223 (1948).

[230] W. Manchot and J. Herzog, *Ann.*, **316**, 331 (1901).

[231] S. Goldschmidt, *Ber.*, **55**, 3199 (1922); S. Goldschmidt and C. Steigerwald, *Ann.*, **438**, 202 (1924); S. Goldschmidt, A. Vogt, and M. A. Bredig, *ibid.*, **445**, 123 (1925).

[232] H. G. Cutforth and P. W. Selwood, *J. Am. Chem. Soc.*, **70**, 278 (1948).

[233] C. D. Cook, *J. Org. Chem.*, **18**, 261 (1953); C. D. Cook and R. C. Wood-worth, *J. Am. Chem. Soc.*, **75**, 6242 (1953). Cf. also C. D. Cook, D. A. Kuhn, and P. Fianu, *ibid.*, **78**, 2002 (1956); C. D. Cook and B. E. Norcross, *ibid.*, **78**, 3797 (1956).

[234] E. Muller and K. Ley, *Z. Naturforsch*, **8b**, 694 (1953); *Chem. Ber.*, **87**, 922 (1954). E. Muller, K. Ley, and W. Kiedaisch, *ibid.*, **87**, 1605 (1954).

trisubstituted phenols containing no benzylic hydrogen give similar radicals.

9·5d   *Reactions of Some Carbanions with Oxygen*

In this section, we will conclude our discussion of autoxidation processes by taking up the rather miscellaneous reactions of carbanions with molecular oxygen, some of which rather obviously involve radical intermediates, and others of which more probably do not.

An example of the first group is provided by the autoxidation of 2-nitropropane in alkaline solution investigated by Russell.[235] The overall reaction is

$$CH_3\overset{\overset{\displaystyle NO_2}{|}}{C}HCH_3 + OH^- + \tfrac{1}{2}O_2 \rightarrow CH_3COCH_3 + NO_2^- + H_2O \quad (133)$$

in excess alkali, and, at lower pH, the symmetric coupled product, 2,3-dinitro-2,3-dimethylbutane, is also formed. The reaction rate increases with pH and is autocatalytic. Here a chain process is evidently taking place, since oxygen uptake is accelerated by small amounts of $FeCl_2$, $FeCl_3$, $CrCl_3$, and Na_2S and retarded by As_2O_3, manganese, and ceric salts.

The reaction path has not really been established but Russell suggests the chain steps

$$\underset{\underset{\displaystyle CH_3 \quad NO_2}{}}{\overset{\overset{\displaystyle CH_3}{}}{C}}\cdot \;+\; O_2 \;\rightarrow\; \underset{\underset{\displaystyle CH_3 \quad NO_2}{}}{\overset{\overset{\displaystyle CH_3 \quad O-O\cdot}{}}{C}} \qquad\qquad (134)$$

$$\underset{\underset{\displaystyle CH_3 \quad NO_2}{}}{\overset{\overset{\displaystyle CH_3 \quad O-O\cdot}{}}{C}} \;+\; \underset{\underset{\displaystyle CH_3 \quad NO_2}{}}{\overset{\overset{\displaystyle CH_3}{}}{C}}^- \;\rightarrow\; \underset{\underset{\displaystyle CH_3 \quad NO_2}{}}{\overset{\overset{\displaystyle CH_3 \quad O-O^-}{}}{C}} \;+\; \underset{\underset{\displaystyle CH_3 \quad NO_2}{}}{\overset{\overset{\displaystyle CH_3}{}}{C}}\cdot \quad (135)$$

where reaction 135 is a rapid electron-transfer process. The actual products are suggested as arising from

$$\underset{\underset{\displaystyle CH_3 \quad NO_2}{}}{\overset{\overset{\displaystyle CH_3 \quad O-O^-}{}}{C}} \;+\; \underset{\underset{\displaystyle CH_3 \quad NO_2}{}}{\overset{\overset{\displaystyle CH_3}{}}{C}}^- \;\rightarrow\; 2\; \underset{\underset{\displaystyle CH_3 \quad NO_2}{}}{\overset{\overset{\displaystyle CH_3 \quad O^-}{}}{C}}$$

$$\rightarrow 2CH_3COCH_3 + 2NO_2^- \quad (136)$$

[235] G. A. Russell, *J. Am. Chem. Soc.*, **76**, 1595 (1954).

The anion of tri-p-nitrophenylmethane also autoxidizes readily in alcoholic alkali at room temperature, although the parent compound is stable, and Hawthorne and Hammond [236] report that products are 59% hydroperoxide plus carbinol and traces of p-nitrophenol. The hydroperoxide can be pictured as arising through steps analogous to 134–135, but, since it is stable in alkali, the carbinol must be formed simultaneously or by reaction of the hydroperoxide with some other species in the system.[237]

The reaction of simpler carbanions with oxygen has been investigated by Doering and Haines,[238] using as a medium t-butyl alcohol, containing excess potassium t-butoxide. In many cases oxygen uptake is rapid, and, although peroxides are considered to be intermediates, the species isolated are non-peroxidic cleavage products, e.g.,

$$\phi CH_2CH_2CO\phi \xrightarrow{O_2} \phi CH_2COOH + \phi COOH \qquad (137)$$

Doering and Haines come to no definite conclusion as to the mechanism of the initial reaction but point out that, in addition to a radical path, reactions such as

$$\underset{\substack{|\\H}}{R-CH^--COR} + O_2 \rightarrow \underset{\substack{|\\H}}{\overset{\substack{OO^-\\|}}{R-C-COR}} \quad \text{or} \quad \underset{\substack{|\\H}}{\overset{\substack{O-O\\|\ \ |}}{R-C-C-R}} \underset{O^-}{|} \qquad (138)$$

are plausible. Subsequent cleavage is undoubtedly a polar reaction.

The reaction of Grignard reagents are for the most part carbanionic in nature even though the carbon metal bond must have considerable covalent character.[239] Their rapid reaction with oxygen to yield alcohols is well known, and in 1920 Porter and Steele [240] suggested that the reaction actually occurs in two steps, via an intermediate hydroperoxide. The correctness of this formulation has been

$$RMgX + O_2 \rightarrow R-O-OMgX \qquad (139)$$

$$ROOMgX + RMgX \rightarrow 2ROMgX \qquad (140)$$

[236] M. F. Hawthorne and G. S. Hammond, *ibid.*, **77**, 2549 (1955).

[237] Hawthorne and Hammond suggest the process $R_3C^- + R_3COOH \rightarrow R_3C \cdot$ $\rightarrow R_3CO \cdot + OH^-$, but the reaction seems unlikely without further evidence, since hydroperoxides are relatively strong acids and must be present chiefly as the anion.

[238] W. E. Doering and R. M. Haines, *J. Am. Chem. Soc.*, **76**, 482 (1954).

[239] Cf. M. S. Kharasch and O. Reinmuth, *Grignard Reactions of Nonmetallic Substances*, Prentice-Hall, New York, 1954. Some radical reactions of Grignard reagents are discussed in Section 10.

[240] C. W. Porter and C. Steele, *J. Am. Chem. Soc.*, **42**, 2650 (1920).

demonstrated by Walling and Buckler,[53] who show that hydroperoxides can be obtained in good yield (30–90%) by the inverse addition of aliphatic Grignard reagents to oxygen-saturated solvents at Dry Ice temperatures. It is tempting to formulate reaction 139 as a chain process similar to reactions 134–135, but the presence of butyraldehyde, or diphenylamine (both of which might be expected to become involved in the autoxidation chain), has no effect on hydroperoxide yields. Although this could be due to the extraordinary rapidity of a chain process involving electron transfer rather than hydrogen abstraction, in what is generally the slow step in autoxidation chains, it is as plausible at present to formulate the reactions as a non-chain process analogous to the usual addition reactions of Grignard reagents.

With aromatic Grignard reagents, phenol yields are low in the reaction as usually run, and although Walling and Buckler were able to detect small amounts (3–9%) of peroxides at −78°, they proved too unstable to isolate. Apparently the high resonance energy of phenoxy radicals, $\phi O \cdot$ (which are analogous to benzyl radicals, cf. also the stable substituted phenoxy radicals just mentioned), makes the O—O bond dissociation energy of aryl hydroperoxides so low that they undergo rapid decomposition. The variety of by-products isolated from the oxidation of aryl Grignard reagents (benzene, ethanol, diphenyl, methylphenylcarbinol, quinones, diphenyl ether, and p,p'-dihydroxydiphenyl) are essentially those to be expected from decomposition of a transiently formed peroxide into radicals which then attack both the aromatic molecules present and the ether solvent (cf. Section 10.2b).

Finally, we may note that the autoxidation of (particularly aryl) Grignard reagents is often strongly chemiluminescent, a characteristic of a number of other oxidation processes of which the most striking example is the oxidation of 3-aminophthalhydrazide (luminol). The origin of this interesting and dramatic phenomenon, however, is not understood in detail.[241]

[241] For a recent discussion, cf. T. Bremer, *Bull. Soc. chim. Belges*, **62**, 569 (1953).

CHAPTER 10

Radical Formation
by Thermal Cleavage
of Covalent Bonds

467

10 · 1   Introduction

In Section 2·1b we have rather briefly enumerated the different types of reaction by which free radicals may be produced in organic systems, and in Section 3·3a we discussed the question of initiator efficiency in polymerization reactions in terms of radical recombinations within a solvent "cage" (the Franck-Rabinowich principle). Since then, we have been concerned chiefly with radical chain processes, and here our major interest has been in the chain propagation steps which determine the products formed rather than the details of chain initiation.

In these final chapters we return to a more detailed consideration of radical-forming processes from the point of view of their mechanisms and their practical use as initiation systems for bringing about radical chain processes. We will also choose this as a convenient point to discuss a number of non-chain radical reactions and certain chain processes in which the initiators themselves are involved.

The basic requirement for the thermal formation of free radicals at ordinary temperatures (0–200°) in the liquid phase is a structure stable to competing heterolytic processes and possessing a covalent bond with a dissociation energy of 20–40 kcal. A variety of such basic structures are known, involving chiefly C—C, N—N, O—O, and S—S bonds and their combinations, and containing various substituent groups which decrease the bond dissociation energies by resonance stabilization of the resulting radicals. When these radicals are particularly stable and unreactive, they are formed reversibly (as in the dissociation of hexaarylethanes) and may be detected by the physical methods described in Chapter 1. More often radical formation is detected by the products formed in such systems, particularly by the initiation of typical radical chain processes such as polymerization, in which the observable effect of radical formation is enormously multiplied.

From the point of view of the practical use of such materials as chain initiators, the resulting radicals must be sufficiently reactive (a requirement which is usually met) and must be produced at convenient, predictable rates. In planning experiments involving radical chain processes it is desirable to select conditions so that the initiator half-life is of the same order of length as the expected reaction time, and Fig. 10·1 indicates the half-life–temperature relation for a number of convenient radical sources which dissociate at approximately the same rate in different media and are not too subject to wastage by becoming involved in subsequent radical processes. Numerous additional examples are discussed in subsequent sections.

468

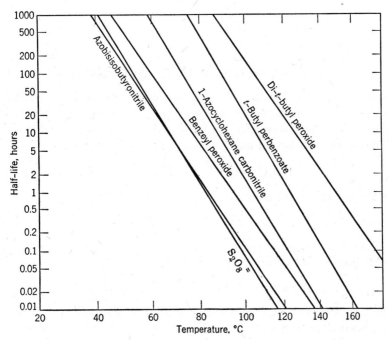

Fig. 10·1 Half-lives of some common initiators. Curves are approximate since rates may vary somewhat with solvent (see text).

10 · 2 The Thermal Decomposition of Peroxides

10·2a Dialkyl Peroxides

Of the dialkyl peroxides, di-t-butyl peroxide has been studied in the most detail. In the gas phase it decomposes by a first-order process, independent of pressure, the rate of which has been studied by a number of workers.[1-6] Results are in reasonable agreement, and Lossing and Tickner [4] have shown that data over the whole range of 116–350°C are fitted by a rate constant of $7 \times 10^{15} e^{-38,000/RT}$. The

[1] J. H. Raley, F. F. Rust, and W. E. Vaughan, *J. Am. Chem. Soc.*, **70**, 88 (1948).

[2] M. Szwarc and J. S. Roberts, *J. Chem. Phys.*, **18**, 561 (1950); **19**, 683 (1951).

[3] R. K. Brinton and D. H. Volman, *ibid.*, **20**, 25 (1952).

[4] F. Lossing and A. W. Tickner, *ibid.*, **20**, 907 (1952).

[5] M. T. Jaquiss, J. S. Roberts, and M. Szwarc, *J. Am. Chem. Soc.*, **74**, 6005 (1952).

[6] G. O. Pritchard, H. O. Pritchard, and A. F. Trotman-Dickenson, *J. Chem. Soc.*, **1954**, 1425.

decomposition occurs in solution in cumene, t-butylbenzene, and tri-n-butylamine, at essentially the same rate as in the gas phase,[7] suggesting as a rate-determining step the simple unimolecular process

$$(CH_3)_3C-O-O-C(CH_3)_3 \rightarrow 2(CH_3)_3C-O \cdot \tag{1}$$

uncomplicated by any sort of induced chain process. However, the overall course of the decomposition is somewhat more complicated, since, as we have seen (Section 9·3b), t-butoxy radicals readily decompose to acetone and methyl radicals:

$$(CH_3)_3C-O \cdot \rightarrow CH_3COCH_3 + \cdot CH_3 \tag{2}$$

In the gas phase, reaction 2 is chiefly followed by

$$2 \cdot CH_3 \rightarrow C_2H_6 \tag{3}$$

yielding ethane and acetone,[1, 8] but, in solution, attack on solvent, e.g., by hydrogen abstraction, may compete with reaction 2.

$$(CH_3)_3C-O \cdot + HR \rightarrow (CH_3)_3C-OH + R \cdot \tag{4}$$

Here the methyl radicals are also consumed by reaction with solvent (cf. Section 10·2c), and little ethane is produced. Since reaction 2 is a radical decomposition which may be expected to occur at a reasonably constant rate at a given temperature independent of medium, comparison of the t-butyl alcohol/acetone ratio in different solvents permits a measure of their reactivity toward t-butoxy radicals. With t-butyl benzene at 125°, the ratio is 0.6, with cumene 4.1, and with tri-n-butylamine approximately 19.[7] In the presence of benzaldehyde, t-butyl alcohol is essentially the sole peroxide residue isolated [9] (cf. Section 6·3c). Additional values on a variety of hydrocarbons have been reported recently,[10] indicating increasing reactivity of C—H bonds in the order primary < secondary < tertiary, with phenyl groups moderately increasing the reactivity of benzyl hydrogens. Since hydrogen abstraction here is an exothermic process,[11] the differences are not large. Since the t-butoxy radical should have electron-acceptor properties, the observed order of hydrocarbon re-

[7] J. H. Raley, F. F. Rust, and W. E. Vaughan, *J. Am. Chem. Soc.*, **70**, 1336 (1948).

[8] N. A. Milas and D. M. Surgenor, *ibid.*, **68**, 205, 643 (1946).

[9] F. F. Rust, F. H. Seubold, Jr., and W. E. Vaughan, *ibid.*, **70**, 3258 (1948).

[10] A. L. Williams, E. A. Oberright, and J. W. Brooks, *ibid.*, **78**, 1190 (1956).

[11] The value of $D(t\text{-}C_4H_7O-H)$ has been estimated as 104 kcal/mole, P. Gray, *Trans. Faraday Soc.*, **52**, 344 (1956).

activities is probably due to the electron-supplying ability of alkyl groups as well as changes in C—H bond dissociation energies. The high reactivity of tri-n-butylamine is almost certainly the result of high electron availability in that molecule.

t-Butyl alcohol is also the major product of decomposition in the presence of methyl linoleate and methyl linolenate,[12] the alkoxy radical resembling the peroxy radicals discussed in Chapter 9 in abstracting hydrogen rather than adding to the double bonds of such substrates (the esters are converted to dehydrogenated dimers, largely with conjugated double bonds, again as in the autoxidation case). On the other hand, alkoxy radicals do add to reactive olefins such as butadiene,[13, 14] and it seems plausible that this is the chief reaction when di-t-butyl peroxide is used as an initiator in polymerizable systems.

In general, values of the t-butyl alcohol/acetone ratio in a given system decrease with temperature, indicating a considerable activation energy for the t-butoxy radical decomposition (reaction 2), higher than that for hydrogen abstraction. A recent estimate of its value is 11.2 ± 2 kcal,[13] although earlier work had suggested larger values as high as 16–18 kcal.[3, 7]

In pure liquid di-t-butyl peroxide, where the peroxide provides its own solvent, there is evidence for appreciable induced decomposition.[15] At 110° the decomposition rate is about five times faster than in other solvents, and the major products are (moles per mole of radicals): t-butyl alcohol 0.25, acetone 0.33, methane 0.31, and isobutylene oxide 0.35. This last product suggests, as chain steps, the reactions

$$R \cdot + (CH_3)_3COOC(CH_3)_3 \rightarrow RH + \cdot CH_2C(CH_3)_2OOC(CH_3)_3 \quad (5)$$

$$R = \cdot CH_3 \text{ or } C_4H_9O \cdot$$

$$\cdot CH_2C(CH_3)_2OOC(CH_3)_3 \rightarrow \overset{O}{\underset{CH_2 \diagup \diagdown C(CH_3)_2}{}} + (CH_3)_3CO \cdot \quad (6)$$

Similar products are obtained in the photochemical decomposition at 17°, except that the isobutylene oxide is largely polymerized and the yield of acetone and methane greatly reduced. Reaction 6 must be a

[12] S. A. Harrison and D. H. Wheeler, *J. Am. Chem. Soc.*, **76**, 2379 (1954).

[13] D. H. Volman and W. M. Graven, *ibid.*, **75**, 3111 (1953).

[14] M. S. Kharasch, D. Schwartz, and W. Nudenberg, *J. Org. Chem.*, **18**, 337 (1953).

[15] E. R. Bell, F. F. Rust, and W. E. Vaughan, *J. Am. Chem. Soc.*, **72**, 337 (1950).

rather slow process, since di-t-butyl peroxide can be chlorinated [16] or converted to the sulfonyl chloride derivative with SO_2—Cl_2 [17] with little decomposition.

Much scantier data are available on other dialkyl peroxides. Di-t-amyl peroxide decomposes 2–3 times as rapidly as di-t-butyl peroxide at 140–150° in the gas phase, but the kinetics are not as strictly first order.[1] The rate constant for the decomposition of dimethyl peroxide has been reported [18] as $4.1 \times 10^{15}e^{-36,900/RT}$ and for diethyl peroxide [19] as $2.1 \times 10^{13}e^{-31,700/RT}$.

The lower dissociation energies for primary dialkyl peroxides are plausible if the resulting alkoxy radicals derive some stabilization from hyperconjugation, but the value for diethyl peroxide is so low that the possibility that the measured process is one involving some induced decomposition must be considered, cf. Section 9·3b and the discussion of benzoyl peroxide below.

In the absence of a reactive solvent, the major products from di-t-amyl peroxide are acetone and derivatives of ethyl radicals, indicating that the more stable ethyl (rather than methyl) radical is split off in the decomposition, i.e.,

$$C_2H_5—C(CH_3)_2O \cdot \; \rightarrow \; \cdot CH_2CH_3 + CH_3COCH_3 \qquad (7)$$

An interesting comparison of the relative stability of alkoxy radicals towards decomposition has been made by Rust, Seubold, and Vaughan [20] by decomposing mixed t-butyl alkyl peroxides in the presence of cyclohexene as a hydrogen donor in the vapor phase at 195° and determining the relative yields of alcohol and other products. Their results give an order of stability methoxy > ethoxy > n-butoxy > isopropoxy > isobutoxy, t-butoxy, but this is only qualitative and assumes, to be significant, that all alkoxy radicals have similar reactivities towards cyclohexene.

Other examples of dialkyl peroxides are known which appear to decompose by free radical paths since they are effective in initiating radical processes. "Cumyl peroxide," di-α,α-dimethylbenzyl peroxide, has been described by Kharasch [21] as a solid, melting point 39°,

[16] W. E. Vaughan and F. F. Rust, U.S. Pat. 2,501,966–7 (March 28, 1950).

[17] F. F. Rust, A. R. Stiles, and W. E. Vaughan, U.S. Pat. 2,536,008 (December 26, 1950).

[18] Y. Takezaki and C. Takeuchi, *J. Chem. Phys.*, **22**, 1527 (1954).

[19] R. E. Rebbert and K. J. Laidler, *ibid.*, **20**, 574 (1952).

[20] F. F. Rust, F. H. Seubold, Jr., and W. E. Vaughan, *J. Am. Chem. Soc.*, **72**, 338 (1950).

[21] M. S. Kharasch, A. Fono, and W. Nudenberg, *J. Org. Chem.*, **15**, 748 (1950).

which cleaves into radicals slowly at above 100°. The resulting alkoxy radical appears to decompose into acetophenone and methyl, although most of the evidence has been obtained from decompositions of the corresponding hydroperoxide.[22] With triarylmethyl peroxides, O—O bond scission also occurs, but the intermediate radicals undergo rearrangement rather than scission, usually followed by dimerization,[23] i.e.,

$$\phi_3C\!-\!OO\!-\!C\phi_3 \rightarrow 2\phi_3C\!-\!O\cdot \longrightarrow 2\phi_2\dot{C}\!-\!O\phi \rightarrow \underset{\phi}{\overset{\phi\quad O\phi\quad\phi}{\underset{/}{\overset{\backslash\ |}{C}}\!-\!-\!-\!\underset{|}{\overset{|}{C}}\!-\!\phi}} \qquad (8)$$

since the rearranged radical is relatively unreactive.

p-Nitrophenyl has been shown by Bartlett and Cotman [24] to migrate in preference to phenyl in such systems in contrast to the situation in non-sterically-controlled rearrangements involving carbonium ions or other electron-deficient species. Kharasch [25] et al. have investigated the similar rearrangement in triarylmethyl t-butyl peroxides, finding that p-biphenyl and α-naphthyl groups migrate some six times as readily as phenyl and p-tolyl. No analogous migration of alkyl groups has been observed (cf. the similar situation with carbon radicals, Section 6·3b), and the non-occurrence of a similar hydrogen migration in the decomposition of α-phenylethyl t-butyl peroxide has been shown by Kornblum and Teitelbaum [26] by decomposing the optically active peroxide in the presence of thiophenol and isolating active α-phenylethanol, i.e.,

$$\underset{H}{\overset{CH_3}{\phi\!-\!\underset{|}{\overset{|}{C}}\!-\!O\cdot}} \ -\|\!\rightarrow\ \overset{CH_3}{\phi\!-\!\underset{|}{\overset{|}{C}}\!-\!OH} \qquad (9)$$

Since good synthetic methods are now available for the synthesis of a wide variety of dialkyl peroxides, much additional information on their radical reactions may be anticipated in the future.[27]

[22] M. S. Kharasch, A. Fono, and W. Nudenberg, *ibid.*, **16**, 113 (1951).

[23] H. Wieland, *Ber.*, **44**, 2553 (1911).

[24] P. D. Bartlett and J. D. Cotman, Jr., *J. Am. Chem. Soc.*, **72**, 3095 (1950).

[25] M. S. Kharasch, A. C. Poshkus, A. Fono, and W. Nudenberg, *J. Org. Chem.*, **16**, 1458 (1951).

[26] N. Kornblum and C. Teitelbaum, *J. Am. Chem. Soc.*, **74**, 3079 (1952).

[27] In contrast to the alkyl peroxides, diaryl peroxides, in general, appear to have O—O bond dissociation energies too low to exist as stable entities. The

At least some transannular peroxides appear to decompose into radicals. Ascaridole explodes on heating to 130° but has occasionally been used as a radical source, and anthracene 9,10-endoperoxide initiates the polymerization of styrene.[28] A puzzling feature of such processes is that the initial product should be a diradical and, as such, should be a rather inefficient initiator, particularly of polymerization (Section 5·1), but little is known about the reactions involved. Ascaridole, for example, on heating in an inert solvent, is reported to yield an epoxyether[29] by what may well be a non-radical process.

$$\text{(10)}$$

Finally, the polyperoxides discussed in Section 9·3a decompose on heating. They are polymerization initiators, and the irreproducible and sometimes violent polymerization of many monomers which have been exposed to air is presumably due to their presence.[30] The decomposition of styrene polyperoxide has been recently studied in some detail by Mayo and Miller,[31] who conclude that at least two sorts of chain process are involved, one yielding benzaldehyde and formaldehyde, and the other α-hydroxyacetophenone, phenylglycol, and phenylglyoxal as primary products.

10·2b Benzoyl and Related Peroxides; Reactions of Phenyl Radicals

The decomposition of benzoyl peroxide provides a classic case of thermal dissociation of an organic molecule in solution into reactive free radicals and has received exhaustive study in the past thirty years. The nature of the products formed in various media was first investigated in detail by Gelissen and co-workers in the 1920's, and the formulation of the reactions as free radical processes by Hey and Waters in 1937[32] provides an important part of one of the crucial

existence of examples of moderately stable substituted phenoxy *radicals* was noted in Section 9·5c.

[28] J. W. Breitenbach and A. Kastell, *Monatsh.*, **85**, 676 (1954).

[29] H. Thoms and W. Dobke, *Arch. Pharm.*, **128**, 268 (1930).

[30] Cf. for example, I. Waltcher, *J. Polymer Sci.*, **14**, 411 (1954).

[31] F. R. Mayo and A. A. Miller, *J. Am. Chem. Soc.*, **78**, 1023 (1956).

[32] D. H. Hey and W. A. Waters, *Chem. Revs.*, **21**, 202 (1937). This paper gives many references to earlier work in addition to those cited below.

papers in the chemistry of free radicals in solution. In spite of this importance of benzoyl peroxide, the complexity of its decomposition makes it not altogether an ideal initiator for mechanism studies, and many of the details of its reactions are still being elucidated.

Kinetically, the decomposition of benzoyl peroxide in most systems follows a first-order law, but rate constants generally increase with concentration, suggesting a combination of first- and higher-order processes. These last arise from an induced decomposition, discussed further below, but even when they are eliminated, either by kinetic analysis [33, 34] or by the use of radical "traps" which inhibit the induced process,[35-38] the rate varies somewhat with solvent, although the activation energy remains within experimental error of 30 kcal/mole. Under increasing high pressure, the decomposition rate first decreases and then rises sharply. The fast reaction is higher than first order and apparently represents an induced decomposition (see below).[39]

The products obtained from benzoyl peroxide decompositions are those which would be expected from the reaction of both benzoyloxy and phenyl radicals,[40] and it now seems clear that the reaction is a two-step process:

$$\phi - \overset{\overset{O}{\|}}{C} - O - O - \overset{\overset{O}{\|}}{C}\phi \rightarrow 2\phi - \overset{\overset{O}{\|}}{C} - O \cdot \tag{11}$$

$$\phi - \overset{\overset{O}{\|}}{C}\diagdown_{O \cdot} \rightarrow \phi \cdot + CO_2 \tag{12}$$

The cleanest demonstration of the initial scission into benzoyloxy radicals comes from a study by Hammond and Soffer [37] of the de-

[33] K. Nozaki and P. D. Bartlett, J. Am. Chem. Soc., 68, 1686 (1946).

[34] B. Barnett and W. E. Vaughan, J. Phys. Colloid Chem., 51, 926 (1947).

[35] C. G. Swain, W. H. Stockmayer, and J. T. Clarke, J. Am. Chem. Soc., 72, 5426 (1950).

[36] G. S. Hammond, ibid., 72, 3737 (1950).

[37] G. S. Hammond and L. M. Soffer, ibid., 72, 4711 (1950).

[38] C. E. H. Bawn and S. F. Mellish, Trans. Faraday Soc., 47, 1216 (1951).

[39] C. Walling and J. Pellon, unpublished work. In allyl acetate at 80° the decomposition rate is decreased 40% at 3000 atmospheres. In acetophenone it goes through a minimum (80% of the rate at atmospheric pressure) at about 1500 atmospheres.

[40] Decomposition in the absence of solvent gives CO_2, biphenyl, and small amounts of phenyl benzoate and benzene; H. Erlenmeyer and W. Schoenaur, Helv. Chim. Acta, 19, 338 (1936).

composition in moist CCl_4 solution in the presence of iodine. The iodine suppresses any induced decomposition but is without other effect on the decomposition rate, and the benzoyl peroxide appears quantitatively as benzoic acid via the plausible sequence

$$\phi-\overset{\displaystyle O}{\underset{\displaystyle O\cdot}{C}} + I_2 \rightarrow \phi-\overset{\displaystyle O}{C}-OI + I\cdot \qquad (13)$$

$$\phi-\overset{\displaystyle O}{C}-OI + H_2O \xrightarrow{\text{Hydrolysis}} \phi-\overset{\displaystyle O}{\underset{\displaystyle OH}{C}} \qquad (14)$$

In the absence of water, the intermediate benzoyl hypoiodite decomposes chiefly to iodobenzene (90%), whereas with iodine in aromatic solvents, benzene and chlorobenzene, a variety of products are obtained, suggested as arising from subsequent polar reaction of the hypoiodite.[41]

As in the case of di-t-butyl peroxide, the amount of breakdown of the intermediate benzoyloxy radical depends upon the relative rates of reaction 12 and attack on other substrates in the reaction system,[42] iodine being a particularly effective radical trap. In the presence of polymerizable monomers, most of either benzoyl peroxide or substituted benzoyl peroxides turns up as benzoate esters groups in the polymer,[42-44] although some CO_2 is evolved, the amount increasing with temperature.[42] The amount of CO_2 increases, in general, for various solvents in the order olefins < paraffins < aromatics < CCl_4, but, before discussing these reactions further, it is necessary to say something about the induced decompositions of benzoyl peroxide

[41] Similarly, in cyclohexene, benzoyl peroxide and iodine give a mixture of cyclohexene dibenzoate and iodobenzoate; A. Perret and A. Perrot, *ibid.,* **28,** 558 (1945).

[42] P. D. Bartlett and S. G. Cohen, *J. Am. Chem. Soc.,* **65,** 543 (1943). Since, in general, yields of CO_2 increase with temperature, the activation energy for reaction 12 must be higher than for most attacks of benzoyloxy radicals on solvent, although the situation is complicated by the induced decompositions discussed below, cf. P. F. Hartman, H. G. Sellers, and D. Turnbull, *J. Am. Chem. Soc.,* **69,** 2416 (1946).

[43] M. M. Koton, T. M. Kiseleva, and M. I. Bessonor, *Doklady Akad. Nauk S.S.S.R.,* **96,** 85 (1954).

[44] M. Takebayashi, T. Shingaki, and Y. Ito, *Bull. Chem. Soc. Japan,* **26,** 475 (1953).

which must play an important role in determining product composi-tions in the concentrated solutions in which product studies are usually carried out.[44a]

The importance of induced chain decompositions of benzoyl per-oxide was deduced by Nozaki and Bartlett [33] and by Cass [45] from the observations that the apparent unimolecular rate constant for decom-position increases with peroxide concentration, and that the rate is increased by added radical sources and decreased by oxygen and typical inhibitors such as quinones and polynitroaromatics. In gen-eral terms, such processes can be written as

$$P \rightarrow 2P\cdot \tag{15}$$

$$P\cdot + P \rightarrow P\cdot \tag{16}$$

$$P\cdot + S \rightarrow S\cdot \tag{17}$$

$$S\cdot + P \rightarrow P\cdot \tag{18}$$

$$2P\cdot \rightarrow X \tag{19}$$

$$P\cdot + S\cdot \rightarrow Y \tag{20}$$

$$2S\cdot \rightarrow Z \tag{21}$$

where P represents peroxide and $P\cdot$ and $S\cdot$ unspecified radicals de-rived from peroxide and solvent. Depending upon the steps chosen, such a scheme can lead to a variety of kinetics. A chain involving only peroxide, reactions 15, 16, and 19, introduces a $\frac{3}{2}$ order term in the kinetics, whereas chains involving solvent, reactions 15, 17, and 18, give $\frac{1}{2}$-, first-, or $\frac{3}{2}$-order kinetics depending upon whether termination is by reaction 19, 20, or 21. A chain involving only peroxide, but occasionally interrupted by reaction 17 to give inert radicals, which terminate the chain (i.e., analogous to degradative chain transfer), gives second-order kinetics.

On the basis of a first-order decomposition plus a $\frac{3}{2}$-order induced reaction, Nozaki and Bartlett [33] have calculated relative contributions from initial (k_d) and induced (k_i) decompositions in a number of

---

[44a] An elegant technique for determining the importance of reaction 12 at high dilution (which should eliminate most of the complications due to induced decomposition) by employing benzoyl peroxide labeled with C^{14} in the car-boxyl group and counting the evolved CO_2 has been described by C. A. Barson and J. C. Bevington, *J. Polymer Sci.*, **20**, 133 (1956). In benzene 90% of the possible CO_2 is evolved, but the amount decreases in the presence of styrene, cumene, or diphenylpicrylhydrazyl.

[45] W. E. Cass, *J. Am. Chem. Soc.*, **68**, 1976 (1946).

TABLE 10·1   THERMAL AND INDUCED DECOMPOSITIONS OF BENZOYL PEROXIDE
AT 80° [33]

Solvent	$k_d \times 10^5$ (sec^{-1})	$k_i \times 10^5$ (liters/mole)$^{1/2}$ sec^{-1}
Carbon tetrachloride	2.08	3.70
Benzene	3.28	4.28
Toluene	3.28	4.28
Nitrobenzene	3.28	4.28
t-Butylbenzene	3.28	15.3
Cyclohexene	1.93	4.64
Ethyl iodide	4.03	6.78
Cyclohexane	6.36	32.5
Ethyl acetate	8.98	36.7
Acetic acid	8.14	51.1
Acetic anhydride	7.50	30.6

solvents, Table 10·1. With most of the systems the induced reactions are only a few per cent of the total decomposition rates at 0.01 M peroxide concentration at 80°, but in acetic anhydride it accounts for about 30% of the total reaction. At higher concentrations, of course, the amount of induced reaction rises markedly. Since the induced reaction usually has a lower activation energy than the thermal cleavage, it is also more important at lower temperatures.

Before leaving the results listed in Table 10·1, it should be pointed out that the analysis used in separating k_d and k_i permits considerable experimental uncertainty, and there is appreciable variation in different workers' estimates of k_d even in the same solvent. Thus, Russell [46] has recently obtained values of k_d in aromatic solvents significantly lower than those reported above.

In several classes of solvent a much more rapid induced decomposition occurs. Thus, in ethyl ether the decomposition of benzoyl peroxide is unimolecular, but its half-life is slightly less than five minutes at 80°, and just under fifteen minutes in isopropyl and n-butyl ethers, compared with 4–6 hours in unreactive solvents.[47] The decomposition in ethers is slowed by oxygen, many typical inhibitors, and polymerizable monomers.[35, 45, 47] The products of the reaction in ethyl ether at 37° have been determined by Cass [48] as (in moles/mole peroxide decomposed): benzoic acid, 0.8; 1-ethoxyethylbenzoate, 0.85–0.95; and CO_2, 0.20–0.25. They suggest, as the major chain, the sequence

[46] G. A. Russell, *J. Am. Chem. Soc.*, **78**, 1044 (1956).
[47] P. D. Bartlett and K. Nozaki, *ibid.*, **69**, 2299 (1947).
[48] W. E. Cass, *ibid.*, **69**, 500 (1947).

$$\phi-C\!\!\begin{array}{c}O\\\diagup\diagup\\\diagdown\\O\cdot\end{array} + CH_3CH_2-OR \rightarrow \phi COOH + CH_3\dot{C}HOR \qquad (22)$$

$$CH_3\dot{C}HOR + \phi COO-OCO\phi \rightarrow CH_3CH(OR)OCO\phi + \phi C\!\!\begin{array}{c}O\\\diagup\diagup\\\diagdown\\O\cdot\end{array} \qquad (23)$$

Similar products were found in dioxane and 1,2-diethoxyethane. Since inhibitors and polymerizable olefins reduce the decomposition rate to essentially that in inert solvents, there is no rapid initiating process between ethers and peroxide and chains can be quite long (~ 50 from Bartlett and Nozaki's data). The first-order kinetics of chain decomposition indicates chain termination between peroxide and ether radicals, reaction 20. Reaction 23 can be formulated either as a radical displacement on oxygen ($R\cdot = CH_2\dot{C}HOC_2H_5$) or addition to

$$R\cdot \rightarrow O\!\!\begin{array}{c}CO\phi\\\diagup\\\diagdown\\OCO\phi\end{array} \rightarrow R-O-CO\phi + \phi COO\cdot \qquad (24)$$

the carbonyl group, followed by decomposition of the intermediate radical. Since the analogous chain process is not observed with di-

$$R\cdot + \phi-CO-O-O-CO-\phi \rightarrow$$

$$[\phi-\overset{\displaystyle OR}{\underset{\displaystyle |}{C}}-OOCO\phi] + \phi-\overset{\displaystyle O}{\underset{\displaystyle ||}{C}}-OR + \phi COO\cdot \qquad (25)$$

alkyl peroxides, reaction 25 is perhaps more plausible.

The origin of the driving force for the sequence 22–23 is interesting. Since copolymerization data, Section 4·1, indicates little resonance stabilization of α-alkoxyalkyl radicals, a polar factor is suggested lowering the activation energy for reaction between the acceptor-type benzoate radical and the potentially electron-donating ether. We have already remarked a similar effect in the radical addition of ethers to negatively substituted olefins, Section 6·4.

A rapid induced decomposition also occurs in primary and secondary alcohols, the half-life of benzoyl peroxide at 80° being only 2–3 minutes in ethyl and isopropyl alcohols, and the decomposition is oxygen inhibited.[47] The analogous sequence would be

$$\phi C\!\!\!\overset{O}{\underset{O\cdot}{\diagdown}}\!\!\!\diagup + R_2CHOH \rightarrow \phi COOH + R_2\dot{C}\!\!-\!\!OH \qquad (26)$$

$$R_2\dot{C}\!\!-\!\!OH + \phi COO\!\!-\!\!OCO\phi \rightarrow R_2C(OH)OCO\phi + \phi\!\!-\!\!C\!\!\!\overset{O}{\underset{O\cdot}{\diagdown}}\!\!\!\diagup \qquad (27)$$

followed by

$$R_2C(OH)OCO\phi \rightarrow R_2C\!\!=\!\!O + \phi COOH \qquad (28)$$

Actually considerable decarboxylation also occurs, so phenyl radicals may also be important chain carriers. Thus, in isobutyl alcohol, aldehyde and benzoic acid are produced, but also 0.7 moles of CO_2 plus other minor products.[49] Radical attack on the C—H rather than O—H bond is indicated by bond dissociation energies and data on radical additions of alcohols to olefins, Section 6·4, and also by the observation that, in t-butyl alcohol, the decomposition rate is about that in cyclohexane.[47]

In the presence of polymerizable olefins, a moderate amount of induced decomposition may occur and has already been discussed in connection with chain transfer processes, Section 4·2b. A rather rapid induced decomposition occurs in the presence of maleic anhydride,[33] and a still faster reaction in maleic anhydride–allyl acetate mixtures.[50] The nature of the induced process is not known with certainty, but the rather complex products obtained with the somewhat analogous diethyl maleate contain both peroxide and olefin residues.[51] The rapid reaction which occurs in the presence of vinyl ethers has already been discussed in Section 6·4.

Two other types of rapid reaction of benzoyl peroxide with solvents are known, one the reaction with amines, discussed further in Section 11·5a, and the other that with phenols. The latter was noted in 1944[52] and the kinetics investigated briefly by Bartlett and Nozaki,[46] who inferred a chain process similar to that shown for the ether and alcohol reactions. The products of these phenol reactions were studied by Cosgrove and Waters[53] and interpreted essentially as the products of various radical coupling processes. However, the reaction has re-

[49] H. Gelissen and P. H. Hermans, *Ber.*, **58B**, 765 (1925).

[50] P. D. Bartlett and K. Nozaki, *J. Am. Chem. Soc.*, **68**, 1495 (1946).

[51] C. S. Marvell, E. J. Prill, and D. F. DeTar, *ibid.*, **69**, 52 (1947).

[52] C. Walling, *ibid.*, **66**, 1602 (1944).

[53] S. L. Cosgrove and W. A. Waters, *J. Chem. Soc.*, **1949**, 3189; **1951**, 388.

cently been investigated by Walling, Hodgdon, and Helmreich,[54] who conclude that the processes are certainly not radical chain reactions, and probably have as an initial step a bimolecular polar process. In fact there seems to be no convincing evidence for free radical production in the reaction at all.[55]

With this background, we can now return to a consideration of the products found in benzoyl peroxide decomposition in some of the solvents which have been investigated, recognizing that they generally arise from combinations of non-chain and chain processes, and that, commonly, the latter may not be clean but may proceed by several paths. In the subsequent discussion, when yields are given, they are in mole %/mole of peroxide decomposed and were generally obtained by heating rather concentrated peroxide solutions to complete decomposition.

In cyclohexane, a typical paraffin,[56-58] the products are largely CO_2 (96%), benzene (50%), benzoic acid (35%), and smaller quantities of cyclohexylbenzene (10%) and phenyl benzoate (3%), all of which could arise by radical coupling, or chain processes involving attack on the peroxy group.

$$\phi - C \overset{\displaystyle O}{\underset{\displaystyle O\cdot}{\big\langle}} \; + \; RH \rightarrow \phi COOH + R\cdot \tag{29}$$

$$\phi\cdot + RH \rightarrow \phi H + R\cdot \tag{30}$$

$$R\cdot + \phi COO\cdot \rightarrow \phi COOR \tag{31}$$

$$R\cdot + \phi\cdot \rightarrow R{-}\phi \tag{32}$$

$$\phi\cdot + \phi COO\cdot \rightarrow \phi COO\phi \tag{33}$$

$$\phi\cdot + Bz_2O_2 \rightarrow \phi COO\phi + \phi COO\cdot \tag{34}$$

$$R\cdot + Bz_2O_2 \rightarrow \phi COOR + \phi COO\cdot \tag{35}$$

[54] C. Walling, R. B. Hodgdon, Jr., and W. Helmreich, *Am. Chem. Soc. Meeting Abstracts,* **128,** 21-O (1955); R. B. Hodgdon, Jr., Thesis, Columbia University, 1957.

[55] Other rapid polar reactions of benzoyl peroxide are also known, including its reaction with iodide and Friedel-Crafts-type reactions in the presence of $AlCl_3$. A rapid decomposition of unknown path in the presence of activated carbon has also been described; J. W. Breitenbach and H. Preussler, *Oesterr. Chem. Ztg.,* **51,** 66 (1950).

[56] H. Gelissen and P. H. Hermans, *Ber.,* **69,** 662 (1926).

[57] P. H. Hermans and J. VanEyk, *J. Polymer Sci.,* **1,** 407 (1946).

[58] J. Boeseken and H. Gelissen, *Rec. trav. chim.,* **43,** 869 (1924).

In addition, however, at least 18% mixed o- and p-cyclohexylbenzoic acids are also found, together with other polycyclic acids, indicating either that some of the induced chain process involves attack on the benzene ring, or that benzoyl peroxide undergoes substitution by the various radical species present (in the same manner as the other aromatic species discussed below) prior to its decomposition.

Decompositions in cyclohexene,[58, 59] a more reactive substrate with labile allylic C—H bonds, gives less CO_2 (30%) and only traces of benzene. The chief product is surprisingly phenyl benzoate (70%), and formation of p-cyclohexenylphenyl benzoate plus polycyclic compounds again indicates ring attack. Similarly, in chloroform and carbon tetrachloride,[58] benzene and chlorobenzene are formed, plus much CO_2, $COCl_2$ (perhaps by autoxidation of the intermediate $CCl_3 \cdot$ radicals), C_2Cl_6, and derivatives of trichloromethylbenzoic acid.

Acetic acid appears to be relatively inert towards the radicals produced by benzoyl peroxide since the major products, CO_2, benzene, benzoic acid, phenylbenzoic acids, and tars,[59-61] are those which should arise from the solvent-independent induced decomposition. However, some 16–18% mixed homophthalic and homoterephthalic acids have been found at 75°, the amounts decreasing at higher temperatures.[61]

Decompositions of benzoyl peroxide in aromatic solvents have received very extensive investigation,[62] the products in general being CO_2, benzoic acid, and (substituted) biphenyls plus smaller quantities of phenyl benzoate, substituted phenyl benzoates, polyphenyls, and considerable tar. At least three initial reactions have been suggested for the substitution processes involved:

$$R \cdot + \text{[benzene ring]} \rightarrow \text{[R-substituted ring]} + H \cdot \qquad (36)$$

$$R \cdot + \text{[benzene ring]} \rightarrow \text{[phenyl radical]} + R—H \qquad (37)$$

[59] H. Gelissen and P. H. Hermans, Ber., 58, 770 (1925).

[60] M. S. Kharasch, E. V. Jensen, and W. H. Urry, J. Org. Chem., 10, 386 (1945).

[61] M. T. Gladstone, J. Am. Chem. Soc., 76, 1581 (1954).

[62] H. Gelissen and P. H. Hermans, Ber., 58, 285, 476, 764 (1925); W. Dietrich, Helv. Chim. Acta, 8, 149 (1925); H. Wieland, S. Shapiro, and H. Metzger, Ann., 513, 93 (1934); D. H. Hey, J. Chem. Soc., 1934, 1966; and subsequent papers cited below.

$$R\cdot + \bigcirc \rightarrow \overset{R}{\underset{H}{\overset{H}{\bigcirc}}} \tag{38}$$

($R = \phi\cdot$ or $\phi COO\cdot$). Of the three, reaction 36 should be strongly endothermic and is the most unlikely. Hydrogen abstraction, reaction 37, is not appreciably endothermic but can probably be ruled out, since, when the decomposition is carried out in solvents such as chlorobenzene, only monosubstituted diphenyls are obtained, and some coupling of the resulting phenyl radicals should certainly be expected. We are thus left with the addition process, reaction 38, which parallels the reaction of halogen atoms with benzene, Section 7·1e, and also the addition of methyl radicals to aromatic nuclei considered below, Section 10·2c.[63] The energetics of such a process are unknown, but the loss of resonance energy of the benzenoid system must be compensated by the formation of a new C—C bond and by the delocalization of the π electron in the resulting allylic radical.

The subsequent path by which the products of reaction 38 are converted to stable aromatic molecules is still conjectural, but dehydrogenation by other radicals (disproportion) is plausible.

$$\overset{R}{\underset{H}{\overset{H}{\bigcirc}}} + R\cdot \rightarrow \overset{R}{\bigcirc} + RH \tag{39}$$

Since such decompositions always give rather high yields of polyphenyls and tars, it seems evident that these do not arise from successive radical attack upon stable aromatic molecules, but rather that highly reactive intermediate species are formed in the decompositions, perhaps through sequences such as

$$2 \overset{R}{\underset{H}{\overset{H}{\bigcirc}}} \rightarrow \cdots + \overset{R}{\bigcirc} + \overset{R}{\underset{H}{\overset{H}{\bigcirc}}} \tag{40}$$

followed by preferential attack by the radicals present.

[63] Cf. also the copolymerization of vinyl acetate and other olefins with aromatic molecules, Section 4·1.

The structure of the biphenyls produced in aromatic solvents has recently received careful study, chiefly by Hey and his group [64] and by Dannley,[65] with the object of determining orienting effects of substituents in reactions with phenyl radicals and (by competitive experiments) the relative sensitivity of different aromatic nuclei to phenyl radical attack. Results are summarized in Table 10·2 and

TABLE 10·2   RELATIVE REACTIVITIES, ISOMER DISTRIBUTIONS, AND PARTIAL RATE FACTORS FOR REACTIVITIES OF AROMATIC MOLECULES WITH PHENYL RADICALS DERIVED FROM BENZOYL PEROXIDE [a]

Molecule	Relative Reactivity	% Ortho		% Meta		% Para	
Benzene	1.00	...					
Fluorobenzene	1.35 [64d,e]		(2.20)		(1.25)		(1.20)
Chlorobenzene	1.44 [64c,d,e]	62.2	(2.7)	24.0	(1.03)	13.8	(1.2)
	1.4 [65b]	64	(2.7)	23	(0.97)	13	(1.1)
Bromobenzene	1.75 [64d,e]	49.2	(2.59)	33.3	(0.75)	17.5	(1.83)
	1.4 [65a,b]	48.5	(2.0)	33	(1.4)	18.5	(1.6)
Iodobenzene	1.80 [64d,e]	51.7	(2.79)	31.6	(1.70)	16.7	(1.80)
	1.7 [65a,b]	55	(2.8)	28	(1.4)	16.5	(1.7)
p-Dichlorobenzene	1.8 [64c,i]						
sym-Trichlorobenzene	4.4 [64c,i]						
Anisole [66a,b]	1.2	67	(2.4)	18	(0.65)	15	(1.1)
Benzonitrile	3.7 [65b]						
Methyl benzoate [65b]		59		15		26	
Nitrobenzene	4.0 [64e]	59.5	(7.5)	8.5	(1.1)	32	(8.0)
Methyl phenyl sulfone	1.5 [65b]	49	(2.2)	20	(0.9)	31	(2.8)
Toluene	1.9 [64i]	71	(4.1)	17	(1.0)	12	(1.4)
		65 [65d]		19 [65d]		16 [65d]	
Ethyl benzene [65d]	...	50		25		25	
Cumene [65d]	...	10		60		30	
t-Butylbenzene	0.87 [64g]	24	(0.63)	49.5	(1.28)	26.5	(1.41)
p-Di-t-butylbenzene	0.93 [64g]						
Benzotrifluoride	0.99 [66b]	20	(0.59)	40	(1.2)	40	(2.4)
Benzotrichloride [65c]	...	0		60		40	
Phenyltrimethylsilane [66b]	1.06	31	(0.99)	45	(1.4)	24	(1.4)
Biphenyl	4 [64f]	48.5	(2.9)	23	(1.4)	28.5	(3.4)
Pyridine	1.04 [64e]	58	(1.91)	26	(0.86)	16	(1.01)
	1.5 [65a,b]	58	(2.6)	28	(1.3)	14	(1.3)
Naphthalene	23.9 [64e]	(α)	(29.9)	(β)	(6.0)		

[a] Partial rate factors are indicated by figures in parentheses.

[66] (a) T. Suehiro, J. Chem. Soc. Japan, Pure Chem. Sect., **72**, 301 (1951); (b) C. S. Rondestvedt and H. S. Blanchard, J. Org. Chem., **21**, 229 (1956).

show that simple aromatic molecules do not differ greatly in reactivity, such increases as are observed resulting chiefly in the acti-

[64] (a) D. R. Augood, D. H. Hey, A. Nechvatal, T. S. Robinson, and G. H. Williams, *Research*, **4**, 386 (1951); (b) D. R. Augood, D. H. Hey, and G. H. Williams, *J. Chem. Soc.*, **1952**, 2094; (c) ibid., **1953**, 44; (d) D. R. Augood, J. I. G. Cadogan, D. H. Hey, and G. H. Williams, ibid., **1953**, 3412; (e) D. H. Hey and G. H. Williams, *Discussions Faraday Soc.*, **14**, 216 (1953); (f) J. I. G. Cadogan, D. H. Hey, and G. H. Williams, *J. Chem. Soc.*, **1954**, 794; (g) ibid., **1954**, 3352; (h) D. H. Hey, B. W. Pengilly, and G. H. Williams, ibid., **1955**, 6; (i) D. H. Hey and G. H. Williams, *J. Chem. Phys.*, **23**, 757 (1955).

[65] (a) R. L. Dannley, E. C. Gregg, Jr., R. E. Phelps, and C. B. Coleman, *J. Am. Chem. Soc.*, **76**, 445 (1954); (b) R. L. Dannley and E. C. Gregg, Jr., ibid., **76**, 2997 (1954); (c) R. L. Dannley and M. Sternfeld, ibid., **76**, 4543 (1954); (d) R. L. Dannley and B. Zaremsky, ibid., **77**, 1588 (1955).

vation of the ortho and para positions.   This is brought out particularly by the partial rate factors (relative reactivities per carbon versus the reactivity per carbon of benzene), indicated in parentheses following the isomer distributions, and correlates reasonably with the expected resonance stabilization of the radicals produced in reaction 38 through o- and p-substitution, e.g.,

$$\hspace{12cm} (41)$$

Hey [64i] also points out that good qualitative correlation exists between partial rate factors and theoretical quantities such as free valencies and localization energies obtained from quantum mechanics.

In alkylbenzenes, side-chain attack is also a possibility.   In toluene, ethylbenzene, and cumene, the ratios of side-chain substitution to diaryl formation are reported to be 0.17, 1.7, and 0.44 respectively,[65d] and side-chain attack has also been noted with p-xylene,[64a, 67] mesitylene,[64a] and benzotrichloride,[65c] but, as we would expect, none occurs with t-butylbenzene.[64g]   Admittedly, as far as being accurate measures of relative reactivities of the different positions in substituted benzenes, the data of Table 10·2 are somewhat qualitative, since the biphenyls are generally obtained in yields of under 40% and the actual yield of any one product or isomer must depend, not only upon the rate of phenyl radical attack, reaction 38, but also upon the relative rates at which the intermediate is dehydrogenated or yields complex products.   A further complication is that, as we have seen in Sections 7·1e and 9·2g, radical reactions with aromatic systems may actually go through initial loose complexes which finally yield stable products by unknown, polymolecular processes.

A further indication of the latter state of affairs comes from an investigation of the reaction in benzene solution between benzoyl peroxide and triphenylmethyl radicals from hexaphenylethane.[68]

[67] J. I. G. Cadogan, V. Gold, and D. P. N. Satchell, J. Chem. Soc., **1955,** 561.

[68] G. S. Hammond, J. T. Rudesill, and F. J. Modic, J. Am. Chem. Soc., **73,** 3929 (1951).

Here a rapid decomposition occurs, apparently via

$$\phi_3 C\cdot + Bz_2O_2 \rightarrow \phi_3C—O—CO\phi + \phi COO\cdot \tag{42}$$

$$\phi COO\cdot + \phi_3 C\cdot \rightarrow \phi_3C—O—CO\phi \tag{43}$$

accounting for 72% of the peroxide. However, in addition, 25% tetraphenylmethane and 24% benzoic acid are produced, with no detectable CO_2, biphenyl, or phenyl benzoate. To account for the tetraphenylmethane under such conditions where there is no evidence of *free* phenyl radicals, Hammond [68] suggests some sort of concerted termolecular process.

$$\phi_3 C\cdot + C_6H_6 + \phi COO\cdot \rightarrow \phi COOH + \phi_4 C \tag{44}$$

Turning to polynuclear hydrocarbons, Hey's data [64e] indicate that naphthalene is some 24 times as reactive as benzene towards phenyl radicals, the chief point of attack being the α position. Dannley and Gippin [69] find that in 1-bromo, 1-chloro, and 1-nitronaphthalene little CO_2 is evolved, and that the isolatable products are chiefly benzoic acid (91–98%) and naphthyl benzoates. With 1-chloronaphthalene, yields are 41% 4-chloro-1-naphthyl benzoate and 20% 5-chloro-1-naphthyl benzoate. With the bromo- and nitronaphthalenes yields of 1,4 and 1,5 isomers are 16 and 14% and 18 and 1% respectively, results suggesting that naphthalene is also much more reactive than benzene towards *benzoyloxy* radicals, so that these species add rather than decarboxylating. Roitt and Waters [70] have compared the reactivities of a number of more complex aromatics towards benzoate radicals by the amount of CO_2 evolved and ester formed on decomposing benzoyl peroxide in their presence, and also have determined product structures. Anthracene, 1,2-benzanthracene, 3,4-benzpyrene, and 9-methylanthracene are substituted in the 9-, 10-, 5-, and 10-positions respectively.

Benzoyl peroxide yields interesting products in the presence of metals, organometallic compounds, and some metal salts in reactions which have been studied by Russian workers. In the presence of mercury in refluxing benzene, 31.5% phenylmercuric benzoate has been obtained,[71] and finely divided tin yields $(\phi COO)_2Sn(OH)_2$ on

[69] R. L. Dannley and M. Gippin, *ibid.*, **74**, 332 (1952).

[70] I. M. Roitt and W. A. Waters, *J. Chem. Soc.*, **1952**, 2695.

[71] G. A. Razuvaev, Y. A. Ol'dekop, and L. N. Grobov, *Doklady Akad. Nauk S.S.S.R.*, **88**, 77 (1953); *Zhur. Obshchei Khim.*, **23**, 589 (1953).

subsequent treatment with NaOH.[72] In the latter case, at least, no rapid induced reaction is involved since no detectable reaction occurs in 150 hours at room temperature. Acetyl peroxide gives similar products and, with antimony, yields antimony triacetate.[72] In contrast, stannous chloride reacts appreciably with benzoyl peroxide, even at room temperature giving $(\phi COO)_2 SnCl_2$, by what must be either an induced process or a direct oxidation-reduction, and $SbCl_3$ also appears to be oxidized.[72] When benzoyl peroxide is decomposed in chlorobenzene in the presence of tetraphenyl lead, some diphenyl lead dibenzoate is produced, and, in CCl_4, a higher yield of diphenyl lead dichloride. Tetraphenyl tin behaves similarly.[73] Although the detailed paths of these reactions are unknown, they certainly suggest radical displacements on the metal atoms.

Several significant investigations have also been made of the decomposition of other diaroyl peroxides. The effect of substitution on the rate of decomposition of benzoyl peroxide was studied by Swain, Stockmayer, and Clarke,[35] carrying out the reaction in dioxane in the presence of 0.2 molar 3,4-dichlorostyrene to inhibit the induced decomposition. The data give a good Hammett $\sigma\rho$ plot (using the sum of the σ values for the substituents), Fig. 10·2, with $\rho = -0.38$. These authors make the plausible inference that the dipole interaction must contribute to lowering the activation energy for

$$\phi - C \overset{O}{\diagup} \quad \overset{O}{\diagdown} C - \phi \tag{45}$$
$$\diagdown O - O \diagup$$

benzoyl peroxide decomposition, and this dipole interaction is necessarily lowered by strongly electron withdrawing groups. Rather similar results (and a similar conclusion) have been obtained by Blomquist and Buselli,[74] working in acetophenone solution, although their data indicate a ρ value of -0.5 to -1.0. Significantly, the tendency to undergo induced decomposition in dioxane (as judged by the amount of styrene or other inhibitor required to reduce the

[72] G. A. Razuvaev, B. N. Moryganov, E. P. Dlin, and Y. A. Ol'dekop, *ibid.*, **24**, 262 (1954).

[73] Y. A. Ol'dekop and R. F. Sokolova, *ibid.*, **23**, 1159 (1953).

[74] A. T. Blomquist and A. J. Buselli, *J. Am. Chem. Soc.*, **73**, 3883 (1951).

decomposition rate to a low constant value) increases with electron-withdrawing substituents,[35] an observation in keeping with the sug-

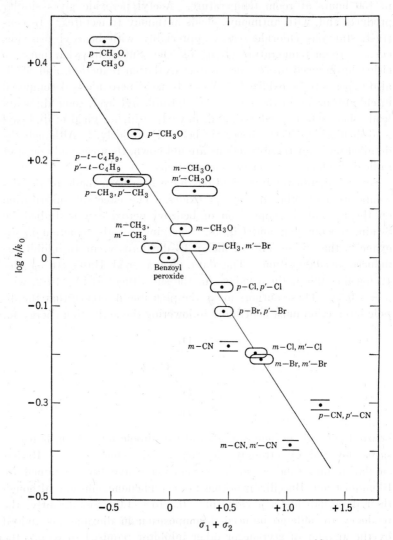

FIG. 10·2 Rates of decomposition of substituted benzoyl peroxides versus sum of Hammett σ values for substituents.[35]

gestion above that a strong polar driving force facilitates this reaction. Similarly, the transfer constants for chain transfer between a series of benzoyl peroxides and styrene increases with electron withdrawal, being over ten times as great with p-cyanobenzoyl peroxide as with benzoyl peroxide itself.[75]

The decomposition of α- and β-naphthoyl peroxides in CCl_4 yields the same types of products as does benzoyl peroxide,[76] but isomer distributions obtained in aromatic solvents from substituted benzoyl peroxides show significant differences. Dannley and Sternfeld [65c] find that in benzotrichloride, using benzoyl, p-chlorobenzoyl, and p-nitrobenzoyl peroxides, the amount of m-substitution increases from 60 to 83 to 100%, a result which they also interpret as a polar effect, the negatively substituted phenyl radicals preferentially attacking points of higher electron availability. Similarly, Cadogan, Hey, and Williams [77] find that p-chlorophenyl radicals attack nitrobenzene only 0.53 times as rapidly as they do benzene, compared with a factor of 4 for phenyl radicals, and advance a similar reason.

Several aroyl peroxides show interesting or anomalous decompositions. DeTar and Hlynsky [78] find that 2-phenoxybenzoyl peroxide yields radicals, since it initiates polymerization, but, in benzene, gives little CO_2, 8–12% o-phenoxybenzoic acid, and 25% phenyl salicylate, which they suggest as arising via the rearrangement

$$(46)$$

No methyl salicylate is formed similarly from o-methoxybenzoyl peroxide, and we have previously noted that phenyl, but not alkyl, groups are able to migrate in other radical reactions. The highly unsymmetric peroxide, 4-nitro-4'-methoxybenzoyl peroxide has been studied by Leffler, who finds the usual radical cleavage in benzene but finds an acid-catalyzed polar decomposition in polar solvents.[79]

The decomposition of the optically active peroxide from 2-(2-methyl-6-nitrophenyl)-benzoic acid has been studied by DeTar and Howard,[80] with results that show clearly the short lives of the inter-

[75] W. Cooper, *J. Chem. Soc.*, **1952**, 2408.

[76] M. S. Kharasch and R. L. Dannley, *J. Org. Chem.*, **10**, 406 (1945).

[77] J. I. G. Cadogan, D. H. Hey, and G. H. Williams, *J. Chem. Soc.*, **1955**, 1425.

[78] D. F. DeTar and A. Hlynsky, *J. Am. Chem. Soc.*, **77**, 4411 (1955).

[79] J. E. Leffler, *ibid.*, **72**, 67 (1950).

[80] D. F. DeTar and J. C. Howard, *ibid.*, **77**, 4393 (1955).

mediate substituted phenyl radicals. In benzene, CCl_4, and CCl_3Br the products retain their configuration to the extent of 25–50, 40–45,

$$Y = C_6H_5, Cl, Br$$

and 90% respectively. Thus, the intermediate radicals react with benzene and CCl_4 at comparable rates but appreciably faster (as would be anticipated) with CCl_3Br.

Recently, cyclic monomeric phthaloyl peroxide has been described [81–83] and its reactions studied. In benzene at 80° $k_d = 7 \times 10^{-5}$, about the same as benzoyl peroxide, but in CCl_4 the decomposition is only $\frac{1}{100}$ as fast.[83] The reaction in aromatic solvents is apparently an induced chain, since it is strongly oxygen inhibited.[82, 83] The major products in benzene are CO_2 (78%), o-phenylbenzoic acid (50%), and "polymeric" acids (25%), plus phthalic acid and phthalic anhydride (7%), benzoic acid (5%), and 3,4-benzocoumarin (0.5%). Since the decomposition rate in CCl_4 is notably slower than that of benzoyl peroxide, there seems to be no particular strain in the six-membered ring, or else the initial scission (up until CO_2 is lost) is highly reversible. Since this peroxide produces a diradical, it is to be expected that it would be an inefficient initiator of polymerization, and Russell [82] observes an apparent efficiency in methyl methacrylate of only 0.1–0.2%.[84] Phthaloyl peroxide also undergoes an acid-catalyzed breakdown in CCl_4 and decomposes rapidly in the presence of olefins (at 0° in styrene $k_d = 2 \times 10^{-5}$).[83] The reaction in the presence of cis- and trans-stilbene has been studied further; [84a] with trans-stilbene it gives derivatives of the dl-glycol.

[81] H. Kleinfeller and K. Rastadter, *Angew. Chem.*, **65**, 543 (1953).

[82] K. E. Russell, *J. Am. Chem. Soc.*, **77**, 4814 (1955).

[83] F. D. Greene, *ibid.*, **78**, 2246 (1956).

[84] Polymeric phthaloyl peroxide, which produces monoradicals, is more effective, cf. H. A. Shah, F. Leonard, and A. V. Tobolsky, *J. Polymer Sci.*, **7**, 537 (1951).

[84a] F. D. Greene, *J. Am. Chem. Soc.*, **78**, 2250 (1956).

$$(48)$$

Kinetics in CCl_4 are first order in peroxide and olefin with $k_d = 13.7 \times 10^{-3}$ liter/mole/sec. at 80°. The reaction with *cis*-stilbene is similar, giving *meso*-glycol derivatives with $k_d = 7.18 \times 10^{-3}$, but whether a radical process is involved is uncertain.

10·2c Acetyl and Related Peroxides

The decomposition of acetyl peroxide in typical "inert" solvents occurs at about the same rate as that of benzoyl peroxide (Table 10·3).[85] Below approximately 0.1 molar, first-order rate constants are independent of initial peroxide concentrations, but at higher concentrations they increase, indicating a certain amount of induced decomposition. In primary and secondary alcohols (and presumably in ethers) rates are relatively high (cf. ethyl alcohol in Table 10·3), again pointing to long induced chains in these solvents. The products isolated from acetyl peroxide decompositions, particularly in solvents giving long induced chains, differ from those obtained from benzoyl peroxide in that larger quantities of CO_2 are produced, and suggest that the acetate radical has a very short life. Thus, in isopropyl alcohol, CO_2 (105%), CH_4 (105%), acetone (89%), acetic acid

---

[85] It is desirable to distinguish between the slow decomposition rate of acetyl peroxide in solution and the violent explosions which readily occur with the solid material. The latter arise from its sensitivity to shock and the large amount of energy per gram liberated in its decomposition.

TABLE 10·3   DECOMPOSITION RATES OF ACETYL PEROXIDE

(References also give data on other solvents and temperatures)

Solvent	Temperature	$k^d \times 10^5$ (sec^{-1})	E_a(kcal/mole)	Footnote
(Gas phase)	85	22.4	29.5	87
Benzene	60	0.5		86
	85.2	16.2	32.3	87
Toluene	60	0.5		86
	73.2	3.07		88
	85.2	15.9	32.0	87
Cyclohexane	85.2	12.7	31.4	87
Carbon tetra- chloride	60	0.3		86
	73.2	1.95		88
	85.2	11.7	33.4	89
Acetic acid	85.2	13.0	29.5	87
t-Butyl alcohol	60	0.31		86
Ethyl alcohol	60	10.1		86

[86] W. M. Thomas and M. T. O'Shaughnessy, *J. Polymer Sci.*, **11**, 455 (1953).
[87] M. Levy, M. Steinberg, and M. Szwarc, *J. Am. Chem. Soc.*, **76**, 5978 (1954).
[88] S. D. Ross and M. A. Fineman, *ibid.*, **73**, 2176 (1951).
[89] F. G. Edwards and F. R. Mayo, *ibid.*, **72**, 1265 (1950).

(54%), and isopropyl acetate (33%) are produced [90] indicating the major chair

$$Ac_2O_2 \rightarrow 2CH_3C \begin{matrix} O \\ \diagdown \\ O \cdot \end{matrix} \tag{49}$$

$$CH_3C \begin{matrix} O \\ \diagdown \\ O \cdot \end{matrix} \rightarrow CH_3 \cdot + CO_2 \tag{50}$$

$$CH_3 \cdot + CH_3\overset{OH}{\underset{|}{C}}HCH_3 \rightarrow CH_4 + CH_3\overset{OH}{\underset{|}{C}}CH_3 \tag{51}$$

$$CH_3\overset{OH}{\underset{|}{C}}CH_3 + Ac_2O_2 \rightarrow CH_3\overset{OH}{\underset{|}{\underset{OAc}{C}}}CH_3 + CH_3C\begin{matrix}O \\ \diagdown \\ O\cdot\end{matrix} \tag{52}$$

followed by decomposition of the hydroxyacetate and partial esterification of acetic acid. The point of attack of the methyl radicals is

[90] M. S. Kharasch, J. L. Rowe, and W. H. Urry, *J. Org. Chem.*, **16**, 905 (1951).

on the C—H rather than the O—H bond, since in $CH_3CDOHCH_3$ CH_3D is produced but not in $CH_3CHODCH_3$.[90] Secondary butyl alcohol reacts similarly and, with primary alcohols, aldehydes and their decomposition products result, but with t-butyl alcohol no clearly defined products of attack on solvent are isolated.[90] Products to be expected from similar chains are also found in isopropyl ether [91] and vicinal glycols.[92]

Even in the presence of iodine, essentially quantitative evolution of CO_2 takes place in the gas phase,[93] in toluene,[93] or moist CCl_4,[94] the major product in the last case being methyl iodide.[94] Since small amounts of ethane are still formed in toluene in the presence of iodine, Rembaum and Szwarc [93] conclude that this ethane represents recombination of methyl radicals still within the solvent cage (Section 3·3a) and that reactions 49 and 50 occur essentially simultaneously. The difference in stability of acetoxy and benzoyloxy radicals must arise from conjugation between the electron systems of the carboxy radical and the benzene ring. In fact, Szwarc finds (from thermochemical data) that reaction 50 is exothermic by 12–14 kcal, whereas the analogous decomposition of benzoyloxy radicals is $endo$thermic by 4 kcal/mole.[95]

From the foregoing, acetyl peroxide provides a convenient source of methyl radicals at temperatures of 60–100° (just as di-t-butyl peroxide may be used at higher temperatures) and has been extensively employed in the study of the liquid-phase reactions of these simple reactive species. From the synthetic point of view, a number of dimerization reactions may be accomplished by decomposing acetyl peroxide in solvents containing specifically reactive C—H bonds and have been investigated by Kharasch and his students. The best known are the dimerization of aliphatic acids and their derivatives via the path

$$R_2CHCOOH + \cdot CH_3 \rightarrow R_2\dot{C}COOH + CH_4 \qquad (53)$$

$$2R_2\dot{C}COOH \rightarrow R_2\overset{\displaystyle COOH}{\underset{\displaystyle COOH}{C-CR_2}} \qquad (54)$$

[91] M. S. Kharasch, H. N. Friedlander, and W. H. Urry, $ibid.$, **16,** 533 (1951).

[92] M. S. Kharasch, H. N. Friedlander, and W. H. Urry, $ibid.$, **14,** 91 (1949).

[93] A. Rembaum and M. Szwarc, $J. Am. Chem. Soc.$, **77,** 3486 (1955).

[94] C. Walling and R. B. Hodgdon, Jr., unpublished work.

[95] M. Szwarc, private communication.

which, with acetic acid, gives succinic acid in high yield [96] and can also be used with more complicated acids and their derivatives.[96–99]

Ketones are similarly linked to yield 1,4-diketones [99, 100] and alkyl chlorides are dimerized (when they possess CHCl structures) to yield vicinal dihalides,[101] as are a whole series of molecules containing benzyl C—H bonds.[102, 103]

The preferential attack of methyl radicals on CO—C—H and CCl—H bonds is in strong contrast to the behavior of halogen atoms (Section 8·3c) and provides one of the best examples of the role of polar effects in determining the course of radical reactions.

A more quantitative measure of the relative reactivity of methyl radicals with different structures may be obtained by competitive reactions, as first shown by Edwards and Mayo,[89] who decomposed acetyl peroxide in mixtures of CCl_4 and various solvents, determining the ratio of CH_4 to CH_3Cl produced by the competitive processes

$$CH_3Cl + \cdot CCl_3$$

$$\overset{CCl_4}{\nearrow}$$

$$\cdot CH_3 \qquad\qquad\qquad\qquad (55)$$

$$\underset{RH}{\searrow}$$

$$CH_4 + R\cdot$$

Results at 100° are shown in Table 10·4.

Since the method detects only hydrogen abstraction processes, the low reactivity of benzene is understandable. The high reactivity of cyclohexane, however, is striking and resembles the situation in chlorination, and the relative reactivities of $CHCl_3$ and CCl_4 were discussed in Section 6·2b.[104]

[96] M. S. Kharasch and M. T. Gladstone, *J. Am. Chem. Soc.*, **65**, 15 (1943).

[97] M. S. Kharasch, E. V. Jensen, and W. H. Urry, *J. Org. Chem.*, **10**, 386 (1945).

[98] M. S. Kharasch, H. C. McBay, and W. H. Urry, *ibid.*, **10**, 394 (1945).

[99] M. F. Ansell, W. J. Hickinbottom, and P. G. Holton, *J. Chem. Soc.*, **1955**, 349.

[100] M. S. Kharasch, H. C. McBay, and W. H. Urry, *J. Am. Chem. Soc.*, **70**, 1269 (1948).

[101] M. S. Kharasch and G. Buchi, *ibid.*, **73**, 632 (1951). However, allyl bromide gives 1-butene as a major product, apparently by addition of a methyl radical to the double bond, followed by bromine atom loss, M. S. Kharasch and G. Buchi, *J. Org. Chem.*, **14**, 84 (1949).

[102] M. S. Kharasch, E. V. Jensen, and W. H. Urry, *J. Org. Chem.*, **10**, 386 (1945).

[103] H. C. McBay, O. Tucker, and A. Milligan, *ibid.*, **19**, 1003 (1954).

[104] At the time of this work, Edwards and Mayo suggested that the radicals involved were actually acetate radicals which lost CO_2 simultaneously with

TABLE 10·4 RELATIVE REACTIVITIES OF SOLVENTS WITH METHYL RADICALS [89]

Solvent	Relative Reactivity	Solvent	Relative Reactivity
Benzene	0.039	1-Octene	3.2
Methyl benzoate	0.062	Cyclohexane	4.8
Acetone	0.40	Chloroform	11.1
Toluene	0.75	Methyl acetate	21
CCl₄	1.00		

It is of interest to compare the data of Table 10·4 with data on relative reactivities of methyl radicals with various substrates in the gas phase. These have been obtained by a variety of techniques and have been reviewed in detail by Trotman-Dickenson,[105] the data of Table 10·5 representing a few examples. The agreement in the

TABLE 10·5 RATE CONSTANTS FOR HYDROGEN ABSTRACTION BY METHYL RADICALS

(All at 182°, units liter/mole/sec × 10^{-3})

Substrate	k	Ratio [a]	Substrate	k	Ratio [a]
Methane	0.17	...	Benzene	1.0	26
Ethane	2.0	...	Toluene	14	19
n-Butane	14	...	Chloroform	100	9
Isobutane	10–22	...	Acetaldehyde	220	...
Cyclohexane	22	4.6	Acetone	10	25
Propylene	12	3.8 [b]	Isopropyl ether	38	...

[a] Ratio of k to relative reactivity in Table 10·4.
[b] Propylene versus 1-octene.

cases where both liquid- and vapor-phase data are available is only fair, but it seems doubtful to this writer that the discrepancies arise entirely from "the usual difficulties with reactions in solution" as Trotman-Dickenson suggests. A noteworthy feature of the extensive gas-phase data is the small spread in rate constants and activation energies (6–12 kcal) for a wide variety of structures, suggesting that one of the major characteristics of methyl radicals is their low selectivity in such systems.

The method of competitive reactions has been elegantly extended

their reaction with solvent. However, the data cited in our previous discussion now make this seem unlikely.

[105] A. F. Trotman-Dickenson, Quart. Revs., 7, 198 (1953).

by Szwarc and his colleagues,[106-112] who have developed techniques for carrying out the decompositions at high dilutions and analyzing the gaseous products on a vacuum line.[107] Under these conditions, in a solvent such as isoöctane, the fragments from acetyl peroxide appear as CO_2, CH_4, and a little ethane presumably formed in the initial solvent cage.[106, 107] If a substance is introduced which reacts with methyl radicals by addition, the yield of methane drops, and, from the decrease, the relative reactivities of solvent and added material towards methyl radicals can be calculated. Although such a scheme may be criticized in that it tells nothing about the fate of the radicals subsequently produced in the system, it should provide a reliable measure of the relative rates of hydrogen abstraction and methyl radical addition going on providing the initial step is not reversible (which is a plausible assumption here).

Results in benzene are particularly interesting, for, since only about 25% of the radicals produced appear as methane, methyl radical addition to the benzene ring must be the chief path of the initial reaction, although the final products have not been established and are probably a complex mixture (cf. our discussion of benzoyl peroxide decompositions, Section 10·2b).[107] With toluene, on the other hand, there is little drop in methane, indicating predominantly side-chain attack.[107] Szwarc has chosen this addition of methyl radicals to benzene as his standard reaction, defining the *methyl affinity* of other substrates as ratios of their reactivities with methyl radicals to that of benzene.

Table 10·6 summarizes data on methyl affinities so defined for a series of aromatic molecules, and Szwarc notes that there is good correlation of his results with both Kooyman's data on reactivities towards ·CCl_3 radicals (Section 6·2c) and spectroscopic measurements of singlet-triplet excitation energies.[113]

[106] M. Levy, M. Steinberg, and M. Szwarc, *J. Am. Chem. Soc.*, **76**, 3439 (1954).

[107] M. Levy and M. Szwarc, *ibid.*, **76**, 5981 (1954).

[108] M. Levy and M. Szwarc, *ibid.*, **77**, 1949 (1955).

[109] M. Levy, M. S. Newman, and M. Szwarc, *ibid.*, **77**, 4225 (1955).

[110] A. Rembaum and M. Szwarc, *ibid.*, **77**, 4468 (1955).

[111] F. Leavitt, M. Levy, M. Szwarc, and V. Stannett, *ibid.*, **77**, 5493 (1955).

[112] M. Szwarc, *J. Polymer Sci.*, **16**, 367 (1955).

[112a] M. Szwarc and F. Leavitt, *J. Am. Chem. Soc.*, **78**, 3590 (1956).

[112b] R. P. Buckley, F. Leavitt, and M. Szwarc, *ibid.*, **78**, 5557 (1956).

[112c] R. P. Buckley and M. Szwarc, *ibid.*, **78**, 5696 (1956).

[113] The correlation with atom localization energies and free valence has been pointed out by C. A. Coulson, *J. Chem. Soc.*, **1955**, 1435, who suggests the possibility of calculating the structures of the expected products on such a basis.

TABLE 10·6 METHYL AFFINITIES OF AROMATIC HYDROCARBONS (85°) [108]

Benzene	1	Anthracene	820
Biphenyl	5	Naphthacene	9250
Naphthalene	22	Pyridine	3
Phenanthrene	27	Quinoline	29
Chrysene	57.5	Isoquinoline	36
Pyrene	125	Acridine	430
Stilbene	183	Benzophenone	11
Benzanthracene	468	Diphenyl ether	2.5

With benzene, pyridine and biphenyl, the results are also in fair agreement with reactivities with phenyl radicals, determined by actual product isolation.

In addition to the data of Table 10·6, methyl affinities of a series of benzo[c]phenanthrenes has been investigated.[109]

$$\left. \begin{array}{c} \end{array} \right\} -CH_3 \qquad (56)$$

The methyl affinity of the parent compound is 64, and 2-, 3-, 4-, 5-, and 6-methyl derivatives all show values between 55 and 73. However, the methyl affinity of the 1-methyl compound is increased to 108, and of the 1,12-dimethyl derivative to 183, a result attributed to the higher energy (and reactivity) of the latter compounds, in which steric hindrance prevents the aromatic system from assuming a planar conformation. A similar enhanced reactivity has also been noted with bisdiphenyleneethylene.[112a]

Methyl reactivities of a series of olefins, Table 10·7, are interesting since they provide reactivities with the simplest possible carbon radical to compare with the extensive data on copolymerization (Section 4·1). The only significant inversion is that methyl methacrylate and acrylonitrile here appear intrinsically more reactive than styrene (contrary to our previous conclusion). The apparent role of steric hindrance in the 2-butenes, stilbene, triphenylethylene, tetraphenylethylene, diethyl maleate, and tetrachloroethylene is also noteworthy. Tetrafluoroethylene proves to be very reactive, the fluorine atoms evidently being too small to interfere with radical attack. Table 10·7 also provides the only direct comparison between the

TABLE 10·7 RELATIVE REACTIVITIES COMPARED WITH ISOÖCTANE AND
METHYL AFFINITIES OF OLEFINS

Olefin	Relative Reactivity		Methyl Affinity
	85°	65°	
Ethylene [112c]	35.5	34.1	...
cis-2-Butene [112b]	...	3.3	...
trans-2-Butene [112b]	...	6.9	...
Isobutylene [112b]	...	36	...
Styrene [111]	651	792	1630
α-Methylstyrene [111]	755	926	1890
trans-Stilbene [111]	84	104.5	205
1,1-Diphenylethylene [111]	895	1590	2240
Triphenylethylene [111]	34	46	85
Tetraphenylethylene [111]	10	10	25
Allyl acetate [112b]	5.7	8.4	...
Tetrafluoroethylene [112c]	273	342	...
Tetrachloroethylene [112c]	...	<0.3	...
Methyl methacrylate [112]	960	1420	...
Vinyl acetate [112]	28	37	...
Diethyl maleate [112]	161	264	...
Acrylonitrile [112]	...	1540	...

reactivities of ethylene and other olefins, and supports our previous conclusion that alkyl or acetoxy groups (in the absence of polar effects) increase olefin reactivities only slightly.

By a more detailed analysis of their data, Buckley, Leavitt, and Szwarc [112b] have also been able to estimate the relative rates of abstraction of allylic hydrogen and methyl radical addition in allyl acetate, cis-2-butene, trans-2-butene, and isobutylene. At 65° the ratios of rates for the two processes are 0.23, 0.95, 0.7, and 0.06, results which certainly confirm our picture of the importance of such side reactions in radical additions to double bonds developed in Chapters 5, 6, and 7.

Finally, Szwarc has determined the methyl affinities of a long series of quinones (Table 10·8). The extraordinary reactivity of these materials is striking and parallels their potency as polymerization inhibitors (Section 4·3). Since completely substituted quinones are relatively unreactive, Szwarc concludes that the preferred initial addition in this case is to the C=C double bond. However, isolated products in other radical-quinone reactions frequently indicate O addition (Sections 4·3c and 6·3c) so that it seems likely that the point of attack depends not only upon the quinone but on the attacking radical as well.

TABLE 10·8   METHYL AFFINITIES OF QUINONES (65°C) [110]

Benzoquinone	15,200	1,4-Naphthoquinone	4,900
2-Methylbenzoquinone	10,400	2-Methyl-1,4-naphthoquinone	3,400
2,5-Dimethylbenzoquinone	6,500	2,7-Dimethylnaphthoquinone	4,100
Duroquinone	790	2,3-Dimethylnaphthoquinone	550
2-Methoxybenzoquinone	8,000	2,3-Dichloronaphthoquinone	90
2-Chlorobenzoquinone	27,000	1,2-Naphthoquinone	3,400
2,5-Dichlorobenzoquinone	39,200	Phenanthraquinone	700
2,6-Dichlorobenzoquinone	38,400	2-t-Butylanthraquinone	90
Chloranil	300		

With certain quinones, C-alkylation by acyl peroxides is established by actual product isolation, sometimes in excellent yield. In 1942 Fieser and Oxford [114] described the alkylation of 2,5-dihydroxybenzoquinone, tribromobenzoquinone, 1,4-naphthoquinone, and 2-alkyl- and 2-hydroxy-1,4-naphthoquinones in good yield by various acyl peroxides, and subsequently the last reaction (57) has been

$$+ CO_2 + RCOOH \quad (57)$$

enormously extended by Fieser and co-workers,[115] who prepared approximately 200 different 3-substituted 2-hydroxy-1,4-naphthoquinones by this route as part of the wartime search for new antimalarial drugs. The reaction mechanism of this particular process has not been investigated, and it may well be a chain reaction. However, the observation that it fails with benzoyl peroxide [114] and the evolution of carbon dioxide certainly point to a radical process. This investigation represents the most extensive preparation of acyl peroxides on record, even though, in some cases, they were used in solution without isolation.

[114] L. F. Fieser and A. E. Oxford, J. Am. Chem. Soc., 64, 2060 (1942).
[115] L. F. Fieser et al., ibid., 70, 3174 (1948) .

Turning now to other aliphatic acyl peroxides, activation energies for gas-phase decomposition of propionyl and butyryl peroxides are 30 and 29.6 kcal/mole respectively, within experimental error the same as for acetyl peroxide.[116] The resulting radicals are apparently somewhat less reactive, for, although, in CCl_4, butyryl and isobutyryl peroxide yield n- and isopropyl chlorides plus CO_2 and C_2Cl_6 as major products,[117] lauroyl peroxide (and also benzoyl peroxide) fail to dimerize acetic acid.[97] Dimethylsuccinic acid has, however, been reported from the decomposition of propionyl peroxide in propionic acid.[118] Induced chain decompositions in more reactive solvents also occur, lauroyl peroxide decomposing about 80 times as fast in ether at 30° as in benzene. The major products are CO_2 (92%), n-undecane (84%), and 1-ethoxyethyl laurate (88%),[119] indicating that CO_2 loss, again, must occur very rapidly, so that the undecyl radical serves as the chain carrier.

DeTar and Weis [119a] have recently made a very detailed study of the products formed in the decomposition of δ-phenylvaleryl peroxide at low concentration (0.004 − 0.016 M) in CCl_4 and benzene. In CCl_4 the major products are CO_2 (84%), acid (4%), ester (17.5%), 1,8-diphenyloctane (21.5%), and 1-chloro-4-phenylbutane (41%). They conclude that CO_2 loss is very rapid, and that all products but the chlorobutane are formed within the solvent cage (or perhaps by a non-radical cyclic path). In benzene similar products result (except for the chloroöctane) plus 28% tetralin, evidently arising from radical attack on its own phenyl group in this less-reactive solvent.

More complex peroxides which, on CO_2 loss, should yield relatively stable radicals, decompose much more rapidly than benzoyl and acetyl peroxide, suggesting that O—O bond scission and CO_2 loss occur simultaneously, with the stability of the resulting radical providing driving force for the reaction. The case of phenylacetyl peroxide has been studied by Bartlett and Leffler,[120] who find that, in toluene, this substance decomposes slightly faster at 0° than benzoyl peroxide at 70°. It initiates the polymerization of styrene at 0°, and

[116] A. Rembaum and M. Szwarc, *J. Chem. Phys.*, **23**, 909 (1955). Decomposition rates in solution are also similar; J. Smid, A. Rembaum, and M. Szwarc, *J. Am. Chem. Soc.*, **78**, 3315 (1956).

[117] M. S. Kharasch, S. S. Kane, and H. C. Brown, *J. Am. Chem. Soc.*, **63**, 526 (1941).

[118] S. Goldschmidt, W. Leicher, and H. Haas, *Ann.*, **577**, 153 (1952).

[119] W. E. Cass, *ibid.*, **72**, 4915 (1950).

[119a] D. F. DeTar and C. Weis, *ibid.*, **78**, 4296 (1956).

[120] P. D. Bartlett and J. E. Leffler, *J. Am. Chem. Soc.*, **72**, 3030 (1950).

its decomposition apparently involves both simple scission and some induced reaction. The activation energy of the former is about 23 kcal, and, because of the low reactivity of benzyl radicals, there seems to be little attack on solvents such as CCl_4. In the presence of acids, a still faster polar decomposition also occurs. Trichloro-acetyl peroxide also decomposes into radicals rapidly even at room temperature,[121] and similarly peroxides of the structure $(H(C_2F_4)_nCOO)_2$ [122] and $(CF_3CCl_2COO)_2$ [123] have been patented as low-temperature polymerization initiators. Here we note that, by analogy to substituted benzoyl peroxides, the *polar* properties of the CX_n- groups should, if anything, stabilize such peroxides.

The decomposition of some bridgehead peroxides are of interest as indicating the existence of non-planar hydrocarbon radicals. The decomposition of apocamphoyl peroxide was studied by Kharasch, Engelmann, and Urry,[124] who found that, in CCl_4, the reaction followed the course

$$(58)$$

The apocamphyl chloride clearly points to the transient presence of the bridgehead apocamphyl radical, and the large yield of ester either suggests that CO_2 loss is slow or (more likely) that there is considerable induced decomposition. Alternatively, some ester may arise from a non-radical reaction via some sort of cyclic intermediate. The rate constant for decomposition of apocamphoyl peroxide has

[121] W. T. Miller, A. L. Dittman, and S. K. Reed, U.S. Pat. 2,580,358 (December 25, 1951); C. Zimmerman, U.S. Pat. 2,580,373 (December 25, 1951).

[122] O. H. Bullitt, Jr., U.S. Pat. 2,559,630 (July 10, 1951).

[123] A. L. Dittman and J. M. Wrightson, U.S. Pat. 2,705,706 (April 5, 1955).

[124] M. S. Kharasch, F. Engelmann, and W. H. Urry, *J. Am. Chem. Soc.,* **65,** 2428 (1943).

been reported [125] as $k_{80} = 23 \times 10^{-5}$ sec^{-1}, slightly faster than acetyl peroxide.

The more complex bridgehead peroxide triptoyl peroxide has been investigated by Bartlett and Greene,[125] who obtain, in benzene, $k_{80} = 14.2 \times 10^{-5}$ sec^{-1}. The reaction gives a mixture of products and is considered to involve both a radical (84%) and a polar (16%) path.

As a more quantitative measure of the relative reactivities of various substrates towards higher alkyl radicals, Szwarc [126] has been able to extend his competitive measurements to ethyl radicals derived from propionyl peroxide, obtaining a series of *ethyl affinities*, comparable to the methyl affinities discussed above. Benzene proves to be about ten times as reactive compared with isoöctane as in the case of methyl radicals, but, if it is again chosen as the reference standard, a reaction series is obtained with a number of aromatics and olefins almost identical with those of Tables 10·7 and 10·8.

Finally, some recent results give information on the stereochemistry of peroxide decompositions. Kharasch, Kuderna, and Nudenberg [127] have decomposed optically active α-methylbutyryl peroxide in benzotrichloride, obtaining *sec*-butyl α-methylbutyrate (30–40%) in which both alcohol and acid residues have retained their configuration. Dauben and Liang [128] have carried out the same decomposition with both optical isomers in CCl$_4$ and CCl$_3$Br, also obtaining the active ester in similar yield plus inactive *sec*-butyl chloride and bromide. The latter workers propose a cyclic, non-radical path to the active ester, but, in view of the high efficiency of recombination within the solvent cage noted in other radical-forming processes in such dense solvents (Sections 3·3a and 11·1b), it may be possible that the ester simply arises from very rapid recombination of radicals before the *sec*-butyl radical has had time to undergo the racemization noted in its slower reaction with solvent.

In any case, the whole question of a cyclic path not involving free radicals remains one of the unsolved problems of peroxide chemistry. However, a similar process has been suggested by Greene [129] involving the transient formation of an unstable peroxide (cf. phenylacetyl

[125] P. D. Bartlett and F. D. Greene, *ibid.*, **76**, 1088 (1954).

[126] J. Smid and M. Szwarc, *ibid.*, **78**, 3322 (1956).

[127] M. S. Kharasch, J. Kuderna, and W. Nudenberg, *J. Org. Chem.*, **19**, 1283 (1955).

[128] H. J. Dauben, Jr., and H. T. Liang, private communication.

[129] F. D. Greene, *J. Am. Chem. Soc.*, **77**, 4869 (1955).

peroxide above) to account for the formation of α-phenylethylhydrotropoate (among a variety of other products) in which both alcohol and acid fragments retain their configuration when optically active hydratropoyl chloride is reacted with cold solutions of sodium peroxide.

$$
2\phi\!-\!\underset{\underset{H}{|}}{\overset{\overset{CH_3}{|}}{C}}\!-\!COCl + Na_2O_2 \rightarrow \left[\phi\!-\!\underset{\underset{H}{|}}{\overset{\overset{CH_3}{|}}{C}}\!-\!CO\!-\!O\!-\!O\!-\!CO\!-\!\underset{\underset{H}{|}}{\overset{\overset{CH_3}{|}}{C}}\!-\!\phi \right]
$$

$$
\rightarrow \phi\!-\!\underset{\underset{H}{|}}{\overset{\overset{CH_3}{|}}{C}}\!-\!O\!-\!CO\!-\!\underset{\underset{H}{|}}{\overset{\overset{CH_3}{|}}{C}}\!-\!\phi + CO_2 \qquad (59)
$$

10·2d Hydroperoxides

Hydroperoxides are among the most easily available organic derivatives of hydrogen peroxide, and their ability to initiate polymerization and autoxidation processes is clear evidence of their ability to split into free radicals. Nevertheless, as was intimated in our discussion of autoxidation processes, these decompositions are extremely complicated and not at all well understood. At least two sorts of processes appear to go on in addition to simple thermal scission of the O—O bond: first, an often very rapid induced decomposition involving only the peroxide; second, induced chains involving solvent. Both of these phenomena are more pronounced than among the acyl peroxides, and, in addition, the rate of the initial scission process evidently varies widely in different solvents.

The decomposition of t-butyl hydroperoxide has been studied in some detail and should be typical of aliphatic tertiary hydroperoxides. The pure material decomposes completely in 24 hours at 95–100°, giving an almost quantitative yield of oxygen and t-butyl alcohol.[130] A similar decomposition occurs at 140° in inert solvents such as chlorobenzene,[131] and Vaughan and his group (cf. Section 9·3b) have suggested the chain process

$$
(CH_3)_3COOH \rightarrow (CH_3)_3CO\cdot + \cdot OH \qquad (60)
$$

[130] N. A. Milas and D. M. Surgenor, *ibid.*, **68**, 205 (1946).

[131] E. R. Bell, J. H. Raley, F. F. Rust, F. H. Seubold, Jr., and W. E. Vaughan, *Discussions Faraday Soc.*, **10**, 242 (1951).

$$(CH_3)_3CO\cdot + (CH_3)_3COOH \rightarrow (CH_3)_3COO\cdot + (CH_3)_3COH \quad (61)$$

$$2(CH_3)_3COO\cdot \rightarrow 2(CH_3)_3CO\cdot + O_2 \quad (62)$$

steps 61 and 62 constituting the chain.

In octane at 150–180° the decomposition is slower (presumably by diversion of the chain through attack on solvent), and first-order rate constants increase with initial concentration. The situation thus resembles the induced decomposition of acyl peroxides, and the rate constant for reaction 60 has been calculated as 1×10^{15} exp $(-39,000/RT)$. The reported activation energy seems low, as *a priori* we might anticipate a valve of about 46 kcal, intermediate between those of hydrogen peroxide and di-t-butyl peroxide, and it is possible that solvent is involved in the cleavage process. The decomposition in a variety of solvents at 73.5° has been studied by Stannett and Mesrobian,[132] who note that in three hours the reaction is undetectable in several aromatic solvents, cyclohexane, CCl_4, and $CHCl_3$. However, appreciable reaction occurs in alcohols, ethers, o-cresol, aniline, and several other media. Evidently chains are involved, benzyl alcohol being oxidized to benzaldehyde, and, even in benzene where decomposition is normally slow, t-butyl hydroperoxide undergoes a faster induced decomposition in the presence of azobisisobutyronitrile.

The behavior of t-butyl hydroperoxide in the presence of olefins is particularly interesting. Here the decomposition rate is relatively high. With styrene the peroxide shows an appreciable transfer constant (0.035 to 0.06),[133–135] so evidently some of the decomposition is due to an induced chain, probably involving the step [134]

$$M\cdot + (CH_3)_3COOH \rightarrow MH + (CH_3)_3COO\cdot \quad (63)$$

However, the actual amount of polymer formed at 70° indicates a rate of chain starting far in excess of that calculated from Vaughan's k_d in isoöctane. This, plus the complex kinetics, both of the decomposition and polymerization, indicate an initial step of radical formation involving both peroxide and olefin for which the process

$$ROOH + CH_2{=}CH\phi \rightarrow ROO\cdot + CH_3\dot{C}H\phi \quad (64)$$

has been suggested.[134]

[132] V. Stannett and R. B. Mesrobian, *J. Am. Chem. Soc.*, **72**, 4125 (1950).
[133] D. H. Johnson and A. V. Tobolsky, *ibid.*, **74**, 938 (1952).
[134] C. Walling and Y. W. Chang, *ibid.*, **76**, 4878 (1954).
[135] R. N. Haward and W. Simpson, *Trans. Faraday Soc.*, **47**, 212 (1951).

Cumene hydroperoxide parallels the behavior of *t*-butyl hydroperoxide in many respects, except that its decomposition at around 100° in certain solvents (acetic or benzoic acids, 2-phenyl-2-propanol) [21] or alone [136] gives high yields of α,α-dimethylbenzyl (α-cumyl) peroxide plus some acetophenone and 2-phenyl-2-propanol. Oxygen is also evolved. It seems probable that the α-cumyl peroxide arises through dimerization of α,α-dimethylbenzyloxy radicals,

$$
2\phi \overset{\displaystyle CH_3}{\underset{\displaystyle CH_3}{-C-}} O \cdot \; \rightarrow \; \phi \overset{\displaystyle CH_3}{\underset{\displaystyle CH_3}{-C-}} O-O \overset{\displaystyle CH_3}{\underset{\displaystyle CH_3}{-C-}} \phi \tag{65}
$$

The high rate of decomposition, compared with that in dilute solution in inert solvents (see below) indicates that some sort of polymolecular or chain process is involved.

Interestingly, when cumene hydroperoxide is heated at 75° in cumene or ethylbenzene in the presence of acetyl peroxide, α-cumyl peroxide or α-cumyl α-phenylethyl peroxides are formed, and *t*-butyl hydroperoxide in cumene gives α-cumyl *t*-butyl peroxide in a similar manner.[21] The latter two products point to radical attack on solvent and perhaps coupling of ROO· and ·R' radicals, although the steps are speculative, and Kharasch [21] gives a somewhat different interpretation. In dilute solution, the rate of decomposition of cumene hydroperoxide varies with solvent, and apparent first-order rate constants increase with concentration.[132,137,138] In aromatic solvents the rate is relatively slow (a half-life of about 25 hours in mesitylene at 113° at concentrations below 0.027 molar).[132] In decane the products are chiefly methane (30%), acetophenone (20%), and 2-phenyl-2-propanol (54%).[138] Evidently considerable breakdown of the intermediate cumyloxy radical occurs.

$$
\phi \overset{\displaystyle CH_3}{\underset{\displaystyle CH_3}{-C-}} O \cdot \; \rightarrow \; \phi -COCH_3 + \cdot CH_3 \tag{66}
$$

Interestingly, in cumene yields of methane and acetophenone are about the same (32–46% and 30–39%) but 78–90% 2-phenyl-2-

[136] J. Lorand and J. E. Reese, U.S. Patent 2,691,683 (October 12, 1954).

[137] J. W. L. Fordham and H. L. Williams, *Can. J. Research*, **B27**, 943 (1949).

[138] M. S. Kharasch, A. Fono, and W. Nudenberg, *J. Org. Chem.*, **16**, 113 (1951).

propanol is produced, indicating radical attack on the cumene, and perhaps transient formation of α-cumyl peroxide. Small amounts of phenol and acetone also appear, the results of polar decomposition.[138]

In dibutyl ether the rate is more rapid and the kinetics complicated, indicating a chain process. In styrene, decomposition is enormously faster (somewhat more rapid at 73.5° than in mesitylene at 113°),[132] and, as in the case of t-butyl hydroperoxide, both decomposition via chain transfer and an initial radical-forming reaction involving solvent must be occurring.[134] Similar high rates are observed in a number of other olefins.[132, 139]

The decomposition of few other tertiary hydroperoxides have been studied in detail. Schmidt and Fisher [140] have noted that pinane hydroperoxide in pinane at 117°, gives as a major product (20%) a ketone, 2,2-dimethyl-3-ethylacetylcyclobutane, via the plausible path

(67)

although chain steps may also be involved. Other examples of such ring-opening processes are also known.

The simplest secondary hydroperoxide which has been investigated is cyclohexyl hydroperoxide, which Farkas and Passaglia [141] find to decompose very slowly in cyclohexane, even at 150° ($k_d = 3.2 \times 10^{-5}$ sec^{-1}, $E_a = 34$ kcal/mole). In 1:1 styrene-benzene the rate is again much faster, $k_d \doteqdot 1.27 \times 10^{-7}$ at 70°, largely (but again not entirely) as a result of chain transfer. Tetralin hydroperoxide undergoes a complex decomposition with a solvent-dependent rate,[142, 143]

[139] T. I. Yurzhenko, D. K. Tolopko, and V. N. Puchin, *Doklady Akad. Nauk S.S.S.R.*, **74**, 85 (1950).

[140] G. S. Schmidt and G. S. Fisher, *J. Am. Chem. Soc.*, **76**, 5426 (1954).

[141] A. Farkas and E. Passaglia, *ibid.*, **72**, 3333 (1950).

[142] K. I. Ivanov, V. K. Savinova, and E. G. Michaelova, *C. R. Acad. Sci., U.R.S.S.*, **25**, 3440 (1939).

[143] A. Robertson and W. A. Waters, *J. Chem. Soc.*, **1948**, 1574.

and the products formed were discussed in Section 9·3b. Cyclohexene hydroperoxide also shows a decomposition rate which varies with solvent, being as much as 40 times faster in olefins than in benzene, and which increases with concentration from first to almost second order. The products in benzene include cyclohexenol (13%), cyclohexene (30%), O_2 (11%), and H_2O (44%), plus 44 weight % of higher boiling residues.[144] Bateman suggests that the decomposition at higher concentrations involves breakdown of a bimolecular complex, and a complicated induced process is certainly indicated.

Finally, Mosher and Wurster [145] have described a remarkable decomposition of primary hydroperoxides in which, for example, *n*-butyl hydroperoxide decomposes in the absence of solvent at 86° to give, as the chief products, hydrogen (43%), butyric acid (50%), butyl butyrate (15%), and water (43%). Although the radical nature of the reaction can only be surmised, and a chain sequence is indicated, we have here one of the few low-temperature organic reactions known giving rise to molecular hydrogen.

10·2e   *Other Peroxides, Inorganic Peroxides, Peresters, Etc.*

A considerable variety of further types of peroxide undergo thermal cleavage into radicals and have been studied in sufficient detail for discussion. The simplest is hydrogen peroxide itself, which long has found some use as a polymerization initiator, but which has had little systematic study. Nandi and Palit,[146] however, have recently described the hydrogen peroxide-initiated polymerization of methyl methacrylate in toluene, ethyl acetate, and methyl ethyl ketone. The reaction occurs at convenient rates between 50 and 115°, but both the kinetics and rates of chain initiation vary with solvent (at 60° $k_i = 0.11 \times 10^{-7}$ in toluene, 2.55×10^{-7} in methylethyl ketone) and there is also evidence for considerable chain transfer (C = ~0.1). Since $D(\mathrm{HO-OH})$ in the gas phase has a value of 54 kcal, radical formation must be only a pseudounimolecular process with solvent in some way involved.

Persulfate ion is a rather more important radical source, widely used as an initiator in emulsion polymerization. Its unimolecular decomposition in water has been studied by Bartlett and Cotman [147]

[144] L. Bateman and Mrs. H. Hughes, *ibid.*, **1952**, 4594; L. Bateman, Mrs. H. Hughes, and A. L. Morris, *Discussions Faraday Soc.*, **14**, 190 (1953).

[145] H. S. Mosher and C. F. Wurster, *J. Am. Chem. Soc.*, **77**, 5451 (1955).

[146] V. S. Nandi and S. R. Palit, *J. Polymer Sci.*, **17**, 65 (1955).

[147] P. D. Bartlett and J. D. Cotman, Jr., *J. Am. Chem. Soc.*, **71**, 1419 (1949).

and by Kolthoff and Miller.[148] The latter have distinguished two processes, one a radical-forming process which is pH independent, and the second a polar reaction which is acid catalyzed. The radical-forming reaction is a simple bond scission

$$^-O_3S-O-O-SO_3^- \rightarrow 2SO_4 \cdot^- \tag{68}$$

with a rate constant of 1×10^{-6} sec^{-1} at $50°$ and an activation energy of 33.5 kcal which in the absence of other substrates is thought to be followed by

$$SO_4 \cdot^- + H_2O \rightarrow HSO_4^- + \cdot OH \tag{69}$$

$$2OH \cdot \rightarrow H_2O + \tfrac{1}{2}O_2 \tag{70}$$

a sequence that accords with the stoichiometry of the reaction and the observation (using O^{18}-labeled materials) that the evolved oxygen is derived from water. The acid-catalyzed process is suggested as

$$S_2O_8^= + H^+ \rightarrow HS_2O_8^- \tag{71}$$

$$HS_2O_8^- \rightarrow HSO_4^- + SO_4 \tag{72}$$

$$SO_4 \rightarrow SO_3 + \tfrac{1}{2}O_2 \tag{73}$$

In strong acid, reaction 73 is replaced by formation of Caro's acid

$$SO_4 + H_2O \rightarrow HSO_5^- \tag{74}$$

Bartlett and Cotman [147] find that in 1 M methanol the rate of the homolytic decomposition increases 25-fold, obeying the rate law

$$-d[S_2O_8^=]/dt = k[MeOH]^{1/2}[S_2O_8^=]^{3/2} \tag{75}$$

and propose the chain process

$$SO_4 \cdot^- + CH_3OH \rightarrow HSO_4^- + \cdot CH_2OH \tag{76}$$

$$\cdot CH_2OH + S_2O_8^= \rightarrow HSO_4^- + SO_4 \cdot^- + CH_2O \tag{77}$$

analogous to the benzoyl peroxide–ether chain with perhaps an additional radical-forming step

$$S_2O_8^= + CH_3OH \rightarrow HSO_4^- + SO_4 \cdot^- + \cdot CH_2OH \tag{78}$$

This decomposition has been investigated in more detail by Kolthoff, Meehan, and Carr,[149] who found that the induced de-

[148] I. M. Kolthoff and I. K. Miller, *ibid.*, **73**, 3055 (1951).

[149] I. M. Kolthoff, E. J. Meehan, and E. M. Carr, *ibid.*, **75**, 1439 (1953). The rapid reaction in the presence of isopropyl alcohol has also been studied by L. S. Levitt and E. R. Malinowski, *J. Am. Chem. Soc.*, **77**, 4517 (1955), but they

composition in alcohols is completely eliminated in the presence of allyl acetate, which interrupts the chain, so that reaction 78 is actually unimportant. The sulfate radicals formed in reaction 68 are evidently very efficient initiators of polymerization, since, if S^{35}-labeled persulfate and styrene are used, essentially all the persulfate decomposed appears attached to polymer.[150] Persulfate is also an efficient oxidant of many other types of organic molecules, although in some cases the process may involve polar rather than radical intermediates.

Other essentially inorganic esters of hydrogen peroxide which are reported to decompose into radicals are bis(methylsulfonyl) peroxide (A),[151] cyclohexylpersulfonic acid and cyclohexylsulfonyl acetyl peroxide (B and C),[152] and pernitrous acid (D) [153]

$$CH_3SO_2\text{—}O\text{—}O\text{—}SO_2CH_3$$

$$A \qquad\qquad B$$

$$C \qquad\qquad D \qquad\qquad HOO\text{—}NO \qquad (79)$$

Pernitrous acid is an extremely reactive and unstable substance which is suggested as decomposing via

$$HO\text{—}ONO \rightarrow \cdot OH + NO_2 \qquad (80)$$

and not only induces vinyl polymerization but attacks a variety of aromatic nuclei.

A number of peresters are known and used as radical sources, t-butyl perbenzoate being the best characterized. In aromatic solvents Blomquist and Ferris find a first-order decomposition with a half-life of about 5.8 hours at 110° and $E_a = 34.5$ kcal/mole with evidence of slight induced decomposition.[154] In alcohols and ethers a rapid

interpret their results as a non-chain process involving SO_4 which is certainly incompatible with Kolthoff's observations.

[150] W. V. Smith, *ibid.*, **71**, 4077 (1949); I. M. Kolthoff, B. R. O'Connor, and J. L. Hanson, *J. Polymer Sci.*, **15**, 459 (1955).

[151] G. D. Jones and R. E. Friedrich, U.S. Pat. 2,619,507 (November 25, 1952).

[152] R. Graf, *Ann.*, **578**, 50 (1952).

[153] E. Halfpenny and P. L. Robinson, *J. Chem. Soc.*, **1952**, 928, 939; J. R. Laville and W. A. Waters, *ibid.*, **1954**, 400.

[154] A. T. Blomquist and A. F. Ferris, *J. Am. Chem. Soc.*, **73**, 3408 (1951).

induced decomposition occurs which is inhibited by styrene.[155]   The
rates of decomposition of a series of p-substituted t-butyl perben-
zoates give a negative value of ρ in a Hammett plot,[156] all properties
(except for the higher O—O bond strength) paralleling that of benzoyl peroxide and with a similar explanation.

The peroxydicarbonates R—O—CO—OO—O—R, with R = CH$_3$
and higher alkyl groups, have been studied by Cohen[157] and by
Strain.[158] In aromatic solvents they decompose at rates which are
somewhat faster than that of benzoyl peroxide and show faster induced rates in alcohols. However, the pure materials are highly
sensitive and hazardous to handle and apparently undergo rapid self-
induced decomposition only a little above room temperature.[158] Their
decomposition is pictured as

$$R\text{—}O\text{—}CO\text{—}OO\text{—}CO\text{—}O\text{—}R \rightarrow 2R\text{—}O\text{—}C{\overset{\displaystyle O}{\underset{\displaystyle O\cdot}{\Big\langle}}} \qquad (81)$$

$$R\text{—}O\text{—}C{\overset{\displaystyle O}{\underset{\displaystyle O\cdot}{\Big\langle}}} \rightarrow R\text{—}O\cdot + CO_2 \qquad (82)$$

with reactions 81 and 82 not simultaneous, since little CO$_2$ is evolved
in the presence of styrene. The nature of the subsequent induced
decompositions has not been worked out in detail. If care is used in
handling the peroxydicarbonates, they provide convenient low-temperature sources of alkoxy radicals and have been investigated for
this purpose by McBay,[103, 159] who has compared the properties of
the latter with those of alkyl radicals.

In addition to the peroxydicarbonates, several other types of per-
oxycarbonates are known,[158, 160] which also decompose into radicals
but have not been studied in detail.

The remaining class of peroxides which have found appreciable use
as radical sources are the ketone-hydrogen peroxide (or hydroperox-

[155] A. T. Blomquist and A. F. Ferris, *ibid.*, **73**, 3412 (1951).

[156] A. T. Blomquist and I. A. Berstein, *ibid.*, **73**, 5546 (1951).

[157] S. G. Cohen and D. B. Sparrow, *ibid.*, **72**, 611 (1950).

[158] F. Strain, W. E. Bissinger, W. R. Dial, H. Rudoff, B. J. DeWitt, H. C.
Stevens, and J. H. Langston, *ibid.*, **72**, 1254 (1950).

[159] H. C. McBay and O. Tucker, *J. Org. Chem.*, **19**, 869 (1954).

[160] A. G. Davies and K. J. Hunter, *J. Chem. Soc.*, **1953**, 1809.

ide) reaction products, but their decomposition rates and products have received little attention. According to Cooper,[161] the cyclohexanone-hydrogen peroxide reaction product (which is chiefly 1-hydroxy-1-hydroperoxy-cyclohexyl peroxide) decomposes smoothly at 130–140° to cyclohexanone, hexanoic acid, adipic acid, and decane 1,10-dicarboxylic acid, evidently by complex processes. A further discussion of the chemistry of such materials has been given by Tobolsky and Mesrobian.[162]

10 · 3   Azo and Diazo Compounds

10·3a   The Azonitriles and Related Materials

Simple aliphatic azo compounds, e.g., azomethane, decompose appreciably only at temperatures near 400°C. However, suitably substituted azo compounds, in which $C-N$ bond dissociation energies are lowered by the stability of the resulting radicals, dissociate at much lower temperatures and provide convenient radical sources. Particularly important are the disubstituted azoacetonitriles, of which azobisisobutyronitrile is the best-known and most studied example. These substances are easily prepared using ketones, hydrazine, and HCN as starting materials,[163] and their use as radical sources was noted independently by several groups of investigators in about 1949.[164–166] Their breakdown in all probability involves the step

$$\underset{\substack{|\\R}}{\overset{\substack{R\\|}}{NC-C}}-N=N-\underset{\substack{|\\R}}{\overset{\substack{R\\|}}{C}}-CN \qquad 2\,NC-\underset{\substack{|\\R}}{\overset{\substack{R\\|}}{C}}\cdot + N_2 \qquad (83)$$

with simultaneous cleavage of both $C-N$ bonds, since no azo compounds have been detected from their decompositions, and the heat of formation of the very stable N_2 molecule is probably required to account for the low activation energy (~ 30 kcal) of the process. The azonitriles make particularly valuable and convenient radical

[161] W. Cooper, ibid., **1951**, 1340; W. Cooper and W. H. T. Davison, ibid., **1952,** 1180.

[162] A. V. Tobolsky and R. B. Mesrobian, Organic Peroxides, Interscience Publishers, New York, 1954, pp. 41–52.

[163] J. Thiele and K. Heuser, Ann., **290,** 1 (1896).

[164] K. Ziegler, Brennstoff-Chem., **30,** 181 (1949).

[165] F. M. Lewis and M. S. Matheson, J. Am. Chem. Soc., **71,** 747 (1949).

[166] C. G. Overberger, M. T. O'Shaughnessy, and H. Shalit, ibid., **71,** 2661 (1949).

sources, since, as noted in Section 3·3a, they decompose by strictly first-order kinetics at essentially the same rate in a variety of solvents, with no evidence of induced chain reactions, and since, by suitable structural changes, substances with a wide variety of decomposition rates are available. Decomposition rates may be followed by nitrogen evolution [165, 166] or spectrophotometrically.[167] Measurements using radical scavengers [168] necessarily give somewhat low results, since as discussed in Section 3·3a, a certain fraction of the radicals formed (generally 20–60%) are wasted by recombination within the solvent cage. Decomposition rates of azobisisobutyronitrile in several solvents are summarized in Table 10·9, and rates for a variety of other azonitriles and related compounds in Table 10·10.

TABLE 10·9   DECOMPOSITION OF AZOBISISOBUTYRONITRILE IN VARIOUS SOLVENTS AT 80°

Solvent	$k \times 10^4$ (sec^{-1})	Footnote
Xylene	1.53	165
Xylene ^{a}	1.50	165
Acetic acid	1.52	165
Dimethyl aniline	1.83	165
Dodecyl mercaptan	1.46	165
Isobutyl alcohol	1.72	166
Toluene	1.60	166
t-Amyl alcohol	1.40	166
Aniline	1.68	166
Nitrobenzene	1.98	169
Toluene	1.55	167

^{a} Containing 0.012 M chloranil.

[167] M. Talat-Erben and S. Bywater, *J. Am. Chem. Soc.*, **77**, 3712 (1955).
[168] C. E. H. Bawn and S. F. Mellish, *Trans. Faraday Soc.*, **47**, 1216 (1951).
[169] K. Ziegler, W. Deparade, and W. Meye, *Ann.*, **567**, 141 (1950).

(*Footnotes, Table 10.10*)

^{a} Data taken from reference number in parentheses when more than one number is given.

^{b} Two stereoisomers.

^{c} Compound is reported to decompose in solution at room temperature and initiate polymerization at 5°C.

^{d} In xylene.

^{e} In nitrobenzene.

^{f} In water.

^{g} 70°.

^{h} 100°.

[170] L. M. Arnett, *J. Am. Chem. Soc.*, **74**, 2027 (1952).
[171] J. W. Breitenbach and A. Schindler, *Monatsh.*, **83**, 724 (1952).
[172] C. G. Overberger and H. Biletch, *J. Am. Chem. Soc.*, **73**, 4880 (1951).
[173] C. G. Overberger, W. F. Hale, M. B. Berenbaum, and A. B. Finestone, *ibid.*, **76**, 6185 (1954).
[174] C. G. Overberger and A. Lebovits, *ibid.*, **76**, 2722 (1954).
[175] C. G. Overberger, H. Biletch, A. B. Finestone, J. Lilker, and J. Herbert, *ibid.*, **75**, 2078 (1953).
[176] D. C. Pease and J. A. Robertson, U.S. Patent 2,565,573 (August 28, 1951).

TABLE 10·10   DECOMPOSITION RATES OF AZONITRILES R—N=N—R [a]

(At 80° in toluene unless indicated)

R	$k \times 10^4 \ \text{sec}^{-1}$	E_{act}, kcal/mole
$(CH_3)_2CCN$	1.53 [d, (165), 166–171]	31.3
$(CH_3)_2CCOOCH_3$	1.09 [d, (165), 169]	35.8
$(CH_3)_2CCOOEt$	1.57 [e, 169]	30.9
$C_2H_5(CH_3)CCN$	0.995 [d, (165), 166]	29.4
$n\text{-}C_5H_{11}(CH_3)CCN$	1.79 [d, 165]	30.2
$HOOC(CH_2)_3C(CH_3)CN$	0.896 [f, 165]	34.0
$n\text{-}C_3H_7C(CH_3)CN$	0.42 [g, 166]	33 ± 4
$Iso\text{-}C_3H_7C(CH_3)CN$	0.26 [b, 166]	32 ± 4
$Iso\text{-}C_4H_9C(CH_3)CN$	1.98 [g, 166]	29 ± 4
$\phi CH_2C(CH_3)CN$	1.16 [172]	...
$p\text{-}Cl\phi CH_2C(CH_3)CN$	0.88 [172]	...
$p\text{-}NO_2\phi CH_2C(CH_3)CN$	1.00 [172]	...
$t\text{-}C_4H_9C(CH_3)CN$	158 [b, 173]	27 ± 1.5
	136 [b, 173]	29 ± 1.5
$(Iso\text{-}C_4H_9)_2CCN$	49.5 [173]	...
$(Iso\text{-}C_3H_7)_2CCN$	1.25 [173]	...
$Iso\text{-}C_3H_7C(C_2H_5)CN$	0.95 [173]	...
$(C_2H_5)_2CCN$	0.84 [e, 168]	34.2
$(n\text{-}C_3H_7)_2CCN$	1.15 [e, h, 169]	...
$Cyclo\text{-}C_3H_5C(CH_3)CN$	33 [174]	...
$Cyclo\text{-}C_4H_7C(CH_3)CN$	1.51 [174]	...
$Cyclo\text{-}C_5H_9C(CH_3)CN$	1.31 [174]	...
$Cyclo\text{-}C_6H_{11}C(CH_3)CN$	2.27 [174]	...
$\overline{(CH_2)_3}CCN$	0.00173 [175]	32.1
$\overline{(CH_2)_4}CCN$	0.726 [175]	33.8
$\overline{(CH_2)_5}CCN$	0.063 [155, 169, (175)]	35.4
$\overline{(CH_2)_6}CCN$	12.2 [175]	27.5
$\overline{(CH_2)_7}CCN$	83.4 [175]	25.9
$\overline{(CH_2)_9}CCN$	18.4 [175]	28.0
$\overline{(CH_2)_4}CCN$ with CHCH$_3$	0.074 [175]	...
$\phi\text{-}C(CH_3)CN$	Very fast [c, 176]	...

(Table 10.10 footnotes on p. 512)

It is worth noting that, although other carboxylic acid derivatives behave much like the disubstituted azonitriles, monosubstituted azonitriles appear to decompose by non-radical paths and are not good radical sources.

From Table 10·10 it is evident that most of the azonitriles decompose at comparable rates, but there are some striking exceptions. Overberger has suggested that the stability of some of the cyclic compounds arises from a lowered resonance energy for radicals attached to small rings,[175] and that the high decomposition rate of compounds such as the methylneopentylacetonitrile derivative is caused by steric repulsion between bulky groups.[178] Similarly, the rapid decomposition of azobis-α-phenylpropionitrile [176] may be due to resonance stabilization of the resulting benzyl-type radical.

The 2-cyanopropyl radical arising from the decomposition of azobisisobutyronitrile is a relatively inactive species (structurally it resembles the radical involved in the polymerization of methacrylonitrile), and in unreactive solvents it disappears largely by a coupling reaction generally presumed to be

$$2(CH_3)_2\overset{\cdot}{C}CN \rightarrow (CH_3)_2\overset{\overset{\displaystyle CN}{\displaystyle |}}{C}\text{—}\underset{\underset{\displaystyle CN}{\displaystyle |}}{C}\cdot(CH_3)_2 \tag{84}$$

In CCl_4, for example, a 90% yield of tetramethylsuccinonitrile has been reported by Hammond.[177] Recently, however, Talat-Erben and Bywater [167,178] have concluded that as much as 33% of the initial recombination is to dimethylketenecyanoisopropylimine, an unstable intermediate which (most probably) rearranges to the nitrile so that

$$2(CH_3)_2CCN \rightarrow (CH_3)_2\overset{\overset{\displaystyle CN}{\displaystyle |}}{C}\text{—}N\text{=}C\text{=}C(CH_3)_2 \tag{85}$$

the reaction is more complex than was formerly assumed.[179]

Methyl α-azobisisobutyrate apparently gives rather more disproportionation to methyl methacrylate and methyl isobutyrate (30–60%).[180] More complex azonitriles also appear to give more

---

[177] G. S. Hammond, J. N. Sen, and C. E. Boozer, *ibid.*, **77**, 3244 (1955).

[178] M. Talat-Erben and S. Bywater, *ibid.*, **77**, 3710 (1955).

[179] J. C. Bevington's observation, *J. Chem. Soc.*, **1954**, 3707, that the apparent amount of disproportionation of 2-cyanoisopropyl radicals decreases with conversion may perhaps be accounted for by this same intermediate.

[180] A. F. Bickel and W. A. Waters, *Rec. trav. chim.*, **69**, 312 (1950).

disproportionation,[181] and, with these, Overberger and Berenbaum [182] have obtained good evidence that the initial dissociation (reaction 83) is actually into *free* radicals. Thus racemic and *meso*-azobis-methylisobutylacetonitrile yield the same mixture of diastereomeric dimethyldiisobutylsuccinonitriles, and decomposition of a mixture of azobisisobutyronitrile and 1-azobiscyclopentanenitrile gives both symmetric and unsymmetric products, i.e.,

$$(CH_3)_2\dot{C}CN + \text{[cyclopentane with CN]} \rightarrow (CH_3)_2C{\overset{CN}{\underset{CN}{\big|}}}\text{[cyclopentane]} \qquad (86)$$

With more reactive substrates, azonitriles not only initiate polymerization efficiently but also attack a variety of other molecules including mercaptans,[177,183] quinones,[184] quinone imides,[185] and polynuclear hydrocarbons such as anthracene,[186] in the last case to give 9,10-di-(2-cyanoisopropyl)-9,10-dihydroanthracene and the dimeric product containing two anthracene residues. Some attack occurs on aldehydes,[187] a few organic halides,[188] and on N-chloroacetanilide.[189] 2-Cyanoisopropyl radicals react rapidly with iodine [190] and oxygen (Section 9·2g) and also with nitric oxide,[185,191] apparently giving α-nitrosoisobutyronitrile as an intermediate, but a trisubstituted hydroxylamine as a final product. Similar phenylhydroxylamine derivatives are obtained from nitrosobenzenes, i.e. (R = $(CH_3)_2CCN$),

[181] C. G. Overberger and M. B. Berenbaum, *ibid.*, **74**, 3293 (1952), have isolated 78% disproportionation products from azobis-*t*-butylmethylacetonitrile. They also noted no isomerization of the intermediate substituted neopentyl radical.

[182] C. G. Overberger and M. B. Berenbaum, *J. Am. Chem. Soc.*, **73**, 4883 (1951).

[183] P. Bruin, A. F. Bickel, and E. C. Kooyman, *Rec. trav. chim.*, **61**, 1115 (1952).

[184] F. J. Lopez Aparicio and W. A. Waters, *J. Chem. Soc.*, **1952**, 4666 (cf. Section 6·3c).

[185] B. A. Gingras and W. A. Waters, *ibid.*, **1954**, 1902.

[186] A. F. Bickel and E. C. Kooyman, *Rec. trav. chim.*, **71**, 1137 (1952); J. W. Engelsma, E. Farenhorst, and E. C. Kooyman, *ibid.*, **73**, 878 (1954); E. Farenhorst and E. C. Kooyman, *Nature*, **175**, 598 (1955).

[187] E. F. P. Harris and W. A. Waters, *J. Chem. Soc.*, **1952**, 3108.

[188] M. C. Ford and W. A. Waters, *ibid.*, **1952**, 2240.

[189] M. C. Ford, L. J. Hunt, and W. A. Waters, *ibid.*, **1953**, 3529. Methyl azobisisobutyrate was actually employed.

[190] M. C. Ford and W. A. Waters, *ibid.*, **1951**, 1851.

[191] B. A. Gingras and W. A. Waters, *Chemistry & Industry*, **1953**, 615.

$$R \cdot + NO \rightarrow R{-}NO \xrightarrow{2R} \underset{\underset{R}{|}}{R{-}N{-}O{-}R} \tag{87}$$

$$\phi NO + 2R \cdot \longrightarrow \underset{\underset{R}{|}}{\phi{-}N{-}O{-}R} \tag{88}$$

10·3b   Other Alkyl and Alkyl Aryl Azo Compounds

A number of azo derivatives of hydrocarbons are known, most of which decompose at higher temperatures than the azonitriles, and which yield radicals by more or less clean-cut first-order processes. Decomposition rate data are summarized in Table 10·11. As Cohen

TABLE 10·11   DECOMPOSITION OF AZO HYDROCARBONS

Compound	Solvent	Temperature	$k \times 10^4 (\text{sec}^{-1})$	E_{act}, kcal/mole	Footnote
$CH_3{-}N{=}N{-}CH_3$	Gas	300°	5.6	50.2	196
$(CH_3)_2CH{-}N{=}N{-}CH(CH_3)_2$	Gas	250°	4.8	40.9	197
$\phi{-}N{=}NC\phi_3$	Benzene	25°	0.042	26.8	192
	Toluene	53°	2.25	...	193
$\phi{-}N{=}N{-}CH\phi_2$	Decalin	54°	1.01	34.0	194
$\phi CH(CH_3){-}N{=}N{-}CH(CH_3)\phi$	Toluene	110°	1.69	32.6	198
$\phi_2CH{-}N{=}N{-}CH\phi_2$	Toluene	64°	3.40	26.6	195
$\phi CH(C_2H_5){-}N{=}N{-}CH(C_2H_5)\phi$	Ethylbenzene	110°	0.72	32.3	198
$\phi CH(\text{iso-}C_4H_9){-}N{=}N{-}CH(\text{iso-}C_4H_9)\phi$	Ethylbenzene	110°	2.42	33.3	198

[192] M. G. Alder and J. E. Leffler, *J. Am. Chem. Soc.*, **76**, 1425 (1954).
[193] S. G. Cohen and C. H. Wang, *ibid.*, **75**, 5504 (1953).
[194] S. G. Cohen and C. H. Wang, *ibid.*, **77**, 3628 (1955).
[195] S. G. Cohen and C. H. Wang, *ibid.*, **77**, 2457 (1955).
[196] O. K. Rice and D. V. Sickman, *J. Chem. Phys.*, **4**, 239, 242, 608 (1936)
[197] H. C. Ramsperger, *J. Am. Chem. Soc.*, **50**, 714 (1928).
[198] S. G. Cohen, S. J. Groszos, and D. B. Sparrow, *ibid.*, **72**, 3947.

has pointed out, considering azomethane as the parent compound, substitution of two methyl and two phenyl groups lower the activation energy for dissociation by 5 and 12 kcal respectively.[199] In addition to the data listed in Table 10·11, Cohen has determined the rates of decomposition of a series of p-substituted phenylazotriphenyl-methanes, finding about a 4-fold decrease in going from p-methyl to p-nitro,[193] and Leffler has investigated the variation in rate with solvent for both phenylazotriphenylmethane [192,200] and p-nitrophenyl-azotri-(p-anisyl)-methane,[201] noting small compensating changes in $\Delta S^{\ddagger}$ and $\Delta H^{\ddagger}$ but very little net difference in rate.

[199] Azotriphenylmethane is reported to be too unstable to isolate, H. Wieland, H. vom Hove, and K. Borner, *Ann.*, **456**, 31 (1926).

[200] J. E. Leffler and R. A. Hubbard, *J. Org. Chem.*, **19**, 1089 (1954).

[201] M. D. Cohen, J. E. Leffler, and L. M. Barbato, *J. Am. Chem. Soc.*, **76**, 4169 (1954).

In general, the azo compounds of Table 10·11 initiate polymerization, although with azodiphenylmethane the efficiency of the process is rather low, the relatively unreactive radicals stopping chains as well.[195] In this regard, an interesting cyclic bis azo compound has been studied by Overberger and Lapkin,[202] which produces diradicals and, as would be anticipated (Section 5·1), is a very poor initiator. In inert solvents it decomposes to tetraphenylcycloeicosane as shown, at a rate, k_{120} 2.2×10^{-4} sec^{-1}, E_{act} 30 kcal/mole, comparable to its analogs in Table 10·11.

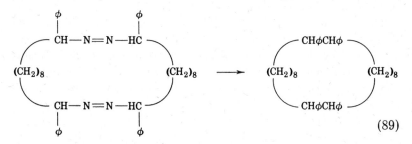

$$(89)$$

In any but the most reactive media, azohydrocarbons yielding solely substituted benzyl radicals give chiefly products of coupling of the initial radicals. However, the phenylazo compounds produce more reactive phenyl radicals which attack solvent in the manner discussed in Section 10·2b.[203-206] The decomposition of acylazotriphenylmethanes also appears to yield radicals, and, in the presence of oxygen, acetylazotriphenylmethane is said to give both acetyl peroxide and triphenylmethyl peroxide.[207] The former product is interesting since the reaction may correspond to the termination step in aldehyde autoxidation, Section 9·2e.[208]

[202] C. G. Overberger and M. Lapkin, *ibid.*, **77**, 4651 (1955).

[203] D. H. Hey, *J. Chem. Soc.*, **1954**, 1966.

[204] H. Wieland, *Ann.*, **514**, 145 (1934).

[205] G. A. Razuvaev and E. T. Fedotova, *Zhur. Obshchei Khim.*, **21**, 1118 (1951).

[206] R. Huisgen and H. Nakatan, *Ann.*, **586**, 70 (1954), have recently discussed the decomposition of phenylazotriphenylmethyl in aromatic solvents in some detail. They conclude that phenyl radicals attack solvent via reaction 38 (hydrogen atom loss), which, however, we have discarded as a possibility in our discussion.

[207] H. Wieland, H. vom Hove, and K. Borner, *ibid.*, **446**, 31 (1926); H. Wieland, A. Hintermaier, and I. Dennstedt, *ibid.*, **452**, 1 (1927).

[208] For a further discussion of the chemistry of azo compounds, cf. W. A. Waters, *The Chemistry of Free Radicals,* second edition, Oxford University Press, Oxford, 1948.

10·3c   Diazo Compounds

Because of their importance, an enormous literature exists on the chemistry of aromatic diazonium compounds and their derivatives.[209] Present evidence indicates that the coupling reactions of diazonium ions to amines and phenols [210] and the majority of processes occurring in acid media are polar reactions.   In neutral or alkaline solution, however, diazonium ions are converted to covalent phenylazo derivatives, hydroxides, cyanides, xanthates, diazoamino compounds, etc., and there are many indications that the subsequent decompositions of these materials may be radical processes.

The behavior of nitrosoacetanilide and its analogs provides a good example.   Such substances initiate polymerization [211] and, in a variety of solvents, yield the products to be anticipated from phenyl radicals.[212]   Huisgen and Horeld [213] have shown that the rate-controlling step in the decomposition is a polar rearrangement to benzene diazoacetate, followed by a rapid breakdown into radicals, since, in the presence of phenols, disappearance of the nitrosoacetanilide occurs at the same rate but the radical decomposition is replaced by the more rapid polar coupling process.   The rearrangement occurs at essen-

$$
\begin{array}{c}
\text{NO} \\
| \\
\phi\text{—N—COCH}_3 \xrightarrow{\text{Slow}} \phi\text{—N}{=}\text{N—OAc}
\end{array}
\quad
\begin{array}{l}
\xrightarrow{\text{AroH}} \phi\text{—N}{=}\text{N—AroH} \\
\\
\searrow \\
\phi\cdot + \text{N}_2 + \cdot\text{OAc}
\end{array}
\tag{90}
$$

tially the same rate in a variety of solvents but varies with substituents on the aryl nucleus and appears to be catalyzed by bases such as piperidine.[214]   A puzzling feature of this formulation, however, is that the presumed acyloxy radical fails to evolve CO_2, and can generally be recovered as the corresponding acid rather than becoming involved in further radical processes.   Evidently the process is more complicated than is indicated by eq. 90.

[209] K. H. Saunders, *The Aromatic Diazo-Compounds,* second edition, Edward Arnold, London, 1949.

[210] H. Zollinger, *Chem. Revs.,* **51,** 347 (1952).

[211] A. T. Blomquist, J. R. Johnson, and H. J. Sykes, *J. Am. Chem. Soc.,* **65,** 2446 (1953); D. H. Hey and G. S. Misra, *Discussions Faraday Soc.,* **2,** 879 (1947); D. F. DeTar and C. S. Savat, *J. Am. Chem. Soc.,* **75,** 5116 (1953).

[212] References and discussion of these reactions are given by Waters, pp. 148–152 of reference cited in footnote 208; cf. also footnote 219.

[213] R. Huisgen and G. Horeld, *Ann.,* **562,** 137 (1949).

[214] R. Huisgen, *Ann.,* **573,** 163 (1951); D. H. Hey, J. Stuart-Webb, and G. H. Williams, *Research,* **4,** 385 (1951); *J. Chem. Soc.,* **1952,** 4657.

Diazoamino compounds, $ArN{=}N{-}NR_2$ or $ArN{=}N{-}NHR$, also initiate polymerization at temperatures in the neighborhood of $100°$,[215] and the decomposition rates of a large number have been studied by Dolgoplosk, Ugryumov, and Krol,[215] who find first-order kinetics. Rondestvedt and Blanchard report that essentially the same mixtures of isomeric substituted diphenyls are obtained when benzoyl peroxide, nitrosoacetanilide, and dimethylaminodiazobenzene, $\phi{-}N{=}N{-}N(CH_3)_2$, are decomposed in a series of alkyl benzenes.[216] Both results suggest a decomposition into radicals, as does the ob-

$$\phi{-}N{=}N{-}NR_2 \rightarrow \phi{\cdot} + N_2 + {\cdot}NR_2 \tag{91}$$

servation that benzylaminodiazobenzene, in the presence of CCl_4 and mercury, yields both phenylmercuric chloride and hexachloroethane.[217]

The Gomberg-Bachmann reaction [218] is another well-authenticated example of a radical decomposition of aryl diazonium derivatives. Here a solution of an aryl diazonium salt is treated with alkali in the presence of an aromatic solvent to yield diphenyl derivatives.[219] It is probable that the reaction involves the steps

$$\phi N_2{}^+ + OH^- \rightarrow \phi N{=}N{-}OH \text{ (aqueous)} \tag{92}$$

$$\phi{-}N{=}N{-}OH \text{ (aqueous)} \rightarrow \phi{-}N{=}N{-}OH \text{ (organic solvent)} \tag{93}$$

$$\phi{-}N{=}N{-}OH \text{ (organic solvent)} \rightarrow \phi{\cdot} + N_2 + {\cdot}OH \tag{94}$$

$$\phi{\cdot} + ArH \rightarrow Ar{-}\phi \tag{95}$$

with the covalent diazohydroxide decomposing into radicals in the non-aqueous phase, since the isomer distribution of substituted diphenyls obtained is the same as that observed when phenyl radicals are produced by other means,[220] but, again, the fate of the presumed $\cdot OH$ radical is obscure.

[215] B. A. Dolgoplosk, P. G. Ugryumov, and V. A. Krol, *Doklady Akad. Nauk S.S.S.R.*, **96**, 757 (1954).

[216] C. S. Rondestvedt, Jr., and H. S. Blanchard, *J. Am. Chem. Soc.*, **77**, 1769 (1955).

[217] G. A. Razuvaev, E. I. Fedotova, and A. G. Orchinnikova, *Zhur. Obshchei Khim.*, **23**, 435 (1953).

[218] M. Gomberg and W. E. Bachmann, *J. Am. Chem. Soc.*, **46**, 2339 (1924).

[219] For examples and experimental techniques, cf. W. E. Bachmann and R. A. Hoffman, *Organic Reactions*, **2**, 224 (1944).

[220] The isomer distribution obtained from a given solvent may, however, vary with different substituted phenyl radicals. Data on the decomposition of nitro-

Other covalent diazonium derivatives can apparently decompose by radical paths; as examples, diazothioethers [221] and even non-covalent diazonium fluoborates [222] serve as polymerization initiators, although the reactions have not been studied in as much detail,[223] and certainly deserve further investigation.[224]

The Sandmeyer and Gattermann reactions have been suggested as radical processes by Waters,[225] although with little direct evidence. A somewhat better case can be made for the Meerwein reaction,[226] in which diazonium chlorides react with (chiefly carbonyl-conjugated) olefins in aqueous acetone in the presence of acetate ion and copper salts with addition of halogen and aryl group to the double bond. This reaction has received extensive recent study,[227, 228] and

$$\text{ArN}_2\text{Cl} + \text{RCH}\!=\!\text{CH}\!-\!\text{COOR}' \rightarrow$$

$$\underset{\displaystyle \text{RCH}-\overset{\displaystyle |}{\underset{\displaystyle |}{\text{CH}}}-\text{COOR}}{\overset{\text{Ar} \quad \text{Cl}}{}} \quad \text{or} \quad \underset{\displaystyle \text{R}-\text{CH}-\text{CH}-\text{COOR}}{\overset{\text{Cl} \quad \text{Ar}}{}} \quad (96)$$

Kochi [228] finds that cuprous ion is the effective catalyst, implying that best yields are obtained with careful exclusion of air. This suggests that a radical process is involved, perhaps a redox system of some sort (see below), and Koelsch and Boekelheide some time ago [229] proposed a radical path involving cupric ion, although this

phenyl diazohydroxides in nitrobenzene are given by D. F. DeTar and A. A. Kazimi, *J. Am. Chem. Soc.*, **77**, 3842 (1955), who note 30–35% ortho substitution and 23–25% meta, compared to 60 and 8% respectively with phenyl radicals, Table 10·2.

[221] W. B. Reynolds and E. B. Cohen, *Ind. Eng. Chem.*, **42**, 1905 (1950); M. Morton, P. Salatiello, and H. Landfield, *ibid.*, **44**, 739 (1952).

[222] C. S. Marvel, H. Z. Friedlander, S. Swann, Jr., and H. K. Inskip, *J. Am. Chem. Soc.*, **75**, 3846 (1953).

[223] Cf. Waters, p. 155 et seq. of reference cited in footnote 208.

[224] An interesting example has recently been noted by D. I. Relyea and D. F. DeTar, *J. Am. Chem. Soc.*, **76**, 1202 (1954), who find that 2-*p*-tolylbenzene-diazonium fluoborate in the presence of CCl_4 and alkali gives both 2′-chloro-4-methylbiphenyl and 2-chloro-4-methylbiphenyl.

[225] W. A. Waters, *J. Chem. Soc.*, **1942**, 266; cf. Waters, p. 162 of reference cited in footnote 208.

[226] H. Meerwein, E. Buchner, and K. van Emster, *J. prakt. Chem.*, **152**, 237 (1939).

[227] C. S. Rondestvedt, Jr., and O. Vogl, *J. Am. Chem. Soc.*, **77**, 2313, 3067, 3401 (1955); *ibid.*, **78**, 3799 (1956).

[228] J. K. Kochi, *ibid.*, **77**, 5090, 5274 (1955); **78**, 1228, 4815 (1956). The first paper lists many earlier references.

[229] C. F. Koelsch and V. Boekelheide, *ibid.*, **68**, 412 (1944).

must require modification in view of Kochi's findings.[228] An interesting aspect of the reaction is that, although methyl crotonate gives methyl β-aryl-α-chlorobutyrates, methyl cinnamate gives methyl α-aryl-β-chlorodihydrocinnamates, a reversal of direction of addition which might be expected in a radical process involving addition of an aryl radical to the double bond.[229]

Finally, we may mention the reactions by which aryldiazonium compounds are reduced to hydrocarbons,[230] two of which appear to be clearly radical chain processes. The first is the reduction by hypophosphorous acid, with an overall reaction

$$ArN_2X + H_3PO_2 + H_2O \rightarrow ArH + H_3PO_3 + HX + N_2 \quad (97)$$

Kornblum, Cooper, and Taylor [231] find that the reaction shows rather erratic rates but is strongly catalyzed by traces of $KMnO_4$, $K_2Cr_2O_7$, $CuSO_4$, $FeSO_4$, and copper ion and less so by a variety of other materials, and is strongly inhibited by benzoquinone. From this they conclude that an initial reaction with hypophosphorous acid occurs, followed by a chain process. [From our consideration of radical

$$ArN{=}N{-}OPOH_2 \rightarrow Ar\cdot + N_2 + (H_2PO_2)\cdot \quad (98)$$

$$(H_2PO_2)\cdot + ArN_2^+ \rightarrow Ar\cdot + N_2 + (H_2PO_2)^+ \xrightarrow{H_2O}$$

$$H_3PO_3 + H^+ \quad (99)$$

$$Ar\cdot + H_3PO_2 \rightarrow ArH + (H_2PO_2)\cdot \quad (100)$$

addition reactions, $(H_2PO_2)\cdot$ should be $\cdot\overset{\nearrow O}{PH}(OH)$.]

As evidence for reaction 98 they note that addition of a small amount of rapidly reduced diazonium ion (i.e., p-nitrophenyldiazonium ion) leads to the rapid reduction of many equivalents of a slow-reacting compound. In the presence of an oxidizing agent additional hypophosphite radicals are produced via reactions such as

$$Cu^{++} + H_2PO_2^- \rightarrow Cu^+ + H_2PO_2\cdot \quad (101)$$

Subsequently Kornblum has found that the much slower reduction of diazonium compounds by phosphorous acid follows a similar pattern.[232]

[230] For a review, cf. N. Kornblum, *Org. Reactions*, **2**, 262 (1944).

[231] N. Kornblum, G. D. Cooper, and J. E. Taylor, *J. Am. Chem. Soc.*, **72**, 3013 (1950).

[232] N. Kornblum, A. E. Kelley, and G. D. Cooper, *ibid.*, **74**, 3074 (1952).

Although the reduction of diazonium compounds by alcohols was described by Griess in 1864,[233] the reaction has always been somewhat limited as to scope and unreliable as to yield.[230] In part, this difficulty may be accounted for by the finding of DeTar and Turetzky [234] that the reduction is a strongly oxygen-inhibited radical chain process. They find that benzenediazonium chloride or fluoroborate, decomposed in methanol under acid conditions, gives anisole in 93% yield. In acetate buffers in the presence of air, reactions are complex, only a portion of the nitrogen is evolved, and anisole, benzene, diphenyl, and azobenzene are produced plus 25–70% of unidentified tarry products. When air is carefully excluded the decomposition is much more rapid, essentially all of the nitrogen is evolved, and the benzene yield rises to 85–90% plus anisole (3–4%) and biphenyl (5%). They suggest a chain process in which the propagation steps are

$$\phi\cdot + CH_3OH \rightarrow \phi H + \cdot CH_2OH \tag{102}$$

$$\cdot CH_2OH + \phi N_2^+ \rightarrow \phi\cdot + N_2 + \overset{+}{C}H_2OH(\rightarrow CH_2O + H^+) \tag{103}$$

That radical attack actually occurs at the H—CH_2OH bond in such systems is shown by the observation by Rekasheva and Miklukhin [235] that decompositions in oxygen-deuterated ethanol, C_2H_5OD, give little deuterium in the aryl hydrocarbons produced.

10·4   Other Thermal Free Radical Sources

10·4a   Sulfur Compounds

In Section 7·3 a variety of reactions were considered which involve sulfur atoms carrying an odd electron, RS·, and we also saw that sulfur itself dissociates appreciably into polysulfide radicals at elevated temperatures, $D(S_x—S_y)$ being only 33.4 kcal. Simple disulfides have relatively strong S—S bonds, $D(CH_3S—SCH_3)$ having a reported value of 73 kcal.[236] However, more complicated substituents, permitting greater resonance stabilization of the resulting radicals, produce lower bond dissociation energies, and a number of cases are known of disulfides which apparently yield radicals at

[233] P. Griess, *Phil. Trans.*, **154**, 683 (1864).

[234] D. F. DeTar and M. N. Turetzky, *J. Am. Chem. Soc.*, **77**, 1745 (1955); *ibid.*, **78**, 3925, 3928 (1956).

[235] A. F. Rekasheva and G. P. Miklukhin, *Doklady Akad. Nauk S.S.S.R.*, **80**, 221 (1951); *Zhur Obschei. Khim.*, **24**, 96 (1954).

[236] J. L. Franklin and H. E. Lumpkin, *J. Am. Chem. Soc.*, **74**, 1023 (1948).

moderate temperatures. Thus, solutions of diphenyl disulfide and α-naphthoyl disulfide $(C_{10}H_7COS—)_2$ reversibly develop a yellow color on heating.[237] 2,2'-Benzothiazyl disulfide behaves similarly, and magnetic susceptibility studies of its solutions in toluene indicate an equilibrium constant for the reaction

$$\tag{104}$$

of 6.07×10^{-5} at 100° and 5.94×10^{-3} at 150°.[238] From these data, $D(RS—SR)$ for this substance is approximately 29 kcal. Several of these more complex disulfides, on dissociation, produce radicals capable of initiating polymerization, including dibenzoyl disulfide,[239] 2,2'-benzothiazyl disulfide,[240] and tetramethylthiuram disulfide.[240, 241] This last compound, $[(CH_3)_2NCS—S—]_2$ has been studied in some detail by Ferington and Tobolsky,[242] who find that the rate of polymerization produced in styrene and methyl methacrylate at 70° by low concentrations is one- to two-tenths that produced by the same concentration of benzoyl peroxide. At higher concentrations, the disulfide behaves both as a transfer agent and retarder. Apparently the radicals produced have rather low reactivity since they fail to initiate polymerization of vinyl acetate.[241]

In simple molecules, C—SR bonds have about the same strength as S—S bonds, $D(CH_3S—CH_3) = 73$ kcal, so sufficiently complex monosulfides might also be expected to dissociate into radicals. Tetramethylthiuram monosulfide, $(CH_3)_2NCS—S—CSN(CH_3)_2$, initiates the polymerization of monomers such as acrylonitrile,[241] and substances such as phenyl triphenylmethyl sulfide react with oxygen to yield diphenyl disulfide and triphenylmethyl peroxide,[243] presumably via dissociation:

$$\phi_3C—S—\phi \rightarrow \phi_3C\cdot + \cdot S\phi \xrightarrow{O_2} \phi_3C—O_2—C\phi_3 + \phi SS\phi \tag{105a}$$

[237] A. Schönberg, E. Rupp, and W. Gumlich, *Ber.*, **66**, 1932 (1933).

[238] H. G. Cutforth and P. W. Selwood, *J. Am. Chem. Soc.*, **70**, 278 (1948).

[239] R. L. Frank, R. J. Blegen, and A. Deutschman, *J. Polymer Sci.*, **3**, 58 (1948).

[240] J. W. Breitenbach and A. Schinder, *Monatsh.*, **84**, 820 (1953).

[241] R. J. Kern, *J. Am. Chem. Soc.*, **77**, 1385 (1955).

[242] T. E. Ferington and A. V. Tobolsky, *ibid.*, **77**, 4510 (1955).

[243] H. Lecher, *Ber.*, **48**, 524 (1915); **55**, 577 (1920).

Barkenbus and Brower [244] have recently suggested that the decomposition of tetraphenylthiodiacetic acid (which occurs in two hours at room temperature in pyridine solution) involves a similar dissociation:

$$
\begin{array}{c}
\text{COOH} \\
| \\
\phi_2C\!-\!S\!-\!C\phi_2 \;\rightarrow\; \phi_2\!-\!\underset{|}{C}\!-\!\text{COOH} \;+\; \phi_2\overset{|}{C}\!-\!S\cdot \\
\end{array} \qquad (105b)
$$

$$
\phi_2\text{CHCOOH} \qquad\qquad CO_2 + \phi_2C\!=\!S
$$

Finally, Hirshon, Gardner, and Fraenkel have noted that many sulfur compounds such as thiophenol and diphenyl disulfide give deeply colored solutions in sulfuric acid (or in the presence of aluminum chloride) which exhibit paramagnetic resonance spectra,[245] although the exact species involved are unknown. Since a great many complex sulfur-containing molecules are readily available and the study of their properties as radical sources has scarcely begun, this is evidently a field which should be of much future interest. The importance of such processes in connection with vulcanization was noted in Section 7·3.

10·4b   *Nitrogen Compounds*

In Section 10·3 we discussed azo compounds as thermal radical sources in which the driving force for the initial dissociation is apparently the formation of the very stable N_2 bond. The value of $D(H_2N\!-\!NH_2)$ in hydrazine is approximately 60 kcal (Table 2·2), little more than $D(HO\!-\!OH)$ in hydrogen peroxide (54 kcal), suggesting that substituted hydrazines should behave as radical sources analogous to the peroxides. The bond dissociation energies for phenylhydrazine, hydrazobenzene, and tetraphenylhydrazine have been calculated as 47.8, 37.7, and 30.5 kcal respectively from thermochemical data by Cole and Gilbert.[246] As first noted by Wieland,[247] tetraphenylhydrazine in non-polar solvents reversibly develops a green color on heating, and the rate of dissociation has been meas-

[244] C. Barkenbus and F. M. Brower, *J. Am. Chem. Soc.*, **77**, 579 (1955).

[245] J. M. Hirshon, D. M. Gardner, and G. K. Fraenkel, *ibid.*, **75**, 4115 (1953). Many oxygen-containing molecules behave similarly; cf. also J. E. Wertz and J. L. Vivo, *J. Chem. Phys.*, **23**, 2193 (1955).

[246] L. G. Cole and E. C. Gilbert, *J. Am. Chem. Soc.*, **73**, 5423 (1951).

[247] H. Wieland, *Ann.*, **381**, 200 (1911).

ured (by rate of uptake of nitric oxide) by Cain and Wiselogle,[248] who find a half-life of 3.1 minutes at 100°, with $E_{act} = 30 \pm 1.5$ kcal. On prolonged heating the intermediate radicals undergo irreversible disproportionation into diphenylamine and diphenyldihydrophenazine, and a number of other polyarylhydrazines behave similarly.[249] Wieland has found that the ease of dissociation of tetraarylhydrazines is increased by electron-supplying groups and decreased by electron-withdrawing ones,[250] and Lewis and Lipkin [251] suggest that the effect is due to the resulting changes in the dipolar repulsion between the two halves of the molecule (cf. the case of the substituted benzoyl peroxides, Section 10·2b). The foregoing suggest that many suitable hydrazines could be used as radical sources for inducing chain reactions, although the matter seems to have had little study from this point of view.[252] Hexaaryltetrazanes, $R_2N—NR—NR—NR_2$, dissociate rapidly into radicals, even at low temperatures,[253] with the radicals slowly undergoing irreversible changes into non-radical products. The rates of dissociation and equilibrium constants for a series of tetraaryldibenzoyltetrazanes have recently been measured in acetone at temperatures near −30° by Wilmarth and Schwartz [254]

$$(106)$$

[248] C. K. Cain and F. Y. Wiselogle, *J. Am. Chem. Soc.*, **62**, 1163 (1940).

[249] H. Wieland and H. Fressel, *Ann.*, **392**, 133 (1912); for a more detailed discussion, cf. Waters,[208] pp. 64–67. The dissociation of triphenylhydrazine at 140° has also been studied by P. F. Holt and B. P. Hughes, *J. Chem. Soc.*, **1955**, 1320, and of tetrafluorenylhydrazine in a range of solvents by T. L. Chu and T. L. Weismann, *J. Am. Chem. Soc.*, **76**, 3787 (1954).

[250] H. Wieland, *Ber.*, **48**, 1078, 1091 (1915); **55**, 1804 (1922).

[251] G. N. Lewis and D. Lipkin, *J. Am. Chem. Soc.*, **63**, 3232 (1941).

[252] A few references to hydrazine derivatives as radical sources appear in the patent literature. Thus, *sym*-dibenzoylhydrazine is claimed as an initiator for high-temperature (200–240°) ethylene polymerization; J. R. Roland and J. Harmon, U.S. Pat. 2,433,015 (December 23, 1947).

[253] S. Goldschmidt, *Ber.*, **53**, 44 (1920).

[254] W. K. Wilmarth and N. Schwartz, *J. Am. Chem. Soc.*, **77**, 4543, 4551 (1955).

TABLE 10·12   DISSOCIATION OF TETRAARYLDIBENZOYLTETRAZANES

(At $-30°$ in acetone)

R_1 [a]	R_2 [a]	$K \times 10^4$	ΔH [b]	$k_1 \times 10^4$	$\Delta H^{\ddagger}$ [b]	k_2	$\Delta H_2^{\ddagger}$ [b]
CH₃	CH₃	53.6	6.8	31.4	15.0	0.59	8.3
CH₃	H	9.46	7.8	16.0	15.8	1.7	8.0
H	H	4.15	8.9	8.29	16.6	2.0	7.4
Br	H	0.625	10.3	6.15	16.6	9.8	5.7
Br	Br	0.170	11.8	4.49	17.2	26.0	6.0
NO₂	H	...	...	0.214	19.3	...	...
NO₂	NO₂	...	...	0.022	21.6	...	...

[a] Cf. reaction 106.
[b] In kcal/mole.

with results shown in Table 10·12. Again both amount and rate of dissociation is increased by electron-supplying groups. A plot of log K versus Hammett σ values for substituents gives $\rho = -1.52$, whereas for k_1, $\rho = -0.55$. Interestingly, recombination here has an appreciable activation energy and is also slowed by a large entropy loss (ΔS for the equilibrium = 18–25 cal/degree). Wilmarth and Schwartz, in effect, attribute the increase in ease of dissociation with electron-supplying substituents to enhanced participation of form II in the resonance hybrid, an additional example of a polar effect in

$$\begin{array}{ccc} \text{R} & & \text{R} \\ \diagdown \ddot{} \; \cdot & & \diagdown \ddot{}^{+} \; \ddot{}^{(-)} \\ \text{N}-\text{N} & \leftrightarrow & \text{N}-\text{N} \\ \diagup \; | & & \diagup \; | \\ \text{R} \quad \text{CO}\phi & \text{R} & \text{CO}\phi \\ \text{I} & & \text{II} \end{array} \qquad (107)$$

a radical process.

The best-known trisubstituted hydrazyl radical is the deep violet substance, diphenylpicrylhydrazyl,[255] which has already been dis-

$$\begin{array}{c} \text{NO}_2 \\ \phi \quad | \\ \diagdown \quad \cdot \quad / \diagup \diagdown \\ \text{N}-\text{N}- \langle \quad \rangle -\text{NO}_2 \qquad (108) \\ \diagup \quad \diagdown \diagup \diagdown \\ \phi \quad | \\ \text{NO}_2 \end{array}$$

cussed in connection with its use as a radical scavenger or counter (Sections 3·3c and 4·3b). Stability is, of course, a relative matter,

[255] S. Goldschmidt and K. Renn, *Ber.*, **55**, 628 (1922).

and diphenylpicrylhydrazyl reacts with a variety of substances other than radicals, for example phenols and easily dehydrogenated olefins [256a] and thiols.[256b] In the presence of oxygen and olefins it is also rapidly decolorized,[257, 258] so its use as a reliable radical counter requires careful techniques, and its value, even then, is in some doubt at present. The chemistry of the reactions of diphenylpicrylhydrazyl is still somewhat mysterious,[259] but with triphenylmethyl one product isolated is the result of the overall process

$$\phi_3C\cdot \ + \ \overset{\phi}{\underset{\phi}{N}}-\overset{\cdot}{N}-Pic \ \rightarrow \ \phi_3C-\underset{}{\bigcirc}-\overset{\phi}{N}-NH-Pic \quad (109)$$

Finally, in discussing $N-H$ bond dissociations, some organic azides appear to decompose thermally into radicals. The decomposition of benzenesulfonylazide,[260] first described by Curtius,[261] apparently yields a radical species, perhaps the benzenesulfonimido diradical

$$\phi-SO_2-N_3 \ \rightarrow \ \phi-SO_2-\overset{\cdot}{N}\cdot \ + \ N_2 \quad (110)$$

since it initiates the polymerization of methyl acrylate and acrylonitrile. Decomposition occurs quite rapidly at 105–120° and, in aromatic solvents, gives N_2, benzenesulfonamide, and mixtures of $N-aryl$ benzenesulfonamides, presumably by attack of the benzenesulfonimide radical on solvent.[260] Phenyl azide also undergoes a unimolecular decomposition in solvents such as tetralin and nitrobenzene,[262] but here the process is obscure, since the reaction is much faster in the presence of methyl methacrylate and styrene, and little polymer is produced. In fact, the whole formulation given above is puzzling since the electronically similar carbene, CH_2, does not, in general, show radical properties; cf. Section 11·1b.

Several reactions are known involving the thermal cleavage of

256 (a) E. A. Braude, A. G. Brook, and R. P. Linstead, J. Chem. Soc., **1954**, 3574; (b) K. E. Russell, J. Phys. Chem., **58**, 437 (1954).

257 K. E. Russell and A. V. Tobolsky, J. Am. Chem. Soc., **75**, 5052 (1953).

258 A. Chapiro, J. Durup, and J. Grosmangin, J. chim. phys., **50**, 482 (1953).

259 For recent work, cf. F. Poirier, E. J. Kanler, and F. Benington, J. Org. Chem., **17**, 1437 (1952); F. Poirier and F. Benington, ibid., **19**, 1157, 1847 (1955); also Section 4·3b.

260 O. C. Dermer and M. T. Edmison, J. Am. Chem. Soc., **77**, 70 (1955).

261 T. Curtius, J. prakt. chem., **125**, 303 (1930).

262 K. E. Russell, J. Am. Chem. Soc., **77**, 3487 (1955).

N—O bonds, the best examples being the decomposition of nitrate and nitrite esters. The chemistry of nitrate esters has recently been reviewed by Boschan, Merrow, and Van Dolah.[263] The best-understood case is that of ethyl nitrate which, according to Levy,[264] decomposes in the gas phase at 160–200° via the sequence

$$EtO-NO_2 \rightarrow EtO\cdot + NO_2 \qquad (111)$$

$$EtO\cdot \rightarrow CH_2O + CH_3\cdot \qquad (112)$$

$$CH_3\cdot + EtO\cdot + NO_2 \rightarrow CO_2 + CO + H_2O + NO \qquad (113)$$

$$NO + EtO \rightarrow EtONO \qquad (114)$$

Thus, a major product (up to 75%) in the early stages of the reaction is ethyl nitrite. From Levy's results $D(EtO-NO_2) = 41.3$ kcal, and we may note that the alkoxy radicals produced are the same as those arising in peroxide decompositions.[265]

The decomposition of 2-octyl nitrite in the liquid phase at 100° has been studied by Kornblum and Oliveto,[266] who find that the major products are 2-octanol (37%), 2-octanone (37%), nitric oxide (37%), and nitrogen (55% based on moles of nitrogen in the starting material). Starting with optically active nitrite, alcohol of the same configuration is obtained, and they accept the mechanism proposed by Rice and Rodowskas.[267]

$$\overset{\displaystyle ONO}{\underset{\displaystyle |}{CH_3CHR}} \rightarrow \overset{\displaystyle O\cdot}{\underset{\displaystyle |}{CH_3CHR}} + NO \qquad (115)$$

$$\overset{\displaystyle O\cdot}{\underset{\displaystyle |}{CH_3CHR}} + \overset{\displaystyle ONO}{\underset{\displaystyle |}{CH_3CHR}} \rightarrow \overset{\displaystyle OH}{\underset{\displaystyle |}{CH_3CHR}} + \overset{\displaystyle ONO}{\underset{\displaystyle |}{CH_3-C-R}} \qquad (116)$$

$$\overset{\displaystyle ONO}{\underset{\displaystyle |}{CH_3-C-R}} \rightarrow \overset{\displaystyle O}{\underset{\displaystyle ||}{CH_3-C-R}} + NO \qquad (117)$$

---

[263] R. Boschan, R. T. Merrow, and R. W. Van Dolah, *Chem. Revs.*, **55**, 485 (1955).

[264] J. B. Levy, *J. Am. Chem. Soc.*, **76**, 3254, 3790 (1954).

[265] Thus tri-(p-nitrophenyl)methyl nitrate gives dinitrobenzophenone, dinitrophenol, tri-p-nitrophenyl carbinol, and the di-p-nitrophenyl ether of tetra-(p-nitrophenyl)ethylene glycol, M. F. Hawthorne, *ibid.*, **77**, 5523 (1955).

[266] N. Kornblum and E. P. Oliveto, *ibid.*, **71**, 226 (1949); cf. also B. A. Gingras and W. A. Waters, *J. Chem. Soc.*, **1954**, 3508.

[267] F. O. Rice and E. L. Rodowskas, *J. Am. Chem. Soc.*, **57**, 350 (1935).

The large amount of nitrogen is thought to arise from subsequent reactions of nitric oxide with the alcohol and ketone.

Among more complex nitrites, Kuhn and DeAngelis [268] find that vicinal dinitrites give high yields of aldehydes when decomposed in a flow system at 260–280°, presumably via the path

$$
\begin{matrix}
\text{ONO} & \text{ONO} & & \text{O·} & \text{ONO} \\
| & | & & | & | \\
\end{matrix}
$$

$$\text{R}-\text{CH}-\text{CHR} \rightarrow \text{R}-\text{CH}-\text{CH}-\text{R} + \text{NO} \qquad (118)$$

$$
\begin{matrix}
\text{O·} & \text{ONO} & & & \text{ONO} \\
| & | & & & | \\
\end{matrix}
$$

$$\text{R}-\text{CH}-\text{CH}-\text{R} \rightarrow \text{R}-\text{CHO} + \cdot\text{CHR} \qquad (119)$$

$$
\begin{matrix}
\text{ONO} \\
| \\
\end{matrix}
$$

$$\cdot\text{CHR} \rightarrow \text{RCHO} + \text{NO} \qquad (120)$$

At lower temperatures, in the liquid phase, more complex products result, including diketones, hydroxyketones, and glycols, apparently through attack of the intermediate radicals on other nitrite molecules (cf. reactions 116 and 117).

The use of nitrites and nitrites as radical sources has been little investigated and suffers from the difficulty that the nitrogen oxides produced are generally efficient radical traps, although at high temperatures they are evidently able to abstract hydrogen from organic molecules as in the vapor-phase nitration of paraffins.[269] However, the resulting processes might be of considerable interest.[270]

Before leaving our discussion of nitrogen radicals we may note that a large number of further quite stable nitrogen free radicals exist. Among these are the radical-ion semiquinone types (Section 9·5b) and substances such as diphenyl nitric oxide, $\phi_2\text{NO}$ (nitrosobenzene is also a free radical, although it seems to dimerize reversibly). Such materials might be of considerable interest as radical counters, but, as their known chemistry is largely old and is reviewed in detail by Waters,[208] they will not be discussed further here.

[268] L. P. Kuhn and L. DeAngelis, *ibid.*, **76**, 328 (1954).

[269] Cf. G. B. Bachman, L. M. Addison, I. V. Hewitt, L. Kohn, and A. Millikan, *J. Org. Chem.*, **17**, 906 et seq. (1952).

[270] Nitryl chloride, NO_2Cl, also has a low bond dissociation energy of 29.5 kcal (Table 2·2), and its apparent radical addition to double bonds was discussed in Section 7·4c. An apparent radical decomposition of benzyl hyponitrite, $\text{RO}-\text{N}=\text{N}-\text{OR}$, has also been reported, since the material initiates methyl methacrylate polymerization; J. Harris, I. Marshall, and K. B. Jarrett, *Nature*, **159**, 843 (1947).

10·4c   *Thermal Scission of C—C Bonds*

C—C bond dissociation energies range from 84 kcal/mole in ethane down to 11 kcal and less in the hexaaryl ethanes. Thus hydrocarbons vary from materials which are stable towards pyrolysis at exceedingly high temperatures to ones which are largely dissociated in solution at room temperature. The latter group, of which hexaphenylethane is typical, have played an extremely important part in the development of the concept of free radicals as actual chemical species (Chapter 1). However, as most of the chemistry of such substances was developed between 1900 and 1940 and has been thoroughly reviewed by Bachmann,[271] by Waters,[208] and by many others, we are only justified in discussing them briefly here.

In solution, hexaphenylethane dissociates into free radicals, via the equilibrium

$$\phi_3C\!-\!C\phi_3 \rightleftharpoons 2\phi_3C\cdot \tag{121}$$

with K at 20° varying from 1.2×10^{-4} in propionitrile to 19.2×10^{-4} in carbon disulfide, but with an essentially constant value of $\Delta H = 11.3 \pm 1$ kcal. The usual methods of determining K (by spectrophotometry or magnetic susceptibility) were discussed in Chapter 1 and, as we saw, are not always in good agreement.

The value of ΔH in reaction 121 necessarily represents the bond dissociation energy (in solution) of hexaphenylethane, and the origin of its low value has been discussed by many workers. Taking the resonance energy of a benzyl radical as 24.5 kcal (Section 2·3c), as a first approximation, the resonance energy of two triphenylmethyl radicals should approach six times this figure, more than enough to make the dissociation in reaction 121 strongly exothermic. However, for such stabilization to be fully developed, the entire triphenylmethyl radical must lie in a single plane (cf. Section 1·4), and inspection of a model shows that, due to steric interference between phenyls, it necessarily has a propeller-like form, with the phenyl groups tipped at an angle. On the other hand, models of hexaphenylethane indicate considerable steric repulsion, both between individual phenyl groups attached to the same carbon and between those on opposite sides of the molecule, providing additional driving force for

[271] W. E. Bachmann, "Free Radicals," in *Organic Chemistry*, Volume I, H. Gilman, editor, John Wiley & Sons, New York, 1943, Chapter 6.

dissociation.[272] In short, at present the lowering of bond dissociation energy appears due to both somewhat damped resonance stabilization of the resulting radicals and steric repulsion in the hexaphenylethane. Although the relative contributions of the two factors cannot be assigned with complete certainty,[273] evidence that each is important comes from data on other hexaarylethanes discussed below.

The dissociation of a large number of other hexaarylethanes has been studied, and a few results are summarized in Table 10·13 taken

TABLE 10·13   EQUILIBRIUM CONSTANTS OF SOME HEXAARYLETHANES [274]

(In benzene, 25° unless noted)

Ethane	$K \times 10^3$
Hexaphenyl	0.22 [a]
Tetraphenyldi-o-tolyl	33
Tetraphenyldi-m-tolyl	1.8
Tetraphenyldi-p-tolyl	1.1
Diphenyltetra-o-tolyl	1500
Tetraphenyldi-o-chlorophenyl	6.5
Tetraphenyldi-m-chlorophenyl	1.8
Tetraphenyldi-p-chlorophenyl	1.1
Hexa-o-anisyl	120
Tetraphenyldi-p-biphenylyl	3.8–4.7 [b]
Diphenyltetra-p-biphenylyl	16
Hexa-p-biphenylyl	Large [c]
Hexa-p-nitrophenyl	Largely dissociated [d]

[a] 22–24°.
[b] 26–28°.
[c] Variously reported as $K = 0.037$ and as completely dissociated.
[d] Solid state.

from Wheland.[274] The increased dissociation of the p-biphenylylethanes and p-nitrophenylethanes points to the role of resonance

[272] The $\phi_3C—C\phi_3$ bond distance in hexaphenylethane is 1.58 A, compared with the normal value of 1.54 A; S. H. Bauer and J. Y. Beach, J. Am. Chem. Soc., **64**, 1142 (1942).

[273] An often quoted measure comes from heats of hydrogenation, H. E. Bent and G. R. Culbertson, J. Am. Chem. Soc., **58**, 170 (1936). For the reaction $C_2H_6 + H_2 \rightarrow 2CH_4$, $\Delta H = -13$ kcal, and for the analogous reaction of hexaphenylethane $\Delta H = -35$ kcal. This suggests that only 22 kcal of the lowering is due to resonance stabilization of the triphenylmethyl radicals (a surprisingly low figure), the remaining 51 kcal being steric in origin.

[274] G. W. Wheland, Advanced Organic Chemistry, second edition, John Wiley & Sons, New York, 1948, p. 694.

stabilization in the process, whereas the very general marked increase in dissociation on ortho substitution certainly suggests the importance of steric hindrance. In fact, even symmetrical tetraphenylethanes with sufficient *ortho*-methyl groups appear to dissociate appreciably,[275] and many other examples of obvious steric effects are known. More complicated ethanes with polycyclic substituents are often highly dissociated,[276] and an interesting example of a radical with evidently enormous resonance stabilization is tetraphenylcyclopentadienyl

(122)

which is monomeric in solution and paramagnetic even in the solid state.[277] An investigation of the dissociation of mixtures of hexa-arylethanes has given interesting results, in that unsymmetrical hexa-arylethanes are relatively undissociated.[278] The explanation is not known with certainty, but similar phenomena are encountered with other unsymmetric radical equilibria,[279] and, in analogy to the increased rate of many crossed coupling reactions (Section 4·1*j*), may have a polar origin.

The rate of dissociation and association in equilibria such as reaction 121 are of considerable interest, the former being measured by the rate of reaction of the newly formed radicals with a reactive species such as nitric oxide. With hexaphenylethane, the activation energy for dissociation is approximately 19 kcal.[208] The rate varies somewhat with solvent, but in chloroform the (extrapolated) rate constant at 20° is 2.5 sec^{-1}. From the values of the equilibrium constant, the recombination of triphenylmethyl radicals has an activa-

[275] W. T. Nauta and P. J. Wuis, *Rec. trav. chim.*, **57**, 41 (1938); J. Coops, W. T. Nauta, M. J. E. Ernsting, and A. C. Farber, *ibid.*, **59**, 1109 (1940); J. Coops, W. T. Nauta, and M. J. E. Ernsting, *ibid.*, **60**, 245 (1941).

[276] Oddly, however, *sym*-tetraphenyldi-α-thienylethane and *sym*-diphenyl-di-α-naphthyl-di-α-thienylethane do not show measurable dissociation; T. L. Chu and T. J. Weismann, *J. Am. Chem. Soc.*, **77**, 2189 (1955).

[277] E. Muller and I. Muller-Rodloff, *Ber.*, **69**, 665 (1936).

[278] C. S. Marvel and C. H. Himel, *J. Am. Chem. Soc.*, **64**, 2227 (1942); C. H. Himel and M. B. Mueller, *ibid.*, **65**, 1654 (1953).

[279] W. E. Bachmann and F. V. Wiselogle, *J. Org. Chem.*, **1**, 354 (1939); H. Wieland, *Ann.*, **381**, 206 (1911); *Ber.*, **48**, 1078 (1915); R. Pummerer and F. Frankfurter, *ibid.*, **47**, 1472 (1914); S. Goldschmidt and W. Schmidt, *ibid.*, **55**, 3197 (1922).

tion energy of about 8 kcal and a rate constant, in chloroform, at 20°
of 3600 liters/mole/sec. Dissociation rates for many other polyaryl-
methanes have also been measured.

Although triarylmethyl radicals in inert solvents are often thought
of as stable species, they tend to undergo various irreversible dis-
proportionations and dimerizations into non-radical products which
are sometimes quite rapid. Thus, triphenylmethyl in the presence
of light decomposes as indicated: [280]

$$6\phi_3 C\cdot \ \rightarrow\ 4\phi_3 CH\ +\ \text{(structure)} \qquad (123)$$

whereas tri-p-tolylmethyl undergoes a series of changes on standing,
considered [281] to involve the sequence

$$2\left(CH_3-\langle\ \rangle-\right)_3 C\cdot \ \rightarrow\ \left(CH_3\langle\ \rangle-\right)_3 CH$$

$$+\ CH_2=\langle\ \rangle=C \begin{matrix} \langle\ \rangle-CH_3 \\ \\ \langle\ \rangle-CH_3 \end{matrix} \qquad \rightarrow\ \text{Polymer} \quad (124)$$

Triarylmethyl radicals also attack all the species such as oxygen
(Section 9·2a), oxides of nitrogen, halogens, sulfur, etc., which react
very rapidly with more reactive radicals. They also react, but rather
slowly, with unsaturated molecules, e.g., with quinone and maleic

$$2\phi_3 C\cdot\ +\ \text{(quinone)}\ \rightarrow\ \text{(structure with O—C}\phi_3\text{)} \qquad (125)$$

[280] J. Schmidlin and A. Garcia-Banus, *Ber.*, **45**, 1344 (1912).
[281] C. S. Marvel, W. H. Rieger, and M. B. Mueller, *J. Am. Chem. Soc.*, **61**, 2769 (1935).

anhydride and other olefins [282,283] The reaction of triphenylmethyl

$$2\phi_3C\cdot + \begin{array}{c} CH-CO \\ \| \quad \diagdown \\ \quad \quad O \rightarrow \\ \| \quad \diagup \\ CH-CO \end{array} \quad \begin{array}{c} \phi_3C-CH-CO \\ | \quad \diagdown \\ \quad \quad O \\ | \quad \diagup \\ \phi_3C-CH-CO \end{array} \quad (126)$$

with diphenyl disulfide has been cited [208] as evidence for the dissocia-

$$2\phi_3C\cdot + \phi-S-S-\phi \rightarrow 2\phi-S-C\phi_3 \quad (127)$$

tion of the disulfide into radicals, but, in view of the ease of radical displacements on sulfur, the evidence seems doubtful.

Because of their relatively slow attack on most substrates and the high concentrations of potential chain terminating radicals present in their solutions, the stable triarylmethyl radicals are of little value as initiators of radical chain processes.[284] Less highly substituted polyarylethanes, e.g., tetrabutyldiphenylethane and many similar compounds which dissociate only very slowly, have been shown by Ziegler [285] to be excellent initiators for the polymerization of acrylonitrile and methyl methacrylate. An interesting feature of such reactions is that, by using somewhat more readily dissociating species such as 2,2,3,3-tetraphenylbutane, radical reactions may be induced at −25 to −30°C. Recently Vansheidt and Gruz [286] have noted that 1,1,1,2,4,4,4-heptaphenylbutane, the product of addition of two triphenylmethyl radicals to styrene, is itself an initiator of styrene polymerization at 100°.

10·4d Other Thermal Radical Sources

The bonds linking metals to carbon are relatively weak even with metals such as mercury and lead, which form stable covalent compounds. The gas-phase pyrolyses of tetraalkylleads, as we have seen (Section 1·1), provide the classic demonstration of the actual existence of free methyl radicals. Cramer, working with tetraethyllead

[282] J. B. Conant and H. W. Scherp, *J. Am. Chem. Soc.*, **53**, 1941 (1931).

[283] C. S. Marvel, J. Dec, and J. A. Corner, *ibid.*, **67**, 1855 (1945).

[284] There is, however, evidence of their inducing autoxidation processes; cf. K. Ziegler, L. Ewald, and A. Seib, *Ann.*, **564**, 182 (1933); K. Ziegler and K. Ganicke, *ibid.*, **551**, 213 (1942).

[285] K. Ziegler, W. Deparade, and H. Kuhlhorn, *Ann.*, **567**, 151 (1950).

[286] A. A. Vansheidt and R. I. Gruz, *Chem. Abstr.*, **47**, 7819 (1953).

in hydrocarbon solvents under pressure at 200–270° has observed the expected reactions of ethyl radicals in these media.[287]

Although the decomposition has been considered too slow at lower temperatures to be of much use in the type of liquid-phase reaction considered in this book, Koton [288] has recently described the use of a number of organolead, -tin, and -mercury compounds as initiators of methyl methacrylate and vinyl acetate polymerization at moderate temperatures. Tetracyclohexyllead and dicyclohexyl and dibenzylmercury were particularly effective, and the topic needs further study. Although organomercuric halides RHgX are quite stable substances, Winstein and his students have obtained evidence [288a] that they may become involved in radical chain processes, e.g., with halogens to yield alkyl halides and HgX_2.

Turning to less stable organometallic compounds, Grignard reagents appear to undergo almost exclusively reactions with polar paths,[289] and those which do involve radicals (e.g., the reactions in the presence of cobalt halides and certain other salts) are probably best classified as redox reactions and are considered in Section 11·4c. The same is true for most of the reactions of organoderivatives of the alkali metals, although the reaction between sodium and the triphenylmethyl radical is apparently a reversible one, shifting to the

$$\phi_3C\cdot + Na \rightleftharpoons \phi_3CNa \qquad (128)$$

left if the sodium is removed by amalgamation.[208] Morton has also obtained evidence of similar reversibility in the decomposition of simpler organosodium compounds,[290] but at present the reactions are not well understood.

Organoderivatives of copper and silver decompose rapidly at -20 to $-50°C$. These compounds are prepared from the corresponding tetraalkylleads and metal nitrates, and their subsequent decomposi-

---

[287] P. L. Cramer, *J. Am. Chem. Soc.,* **56**, 1234 (1934); **60**, 1406 (1938); there are also a number of references in the patent literature to the use of tetraethyllead as a polymerization initiator at high temperatures and pressures.

[288] M. M. Koton, *Doklady Akad. Nauk S.S.S.R.,* **88**, 991 (1953).

[288a] J. Keller, thesis, University of California in Los Angeles (1948); S. Winstein and T. G. Traylor, *J. Am. Chem. Soc.,* **78**, 2597 (1956).

[289] Their pyrolyses at higher temperatures may be an exception, but little is known about such processes.

[290] A. A. Morton and E. F. Cluff, *J. Am. Chem. Soc.,* **74**, 4056 (1952); A. A. Morton and E. J. Lanpher, *J. Org. Chem.,* **21**, 93 (1956).

tion to metal and hydrocarbon is believed to be a radical process.[291] The decomposition of isobutenylsilver in alcohol has recently been studied in more detail by Glocking,[292] who finds it a rather complex process in which the alcohol is oxidized to aldehyde.

An organotitanium compound, ϕ—Ti(O—C_3H_7)$_3$, has recently been described which apparently undergoes radical decomposition as it initiates the polymerization of styrene.[293] Diborane also appears to be a polymerization initiator.[294]

Lead tetraacetate is another type of organometallic derivative which, under some conditions, apparently decomposes to free radicals.[295] The well-known reaction in which lead tetraacetate cleaves vicinal glycols in the cold appears to be a polar process, most probably involving an intermediate cyclic ester.[296] On the other hand, Fieser has found that naphthoquinones[297] and nitrobenzenes[298] are *methylated* on boiling with lead tetraacetate in acetic acid, a process best formulated as involving formation of acetate radicals (which immediately decarboxylate) by thermal decomposition of the lead tetraacetate. Hey[299] has recently described similar phenylation reactions using lead tetrabenzoate at 130°. Rather more equivocal are the reactions in hot acetic acid by which lead tetraacetate introduces acetoxy groups into compounds such as ketones and toluene, or converts olefins to glycol diacetates. However, in view of our conclusion that acetate radicals have vanishingly short lives under these conditions, it seems reasonable to conclude that these are polar processes as well.[300] The possibility of a radical path for the high-

[291] C. E. H. Bawn and F. J. Whitby, *Discussions Faraday Soc.,* **2,** 228 (1947).

[292] F. Glocking, *J. Chem. Soc.,* **1955,** 716.

[293] D. F. Herman and W. K. Nelson, *J. Am. Chem. Soc.,* **74,** 2693 (1952); **75,** 3877, 3882 (1953).

[294] R. G. Heiligmann and F. Benington, U.S. Pat. 2,685,575 (August 3, 1954).

[295] For a recent review, cf. W. A. Waters in Volume IV of *Organic Chemistry,* H. Gilman, editor, John Wiley & Sons, New York, 1953, pp. 1185–1195.

[296] R. Criegee and E. Buchner, *Ber.,* **73,** 563 (1940); R. Criegee, E. Buchner, and W. Walther, *ibid.,* **73,** 571 (1940).

[297] L. F. Fieser and F. C. Chang, *J. Am. Chem. Soc.,* **64,** 2042 (1942).

[298] L. F. Fieser, R. C. Clapp, and W. H. Daudt, *ibid.,* **64,** 2052 (1942).

[299] D. H. Hey, C. J. N. Stirling, and G. H. Williams, *J. Chem. Soc.,* **1954,** 2747; **1955,** 3963. Significantly, essentially the same mixture of isomeric phenylpyridines are obtained in pyridine as when benzoyl peroxide or nitrosoacetanilide are decomposed.

[300] W. A. Mosher and C. L. Kehr, *J. Am. Chem. Soc.,* **75,** 3172 (1953), have also concluded that the reactions of lead tetraacetate in acetic acid are polar processes on other grounds.

temperature decomposition of carboxylic acid salts of polyvalent metals to ketones has been discussed by Reed.[301]

Finally, we may mention a few examples of radical formation by thermal scission of carbon halogen bonds. A rather slow initiation of vinyl chloride polymerization by carbon tetrabromide at 70° was noted by Breitenbach and Schindler,[240] from which they calculated a half-life of 300 years at that temperature, a plausible value for a substance with a C—Br bond dissociation energy of 49 kcal (Table 2·3). The purely thermal high-temperature addition of CF_3I to numerous olefins described by Haszeldine (Section 6·2a) probably involves similar scission of the CF_3—I bond. Inspection of Table 2·3 certainly suggests that allyl and benzyl iodides should act as effective initiators of radical chain processes at 150–200°, as should (Table 2·1) various species with N—, O—, and S—halogen bonds.

[301] R. I. Reed, *J. Chem. Phys.*, **21**, 377 (1953).

CHAPTER 11

Radical Production by Photochemical, High-Energy-Radiation, and Oxidation-Reduction Processes

11 · 1   Photochemical Production of Radicals

11·1a   General Aspects of Photochemical Reactions

In Section 2·1b we saw that absorption of radiation frequently leads to dissociation of molecules into free radicals, and subsequently we have made frequent note of the photoinitiation of radical processes, the most important occasions being the use of intermittent photoinitiation to produce non-steady-state conditions for the determination of rate constants of the individual steps in radical chain processes. We now undertake a more detailed survey of the photochemical production of free radicals, beginning with a brief summary of some of the general properties of photochemical processes. Since a detailed presentation of this topic is far beyond the scope of this book (and the capabilities of this author) the treatment must, of necessity, be both brief and qualitative.[1]

Basically, the properties of photochemical processes arise from the quantization of the energy of electromagnetic radiation and the quantum mechanical nature of its interaction with matter. As is well known, light of a given vibration frequency can only be emitted or absorbed in units of energy given by the relation

$$E = h\nu \tag{1}$$

where ν is the frequency and h is Planck's constant, a relation which may also be usefully expressed in the form

$$2.8579 \times 10^8/\text{wave length in A} = E \text{ in cal/mole} \tag{2}$$

As a consequence, light of a given frequency can only be absorbed (or emitted) by a molecule if it can simultaneously undergo an energy change equal to $h\nu$, and it is an obvious postulate of photochemistry

---

[1] For a more detailed treatment, cf. W. A. Noyes, Jr., and D. A. Leighton, *The Photochemistry of Gases,* Reinhold Publishing Corp., New York, 1941; E. J. Bowen, *The Chemical Aspects of Light,* second edition, Clarendon Press, Oxford, 1946. More recent work is covered in *Annual Reviews of Physical Chemistry,* Annual Reviews, Inc., Stanford, California, 1950 et seq.

(noted by Grotthuss in 1817) that only light which is absorbed can be effective in bringing about a chemical process. In general, energy is stored in molecules as kinetic (translational, rotational, and vibrational) and electronic energy, and the processes which are important in photochemistry are those in which light absorption leads to changes in electronic states, i.e., in which absorption elevates one or more electrons in the system from a ground to an excited state. Such absorption usually occurs in the ultraviolet or visible spectrum, and, since, from eq. 2, light at wave lengths of 6000, 4000, and 2000 A is quantized in packages of energy amounting to 47.6, 71.4, and 142.8 kcal/mole respectively, it is evident that such absorption frequently introduces enough energy into molecules to bring about complete rupture of covalent bonds. However, the actual production of radicals from such *photoexcited* molecules is considerably more complicated than is implied by the above calculation and can best be discussed by considering the case of a diatomic molecule.[2]

The initial consequences of light absorption by a diatomic molecule are shown schematically in Fig. 11·1 for three possible cases which can be distinguished spectroscopically and which illustrate an important restriction upon such processes. This is the *Franck-Condon principle*, which, taking into account the fact that molecular vibrations or other displacements of atomic nuclei are slow compared to the time required for light absorption or emission, may be stated as follows: *Electronic transitions brought about by light are restricted to those in which there is no displacement of the atomic nuclei.* (As in other quantum mechanical situations the accurate statement is more indeterminate: other transitions are much less probable.) In case A excitation is to a repulsive state and leads to immediate dissociation. Case B is to a bonding excited state, but the molecule now possesses enough energy to dissociate into *excited* fragments. Case C is more interesting, for, although the molecule has ample energy for dissociation, it is in a metastable state and has no easy way of coming apart. Instead it may lose its energy by re-emission of light, dropping down to one of the vibrational levels of its lowest electronic state (the phenomenon of *fluorescence*), or divide its energy with another molecule by collision. (If conditions are right, the molecule may be left with enough energy to dissociate after collision.) If the excitation in C is a probable one (i.e., associated with a strong ab-

[2] A good discussion of the interpretation of absorption spectra of unsaturated molecules is given by G. W. Wheland, *Resonance in Organic Chemistry*, John Wiley & Sons, New York, 1955, Chapter 6.

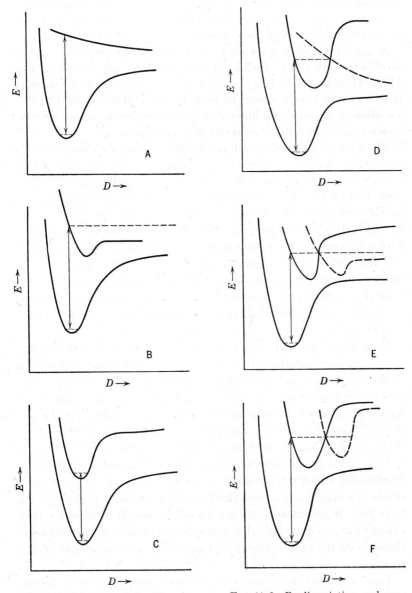

FIG. 11·1 Diagram of the Franck-Condon principle and photoexcitation to a metastable state.

FIG. 11·2 Predissociation and conversion of a photoexcited molecule to a triplet state.

sorption band) fluorescence is also probable, with a half-time of 10^{-8} sec or less. Collision with another molecule before this time can thus lead to the important phenomenon of *quenching* of fluorescence.

A third possibility for case C exists if another electronic energy level intersects the excited level, and examples are shown in Fig. 11·2. Here the two levels perturb each other, and the molecule may pass over to the new state. In both D and E this will lead to dissociation, a phenomenon known to spectroscopists as *predissociation* which complicates the interpretation of their spectra.

The situation in saturated polyatomic molecules appears to be similar; but the energy diagrams are harder to draw, and the spectra of very few molecules have been analyzed in detail. In unsaturated molecules an additional phenomenon may occur. Absorption of light by the π electron system appears usually to lead to an excited state in which the electrons are still paired, but one is in an excited state with a different (often more highly polarized) distribution in space.[2] However, a triplet diradical state may also exist into which the excited state may pass, even though its direct photoexcitation to a diradical is forbidden by transition rules. Such a situation is depicted in F of Fig. 11·2, and such processes are discussed further in Section 11·1c.

A final path by which radicals may be produced photochemically is by photosensitization: the energy absorbed by one molecule is transferred to another by collision and leads to dissociation of the latter. Such processes are well established in the gas phase, as in the mercury-sensitized dissociation of hydrogen molecules, but the situation in solution is more equivocal. Many processes which have been described loosely as photosensitization are actually chain processes induced by dissociation of the absorbing species. Non-chain reactions in which the sensitizer is not destroyed (as in the chlorophyll- or methylene blue-sensitized autoxidations described in Section 9·4) may represent such energy transfers, but in some cases they evidently proceed through alternate oxidation and reduction (or other chemical change) of the absorbing molecule rather than simple energy transfer.

Two significant differences exist between photochemical processes in the gas phase (on which most of the preceding picture is based) and in solution. First, since molecules in solution are continually undergoing collisions, the likelihood of metastable excited states such as B in Fig. 11·1 is reduced (although fluorescence and the formation

Photochemical and Oxidation-Reduction Processes 543

of triplet diradicals certainly both occur). Second, since dissociation in solution leads to the production of two radicals within the same solvent cage, primary recombination (Section 3·3b) may significantly reduce the quantum efficiency (number of radicals produced, or molecules reacting per quantum of light absorbed) in photochemical processes.

A good example of this phenomenon has been provided by Lampe and Noyes,[3] who investigated the quantum yields obtained in the photodissociation of iodine in various solvents with results shown in Table 11·1. Their technique involves measuring the additional iodine

TABLE 11·1   QUANTUM YIELDS IN PHOTODISSOCIATION OF IODINE [3]

Solvent	Temperature, °C	ϕI_2
Hexane	15	0.50 ± 0.04
	25	0.66 ± 0.04
Carbon tetrachloride	17.5	0.11 ± 0.01
	25	0.14 ± 0.01
	38	0.21 ± 0.02
Hexachlorobutadiene	15	0.042 ± 0.006
	25	0.075 ± 0.009
	35	0.15 ± 0.02

formed in the presence of oxygen and allyl iodide, conditions under which each pair of iodine atoms that escapes from the initial cage reacts quantitatively with allyl iodide and oxygen to produce an additional mole of I_2. The decrease in quantum yield in dense solvents composed of heavy molecules parallels our observations of the efficiency of thermal initiation processes in Section 3·3b.

Finally, we may note that, although the bulk of our picture of the photochemical production of radicals is inferred from their subsequent chemical reactions, two techniques are now available for their direct observation. The first is carrying out the irradiation in a glassy medium (usually at low temperatures), developed by Lewis and Kasha,[4,5] in which the radicals are trapped and prevented from recombining. The second is the technique of flash photolysis de-

[3] F. W. Lampe and R. M. Noyes, J. Am. Chem. Soc., 76, 2140 (1954). Qualitatively similar results are obtained in the photolysis of acetone, the quantum yield of decomposition products being greatly reduced in the liquid phase over those observed in the vapor; R. Pieck and E. W. R. Steacie, Can. J. Chem., 33, 1304 (1955).

[4] G. N. Lewis and M. Kasha, ibid., 66, 2100 (1944).
[5] M. Kasha, Chem. Revs., 41, 401 (1947).

veloped by Norrish and Porter,[6] in which a very intense pulse of light produces such a high concentration of radicals that they can be examined spectroscopically with the aid of suitable electronic scanning circuits. Examples of both techniques will occur in our later discussion.

11·1b   Photodissociation; Photoinitiation of Chain Processes

Most substances which dissociate thermally into radicals at moderate temperatures (Chapter 10) also dissociate on absorption of ultraviolet light, and the resulting radicals undergo the same types of reactions as when they are produced thermally. Thus, in the gas phase di-t-butyl peroxide gives ethane, acetone, and t-butyl alcohol,[7] and in carbon tetrachloride t-butyl hydroperoxide undergoes a chain decomposition to t-butyl alcohol and oxygen.[8] A great number of examples of the use of peroxides as photoinitiators of polymerization have been reported (Chapter 3), but they suffer from the drawback that they show appreciable absorption only below 3200 A and accordingly cannot be used efficiently in ordinary glass equipment. Azobisisobutyronitrile, in contrast, shows an absorption peak at 3450 A ($\epsilon = 14.65$) and appreciable absorption all the way to 4000 A. It and its analogs are efficient photoinitiators for radical chain processes,[9] and the efficiency of the primary decomposition has recently been studied by Back and Sivertz,[10] who report a quantum yield of 0.43 in benzene solution. The simpler azo compound 2-azobispropane is apparently a less efficient radical source under near-ultraviolet light, giving quantum yields for the polymerization of styrene and vinyl acetate only 5–20% as large as the azonitrile.[9] Other azo compounds presumably can also be used as photoinitiators of radical processes, although they have received less investigation. A very interesting gas-phase photolysis of perfluoroazomethane has been described by Prichard and Prichard,[11] who find that the major products are those of addition of ·CF_3 to the double bond of undecomposed azo compound, a striking result which has no analogy among non-fluorinated materials.

[6] R. G. W. Norrish and G. Porter, *Nature,* **164,** 658 (1949), and subsequent papers.

[7] L. M. Dorfman and Z. W. Salsburg, *J. Am. Chem. Soc.,* **73,** 255 (1951).

[8] J. T. Martin and R. G. W. Norrish, *Proc. Roy. Soc. London,* **A220,** 322 (1953).

[9] F. M. Lewis and M. S. Matheson, *J. Am. Chem. Soc.,* **71,** 747 (1949).

[10] R. Back and C. Sivertz, *Can. J. Chem.,* **32,** 1061 (1954).

[11] G. O. Pritchard and H. O. Pritchard, *Chemistry & Industry,* **1955,** 564.

$$CF_3\text{—}N\text{=}N\text{—}CF_3 \xrightarrow{h\nu} N_2 + 2\ \cdot CF_3 \qquad (3a)$$

$$2\ \cdot CF_3 + CF_3\text{—}N\text{=}N\text{—}CF_3 \longrightarrow \quad \begin{array}{c} F_3C \quad\quad\quad CF_3 \\ \diagdown\quad\quad\diagup \\ N\text{—}N \\ \diagup\quad\quad\diagdown \\ F_3C \quad\quad\quad CF_3 \end{array} \qquad (3b)$$

$$2\ \cdot CF_3 + 2CF_3\text{—}N\text{=}N\text{—}CF_3 \longrightarrow \quad \begin{array}{c} F_3C \quad\quad CF_3 \quad CF_3 \\ \diagdown\quad\diagup\quad\quad\diagup \\ N\text{—}N\text{—}N\text{—}N \\ \diagup\quad\quad|\quad\quad\diagdown \\ F_3C \quad\quad CF_3 \quad CF_3 \end{array} \qquad (3c)$$

Many other substances structurally similar to the aliphatic azo compounds are readily decomposed by light, but the processes do not always take radical paths. Thus, the photolysis of diaroylazo compounds $RCO\text{—}N\text{=}N\text{—}COR$ fails to initiate the polymerization of acrylonitrile,[12] and the ready decomposition of many diazonium ions in aqueous solution yields phenols (or, in alcohols, alkyl aryl ethers),[13] the expected products of *polar* decomposition. Again, the photolysis of diazomethane and its homologs appears to yield a *carbene*.

$$\begin{array}{c} R \\ \diagdown \\ \quad CN_2 \xrightarrow{h\nu} \\ \diagup \\ R \end{array} \quad \begin{array}{c} R \\ \diagdown \\ \quad C\colon + N_2 \\ \diagup \\ R \end{array} \qquad (4)$$

Although the electronic structure of such species is not known with certainty, it is somewhat analogous to carbon monoxide, and most of their subsequent reactions, e.g., additions to aromatic [14] or unsaturated [15] systems or rearrangement,[16] are those of electron-deficient electrophilic entities rather than free radicals.[17]

Another class of substances which readily decompose into radicals by both thermal and photochemical paths is organometallic compounds such as dimethylmercury and tetraethyllead. Both of these compounds absorb below 2800 A and have been extensively investi-

[12] L. Horner and W. Naumann, *Ann.*, **587**, 93 (1954).

[13] K. H. Saunders, *The Aromatic Diazo-Compounds*, Edward Arnold & Co., London, 1949, Chapter X.

[14] W. Von E. Doering and L. H. Knox, *J. Am. Chem. Soc.*, **72**, 2305 (1950).

[15] W. Von E. Doering and A. K. Hoffmann, *ibid.*, **76**, 6162 (1954).

[16] L. Horner and E. Spietschka, *Chem. Ber.*, **85**, 225 (1952).

[17] However, note the apparent radical photoaddition of diazomethane to CCl_4 (Section 6·2c).

gated in the gas phase and occasionally in solution. Since the processes involved have been discussed in detail by Steacie [18] and add little to our picture of radical processes in solution, they will not be considered further.

Of the materials which dissociate photochemically but not thermally (except at very high temperatures) carbonyl compounds have received by far the most study. Again, the bulk of the work has been on the gas-phase process,[18a] but their photochemistry is sufficiently important to summarize the gas-phase results at least briefly. As a typical example, acetone shows an absorption peak at 2700 A which is evidently due to excitation of a π electron of the carbonyl group to an excited, but non-radical, state. From here the molecule can apparently drop to a triplet diradical state, which is important in some of the processes discussed below, or finally the stored energy may lead to dissociation

$$CH_3COCH_3 \xrightarrow{h\nu} CH_3COCH_3 \; excited \rightarrow CH_3\cdot + CH_3CO\cdot \quad (5a)$$

subsequent reactions being those expected from methyl and acetyl radicals. Methyl ethyl ketone dissociates similarly, although in chloroacetone a chlorine atom is apparently lost.[19]

$$CH_3COCH_2Cl \xrightarrow{h\nu} CH_3COCH_2\cdot + Cl\cdot \quad (5b)$$

The photoexcited states of more complex ketones appear to lose their energy by more than one path. The subject has recently been clarified and reviewed by Martin and Pitts,[20] who find that the major products of the photolysis of methyl neopentyl ketone are acetone and isobutylene. They formulate the process as involving a rearrangement of the excited polar state, but the rearrangement could

$$
\begin{array}{ccc}
\underset{|}{CH_2}\text{—H } \underset{\parallel}{O^*} & \underset{\parallel}{CH_2} & H\text{—O} \\
CH_3\text{—}\underset{|}{C}\text{—}CH_2\underset{}{C}\text{—}CH_3 \rightarrow CH_3\text{—}C + CH_2\text{=}\underset{|}{C}\text{—}CH_3 \\
\underset{}{CH_3} & & CH_3 \\
& \rightarrow CH_3COCH_3 & (6)
\end{array}
$$

also occur through a metastable diradical state (see below).

[18] E. W. R. Steacie, *Atomic and Free Radical Reactions,* second edition, Reinhold Publishing Corp., New York, 1954.

[18a] W. A. Noyes, Jr., G. B. Porter, and J. E. Jolley, *Chem. Revs.,* **56,** 49 (1956).

[19] A. N. Strachan and F. E. Blacet, *J. Am. Chem. Soc.,* **77,** 5254 (1954).

[20] T. W. Martin and J. N. Pitts, Jr., *ibid.,* **77,** 5465 (1955).

Several other ketones give similar products,[21] suggesting that they should make only poor photoinitiators. With acetaldehyde the initial dissociation is probably chiefly into $\cdot CH_3$ and $\cdot CHO$, whereas with biacetyl two acetyl radicals are produced. Since biacetyl is

$$CH_3CO—COCH_3 \rightarrow 2CH_3C\overset{O}{\diagup}\cdot \qquad (7)$$

dissociated by light in the neighborhood of 3600 A, it has found appreciable use as a photoinitiator of chain processes.

Another group of carbonyl compounds which yield radicals on near-ultraviolet irradiation are benzoin and its derivatives. These too have found use as photoinitiators, and Mochel, Crandall, and Peterson have reported that C^{14}-labeled benzoin methyl ether not only initiates the polymerization of methyl methacrylate but that 12–15 benzoin units are incorporated in each polymer molecule, even though no such "copolymerization" occurs in the dark.[22]

The photodissociation of halogens has been discussed in Chapter 8, and alkyl halides are also readily photolyzed with dissociation of the C—halogen bond. Again, such processes are reviewed by Steacie, and, as examples of more recent work, the photolysis of 1-chlorocyclohexene has been identified as a radical chain process by Lindsey and Ingraham [23] and the reactions with olefins of radicals from photolyzed isopropyl bromide studied by Kharasch.[24] Further information is also available on the liquid-phase photolysis of alkyl iodides,[25] including the apparent trapping of iodine atoms in glassy media.[26] We may note that, although simple alkyl iodides are dissociated rather inefficiently by light at 3130 A and chlorides and bromides require still shorter wave lengths, carbon tetrabromide apparently produces radicals on illumination with an ordinary incan-

[21] A. J. C. Nicholson, *Trans. Faraday Soc.*, **50**, 1067 (1954).

[22] W. E. Mochel, J. L. Crandall and J. H. Peterson, *J. Am. Chem. Soc.*, **77**, 494 (1955). One wonders whether this represents a copolymerization with photoexcited benzoin molecules, although the authors reject this idea.

[23] R. V. Lindsey, Jr., and J. N. Ingraham, *ibid.*, **75**, 5613 (1953).

[24] M. S. Kharasch, D. Schwartz, and W. Nudenberg, *J. Org. Chem.*, **18**, 337 (1953).

[25] E. L. Cochran, W. H. Hamill and R. R. Williams, Jr., *J. Am. Chem. Soc.*, **76**, 2145 (1954); C. E. McCauley, W. H. Hamill and R. R. Williams, Jr., *ibid.*, **76**, 6263 (1954).

[26] I. Norman and G. Porter, *Nature*, **174**, 508 (1954); *Proc. Roy. Soc. London*, **A230**, 399 (1955).

descent lamp in Pyrex apparatus.[27] Disulfides also act as photo-initiators,[28] and some of their photochemical reactions were discussed in Section 7·3b. Recently the production of benzyl radicals in the vapor phase by flash photolysis of toluene, benzyl chloride, and similar materials has been described by Porter and Wright.[29] The benzyl radical has a well-defined absorption spectrum at around 3000 A with the strongest band at 3058 A. Its half-life in the gas phase is under 10^{-4} sec, but, when produced by the irradiation of the same substrates in a glassy medium at liquid nitrogen tempera-tures, it has a long life.[26] Phenoxy and ϕ—ṄH radicals from phenol and aniline have been observed in the same way.[29]

Although the detailed mechanism of photoinitiation of polymeri-zation of pure monomers, i.e., in the absence of specific photosensitive initiators, is unknown, there seems little doubt that, at some point, dissociation of the olefin into similar radical fragments occurs, since the difficulties of diradical initiation processes have already been pointed out (Section 5·1). More specifically, in the case of styrene at least, the molecular weight–rate relation in the photoinitiated processes has been shown to be identical with that produced by thermally formed monoradicals.[30]

A number of more complex molecules are also able to initiate radical chains, although the processes involved are obscure. The initiation of the autoxidation of tetralin and the polymerization of styrene by a series of vat dyes in the presence of visible light (>3600 A) was noted by Bamford and Dewar in 1949,[31] and subse-quently a number of other dye-photosensitized polymerizations have been described,[32,33,34] including the chlorophyll-sensitized polymeri-

[27] M. S. Kharasch, E. V. Jensen, and W. H. Urry, *J. Am. Chem. Soc.*, **69**, 1100 (1947).

[28] M. S. Kharasch, W. Nudenberg, and T. H. Meltzer, *J. Org. Chem.*, **18**, 1233 (1953); K. E. Russell and A. V. Tobolsky, *J. Am. Chem. Soc.*, **76**, 345 (1954). Photoinitiation by metal mercaptides and xanthate esters has also been reported in the patent literature: R. Kern, U.S. Pat. 2,738,319 (March 13, 1956); and V. A. Engelhardt and M. L. Peterson, U.S. Pat. 2,716,633 (August 30, 1955), respectively.

[29] G. Porter and F. J. Wright, *Trans. Faraday Soc.*, **51**, 1469 (1955).

[30] D. H. Johnson and A. V. Tobolsky, *J. Am. Chem. Soc.*, **74**, 938 (1952).

[31] C. H. Bamford and M. J. S. Dewar, *Nature*, **163**, 214 (1949); cf. also C. H. Bamford and M. J. S. Dewar, *Proc. Roy. Soc. London*, **A198**, 252 (1949).

[32] M. Koizomi, Z. Kuroda, and A. Watanabe, *Chem. Abstr.*, **46**, 4951 (1952); M. Koizumi, A. Watanabe, and Z. Kuroda, *Nature*, **175**, 770 (1955).

[33] N. Uri, *J. Am. Chem. Soc.*, **74**, 5808 (1952).

[34] G. Oster, *Nature*, **173**, 300 (1954).

zation of methyl methacrylate.[33]   In some cases polycomponent systems have been employed, and it is very interesting that the decomposition of acetyl peroxide photosensitized by anthracene or naphthacene (which should permit a sort of two-step chain photoinitiation process) has been described by Luner and Szwarc.[35]

Finally, photoinitiations of polymerization are known involving the photolysis of inorganic ions.   The most-studied example is the photolysis of ferric complexes by ultraviolet light investigated by Evans, Santappa, and Uri,[36] apparently involving an initial step such as

$$FeOH^{++} \xrightarrow{h\nu} Fe^{++} + OH \cdot \qquad (8)$$

The resulting hydroxyl radicals not only initiate polymerization but also hydroxylate aromatic nuclei and oxidize aromatic side chains.[37] Polymerization is similarly initiated by the photolysis of the trioxalatocobaltate(III) complex.[38]

11·1c Photochemical Non-Chain Processes

In addition to photodissociations, evidenced by the initiation of radical chain processes, numerous other photochemical reactions are known, many of which appear to be radical reactions involving triplet states of unsaturated molecules, arising through the sort of process described in Section 11·1a.   However, since in most cases actual identification of the reactions as radical processes is at best rather tenuous, our treatment of the subject will have to be chiefly descriptive and rather brief.

The photochemistry of anthracene provides a good starting point. The triplet state in glassy media at low temperature is here well recognized,[5] and its absorption spectrum has also been detected by flash-photolysis methods in the vapor state,[39] and in hexane solution[40] where it has a half-life of 5.8×10^{-5} sec.   In solution the excited state reacts readily with oxygen, and also undergoes dimeri-

[35] C. Luner and M. Szwarc, J. Chem. Phys., **23**, 1978 (1955).

[36] M. G. Evans and N. Uri, Nature, **164**, 404 (1949); M. G. Evans, M. Santappa, and N. Uri, J. Polymer Sci., **7**, 243 (1951).

[37] H. G. C. Bates and N. Uri, J. Am. Chem. Soc., **75**, 2754 (1953); J. Saldick and A. O. Allen, ibid., **77**, 1388 (1955).

[38] T. B. Copestake and N. Uri, Proc. Roy. Soc. London, **A228**, 252 (1955).

[39] G. Porter and F. J. Wright, Trans. Faraday Soc., **51**, 1205 (1955).

[40] G. Porter and M. W. Windsor, J. Chem. Phys., **21**, 2088 (1953); Discussions Faraday Soc., **17**, 178 (1954).

zation. The interrelation between these processes and fluorescence has been considered by Bowen.[41] The photosensitization of peroxide decomposition by photoexcited anthracene has already been mentioned, and it also reacts with carbon tetrachloride, apparently to give chlorine-containing 9,10-dihydroanthracene derivatives.[42] The structures of the photodimers of anthracene and a number of substituted anthracenes which form similar products involves linking together of the two nuclei through the 9,10-positions, and, in the case of a series of 9-substituted anthracenes, the products have been shown by Greene to have a head-to-head structure.[43] Such a structure is

$$R = -CHO, -COOEt, -CH_2OH \tag{9}$$

consistent with a process in which an excited anthracene molecule exists as a diradical with the odd electrons localized at the 9,10-positions, and reacts on collision with another unexcited molecule, a formulation also consistent with the kinetics of the dimerization process.

Many other unsaturated molecules undergo similar photoinduced dimerizations. Such processes have been reviewed by Mustafa,[44] and on a basis of product structure fall chiefly into two classes. First are dimerizations analogous to that of anthracene that occur with a variety of polynuclear carbocyclic and heterocyclic aromatics. Many of these (including that of anthracene itself) are reversible, redissociation occurring at elevated temperatures in the dark. A second and larger group leads to cyclobutane derivatives, a well-known example being the photodimerization of cinnamic acid to α-truxillic acid:

[41] E. J. Bowen, *ibid.*, **14**, 143 (1953); E. J. Bowen and D. W. Tanner, *Trans. Faraday Soc.*, **51**, 475 (1955).

[42] E. J. Bowen and K. K. Rohatgi, *Discussions Faraday Soc.*, **14**, 146 (1953).

[43] F. D. Greene, S. L. Misrock, and J. R. Wolfe, Jr., *J. Am. Chem. Soc.*, **77**, 3852 (1955). This paper also reviews evidence for the dimerization mechanism given above; but, for another point of view, cf. C. A. Coulson, L. E. Orgel, W. Taylor, and J. Weiss, *J. Chem. Soc.*, **1955**, 2961.

[44] A. Mustafa, *Chem. Revs.*, **51**, 1 (1952).

$$2 \quad \begin{array}{c} H \\ \diagdown \\ \phi \end{array} C{=}C \begin{array}{c} COOH \\ \diagup \\ \diagdown \\ H \end{array} \quad \rightarrow \quad \begin{array}{c} HOOC{-}CH{-}CH{-}\phi \\ | \qquad | \\ \phi{-}CH{-}CH{-}COOH \end{array} \qquad (10)$$

This process occurs only with the solid acid (in bulk or in aqueous suspension), and the structure of the product is apparently determined by the orientation of molecules in the crystal. Other substances, e.g., stilbene, acenaphthene, and benzalacetophenone, also dimerize in solution, and, in the last case, the reaction in solution follows the course

$$2\phi CH{=}CHCO\phi \quad \rightarrow \quad \begin{array}{c} \phi{-}CH{-}CH{-}CO\phi \\ | \qquad | \\ \phi{-}CH{-}CH{-}CO\phi \end{array} \qquad (11)$$

with the same sort of head-to-head structure as in the 9-substituted anthracene dimerization, presumably for the same reason, i.e., maximum resonance stabilization of the intermediate dimer diradical. Many other similar dimerizations are summarized by Mustafa,[43] and recently a similar dimerization of benzothiophene dioxide and some of its substituted analogs has been noted,[45] presumably following the course

$$\qquad (12)$$

Again many of the processes are reversible.

The analogy of these processes to thermal Diels-Alder-type reactions which sometimes also yield cyclobutane structures (Section 5·1c) is worth noting and may be taken as one of the arguments for a diradical structure of the transition state in the latter process. We may also observe that the photoexcited state involved is presumably the same one involved in the well-known photochemical *trans-cis* interconversion of such olefins.

A further group of photochemical processes involves the addition of a photoexcited molecule to an unsaturated substrate of different structure.[46] Typical is the formation of oxetanes (trimethylene oxides) from carbonyl compounds and tri- or tetrasubstituted olefins

[45] W. Davies and F. C. James, *J. Chem. Soc.,* **1955**, 314; A. Mustafa, *Nature,* **175**, 992 (1955).

[46] The non-chain photooxidations discussed in Section 9·4 may properly belong to this class.

first noted by Paterno and Chieffi [47] and studied more recently by Büchi.[48] An example is the reaction of benzaldehyde with 2-methyl-2-butene which Büchi suggests as following the path

$$
\phi CHO \xrightarrow{h\nu} \phi - \underset{H}{\overset{\overset{\textstyle O \cdot}{|}}{C}} \cdot \xrightarrow{C_5H_{10}} \phi - \underset{H}{\overset{\overset{\textstyle O-CHCH_3}{|}}{C}} \cdot \underset{CH_3}{\overset{|}{C}} - CH_3 \rightarrow \phi - \underset{H}{\overset{\overset{\textstyle O-CHCH_3}{|}}{C}} - C(CH_3)_2 \quad (13)
$$

Acetophenone yields a similar product, and Büchi points out that the structures are those expected on the principle of maximum resonance stabilization of the intermediate diradical. Such processes with aliphatic aldehydes necessarily compete with the radical chain addition of aldehydes to olefins (Section 6·3a) and Büchi makes the interesting suggestion that the n-butyraldehyde-2-methyl-2-butene reaction, which yields an "inverted" product, follows a quite different path involving a radical chain.

$$
RC \overset{\nearrow O}{\cdot} + CH_3CH = C(CH_3)_2 \longrightarrow \underset{O \cdot C(CH_3)_2}{\overset{R-C-CHCH_3}{\overset{||\ |}{}}} \longrightarrow \underset{O-C(CH_3)_2}{\overset{R-\overset{\cdot}{C}-CHCH_3}{\overset{|\ |}{}}}
$$

$$
\cdots\cdots\cdots RC\overset{\nearrow O}{\cdot} \quad + \quad \underset{O-C(CH_3)_2}{\overset{RCH-CHCH_3}{\overset{|\ |}{}}} \quad \overset{RCHO}{\swarrow} \quad (14)
$$

Büchi has recently described two extensions of this sort of reaction in which he believes similar intermediates are involved that undergo rearrangement to yield finally rather different products. In one, a disubstituted acetylene reacts with a carbonyl compound on irradiation to yield an α,β unsaturated ketone via the suggested path [49]

$$
\phi COR \xrightarrow{h\nu} \phi - \underset{R}{\overset{\overset{\textstyle O \cdot}{|}}{C}} \cdot \xrightarrow{R'C \equiv CR'} \left[\phi - \underset{R}{\overset{|}{C}} - \underset{R'}{\overset{\overset{\textstyle O-C}{|}}{C}} \overset{R'}{\underset{}{\overset{||}{}}} \right] \rightarrow \underset{R}{\overset{\phi}{\diagdown}} C = C \overset{R'}{\underset{COR'}{\diagup}} \quad (15)
$$

$$
R = CH_3 \text{ or } H \quad R' = n\text{-}C_4H_9
$$

In the other, photoexcited nitrobenzene reacts with 2-methyl-2-butene to give a variety of products including acetone, acetaldehyde,

[47] E. Paterno and G. Chieffi, *Gazz. chim. ital.*, **39**, 341 (1909).

[48] G. Büchi, C. G. Inman, and E. S. Lipinsky, *J. Am. Chem. Soc.*, **76**, 4327 (1954).

[49] G. Büchi, J. T. Kofron, E. Koller, and D. Rosenthal, *ibid.*, **78**, 876 (1956).

acetanilide, azobenzene, and a neutral product of incompletely determined structure, all proposed as arising by plausible paths from decomposition of an intermediate cyclic material.[50] A number of

$$\phi\text{—}NO_2 + CH_3CH\text{=}C(CH_3)_2 \rightarrow \phi\text{—}N \underset{O\text{—}CHCH_3}{\overset{O\text{—}C(CH_3)_2}{\diagdown\diagup}} \rightarrow \text{Products} \tag{16}$$

intramolecular reactions of nitroolefins are known which may have similar paths; as an example, the photolysis of o-nitrostilbenes has been studied by Splitter and Calvin, who also review earlier literature.[51] Another variant of the photochemical reaction between carbonyl compounds and olefins occurs with 1,2-diketones, particularly orthoquinones and aryl-substituted olefins. Here dioxane-type structures are produced, as in the case of stilbene and phenanthraquinone.[52]

$$\tag{17}$$

Many other examples have been summarized by Schönberg and Mustafa.[53] Although the process has been suggested as involving a diradical it is not at present clear whether the quinone or the olefin undergoes photoexcitation.[54] The photoinduced reaction between quinones and many aldehydes to give monoacylhydroquinones has already been discussed in Section 6·3c, where the process was suggested as a radical *chain* since it occurs with para- as well as orthoquinones.

A third major group of photoinduced reactions are patently oxidation-reduction processes. Many involve carbonyl compounds and have been reviewed by Schönberg and Mustafa.[53] As typical examples, benzophenone is reduced by isopropyl alcohol whereas, with

[50] G. Büchi and D. E. Ayer, *ibid.*, **78**, 689 (1956).

[51] J. S. Splitter and M. Calvin, *J. Org. Chem.*, **21**, 1086 (1955).

[52] A. Schönberg and A. Mustafa, *J. Chem. Soc.*, **1944**, 387; **1948**, 2126.

[53] A. Schönberg and A. Mustafa, *Chem. Revs.*, **40**, 181 (1947).

[54] A. Schönberg, W. I. Awad, and G. A. Mousa, *J. Am. Chem. Soc.*, **77**, 3850 (1955).

$$2\phi CO\phi + CH_3\overset{\displaystyle OH}{\underset{\displaystyle |}{CH}}CHCH_3 \xrightarrow{h\nu} \overset{\displaystyle \phi\;\;OH\;\;\phi}{\underset{\displaystyle \phi\;\;\;HO\;\;\phi}{C-C}} + CH_3COCH_3 \quad (18)$$

xanthopinacol, the reaction runs in the reverse direction. Quinones

$$O\overset{\displaystyle C_6H_4}{\underset{\displaystyle C_6H_4}{\Big\langle}}\overset{\displaystyle OH}{\underset{\displaystyle HO}{C}}\!-\!\overset{\displaystyle C_6H_4}{\underset{\displaystyle C_6H_4}{C}}\Big\rangle O + CH_3COCH_3 \xrightarrow{h\nu}$$

$$2\,O\overset{\displaystyle C_6H_4}{\underset{\displaystyle C_6H_4}{\Big\langle}}C\!=\!O + CH_3CHOHCH_3 \quad (19)$$

similarly oxidize alcohols, cleave pinacols, and even lead to the di-

$$+ CH_3OH \xrightarrow{h\nu} + CH_2O \qquad (20)$$

$$\xrightarrow{h\nu} + 2\phi\!-\!CO\!-\!\phi \qquad (21)$$

merization of diarylmethanes. The photodecomposition of diaryl azo

$$2\phi_2CH_2 + \xrightarrow{h\nu} \phi_2CHCH\phi_2 + \qquad (22)$$

compounds also involves reduction, initially to hydrazo compounds and later to amines,[55] with hydrogen abstraction from solvents such as isopropyl alcohol or isoöctane. Interestingly, such azo compounds

[55] B. E. Blaisdell, *J. Soc. Dyers and Colourists*, **65**, 618 (1949).

$$\phi\text{---}N{=}N\text{---}\phi + CH_3CHOHCH_3 \rightarrow$$

$$\phi\text{---}NH\text{---}NH\text{---}\phi + CH_3COCH_3 \quad (23)$$

also act as efficient photosensitizers for the oxidation of solvents such as isopropyl alcohol by molecular oxygen, the azo compound itself being protected against reduction as long as oxygen is present.[55]

Such oxidation-reduction processes are of great interest since they evidently play a role in the process of photosynthesis [56] and are of technical importance in connection with the fading of dyes.[57] Without going into the subject in detail, the fading of most dyes evidently involves photoinduced reaction with the substrate to which they are applied, since fading rates vary markedly with different fabrics (and even with the amount of moisture present), and since many dyes also produce notable photochemical degradation of fiber molecules.

The detailed mechanisms of these photochemical oxidation-reductions has received a great deal of discussion [58] and is not yet entirely clear. However, Bolland and Cooper [59] have recently made a rather complete analysis of the situation occurring in the photosensitized oxidation of ethanol by anthraquinone-2,6-disulfonate ion. In the absence of oxygen, hydroquinone and aldehyde are produced by the sequence

---

[56] Cf., for example, S. Korkes, *Ann. Revs. Biochem.*, **25**, 728 (1956).

[57] An interesting summary of this problem appears in the proceedings of a symposium held at Harrowgate, September, 1949; cf. *J. Soc. Dyers and Colourists*, **65**, 585 et seq. (1949).

[58] Cf. for example, footnote 57; also R. Livingston, *Record Chem. Progress*, **16**, 13 (1955).

[59] J. W. Bolland and H. R. Cooper, *Proc. Roy. Soc. London*, **A225**, 405 (1954).

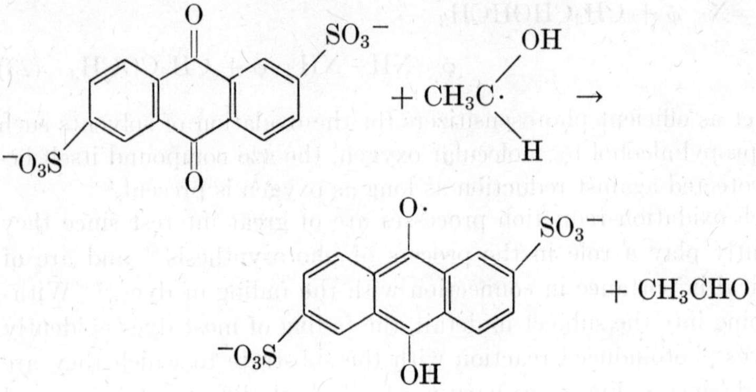

$$+ CH_3\overset{\cdot}{C}\diagdown H \rightarrow$$

$$+ CH_3CHO \quad (25)$$

$$2$$

$$\rightarrow$$

$$+$$

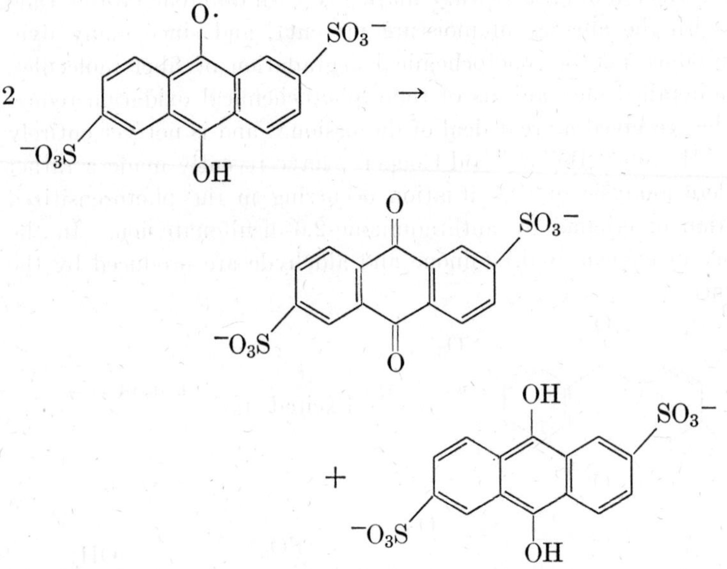

$$(26)$$

In the presence of oxygen, a very efficient induced autoxidation occurs by the additional steps

$$\cdot AH + O_2 \rightarrow A + HO_2\cdot$$
$$R\cdot + O_2 \rightarrow RO_2\cdot$$
$$2RO_2\cdot \rightarrow 2CH_3COOH + H_2O_2 \quad (27)$$
$$2HO_2\cdot \rightarrow H_2O_2 + O_2$$
$$HO_2\cdot + RO_2\cdot \rightarrow CH_3CHO + O_2 + H_2O_2$$

introducing the abbreviations $A = I$, $\cdot AH = II$, $R = III$, and $RO_2 \cdot$ = $CH_3CH(OH)OO\cdot$. In these steps the quinone is continuously regenerated and aldehyde and acid are produced concurrently. The kinetics of this autoxidation have been studied in detail and not only support this formulation but the oxygen-free reaction as well.

Similar schemes might be written for the processes of reactions 18–23, and the formation of symmetric coupled products in many cases certainly points to their occurrence via free radical paths. In concluding our discussion of photochemical processes we may point out that a rather remarkable variety of additional reactions are known. Thus, the photodimerization of o-phthalaldehyde is suggested as going via the path [60]

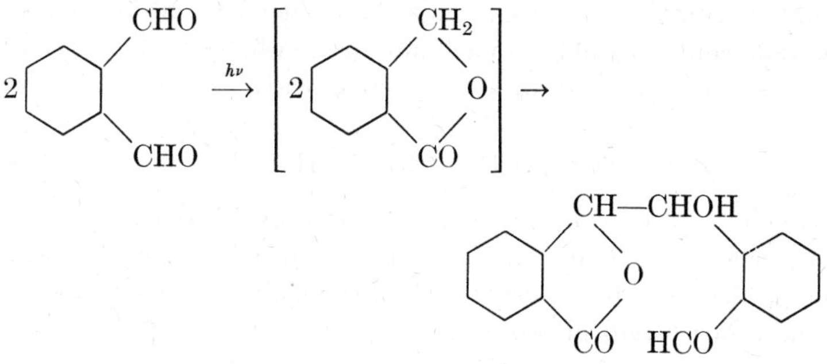

(28)

4-(o-nitrophenyl)dihydropyridines undergo internal oxidation reduction to nitrosopyridines.[61] Azoxybenzenes rearrange to o-hydroxyazo

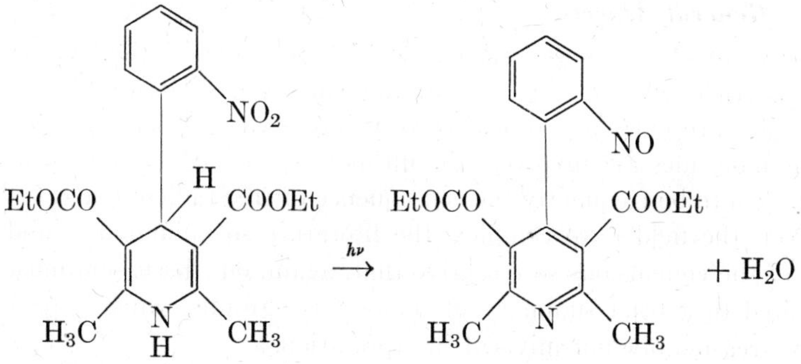

$+ H_2O$ (29)

compounds,[62] 4-alkyl-N-chloropiperidines undergo a remarkable

---

[60] A. Schönberg and A. Mustafa, J. Am. Chem. Soc., **77**, 5755 (1955).
[61] J. A. Berson and E. Brown, ibid., **77**, 447 (1955).
[62] G. M. Badger and R. G. Buttery, J. Chem. Soc., **1954**, 2243.

$$(30)$$

cyclization (the Löffler-Freytag reaction),[63] *cis*-stilbene not only is

$$+ \; HCl \qquad (31)$$

equilibrated with the *trans* isomer and dimerized but, in dilute hexane solution, converted in 95% yield into phenanthrene,[64] and, finally, SO_2 and saturated hydrocarbons react directly to yield sulfinic acids.[65]

$$SO_2 + RH \rightarrow R-SO_2H \qquad (32)$$

The foregoing are only a few suggestive examples from the recent literature, chosen to give some idea of the range of photochemical reactions which have been described, and certainly do not imply that all are necessarily radical processes.

11 · 2   Radical Production by High-Energy Radiation

11·2a   General Aspects

The chemical reactions induced by high-energy radiation, i.e., α and β particles, X and γ radiation, and (in the gas phase) electric discharges, are currently receiving very intensive study, and, where organic molecules are involved, the ultimate chemical reactions produced seem to be frequently the consequence of free radical reactions. However, the field is so complex, the literature so voluminous, and many of the conclusions so tentative that, again, our discussion must be limited to a brief summary of some of the results which appear to have reasonably unequivocal interpretation.[66]

[63] S. Wawzonek, M. F. Nelson, Jr., and P. J. Thelen, *J. Am. Chem. Soc.*, **73**, 2806 (1951); R. Lukes and M. Ferles, *Chem. Listy*, **49**, 510 (1955).

[64] R. L. Buckles, *J. Am. Chem. Soc.*, **72**, 1040 (1955).

[65] F. S. Dainton and K. J. Ivin, *Trans. Faraday Soc.*, **46**, 374, 382 (1950).

[66] For more detailed treatment, cf. G. Friedlander and J. W. Kennedy, *Nuclear and Radiochemistry*, John Wiley & Sons, New York, 1955; E. Collinson

The major primary path by which any high-energy particles or photons interact with matter is by interaction with the electron shells of molecules. Energy is absorbed and electrons ejected to produce ions. To an unknown extent, final products may arise from reactions of these ions. However, these ions are unstable and decompose with the ultimate result that much of the energy is very quickly degraded with the formation of excited molecules and radicals, and it is these species which undergo the reactions which account for many of the products that are ultimately observed. Thus, in the case of water, the overall process may conveniently be written symbolically as

$$H_2O \rightsquigarrow H \cdot + \cdot OH + H_2O_2 + H_2 \text{ (+ perhaps other products)} \quad (33)$$

The number of radicals produced for a given amount of radiation in any system is commonly measured as a G value (radicals per 100 electron-volts of input energy absorbed), which, for non-chain processes, has a value near unity. This value is frequently almost independent of the form of high-energy radiation employed but varies considerably with the material irradiated. In particular, purely aromatic compounds are quite resistant to radiation-induced decomposition, apparently because much of the energy is used up in elevating them to excited states from which they can descend by fluorescence or some other path without decomposition.

The physical or chemical processes resulting from excited state or radical production, in turn, provide some of the most important means of measuring radiation intensity. Thus the fluorescence induced in aromatic molecules is employed in scintillation counters, and the oxidation of ferrous ion in air-saturated 0.8 N H_2SO_4 provides another important standard, G for ferric ion production by Co^{60} γ radiation having a value of about 15.5, and having essentially the same value with other X, γ, or β radiation, but a lower value for α particles.[67]

The practical use of high-energy radiation in inducing free radical processes has received much hopeful discussion by those conscious of the enormous amount of radioactive material potentially available from the operation of nuclear reactors, and for certain purposes, such as the production of radicals in solid plastics or in the sterilization

and A. J. Swallow, *Quart. Revs.*, **9**, 311 (1955); E. Collinson, *Chem. Revs.*, **56**, 471 (1956); and chapters on radiochemistry in *Annual Reviews of Physical Chemistry*, Annual Reviews, Inc., Stanford, California, 1950 et seq.

[67] Cf. E. J. Hart, *Ann. Revs. Phys. Chem.*, **5**, 142 (1954).

of biological materials, the method has unique advantages.[68] However, some simple calculations point out obvious laboratory and commercial difficulties. A one kilocurie Co^{60} source (undergoing disintegration at the rate of 3.7×10^{13} atoms per second) emits most of its energy as approximately 1.2 Mev (million electron volt) γ radiation; two photons being produced per disintegration. If this were completely absorbed in a system, producing radicals with a G value of 5, radical production would be at the rate of 7.4×10^{-6} moles/ sec. This is the same rate as that produced by a lamp giving 1.2 watts of ultraviolet light at 3600 A, which dissociates a photoinitiator with unit quantum efficiency, or by a solution of approximately 0.1 moles of benzoyl peroxide at 80°C. When one considers the elaborate equipment and shielding required for the Co^{60}, plus the incomplete absorption of energy except in a very large system, the drawbacks of radiation-induced processes are rather obvious.

On the other hand, as a research tool, radiation chemistry is an attractive means of studying many radical reactions, particularly since, as in photochemistry, the radical-producing process is temperature independent. Conversely, when applied to systems where the resulting radical processes are well understood, it can be used to study the nature of the initial, radical-producing process.

Some rather simple considerations also indicate the type of systems in which studies of radiation-induced processes should give the most useful information. Initial radical production appears to be a highly indiscriminate process, the number of radicals produced from any component being roughly proportional to the weight fraction present in a system. Accordingly, studies of the reactions of a dilute solution of a reactive substrate in an unreactive solvent are chiefly those of the solvent radicals with the substrate and may be relatively easy to interpret. A good example is a dilute aqueous solution in which the primary radicals are $\cdot OH$ and $\cdot H$ produced via reaction 33. In contrast, irradiation of a single complex organic molecule (or the mixtures found in biochemical systems) may give results of at present almost meaningless complexity.

As a final point, as a high-energy particle or photon passes through a system radicals are produced along its track, and this non-randomness of distribution could produce complexities in the results similar to the consequences of radical production in pairs discussed in Sec-

---

[68] Such technical applications are discussed further by E. J. Henley and N. F. Barr, *Advances in Chemical Engineering*, Vol. I, Academic Press, New York, 1956.

tion 3·3a. This is particularly true with heavy species such as α particles where paths are short and relatively dense concentrations of fragments are produced. Actually, the significance of this complication has not been established in detail, and in many cases it appears unimportant.

11·2b Radiation-Induced Chain Processes

Initiation of radical chain processes provides one of the most unequivocal demonstrations of radical production by high-energy radiation. Olefin polymerization has received the most attention since polymer is readily detected and the details of the chain process are so well understood. The polymerization of ethylene in the gas phase by α particles was described as long ago as 1925.[69] Low molecular weight products are obtained, but at high pressures high polymers result.[66] Many examples of liquid-phase polymerization are known, involving essentially all the types of monomers which undergo polymerization initiated by other radical sources.[70] Several observations support the idea that the normal radical chain process is involved. Inhibitors such as quinones and oxygen are effective. In many systems including styrene,[70] acrylonitrile,[71, 73] methyl methacrylate,[72] vinyl chloride,[73] and acrylamide [74] rates are proportional to the square rate of "dose rate" (radiation intensity). Finally, the copolymerization of styrene and methyl methacrylate, initiated by β radiation, gives monomer reactivity ratios (Section 4·1b) indistinguishable from those obtained using other radical sources.[75]

When monomers with known polymerization constants are known, G values for chain initiation can be calculated from the relation between polymerization and dose rates. This has been done by Seitzer and Tobolsky using β radiation, obtaining $G = 0.22$ for styrene and

[69] W. Mund and W. Koch, Bull. soc. chim. Belg., 34, 117 (1925); S. C. Lind, D. C. Bardwell, and J. H. Perry, J. Am. Chem. Soc., 48, 1556 (1926).

[70] A. Chapiro, J. chim. phys., 47, 764, 747 (1950); A. Chapiro and P. Wahl, Compt. rend., 238, 1803 (1954).

[71] A. Prevot, ibid., 230, 288 (1950).

[72] A. Chapiro and E. Migirdicyan, J. chim. phys., 52, 439 (1955).

[73] A. Chapiro, M. Magat, A. Prevot-Bernas, and J. Serban, ibid., 52, 689 (1955).

[74] R. Schulz, G. Renner, A. Henglein, and W. Kern, Makromol. Chem., 12, 20 (1954).

[75] W. H. Seitzer, R. H. Goeckermann, and A. Tobolsky, J. Am. Chem. Soc., 75, 755 (1953).

$G = 3.14$ for methyl methacrylate,[76] a result paralleling the stability of aromatic systems in general to irradiation mentioned above. The G values for these monomers have also been measured in a variety of solvents and range from 0.4 in toluene to 10.2 in carbon tetrachloride, a very significant index of the variation in efficiency of radical production in various media. The possibility of using pulsed beams of electrons as a means of studying polymerization under non-steady-state conditions has been investigated by Majury,[77] although with as yet inconclusive results.

One difficulty with much of the work on radiation-induced polymerization is that it has been carried out in systems from which the polymer precipitates as formed, e.g., with aqueous solutions of acrylonitrile. This introduces the complications in interpreting results mentioned in Section 5·3b and, in particular, as pointed out by Chapiro et al.[73] obscures the possible importance of inhomogeneity of radical concentrations mentioned above.

In addition to polymerization, a few other radiation-inducing long-chain processes are known including autoxidation and halogenation,[66] but too few data are available for detailed discussion.

11·2c   Non-Chain Processes

Considerable work has been done on the effect of various forms of high-energy radiation on dilute aqueous solutions of both inorganic and simple organic substrates, both in the presence and absence of oxygen.[66] The results have been in general interpreted as processes initiated by hydroxyl radicals and hydrogen atoms, perhaps complexed with protons

$$H^+ + H\cdot \rightleftharpoons H_2^+\cdot \tag{34}$$

Results by Garrison et al.[78] with helium and deuterium ions in aqueous acetic acid are interesting in that yields of succinic acid go through a maximum ($G = 0.7$) at about 2 molar, whereas yields of CO_2, CH_4, C_2H_6, and CO rise continually to pure acetic acid. The succinic acid evidently arises from attack of water fragments on

---

[76] W. H. Seitzer and A. Tobolsky, *ibid.*, **77**, 2687 (1955). Earlier results gave lower values.[75]

[77] T. G. Majury, *J. Polymer Sci.*, **15**, 297 (1955).

[78] W. M. Garrison, H. R. Haymond, D. C. Morrison, B. M. Weeks, and J. Gile-Melchert, *J. Am. Chem. Soc.*, **75**, 2459 (1953); W. M. Garrison, W. Bennett, S. Cole, H. R. Haymond, and B. M. Weeks, *ibid.*, **77**, 2720 (1955).

acetic acid, whereas the other products largely originate from initial destruction of the acetic acid.

In pure organic systems not subject to specific induced chain reactions, again indiscriminate production of radicals produces very complex mixtures of products.[79] However, by introducing radical traps such as diphenylpicrylhydrazyl, Bouby and Chapiro [80] have been able to obtain significant results on the rates of initial radical production in various media.

Finally, an experiment by Miller [81] should be mentioned in which a gaseous mixture of CH_4, NH_3, H_2O, and H_2 was subjected to electric discharge. The situation was intended to simulate primitive earth conditions; it indicated a means by which complex organic compounds might arise, and led to the formation of detectable quantities of a number of organic acids, hydroxy acids, and amino acids plus other products, a remarkable result which will undoubtedly receive further investigation.

11·2d Hot Atom Chemistry

When a nuclear reaction occurs, either as a result of neutron or similar bombardment or by radioactive decay, the resulting atom is generally left with a kinetic *recoil energy* far in excess of ordinary chemical bond dissociation energies. Accordingly, if the atom in question was part of a covalently bonded molecule, it is ejected with a high velocity and, after losing its energy by successive collisions, undergoes a series of reactions by which it is finally converted to some stable product. This phenomenon was first observed by Szilard and Chalmers in 1934, who noted that, when ethyl iodide was irradiated with neutrons, most of the resulting radioactive iodine could be extracted from the ethyl iodide by water. This technique by which radioisotopes may be concentrated is known as the *Szilard-Chalmers process*, and the reactions which the ejected high-energy atoms undergo make up the field of *hot atom chemistry*. Much of the work has been with organic halogen compounds, and here the ultimate reactions must be largely those of halogen atoms and alkyl radicals with organic substrates. Recent results have been reviewed

[79] Cf. for example the products obtained from aliphatic alcohols, W. R. McDonell and A. S. Newton, *ibid.*, **76**, 4651 (1954), or benzene, W. N. Patrick and M. Burton, *ibid.*, **76**, 2626 (1954).

[80] L. Bouby and A. Chapiro, *J. chim. phys.*, **52**, 645 (1955). This paper also reviews earlier work which, however, was not carried out in the absence of air.

[81] S. L. Miller, *J. Am. Chem. Soc.*, **77**, 2351 (1955).

by Hart,[68] and, although knowledge of radical processes gained from other sources should be useful in interpreting experimental observations, we must note that the picture is greatly complicated by two factors: first, the fragments have excess energy and may undergo reactions not available to radicals with purely thermal energy, and, second, since only minute amounts of radicals are produced, radicals should have very long lives (unless non-random distribution of fragments is important) and the systems involved must be extraordinarily sensitive to minute traces of any impurities which undergo ready radical attack. Because of these difficulties, and because of the specialized nature of such processes, we will not consider them further here.

11·3   Redox Systems Involving Inorganic Ions

11·3a   General Survey

An important and extremely versatile means of producing free radicals (chiefly in aqueous systems) and inducing radical chain processes is by the use of partially or wholly inorganic oxidation-reduction systems. An early example is the use of Fenton's reagent, ferrous ion and hydrogen peroxide, for the oxidation of a variety of organic substrates, first described by Fenton [82] in 1894. A variety of similar systems are known, as well as radical chain processes involving solely inorganic reagents such as the metal ion-catalyzed autoxidation of sulfite ion elucidated by Haber and Wilstätter [83] and by Bäckström [84] in the early 1930's. However, the most important development in the field has been in the initiation of vinyl polymerization, a technique variously known as *reduction activation, redox catalysis,* and *redox polymerization.* By extension the term *redox systems* is conveniently applied to all such systems producing free radicals or inducing radical chain processes by one-electron oxidation-reduction reactions.

As often occurs, the technique of initiating vinyl polymerization by redox systems was discovered empirically and independently in several places, in this case in Germany,[85] England,[86] and the United

[82] H. J. H. Fenton, *J. Chem. Soc.,* **65,** 899 (1894).

[83] F. Haber and R. Wilstätter, *Ber.,* **64,** 2844 (1931).

[84] H. L. J. Bäckström, *Z. physik. Chem.,* **B25,** 122 (1934).

[85] W. Kern, *Makromol. Chem.,* **1,** 209, 249 (1948); **2,** 48 (1948).

[86] R. G. R. Bacon, *Trans. Faraday Soc.,* **42,** 140 (1946).

States.[87] Since then the method has had enormous development, particularly for the low-temperature emulsion polymerization of butadiene with styrene in the manufacture of synthetic rubber. This, in turn, has led to the empirical formulation of extraordinarily complex (and aptly named) "recipes" in which the role of the individual components is largely a matter of conjecture, although the fact of overall production of free radicals is beyond doubt. The basic advantage of such systems has been pointed out by Dainton: [88] in general the activation energy for radical formation by redox systems is about 10 kcal compared with 30 kcal or higher for thermal dissociation of radical sources such as peroxides (Chapter 10). Accordingly, redox systems can be used at lower temperatures and over wider temperature ranges. Further, since radical formation is usually the consequence of a bimolecular reaction between oxidant and reductant, its rate can be adjusted almost at will by suitable variation of reactant concentrations.

Because of the complexity of most technical recipes and the obscure nature of the processes involved, only a few simpler examples will be considered here. More technical surveys have been given by Bovey, Kolthoff, Medalia, and Meehan [89] and by Whitby.[90]

11·3b   The Ferrous Ion–Peroxide System

The reactions occurring between ferrous ion and hydrogen peroxide in acid solution were first worked out by Haber and Weiss [91] in connection with the iron-catalyzed decomposition of hydrogen peroxide. For this process they proposed the reaction sequence

$$Fe^{++} + H_2O_2 \rightarrow Fe^{+++} + OH^- + \cdot OH \tag{35}$$

$$\cdot OH + Fe^{++} \rightarrow OH^- + Fe^{+++} \tag{36}$$

$$HO\cdot + H_2O_2 \rightarrow H_2O + \cdot OOH \tag{37}$$

$$\cdot OOH + H_2O_2 \rightarrow O_2 + H_2O + \cdot OH \tag{38}$$

[87] W. D. Stewart, U.S. Pat. 2,380,476 (1945).

[88] F. S. Dainton, *Trans. Faraday Soc.*, **42**, 190 (1946).

[89] F. A. Bovey, I. M. Kolthoff, A. I. Medalia, and E. J. Meehan, *Emulsion Polymerization,* Interscience Publishers, New York, 1955.

[90] *Synthetic Rubber,* G. S. Whitby, editor in chief, John Wiley & Sons, New York, 1954.

[91] N. Uri, *Chem. Revs.*, **50**, 375 (1952). This comprehensive review of redox processes covers many points which cannot be examined here in detail.

although it now appears [91] that reaction 38 should be replaced by

$$\cdot OOH \rightleftharpoons O_2 \cdot^- + H^+ \tag{39}$$

$$O_2 \cdot^- + H_2O_2 \rightarrow O_2 + OH^- + \cdot OH \tag{40}$$

and reactions 35 and 36 perhaps written as

$$Fe^{++} + H_2O_2 \rightarrow FeOH^{++} + \cdot OH \tag{41}$$

and

$$\cdot OH + Fe^{++} \rightarrow FeOH^{++} \tag{42}$$

Although such modifications are not taken into account in our subsequent discussion, they illustrate an important point which enormously complicates any chemistry of inorganic ions; namely, that the ions actually exist as solvated or complexed species or often several such species in rapid equilibrium. Here we can do little more than ignore this complication. It will be noted that reactions 37, 39, and 40 constitute a chain process, important at high H_2O_2/Fe^{++} ratios. However, at lower H_2O_2/Fe^{++} ratios only reactions 35 and 36 are important, each molecule of peroxide oxidizing two Fe^{++} ions.

Although the above scheme has been accepted by most investigators, Bray and Gorin [92] have suggested the alternate path involving tetravalent iron, which has been supported by Cahill and Taube [93]

$$Fe^{++} + H_2O_2 \rightarrow FeO^{++} + H_2O \tag{43}$$

$$FeO^{++} + H_2O_2 \rightarrow Fe^{+++} + H_2O + O_2 \tag{44}$$

on the basis of oxygen exchange phenomena in some inorganic systems. However, the actual incorporation of HO— (or RO—) fragments into organic molecules and the products obtained from hydroperoxide decomposition (see below) make the Haber-Weiss scheme more attractive.

The salient feature of the Haber-Weiss sequence is the production of hydroxyl radicals in reaction 35 since these are the species which are presumed to attack organic substrates. The initiation of vinyl polymerization by ferrous ion plus hydrogen peroxide has been elegantly examined by Baxendale, Evans, and Park [94] using somewhat

[92] W. C. Bray and M. Gorin, *J. Am. Chem. Soc.*, **54**, 2134 (1932).

[93] A. E. Cahill and H. Taube, *ibid.*, **74**, 2312 (1952).

[94] J. H. Baxendale, M. G. Evans, and G. S. Park, *Trans. Faraday Soc.*, **42**, 155 (1946).

water-soluble monomers such as acrylonitrile and methyl acrylate. The initiation process is apparently reaction 35 followed by

$$\cdot OH + CH_2{=}CHR \rightarrow HOCH_2\dot{C}HR \qquad (45)$$

since, in the presence of monomer, no oxygen is evolved, even in the presence of excess peroxide, and only one molecule of ferrous ion is oxidized per mole of peroxide consumed. By work at very high dilutions, the rate of hydroxyl radical formation, reaction 35, has been found [95] to obey the bimolecular rate expression

$$k_{35} = 4.45 \times 10^8 e^{-9400/RT} \qquad (46)$$

with a rate of 12.6 liters/mole/sec at 0°C. By varying the Fe^{++}/ olefin ratio and determining the corresponding Fe^{++}/H_2O_2 stoichiometry, it should be possible also to determine the relative rates of reactions 36 and 45, but here results are in poor agreement,[36, 94] perhaps because of competing oxidation of the olefin. A number of other observations on $Fe^{++} + H_2O_2$-initiated systems have also been made by Baxendale, Evans, and their co-workers.[96]

The reaction of ferrous ion with a number of substituted peroxides has also been observed to initiate polymerization. With persulfate,[97, 98, 99] the process is postulated as

$$Fe^{++} + S_2O_8^{=} \rightarrow Fe^{+++} + SO_4^{=} + SO_4 \cdot^{-} \qquad (47)$$

$$SO_4 \cdot^{-} + CH_2{=}CHR \rightarrow {}^{-}SO_4{-}CH_2{-}\dot{C}HR \qquad (48)$$

Of greater practical importance, since they have found wide use in synthetic rubber manufacture, are the reactions of ferrous ion with various organic hydroperoxides, notably cumene hydroperoxide. Here the initial step is evidently

$$ROOH + Fe^{++} \rightarrow Fe^{+++} + OH^{-} + RO\cdot \qquad (49)$$

since, when the decomposition is carried out rapidly in the presence of butadiene, products of the structure $RO{-}(CH_2{-}CH{=}CH{-}$

[95] W. G. Barb, J. H. Baxendale, P. George and K. R. Hargrave, *ibid.*, **47**, 462, 591 (1951).

[96] J. H. Baxendale, S. Bywater, and M. G. Evans, *ibid.*, **42**, 675 (1946); J. H. Baxendale, M. G. Evans, and J. K. Kilham, *ibid.*, **42**, 668 (1946); J. H. Baxendale and M. G. Evans, *ibid.*, **43**, 210 (1947); J. H. Baxendale, S. Bywater, and M. G. Evans, *J. Polymer Sci.*, **1**, 237 (1946); J. H. Baxendale, M. G. Evans, and J. K. Kilham, *ibid.*, **1**, 446 (1947); M. G. Evans, *J. Chem. Soc.*, **1947**, 266.

[97] J. H. Merz and W. A. Waters, *Discussions Faraday Soc.*, **2**, 179 (1947).

[98] J. W. L. Fordham and H. L. Williams, *ibid.*, **73**, 1634, 4855 (1951).

[99] I. M. Kolthoff, A. I. Medalia, and H. P. Raaen, *J. Am. Chem. Soc.*, **73**, 1733 (1951).

$CH_2)_2$—OR are obtained in yields as high as 85%.[100] Further, in the absence of reactive substrates, a major product from cumene hydroperoxide is acetophenone,[100a] arising from the well-established decomposition (Section 10·2a)

$$R-\overset{\overset{\displaystyle CH_3}{|}}{\underset{\underset{\displaystyle CH_3}{|}}{C}}-O\cdot \ \rightarrow RCOCH_3 + CH_3\cdot \qquad (50)$$

E_a and PZ for reaction 49 have been determined for several hydroperoxides and are listed in Table 11·2, together with data on H_2O_2

TABLE 11·2   FERROUS ION–PEROXIDE REACTIONS

Peroxide	$PZ \times 10^{-9}$	E_a, kcal	Footnote
H_2O_2	0.445	9.4	95
$S_2O_8^=$	100	12.1	98
Cumene hydroperoxide	1.07	12.1	98
p-Isopropylcumene hydroperoxide	4.0	10.8	101
p-t-Butylcumene hydroperoxide	1.8	9.9	101
p-Nitrocumene hydroperoxide	80	13.1	102
p-Methane hydroperoxide	6.3	11.1	102
1-Phenylcyclohexyl hydroperoxide	2.4	10.0	102

[101] R. J. Orr and H. L. Williams, *Can. J. Chem.*, **30**, 985 (1952).
[102] R. J. Orr and H. L. Williams, *J. Phys. Chem.*, **57**, 925 (1953).

and persulfate. The efficiency of chain starting by the radicals produced from a number of hydroperoxides, and also persulfate, has been studied by Orr and Williams,[103] who find that with acrylonitrile and similar monomers in the competition between the processes

$$RO\cdot + Fe^{++} \rightarrow RO^- + Fe^{+++} \qquad (51)$$

$$RO\cdot + CH_2{=}CHR' \rightarrow ROCH_2\dot{C}HR' \qquad (52)$$

$$RO\cdot + HOOR \rightarrow ROH + ROO\cdot \qquad (53)$$

TABLE 11·3   A TYPICAL REDOX RECIPE FOR GR—S POLYMERIZATION [104]

(All components in parts by weight)

Butadiene	75	NaOH	0.061
Styrene	25	Cumene hydroperoxide	0.17
Water	180	$FeSO_4$	0.017
Dresinate 731	5	$Na_4P_2O_7 \cdot 10H_2O$	1.5
t-Mercaptan	0.5	Fructose	0.5

[100] M. S. Kharasch, F. S. Arimoto, and W. Nudenberg, *J. Org. Chem.*, **16**, 1556 (1951). With H_2O_2, 23% of 1,8-dihydroxyoctadiene-2,6 is obtained.
[100a] M. S. Kharasch, A. Fono, and W. Nudenberg, *ibid.*, **15**, 763 (1950).
[103] R. J. Orr and H. L. Williams, *J. Am. Chem. Soc.*, **77**, 3715 (1955).

k_{51}/k_{52} has values of 10^{-3} to 10^{-2}, and k_{53}/k_{51} is also smaller than unity.

Turning briefly now to recipes in which ferrous ion and peroxides are used to initiate technical polymerizations, Table 11·3 gives a typical early formulation,[104] in which at least the presumed role of the components may be indicated. The components in the first column are simply monomers, water, emulsifying agent (a disproportionated rosin soap), and mercaptan that is primarily present to control polymer molecular weight. Hydroperoxide and $FeSO_4$ are the primary redox components, pyrophosphate is present to solubilize the iron in the strongly alkaline medium, and the fructose is believed to act by re-reducing ferric ion to the ferrous state so that it may be reused. The resulting type of cycle has been depicted in the same manner as a biochemical process by Patrick,[105] Fig. 11·3, but actually little is known conclusively about the individual steps. The reaction of cumene hydroperoxide with ferrous ion, present as ferrocyanide in alkaline solution, has been studied by Boardman,[106] who finds a bimolecular reaction to yield acetophenone but which is pH dependent, and Orr and

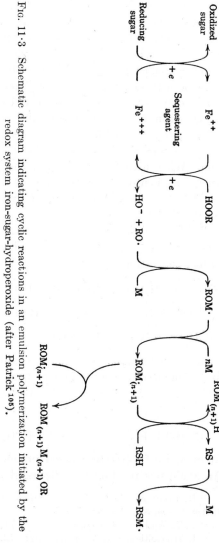

FIG. 11·3 Schematic diagram indicating cyclic reactions in an emulsion polymerization initiated by the redox system iron-sugar-hydroperoxide (after Patrick[105]).

[104] E. J. Vandenberg and G. E. Hulse, *Ind. Eng. Chem.*, **40**, 932 (1948).

[105] R. L. Patrick, *J. Polymer Sci.*, **9**, 467 (1952).

[106] H. Boardman, *J. Am. Chem. Soc.*, **75**, 4268 (1953).

Williams [107] have obtained less conclusive results on the reaction between cumene hydroperoxide and traces of iron in the presence of various polyethylenepolyamines $NH_2(C_2H_4NH)_nC_2H_4NH_2$. Wall and Swoboda [108] have proposed a detailed scheme for the path of reaction of the benzoyl–ferrous pyrophosphate–soap system which, however, has been criticized by Kolthoff and Youse.[109] Finally, the other components present in the system (thiol, reducing sugar, etc.) may be attacked by radicals or react with iron to produce further complications which are too involved to consider here but which are discussed in detail by Bovey et al.[89]

The second major class of reactions of ferrous ion–peroxide systems with organic substrates are oxidations involving hydrogen abstraction. When used for this purpose the $H_2O_2 + Fe^{++}$ combination is known as Fenton's reagent after its discoverer [82,110] and has found synthetic use in the oxidation of hydroxy compounds, particularly sugars.[111]

The first consideration of the reaction in terms of the Haber-Weiss reaction scheme is due to Merz and Waters [97,112] and Weiss,[113] the former suggesting the sequence

$$\cdot OH + RCH_2OH \rightarrow R\dot{C}HOH + H_2O \tag{54}$$

$$R\dot{C}HOH + H_2O_2 \rightarrow \cdot OH + R\!-\!CH(OH)_2 (\rightarrow RCHO + H_2O) \tag{55}$$

$$R\dot{C}HOH + \cdot OH \rightarrow RCH(OH)_2 (\rightarrow RCHO + H_2O) \tag{56}$$

Reactions 54 and 55 constitute a chain reminiscent of that involved in the induced decomposition of benzoyl peroxide (Section $10 \cdot 2b$). Kolthoff and Medalia [114] have investigated the oxidation of ethanol and suggested as alternative to reaction 55 the reaction

$$R\dot{C}HOH + Fe^{+++} \rightarrow Fe^{++} + R\dot{C}HOH \rightarrow RCHO + H^+ \tag{57}$$

followed by fresh $\cdot OH$ radical production by the Fe^{++} produced. An analogous reaction was discussed in Section $4 \cdot 3b$ in connection

[107] R. J. Orr and H. L. Williams, *Discussions Faraday Soc.*, **14**, 170 (1953); *J. Am. Chem. Soc.*, **76**, 3321 (1954).

[108] F. T. Wall and T. J. Swoboda, *ibid.*, **71**, 919 (1949).

[109] I. M. Kolthoff and M. Youse, *ibid.*, **72**, 3431 (1950).

[110] H. J. H. Fenton and H. Jackson. *J. Chem. Soc.*, **75**, 1 (1899); H. J. H. Fenton and H. O. Jones, **77**, 69 (1900).

[111] R. S. Morrell and M. J. Crofts, *ibid.*, **77**, 1219 (1900).

[112] J. H. Merz and W. A. Waters, *ibid.*, **1949**, S15.

[113] J. Weiss, *Discussions Faraday Soc.*, **2**, 188 (1947).

[114] I. M. Kolthoff and A. I. Medalia, *J. Am. Chem. Soc.*, **71**, 3777 (1949).

with the ferric ion inhibition of radical polymerization, cf. also Section 10·3c. This alternative is now generally accepted, and in any case, there is no doubt of the existence of a chain process with many substrates, i.e., primary and secondary alcohols, aldehydes, and ethers, since the decomposition of peroxide is accelerated, and since several moles of substrate are oxidized for every mole of ferrous ion originally present. However, with other substrates chains apparently do not occur, Merz and Waters proposing processes such as reaction 56 in their place.

Merz and Waters [97,112] have attempted a detailed kinetic analysis of Fenton's reagent reactions and have calculated ratios of k_{54}/k_{35} for several systems. For primary and secondary alcohols they obtain values of 2–3, which seem implausibly high. Their treatment has also been criticized by Uri,[91] and the whole problem needs further investigation. Another interesting observation [97,112,114] is that certain substances such as acetic acid and acetone interfere with the Fenton reagent chains. Here processes such as

$$\cdot OH + CH_3COOH \rightarrow CH_3COO\cdot \qquad (58)$$

$$CH_3COO\cdot + Fe^{++} \rightarrow CH_3COO^- + Fe^{+++} \qquad (59)$$

have been suggested, although

$$CH_3COOH + \cdot OH \rightarrow \dot{C}H_2COOH \qquad (60)$$

is a plausible alternative since the product radical could also readily act as an oxidizing agent to give a relatively stable enolate anion.

The reaction of Fenton's reagent with other substrates has also been investigated. With benzene, phenol and biphenyl are produced.[115,116] Such processes are probably as complicated as the substitution of aromatic nuclei by other radicals (Section 10·2b) but other aromatic systems are also hydroxylated, and with toluene both ring and side-chain attack occurs. Phenols [117] and amines [118] also yield complex products. Weiss [113] has shown that the oxidation of oxalic acid is similarly a chain process.

Ferrous ion–hydroperoxide reactions may lead to other interesting

[115] J. H. Merz and W. A. Waters, *J. Chem. Soc.*, **1949**, 2427.

[116] J. H. Baxendale and J. Magee, *Discussions Faraday Soc.*, **14**, 160 (1953).

[117] S. L. Cosgrove and W. A. Waters, *J. Chem. Soc.*, **1951**, 1726; R. G. R. Bacon, R. Grime, and D. J. Munro, *ibid.*, **1954**, 2275.

[118] D. G. H. Daniels, F. T. Naylor, and B. C. Saunders, *ibid.*, **1951**, 3433.

products. Thus 1-hydroxycyclohexyl hydroperoxide gives a C_{12} dibasic acid [119] via the sequence

$$HOOC(CH_2)_{10}COOH \quad (61)$$

whereas in the presence of butadiene the product $HOOC(CH_2)_5$ $(CH_2-CH{=}CH-CH_2)_2(CH_2)_5COOH$ is obtained in up to 75% yield.[120] Kharasch, Kawahara, and Nudenberg [121] have also obtained products from hydroperoxide-butadiene-quinone systems containing all three units, e.g.,

$$(62)$$

cf. Section 4·3.

Finally, it should be noted that halide ions commonly interfere with ferrous ion–peroxide systems via the process [91]

$$\cdot OH \text{ (or } \cdot OR) + X^- \rightarrow HO^- + X\cdot \qquad (63)$$

Accordingly subsequent reactions with organic substrates should be those of halogen atoms.

11·3c   Other Metal Ion–Peroxide Systems

A number of other metal ions able to undergo one-electron-oxidation process appear to react with peroxides in a manner analogous to ferrous ion, e.g.,

$$M^{n+} + HOOH \rightarrow M^{(n+1)+} + HO^- + \cdot OH \qquad (64)$$

The energetics of such processes have been reviewed by Uri.[91] At present, the best characterized system is that involving silver ion and

[119] E. G. E. Hawkins, *ibid.*, **1955**, 3463; N. Brown, M. J. Hartig, M. J. Roedel, A. W. Anderson, and C. E. Schweitzer, *J. Am. Chem. Soc.*, **77**, 1756 (1955).

[120] M. S. Kharasch and W. Nudenberg, *J. Org. Chem.*, **19**, 1921 (1954).

[121] M. S. Kharasch, F. Kawahara, and W. Nudenberg, *ibid.*, **19**, 1977 (1954).

persulfate. The catalytic effect of silver ion on persulfate oxidation of oxalic acid was described by Kempf in 1905,[122] who also studied a number of other reactions.[123] Such processes have been surveyed more recently by Bacon et al.,[124] who noted the oxidation of toluene to benzaldehyde, benzoic acid, and bibenzyl, and of phenols to various complex products. Greenspan and Woodburn [125] have also recently described the oxidation of primary and secondary alcohols and aldehydes and the cleavage of glycols, noting that the rate of persulfate decomposition increases greatly in the presence of such oxidizable substrates.

The kinetics of the oxidation of ethanol have been studied by Bawn and Margerison,[126] who conclude that an initial bimolecular

$$Ag^+ + S_2O_8^= \rightarrow Ag^{++} + SO_4^= + SO_4 \cdot^- \qquad (65)$$

$$Ag^{++} + OH^- \rightarrow Ag^+ + \cdot OH \qquad (66)$$

reaction is succeeded by an induced chain analogous to that occurring in the absence of metal ion (Section 10·2e). By introducing diphenylpicrylhydrazyl to inhibit the chain, they obtain

$$k_{65} = 3.1 \times 10^{11}e^{-17,900/RT} \qquad (67)$$

It is reasonable to assume that other oxidations are initiated similarly.

Other similar metal ion–peroxide systems have been examined in less detail. To mention a few examples, cupric ion also catalyzes the oxidation of ethanol by persulfate, although the kinetics are complex,[126] and leads to the hydroxylation of phenol and benzoic acid by hydrogen peroxide.[127] The ability of V_2O_5 to catalyze the oxidation of a variety of olefins by hydrogen peroxide has been studied by Triebs,[128] and Mugdan and Young [129] have determined the catalytic effect of a whole series of heavy metal ions on the hy-

[122] R. Kempf, *Ber.*, **38**, 3963 (1905); cf. T. L. Allen, *J. Am. Chem. Soc.*, **73**, 3589 (1951).

[123] R. Kempf, *Ber.*, **38**, 3966, 3977, **39**, 3715 (1906).

[124] R. G. R. Bacon, R. W. Bolt, R. J. Doggart, R. Grime, and D. J. Munro, *Chemistry & Industry*, **1953**, 897.

[125] F. P. Greenspan and H. M. Woodburn, *J. Am. Chem. Soc.*, **76**, 6345 (1954).

[126] C. E. H. Bawn and D. Margerison, *Trans. Faraday Soc.*, **51**, 925 (1955).

[127] J. O. Konecny, *J. Am. Chem. Soc.*, **76**, 4993 (1954).

[128] W. Triebs, G. Franke, G. Leichsenring, and H. Röder, *Chem. Ber.*, **86**, 616 (1953).

[129] M. Mugdan and D. P. Young, *J. Chem. Soc.*, **1950**, 2988.

droxylation of allyl alcohol by hydrogen peroxide. Several examples of metal ion–peroxide systems in redox polymerization are given by Bovey et al.[89]

A second group of metal ion–peroxide reactions are those in which the metal ion is reduced and peroxy radicals are formed. Such processes are important in the heavy metal ion-catalyzed decomposition of hydrogen peroxide, and their energetics are discussed by Uri.[91] They have already been mentioned in connection with metal ion catalysis of autoxidation (Section 9·2f). The most important example is that of cobaltic ion, and here a number of interesting synthetic reactions involving hydroperoxides have been described by Kharasch, Pauson, and Nudenberg,[130] e.g.,

$$\text{(cyclohexene)} + (CH_3)_3COOH \xrightarrow{Co^{++}} \text{(cyclohexenyl } OOC_4H_9) + C_4H_9OH \qquad (68)$$

$$C_6H_{13}CH{=}CH_2 + (CH_3)_3COOH \xrightarrow{Co^{++}}$$
$$C_5H_{11}CH{=}CH{-}CH_2OOC_4H_9 \qquad (69)$$

$$CH_2{=}CH{-}CH{=}CH_2 + (CH_3)_3COOH \xrightarrow{Co^{++}}$$
$$C_4H_9OOCH_2{-}CH{=}CH{-}CH_2OOC_4H_9$$
$$+ CH_2{=}CH{-}CH(OOC_4H_9)CH_2OOC_4H_9 \qquad (70)$$

Here the peroxy radicals are apparently generated by a cyclic process:

$$ROOH + Co^{++} \rightarrow RO\cdot + OH^- + Co^{+++} \qquad (71)$$

$$Co^{+++} + ROOH \rightarrow ROO\cdot + Co^{++} + H^+ \qquad (72)$$

$$RO\cdot + ROOH \rightarrow ROH + ROO\cdot \qquad (73)$$

and, for reactions 68 and 69, Kharasch suggests

$$ROO\cdot + CH_2{=}CH{-}CH_2R' \rightarrow ROOCH_2{-}\dot{C}H{-}CH_2R' \qquad (74)$$
$$ROOCH_2{-}\dot{C}H{-}CH_2R' + Ox \rightarrow ROOCH_2{-}CH{=}CH{-}R' + OxH \qquad (75)$$

where Ox is one of the oxidizing species in the system, since in reaction 69 complete double bond migration occurs.

[130] M. S. Kharasch, P. Pauson, and W. Nudenberg, *J. Org. Chem.*, **18**, 322 (1953).

A similar peroxy radical addition occurs to certain 2,4,6-trialkyl-phenols,[131] e.g.,

$$(76)$$

11·3d   Other Inorganic Redox Systems

A number of other inorganic redox systems are known which induce organic radical chain reactions, and it is of historical interest that redox polymerization processes were actually first discovered by adding small quantities of reducing agents to peroxide-containing systems in the hope of eliminating the induction period due to molecular oxygen.[89]   Thus Bacon in 1946 described a number of persulfate–reducing agent combinations, in general further promoted by traces of heavy-metal ions.[86]   An example, which has received further study, is the combination persulfate and thiosulfate.   The process in the absence of organic substrate has been studied by Sorum and Edwards,[132] who propose a chain reaction initiated either by thermal dissociation of persulfate or, in the presence of copper ion, a redox reaction with a cuprous thiosulfate complex.   Using S^{35}-labeled reagents, Berry and Peterson[133] have studied the initiation of tetra-fluoroethylene polymerization.   No persulfate fragments were found in the polymer, perhaps because of the ready hydrolysis of the $-CF_2OSO_3^-$ group.

Sulfite behaves in a similar manner to thiosulfate, and sulfite fragments appear in the polymer.[133]   Sulfite may also be used with other

[131] T. W. Campbell and G. M. Coppinger, *J. Am. Chem. Soc.*, **74**, 1469 (1952); A. F. Bickel, E. C. Kooyman, C. LaLau, W. Roest, and P. Piet, *J. Chem. Soc.*, **1953**, 3211.

[132] C. A. Sorum and J. O. Edwards, *J. Am. Chem. Soc.*, **74**, 1204 (1952).

[133] K. L. Berry and J. H. Peterson, *ibid.*, **73**, 5195 (1951).

oxidizing agents including molecular oxygen [134] (cf. Section 7·3a). In addition to inducing polymerization, sulfite plus persulfate leads to the hydroxylation of naphthionic acid,[135] whereas sulfite plus nitrite introduces sulfonic acid groups into 2-naphthol and 3-hydroxy-2-naphthoic acid.[136] A number of other redox polymerization recipes involving sulfur compounds and oxidizing agents are discussed by Bovey et al.[89] However, Cristol and Reynolds [137] have obtained no evidence for radical formation in the reaction of cumene hydroperoxide and NaHS, and Soloway and Friess [138] have made the interesting observation that the reaction products of peracids and bisulfite are able to acylate amines, which suggests a polar reaction such as

$$
\underset{\parallel}{RC} \overset{O}{\parallel} -OOH + SO_3^= \rightarrow R-\underset{\diagdown}{C}\overset{O}{\diagup} \quad + OH^-
$$
$$
OSO_3^-
$$

$$
\overset{\phi NH_2}{\longrightarrow} R-\underset{\diagdown}{C}\overset{O}{\diagup} \quad + HSO_4^- \quad (77)
$$
$$
NH\phi
$$

The well-known reduction of peroxides by iodide ion is also presumably a simple polar displacement, followed by decomposition of the resulting hypoiodite.

The nitrogen analogs of hydrogen peroxide, hydroxylamine and hydrazine, might be expected to undergo comparable reactions with oxidizable metal ions, and Davis, Evans, and Higginson [139] have proposed for the hydroxylamine–titanous ion reaction in acid solution the process

$$
Ti^{3+} + NH_3OH^+ \rightarrow Ti^{4+} + \cdot NH_2 + H_2O \quad (78)
$$

since the combination induces polymerization. Other metal ions (Cr^{++}, V^{++}, Mo^{+++}, and Fe^{++}) behave similarly, and in the presence of benzene and cyclohexene some aniline and cyclohexyl-

[134] B. D. Sully, *J. Chem. Soc.,* **1950,** 1498.

[135] E. Bamann and K. Schriever, *Chem. Ber.,* **86,** 996 (1953).

[136] S. V. Bogdanov and N. N. Karandasheva, *J. Gen. Chem. U.S.S.R.,* **16,** 1613 (1946).

[137] S. J. Cristol and R. D. Reynolds, *J. Am. Chem. Soc.,* **77,** 1284 (1955).

[138] A. H. Soloway and S. L. Friess, *ibid.,* **73,** 5000 (1951).

[139] P. Davis, M. G. Evans, and W. C. E. Higginson, *J. Chem. Soc.,* **1951,** 2563.

amine are produced.[140]   Again, in analogy to hydrogen peroxide, the reaction of ferrous citrate complex with disulfides has been suggested by Koltoff [141] as

$$Fe^{++} \text{ (complex)} + RSSR \rightarrow Fe^{+++} \text{ (complex)} + RS^- + RS \cdot \quad (79)$$

and of ferric ion with hydrazine [142] as

$$Fe^{+++} + NH_2\text{—}NH_2 \rightarrow Fe^{++} + H^+ + NH_2\text{—}\dot{N}H \quad (80)$$

Halogens also react directly with ferrous ion to produce halogen atoms,

$$Fe^{++} + Br_2 \rightarrow Fe^{+++} + Br^- + Br \cdot \quad (81)$$

and thus bring about reactions such as the isomerization of maleic acid [143] (Section 7·1d), the oxidation of oxalic acid,[144] and the initiation of polymerizations (hypobromous acid behaves similarly).[145]

Turning now to reactions in which radicals might be produced by the direct reaction between inorganic ions and organic molecules, it is now well recognized that the oxidation of organic molecules by such reagents divide sharply into two classes, those involving single- and those involving two-electron transfer processes.   However, in spite of the importance of this generalization, the unequivocal classification of even the most common types of oxidation systems has only been begun.   Accordingly, only a brief survey will be given here.[146]

Evidently, the formation of organic free radicals should be a consequence of oxidation processes involving single-electron transfers and are to be anticipated in reactions involving inorganic ions undergoing one-unit changes in valence in the overall reaction, although even this generalization must be handled with care, since a two-unit change to an unstable intermediate ion is conceivable in many cases. In this class, oxidations by cobaltic ion have recently been studied

[140] H. Seaman, P. J. Taylor, and W. A. Waters, *ibid.*, **1954**, 4690.

[141] I. M. Kolthoff, W. Stricks, and N. Tanaka, *J. Am. Chem. Soc.*, **77**, 5215 (1955).

[142] W. C. E. Higginson and P. Wright, *J. Chem. Soc.*, **1955**, 1551.

[143] D. H. Derbyshire and W. A. Waters, *Trans. Faraday Soc.*, **45**, 749 (1949).

[144] I. L. Hochhauser and H. Taube, *J. Am. Chem. Soc.*, **69**, 1582 (1950).

[145] M. G. Evans, J. H. Baxendale, and D. J. Cowling, *Discussions Faraday Soc.*, **2**, 206 (1947).

[146] A general survey is given by W. A. Waters, "Oxidation Processes," in *Organic Chemistry*, Vol. IV, H. Gilman, editor, John Wiley & Sons, New York, 1953.

by Bawn and White [147,148] and Hargreaves and Sutcliffe,[149] who conclude that hydroxyl radicals are formed from water, although the

$$Co^{+++} + H_2O \rightarrow Co^{++} + H^+ + \cdot OH \qquad (82)$$

overall process is complex, and radicals are also produced in the oxidation of formic acid, alcohols, and aldehydes. Hargreaves and Sutcliffe [149] also deduce a radical path for the oxidation of formaldehyde by ceric ion,[150] and it seems plausible that radicals may be involved in oxidation of many organic substrates by ferric, cupric, and manganic ions.[151] However, in many cases, the overall process appears to involve the decomposition into radicals of an intermediate chelate complex, as in the Mn^{3+}-oxalate reaction,[152] and similar processes.[153]

Many of the common oxidizing agents undergo larger changes in oxidation state, and here the organic substrate may participate in a two-electron transfer process without radical formation. The initial steps in the chromic acid oxidation of isopropyl alcohol have been elegantly shown by Westheimer to involve proton loss from an intermediate chromate ester without radical formation.[154] It is reasonable to assume that other chromic acid oxidations have similar paths, but tetravalent chromium is produced in the oxidation step outlined above and small amounts of apparent radical products are produced in some oxidations, e.g., tetraphenylethane from diphenylmethane,[155] and chromate ion has been used as a component in redox polymerization formulations.[156]

The situation with permanganate is even more complex. In acid solution, the Mn^{3+} ion appears to be an important intermediate in

[147] C. E. H. Bawn and A. G. White, *J. Chem. Soc.*, **1951**, 331, 339, 343.

[148] C. E. H. Bawn, *Discussions Faraday Soc.*, **14**, 181 (1953).

[149] G. Hargreaves and L. H. Sutcliffe, *Trans. Faraday Soc.*, **51**, 786 (1955).

[150] Examples of polymerization initiation are given by J. Saldick, *J. Polymer Sci.*, **19**, 73 (1956).

[151] Some metal-catalyzed autoxidations not involving hydroperoxide chains also appear to involve actual oxidation by metal ions, the oxygen serving simply to return the metal to its higher oxidation state; cf. Section 9·5.

[152] F. R. Duke, *J. Am. Chem. Soc.*, **69**, 2885 (1947).

[153] A. Y. Drummond and W. A. Waters, *J. Chem. Soc.*, **1954**, 2456, 3119; P. Levesley and W. A. Waters, *ibid.*, **1955**, 217.

[154] F. H. Westheimer, *Chem. Revs.*, **45**, 419 (1949), and subsequent papers.

[155] R. Slack and W. A. Waters, *J. Chem. Soc.*, **1948**, 1666.

[156] I. M. Kolthoff and E. J. Meehan, *J. Polymer Sci.*, **9**, 327 (1952).

the oxidation of species such as oxalate ion,[157] and, as noted above, its subsequent reduction can involve one-electron transfer. However, the well-known oxidation of olefins to *cis*-glycols probably involves some sort of cyclic intermediate formed by a strictly non-radical process. In alkaline solution the formation of hydroxyl radicals has been suggested as an initial step,[158] and alkaline permanganate has been found to initiate the polymerization of acrylonitrile.[159]

Finally, to mention two other important inorganic oxidizing agents, the relative roles of radical and non-radical paths in lead tetraacetate oxidations has been discussed in Section 10·4d. The analogous splitting of glycols by periodate seems to be a polar process,[160] but the decomposition of periodate by either light or ferrous ion evidently produces radicals, since the system induces the polymerization of acrylonitrile.[161]

Although in the above discussion we have not attempted to cover all available references, it must be evident that many of our commonest oxidizing agents react by complex and varied paths, the formation of radical intermediates depending very much on the particular substrates involved. Plainly the whole topic offers an important field for future research.

11 · 4   Reactions at Electrodes and Metal Surfaces

11·4a   Electrode Processes

The reactions occurring at electrodes involve the addition or removal of electrons from solvent, solute ions, or solute molecules, and thus, if organic substrates are involved and single electron transfers take place, organic free radicals may be produced. They may also be formed indirectly from inorganic radicals or inorganic oxidizing or reducing species produced at the electrode which then attack an organic substrate by the processes outlined in previous sections.

[157] Recent data and a review of earlier work is given by S. J. Adler and R. M. Noyes, *J. Am. Chem. Soc.*, **77**, 2036 (1955). For data on oxidation of other substrates, cf. A. Y. Drummond and W. A. Waters, *J. Chem. Soc.*, **1953**, 435, 440, 3119; **1954**, 2456.

[158] F. R. Duke, *J. Am. Chem. Soc.*, **70**, 3975 (1948); K. B. Wiberg and R. Stewart, *ibid.*, **77**, 1786 (1955).

[159] M. C. R. Symons, *Research*, **6**, 5S (1953).

[160] F. R. Duke, *J. Am. Chem. Soc.*, **69**, 3054 (1947).

[161] M. C. R. Symons, *J. Chem. Soc.*, **1955**, 2594.

Here we will be concerned chiefly with reactions in which radicals are produced in synthetically significant quantities, but it should be noted that polarographic techniques may also be used to detect radicals formed at electrodes, providing they are of considerable stability (e.g., semiquinones or polyarylmethyl radicals).[162]

The reactions occurring at *anodes* involve *oxidation* by electron removal, and loss of a single electron from an organic anion should produce a free radical. The best example of what appears to be such a process is the Kolbe reaction, in which dimerized hydrocarbons are produced by the electrolysis of salts of carboxylic acids. The re-

$$2RCOO^- \rightarrow 2e + 2CO_2 + R\!-\!R \qquad (83)$$

action was first described by Faraday in 1834 and has found considerable synthetic use, most recently by Linstead, Weedon, and co-workers for the preparation of complex naturally occurring acids.[163] A comprehensive review has recently been given by Weedon.[164]

From the synthetic point of view, the reaction is usually best carried out in methanol solution using smooth platinum electrodes at high current densities. Yields are generally good (over 50%) for aliphatic acids lacking substituents on the α carbon but the reaction fails with α,β- or β,γ-unsaturated and aromatic acids, ArCOOH. By using mixed acids, cross-coupled products are obtained (plus symmetric products), and the reaction has been used very successfully to prepare long-chain acids by the electrolysis of mixtures of a monobasic acid and a half-ester of a dibasic acid.[164] Major side reactions include the formation of non-dimeric paraffins and olefins, esters, alcohols, and ethers (the Hofer-Moest reaction) and attack on solvent or other organic species present.

Several mechanisms for the Kolbe reaction have been proposed, including the intermediate formation of diacyl peroxides [165] and of hydrogen peroxide (in aqueous solution),[166] and the direct formation of radicals by the discharge of the carboxylate anion.[167]

[162] I. M. Kolthoff and J. J. Lingane, *Polarography*, second edition, Interscience Publishers, New York, 1952.

[163] B. W. Baker, R. P. Linstead, and B. C. L. Weedon, *J. Chem. Soc.*, **1955**, 2218 and preceding papers.

[164] B. C. L. Weedon, *Quart. Revs.*, **6**, 380 (1952).

[165] C. Schall, *Z. Elektrochem.*, **3**, 83 (1896).

[166] S. Glasstone and A. Hickling, *J. Chem. Soc.*, **1934**, 1878.

[167] A. C. Brown and J. Walker, *Ann.*, **261**, 107 (1891). Recent kinetic evidence in support of this formulation is given by C. L. Wilson and W. T. Lippincott, *J. Am. Chem. Soc.*, **78**, 4290 (1956).

$$RCOO^- \rightarrow RCOO\cdot + e \qquad (84)$$

The weaknesses in the first two schemes have been pointed out by Weedon,[164] and, as we have seen (Section 10·2c), aliphatic acyloxy radicals should immediately lose CO_2 to give alkyl radicals, which, produced in high concentration near the electrode, should have an excellent chance of dimerizing.[168] The formation of some non-dimeric hydrocarbons, particularly at lower current densities, could arise from either disproportionation or hydrogen abstraction from solvent. In addition, the observation that the Kolbe products from optically active α-methylbutyric acid are inactive [169] is consistent with other radical processes, as is the formation of phenylpyridines on the electrolysis of benzoic acid in pyridine [170] and of trinitroxylene from sodium acetate in the presence of trinitrotoluene.[171]

The Hofer-Moest reaction path giving alcohols (or ethers and esters) is harder to interpret as a radical reaction, but a suggestion is that it involves the further oxidation of the intermediate radicals to carbonium ions which then attack solvent.

$$R\cdot \rightarrow e + R^+ \xrightarrow{R'OH} ROR' \qquad (85)$$
$$R' = -OH, \quad -OCH_3, \quad -OCOR$$

Experimentally, this sort of process is favored by strongly alkaline solutions and the presence of various inorganic ions, and is relatively important with α-branched acids. Consistent with this interpretation are recent results by Dauben and Muhs,[172] who find that, in the electrolysis of 1-methylcyclohexane acetic acid in methanol, in addition to 58% of unrearranged Kolbe dimer, 11% 1-methylcycloheptene and 13% 1-methylcycloheptyl methyl ether are formed, plausible products from the rearrangement of an intermediate carbonium ion.

(86)

---

[168] The good parallel between the products of Kolbe reactions and the decomposition of the corresponding diacyl peroxides really suggests more that the two processes have common paths than that peroxides are intermediates in the former. Cf. S. Goldschmidt and M. Minsinger, *Chem. Ber.*, **87**, 956 (1954), and preceding papers.

[169] E. S. Wallis and F. H. Adams, *J. Am. Chem. Soc.*, **55**, 3838 (1933).

[170] F. Fichter and H. Stenzl, *Helv. Chim. Acta*, **17**, 535 (1934).

[171] L. F. Fieser, R. C. Clapp, and W. H. Daudt, *J. Am. Chem. Soc.*, **64**, 2052 (1942).

[172] H. J. Dauben, Jr., and M. A. Muhs, private communication.

Similarly 1-methylcyclopentylacetic acid gives unrearranged dimer plus 1-methylcyclohexene and 1-methylcyclohexyl methyl ether, and *t*-butylacetic acid unrearranged dimer plus *t*-amyl methyl ether. Dauben and Liang [173] also find that the small amount of *sec*-butyl methyl ether formed from active α-methylbutyric acid is inactive.

A second group of anodic oxidations that apparently involve single-electron transfer occurs in the electrolyses of Grignard reagents, which have been investigated extensively by Evans and his students.[174] In ether solution Grignard reagents apparently exist as mixtures of a variety of complex ions which are discharged at the cathode to deposit magnesium and at the anode to produce alkyl or aryl radicals. Alkyl radicals disproportionate or dimerize, and thus from *n*-propyl-magnesium bromide propane, propylene, and *n*-hexane are produced. In addition, hydrogen abstraction from the ether solvent occurs to give further products including CO_2, ethylene, ethyl alcohol, and pentanol-2, the last perhaps via the sequence (cf. Section 6·4)

$$C_3H_7\cdot + C_2H_5OC_2H_5 \longrightarrow C_3H_8 + CH_3\overset{..}{C}H-OC_2H_5$$

$$\begin{array}{c} \downarrow \\ \end{array} \tag{87}$$

$$\underset{\underset{CH_3\overset{|}{C}HC_3H_7}{|}}{OMgX} \xleftarrow{C_3H_7MgX} CH_3CHO + C_2H_5\cdot$$

When phenylmagnesium bromide is electrolyzed, the products include bi- and polyphenyls, together with a little styrene presumably arising from subsequent dehydration of α-phenylethanol formed by reactions analogous to reaction 87.

A number of other anodic oxidations of organic molecules are known. The bulk of the work is rather old and has been reviewed to 1942 by Fichter.[175] In most cases, it is not clear whether one- or two-electron processes are involved, or, if organic radicals are intermediates, whether they are primary or secondary products. However, the hydroxylation of benzene and dimerization of cresols at least suggest one-electron processes. Recently an interesting anodic reduction of benzophenone to benzopinacol in pyridine containing sodium iodide using a magnesium anode has been described by

[173] H. J. Dauben, Jr., and H. T. Liang, private communication.

[174] W. V. Evans and R. Pearson, *ibid.*, **64**, 2865 (1942); W. V. Evans, R. Pearson, and D. Braithwaite, *ibid.*, **63**, 2574 (1941), and preceding papers.

[175] F. Fichter, *Organische Elektrochemie*, Verlag von Theodor Steinkopff, Dresden, 1942.

Rausch, McEwen, and Kleinberg.[176]   This they suggest as involving the formation of an intermediate unstable Mg^+ ion which acts as the reducing species.

Reactions occurring at *cathodes* involve reduction by electron removal, and the most plausible cases of one-electron processes are examples of dimerizations on reduction of unsaturated molecules.   The best-known examples are probably the reduction of ketones to pinacols and aldehydes to glycols, usually in acid solution at lead or mercury cathodes and many are described by Fichter.[175]   Alcohols and hydrocarbons are also produced, and the formation of mercury dialkyls [177] and lead di- and tetraalkyls [177a] as by-products (using mercury and lead cathodes respectively) suggests radical intermediates in these further reductions as well.

In the many other types of electrolytic reductions which have been described, there seems to be little direct evidence for radical intermediates of sufficient life for their characteristic reactions to be observed, although the initiation of polymerization of methyl methacrylate and methacrylic acid at a mercury cathode has been noted.[178]   However, the process is complex and appears to require traces of peroxide.[179]   Examples of radical formation in non-electrolytic reductions at metal surfaces are discussed below.

11·4b   Other Reactions at Metal Surfaces

Reactive metals, alkali metals and amalgams, magnesium, zinc, tin, or iron and acid, are among the most important reducing agents in organic chemistry, and the close parallel between their action and cathodic reductions has been noted for many years and was strongly pointed by Wilson in 1939.[180]   The mechanisms of such processes recently had illuminating review by Birch [181] and subsequently more briefly by Brewster,[182] and much of the discussion here is a summary of the conclusions of these workers.

[176] M. D. Rausch, W. E. McEwen, and J. Kleinberg, *J. Am. Chem. Soc.*, **77**, 2093 (1955).

[177] J. Tafel, *Ber.*, **39**, 3628 (1906).

[177a] J. Tafel, *ibid.*, **44**, 327 (1911).

[178] (a) C. L. Wilson, *Record of Chem. Progr.*, **10**, 25 (1949); E. Dineen, T. C. Schwan, and C. L. Wilson, *Trans. Electrochem. Soc.*, **96**, 220 (1949).   (b) G. Parravano, *J. Am. Chem. Soc.*, **73**, 628 (1951).

[179] C. D. Cook, Jr., thesis, Ohio State University (1954).

[180] C. L. Wilson, *Trans. Electrochem. Soc.*, **75**, 353 (1939).

[181] A. J. Birch, *Quart. Revs.*, **4**, 69 (1950).

[182] J. A. Brewster, *J. Am. Chem. Soc.*, **76**, 6361, 6364, 6368 (1954).

A number of examples are available of the initiation of organic radical reactions by processes occurring at metal surfaces. The initiation of the abnormal (radical) addition of hydrogen bromide to allyl bromide by finely divided iron, nickel, and cobalt was noted by Urushibara and Takebayashi [183] and studied further by Kharasch, Haefele, and Mayo.[184] The possible role of metal surfaces has frequently been mentioned in technical oxidation studies, and Inoue and his colleagues [185] have reported the polymerization of methyl methacrylate in aqueous solution in the presence of formic acid and a variety of metals, of which copper was the most active.

Alkyl halides are also apparently able to react with metals to produce organic radicals. The initiation of the addition of CCl_3Br to olefins by magnesium plus traces of iodine was noted by Kharasch in 1947,[186] and recently he has described a whole series of reactions between alkyl or aryl halides, sodium or magnesium, and dienes to yield coupled symmetric products.[187] Typically, with t-butyl bromide, isoprene, and sodium sand in the presence of a little ether the following reaction occurs, which Kharasch interprets plausibly as involving the initial formation of t-butyl radicals:

$$C_4H_9Br + Na + CH_2{=}C(CH_3)CH{=}CH_2 \nearrow \!\!\!\!\!\!\!\!\searrow$$

$$
\begin{array}{c}
CH_3\\
|\\
C_4H_9{-}CH_2{-}C{=}CH{-}CH_2{-}C_4H_9 \quad (31\text{-}33\%)\\[1em]
CH_3\\
|\\
(C_4H_9{-}CH_2{-}C{=}CH{-}CH_2{-})_2 \quad (21\text{-}32\%)
\end{array}
$$

(88)

Turning now to metal reductions, treatment of non-enolizable ketones with sodium in inert solvents gives rise to deeply colored metal *ketyls*,[188] which are paramagnetic [189] and usually formulated as $R_2\dot{C}{-}ONa$. However, complex equilibria actually exist in such solutions,[190] the ke-

[183] Y. Urushibara and M. Takebayashi, *Bull. Chem. Soc. Japan*, **11**, 692 (1936); **12**, 51 (1937).

[184] M. S. Kharasch, W. R. Haefele, and F. R. Mayo, *J. Am. Chem. Soc.*, **62**, 2047 (1940).

[185] R. Inoue and T. Yamauchi, *Bull. Chem. Soc. Japan*, **26**, 135 (1953); R. Inoue, T. Yamauchi, and T. Ozeki, *J. Chem. Soc. Japan, Ind. Chem. Sect.*, **57**, 645 (1954).

[186] M. S. Kharasch, O. Reinmuth, and W. H. Urry, *J. Am. Chem. Soc.*, **69**, 1105 (1947).

[187] M. S. Kharasch, P. G. Holton, and W. Nudenberg, *J. Org. Chem.*, **19**, 1600 (1954); *ibid.*, **20**, 920 (1955).

[188] E. Beckmann and T. Paul, *Ann.*, **266**, 1 (1891).

[189] S. Sugden, *Trans. Faraday Soc.*, **30**, 23 (1934).

[190] W. E. Bachmann, *J. Am. Chem. Soc.*, **55**, 1179 (1933); C. B. Wooster, *ibid.*, **56**, 2436 (1934); **59**, 377 (1937).

tyl apparently being a dissociable ion pair and also capable of dimerization.

$$R_2\dot{C}\!-\!O^- + Na^+ \rightleftharpoons R_2\dot{C}\!-\!ONa \rightleftharpoons \underset{\underset{\displaystyle ONa}{|}}{\overset{\overset{\displaystyle ONa}{|}}{R_2C}}\!-\!CR_2$$

$$\rightleftharpoons \underset{\underset{\displaystyle O^-}{|}}{\overset{\overset{\displaystyle O^-}{|}}{R_2C}}\!-\!CR_2 + Na^+ \qquad (89)$$

Proton donors convert the dimers to pinacols, and a similar reaction sequence is plausible for the ordinary pinacol reduction of ketones with magnesium. The monomeric reduction of carbonyl compounds with metal and acid to alcohols or hydrocarbons may well involve a similar initial radical ion, except that here it picks up a proton and is further reduced (perhaps while still adsorbed on the metal surface) before dimerization can occur.[181, 182]

The reduction of esters seems to follow a similar course. As shown by Kharasch,[191] in liquid ammonia one mole equivalent of sodium yields chiefly diketones, and two mole equivalents chiefly acyloins plus aldehydes or, on addition of alkyl halides, unsymmetric ketones. The various equilibria have been formulated as follows by Birch: [181]

$$2RCOOEt + 2Na \rightarrow 2R\overset{\displaystyle O}{\underset{\displaystyle |}{C}}\!\!\overset{\diagup}{\cdot} + NaOEt \rightleftharpoons RCOCOR + 2NaOEt$$

$$RCHO \qquad \qquad ONa\ ONa$$

$$2RC\!\!=\!\!O \rightleftharpoons R\underset{\underset{\displaystyle Na}{|}}{\overset{\overset{\displaystyle |}{C}}{C}}\!\!=\!\!\overset{\overset{\displaystyle |}{C}}{C}R \xrightarrow{H^+} RCOCHOHR$$

$$RCOEt \qquad\qquad\qquad\qquad\qquad\qquad\qquad (90)$$

Further evidence for intermediate radicals in the acyloin condensation has been cited by Van Heyningen,[192] who has obtained dimeric hydrocarbons from 1-phenyl-1-carbethoxycyclopentane by a sequence which may be formulated as

[191] M. S. Kharasch, E. Sternfeld, and F. R. Mayo, *J. Org. Chem.*, **5**, 362 (1940).
[192] E. Van Heyningen, *J. Am. Chem. Soc.*, **74**, 4861 (1952).

$$\text{(cyclopentyl-}\phi\text{-COOEt)} + Na \rightarrow NaOEt + \text{(cyclopentyl-}\phi\text{-C=O)}$$

$$\text{(product)} \leftarrow \text{(cyclopentyl-}\phi\text{ radical)} + CO \qquad (91)$$

Similar products are obtained from a β,γ-unsaturated ester.[193]

$$
\begin{array}{c}
CH_3 \quad\quad CH_3 \ \ CH_3 \\
\diagdown \quad | \quad\quad | \\
C\!=\!C\!-\!-\!\!-\!C\!-\!COOEt \rightarrow \\
\diagup \quad\quad\quad | \\
CH_3 \quad\quad\quad CH_3
\end{array}
$$

$$
CO + \ \
\begin{array}{c}
CH_3 \quad\quad CH_3 \ \ CH_3 \\
\diagdown \quad | \quad\quad | \\
C\!=\!C\!-\!-\!CH + \\
\diagup \quad\quad\quad | \\
CH_3 \quad\quad\quad CH_3
\end{array}
\left[
\begin{array}{c}
CH_3 \quad\quad CH_3 \ \ CH_3 \\
\diagdown \quad | \quad\quad | \\
C\!=\!C\!-\!-\!C\!-\! \\
\diagup \quad\quad\quad | \\
CH_3 \quad\quad\quad CH_3
\end{array}
\right]_2 \qquad (92)
$$

In both cases the driving force for the decarbonylation seems to be the stable benzyl- or allyl-type radical produced.

In the sodium and alcohol reduction of esters the intermediate radicals are rapidly reduced further to alcohols. An interesting aspect of the above processes is that, in many cases, the additions of sodium (or of electrons, if we regard the sodium derivatives as ion pairs) are reversible and perhaps strongly influenced by the solvating ability of the media.

An important example of such solvation occurs in the reaction of sodium with many aromatic molecules. In solvents such as *sym*-dimethoxyethane, Scott, Walker, and Hansley [194] have shown that naphthalene takes up one atom of sodium which is reprecipitated on addition of diethyl ether. The deep-colored product formed in the first solvent is evidently a radical ion, i.e.,

$$\text{(naphthalene)} + Na \rightarrow \text{(naphthalene radical anion)} \leftrightarrow \text{(naphthalene radical anion)} \quad etc., + Na^+ \qquad (93)$$

[193] E. Van Heyningen, *ibid.*, **77**, 4016 (1955).
[194] N. D. Scott, J. F. Walker, and V. L. Hansley, *ibid.*, **58**, 2442 (1936).

A similar reaction occurs in tetrahydrofuran and also with a variety of other aromatic molecules. The radical nature of the products has been extensively confirmed by magnetic susceptibility measurement [195] and paramagnetic resonance spectroscopy.[196] In liquid ammonia, naphthalene readily takes up two atoms of sodium, and on hydrolysis, yields a dihydro derivative. Many other aromatics behave similarly, the reaction providing an extremely useful reduction method which has been extensively developed by Birch [181] and has had broad synthetic application.

Reductions of conjugated dienes and acetylenes by various metal combinations, and of nitro compounds and other molecules, show less evidence of intermediate one-electron transfers and can be given little discussion here.

Reactions occurring at the surface of metals which are typical hydrogenation catalysts appear to follow a somewhat different path, reduction occurring by transfer of adsorbed hydrogen to the adsorbed molecule.[197] However, there are scattered examples of the formation of symmetric dimers in catalytic hydrogenation, suggesting the formation of intermediate (perhaps adsorbed) radicals, for example, in the reduction of polyhaloalkanes over Adams' platinum catalyst in the presence of alcoholic ammonia.[198]

$$2Cl(CH_2)_4CCl_3 \xrightarrow{H_2} Cl(CH_2)_4CCl_2CCl_2(CH_2)_4Cl \qquad (94)$$

Parravano has also reported the polymerization of methyl methacrylate initiated by the decomposition of hydrazine on palladium,[199] and of formic acid on palladium and platinum,[200] although the process is apparently very inefficient. Polymerization was also noted with palladium, platinum, ruthenium, and nickel which had been saturated with chemisorbed hydrogen alone.[178b]

[195] T. L. Chu and S. C. Yu, *ibid.*, **76**, 3367 (1954); W. A. Holmes-Walker and A. R. Ubbelohde, *J. Chem. Soc.*, **1954**, 720.

[196] D. Lipkin, D. E. Paul, J. Townsend, and S. I. Weissman, *Science,* **117,** 534 (1953); S. I. Weissman, J. Townsend, D. E. Paul, and G. E. Pake, *J. Chem. Phys.*, **21**, 2227 (1953).

[197] Thus, where such an effect is distinguishable, hydrogen is generally introduced *cis* on the side of the molecule which can most easily come in contact with the catalyst surface; cf. R. P. Linstead, W. E. Doering, S. B. Davis, P. Levine, and R. H. Whetstone, *J. Am. Chem. Soc.*, **64**, 1985 (1942).

[198] E. C. Ladd and H. Sargent, U.S. Pat. 2,644,835 (July 7, 1953).

[199] G. Parravano, *J. Am. Chem. Soc.*, **72**, 3856 (1952).

[200] G. Parravano, *ibid.*, **72**, 5546 (1952).

11·4c Grignard Reagent–Metal Salt Reactions

In this section we will take up a still rather mysterious series of reactions between Grignard reagents and various substrates which are catalyzed by small quantities of polyvalent metal salts. These have, in general, been investigated by Kharasch and his students in the period since 1941 and are reviewed in somewhat greater detail in his monograph.[201] Typical is the reaction with alkyl and aryl halides catalyzed by iron, nickel, chromium, and cobalt salts ($CoCl_2$ appears to be most effective).[202] Although mixtures of simple alkyl or aryl halides and Grignard reagents are stable for long periods, addition of a few per cent of cobaltous chloride produces a violent reaction leading to high yields of coupling or disproportionation products from both reactants. Thus, phenylmagnesium bromide and aryl or alkyl halides gives up to 86% yields of biphenyl,[202] and the alkyl halides are converted to disproportionation products. On the other hand, benzyl-type halides give dimeric products (3,4-dianisylhexane is obtained in 41% yield from anethole hydrobromide and phenylmagnesium bromide) [203]

$$2MeO\!\!\left\langle\bigcirc\right\rangle\!\!CHBrC_2H_5 \xrightarrow[CoCl_2]{\phi MgBr} MeO\!\!\left\langle\bigcirc\right\rangle\!\!\overset{\overset{\displaystyle C_2H_5}{|}}{CH}\!\!-\!\!\overset{\overset{}{}}{\underset{\underset{\displaystyle C_2H_5}{|}}{CH}}\!\!\left\langle\bigcirc\right\rangle\!\!OMe \tag{95}$$

although vinyl halides yield unsymmetrically coupled products.[204]

$$\phi MgBr + CH_2\!\!=\!\!CHCl \xrightarrow{CoCl_2} \phi CH\!\!=\!\!CH_2 \quad (50\text{--}75\%) \quad (96)$$

There is little doubt that radical intermediates occur in these processes since, as examples, reactions in the presence of cumene yield dicumene [205]

$$2R\cdot + 2\phi CH(CH_3)_2 \rightarrow 2RH + \phi C(CH_3)_2\!\!-\!\!C(CH_3)_2\phi \tag{97}$$

and β-phenoxyethyl bromide and isopropylmagnesium bromide plus isoprene yield typical coupled dimeric products.[206]

[201] M. S. Kharasch and O. Reinmuth, *Grignard Reactions of Nonmetallic Substances,* Prentice-Hall, New York, 1954.

[202] M. S. Kharasch and E. K. Fields, *J. Am. Chem. Soc.,* **63,** 2316 (1941), and subsequent papers.

[203] M. S. Kharasch and M. Kleiman, *ibid.,* **65,** 491 (1943).

[204] M. S. Kharasch and C. F. Fuchs, *ibid.,* **65,** 504 (1943).

[205] M. S. Kharasch and W. H. Urry, *J. Org. Chem.,* **13,** 101 (1948).

[206] M. S. Kharasch, R. D. Mulley, and W. Nudenberg, *ibid.,* **19,** 1477 (1955).

$$CH_3$$
$$|$$
$$[\phi O(CH_2)_3 C = CH - CH_2 -]_2$$

and

$$CH_3 \qquad\qquad CH_3$$
$$| \qquad\qquad\qquad |$$
$$\phi O(CH_2)_3 C = CHCH_2CH_2CH = CCH_2CH(CH_3)_2 \qquad (98)$$

Kharasch has proposed a cyclic mechanism for the process involving an intermediate cobaltous subhalide together with the expected sub-

$$RMgX + CoCl_2 \rightarrow RCoX + MgX_2 \qquad (99)$$

$$RCoX \rightarrow R\cdot + CoX \qquad (100)$$

$$CoX + R'X \rightarrow CoX_2 + R'\cdot \qquad (101)$$

sequent reactions of the radicals produced.

This scheme has been criticized by Wilds and McCormack [207] on several grounds, perhaps most cogent that there is no independent evidence for univalent cobalt and that a Grignard reagent–$CoCl_2$ reaction product retains its ability to react with alkyl halides even after long standing or heating, conditions expected to destroy the unstable intermediate. They propose an alternate path in which finely divided, active cobalt is the reactive intermediate.

$$2RMgX + CoX_2 \rightarrow 2MgX_2 + CoR_2$$

$$\rightarrow Co + 2R\cdot \qquad (\text{or } R - R) \qquad (102)$$

$$Co + 2R'X \rightarrow CoX_2 + 2R\cdot \qquad (\text{or } R - R) \qquad (103)$$

This alternative seems preferable to the writer, particularly since Chu and Friel [208] have shown that the sodium-naphthalene radical ion instantly reduces $CoCl_2$ to metallic cobalt in a very reactive, colloidal form which reacts with air and reduces cupric ion to the cuprous state.

Grignard reagents in the presence of $CoCl_2$ also produce dimerization reactions with acyl chlorides [209] and lead to the almost quantitative conversion of benzophenone to benzpinacol.[210] Benzyl ethers are attacked,[211] and a number of other processes have been observed.[201]

[207] A. L. Wilds and W. B. McCormack, *ibid.*, **14**, 45 (1949).

[208] T. L. Chu and J. V. Friel, *J. Am. Chem. Soc.*, **77**, 5838 (1955).

[209] M. S. Kharasch, W. Nudenberg, and S. Archer, *ibid.*, **65**, 495 (1943); M. S. Kharasch, R. Morrison, and W. H. Urry, *ibid.*, **66**, 368 (1944).

[210] M. S. Kharasch and F. L. Lambert, *ibid.*, **63**, 2315 (1941).

[211] M. S. Kharasch and R. L. Huang, *J. Org. Chem.*, **17**, 669 (1952).

11 · 5   Some Organic Redox Systems

11·5a   Amine-Peroxide Reactions

A complex series of reactions occurs between peroxides and amines which in some cases gives rise to free radicals. Thus suitable systems, for example, benzoyl peroxide and dimethyl aniline, induce polymerization of monomers such as styrene and methyl methacrylate. However, as we shall see, radical production does not appear to be the primary process in peroxide-amine reactions but rather arises from the breakdown of unstable intermediates arising from an initial polar reaction.

The products of reaction of benzoyl peroxide with a series of primary, secondary, and tertiary amines were first investigated by Gambarjan [212] in the period 1925–1933, and the kinetics of the process surveyed by Bartlett and Nozaki in 1947,[213] who noted that the reaction was very rapid compared with the ordinary thermal decomposition of the peroxide. In the case of benzoyl peroxide and triphenylamine, the rate appeared to be approximately first order in each. However, most of our information at present is the result of detailed studies by Horner and his students since 1949.[214]

Radical formation has been most clearly demonstrated in diacyl peroxide–t-amine systems, of which benzoyl peroxide plus dimethyl aniline is typical. The products of this reaction, run in dilute solution in solvents such as chloroform,[215] are an almost quantitative yield of benzoic acid, plus, from the amine, monomethyl aniline, formaldehyde, and small amounts of p-benzoyloxydimethylaniline and p,p'-di(dimethylamino)diphenylmethane.[216]   Horner [214, 216, 217] has proposed essentially the following reaction scheme for the decomposition:

[212] S. Gambarjan, *Ber.,* **58B,** 1775 (1925); S. Gambarjan and O. Cialtician, *ibid.,* **60B,** 390 (1927); S. Gambarjan, O. Cialtician, and A. Babajan, *Bull. inst. sci., R. S. S. Arménie,* **1931,** 265; S. Gambarjan and L. Kazarian, *J. Gen. Chem. U.S.S.R.,* **3,** 222 (1933).

[213] P. D. Bartlett and K. Nozaki, *J. Am. Chem. Soc.,* **69,** 2299 (1947).

[214] L. Horner and E. Schwenk, *Angew. Chem.,* **61,** 411 (1949); *Ann.,* **566,** 69 (1949), and subsequent papers.

[215] L. Horner and C. Betzel, *Ann.,* **579,** 175 (1953).

[216] This substance was earlier identified as 2,2′-di(dimethylamino)biphenyl; L. Horner and E. Schwenk, *ibid.,* **566,** 69 (1950).

[217] L. Horner, *J. Polymer Sci.,* **18,** 438 (1955).

$$\text{(cyclohexyl-ring)}-\overset{\overset{\displaystyle CH_3}{|}}{N}-CH_3 + Bz_2O_2 \rightarrow \left[\text{(cyclohexyl-ring)}-\overset{\overset{\displaystyle CH_3}{|}}{\underset{\underset{\displaystyle CH_3}{|}}{N^+}}-OCO\phi \right] [\phi COO^-] \quad (104)$$

$$\text{I}$$

$$\text{I} \rightarrow \text{(cyclohexyl-ring)}-\overset{\overset{\displaystyle CH_3}{|}}{\underset{\underset{\displaystyle CH_3}{|}}{\overset{\displaystyle \cdot +}{N}}} + \phi COO\cdot + \phi COO^- \quad (105)$$

$$\text{II}$$

$$\text{II} \rightarrow \text{(cyclohexyl-ring)}-\overset{\overset{\displaystyle CH_3}{|}}{\underset{\underset{\displaystyle CH_2OCO\phi}{|}}{N}} + \phi COOH \xrightarrow{H_2O} \text{(cyclohexyl-ring)}-\overset{\overset{\displaystyle CH_3}{|}}{NH} + CH_2O \quad (106)$$

$$\text{II} \rightarrow \underset{\phi COO}{\text{(cyclohexyl-ring)}}-\overset{\overset{\displaystyle CH_3}{|}}{\underset{\underset{\displaystyle CH_3}{|}}{N}} + \phi COOH \quad (107)$$

A number of pieces of evidence support the initial polar formation of the quarternary hydroxyamine derivative, I, and its subsequent cleavage into radicals. Thus, the rate of peroxide decomposition is greatly accelerated by electron-supplying groups on the dimethylaniline, and is retarded by electron withdrawal, the half-life of 0.01 M peroxide in the presence of 0.01 M amine in $CHCl_3$ at 20° being 5 minutes for p-methyldimethylaniline, 13 minutes for dimethylaniline, and 6 days for p-cyanodimethylaniline.[218] Similarly, electron-withdrawing groups on the peroxide accelerate reaction, the compound $\phi SO_2-OO-CO\phi$ reacting almost instantly even with p-nitro-dimethylaniline.[219] Evidence for radical production is supplied not only by the initiation of polymerization (see below) but also by the observation that the system rapidly absorbs oxygen [215] (evidently to form peroxides, since the peroxide titre remains high [220]) and nitric oxide.[215] Further, initiation of polymerization by the acetic anhydride–dimethylaniline oxide system, which presumably gives rise to a similar intermediate (reaction 108), has been reported by Boekel-

[218] L. Horner and K. Sherf, *Ann.*, **573**, 35 (1951).

[219] L. Horner and W. Kirmse, *ibid.*, **567**, 48 (1955).

[220] L. Horner and H. Junkermann, *ibid.*, **591**, 53 (1955).

$$\underset{\overset{|}{CH_3}}{\overset{\overset{\displaystyle CH_3}{|}}{\bigcirc\!\!-\!N\!\rightarrow\!O}} + Ac_2O \rightarrow \left[\underset{\overset{|}{CH_3}}{\overset{\overset{\displaystyle CH_3}{\overset{|+}{}}}{\bigcirc\!\!-\!N\!-\!OCOCH_3}} \right] [AcO^-] \quad (108)$$

heide and Harrington.[221] The kinetics of the reaction have been studied by several groups,[220, 222, 223] all of whom find a rate proportional to amine and peroxide consistent with an initial bimolecular process. By following simultaneously peroxide decomposition and appearance of benzoic acid, Horner and Junkermann [220] have concluded that they have evidence for a small amount of unstable intermediate, perhaps I in reaction 104.

Turning now to polymerization initiation as a means of counting radicals, careful studies by several groups [223, 224, 225] with a variety of monomers indicate relations of the form

$$R_p = k[Bz_2O_2]^{1/2}[Amine]^{1/2} \qquad (109)$$

consistent with a bimolecular radical-forming process, and qualitative results have also been reported for various other peroxide–t-amine systems.[214, 216, 226]

Meltzer and Tobolsky have made the important observation that with styrene the relation between polymerization rate and polymer molecular weight is precisely that calculated for a process in which all chain termination is the usual interaction of growing polymer chains. In short, although radicals from the peroxide-amine system initiate polymerization, neither they nor any of the other species produced interact thereafter with the growing chains. In connection with this observation, it may be noted that various workers [226] have reported rapid initial induction of polymerization by peroxide-amine systems, after which reaction slows and stops short of complete conversion. This apparently does not involve the buildup of some sort of polymerization inhibitor but rather the quick exhaustion of peroxide by rapid reaction with amine, cf. the half-lives cited above.

[221] V. Boekelheide and D. L. Harrington, *Chemistry & Industry*, **1955**, 1423.

[222] M. Imoto and S. Choe, *J. Polymer Sci.*, **15**, 485 (1955).

[223] C. Walling and N. Indictor, unpublished work.

[224] T. H. Melzer and A. V. Tobolsky, *J. Am. Chem. Soc.*, **76**, 5178 (1954).

[225] M. Imoto, T. Otsu, and K. Kimura, *J. Polymer Sci.*, **15**, 475 (1955); M. Imoto and K. Takemoto, *ibid.*, **18**, 377 (1955); M. Imoto, T. Otsu, and T. Ota, *Makromol. Chem.*, **16**, 10 (1955); M. Imoto, S. Chao, and H. Takasugi, *J. Chem. Soc. Japan, Ind. Chem. Sect.*, **58**, 451 (1955).

[226] K. Noma, O. Nishiura, and A. Ichiba, *Chem. High Polymers Japan*, **10**, 231 (1953); J. Lal and R. Green, *J. Polymer Sci.*, **17**, 403 (1955).

The nature of the polymerization-initiating radical has been looked at by Horner and Schwenk,[216] who conclude that it is primarily the benzoyloxy radical formed in reaction 105, since polystyrene initiated by benzoyl peroxide and dimethyl aniline contains negligible nitrogen but 3–6% oxygen, 50–90% of which can be recovered as benzoic acid on hydrolysis. Initiator efficiency, however, is low, Imoto[225] obtaining a figure of about 25% (assuming only benzoyloxy radicals start chains). Results in this laboratory, however, indicate only 2–5%.[223]

In spite of the rather extensive evidence for reactions 104 and 105 above, Horner's subsequent steps seem less well substantiated. Thus, dealkylation could also arise by hydrogen abstraction from the aminium radical ion or by loss of a proton from the quarternary hy-

$$\text{(Cy)}-\underset{\underset{CH_3}{|}}{\overset{\overset{CH_3}{|}}{N}}\cdot^+ \xrightarrow{BzO\cdot} \text{(Cy)}-\underset{\underset{CH_2}{\|}}{\overset{\overset{CH_3}{|}}{N}}{}^+ \xrightarrow{H_2O} \text{(Cy)}-\overset{\overset{CH_3}{|}}{NH} + CH_2O \quad (110)$$

droxylamine rather than by a radical process, and the low efficiency

$$\text{(Cy)}-\underset{\underset{CH_3}{|}}{\overset{\overset{CH_3}{|}}{N}}{}^+-OCO\phi \rightarrow \text{(Cy)}-\underset{\underset{CH_2}{\|}}{\overset{\overset{CH_3}{|}}{N}}{}^+ + \phi COOH \quad (111)$$

of the system as a polymerization initiator certainly suggests that some of the reaction may go entirely by a non-radical path. Horner and Kirmse[219] have made an extensive study of the relative ease of loss of alkyl groups from unsymmetric amines, although with results which lead to no firm conclusions about mechanism. Primary alkyl groups are eliminated more easily than secondary, and secondary more easily than methyl. Benzyl is little different than ethyl, but —CH$_2$CO— is preferentially lost, diethylaminoacetone giving methylglyoxal. As a technique for degrading tertiary amines, the reaction would seem to have some promise.[227]

Another puzzling feature of the reaction is the considerable variation in rate with solvent. A pronounced acceleration in the presence of pyridine was noted by Horner,[220] and work at Columbia[223] indicates that reaction is slow in acetone and intermediate in benzene.

[227] Actually, the dealkylation by reacting t-amine oxides with acetic anhydride has long been known; M. Polonovski and M. Polonovski, *Compt. rend.*, **184**, 331 (1927).

In "fast" solvents it is greatly depressed by small quantities of styrene, suggesting some chain decomposition, and it seems a fair statement to say that all details of the reaction are far from understood.

Secondary amines also react readily with benzoyl peroxide, methylaniline several times as rapidly as dimethylaniline. The products are chiefly benzoic acid and O-benzoylhydroxylamines,[212, 228] or, in the case of arylamines, o-hydroxybenzanilides, arising from the well-known rearrangement of the intermediate hydroxylamine derivatives. Thus Edward[229] has described the oxidation of a whole series of N-alkyl arylamines to the corresponding o-hydroxy compounds in yields of 8–40%. The reaction can most plausibly be formulated as a bimolecular polar displacement followed by proton loss. In keep-

$$\begin{matrix} R_1 \\ \diagdown \\ N{-}H + Bz_2O_2 \rightarrow \\ \diagup \\ R_2 \end{matrix} \qquad \begin{matrix} R_1 \quad H \\ \diagdown \diagup \\ N^+ \\ \diagup \diagdown \\ R_2 \quad OCO\phi \end{matrix} + BzO^-$$

$$\rightarrow \begin{matrix} R_1 \\ \diagdown \\ N{-}OBz + BzOH \\ \diagup \\ R_2 \end{matrix} \qquad (112)$$

ing with this formulation, dibenzylamine and benzoyl p-nitrobenzoyl peroxide give nitrobenzoic acid and the O-benzoylhydroxylamine.[228]

In general there is no evidence for radical formation, secondary amine–peroxide systems neither initiating polymerization nor absorbing oxygen.[228] However, Horner[228] has noted that the diethyl amine–benzoyl peroxide system does absorb nitric oxide to give a little nitrosodiethylamine (by a path which is unclear) and states that diethylamine and alkanesulfonyl acetyl peroxides, $RSO_2{-}OO{-}OAc$ initiate the polymerization of acrylonitrile and evolve CO_2.

Primary amines and benzoyl peroxide give a complex mixture of products,[212, 228] including, from aniline,[228] benzoic acid, benzanilide, azobenzene, and a little o-hydroxybenzanilide. Presumably the same sort of initial process is involved, but little can be said about subsequent steps.

There is relatively little known about radical formation in the reaction of amines with other types of peroxides (however, cf. Section

[228] C. W. Capp and E. G. E. Hawkins. *J. Chem. Soc.,* **1953**, 4106.
[229] J. T. Edward, *ibid.,* **1954**, 1464.

9·2g). Hydroperoxides react rapidly and are reduced to the corresponding alcohols in good yield (72–100%),[229] and we may note that the usual process for preparing tertiary amine oxides from amines and hydrogen peroxides or peracids can be formulated in precisely the same manner as reactions 104 and 112.

$$R_3N + H_2O_2 \rightarrow [R_3N^+\!\!-OH][OH^-] \rightarrow R_3NO + H_2O \quad (113)$$

11·5b   Other Organic Redox Systems

As in the case of inorganic redox systems, other organic oxidation-reductions may involve either one or two electron transfers. However, in many cases even where the intermediate radicals may have some stability, two-electron transfer seems to be preferred. Thus, Linstead has concluded that dehydrogenations by quinones are two-electron processes,[230] and in Section 10·2b we noted that there is little evidence for radical formation in peroxide-phenol reactions. On the other hand, however, Hünig and Daum [231] have concluded that the oxidative coupling of p-aminodimethylaniline and phenols

$$(114)$$

(an important reaction in the chemistry of color photography) involves the intermediate Wurster radical cation of the amine.

Other examples of one-electron transfer with radical formation are scattered, and the field has had little exploration. Leffler [232] has noted that tris-(p-nitrophenyl)methyl bromide reacts with p-nitrobenzoate ion, pyridine, dimethylaniline (and a variety of inorganic reagents) to give the tris-(p-nitrophenyl)methyl radical, and Lal and Green [233] have reported polymerization initiation by combinations of saccharin and N,N-dialkylanilines.

[230] E. A. Braude, L. M. Jackman, and R. P. Linstead, ibid., **1954**, 3548, 3564.
[231] S. Hünig and W. Daum, Ann., **595**, 131 (1955).
[232] J. E. Leffler, J. Am. Chem. Soc., **75**, 3598 (1953).
[233] J. Lal and R. Green, J. Polymer Sci., **18**, 430 (1955).

Recently Ramirez and Dershowitz [234] have investigated the reaction of triphenylphosphine and chloranil and find that it yields an intermediate product which possesses a paramagnetic resonance spectra different from that of chloranil semiquinone and which they believe to be the species $\phi_3 P \cdot {}^+$. Paramagnetic reaction products from p-phenylenediamine and chloranil, bromanil, and tetraiodobenzoquinone have also been reported by Kainer, Bijl, and Rose Innes.[235] Here the usual product would be a diamagnetic molecular compound, but it is suggested that, in these systems, singlet and triplet states lie close enough together so that both may be present in significant concentrations at equilibrium.

Finally, the polymolecular thermal initiation of polymerization of monomers such as styrene (Section 5·1) might be regarded as radical-forming one-electron oxidation-reductions.

[234] F. Ramirez and S. Dershowitz, *J. Am. Chem. Soc.*, **78**, 5614 (1956).

[235] H. Kainer, D. Bijl, and A. C. Rose Innes, *Naturwissenschaften*, **211**, 303 (1954).

Author Index

Abbott, D. C., 390
Abell, P. I., 295
Adam, J., 384
Adams, F. H., 581
Adams, R. M., 131
Addison, L. M., 529
Adkins, H., 368
Adler, S. J., 579
Agallidis, E., 19
Aggarwal, S. L., 112
Agron, P., 111
Alder, K., 181, 186, 188
Alder, M. G., 516
Alderman, D. M., 153, 319
Alekseeva, E., 150, 201
Alexander, E. R., 28
Alexander, P., 31, 222
Alexander, W. A., 447
Alfrey, T., Jr., 99, 101, 103, 106, 111, 112, 113, 127, 130, 131, 132, 140
Allen, A. O., 549

Allen, P. W., 169, 171
Allen, T. L., 573
Altier, M. W., 208
Altshul, R., 160, 175
Alumbaugh, R. L., 201
Alyea, H. N., 430
Amedon, R. W., 188
Anbar, M., 386, 388
Andersen, H. C., 42, 374
Anderson, A. W., 225, 393, 413, 572
Anderson, H. R., 50, 374
Anderson, R. C., 340
Anderson, W. S., 122
Andrews, W., 322
Angier, D. F., 222
Ansell, M. F., 494
Archer, S., 589
Arcus, C. L., 390
Arimoto, F. S., 568
Arlman, E. J., 146, 147
Armstrong, E. C., 339

597

Subject Index

621